California Real Estate Principles and License Preparation
2nd Edition

by

Jim Bainbridge, J.D.

Member of the California State Bar
and
California Real Estate Broker

City Breeze Publishing

Marina del Rey, California

© 2014

City Breeze Publishing
P.O. Box 12650
Marina del Rey, California 90295

ISBN: 978-1-939526-12-0

PRINTED IN THE UNITED STATES OF AMERICA

Introduction

Though the fundamental principles of real estate in California are based on English common law that has been in use for centuries, in recent years many consumer protection statutes at the federal, state, and local levels have dramatically expanded the number and complexity of laws that impact real estate practice. The need for educating anyone interested in becoming a real estate professional has thereby also grown dramatically. Contemporary real estate agents must acquire an adequate working knowledge in a wide variety of subjects: contract law, agency relationships, real estate financing, real estate appraisal, land use control, fair housing, and truth-in-lending laws, to name a few.

This textbook presents a comprehensive college-level course covering the theoretical and practical aspects of California real estate principles and practice needed by today's aspiring real estate licensees and other real estate professionals. Special features of this text include:

- 600 questions of the type used on California salesperson and broker examinations are included. These questions come at the end of each chapter and in the 150-question practice examination that is located near the end of the book. Rather than merely indicating which of the possible answers is correct, a detailed answer to each question is presented, allowing the reader to assess his or her strengths and weaknesses — and to hone test-taking skills — before exam day.

- Keywords used in each chapter are listed at the end of each chapter, and each of these important keywords is defined in the extensive glossary.

- Many helpful figures and tables are presented throughout the book to assist readers in visualizing the real estate principles discussed in the text.

- Numerous forms that real estate agents will use in their practice, such as the listing agreement and the residential purchase agreement, are presented and discussed.

About the Author

Jim Bainbridge is a graduate of Harvard Law School and has been an active member of the California Bar for more than 30 years. He is a licensed California real estate broker, and a past recipient of a National Science Foundation Fellowship for graduate studies in mathematics at UC Berkeley. He is the author of *California Real Estate Broker Practice Exams for 2014, California Real Estate Salesperson Practice Exams for 2014,* and numerous works that have been published in more than 50 journals in the USA, UK, Canada, Australia, Japan, and the Netherlands.

Mr. Bainbridge has also received recognition as a Certified Distance Education Instructor by IDECC, which is a function of the Association of Real Estate License Law Officials.

NEW TO THIS EDITION

- The text has been updated to incorporate recently passed state and federal real estate laws, including:

  - the IRS and California Franchise Tax Board clarifications made late in 2013 that a California taxpayer involved in a short sale pursuant to CCP §580e would not be subject to state or federal income taxation of the short sale debt cancellation, even after the expiration of the Mortgage Forgiveness Debt Relief Act of 2007 on December 31, 2013,

  - the ATR/QM rules effective January 10, 2014, and

  - the reduced maximum loan amount for 2014 that the FHA will insure for California single-family homes.

- Numerous revisions to the text material in the prior edition have been made to provide greater clarity and precision to the concepts discussed.

- Additional questions and answers have been added to the quizzes at the end of several chapters.

- Numerous terms important to California real estate principles have been added in both the text and in the glossary.

- Forms reproduced with permission from the California Association of Realtors® have been updated.

Abbreviations Used in this Book*

B&PC — California Business and Professions Code

CC — California Civil Code

CCP — California Code of Civil Procedure

CR — Commissioner's Regulations

FC — California Family Code

GOV — Government Code

HSC — Health and Safety Code

PC — California Probate Code

*__Note__: References to code sections that appear throughout this text are given to assist those who may wish to pursue the subjects being discussed to their statutory sources. Neither the name nor the number of these code sections has to be memorized for the purpose of preparing to pass the real estate license examinations.

CONTENTS

CHAPTER 4: WAYS OF OWNING REAL PROPERTY 71

CHAPTER 5: INVOLUNTARY LIENS AND HOMESTEADS.87

CHAPTER 6: PROPERTY LISTING AND SALES CONTRACTS 111

CHAPTER 10: THE PRIMARY & SECONDARY MORTGAGE MARKETS 281

CHAPTER 11: REAL ESTATE VALUATION AND APPRAISAL

CHAPTER 12: ESCROW AND CLOSING ....

CHAPTER 13: LANDLORD/TENANT RELATIONS AND PROPERTY MANAGEMENT 355

CHAPTER 14: PUBLIC LIMITATIONS ON USE OF REAL ESTATE 397

CHAPTER 15: TAXATION AND REAL ESTATE 435

CHAPTER 16: HOME STYLES AND BENEFITS OF INVESTMENT VS. RENTING 459

CHAPTER 17: OBTAINING AND MAINTAINING A REAL ESTATE LICENSE 475

The Concept of Property

BRIEF HISTORY OF CALIFORNIA LAND

California history can be divided into several periods:

1. The Native American period, which began over 10,000 years ago;
2. The period of European exploration, 1542-1769, when Spanish explorers first arrived in what is now California and the land was claimed by the King of Spain;
3. The Spanish colonial period, 1769-1821, during which Spanish settlers began colonizing California, ultimately establishing forts called *presidios*, towns called *pueblos*, and ranches called *rancheros*;
4. The Mexican period, 1821-1848, began when Mexico won Independence from Spain and ended when the ***Treaty of Guadeloupe Hidalgo*** ended the Mexican-American War (1846-48) and California was annexed to the United States;
5. California as a U.S. territory, 1848-1850, during which time gold was discovered and the non-Native American, non-Hispanic population rose to over 100,000; and
6. California statehood, 1850 to the present.

The Treaty of Guadalupe Hidalgo provided that the property rights of Mexican citizens would be recognized. California thereby adopted **community property**, a Spanish concept regarding the earnings and accumulations of property during marriage. Contemporary community property law will be discussed in greater detail in a subsequent chapter.

THE NATURE OF PROPERTY

Though historically the prevailing idea was that property existed independently of law and could not be taken away or substantially limited by law (the "natural rights doctrine"), the accepted modern view is that property is a creation of law. Property in this modern view is nothing more than a thing to which a

bundle of rights, created and protected by law, is attributed. This bundle of rights may include the right to possess, use, enjoy, encumber, sell, and/or exclude from others. And because these rights are created by law, they can be changed or even abolished by law — sometimes with, sometimes without, compensation to their former owner(s).

REAL VS. PERSONAL PROPERTY

Property comes in two, and only two, mutually exclusive kinds: real and personal. "Every kind of property that is not real is personal." CC §663. Each kind of property can, under certain circumstances, be transformed into the other kind. A wood board being carried by a carpenter toward a house that is being built is personal property. Moments later, once the carpenter permanently affixes it to the house as part of a wall or floor, the board becomes real property. If sometime later during remodeling the board is removed from the house, it again becomes personal property. As a general rule, the distinction boils down to this: personal property is considered movable; real property, immovable. Knowing the distinction between real property and personal property is important because the laws relating to the acquisition and transfer of real property differ considerably from the laws relating to the acquisition and transfer of personal property.

LEGAL DISTINCTIONS BETWEEN REAL AND PERSONAL PROPERTY

1. As a general rule, to be enforceable an agreement for the sale of real property must be in writing signed by the selling party. Transfer of real property is completed by the delivery of a written ***deed***. An agreement for the sale of personal property must be in writing if the amount of the sale or the value of the property exceeds $500. Personal property is usually transferred by a ***bill of sale***.
2. As a general rule, the laws of the state in which real property is situated govern the transfer of title of the property. Personal property, on the other hand, is normally regulated by the law of the owner's permanent residence (the owner's "***domicile***"), regardless in which state the property is actually located.
3. California law has a system for recording documents or instruments affecting the title or interest in real property.
4. Real and personal property are often subject to substantially different tax laws.

CONSTITUENTS OF REAL PROPERTY

The three broad categories of real property are:

1. Land;
2. Appurtenances; and
3. Things affixed to the land.

LAND

Though land is commonly thought of as surface ground, the code definition of land is broader: "Land is the material of the earth, whatever may be the ingredients of which it is composed, whether soil, rock, or other substance, and includes free or occupied space for an indefinite distance upwards as well as downwards, subject to limitations upon the use of airspace imposed, and rights in the use of airspace granted, by law." CC §659.

APPURTENANCES

In addition to the basic material ingredients of which land is composed, a landowner has certain appurtenant rights. An **appurtenance** is an object, right, or interest that is incidental to the land and goes with or pertains to the land. "A thing is deemed to be incidental or appurtenant to land when it is by right used with the land for its benefit, as in the case of a way, or watercourse, or of a passage for light, air, or heat from across the land of another." CC §662.

Air rights

Traditionally, a land owner could claim unlimited rights to the airspace above his or her property, no matter how high above the land. However, recognizing the need for air travel, contemporary law gives the landowner only a "reasonable" amount of airspace to use above his or her land. What constitutes "reasonable" in this context is often difficult to decide and is determined on a case-by-case basis whenever a lawsuit arises between parties.

Airspace is also something that can be sold separate from the surface of one's land. Condominiums, for example, involve the selling of the exclusive ownership of a certain volume of airspace together with non--exclusive rights to common areas, such as halls, elevators, and recreational facilities.

Water rights

The shortage of water in many areas of California makes water law an important topic. There are three main categories of water rights:

1. Underground water rights;
2. Riparian and littoral rights; and
3. Right of appropriation.

Underground Water Rights

Underground waters are underground streams and water collected in porous ground layers called aquifers. In California, both underground and surface waters are owned by the State, and a landowner may take only a "reasonable" amount of underground water for his or her beneficial use. What is "reasonable" in this context is determined on a case-by-case basis.

Riparian and Littoral Rights

Riparian rights are the rights of a landowner to the reasonable use of water that flows through or adjacent to his or her property. **Littoral rights** are the rights of a landowner to reasonable use of water from lakes, seas, or oceans (non-flowing water) adjacent to his or her property. Such landowners do not own the water but do have the right, along with other riparian landowners, to make "reasonable" use of the waters. What is "reasonable" is a question of fact to be decided on a case-by-case basis.

In general, a riparian landowner has the right to an amount of water in proportion to the amount of land that borders the water, but only after taking into consideration the rights and needs of others. Water law gives preference to domestic use of water over use for irrigation.

If a stream is navigable, the State owns the land under the stream; however, if the stream is not navigable, the riparian landowner owns the land under the stream to the midpoint of the stream.

Right of Appropriation

Landowners have appropriation rights to surface water that does not lie adjacent to their property. To obtain such appropriation rights, one must apply for a permit to the State Water Resources Control Board. In general, the first person who takes water by the right of appropriation has the right to continue to take the same reasonable amount of water from the same source year after year. The second person to take water from the same source is second in priority, and so on. In other words, appropriation water rights are permitted on a first-in-time, first-in-right basis.

Mineral Rights

Landowners have certain rights in minerals that lie directly beneath the surface of their property and may sell their mineral rights separately from the rest of their property. As part of the purchase of such mineral rights, the buyer acquires the right to enter the land under which the minerals lie in order to extract the minerals. This automatically acquired right to enter the land for purposes of mineral extraction is an *implied easement* called a *profit á prendre*.

Solid Mineral Rights

Solid minerals, such as coal and metal ores, are owned by the landowner below whose property the minerals lie and are considered real property until they are extracted from the earth, at which time they become personal property. Upon the sale of real estate, the landowner's rights to the minerals that lie beneath the property automatically pass with the deed, unless specifically excluded.

Liquid Mineral Rights

Oil, gas, and geothermal steam are subject to the *law of capture*. During the time that such minerals lie in their natural state below the surface of land, they are not owned by the owner of the land — the owner of the land (or of the drilling rights to these minerals beneath the land) merely has the right to drill from the surface of the land down to these types of minerals, which lie trapped in natural underground reservoirs. Only when these minerals are "captured" by being brought to the surface do they become property — personal property, not real property.

When a reservoir of these minerals is drilled into and pumping of the minerals to the surface begins, such minerals begin to flow toward the pump, even from areas that do not lie directly below the land on which the drilling rights exist. Because there is no ownership in these underground minerals (as distinct from ownership of rights to drill for these minerals), the owner of the drilling rights may extract all of these transitory minerals in the underground reservoir, even if such extraction depletes the minerals under neighboring lands. Obviously, an effect of this "law of capture" is to stimulate rapid oil and gas production: capture it or lose it.

Other Appurtenant Rights

In addition to air, water, and mineral rights, real property includes other things and rights that are appurtenant to the land. Such additional appurtenances include:

1. Support rights;
2. Stock in mutual water companies; and
3. Easements.

Support Rights

Every piece of land is supported by land beneath and to the sides of it. A landowner has the right to have maintained both **lateral support** from adjacent properties and **subjacent support** from the ground below. Anyone who excavates land, as for the purpose of leveling the land to build upon or for the purpose of building underground parking, must take care not to reduce the lateral support of a neighbor's land to such a degree as to cause damage to the neighbor's property. A property owner must also be careful that his or her improvements or buildings do not cause or contribute damage through subsidence to a neighbor's land or buildings by reducing the subjacent ground support of that neighbor's land.

Stock in a Mutual Water Company

A mutual water company is a nonprofit company created to provide adequate water supplies for property owners in a specific district. The company shares are issued to property owners within the district, and each share is considered to be appurtenant to a specific piece of property. Ownership of a share in a mutual water company may not be transferred unless the land to which the share is appurtenant is transferred with it.

Easements

An easement is a non-possessory right to use a portion of another property owner's land for a specific purpose, as for a right-of-way, without paying rent or being considered a trespasser. Typical easements are right-of-way easements to access otherwise landlocked property and easements to lay power, cable, telephone, or water lines. The owner of an easement has the duty to maintain it.

The land that is **encumbered** by an easement is called the **servient tenement** — it serves the purpose of the easement. If the easement benefits other land (as in the case of a right-of-way easement), the land benefited is called the **dominant tenement**, and such an easement is called an **easement appurtenant**— it is appurtenant to the dominant land and cannot be sold separately from it.

If the easement benefits not other land but a legal person (including a business entity), such as an easement to erect and maintain telephone poles and lines, the easement is called an **easement in gross**. Because an easement in gross is not appurtenant to any dominant land, it is considered personal in nature. Such an easement is (in California) assignable unless it was expressly or implicitly created to benefit one particular legal person and no other.

Easements can be created in many ways — some voluntarily on the part of the owner of the servient tenement, some involuntarily. The most important methods of easement creation are by:

1. *express grant*: the owner of the servient tenement expressly grants someone else the right to use the servient land for some purpose;

2. *express reservation*: the owner of the servient tenement expressly reserves the right to use a portion of the servient tenement (such as when the owner of the servient tenement sells the land but wishes to retain the right to use a private road);

3. *implication*: an implied easement arises by implication, as when a buyer of a parcel of land discovers that the land he or she just purchased has no access except *over the land of the person from whom the parcel was purchased*;

4. *necessity*: an easement by necessity arises as a creation of a court of law in certain cases were justice so demands, as in the case where a buyer of a parcel of land discovers that the land he or she just purchased has no access *except over the land of someone other than from the person from whom the parcel was purchased.*

5. *prescription*: such as when, under certain circumstances, one uses another's land for at least five years without permission. Prescriptive easements are discussed in Chapter 3, where they are compared and contrasted with adverse possession.

Easements can be terminated in many ways, including

1. by the person who benefits from the easement acquiring the servient tenement — a person cannot have an easement over his or her own estate;

2. by the dominant tenement and servient tenement becoming owned by the same person (this is referred to as merger of titles or merger of estates);

3. by the destruction of the servient tenement; and

4. in the case of a prescriptive easement, by nonuse (an easement created by express grant or by express reservation cannot be terminated by nonuse).

THINGS AFFIXED TO THE LAND

The third broad category of real property is "that which is affixed to the land," such as:

1. Things attached to the land by roots, such as trees;
2. Things imbedded in the land, such as walls;
3. Things permanently resting upon the land, such as buildings; and
4. Things "permanently attached to what is thus permanent, as by means of cement, plaster, nails, bolts, or screws." CC §660.

Natural attachments, such as natural trees and vines, that are attached to the earth by roots are considered to be part of the land. However, once such natural vegetation is severed from the land or harvested it becomes personal property. Trees, shrubs, vines, and other plantings by humans are also considered real property, but the crops growing on such plantings are treated as personal property.

Growing crops, such as grapes, avocados, and apples, that are produced seasonally through a tenant farmer's labor and industry are called **emblements**. Emblements are considered the personal property of the tenant farmer, and the **doctrine of emblements** holds that even if the tenancy expires before harvest, the tenant may harvest and remove the crops he or she had planted. Unless otherwise specified, upon transfer of the land, growing plants, natural or human-planted, would transfer with the land, but a tenant farmer would still be able to remove that season's crops.

Fixtures

A fixture is a thing, originally personal property, that is attached to the land in such a manner as to be considered real property. For example, lumber, which is personal property, becomes a fixture when it is used to build a pergola. Sometimes — as with lumber being used to construct shelving — it is not altogether clear whether the item has become a fixture or remains personal property. The courts have established five **tests of a fixture** to determine whether an item of personal property is a fixture. It might be of help to remember these five tests by the mnemonic, "MARIA": method of attachment, adaptability, relationship of the parties, intent, and agreement between the parties.

Method of Attachment

The degree of permanence of the fixed item is significant. An item attached by cement or plaster, for example, is likely to be classified as a fixture. Thus, a bookcase built into a wall and securely nailed or bolted thereto is a fixture; but a freestanding bookcase remains personal property. Also, fixtures that have been temporarily removed for repair remain fixtures — as, for example, a built-in dishwasher that has been sent out for repairs.

Adaptability of the Attached Item

If an item of personal property is attached to real property and is well adapted for use with that real property, the item is probably a fixture. Wall-to-wall carpeting, for example, is cut specifically for a room or rooms of a specific property, is well adapted for use on that property, and would, therefore, be a fixture. Even an item of personal property that is not physically attached to real property may be so well and specifically suited for use on the property as to be considered "constructively attached" and therefore a fixture of the real property — as, for example, a key to the front door.

Relationship of the Parties

Also of significance is the relationship between the person who installs an item of personal property on real property and the person with whom a dispute arises as to whether the installed item is a fixture. Such a situation would usually involve a tenant and landlord or a seller and buyer. All other considerations being equal, it is generally held that a tenant who installs an item, such as a chandelier, intends to remove the item at the expiration of the lease. However, an owner who installs the same chandelier likely did so with the intention of improving the property, thus making this chandelier a fixture. Following similar reasoning, buyers are usually favored over sellers and lenders are favored over borrowers when it comes to deciding whether an item is a fixture. It should be obvious that to avoid disagreements, and possibly expensive litigation, over what is or is not a fixture, tenants and landlords — and sellers and buyers — should carefully put in writing what they deem to be personal property or fixtures.

Intent of the Person Attaching the Item

The intention of the person incorporating an item into the land is considered to be the most significant test for determining whether the item is a fixture. Each of the other tests of a fixture is used as evidence of the incorporator's intention. For example, cementing a bench into the foundation of an outdoor patio would be evidence that the owner intended to make the bench a permanent fixture, whereas merely setting a bench out onto the patio would not.

Agreement Between the Parties

The courts look to any agreement between the parties involved to determine the nature of items affixed to the land. Such agreements can be manifested in real estate listings and in purchase or lease contracts. Even informal correspondence between the parties can be evidence of agreement.

Exceptions to the Removability of Fixtures

There are two exceptions to the general rule that fixtures are part of real property and may not be removed.

Trade Fixtures

A **trade fixture**, often called a "chattel" fixture, is an object that a tenant attaches to real property for use in the tenant's trade or business. Trade fixtures differ from other fixtures in that, even though they are attached with some permanence to real property, they may be removed at the end of the tenancy of the business. Examples include store shelves, display counters, and machining equipment, even if cemented into the property's foundation. However, the business tenant must compensate the real property owner for any damage caused by the removal of trade fixtures.

Encroachments — Good-Faith Improvers

An **encroachment** is a thing affixed under, on, or above the land of another without permission. If the one who affixed the improvement did so knowing that he or she was trespassing on the property of another, the thing so affixed would belong to the owner of the land.

If, however, as is usually the case, the encroachment was done by a person in good faith and erroneous belief because of a mistake of law or fact that he or she had the right to do so, then the person who fixed the thing to the land of another has the right to remove it upon payment of damages to the owner of the land. *CC §1013.5.* If the injury to the land upon which the improvement was made is slight and the cost of removing the improvement great, a court of equity (in action of **ejectment** brought by the owner of the land) may order that only damages be paid and that the **good-faith improver** may keep the improvements in place and not have to remove them.

In the case of an encroachment *on land* by a good-faith improver, there is a three-year statute of limitation to bring an ejectment action. If the landowner fails to bring an ejectment action within three years of learning of the encroachment (or within three years of the time that he or she should have become aware of the encroachment), then the right to sue for damages or removal would be lost. However, in the case of an encroachment *above land*, such as the encroachment of an overhanging tree limb or an overhanging balcony, there is no statute limitation, and a suit to remove can be brought at any time.

Limitations on the Right to Use and Enjoy One's Property

The right to use and enjoy one's property does not mean that one may use and enjoy it without restriction in any manner one wishes.

Nuisance

Just as a property owner's water rights are limited to reasonable use in the context of the reasonable use of water by others, a person may not commit a **nuisance**, defined as anything that is "indecent or offensive to the senses, or an obstruction to the free use of property, so as to interfere with the comfortable enjoyment of life or property..." CC §3479.

An action to remedy a private nuisance may be for money damages, injunctive relief, or removal (**abatement**) of the nuisance. If a person can remove the nuisance without entering another's land, as, for example, if tree roots or vines have crept onto the person's property, the person may remove or if necessary destroy the thing causing the nuisance without first seeking court action. But if the thing causing the nuisance cannot be removed without entering upon another's land, one must bring an abatement action, during which the court will balance the proposed remedies of removal or injunction against the damages caused by the nuisance. In making such a determination, the court will also take into consideration the motives of the parties who are causing the nuisance or are seeking to abate the nuisance.

Private Restrictions

Individuals who wish to limit the use of their land generally may do so unless such restrictions are against the law. Examples of private restrictions include the giving of land to a conservation group with the restriction that it not be developed, or an agreement between neighbors that neither will build a swimming pool on his or her land. Examples of unenforceable restrictions due to illegality include agreements to restrict the sale of property to persons of a particular race, ethnicity, or religion. If a private restriction and a zoning ordinance are at variance, whichever is more restrictive will prevail.

Private restrictions (also referred to as deed restrictions) are either **covenants** or **conditions**. A covenant is a promise placed in a deed, stating that the owner will do or not do something. Remedies for breach of a covenant are either monetary or injunctive relief.

Conditions (often called **conditions subsequent**) that are placed in a deed can have more serious consequences if breached; namely, forfeiture of title. An example would be where A sells to B a parcel of land "on the condition" that the land never be used for the sale of alcoholic beverages. If B subsequently uses that parcel of land to sell alcoholic beverages, a court may order a forfeiture of the parcel back to A. However, the law "abhors forfeiture" (an English common law maxim of equity). Courts, therefore, will often try to construe a restriction as being a covenant rather than a condition (such as in a case of ambiguous language) and impose monetary or injunctive relief for a breach rather than forfeiture of title.

Most private restrictions are applied to entire subdivisions (including condominiums) and are known as **CC&Rs** ("covenants, conditions, and restrictions"). CC&Rs generally are negative covenants (not conditions) whereby persons agree to limit certain things, such as the color of paint on houses or the type of architecture used to build or remodel houses.

LAND DESCRIPTIONS

A land description (also known as a "legal description") is a description that properly delineates and identifies a piece of property and which describes no other piece of property. A requirement of a transfer of real property is that the instrument of conveyance (the deed) include a legal description of the property.

There are three main methods of describing real property:

1. The **recorded map method**;
2. The U.S. Government **sections and township method**; and
3. The **metes and bounds method**.

RECORDED MAP METHOD

The recorded map method (also called the "lot, block, and tract" method) is the most recently developed method of land description and is the simplest of the three land description methods to understand. A **subdivision** is what results when a large parcel of land is divided into smaller parcels. The California Map Act requires a mapping of all new subdivisions. The subdivision map describes the subdivision by reference to a particular lot and block in a particular city and county.

> **Example:** "All of Lot 6 of Block A of Tract number 355 in the city of San Bernardino, County of San Bernardino, State of California, as per map recorded in Book 23, page 67, of maps in the office of the county recorder of said county." (See Fig. 1.1)

SECTIONS AND TOWNSHIP METHOD

California has three sets of horizontal *base lines* and vertical *meridians*:

1. The *Humboldt Base Line and Meridian* in the northern part of the state;
2. The *Mt. Diablo Base Line and Meridian* in the central part of the state; and
3. The *San Bernardino Base Line and Meridian* in the southern part of the state.

The U.S government section and township method establishes a grid of horizontal lines (*township lines* or *tier lines*) that run parallel to the base lines, and vertical lines (*range lines*) that run parallel to the meridians. The township lines are 6 miles apart, as are the range lines.

The description "township 3 north, range 2 east, Mt. Diablo Base Line and Meridian" (typically abbreviated as "T3N, R2E, MDBL&M") is a description of the township that is 3 townships north from the Mt. Diablo Base Line and 2 townships east from the Mt. Diablo Base Meridian.

A *section* is an area one square mile, containing 640 acres. Creating sections of 640 acres makes for ease of dividing into halves, quarters, and so on through seven divisions, down to 5 acres. A township is a six mile square parcel of land consisting of 36 sections. The sections in each township are uniformly numbered from 1 to 36, with Section 1 located in the northeast corner and the Section 36 located in the southeast corner. (See Fig. 1.2)

Measurement Anomalies

Due to such factors as the curvature of the earth and early survey measurement errors, it is not uncommon for sections of certain townships to differ from the ideal of one square mile. In such cases, distortions and errors are distributed to the northern row and western column of sections of the township.

When working with land measurements, it is often helpful to remember the following:

- 1 acre = 43,560 square feet
- 1 square acre ≈ 208.7 ft. x 208.7 ft.
- 1 mile = 5,280 feet or 320 rods
- 1 rod = 16½ ft.
- A *commercial acre* = the buildable part of an acre that remains after subtracting land needed for streets, sidewalks, and curbs.
- 1 township = 6 mi. x 6 mi. = 36 sections
- 1 section = 1 mi. x 1 mi. = 640 acres

METES AND BOUNDS METHOD

Metes and bounds is a method of describing a parcel of land that uses physical features of the locale, along with directions and distances, to define the boundaries of the parcel. **Metes** is a term referring to the measurement of length, in units such as feet, meters, and miles. **Bounds** refers to boundaries such as rivers and roads. Starting with a **point of beginning**, such as an iron stake, an old oak tree, or the intersection of two walls, the boundaries of a parcel are described, working in sequence around the parcel, and finally ending at the beginning point.

The metes and bounds method of describing land may be used when the property is not covered by a recorded map or has irregular contours, such as in mountainous areas. A difficulty with this method of describing land is that old oak trees can be cut down, walls can be removed, and even rivers can change course.

Fig. 1.1	Lot 6 of Block A of Tract number 355	
1	2	3
4	5	6*
7	8	9

Fig. 1.2	A theoretical township showing numbered sections (large type) and adjacent township sections (smaller type).						
36	31	32	33	34	35	36	31
1	**6**	**5**	**4**	**3**	**2**	**1**	6
12	**7**	**8**	**9**	**10**	**11**	**12**	7
13	**18**	**17**	**16**	**15**	**14**	**13**	18
24	**19**	**20**	**21**	**22**	**23**	**24**	19
25	**30**	**29**	**28**	**27**	**26**	**25**	30
36	**31**	**32**	**33**	**34**	**35**	**36**	31
1	6	5	4	3	2	1	6

Key Terms for Chapter 1

abatement — a legal action to remove a nuisance.

appropriation, right of — the legal right to take possession of and use for beneficial purposes water from streams or other bodies of water.

appurtenance — an object, right or interest that is incidental to the land and goes with or pertains to the land.

base lines — in the Sections and Township method of land description, California has three sets of base lines, which are east-west lines, and meridians, which are north-south lines.

bill of sale — a written document given by a seller to a purchaser of personal property.

bundle of rights — rights the law attributes to ownership of property.

capture, law of — the legal right of a landowner to all of the gas, oil, and steam produced from wells drilled directly underneath on his or her property, even if the gas, oil, or steam migrates from below a neighbor's property.

commercial acre — the buildable part of an acre that remains after subtracting land needed for streets, sidewalks, and curbs.

condition subsequent — a condition that, upon its occurrence, can result in the forfeiture of an interest in property.

covenant — a contractual promise to do or not do certain acts, the remedy for breach thereof being either monetary damages or injunctive relief, not forfeiture.

CC&Rs — an abbreviation of "covenants, conditions, and restrictions" — often used to refer to restrictions recorded by a developer on an entire subdivision.

deed — a document that when signed by the grantor and legally delivered to the grantee conveys title to real property.

dominant tenement — land that is benefited by an easement appurtenant.

easement — a non-possessory right to use a portion of another property owner's land for a specific purpose, as for a right-of-way, without paying rent or being considered a trespasser.

easement appurtenant — an easement that benefits, and is appurtenant to, another's land.

easement by necessity —arises as a creation of a court of law in certain cases were justice so demands, as in the case where a buyer of a parcel of land discovers that the land he or she just purchased has no access except over the land of someone other than from the person from whom the parcel was purchased.

easement in gross — an easement that benefits a legal person rather than other land.

ejectment — a legal action to recover possession of real property from a person who is not legally entitled to possess it, such as to remove an encroachment or to evict a defaulting buyer or tenant.

emblements — growing crops, such as grapes, avocados, and apples, that are produced seasonally through a tenant farmer's labor and industry.

encroachment — a thing affixed under, on, or above the land of another without permission.

encumber — To place a lien or other encumbrance on property.

encumbrance — A right or interest held by someone other than the owner the property that affects or limits the ownership of the property, such as easements and liens.

fixture — an object, originally personal property, that is attached to the land in such a manner as to be considered real property.

good-faith improver — a person who, because of a mistake of law or fact, makes an improvement to land in good faith and under erroneous belief that he or she is the owner of the land.

implied easement — an easement arising by implication, as when a purchaser of mineral rights automatically acquires an implied right to enter the property to extract the minerals.

lateral support — the support that soil receives from the land adjacent to it.

lot, block, and tract land description — (see "recorded map land description")

metes and bounds land description — a method of describing a parcel of land that uses physical features of the locale, along with directions and distances, to define the boundaries of the parcel.

meridians — (see and compare "base lines")

nuisance — anything that is indecent or offensive to the senses, or an obstruction to the free use of property, so as to interfere with the comfortable enjoyment of life or property.

point of beginning — the fixed starting point in the metes and bounds method of land description.

profit á prendre — the right to enter another's land for such purposes as to drill for oil, mine for coal, or cut and remove timber.

recorded map land description — a method of land description that states a property's lot, block, and tract number, referring to a map recorded in the county where the property is located.

riparian rights — the rights of a landowner to use water from a stream or lake adjacent to his or her property, provided such use is reasonable and does not injure other riparian owners.

section — one square mile, containing 640 acres.

sections and township land description — a method of land description based on a grid system of north-south lines ("ranges") and east-west lines ("tier" or "township" lines) that divides the land into townships and sections.

servient tenement — land that is burdened by an easement.

subjacent support — the support that soil receives from land beneath it.

township — six square miles, containing 36 sections.

trade fixtures — objects that a tenant attaches to real property for use in the tenant's trade or business. Trade fixtures differ from other fixtures in that, even though they are attached with some permanence to real property, they may be removed at the end of the tenancy of the business.

Treaty of Guadalupe Hidalgo —the treaty that ended the Mexican-American war (1846-48), annexed California to the United States, and provided for the recognition of community property rights in California.

Quiz for Chapter 1

1. The treaty that ended the Mexican-American War is
   a. the Treaty of Paris
   b. the Treaty of Ghent
   c. the Treaty of Guadalupe Hidalgo
   d. the Treaty Versailles
2. California became a state in what year?
   a. 1850
   b. 1848
   c. 1822
   d. 1864
3. The support that soil receives from the land adjacent to it is called
   a. a fixture
   b. subjacent support
   c. an emblement
   d. lateral support
4. A person who, because of a mistake of law or fact, makes an improvement to land in good faith and under erroneous belief that he is the owner of the land is called
   a. a trespasser
   b. a licensee
   c. a good-faith improver
   d. a tenant
5. An item that remains the personal property of a tenant who uses the item in a trade or business is called
   a. a fixture
   b. real property
   c. a trade fixture
   d. an appurtenance
6. An object, right or interest that is incidental to the land and goes with or pertains to the land is called
   a. lateral support
   b. an emblement
   c. an appurtenance
   d. a trade fixture
7. An area six miles square, containing 36 sections is a
   a. tract
   b. township
   c. rural acre

    d. meridian

8. Mineral rights that are sold separate from the land
    a. are personal property
    b. are real property
    c. carry an implied right to enter the land for extraction
    d. both b and c

9. The rights of a landowner to use water from a stream or lake adjacent to his or her property are
    a. bounds
    b. points of beginning
    c. riparian rights
    d. personal property

10. The law of capture states that oil in its natural state below a parcel of land
    a. is always owned by the owner of the land
    b. is sometimes owned by the owner of the land
    c. is never owned by the owner of the land
    d. none of the above

11. A landowner owns all of the airspace above his or her land
    a. up to tree height
    b. up to a reasonable height
    c. up to a distance of 1/2 mile
    d. up to a distance of 1 mile

12. A property described as the W 1/2 of the NW 1/4 and the SW 1/4 of the SE 1/4 of the E 1/2 of Section 2 contains how many acres?
    a. 100
    b. 80
    c. 120
    d. none of the above

13. The most significant test for determining whether an item is a fixture is
    a. the relationship between the parties
    b. how adaptable the item is to the real property
    c. the method of attachment
    d. the intention of the person attaching the item

14. Trade fixtures are sometimes referred to as
    a. real property
    b. chattel fixtures
    c. appurtenances
    d. metes

15. A key to the front door of a residence is
    a. personal property
    b. a metal object
    c. a common and inexpensive item
    d. real property

16. A method of land description that states a property's lot, block, and tract number, referring to a map recorded in the county where the property is located
    a. Sections and Township land description
    b. U.S. Government Homestead land description
    c. County Map land description
    d. Recorded Map land description
17. In a township, how far is section number 4 from section number 33?
    a. 3 miles
    b. 4 miles
    c. 5 miles
    d. 6 miles
18. For determining whether an item is a fixture, the "relationship of the parties" test favors
    a. the tenant over the landlord
    b. the seller over the buyer
    c. the borrower over the lender
    d. both a and c
19. Which of the following is considered part of real estate?
    a. harvested crops
    b. trade fixtures
    c. oil and gas deposits below the land
    d. none of the above
20. In order for an easement appurtenant to exist, there must be
    a. a servient tenement
    b. a dominant tenement
    c. both a and b
    d. neither a nor b
21. Smoke wafting over one person's property from another's property is most likely
    a. an encroachment
    b. a nuisance
    c. a servient easement
    d. a temporary lien
22. An easement created by reservation would be terminated through
    a. extended nonuse
    b. the owner of the dominant tenement acquiring the servient tenement
    c. destruction of the servient tenement
    d. both b and c
23. All of the following are nuisances except
    a. and overhanging balcony
    b. radiation from a power line
    c. smell from a factory
    d. each of a, b, and c would be considered a nuisance

24. A cable company has the right to enter your front yard to maintain its cable lines. The cable company probably has
    a. a license
    b. a dominant tenement
    c. an easement appurtenant
    d. an easement in gross
25. A wind chime hanging by twine from a tree branch is
    a. a fixture
    b. real property
    c. personal property
    d. both a and c

Answers for Chapter 1

1. c. The Treaty of Guadalupe Hidalgo ended the Mexican-American war (1846-48), annexed California to the United States, and provided for the recognition of community property rights in California.

2. a. Though California was annexed to the United States in 1848, it did not become a state until 1850.

3. d. Neighboring lands provide lateral support to a property, whereas subjacent support is provided by earth beneath a property.

4. c. A good-faith improver is a person who, because of a mistake of law or fact, makes an improvement to land in good faith and under erroneous belief that he or she is the owner of the land.

5. c. Trade fixtures are objects that a tenant attaches to real property for use in the tenant's trade or business. Trade fixtures differ from other fixtures in that, even though they are attached with some permanence to real property, they may be removed at the end of the tenancy of the business.

6. c. An appurtenance is an object, right or interest that is incidental to the land and goes with or pertains to the land.

7. b. A township is an area of six miles square, containing 36 sections.

8. d. The minerals themselves might not be real property (such as is the case with oil) but the mineral *rights* that go with the land are considered real property.

9. c. Riparian rights refer to the rights of a landowner to use water from a stream or lake adjacent to his or her property, provided such use is reasonable and does not injure other riparian owners.

10. c. By the law of capture, no person owns oil in its natural state until it is captured.

11. b. Though in the days before flying machines came into being the owner of land was considered to own airspace indefinitely high, contemporary law states that an owner owns all of the airspace above his or her land up to a reasonable height — reasonable to be determined on a case-by-case basis.

12. a. Since Section 2 contains 640 acres, the northwest quarter of Section 2 contains 160 acres and the west half of that parcel contains 80 acres. Similarly,

the east half of Section 2 contains 320 acres, a quarter of that is 80 acres, and a quarter of that is 20 acres. Combining the two parcels, 80+20, gives us 100 acres.

13.   d. As a general rule, courts find that the most significant test for determining whether an item is a fixture is the intention of the person who attached the item to the land.

14. b. Though the word "chattel" refers to personal property that is not sufficiently affixed to real property so as to be considered a fixture, a trade fixture, while being a fixture, is nevertheless considered to be personal property, and as such is sometimes referred to as a "chattel fixture."

15. d. A key to a house is uniquely adapted to the house and is a fixture. [Note: always choose the best answer — a high-tech key need be neither metal nor inexpensive.

16. d. The Recorded Map land description is also referred to as the Lot, Block, and Tract system of land description.

17. b. Looking at figure 1.2 and counting from the bottom of section number 4 to the top of section number 33, one finds that they are 4 miles apart.

18. a. The relationship of the parties test favors the tenant over the landlord, the buyer over the seller, and the lender over the borrower.

19. d. Oil and gas deposits are not owned until "captured." However, the rights to drill for oil and gas are considered real property.

20. c. An easement appurtenant requires both a servient tenement to burden and a dominant tenement to benefit.

21. b. Smoke would not be considered an encroachment because it is transient, not affixed to property.

22. d. An easement created by reservation cannot be terminated by nonuse, unless expressly so stated in the reservation.

23. a. An overhanging balcony would be considered an encroachment, not a nuisance.

24. d. Because there is no indication in the question that the cable company owns adjacent land, there is no dominant tenement here; therefore, the easement is one that benefits a legal person (the cable company) rather than other land.

25. c. A wind chime so attached has not become permanently affixed to the land and so is not a fixture.

Estates in Land

CHARACTERISTICS OF AN ESTATE

Buyers, renters, and lenders are concerned not only in what property (bundle of rights) they are acquiring an interest in; they are also concerned with the measure of the quality and the quantity of the rights they are obtaining. An *estate* refers to the degree, quantity, nature, duration, or extent of interest one has in real property — though, as we shall see in subsequent chapters, not all interests in property, such as mortgages, are considered estates.

The primary characteristic of an estate is its duration. If the estate's duration is potentially indefinite or for the length of someone's life (not necessarily for the estate holder's life), the estate is called a *freehold estate*. Freehold estates include *fee simple estates* and *fee simple defeasible estates* as well as *life estates* and their future interests. All other estates are called *less-than-freehold estates*. Less-than-freehold estates include *estates for years*, *estates from period to period*, *estates at will*, and *estates at sufferance*. (See Fig. 2.1)

FREEHOLD ESTATES

The characteristic that distinguishes a freehold estate from a less-than-freehold estate is its indefinite duration. How long an individual's freehold estate will last is unknown, because it may be transferred whenever the owner wishes. Freehold estates (other than life estates) are sometimes referred to as *estates of inheritance* because they can be inherited. (See Fig. 2.2)

FEE SIMPLE ABSOLUTE

The fee simple absolute estate is the greatest estate that the law permits in land. It is "the best you can get," and when a buyer purchases land, he or she generally purchases a fee simple absolute estate. Indeed, the law presumes that a fee simple absolute is being transferred unless specific words limiting the rights transferred are used at the time of conveyance.

The description "absolute" is perhaps a bit inflated, because the estate can still be subject to other restrictions, such as zoning codes and building restrictions. These governmental restrictions do not, however, affect title, and they are not found in the deed.

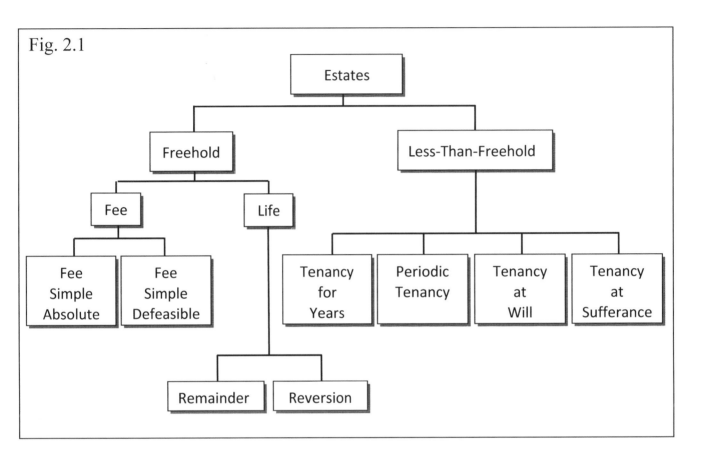

Fig. 2.1

FEE SIMPLE DEFEASIBLE

Fee simple defeasible refers to a fee estate that is qualified by some condition that, if violated, may "defeat" the estate and lead to its loss and reversion to the grantor. Such conditions, called **conditions subsequent,** are infrequently used today as a means of private land restriction. To enforce a condition subsequent, the condition must be valid and the grantor must timely file a lawsuit to get the property back.

Many attempts at private land restriction that were used in the past, such as transfer restrictions relating to race or ethnicity, are considered void by modern law, and the grantee of a deed containing such restrictions may petition the courts to have such restrictions stricken from the deed.

Fig. 2.2

Type of a freehold estate transferred by Grantor A	Words typically used in the deed to create	Future interest in the estate	Action needed to create the future interest
Fee simple absolute	Grant to B and his/her heirs	B has all present and future interests	N/A
Fee simple defeasible	To B on the condition that	B's estate may be terminated upon the happening of the condition	A may terminate B's estate but must do so timely
Life estate	To B for life	Reversion	Future interest automatically reverts to A
	To B (or A) for life, then to C	Remainder	All interests automatically go to C

LIFE ESTATES

A life estate is a freehold estate the duration of which is measured by the life of a natural person — either by the life of the person holding the estate, or by the life or lives of one or more other persons. There are two recognized categories of life estates. If, at the end of the estate, the future interest reverts to the grantor, the residue of the estate is called a *reversion*. If, at the end of the estate, the future interest arises in a third person C, the residue of the estate is called a *remainder* and C is called a *remainderman*. Probably the most common use of life estates is for Grantor A to keep a life estate interest in the property for his/her life, granting the remainder to an heir or heirs. (See Fig. 2.3)

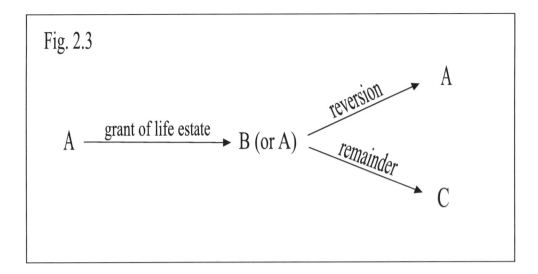

Fig. 2.3

The owner of a life estate possesses most of the rights in the property as does an owner of a fee simple absolute estate. Unless expressly restrained in the grant of the life estate, the life tenant may rent, encumber, or sell his or her interest. Of course, once the life estate terminates, any such lease, encumbrance, or transfer of rights by the life tenant also terminates.

A life tenant has certain duties and obligations, such as the making of necessary repairs to structures and the paying of taxes. Additionally, a life tenant is obligated to act reasonably to avoid harming ("wasting") the value of the future interest of the property.

LESS-THAN-FREEHOLD ESTATES

The holder of a less-than-freehold estate (also known as a **nonfreehold estate** or a **leasehold estate**) has the exclusive right to possession of land for a length of time. The holder of a less-than-freehold estate is usually referred to as a **lessee** (or tenant); the owner of the property is referred to as the **lessor** (or landlord). When referring to leasehold estates, the terms "tenancy" and "estate" are used interchangeably. The four types of leasehold estates differ according to their characteristics, creation, duration, limitation on term, and termination. Though defined here, leasehold estates are discussed in greater detail in Chapter 13, "Landlord/Tenant Relations and Property Management."

An **estate for years** is a leasehold that continues for a fixed period of time. Unlike what the name implies, the lease need not be for a period measured in years — it only need be for a definite period, whether for days, months, or years. The term of a lease for agricultural or horticultural purposes cannot exceed 51 years; the term of a lease for a city lot cannot exceed 99 years; and the term of a lease for the production of oil, gas, or minerals cannot exceed 99 years.

An ***estate from period to period*** (commonly called a ***periodic tenancy***) continues from period to period, whether by days, months, or years, until terminated by proper notice.

An ***estate at will*** has no specified duration, though it may only be terminated by the owner of the property upon giving proper notice. An estate at will arises when a tenant takes possession of a property while negotiating a lease or under a void contract or lease. If, during an estate at will, the owner accepts rent, the estate automatically becomes a periodic tenancy.

An ***estate at sufferance*** arises when a lessee who legally obtained possession of a property remains on the property after the termination of the lease without the owner's consent. Such a holdover tenant can be evicted like a trespasser, but if the owner accepts rent, the estate automatically becomes a periodic tenancy. (See Figure 2.4).

LICENSE TO USE

A ***license***, unlike a lease or an easement, is not a real property interest; it is a right to use that is merely personal to the licensee.

> **Example:** Owner A of a storage unit may give a friend B the right to store some of B's belongings in A's storage unit, but B (unlike a leaseholder) does not have *exclusive* possession of the storage unit. Similarly, a hotel gives the right to use one of its rooms to a guest, but the guest (unlike a leaseholder) does not have the right to exclusive possession of the room, as the hotel reserves the right of inspection and maid service.

In the above examples, the friend of the storage unit owner and the hotel guest have a personal right to use the property. The important differences between a lease and a license are that the lessee has the exclusive right to possession of the property (the licensee only has the non-exclusive right to use) and the lessee has a statutory right to be given written notice that his or her rights in the property are being revoked (the licensee does not).

A license is not considered an estate; it does not run with the land. If ownership of the property that the licensee has permission to use is transferred, the license is automatically revoked.

Fig. 2.4   Less-Than-Freehold Estates

	Estate for years	Estate from period to period	Estate at will	Estate at sufferance
Characteristics	Continues for a definite term — a fraction or a multiple of a year — with definite beginning and ending dates.	Continues for an indefinite term, but with a definite beginning date and definite duration of each period. Conditions of the lease carryover from period to period.	Indefinite term. Begins with permission under a now terminated contract or lease. Continues only with the consent of landlord.	No term at all. Begins with a now terminated contract or lease, but occupant is holding over without permission.
Creation	If the term is greater than one year, then by written lease; otherwise, an oral lease is permitted.	Presumed by law; by agreement; or by accepting the rent at the end of a fixed lease period.	By taking possession while negotiating a lease or under a void contract or lease.	Remaining in possession after the end of a lease term.
Duration	Definite term stated in lease as so many days, weeks, months, or years.	Indefinite term continuing period to period until terminated.	Statutory minimum notice of 30 days must be given.	No duration
Limitation on term	The term may not exceed 99 years for city lots or 51 years for agricultural land.	Presumed to be month to month for city lots unless otherwise stated in writing.	Acceptance of rent creates a month-to-month tenancy, or as otherwise agreed.	Acceptance of rent creates a month-to-month tenancy, or as otherwise agreed.
Termination	Automatically terminates at the end of the term.	By giving proper notice, or as agreed in the lease.	By giving 30-day notice.	By action of a court through an eviction proceeding.

Key Terms for Chapter 2

condition subsequent — a condition written into the deed of a fee estate that, if violated, may "defeat" the estate and lead to its loss and reversion to the grantor.

estate — the degree, quantity, nature, duration, or extent of interest one has in real property.

estate at sufferance — a leasehold that arises when a lessee who legally obtained possession of a property remains on the property after the termination of the lease without the owner's consent. Such a holdover tenant can be evicted like a trespasser, but if the owner accepts rent, the estate automatically becomes a periodic tenancy.

estate at will — a leasehold that has no specified duration, though it may only be terminated by the owner of the property upon giving proper notice. An estate at will arises when a tenant takes possession of a property while negotiating a lease or under a void contract or lease.

estate for years — a leasehold that continues for a definite fixed period of time, measured in days, months, or years.

estate from period to period — a leasehold that continues from period to period, whether by days, months, or years, until terminated by proper notice.

estate of inheritance — a freehold estate other than a life estate.

fee simple defeasible estate — a fee estate that is qualified by some condition that, if violated, may "defeat" the estate and lead to its loss and reversion to the grantor.

fee simple absolute estate — the greatest estate that the law permits in land. The owner of a fee simple absolute estate owns all present and future interests in the property.

freehold estate — an estate in land whereby the holder of the estate owns rights in the property for an indefinite duration.

leasehold estate — a less-than-freehold estate.

lessee — a person (the tenant) who leases property from another.

lessor — a person (the landlord) who leases property to another.

less-than-freehold estate — an estate in which the holder has the exclusive right to possession of land for a length of time. The holder of a less-than-freehold estate is usually referred to as a lessee or tenant.

license to use —a personal right to use property on a nonexclusive basis. A license to use is not considered an estate.

life estate — a freehold estate the duration of which is measured by the life of a natural person — either by the life of the person holding the estate, or by the life or lives of one or more other persons.

periodic tenancy — an estate from period to period.

remainder — the residue of a freehold estate where, at the end of the estate, the future interest arises in a third person.

remainderman — a person who inherits or is entitled to inherit property held as a life estate when the person whose life determines the duration of the life estate passes away.

reversion — the residue of a freehold estate where at the end of the estate, the future interest reverts to the grantor.

Quiz for Chapter 2

1. Of the following, which is not an estate?
   a. fee simple defeasible
   b. lease
   c. mortgage
   d. fee simple absolute
2. Nonfreehold estates include which of the following?
   a. fee simple defeasible
   b. estate for years
   c. estate at will
   d. both b and c
3. A lease for 25 days would describe a(n)
   a. periodic tenancy
   b. estate for years
   c. estate at will
   d. estate at sufferance
4. A conveyance of title with the condition that the premises not be used for the sale of alcoholic beverages creates a(n)
   a. estate at will
   b. less-than-freehold estate
   c. estate at sufferance
   d. fee simple defeasible
5. Jane was granted a residence for the term of her life. Which of the following is correct?
   a. Jane has a fee simple defeasible
   b. Jane has a reversionary interest
   c. Jane has a less-than-freehold estate
   d. if Jane leases the residence to Susan, the lease will terminate if Jane dies during the term of the lease
6. Bob, a life tenant, decides to tear down the detached guesthouse and construct a memorial for his recently deceased mother. Joe, the grantor who owns the reversionary interest in the property, can stop Bob from demolishing the guesthouse because
   a. under no circumstances can a life tenant demolish an existing guesthouse
   b. Joe's interest is superior to Bob's because Joe granted the life estate and owns the reversionary interest
   c. a life tenant cannot commit waste

   d. Joe cannot stop Bob because Bob has exclusive possession for life
      and has no use whatsoever for a guesthouse

7. An estate at will can be terminated
   a. upon giving 10 days notice
   b. by either party at any time
   c. upon giving 30 days notice
   d. only after a court orders eviction

8. A lease from June 1 to June 30 is a(n)
   a. estate for years
   b. periodic tenancy
   c. estate at will
   d. estate at sufferance

9. If Ann dies before Joe, an estate in which Bob granted to Ann an estate
   for the life of Joe
   a. reverts to Bob
   b. vests in Joe for his life
   c. vests in whoever is entitled to Ann's interest in the estate for the life
      of Joe
   d. ceases to exist

10. A freehold estate is also known as a(n)
    a. estate of inheritance
    b. estate at remainder
    c. estate in full
    d. estate at will

11. The holder of a title subject to a condition owns a(n)
    a. fee simple absolute
    b. estate in restriction
    c. estate at will
    d. fee simple defeasible

12. A leasehold estate is a(n)
    a. less-than-freehold estate
    b. fee simple defeasible
    c. estate in remainder
    d. estate at term

13. If Jane rents an apartment to Susan "for $700 a month," Susan is
    presumed to have a(n)
    a. estate at will
    b. estate for years
    c. periodic tenancy
    d. fee simple defeasible

14. A grants to B a life estate for the life of C, remainder to D. D is a(n)
    a. remainderman
    b. life tenant
    c. licensee

    d. owner of an estate for years

15. A periodic tenancy is a(n)
    a. fee simple defeasible
    b. erratic tenancy
    c. estate at will
    d. estate from period to period

16. A condition subsequent is
    a. a reversion
    b. a remainder
    c. a license to use
    d. none of the above

17. The estate constituting the greatest degree of ownership in property is a(n)
    a. life estate
    b. fee simple absolute
    c. inheritance
    d. none of the above

18. Joe has leased a house from Bob on a year-to-year basis for the past 10 years. Near the end of the 10th year, Bob gives Joe proper notice to quit, but Joe refuses to leave and Bob refuses to accept Joe's continued lease payments. Joe has a(n)
    a. estate at will
    b. month-to-month tenancy
    c. year grace period as long as he offers proper lease payments
    d. estate at sufferance

19. A remainderman is
    a. the grantor who receives property back at the end of a life estate
    b. the owner of a life estate
    c. the owner of an estate at will
    d. none of the above

20. Bob gives Joe permission to store some of Joe's excess stuff in Bob's garage at no charge. Joe has a(n)
    a. estate at will
    b. estate at sufferance
    c. a good friend
    d. license to use

Answers for Chapter 2

1. c. Though a mortgage is an interest in land, it is not considered an estate.
2. d. Nonfreehold estates are leaseholds such as an estate for years and an estate at will.
3. b. The lease is for a fixed period with a definite beginning and ending.
4. d. A fee simple defeasible estate is a fee estate that is qualified by some condition that, if violated, may "defeat" the estate and lead to its loss and reversion to the grantor.
5. d. The life estate ended at Jane's death. A life estate cannot be extended by a lease.
6. c. Though Bob owns a life estate in the property, he may not commit waste to the property. Tearing down a guesthouse would be considered waste unless the guesthouse was worthless or perhaps a nuisance by, for example, being a fire hazard.
7. c. The estate can be terminated by giving 30 days notice; but if the tenant refuses to leave after proper notice and lease termination, the tenant would have an estate at sufferance and may have to be evicted by court order. "Self-help evictions" are not permitted in California, as they may lead to violent confrontations between the landlord and tenant.
8. a. Because this lease is for a definite period of time, it is an estate for years.
9. c. The life estate continues for the duration of Joe's life, regardless of the duration of the life tenant's life
10. a. A freehold estate is an estate in land whereby the holder of the estate owns rights in the property for an indefinite duration, and those rights can be passed through inheritance.
11. d. A fee simple defeasible estate is a fee estate that is qualified by some condition that, if violated, may "defeat" the estate and lead to its loss and reversion to the grantor.
12. a. A less-than-freehold estate is an estate in which the holder has the exclusive right to possession of land for a length of time. The holder of a less-than-freehold estate is usually referred to as a lessee or tenant.
13. c. Unless a lease clearly specifies otherwise, it is presumed to be periodic.
14. a. A remainderman is a person who inherits or is entitled to inherit property held as a life estate when the person whose life determines the duration of the life estate passes away.
15. d. A leasehold estate that goes from period to period is referred to as a periodic tenancy.

16. d. A condition subsequent is a condition written into the deed of a fee estate that, if violated, may "defeat" the estate and lead to its loss and reversion to the grantor.

17. b. A fee simple absolute estate is the type of estate that constitutes the greatest degree of ownership in real property.

18. d. Because Joe is remaining on the property after the end of the lease, he has an estate at sufferance. If Bob had accepted a rent check, then Joe would have had a month-to-month, periodic tenancy.

19. d. A remainderman is a person who inherits or is entitled to inherit property held as a life estate when the person whose life determines the duration of the life estate passes away. A grantor who receives property back at the end of a life estate does so not because of inheritance, but because he retained a reversionary interest in the life estate.

20. d. Because Bob and Joe share the use of Bob's garage and there is no indication that Bob gave Joe exclusive possession and use of a specific part of the garage, Joel merely has a license to use.

Ways of Transferring and Acquiring Real Property

Civil Code §1000 states five basic ways of transferring or acquiring property:

1. Will;
2. Succession;
3. Accession;
4. Occupancy; and
5. Transfer.

TRANSFERS OF PROPERTY UPON DEATH

Upon death, an owner's property can be transferred voluntarily to **devisees** by **will**, involuntarily to **heirs** by **intestate succession**, or involuntarily to the state by **escheat**.

WILLS

A person may designate by will (also known as a **testament**) how the property he or she accumulated during life will be transferred upon death. The person who makes the will is called a **testator** ("**testatrix**" was previously used to designate a female testator). A testator **bequeaths** personal property to **legatees**, but **devises** real property to **devisees**. Directions contained in a will are performed by an **executor** ("**executrix**" was previously used to designate a female executor) named in the will, under the supervision of a probate court (in California, probate is handled by superior courts) in a process called **probate**. If no executor was named in the will, the court appoints an **administrator** ("**administratrix**" was previously used to designate a female administrator) to carry out the directions contained in the will. A will may be changed at any time prior to the testator's death, and is therefore said to be an **ambulatory instrument**.

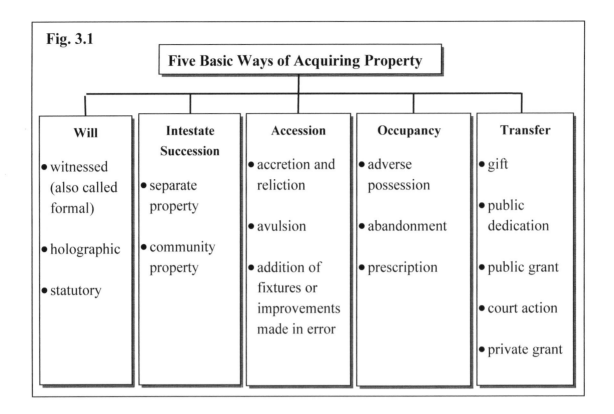

Fig. 3.1

Five Basic Ways of Acquiring Property

Will	Intestate Succession	Accession	Occupancy	Transfer
• witnessed (also called formal) • holographic • statutory	• separate property • community property	• accretion and reliction • avulsion • addition of fixtures or improvements made in error	• adverse possession • abandonment • prescription	• gift • public dedication • public grant • court action • private grant

Witnessed (or Formal) Will

A **witnessed will** generally must be

1. In writing;
2. Signed by a competent testator; and
3. Attested to by at least two competent witnesses.

In Writing

A will must be in writing. Oral wills (also called **nuncupative wills**) are no longer valid in California.

Signed

A will must be signed by the testator. If the testator (who must be mentally competent) cannot sign his or her name (for example, because of physical weakness), the testator may satisfy the signature requirement by making a mark, in which case a witness prints or types the testator's name next to the mark, with the witness signing beside the testator's name. A minor who is not emancipated must have a custodial parent or legal guardian sign the minor's will on behalf of the minor.

Witnessed

With the exception of a ***holographic will*** (discussed below), all wills must be witnessed by at least two competent persons who must also sign the will. The witnesses must either witness the testator signing the will or must ensure that the testator acknowledges his/her signature in their presence. A beneficiary of the will should not be a witness.

Holographic Wills

Though all other types of wills must be witnessed to be valid, a holographic will need not be witnessed "if the signature and the material provisions are in the handwriting of the testator." PC §6111. An undated holographic will is invalid unless evidence can establish the testator's competency at the time of the making of the will. An undated holographic will is also invalid if another will made by the testator exists and it cannot be shown that the undated holographic will was made and signed last.

Statutory Wills

California law provides a statutory will form (PC §6240) for people with relatively small estates. The will is a pre-printed "fill-in-the-blanks" form that must be signed in the presence of two competent witnesses.

INTESTATE SUCCESSION

When a person dies leaving no will, property is distributed to his or her heirs according to the laws of intestate succession. All of the community property of any intestate decedent passes to the decedent's spouse or registered domestic partner, while an intestate decedent's separate property passes as follows, pursuant to PC §§6401 and 6402:

- If the decedent leaves one child and a spouse or domestic partner — 1/2 to the spouse or domestic partner, 1/2 to the child;

- If the decedent leaves two or more children and a spouse or domestic partner — 1/3 to the spouse or domestic partner, 2/3 divided equally among the children;

- More complicated divisions are made (usually to parents or blood relatives) if the decedent leaves no spouse or domestic partner and no children.

PROBATE

Probate is a legal procedure whereby a superior court in the county where the real property is located or where the deceased resided oversees the distribution of the decedent's property in accordance with the will or, if no will, the laws of intestate succession. If it is in the best interest of the decedent's estate, the court may order the sale of some or all of the estate property. Such a sale must follow certain guidelines, summarized as follows:

- An initial offer to purchase must be for a price not less than 90% of the appraised value of the property.

- The initial bids are usually taken to the supervising court for an approval hearing, wherein the court may accept late bids, which must be at least 10% higher than the first $10,000 plus 5% higher than the balance of the highest bid being considered. (See Figure 3.2 for an example).

- The court may, at its discretion, set increments for further bids, and then confirm the sale.

- If a broker was involved in the sale, the court will grant a commission, usually at prevailing rates.

Fig. 3.2

If the bid being considered by the probate court were for $300,000, the first late overbid would need to be at least $315,500:

10% of $10,000 = $1,000
5% of $290,000 = $14,500
          $15,500   (minimum acceptable increase)
   + $300,000 (bid being considered)
     $315,500 (minimum late overbid)

ACCESSION

Accession is the acquisition of additional property by the natural processes of accretion, reliction, or avulsion, and by the human processes of the addition of fixtures or improvements made in error.

ACCRETION AND RELICTION

Accretion is a natural process by which the owner of riparian or littoral property acquires additional land by the gradual accumulation of soil through the action of water. Such addition to land is called *alluvium*. Title to alluvium belongs to the owner of the property to which it is joined.

Reliction is a natural process by which the owner of riparian or littoral property acquires additional land that has been covered by water but has become permanently uncovered by the gradual recession of water.

AVULSION

Avulsion occurs when a river or stream suddenly carries away a part of a bank and deposits it downstream, either on the same or opposite bank. The owner of the carried-away property may, within one year, reclaim his or her property; otherwise, it becomes part of the property onto which it settled.

The law relating to accession by addition of fixtures and by improvements made in error by a good-faith improver is covered in the section "Exceptions to the Removability of Fixtures" of Chapter 1.

OCCUPANCY

Real property or its use may be acquired through *adverse possession*, *abandonment*, or *prescription*.

ADVERSE POSSESSION

Adverse possession is the process by which unauthorized possession and use of another's property can ripen into ownership of that other's property without compensation. In California, five conditions that must be met before legal title through adverse possession can be acquired:

1. There must be *actual, open, and the notorious possession*. This means that the possession must not be kept secret; it must be of a kind such that the true owner of the property could discover the unauthorized possession if he or she used due diligence to inspect the property occasionally. This requirement of possession does not imply the necessity of residence on the land; exclusive use, such as by fencing off the property or by the use of the property for the cultivation of crops, will suffice. (See Figure 3.3).

2. The possession must be *exclusive and hostile* to the owner. As the word is used in adverse possession law, "hostile" does not imply physical or verbal confrontation; it means that the possession is adverse to the owner's rights or interests in the property. Therefore, permission by the owner would defeat this second requirement for adverse possession.

3. There must be a *claim of right or color of title*. If, in good faith, the possessor claims the land because of a forged or otherwise defective document, the possession is under *color of title*. Possession is by *claim of right* if the possessor, perhaps even knowing that he or she is trespassing, possesses the property with the intent to claim ownership of it and can establish evidence through action of that intention.

4. The possession must be *continuous and uninterrupted for five years*.

5. The possessor must *pay all real property taxes* during the five-year period — a requirement that makes acquisition of property by adverse possession an uncommon occurrence.

It is not possible to acquire title to government property or to property owned by an incompetent through adverse possession.

ABANDONMENT

Acquisition of title to real property by abandonment results from the extinguishment of a right or interest in the property held by one person and the concomitant acquisition of that right or interest in the property by another.

Abandonment of a Lease

If a tenant leaves the premises before the end of the lease, the landlord has the obligation of establishing that the tenant has permanently vacated (abandoned) the premises and is not just temporarily away, as, for example, merely on a vacation. California law (CC §1951.3) provides a way for the landlord to terminate the lease in case of abandonment and to re-establish control over the premises and title to any improvements that the tenant may have made.

A more in-depth discussion of a landlord's rights, duties, and obligations regarding acquisition of a lease through abandonment is contained in the subsequent chapter on landlord and tenant relations.

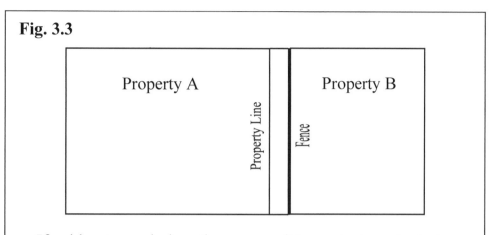

Fig. 3.3

If, without permission, the owner of Property A exclusively, continuously, and uninterruptedly occupies and pays property taxes on all of the strip of land between the property line and the fence for a period of five years and does so with the intention of laying claim to that strip of land, that strip of land would likely be acquired by the owner of Property A by adverse possession.

Abandonment of an Easement

An *easement* is a right or interest in the land of another for a particular use; for example, for use as an access road or driveway, or for installing power or water lines. The rights or interests that compose an easement can be abandoned (and thereby acquired by another) if during the past 20 years the easement was not used, no property tax was paid for the easement, and no instrument evidencing the easement was recorded. CC §887.050. An exception is a prescriptive easement (discussed below), which can be abandoned after 5 years of nonuse.

PRESCRIPTION

Similar to adverse possession, a *prescriptive easement* can be acquired when someone uses another's property for a long time. As with adverse possession, the use must be open and notorious, hostile to the true owner's title, under claim of right or color of title, and continuous and uninterrupted for a period of five years. Also like adverse possession, a prescriptive easement cannot be obtained on government land. However, unlike adverse possession, one can obtain a prescriptive easement without the payment of taxes and without exclusive use or possession. See Figure 3.4 for a comparison of adverse possession and prescriptive easement.

TRANSFER

Property is acquired most commonly by transfer when title to the property is conveyed from one person to another by an act of the owner or of law. The act of transferring title to real property is called *alienation*, and occurs in five basic types:

1. gift;
2. public dedication;
3. public grant;
4. court action; and
5. private grant.

GIFT

The owner of property may voluntarily transfer property to another person or organization without demanding or receiving tangible consideration (affection is the ostensible consideration for a gift). If the gift is real property, transfer would normally be conveyed by gift deed, which would be valid despite the lack of tangible consideration unless the transfer was made to defraud creditors, in which case it can be voided.

PUBLIC DEDICATION

A *public dedication* is a gift of an interest in land to a public body for public use, such as for a street, a park, or an easement to access a beach. A public dedication is not valid unless the public body accepts, either expressly or implicitly, the dedication.

PUBLIC GRANT

Public land can be conveyed, such as to railroads, universities, or individuals, through a *public grant*. The *Homestead Act of 1862*, which was signed into law by Abraham Lincoln, gave individual applicants land, typically in the amount of 160 acres (a quarter section) each. The applicant had to file an application, improve the land, live on the land for five years, and pay a small fee before receiving a *land patent* from the government that gave the applicant freehold title to the land. A 1976 federal act ended homesteading in all states except Alaska, where homesteading ended in 1986.

Fig. 3.4   Comparison of Adverse Possession and Prescriptive Easement

Adverse Possession	Prescriptive Easement
<u>Rights acquired:</u> title; ownership of property	<u>Rights acquired:</u> nonexclusive use of property
<u>Elements:</u>	<u>Elements:</u>
1. actual, open, and notorious possession	1. notorious use (not necessarily possession)
2. exclusive and hostile	2. hostile
3. under claim of right or color of title	3. under claim of right or color of title
4. continuous and uninterrupted for five years	4. continuous and uninterrupted for five years
5. payment of all real property taxes	5. no requirement to pay taxes

COURT ACTION

Legal title to land can be transferred by court order in many ways, such as through foreclosure sales, sheriff's sales, tax sales, and partition actions. Such court-ordered transfers will be considered in subsequent chapters. Three types of court-ordered transfers are considered briefly here: escheat, eminent domain, and bankruptcy.

Escheat

Escheat is a process whereby property passes to the state if a person owning the property dies intestate without heirs. If no heirs of a decedent can readily be found, publication is made to locate heirs, but if none comes forward to claim the property within five years, the court will order an escheat of the property to the state.

Eminent Domain

Eminent domain is a right of the state to take, through due process proceedings (often referred to as ***condemnation proceedings***), private property for public use upon payment of just compensation. To exercise eminent domain, an appropriate governmental body must satisfy three basic requirements:

1. the property must be taken for the public good;

2. the property must be necessary for the public purpose for which it is supposedly being taken; and

3. the owner of the property must be paid just compensation, which is usually what a governmental agency or, ultimately, a court determines is the fair market value of the property

Eminent domain has recently been construed quite liberally by the courts, even permitting a state to condemn large parcels of privately held land, acquire title through eminent domain, and then sell the land to private developers.

One should be careful to distinguish eminent domain, for which just compensation must be made, from ***police power***, which is the power of a government to impose restrictions on private rights, including property rights, for the sake of public welfare, health, order, and security, for which no compensation need be made. Examples of the use of police power in regard to real property include the creation and enforcement of zoning codes, building codes, and property setback lines.

Bankruptcy

If a person becomes insolvent, that person can voluntarily institute bankruptcy proceedings in a United States District Court or can be involuntarily forced into bankruptcy by creditors. During bankruptcy proceedings, title to the bankrupt's property is vested in a court-appointed trustee, who, under court supervision, may sell the bankrupt's property to pay creditors. As we shall see in a subsequent chapter that discusses homestead law, a family home may, under certain circumstances, be protected from sale through bankruptcy.

PRIVATE GRANT

Most individuals acquire or transfer title to real property by means of a ***grant deed***, "grant" being a word designated by statute as a word of conveyance. Because there are other deeds, we will discuss the essentials of a deed in general before taking a closer look at private grant deeds.

Deeds in General

A **deed** is a written document that, when properly signed, delivered, and accepted, conveys title to real property from a **grantor** to a **grantee**. The deed will transfer title to property only if it is valid. There are several essential elements to a valid deed:

- in writing
- signed by the grantor
- the grantor must be competent
- the grantee must be capable of holding title
- the parties must be properly described
- the property must be adequately described
- the deed must contain a granting clause
- the deed must be delivered to the grantee
- the deed must be accepted by the grantee

In Writing

According to the Statute of Frauds, nearly any transfer of an interest in real property must be in writing. An exception is a lease for one year or less. Note, however, that a lease for 10 months that does not begin until 3 months after the execution of the lease (i.e., whose term does not expire in one year or less) is a lease that falls within the purview of the Statute of Frauds and must be in writing to be enforceable.

Signed by the Grantor

The deed must be signed by all of the grantors named on the deed, who must use the same names as they did when they took title. For example, a person who used a different name before marriage and took title in that name must use that prior name when signing the deed. Though the grantor(s) must sign the deed, the grantee(s) do not sign the deed unless they are taking the property as community property with right of survivorship. (See the section on *community property with right of survivorship* in the next chapter). If the grantor's signature is forged, the deed is void.

Grantor must be Competent

The grantors must have legal capacity to sign the deed. Unemancipated minors and incompetents are not competent to sign deeds, and any deed signed by them is void. (Legal competency is discussed in the chapter on real estate contracts).

Grantee must be Capable of Holding Title

All grantees must be living (or existing in the case of business organizations) and all such existing legal persons (except unincorporated associations) may hold title to real property.

Parties must be Properly Described

The identities of the grantors and grantees must be adequately described. To ensure that there will be no confusion in the future as to the identity of the grantees, their identities must be designated in a way so as to be determined with certainty.

Property must be Adequately Described

The property must be described specifically enough so that it can be located with certainty. As a general rule, one of the legal land descriptions discussed in Chapter 1 (recorded map, U.S. government survey, or metes and bounds) is used.

Granting Clause

The deed must contain a clause with operative words of conveyance, such as "I hereby transfer," "I hereby grant," or "I hereby convey."

Delivered to the Grantee

A deed is not effective until it is legally delivered to the grantee. Delivery of a deed in this context is a legal, not a physical, concept. Actual physical delivery is not sufficient; there must be an unconditional intent on the part of the grantor to pass title *immediately* to the grantee. Therefore, physical delivery of the deed to escrow is not effective to transfer title because there is no intention on the part of the grantor to pass title immediately. Nor would the physical delivery to a grantee of a deed properly filled out in every way be effective if the intention of the grantor were that the grantee would not take title until some future date, such as upon the grantor's death — a deed cannot take the place of a will. Because the past intention of a party is often difficult to determine, legal delivery is probably the most litigated issue concerning the validity of deeds.

California law provides certain (rebuttable) presumptions as to the legal delivery of a deed. Legal delivery is presumed if:

- the deed is found in the possession of the grantee; or
- the deed is recorded, unless it was recorded after the grantor's death.

Conversely, finding the deed in the grantor's possession raises the (also rebuttable) presumption of nondelivery.

Accepted by the Grantee

Acceptance must be voluntary, unconditional, and accomplished during the grantor's lifetime. Acceptance by the grantee can be evidenced by acts, words, or by conduct such as by recording a deed.

ACKNOWLEDGMENT

The essential elements of a valid deed do *not* include having to be dated or recorded. However, it is wise to do both.

In order to be recorded, the deed must first be acknowledged. An **acknowledgment** is a formal declaration made by the grantor before a duly authorized public official (such as a notary public), that states that the grantor voluntarily signed the deed and that the signature on the deed is the grantor's.

GRANT DEED

A **grant deed** (Figure 3.7) is the most commonly used deed in California. It has two implied warranties that are enforced whether or not they are expressly stated in the deed:

1. the grantor has not transferred title to anyone else; and

2. the property at the time of execution is free from any encumbrances made by the grantor, except for those disclosed.

Note that these implied warranties do *not* warrant that the grantor is the owner of the property or that there are no other liens or encumbrances that exist against the property — good reasons why a grantee should insist upon the acquisition of title insurance as a condition of closing.

Grant deeds convey **after-acquired title** (all interests in the property acquired by the grantor subsequent to the conveyance of the deed automatically pass to the grantee) and are presumed to be fee simple unless the deed states otherwise.

QUITCLAIM DEED

A **quitclaim deed** (Figure 3.8) contains no warranties of any kind, no after-acquired title provisions, and provides the grantee with the least protection of any deed. It merely provides that any interest (if there is any) that the grantor has in the property is transferred to the grantee.

Typically, a quitclaim deed is used to clear some "cloud on the title" to the property, such as to eliminate a presumption of community property if the grantee is married, or to remove an easement.

WARRANTY DEED

A *warranty deed* provides that the grantor is warranting that the title being conveyed is good and free from defects or encumbrances, and that he or she will defend the title against anyone who challenges it. Warranty deeds are seldom used in California because grantors are seldom willing to take on such liability, insisting, rather, that such liabilities be covered by purchasing title insurance.

TRUST DEED

A *trust deed* (or *deed of trust*) is a three-party security device. The three parties are the borrower (*trustor*), the lender (*beneficiary*), and a third-party, referred to as the *trustee*, to whom "bare legal title" is conveyed. (See Figure 3.5) This "bare legal title" entails no right of use or possession in the property; it merely gives the trustee (1) the legal title to hold as security for the lender and (2) the power to sell the property if the borrower does not fulfill all of the obligations set out in the instrument and in the promissory note given by the borrower to the lender. Deeds of trust will be considered in greater detail in a subsequent chapter.

RECONVEYANCE DEED

A *reconveyance deed* (Figure 3.9) is executed by the trustee of a deed of trust after the promissory note is paid off in full by the borrower and the lender instructs the trustee to so execute the reconveyance deed, which reconveys legal title to the borrower.

SHERIFF'S DEED

A *sheriff's deed* is a deed given at the foreclosure of a property, subsequent to a judgment for foreclosure of a money judgment against the owner or of a mortgage against the property. A sheriff's deed contains no warranties and transfers only the former owner's interest in the property. CCP §701.640.

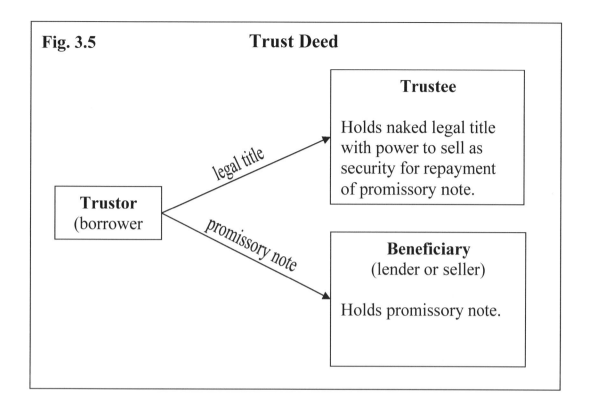

Fig. 3.5   **Trust Deed**

Trustor (borrower

legal title

promissory note

Trustee

Holds naked legal title with power to sell as security for repayment of promissory note.

Beneficiary (lender or seller)

Holds promissory note.

GIFT DEED

A *gift deed* is used to convey title when no tangible consideration (other than "affection") is given. The gift deed is valid unless it was used to defraud creditors, in which case such creditors may bring an action to void the deed.

RECORDING THE TRANSFER

California's recording system provides a person who has acquired real property with a method of protecting his or her interests in the property by recording the document of conveyance with the county recorder. Recording also provides access to information regarding ownership of the property and imparts **constructive notice** to subsequent purchasers or encumbrancers. Constructive notice (as distinct from **actual notice**, which is express notice of information given in fact) refers to notice given to the public by the records available to the public.

There is no requirement of a valid deed that it be recorded; however, if the conveyance is not recorded, it will be considered void as against subsequent purchasers or encumbrancers who act in good faith without actual knowledge of the prior, unrecorded conveyance. *CC §1214.*

TITLE INSURANCE

Real estate is expensive, and real estate transactions are complex, so it behooves a property buyer to obtain a complete chronological history of all of the documents affecting title to the property (referred to as a *chain of title*) and have it examined by an attorney. But even a thorough examination and analysis of the chain of title would not offer protection to the buyer against latent or undiscovered defects in the documents affecting title (for example, a forged deed).

To help protect their interests in the property, a buyer should acquire title insurance. This admonition to acquire title insurance to protect one's interest in property is even emblazoned in all capital letters in a California statute that provides that the agent who handles escrow for the real estate transaction must obtain the buyer's signature on a written notice that contains the following warning:

"IMPORTANT: IN A PURCHASE OR EXCHANGE OF REAL PROPERTY, IT MAY BE ADVISABLE TO OBTAIN TITLE INSURANCE IN CONNECTION WITH THE CLOSE OF ESCROW SINCE THERE MAY BE PRIOR RECORDED LIENS AND ENCUMBRANCES WHICH AFFECT YOUR INTEREST IN THE PROPERTY BEING ACQUIRED. A NEW POLICY OF TITLE INSURANCE SHOULD BE OBTAINED IN ORDER TO ENSURE YOUR INTEREST IN THE PROPERTY THAT YOU ARE ACQUIRING." CC §1057.6.

In most real estate transactions, the lender requires that the buyer pay for a *lender's policy* of title insurance that protects the lender up to the amount being loaned. As for the *owner's policy*, which insurers the title of the buyer, either the seller or the buyer pays for the title policy — a point of negotiation between them.

When requested to provide title insurance on the property, a title insurance company usually utilizes their own set of records (called *title plants*) to examine the condition of title before issuing a *preliminary report*, which is a statement by the title insurance company of the condition of the title and of the terms and conditions upon which it is willing to issue a policy.

There are many ways in which title may be adversely affected, and, consequently, there are different policies of title insurance to cover various possible defects. The two main title insurance policies are the *standard coverage* (sometimes called a *CLTA policy*, after the California Land Title Association) and the *extended coverage* (sometimes called an *ALTA policy*, after the American Land Title Association). The coverage of these two types of policies is summarized in Figure 3.6.

Neither the standard coverage nor the extended coverage offers protection regarding governmental regulations concerning occupancy and use (which affect the condition of the property rather than the condition of the title) or regarding defects that the buyer knew as of the date of policy issuance.

Fig. 3.6   **Comparison of Standard and Extended Title Policies**

Standard Coverage	Extended Coverage

A: Marketable title vested in the insured
 	
B: Latent defects in title
  • forged deed
  • incompetent grantor
  • legal delivery problems
 	
C: Loss from federal estate tax liens
 	
D: Expenses incurred in defending the title in case of a lawsuit
	Everything covered by the standard coverage policy, plus
	
	• Rights of parties in possession, such as tenants and adverse possessors
	• Matters that a survey would disclose, such as encroachments and boundary lines
	• unrecorded physical easements and mechanics liens
	• Certain mining and water claims

Fig. 3.7

RECORDING REQUESTED BY

AND WHEN RECORDED MAIL DOCUMENT AND
TAX STATEMENT TO:

NAME

STREET
ADDRESS

CITY, STATE &
ZIP CODE

TITLE ORDER NO.   ESCROW NO.   SPACE ABOVE THIS LINE FOR RECORDER'S USE ONLY

GRANT DEED

APN:

The undersigned grantor(s) declare(s) _____
DOCUMENTARY TRANSFER TAX $
☐ computed on full value of property conveyed, or
☐ computed on full value less liens and encumbrances remaining at time of sale.
☐ Unincorporated Area   City of_____

FOR VALUABLE CONSIDERATION, receipt of which is hereby acknowledged, I (We)

hereby remise, release and grant to

the following described real property in the City of_____, County of_____
State of California, with the following legal description:

_____
Date

_____

_____

STATE OF _____

COUNTY OF _____

On _____ before me, _____,
        (Date)   (Name and title of the officer)

personally appeared _____, who proved to me on the basis of
                     (Name of person signing)
satisfactory evidence to be the person(s) whose name(s) is/are subscribed to the within instrument and acknowledged to me that
he/she/they executed the same in his/her/their authorized capacity(ies), and that by his/her/their signature(s) on the instrument the
person(s), or the entity upon behalf of which the person(s) acted, executed the instrument.

I certify under PENALTY OF PERJURY under the laws of the State of California that the foregoing paragraph is true and correct.

WITNESS my hand and official seal.

_____
Signature of officer

(Seal)

MAIL TAX STATEMENT AS DIRECTED ABOVE

* There are various types of deed forms depending on each person's legal status. Before you use this form you many want to consult an
attorney if you have questions concerning which document form is appropriate for your transaction.

Fig. 3.8

RECORDING REQUESTED BY

AND WHEN RECORDED MAIL DOCUMENT AND
TAX STATEMENT TO:

NAME

STREET
ADDRESS

CITY, STATE &
ZIP CODE

TITLE ORDER NO.   ESCROW NO.   SPACE ABOVE THIS LINE FOR RECORDER'S USE ONLY

QUITCLAIM DEED

APN:

The undersigned grantor(s) declare(s) _____
DOCUMENTARY TRANSFER TAX $
☐ computed on full value of property conveyed, or
☐ computed on full value less liens and encumbrances remaining at time of sale.
☐ Unincorporated Area   City of _____

FOR VALUABLE CONSIDERATION, receipt of which is hereby acknowledged, I (We)

hereby remise, release and quitclaim to

the following described real property in the City of _____, County of _____
State of California, with the following legal description:

_____
Date

_____

_____

STATE OF _____

COUNTY OF _____

On _____ before me, _____,
        (Date)   (Name and title of the officer)

personally appeared _____, who proved to me on the basis of
                    (Name of person signing)
satisfactory evidence to be the person(s) whose name(s) is/are subscribed to the within instrument and acknowledged to me that
he/she/they executed the same in his/her/their authorized capacity(ies), and that by his/her/their signature(s) on the instrument the
person(s), or the entity upon behalf of which the person(s) acted, executed the instrument.

I certify under PENALTY OF PERJURY under the laws of the State of California that the foregoing paragraph is true and correct.

WITNESS my hand and official seal.

_____
Signature of officer

(Seal)

MAIL TAX STATEMENT AS DIRECTED ABOVE

* There are various types of deed forms depending on each person's legal status. Before you use this form you many want to consult an
attorney if you have questions concerning which document form is appropriate for your transaction.

Fig. 3.9

RECORDING REQUESTED BY

_____

AND WHEN RECORDED MAIL THIS DEED AND, UNLESS
OTHERWISE SHOWN BELOW, MAIL TAX STATEMENT TO:

NAME   _____

STREET
ADDRESS   _____

CITY, STATE &
ZIPCODE   _____

TITLE ORDER NO _____ ESCROW NO _____

SPACE ABOVE THIS LINE FOR RECORDER'S USE

DEED OF FULL RECONVEYANCE

_____, the

Trustee ___ under the Deed of Trust dated _____ _____, made and executed by

_____ as Trustor(s), and recorded

as Instrument No. _____ On _____ _____, in Book _____ at Page _____, of the
Official Records in the Office of the Recorder of _____ County, State of _____
having received from the Beneficiar ___ under said Deed of Trust a written request to reconvey, reciting that
all sums secured by said Deed of Trust have been fully paid, and said Deed of Trust and the note or notes
secured thereby having been surrendered to the Trustee ___ for cancellation, do ___ hereby reconvey, without
warranty, to the person or persons legally entitled thereto, all right, title and interest heretofore acquired and
now held by said Trustee under said Deed of Trust, in the real property commonly known as _____

situated in the County of _____, State of ____, and more particularly described as follows:

_____

_____

_____

Dated: _____ _____

_____

_____, as Trustee ___

STATE OF _____

COUNTY OF _____

On _____ before me, _____
                                        [here insert the name and title of the officer]

personally appeared _____
who proved to me on the basis of satisfactory evidence to be the person(s) whose name(s) is/are subscribed
to the within instrument and acknowledged to me that he/she/they executed the same in his/her/their
authorized capacity(ies), and that by his/her/their signature(s) on the instrument the person(s), or the entity
upon behalf of which the person(s) acted, executed the instrument.

I certify under PENALTY OF PERJURY under the laws of the State of California that the foregoing
paragraph is true and correct

WITNESS my hand and official seal.

_____
        (SIGNATURE OF NOTARY)

Key Terms of Chapter 3

abandonment — failure to occupy or use property that may result in the extinguishment of a right or interest in the property.

accession — the acquisition of additional property by the natural processes of accretion, reliction, or avulsion, or by the human processes of the addition of fixtures or improvements made in error.

accretion — a natural process by which the owner of riparian or littoral property acquires additional land by the gradual accumulation of soil through the action of water.

administrator — a person appointed by a probate court to conduct the affairs and distribute the assets of a decedent's estate when there was no executor named in the will or there was no will.

adverse possession — the process by which unauthorized possession and use of another's property can ripen into ownership of that other's property without compensation.

after-acquired interests — all interests in a property acquired subsequent to a transfer of the property.

alluvium — addition to land acquired by the gradual accumulation of soil through the action of water.

ALTA policy — an extended title insurance policy developed by the American Land Title Association.

ambulatory instrument — a document that can be changed or revoked, such as a will.

avulsion — a process that occurs when a river or stream suddenly carries away a part of a bank and deposits it downstream, either on the same or opposite bank.

beneficiary — (1) the lender under a deed of trust, (2) one entitled to receive property under a will, (3) one for whom a trust is created.

bequeath — to transfer personal property by a will.

bequest — a gift of personal property by will.

chain of title — a complete chronological history of all of the documents affecting title to the property.

CLTA policy — a standard title insurance policy developed by the California Land Title Association.

constructive notice — (1) notice provided by public records; (2) notice of information provided by law to a person who, by exercising reasonable diligence, could have discovered the information.

devise — (1) (noun) a gift of real property by will; (2) (verb) to transfer real property by a will.

devisee — a recipient of real property through a will.

eminent domain — right of the state to take, through due process proceedings (often referred to as condemnation proceedings), private property for public use upon payment of just compensation.

escheat — a process whereby property passes to the state if a person owning the property dies intestate without heirs.

executor — a person named in a will to carry out the directions contained in the will.

gift deed — a deed used to convey title when no tangible consideration (other than "affection") is given. The gift deed is valid unless it was used to defraud creditors, in which case such creditors may bring an action to void the deed.

grant deed — the deed most commonly used in California. It has two implied warranties that are enforced whether or not they are expressly stated in the deed: the grantor has not transferred title to anyone else, and the property at the time of execution is free from any encumbrances made by the grantor, except for those disclosed.

grantee — one who acquires an interest in real property from another.

grantor — one who transfers an interest in real property to another.

heir — a person entitled to obtain property through intestate succession.

holographic will — a will written, dated, and signed by a testator in his or her own handwriting.

intestate — not having made, or not having disposed of by, a will.

intestate succession — transfer of the property of one who dies intestate.

legatee — one who acquires personal property under a will.

nuncupative will — an oral will; nuncupative wills are no longer valid in California.

patent, land — an instrument used to convey government land.

police power — the power of a government to impose restrictions on private rights, including property rights, for the sake of public welfare, health, order, and security, for which no compensation need be made.

preliminary title report — a statement by a title insurance company of the condition of the title and of the terms and conditions upon which the company is willing to issue a policy.

prescription — a method of acquiring an interest in property by use and enjoyment for five years.

prescriptive easement — an easement acquired by prescription.

probate — a legal procedure whereby a superior court in the county where the real property is located or where the deceased resided oversees the distribution of the decedent's property.

public dedication — a gift of an interest in land to a public body for public use, such as for a street, a park, or an easement to access a beach.

public grant — public land conveyed, usually for a small fee, to individuals or to organizations, such as to railroads or universities.

quitclaim deed — a deed that contains no warranties of any kind, no after-acquired title provisions, and provides the grantee with the least protection of any deed; it merely provides that any interest (if there is any) that the grantor has in the property is transferred to the grantee.

reconveyance deed — a deed executed by the trustee of a deed of trust after the promissory note is paid off in full by the borrower and the lender instructs the trustee to so execute the reconveyance deed, which reconveys legal title to the borrower

reliction — a natural process by which the owner of riparian or littoral property acquires additional land that has been covered by water but has become permanently uncovered by the gradual recession of water.

sheriff's deed — a deed given at the foreclosure of a property, subsequent to a judgment for foreclosure of a money judgment against the owner or of a mortgage against the property. A sheriff's deed contains no warranties and transfers only the former owner's interest in the property.

statutory will — a pre-printed "fill-in-the-blanks" will provided by statute that must be signed in the presence of two competent witnesses.

testament — a will.

testator — one who dies leaving a will.

title plant — a duplicate of county title records maintained at title insurance companies for use in title searches.

trust deed — a three-party security device, the three parties being the borrower (trustor), the lender (beneficiary), and a third-party (trustee) to whom "bare legal title" is conveyed.

trustee — a person who holds something of value in trust for the benefit of another; under a deed of trust, a neutral third-party who holds naked legal title for security.

trustor — a borrower who executes a deed of trust.

warranty deed — a deed in which the grantor warrants that the title being conveyed is good and free from defects or encumbrances, and that the grantor will defend the title against all suits.

will — a document that stipulates how one's property should be distributed after death; also called a testament.

Quiz for Chapter 3

1. Which deed contains the fewest warranties?
   a. warranty deed
   b. quitclaim deed
   c. grant deed
   d. they all contain the same warranties
2. Which of the following is a valid will?
   a. nuncupative will
   b. holographic will
   c. quitclaim will
   d. grant will
3. If Joe were primarily concerned about protecting against a forged deed in the chain of title to a property he is acquiring, he would probably obtain
   a. a CLTA policy
   b. an ALTA policy
   c. both a and b
   d. neither a nor b
4. Eminent domain is
   a. a public grant
   b. considered a police power of the state
   c. is property taken for the private good
   d. none of the above
5. A holographic will
   a. may be signed by having the testator make an X if a witness prints or types the testator's name next to the mark, with the witness signing beside the testator's name.
   b. must be dated to be valid
   c. need not be witnessed
   d. both a and c
6. Which, if any, of the following is misspelled?
   a. noncupative
   b. avulsion
   c. escheat
   d. none of the above are misspelled
7. A minor is likely
   a. is a competent grantor
   b. is a competent grantee
   c. both a and b
   d. neither a nor b

8. Delivery of a deed most importantly rest on
   a. acknowledgment
   b. signing of the deed
   c. intent of the grantor
   d. physical conveyance

9. The administrator of an estate brings a high bid of $150,000 to probate court. The probate court will not accept late bids for less than
   a. $151,000
   b. $165,000
   c. $158,450
   d. none of the above

10. After Joe died, both a signed will giving his house to his friend Jane and a deed granting his house to his daughter Susan were discovered in his safe. If the deed was signed later than the will, who will probably acquire the house?
    a. Susan because a deed signed during the grantor's life has priority over a will
    b. Susan because the deed was signed later than the will
    c. Susan because blood relatives have priority over friends
    d. none of the above

11. Which of the following terms least belongs with the others?
    a. bequest
    b. real property
    c. legacy
    d. gift

12. Bob's home has been in the family for three generations. Nevertheless, the city wants to demolish it to make room for a public park. By which power will the city proceed to acquire Bob's home?
    a. eminent domain
    b. power reconveyance
    c. police power
    d. public grant

13. Bob dies intestate leaving a spouse and three children. What portion of Bob's separate property would each child receive?
    a. 1/3
    b. 2/3
    c. 2/9
    d. none of the above

14. The implied warranties in a grant deed include
    a. that the grantor owns the title
    b. that the grantor will defend the title against all suits
    c. that the grantor has not transferred the title to anyone else
    d. both a and c

15. For a deed to be recorded it must be

    a. witnessed
    b. acknowledged
    c. free from encumbrances
    d. both a and b

16. Which of the following concepts least belongs with the others?
    a. after-acquired interests
    b. grant deed
    c. two implied warranties
    d. no warranties

17. Escheat is
    a. the estate tax paid to the state
    b. the estate tax paid to the federal government
    c. what happens to an intestate's property
    d. none of the above

18. You might be able to acquire property by adverse possession in which of the following situations?
    a. both you and your neighbor have regularly used your neighbor's back lot to park your cars on for five years
    b. you and your children have been playing basketball in a public street that hasn't been used by the public in over five years
    c. you have been exclusively cultivating a strip of land owned by your neighbor for over five years
    d. both b and c

19. The sudden carrying away of land by the action of a river or stream is called
    a. avulsion
    b. accretion
    c. alluvium
    d. none of the above

20. Which of the following terms least belongs with the others?
    a. adverse possession
    b. abandonment
    c. eminent domain
    d. prescription

21. Bob conveys a vacant lot to the city for the use as a public park. This is an example of a
    a. public grant
    b. land patent
    c. prescription
    d. none of the above

22. Which of the following statements is incorrect?
    a. a statutory will uses a form approved by the state
    b. an ALTA policy is an extended title insurance policy
    c. to die intestate means to die without leaving a will

    d. both a and b are incorrect

23. Adverse possession requires
    a. payment of taxes
    b. exclusive possession for at least six years
    c. claim of title or color of right
    d. both a and c

24. A valid deed must be
    a. recorded
    b. witnessed
    c. dated
    d. none of the above

25. A river gradually deposits soil on Jane's land. This is an example of
    a. reliction
    b. accretion
    c. avulsion
    d. none of the above

26. If you discover that someone has been on your property for four years, you can stop that person from acquiring the property by adverse possession by
    a. being sure that you timely pay the property taxes on the property
    b. complaining about the situation in an e-mail to your best friend
    c. immediately sending the trespasser a letter giving him or her the right to stay on your property for another two years
    d. either a or c

27. After-acquired interests are conveyed with
    a. grant deeds
    b. warranty deeds
    c. quitclaim deeds
    d. both a and b

28. One who inherits a house has received a
    a. bequest
    b. legacy
    c. devise
    d. testament

29. A quitclaim deed
    a. warrants that the grantor has not granted the property to anyone else
    b. warrants that the grantor has disclosed all of the material defects in the title that he or she knows of
    c. warrants that, at a minimum, the grantor owns the property
    d. none of the above

30. A is selling her residence to B. B will acquire title at the time
    a. A signs the grant deed
    b. A acknowledges the grant deed
    c. A delivers the deed to B

d. either a or b

Answers to Chapter 3 Quiz

1. b. A quitclaim deed contains no warranties of any kind, no after-acquired title provisions, and provides the grantee with the least protection of any deed; it merely provides that any interest (if there is any) that the grantor has in the property is transferred to the grantee.

2. b. A nuncupative will is no longer valid in California.

3. a. A CLTA policy covers forgery and is less expensive than an ALTA policy

4. d. Eminent domain refers to the right of the state to take, through due process proceedings, private property for public use upon payment of just compensation.

5. c. A holographic will does not need to be dated or witnessed to be valid. It does, however, have to be written in the testator's handwriting; therefore, since the testator can write, there is no reason for the testator to make an X rather than to sign his or her name.

6. a. The correct spelling is "nuncupative."

7. b. A competent minor can receive real property but may not transfer real property to another. If property that the minor owns is to be transferred, the deed transferring the property must be signed by the minor's guardian.

8. c. Though a deed needs to be signed by the grantor to be valid, the most important element for legal delivery of the deed is the grantor's intent.

9. d. The next highest bid needs to be the original bid ($150,000) plus at least 10% of the first $10,000 ($1,000) plus 5% of the remaining $140,000 ($7,000), which equals $157,000.

10. d. The only way that Susan could acquire the property is if she could prove that the deed had been delivered to her by Joe during Joe's lifetime. The fact that the deed was found in Joe's safe creates a presumption that the deed was never delivered. In any case, the reasons given in a, b, and c are all faulty.

11. b. A bequest and a legacy are gifts of personal property.

12. a. A city wanting to take private property for public use must do so through the power of eminent domain.

13. c. The separate property of a person who dies intestate leaving a spouse and two or more children goes 1/3 to the spouse and 2/3 to the children, to be apportioned among them equally.

14. c. The implied warranties in a grant deed include neither that the grantor owns the property nor that the grantor will defend the title against all suits.

15. b. A deed need not be witnessed or free from encumbrances to be recorded, but it must be acknowledged by the grantor.

16. d . A grant deed conveys two implied warranties and after-acquired interests.

17. d. There would not be an escheat of an intestate's property unless no heirs could be found during a five-year period. Note: when presented with questions such as this, do not assume unstated facts.

18. c. You could not lay claim to your neighbor's back lot by adverse possession because your possession had not been exclusive. You could not lay claim to the street because government property cannot be acquired by adverse possession.

19. a. Avulsion refers to the process that occurs when a river or stream suddenly carries away a part of a bank and deposits it downstream, either on the same or opposite bank.

20. c. Private persons can acquire interests in property through adverse possession, abandonment, and prescription — not through eminent domain, which is a governmental power.

21. d. This is an example of a public dedication.

22. d. The only incorrect statement here is d.

23. d. Adverse possession requires exclusive possession for five years, not six.

24. d. A valid deed need not be recorded, witnessed, or dated.

25. b. Accretion is a natural process by which the owner of riparian or littoral property acquires additional land by the gradual accumulation of soil through the action of water.

26. c. Because adverse possession requires that the possession be hostile to the owner's interests, an owner's permission negates this "hostile" requirement. Your paying taxes would not necessarily prevent the trespasser from also paying taxes on the property, thereby satisfying the requirement that to acquire property by adverse possession the trespasser must pay the real property taxes on the property.

27. d. Though after-acquired interests are conveyed by grant deeds and warranty deeds, quitclaim deeds convey neither warranties nor after-acquired interests

28. c. A devise is a gift of real property by will; a bequest is a gift of personal property by way of will.

29. d. A quitclaim deed carries no warranties of any kind

30. c. A purchaser does not acquire title to a deed until it is legally delivered.

Chapter 4

Ways of Owning Real Property

When people acquire real property, they must decide in what legal form that ownership should be. This decision as to the form of ownership is important because it undoubtedly will have significant tax, inheritance, and liability consequences.

There are two general types of private ownership: ***ownership in severalty*** (the property is owned by one person only) and ***joint ownership*** or ***co-ownership*** (the property is owned by two or more persons).

OWNERSHIP IN SEVERALTY

When one person is the sole owner of property, the property is owned in severalty. "Severalty" is a term derived from "sever" and refers to keeping the bundle of rights that is this solely owned property entirely separate from the rights of others.

JOINT OWNERSHIP

Joint ownership or co-ownership refers to simultaneous ownership of property by two or more persons. The California Civil Code recognizes five types of joint ownership, as depicted in Figure 4.1.

A table comparing the first four methods of holding real property in joint tenancy (tenancy in partnership is not included) is shown in Figure 4.2.

JOINT TENANCY

A joint tenancy "is one owned by two or more persons in equal shares, by a title created by a single will or transfer, when expressly declared in the will or transfer to be a joint tenancy…" CC §683.

As a general rule, to create a joint tenancy it is only necessary to state in the deed that the grantees will hold title "as joint tenants." However, California appellate courts have long accepted and enforced the common law rule that if any of the **four unities** is missing, a tenancy in common, rather than a joint tenancy, exists. The four unities are:

Unity of possession — each of the joint tenants must have an equal, undivided right to possession of the entire property;

Unity of time — each of the joint tenants must acquire his/her interest in the property at the same time;

Unity of interest — the joint tenants must have equal interests in the property; and

Unity of title — the joint tenants must receive their ownership in the property from the same deed.

Because the modern statutory definition of joint tenancy and the common law rule of the four unities do not precisely coincide (in particular, with regard to the unity of time), consultation with knowledgeable counsel is recommended with respect to creation, termination, and other issues regarding joint tenancy.

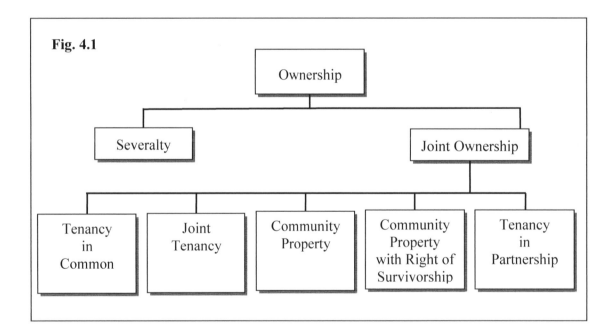

Fig. 4.1

Right of Survivorship

The most important feature distinguishing a joint tenancy from a tenancy in common is the **right of survivorship**. On the death of one of the joint tenants, the surviving joint tenants receive in equal shares the decedent's interest in the property, free from probate; hence, the decedent's inclusion of his/her joint tenancy interest in a will would have no legal force and effect, provided that at least one joint tenant survives the decedent. This consequence is the result of the legal fiction that each joint tenant holds the (single) title to the entire property. An exception is that if a joint tenant murders another joint tenant, the murderer would not receive the decedent's interest in the joint tenancy.

A corporation may not be a joint tenant because the law regards a corporation as having potentially infinite duration, and infinite duration would result in the right of survivorship having no consequence.

Along with the right of survivorship, joint tenancy has another significant characteristic: any lien against a decedent's interest in a joint tenancy that was placed on the decedent's interest during joint tenancy is extinguished upon death, and the surviving joint tenant(s) receive the title unencumbered by the decedent's liens. No other form of property transfer has this characteristic. A creditor's right to payment continues against the decedent's estate as an unsecured claim, but the decedent's joint tenancy interest does not go through probate, the lien simply evaporates, and the remaining joint tenants have no obligation whatsoever to pay the debt. Needless to say, creditors would be wise to think twice before accepting a joint tenant's interest as security for a loan.

Transferring a Joint Tenancy Interest

A joint tenant's interest may be severed from the joint tenancy either by voluntary or involuntary conveyance. The grantee of such a conveyance would take title as a tenant in common with the remaining tenants (if there had been more than one), who continue as joint tenants with respect to their interests among themselves.

Terminating a Joint Tenancy

A joint tenancy may be terminated either by agreement among the joint tenants through a **voluntary partition**, or, if no voluntary agreement can be reached, by a judicial determination after the filing of a **partition action** by one or more of the joint tenants. Of course, it is often impossible or impractical to divide real property into parts that are solely owned, so the termination of a joint tenancy through partition, whether voluntary or involuntary, usually requires the selling of the property.

TENANCY IN COMMON

A tenancy in common "is one owned by several persons, not in joint ownership or partnership." CC §685.

When two or more persons who are neither married nor registered domestic partners own undivided interests in property and the deed does not specify the form of co-ownership, the property is presumed to be held as a tenancy in common. Tenants in common may hold unequal interests; however, if the deed does not specify fractional interests among the tenants, the interests will be presumed to be equal.

Tenants in common are said to have an ***undivided interest*** in the property, which, as in joint tenancy, means that each owner has the right of possession of the entire property and may not exclude the other owners from any portion by claiming that any specific portion of the property is his or hers alone. All income and expenses related to the property are to be divided proportionally among all of the tenants in common. And as we saw in Chapter 2 regarding a life tenant, a tenant in common may not physically damage the property (commit ***waste***).

Transferring a Tenancy in Common Interest

A tenant in common may freely mortgage, sell, gift, or will his/her interest to another, who becomes a tenant in common with the others. There is no right of survivorship for tenants in common — the interest of a deceased tenant in common passes to the beneficiaries the decedent's estate, who take the decedent's place as tenant(s) in common with the other co-tenants.

Terminating a Tenancy in Common

As in the case of joint tenancy, a tenancy in common may be terminated either by agreement among the co-tenants by a voluntary partition, whereby each co-tenant receives an agreed-upon fraction of the property, or, if no voluntary agreement can be reached, by a judicial determination after the filing of a partition action by one or more of the co-tenants.

COMMUNITY PROPERTY

Only nine states — California, Arizona, Idaho, Louisiana, Nevada, New Mexico, Texas, Washington, and Wisconsin — have community property systems. As we saw in Chapter 1, the concept of community property derived from Spanish law and was recognized in California pursuant to the Treaty of Guadalupe Hidalgo.

Fig. 4.2	Forms of Joint Ownership (excluding Tenancy in Partnership)			
	Tenancy in Common	**Joint Tenancy**	**Community Property**	**Community Property with Right of Survivorship**
Definition	Property owned by two or more persons having undivided interests; no right of survivorship.	Property held by two or more persons, with right of survivorship.	Property held only by a married couple or registered domestic partners.	Property held only by a married couple or registered domestic partners, with right of survivorship.
Creation	Property acquired by unmarried persons that fails as joint tenancy or fails to state the type of tenancy; or by expressly so stating.	By satisfying the four unities and unequivocally expressing the intention to create a joint tenancy.	Property acquired during marriage or domestic partnership, unless acquired as separate property or joint tenancy.	By expressly so stating, and spouses or domestic partners must sign the deed accepting this form of title.
Unities	Possession (undivided).	Time (created at the same time); Title (created by the same deed); Interests (equal); Possession (undivided).	Not applicable.	Not applicable.
Presumption	Yes, unless a married couple.	None.	Yes if married or reg. domestic partner.	Never presumed.
Ownership	Each tenant owns separate title to his/her interest. If the deed fails to recite tenant's interest, interest presumed equal.	Each tenant is fictionally considered the owner of the single title to the property.	Although there is only one title, each owns one-half interest in the property.	Although there is only one title, each owns one-half interest in the property.
Transferred to new party	Each tenant can convey own interest.	Severs joint tenancy as to that tenant's interest; does not affect the continued joint tenancy of any two other owners.	Each must join in the conveyance, encumbrance, or leasing of community property.	Each must join in the conveyance, encumbrance, or leasing of community property.
New Purchaser	Will be a tenant in common with the other owner(s).	Will be a tenant in common with the other owner(s).	One member of the pair cannot convey separately.	One member of the pair cannot convey separately.
Death of One Party	Interest passes through probate according to the decedent's will or by intestacy.	Interest passes to other joint tenant(s) outside of probate, free from decedent's debts.	Interest passes per will; otherwise to survivor. Probate, unless survivor elects otherwise.	Interest passes to survivor. No probate; no passing by terms of a will.
Amount in Decedent's Estate	Decedent's separate fractional interest	Interest passes equally to the other joint tenant(s).	Half of the property.	Half of the property.

Community property law in California applies both to married couples and to registered domestic partners: "Registered domestic partners shall have the same rights, protections, and benefits, and shall be subject to the same responsibilities, obligations, and duties under law…" as traditional spouses who are married. FC §297.5(a).

Although there is only one title to property held as community property, each spouse owns one-half interest in the property.

Separate Property

California law presumes that "all property, real or personal, wherever situated, acquired by a married person during the marriage while domiciled in the state is community property." FC §760. There is a class of property called *separate property* that is excluded from community property. The separate property of a married person includes:

1. "All property owned by the person before marriage.
2. All property acquired by the person after marriage by gift, bequest, devise, or descent.
3. The rents, issues, and profits of the property described" in 1 and 2 above. FC §770
4. "The earnings and accumulations of a spouse… while living separate and apart from the other spouse…" FC §771.

Property Owned Before Marriage

The property that a spouse acquires before marriage is his/her separate property.

> **Example:** If Jane owned an office building before marrying Bob, the office building would remain Jane's after marriage. Furthermore, if Jane were to sell the office building after marrying Bob and were to use the proceeds to purchase some other property, this other property would also remain Jane's separate property.
>
> Caveat: if Jane wants her separate property to remain entirely separate during marriage, she must be careful not to use community property or her own personal efforts to manage, maintain, or improve her separate property, because if she does, she risks losing part or all her property's separate-property status

or the separate-property status of the property's income and appreciation. In divorce proceedings, these kinds of factual situations can, and often do, lead to byzantine legal and accounting arguments with uncertain outcomes.

To avoid risking her property's separate-property status, Jane should maintain a separate checking account funded only with her separate funds, hire a property management company to manage the property, deposit her property's rental income into her separate checking account, and pay the management fees from this same account.

Gifts and Inheritances

Property acquired during marriage by way of gift or inheritance is separate property. Even gifts purchased with community property, such as birthday or anniversary gifts, are considered the separate property of the spouse who receives the gifts.

Commingling

If a spouse mixes (*commingles*) his or her separate property to such an extent that a court cannot distinguish or trace which is which, the result will be that it all becomes community property.

Management and Control of Community Property

As a general rule, both spouses have equal rights in managing community property. However, if one spouse is the primary manager of a business or business interest (such as a real estate agent business), the other spouse has no right to participate in its management, though this other spouse may object to a sale or mortgage of substantially all of the business assets. FC §1100(d). Furthermore, both spouses must agree in writing to all transfers of, or encumbrances on, community real property or on the furniture or furnishings of the family home. FC §1100(b).

COMMUNITY PROPERTY WITH RIGHT OF SURVIVORSHIP

Becoming operative July 1, 2001, CC §682.1 created a new form of property ownership — *community property with right of survivorship* — that allows title to pass directly to a surviving spouse without probate. This form of ownership provides benefits of both joint tenancy and community property. The surviving spouse takes title to this type of property automatically, regardless of what is stated in the decedent's will. To create this type of property, the deed must state "community property with right of survivorship" and, *unlike all other deeds*, must be signed by the grantees.

TENANCY IN PARTNERSHIP

California also recognizes a form of joint ownership called **tenancy in partnership**, which exists when two or more persons combine their assets and efforts in a business venture in exchange for a partnership interest in the venture. The corporate form of such business ventures can be **general partnerships** or **limited partnerships**.

The primary difference between a general partnership and a limited partnership is that each of the partners of a general partnership is personally liable for all of the debts of the partnership, whereas only the general partners of a limited partnership (there must be at least one) are personally liable for partnership debts — the limited partners have no liability beyond their investment in, and pledges to, the partnership.

The primary real estate characteristics of a tenancy in partnership are:

1. Each partner has an equal right to possession of partnership property for partnership purposes; however, unless all of the partners agree, no partner has the right to use or possess partnership property for any other purpose.
2. A partner's interest in partnership property is not assignable except in connection with the assignment of all partners' interests in the same property.
3. A partner's interest in partnership property is not subject to attachment or execution, except on a claim against the partnership.
4. When a partner dies, title to the partnership rests entirely in the surviving partners. The decedent's estate or heirs acquire no direct interest in the property of the partnership or in its management. The decedent's estate or heirs do, however, have a right to an accounting and a share of the partnership profits and value upon dissolution.

Key Terms of Chapter 4

commingling — the mixing of separate and community property. If a spouse or registered domestic partner commingles his/her separate property to such an extent that a court cannot distinguish or trace which is which, the result will be that it all becomes community property.

community property — property owned jointly by a married couple or by registered domestic partners, as distinguished from separate property. As a general rule, property acquired by a spouse or registered domestic partner through his/her skills or personal efforts is community property.

community property with right of survivorship — property that is community property and that has a right of survivorship. Upon the death of a spouse or registered domestic partner, community property with right of survivorship passes to the surviving spouse or domestic partner without probate.

co-ownership — joint ownership

four unities — refers to the common law rule that a joint tenancy requires unity of possession, time, interest, and title.

general partnership — a partnership in which each partner has the equal right to manage the partnership and has personal liability for all of the partnership debts.

joint ownership — ownership of property by two or more persons.

joint tenancy —a form of joint ownership which has unity of possession, time, interest, and title.

limited liability partnership — a partnership in which there is at least one general partner and one or more limited partners. The limited partners have no liability beyond their investment in and pledges to the partnership.

partition —a court-ordered or voluntary division of real property held in joint ownership into parcels owned in severalty.

right of survivorship — the right to succeed to the interest of a joint tenant or, if community property with right of survivorship, to succeed to the interest of a spouse or registered domestic partner. Right of survivorship is the most important characteristic of joint tenancy.

separate property — property that is owned in severalty by a spouse or registered domestic partner. Separate property includes property acquired before marriage or the registering of domestic partnership, and property acquired as a gift or by inheritance during marriage or registered domestic partnership.

severalty — ownership of property by one person.

tenancy in common — a form of joint ownership that is presumed to exist if the persons who own the property are neither married nor registered domestic partners and they own undivided interests in property. Tenants in common may hold unequal interests; however, if the deed does not specify fractional interests among the tenants, the interests will be presumed to be equal.

tenancy in partnership — a form of joint ownership in which the partners combine their assets and efforts in a business venture.

undivided interest — an ownership interest in property in which an owner has the right of possession of the entire property and may not exclude the other owners from any portion by claiming that a specific portion of the property is his or hers alone.

unity of interest — in reference to joint ownership, refers to each of the owners having equal interests in the property.

unity of possession — in reference to joint ownership, refers to each of the owners having an equal, undivided right to possession of the entire property.

unity of time — in reference to joint ownership, refers to each of the owners having acquired his/her interest in the property at the same time.

unity of title — in reference to joint ownership, refers to each of the owners having received ownership in the property from the same deed.

Quiz for Chapter 4

1. Ownership in severalty refers to
   a. ownership in property can take many forms
   b. ownership by several persons
   c. ownership by one person only
   d. several persons in a partnership

2. When a brother and sister inherit property from their parents, they might own the property as
   a. joint tenants
   b. community property
   c. tenants in common
   d. either a or c

3. A, B, and C own property as tenants in common. After A dies and B sells his interest to C, the property is owned
   a. by C only
   b. by C and the heirs of A as joint tenants
   c. by C and the heirs of A as a partnership in tenancy
   d. none of the above

4. The most important characteristic of joint tenancy is
   a. equal right of possession
   b. equal right to convey
   c. unity of time
   d. right of survivorship

5. A, B, and C are joint tenants. A wills her interest to D. A dies. Regarding the interests of B, C, and D
   a. they are tenants in common
   b. they are joint tenants
   c. B and C are joint tenants, but D is a tenant in common
   d. none of the above

6. While they were single, Jane and Bob each owned a condo. After they married, the two condos were held as

    a. community property

    b. joint tenancy

    c. separate property, unless otherwise agreed

    d. community property with right of survivorship

7. Jane is a real estate agent. She saved $40,000 during her seven-year marriage to Bob, a "house-husband" who took care of the children, cooked the meals, etc. Pursuant to which rule does the divorce court award half of Jane's savings to Bob?

    a. community property

    b. equal pay for equal work

    c. joint tenancy

    d. tenancy in partnership

8. Joint tenants do not have

    a. the right of survivorship

    b. the right to sell their interest to another

    c. the right to will good title to another

    d. equal possession rights

9. A corporation may hold title as

    a. community property

    b. a joint tenant

    c. a tenant in common

    d. both b and c

10. A joint tenant may sever his/her interest

    a. never

    b. only if all of the other joint tenants agree

    c. by selling his/her interest to another

    d. none of the above

11. California's community property law originated in

    a. federal law

    b. common law

    c. Spanish law

    d. French law

12. A tenancy in common requires the unity of

    a. title and possession

    b. possession

    c. time and possession

    d. interest, time, and possession

13. Bob and his nephew Joe own three-quarters and one-quarter interest, respectively, in an office building. They might be holding title as
    a. joint tenants
    b. tenants in common
    c. community property
    d. tenancy at sufferance

14. Without contrary evidence, it is presumed that married couples and registered domestic partners hold title in real estate as
    a. joint tenants
    b. tenants in common
    c. community property with right of survivorship
    d. none of the above

15. A husband may sell the couple's residence for $200,000
    a. without his wife's approval
    b. only if $200,000 represents the fair market value of the residence
    c. if his wife joins in the conveyance in writing
    d. both b and c are true

16. Separate property consists of property acquired
    a. before marriage
    b. by inheritance after marriage
    c. both a and b
    d. not both a and b

17. All owners must have undivided rights to possession except in which form of ownership
    a. joint tenancy
    b. tenancy in partnership
    c. tenancy in common
    d. all of the above have undivided rights to possession

18. Jane and Bob are neither married nor registered domestic partners. If they acquire real property together, title is presumed to be held as
    a. tenants in common
    b. joint tenants
    c. community property
    d. there is no presumption as to the form of property ownership in this case

19. Which kind of property is not usually subject to disposition by a will?
    a. tenancy in common
    b. community property
    c. joint tenancy
    d. both b and c

20. Jane is married to Bob. During their marriage, Jane inherits a condo from Bob's father. The condo is acquired as
    a. community property
    b. joint tenancy
    c. tenancy in common
    d. separate property

Answers to Chapter 4 Quiz

1. c. Ownership in severalty refers to ownership of property by one person.

2. d. A brother and sister cannot become spouses or domestic partners, so they could not own what was formerly community property as community property.

3. d. When A dies and B sells B's interest to C, A's interest goes to A's heirs or devisees who take an interest in the property as tenants in common with C.

4. d. Right of survivorship is considered the most important characteristic of joint tenancy.

5. d. Joint tenant A cannot will his/her joint interest because there is right of survivorship in a joint tenancy. Therefore, D acquires no interest in the property.

6. c. Unless they agree otherwise or unless they use community property to maintain each of their separate properties, the condos that they owned before marriage will be considered their separate property after marriage.

7. a. The income from a spouse's labor is community property.

8. c. Because joint tenancy carries with it the right of survivorship, a joint tenant may sell but not will his or her interest in the joint tenancy.

9. c. A corporation may not be a joint tenant, as the law deems a corporation to have potentially infinite duration, thereby making the right of survivorship without consequence.

10. c. Though a joint tenant may not convey good title to his/her interest through a will, a joint tenant may sell his/her interest.

11. c. California's community property law is derived from Spanish law via the Treaty of Guadalupe Hidalgo.

12. b. Tenancy in common requires only the unity of possession.

13. b. Because Bob and Joe do not own equal interests in the property, they could not be joint tenants.

14. d. Married couples and registered domestic partners are presumed to hold real estate as community property. To have community property

with right of survivorship requires that the deed contain the words "community property with right of survivorship."

15. c. Real estate need not always be sold at fair market value.

16. c. Property acquired before marriage or by inheritance is separate property unless there is an agreement otherwise or unless community property is used to maintain the acquired properties.

17. d. Joint tenancy, tenancy in partnership, and tenancy in common all entail undivided rights to possession by each of the owners.

18. a. Under these circumstances, unless there is an agreement otherwise, acquisition of real property by two or more persons is presumed to be to create a tenancy in common.

19. c. As a general rule, tenancy in common and community property may be disposed of by will.

20. d. Property acquired by way of inheritance is acquired as separate property regardless of from whom.

Chapter 5

Involuntary Liens and Homesteads

A *lien* is an official charge against property as security for the payment of a debt or an obligation owed for services rendered. A lien can be either a **voluntary lien** (such as a deed of trust) or an **involuntary lien**, which is a lien created by operation of law, not by the voluntary acts of the debtor. To satisfy a lien, real estate can be foreclosed on. In this chapter we will look at involuntary liens against real property.

JUDGMENT LIENS

A *judgment* is a court's final determination of the rights and duties of the parties in an action before it. A judgment that includes a monetary award does not automatically create a lien; however, the winner of the monetary award may record the judgment, or a summary of the judgment referred to as an **abstract of judgment**, which creates a **general lien** against the (nonexempt) property (real or personal) of the loser (the debtor) in the county (or counties) in which the judgment or abstract of judgment is recorded. CCP §697.310 (a). This judgment lien would be good for 10 years *from the time of entry of judgment*, not from its recording. CCP §697.310 (b).

RENEWAL AND TERMINATION OF A JUDGMENT LIEN

A judgment lien against real property remains valid even if the property is transferred. Furthermore, judgment creditors may renew their judgment liens for another 10 years if the renewal is filed prior to the expiration of the 10-year statute of limitations period (except for liens based on child support, which have no statutory limitation period).

A judgment lien can be terminated in one of the following ways:

1. Discharge of the debt in a bankruptcy proceeding;
2. Payment of the amount owed on the lien. Once the lien is paid off in full, the judgment creditor "shall immediately" issue an **acknowledgement of**

satisfaction and file it with the court, thereby clearing the lien from the title to the property (CCP §724.040);

3. Expiration of the 10-year statute limitation period and any renewal thereof.

NOTICE OF PENDENCY OF ACTION (LIS PENDENS)

When a lawsuit is pending that may affect title to real property, the plaintiff may file a *notice of pendency of action*, formerly known and still often referred to as a *lis pendens*. Though a notice of pendency of action is not a lien, it serves as constructive notice to prospective purchasers or encumbrancers of the property identified in the notice of pendency of action of the pending lawsuit, and such person would, therefore, be bound by any judgment resulting from the lawsuit. If the claimant who filed the notice of pendency of action is successful in the lawsuit and obtains a judgment lien against the property, that judgment lien would have priority relating back to the date of the recording of the notice.

ATTACHMENT LIENS

When a lawsuit *based on a commercial contract where a claim of $500 or more* is filed, there is a danger that the *defendant* (the one sued) will attempt to transfer, encumber, dissipate, or conceal assets that might be used to satisfy a *money* judgment that the *plaintiff* (the one who brought the lawsuit) may obtain. To prevent such actions on the part of the defendant, the plaintiff may request the court to issue a *writ of attachment*, which directs the sheriff to seize enough of the defendant's property to satisfy the amount of the judgment that the plaintiff is seeking.

Once recorded, the writ of attachment creates an *attachment lien* on certain (nonexempt) property owned by the defendant in the county (or counties) in California in which the writ is recorded. An attachment lien cannot be foreclosed; it is merely used to hold the property attached until a judgment is entered. An attachment lien expires three years after its issuance unless it is sooner terminated by discharge or by entry of judgment. It can be renewed for an additional one year at the discretion of the court. CCP §488.510.

Attachments can only be awarded against California resident defendants that are business entities or are individuals who engaged in a trade or business in a manner that formed the basis of the lawsuit. Therefore, a broker would *not* be able to obtain an attachment against the property of a principal who fails to pay a commission owed to the broker, unless the principal is found to have been in the business of buying and selling real estate.

WRIT OF EXECUTION

Once a money judgment has been rendered and a judgment lien has attached to a property, the debtor must pay the amount of the judgment to remove the lien from the property. If the amount of the lien is not paid, the creditor may request the court to issue a *writ of execution*, which directs the sheriff to seize and sell the property to satisfy the judgment.

TAX LIENS

Federal, state, and local governments have the power to place liens on a person's assets to ensure the payment of taxes. Liens placed on real property to enforce the collection of real property taxes are *specific liens*, in that they attach only to the specific property on which the taxes are due, whereas liens to collect unpaid income taxes are general liens.

MECHANICS LIENS

Provided that certain requirements are met and strict procedures followed, persons who provide materials, labor, or other services that are used to improve property may apply for a *mechanics lien*. The right of an improver of property to obtain a mechanics lien is provided for in Article XIV, Section 3 of the California Constitution, but the manner in which the improver must perfect a mechanics lien to ensure that the lien is valid and enforceable is based on statutes. If the strict statutory requirements to perfect a mechanics lien are not met, such as if a deadline is missed, the lien would be extinguished. However, if because of failure to meet statutory requirements a mechanics lien is lost, the claimant may still have the right to sue for breach of contract if the owner of the property refuses to pay for the services or material supplied.

A mechanics lien is a specific lien, attaching only to the property improved. An unlicensed contractor cannot apply for a mechanics lien.

PRELIMINARY NOTICE

As a prerequisite to the validity of a mechanics lien, a *preliminary notice* (see Figure 5.2) must be given by all persons, except wage earners, who furnish service, equipment, or material used for improvements of a property. This preliminary notice *must be given within 20 days after first providing the labor or materials* in order to preserve the right of the claimant to obtain a lien once the job is completed. The purpose of requiring this notice is to prevent secret liens or secret claims.

The persons who must receive a preliminary notice are the owner, the contractor to whom the claimant provides work, and the construction lender, if any. A claimant who has a direct contractual relationship with the owner is required to give notice only to the construction lender, if any.

> **Example:** A general contractor probably has a contract with the owner, so would have to give a preliminary notice only to the construction lender. A plumber or electrician, on the other hand, probably is an independent contractor who supplies labor to the general contractor or to a subcontractor. Such a plumber or electrician would have to give a preliminary notice to the owner, to the contractor or subcontractor, and to the construction lender, if any.

As of July 1, 2012, the preliminary notice served on the owner must contain in boldface type a "NOTICE TO PROPERTY OWNER" that contains language specifically provided for in CC §8202. This special notice to the owner explains that even though the owner may have paid the contractor in full, if the person who serves the owner with the preliminary notice is not paid in full by the contractor, a mechanics lien may be placed on the property to enforce the payment of any amounts owed to the claimant. Therefore, before giving a final payment to the contractor, it would be wise for a property owner to obtain releases from all persons who sent the owner a preliminary notice, stating that they have been paid in full for their work on the property.

NOTICES OF COMPLETION OR CESSATION

If work on the property stops for any reason (such as if there is a dispute with the general contractor, or if the project has been completed) the owner may obtain some protection by signing and recording at the county recorder's office a *notice of completion* (see Figure 5.3) or a *notice of cessation*. A notice of completion must be recorded within 15 days of completion of the work of improvement. A notice of cessation may be recorded by the owner if there has been a continuous cessation of labor on the work of improvement for at least 30 days prior to the recordation. These notices shorten the time claimants have to file a mechanics lien.

RECORDING THE LIEN

To enforce a mechanics lien, a direct contractor (any person who has a direct contract with the owner, usually the general contractor) must record the lien (see Figure 5.4) before the earlier of:

   a) 90 days after completion of the work of improvement
   b) 60 days after the owner records a notice of completion or cessation

Persons other than a direct contractor must record the lien within the following times:

    a) after the claimant ceases to provide work
    b) before the earlier of the following times:
       1) 90 days after completion of the work of improvement
       2) 30 days after the owner records a notice of completion or cessation.

FORECLOSURE ACTION

Unless the holder of the mechanics lien grants and records a written extension of credit to the owner of the property, the lien holder must file a lien foreclosure action within 90 days after recordation of the lien. If the lien holder does not commence foreclosure action within that time, the lien expires and is unenforceable. It is now also mandatory that the claimant record a notice of pendency of action (lis pendens) within 20 days of filing the foreclosure action.

TERMINATION OF MECHANICS LIENS

A mechanics lien is terminated when the lien debt is paid, when the owner files a release bond of 125% of the amount of the lien claim, or if and when the lien is found to be invalid by a court upon petition by the owner.

NOTICE OF NONRESPONSIBILITY

Suppose an owner's tenant contracts to have improvements made on the property and, after completion of the work, refuses to pay the improver. Would the owner be responsible to pay the improver in this situation? The answer is "yes" if the owner had (or should have) discovered the unauthorized work being done and failed to give notice that he or she was not responsible for the work.

An owner can obtain protection from such vicarious responsibility by serving on the improver a *notice of nonresponsibility* (see Figure 5.5). To be effective, the notice of nonresponsibility must be posted on the property and recorded by the owner within 10 days of discovery of the work of improvement.

PRIORITY OF LIENS

At any given time, a piece of real property might have several liens recorded against it: a deed of trust, a mechanics lien, a tax lien, a special assessment lien, a judgment lien — all vying to obtain priority over the others in case of a default where the property is worth less than the sum of the existing valid liens. The order in which lien holders are paid is known as *lien priority*.

As a general rule, the order of payment is determined by the order of lien recording; in other words, first to record, first in priority. However, some types of liens are given special priority: property tax liens and special assessment liens have priority over all other liens, and mechanics liens attach as of the date the work of improvement *commenced* (even though the liens were recorded later). Mechanics liens also have priority over any private lien that was unrecorded on the date the work of improvement commenced and of which the claimant had no notice.

Note that for mechanics lien priority, the date of attachment of the lien is the date on which the work of improvement began — not the date on which the claimant began furnishing labor or materials for the work of improvement. Therefore, all mechanics liens relating to the same work of improvement have equal priority, and each mechanics lien holder is entitled to collect his or her pro rata (proportional) share of the work furnished.

DECLARATION OF HOMESTEAD

If a homeowner is sued and a judgment is rendered against the homeowner, California's homestead law provides limited protection of the homeowner's equity in the homestead from levy by creditors. The protection was adjusted as of January 1, 2013 (CCP §704.730), and is as follows:

- $75,000 for an individual;

- $100,000 if the homeowner lives with at least one family member who has no interest other than a community property interest with the judgment debtor in the house (in other words, if the homeowner is a "head of the household";

- $175,000 if the homeowner is 65 years of age or older;

- $175,000 if the homeowner is physically or mentally disabled and as a result of that disability is unable to engage in substantial employment;

- $175,000 if the homeowner is 55 years of age or older and single with an annual income of $25,000 or less, and the sale is an *involuntary* sale;

- $175,000 if the homeowner is 55 years of age or older, married, and the combined annual income of the couple is $35,000 or less, and the sale is an *involuntary* sale.

Fig. 5.1   Summary of Important Mechanics Lien Dates
(effective July 1, 2012)

Direct Contractors	All Other Furnisher's of Work or Materials	Owner of Property

Preliminary Notice:
• served within 20 days of beginning work
 	
• served to:
   construction lender
 	
Mechanics Lien:
• filed earlier of
   a)   90 days after completion of the work
   b)   60 days after the owner records a notice of completion or cessation
 	
Foreclosure Action:
• filed within 90 days of recordation of lien
 	
Lis Pendens:
• filed within 20 days of filing foreclosure action
	Preliminary Notice:
	• served within 20 days of beginning work (wage earners are exempt from the requirement to serve a preliminary notice)
	• served to:
	   a) owner
	   b) contractor to whom the claimant provides work
	   c) construction lender
	
	Mechanics Lien:
	• filed earlier of
	   a) 90 days after completion of the work
	   b) 30 days after the owner records a notice of completion or cessation
	
	Foreclosure Action:
	• within 90 days of recordation of lien
	
	Lis Pendens:
	• within 20 days of filing foreclosure action
		Notice of Completion:
		• recorded within 15 days of completion of work
		
		Notice of Cessation:
		• recorded at least 30 days after work ceased
		
		Notice of Nonresponsibility:
		• posted and recorded within 10 days of discovery of the work of improvement

Example: If the home of someone who is single, lives alone, and is not disabled has a value of $500,000 and a mortgage balance against it of $400,000, then $75,000 of the $100,000 equity in the home would be protected from creditors, regardless of whether the homeowner was in or out of bankruptcy.

Anyone who lives in their own home automatically has an automatic homestead, without having to sign or file anything. However, by having a declared homestead, a homeowner can obtain significant advantages over having merely an automatic homestead.

A *homestead declaration* (see Figure 5.6) is a legal form that claims a particular dwelling (such as a house, condominium, boat, or mobile home) as the homeowner's principal residence. The form must be signed by the homeowner, notarized, and recorded at the county recorder's office. The declaration must contain:

1. the name of the homestead owner;

2. a description of the homestead sufficient to identify it;

3. a statement that the claimant is an owner of the homestead property;

4. a statement that the homestead is the principal dwelling of the claimant or of the claimant's spouse; and

5. a statement that the claimant or the claimant's spouse is currently residing in the declared homestead.

BENEFITS OF A DECLARED HOMESTEAD

Though the same monetary limits listed above apply to both declared and automatic homesteads, and though in either case the owner can claim the homestead protection on only one home at a time, the owner who has filed a declaration of homestead has the following advantages over a homeowner who merely has an automatic homestead:

- The owner who files a *declared* homestead can choose which of several dwellings will be protected as the person's home; the owner of an *automatic* homestead has protection only on the home in which he or she currently resides.

- The owner who files a *declared* homestead can move to a new residence and still have the homestead protection continue to apply to his or her former residence (for example, if the owner continues to own the former residence and after moving rents it to someone else); the owner of an *automatic* homestead would lose the homestead exemption on the home from which he or she moved.

- The owner who files a *declared* homestead has the homestead protection even in the case of a voluntary sale; the owner of an *automatic* homestead is only protected in the case of an involuntary sale.

- The proceeds of a sale of a home on which a *declared* homestead has been recorded may be used (up to the dollar limits of the homestead law) to purchase another home within six months of the sale (the so-called **"*six-month rule*"**) with the exemption that applied to the sold house applying to the new house; the owner of an *automatic* homestead does not have this six-month protection from creditors.

The homestead exemption, whether declared or automatic, protects the owner's equity only against judgment liens, not against

- liens held by secured creditors (such as deeds of trust);
- mechanics liens;
- tax liens;
- liens for child support or alimony; or
- liens imposed by condominiums or by homeowners associations.

If the equity in a home does not exceed the amount of the applicable homestead exemption, then the home would not be subject to a forced sale by a judgment lien holder. However, if the equity in the home exceeds the applicable homestead exemption, then a judgment lien holder can force the sale of the home, and the proceeds of the sale would be distributed in the following order:

1. to discharge all liens and encumbrances exempt from the homestead protection;

2. to the judgment debtor in the amount of any applicable homestead exemption;

3. to pay the costs of the execution sale;

4. to the judgment creditor to satisfy the judgment debt;

5. to the judgment debtor in the amount remaining.

Fig. 5.2

California Preliminary Notice

NOTICE TO PROPERTY OWNER

EVEN THOUGH YOU HAVE PAID YOUR CONTRACTOR IN FULL, if the person or firm that has given you this notice is not paid in full for labor, service, equipment, or material provided or to be provided to your construction project, a lien may be placed on your property. Foreclosure of the lien may lead to loss of all or part of your property. You may wish to protect yourself against this by (1) requiring your contractor to provide a signed release by the person or firm that is giving you this notice before making payment to your contractor, or (2) any other method that is appropriate under the circumstances.

This notice is required by law to be served by the undersigned as a statement of your legal rights. This notice is not intended to reflect upon the financial condition of the contractor or the person employed by you on the construction project.

If you record a notice of cessation or completion of your construction project, you must within 10 days after recording, send a copy of the notice of completion to your contractor and the person or firm that has given you this notice. The notice must be sent by registered or certified mail. Failure to send the notice will extend the deadline to record a claim of lien. You are not required to send the notice if you are a residential homeowner of a dwelling containing four or fewer units.

Please take notice that_____, whose address is at

_____ has furnished or will furnish labor,

service, equipment or material to the work of improvement located at _____

_____ as follows: _____

_____

_____

_____

Signature   Title   Date

The name and address of the person who, or the business that, contracted for the labor, services, or equipment described above is_____.

This preliminary notice is being served on the following persons and businesses at the indicated addresses:

☐ Owner or Reputed Owner
(name) _____
(address) _____

☐ Direct Contractor or Reputed Direct Contractor (to which the claimant provides work, either directly or through one or more subcontractors)
(name) _____
(address) _____

☐ Construction Lender or Reputed Construction Lender, if any
(name) _____
(address) _____

Estimated Price of the labor, services, equipment or materials described above is $ _____.

Name of the claimant who is providing this notice is _____.

Fig. 5.3

RECORDING REQUESTED BY:

AND TO BE RETURNED TO:

NAME:

ADDRESS:

CITY:

STATE & ZIP:

NOTICE of COMPLETION

Pursuant to California Civil Code, Section 8182, notice is hereby given that:

1. The undersigned is an owner of a property interest or estate in the property hereinafter described.
2. The full name of the owner is_____
3. The address of the owners _____
4. The nature of the interest or estate of the undersigned : _____
(e.g. fee simple, leasehold interest, etc.)
5. A description of the property sufficient for identification is:_____
_____
6. The street address of said property is _____
7. The full names and addresses of all persons who hold an interest or estate with the owner as joint tenants or as tenants in common are:

NAMES: ADDRESSES:

_____   _____

_____   _____

8. The full names and addresses of the predecessors in interest of the owner of the property if the property was transferred after the work or improvement referred to in this notice began:

NAMES: ADDRESSES:

_____   _____

_____   _____

9. A work of improvement on the property described above was completed on _____
10. The work of improvement completed is described as follows: _____
_____
11. The name of the original contractor, if any, for the work of improvement is _____

VERIFICATION

I, the undersigned, declare under penalty of perjury under the laws of the State of California that:

I am the_____ of the interest or estate, described above.
       (Owner, officer of owning entity, agent of owner, etc.)

I have read the foregoing notice and know and understand the contents of it. The facts stated in it are true and correct.

DATE:_____   _____
                                       SIGNATURE OF OWNER OR AGENT OF OWNER

Fig. 5.4

Recording Requested By And When Recorded Mail To:

CLAIM OF MECHANICS LIEN

NOTICE IS HEREBY GIVEN that Claimant, whose full name is _____ and whose full address is _____ furnished labor, service, equipment, or materials for improvements to real property situated in the County of_____, State of California. Said real property is described as

STREET, CITY, ZIP ADDRESS: _____

    and/or

LEGAL DESCRIPTION: _____

_____

This lien is claimed for the following labor and material furnished: _____

_____. Claimant is owed $_____ for labor, service, equipment, or materials furnished for the work of improvement, after deducting all credits and offsets, plus interest at the legal rate from the date of this lien.

The name of the person or company by whom claimant was employed or to whom the claimant furnished work is: _____

The name and address of the owner or reputed owner of the real property is:

_____

Date:_____   Name of Claimant: _____
                                      (Claimant's Printed Name)

                    By: _____
                                        (Claimant's Signature)

Verification

I, the undersigned, declare: I am the claimant of the foregoing mechanics lien. I have read the foregoing claim of mechanics lien and know the contents thereof, and the same is true of my knowledge. I declare under penalty of perjury under the laws of the State of California that the foregoing is true and correct.

Executed on_____, 20___at_____ California.

_____
          Signature of Claimant

<u>NOTICE OF MECHANICS LIEN</u>
ATTENTION!

Upon the recording of the enclosed MECHANICS LIEN with the County Recorder's Office of the county where the property is located, your property is subject to the filing of a legal action seeking a court-ordered foreclosure sale of the real property on which the lien has been recorded. That legal action must be filed with the court noted later than 90 days after the date the mechanics lien is recorded.

The party identified in the mechanics lien may have provided labor or materials for improvements to your property and may not have been paid for these items. You are receiving this notice because it is a required step in filing a mechanics lien foreclosure action against your property. The foreclosure action will seek a sale of your property in order to pay for unpaid labor, materials, or improvements provided to your property. This may affect your ability to borrow against, refinance, or sell the property until the mechanics lien is released.

BECAUSE THE LIEN AFFECTS YOUR PROPERTY, YOU MAY WISH TO SPEAK WITH YOUR CONTRACTOR IMMEDIATELY, OR CONTACT AN ATTORNEY, OR FOR MORE INFORMATION ON MECHANICS LIENS GO TO THE CONTRACTORS STATE LICENSE BOARD WEBSITE AT www.cslb.ca.gov.

PROOF OF SERVICE AFFIDAVIT

Pursuant to the California Civil Code, service of the Claim of Mechanics Lien and Notice of Mechanics Lien shall be by registered mail, certified mail, or first-class mail, evidenced by a certificate of mailing, postage prepaid, addressed to the owner or reputed owner at the owner's or reputed owner's residence or business address. If the owner or reputed owner cannot be served by this method, then a copy of the Claim of Mechanics Lien and Notice of Mechanics Lien may be given by the same methods as if to the owner but addressed to the construction lender or to the original contractor.

Affidavit For Service On The Owner

I,_____ (full name), declare that I served a copy of this Claim of Mechanics Lien and Notice of Mechanics Lien by registered mail, certified mail, or first-class mail, evidenced by a certificate of mailing, postage prepaid, addressed as follows to the owner or reputed owner of the property:

Name and title or capacity of persons served: _____

Service address: _____

Executed on this_____ (day)_____ (month)_____ (year)

at_____ (city), California.

By:_____

(signature of person making service)

Affidavit For Service On The Construction Lender Or Original Contractor

I,_____ (full name), declare that the owner or reputed owner cannot be served with a copy of this Mechanics Lien and Notice of Mechanics Lien by registered mail, certified mail, or first-class mail. Alternatively, I served a copy of this Claim of Mechanics Lien and Notice of Mechanics Lien by registered mail, certified mail, or first-class mail, evidenced by a certificate of mailing, postage prepaid, addressed as follows to the construction lender or original contractor:

Name and title or capacity of persons served: _____

Service address: _____

Executed on this_____ (day)_____ (month)_____ (year)

at_____ (city), California.

By:_____

(signature of person making service)

Fig. 5.5

Recording Requested By
And When Recorded Mail To:

NOTICE OF NONRESPONSIBILITY

NOTICE IS HEREBY GIVEN PURSUANT TO CALIFORNIA CIVIL CODE, SECTION 8444 THAT:

1. I,_____ (full name), the undersigned, am the _____ (specific nature of title or interest in the property of the person giving the notice, e.g., owner) of the property located at:

Street Address:_____

City of_____, California.

2. On_____ (month, day, year) I first obtained knowledge of that a work of improvement was being constructed on the above-described property.

3. Not more than 10 days elapsed since I obtained that knowledge.

4. I did not cause the above work of improvement to be performed and will not be responsible for any claims arising from the work of improvement.

5. The name of the purchaser under contract or the lessee of the above property is:

_____ (full name).

Date:_____   By:_____
                                          (signature)

_____
(print name)

VERIFICATION

I, the undersigned, declare: I am the person who signed the foregoing notice. I have read that notice and know its contents and the facts stated therein, and the same is true of my own knowledge. I declare under penalty of perjury under the laws of the State of California that the foregoing is true and correct.

Executed at_____, California.

Date:_____   By:_____
                                          (signature)

_____
(print name)

Fig. 5.6

RECORDING REQUESTED BY

AND WHEN RECORDED MAIL TO:

NAME

STREET
ADDRESS

CITY, STATE &
ZIP CODE

SPACE ABOVE THIS LINE FOR RECORDER'S USE ONLY

DECLARATION OF HOMESTEAD

I, _____
(Full Name of Declarant)

do hereby certify and declare as follows:
(1) I hereby claim as a declared homestead the premises located in the City of _____

County of _____, State of _____

commonly known as _____
(Street Address)
and more particularly described as follows: [Give complete legal description]

(2) I am the declared homestead owner of the above declared homestead.
(3) I own the following interest in the above declared homestead:
(4) The above declared homestead is [strike inapplicable clause] my principal dwelling   and
                                                       the principal dwelling of my spouse

[strike inapplicable clause] I am   currently residing on that declared homestead.
                              my spouse is

(5) The facts stated in this Declaration are true as of my personal knowledge.

_____   _____
Date   (Signature of Declarant)

STATE OF _____

COUNTY OF _____

On _____ before me, _____,
(Date)   (Name and title of the officer)

personally appeared _____, who proved to me on the basis of
(Name of person signing)
satisfactory evidence to be the person(s) whose name(s) is/are subscribed to the within instrument and acknowledged to me that he/she/they executed the same in his/her/their authorized capacity(ies), and that by his/her/their signature(s) on the instrument the person(s), or the entity upon behalf of which the person(s) acted, executed the instrument.

I certify under PENALTY OF PERJURY under the laws of the State of California that the foregoing paragraph is true and correct.

WITNESS my hand and official seal.

_____
Signature of officer

(Seal)

* There are various types of homestead forms depending on each person's legal status. Before you use this form you many want to consult an attorney if you have questions concerning which document form is appropriate for your transaction.

Key Terms for Chapter 5

acknowledgment — a written declaration signed by a person before a duly authorized officer, usually a notary public, acknowledging that the signing is voluntary.

acknowledgment of satisfaction — a written declaration signed by a person before a duly authorized officer, usually a notary public, acknowledging that a lien has been paid off in full and that the signing is voluntary.

attachment lien — a prejudgment lien on property, obtained to ensure the availability of funds to pay a judgment if the plaintiff prevails.

automatic homestead —a homestead exemption that applies automatically to a homeowner's principal residence and that provides limited protection for the homeowner's equity in that residence against a judgment lien foreclosure.

declared homestead — the dwelling described in a homestead declaration.

defendant — the one against whom a lawsuit is brought.

dwelling house homestead — an automatic homestead.

general lien — a lien that attaches to all of a person's nonexempt property.

homestead declaration —a recorded document that claims a particular dwelling (such as a house, condominium, boat, or mobile home) as the owner's principal place of residence and that provides limited protection for the claimant's equity in the dwelling.

homestead exemption — the amount of a homeowner's equity that may be protected from unsecured creditors.

involuntary lien — a lien created by operation of law, not by the voluntary acts of the debtor.

judgment — a court's final determination of the rights and duties of the parties in an action before it.

lien —an encumbrance against real property that is used to secure a debt and that can, in most cases, be foreclosed.

lien priority — the order in which lien holders are paid.

lis pendens — (Latin for "action pending") a notice of pendency of action.

mechanics lien — a specific lien claimed by someone who furnished labor or materials for a work of improvement on real property and who has not been fully paid.

notice of cessation — a written form that notifies that all work of improvement on a piece of real property has ceased, and that limits the time in which mechanics liens may be filed against the property.

notice of completion — a written form that notifies that a work of improvement on real property has been completed, and that limits the time in which mechanics liens may be filed against the property.

notice of nonresponsibility — a written notice that a property owner may record and post on the property to shield the owner from any liability for a work of improvement on the property that a lessee or a purchaser under a land sales contract authorized.

notice of pendency of action — a notice that provides constructive notice to potential purchasers or encumbrancers of a piece of real property of the pendency of a lawsuit in which an interest in that piece of real property is claimed.

plaintiff — the one who brings a lawsuit.

preliminary notice — a notice sent by someone who furnishes work or materials for a work of improvement on real property that creates a right to file a mechanics lien against the property.

specific lien — a lien that attaches only to specific property.

voluntary lien — a lien obtained through the voluntary action of the one against whose property the lien attaches.

writ — a court order commanding the person to whom it is directed to perform an act specified therein.

writ of attachment — a writ ordering the seizure of property belonging to a defendant to ensure the availability of the property to satisfy a judgment if the plaintiff wins.

writ of execution — a writ directing a public official (usually the sheriff) to seize and sell property of a debtor to satisfy a debt.

Quiz for Chapter 5

1. Bob was awarded a money judgment in 2002. Bob recorded the judgment in 2011. The judgment lien Bob received is good until
   a. sometime in 2022
   b. sometime in 2012
   c. sometime in 2017
   d. none of the above
2. Sally files a notice of cessation regarding a construction project on her property. Bob, a laborer, has how long to file a mechanics lien?
   a. 30 days
   b. 45 days
   c. 60 days
   d. 90 days
3. Sally files a notice of cessation regarding a construction project on her property. A direct contractor has how long to file a mechanics lien?
   a. 90 days
   b. 60 days
   c. 30 days
   d. none of the above
4. Which of the following may arise after the outcome of a lawsuit?
   a. mechanics lien
   b. judgment lien
   c. lis pendens
   d. prejudgment attachment lien
5. A subcontractor must file a lis pendens within how many days of foreclosing on a mechanics lien?
   a. 10
   b. 20
   c. 30
   d. 60
6. In order to be protected from liability, the owner of a property must post and record a notice of nonresponsibility within how many days of discovery of the work of improvement?
   a. 10
   b. 20
   c. 30
   d. 60

7. Sally was awarded a judgment against Janet for $10,000 in 2000. Sally recorded the judgment in 2012. Sally's lien would be good until
   a. 2022
   b. Sally never received a lien
   c. 2017
   d. 2022 or 2032

8. A mechanics lien can be terminated when
   a. the lien debt is paid
   b. the owner files a notice of nonresponsibility
   c. the owner files a notice of cessation
   d. none of the above

9. If the owner of a property does not file a notice of completion or a notice of cessation, how long after the completion of work does a direct contractor have to file a mechanics lien?
   a. 90
   b. 60
   c. 30
   d. none of the above

10. A notice of pendency of action may be filed in which of the following actions?
    a. an action to recover possession of a car
    b. an action to collect on a promissory note
    c. an action to determine who has title to a house
    d. none of the above

11. In order to preserve his or her right to file a mechanics lien, a wage earner must file a preliminary notice within how many days of beginning to furnished work for a work of improvement?
    a. 10
    b. 20
    c. 30
    d. none of the above

12. An involuntary lien can be which of the following?
    a. a mechanics lien
    b. a judgment lien
    c. a tax lien
    d. all of the above

13. Which of the following words is least related to the others?
    a. notice of nonresponsibility
    b. general lien
    c. mechanics lien
    d. preliminary notice

14. A declared homestead can give protection from all of the following except
    a. federal income tax liens

    b. mechanics liens

    c. a deed of trust foreclosure

    d. none of the above

15. An attachment lien may be obtained in which of the following actions?

    a. an action arising from the business dealings of an individual, where the amount of the claim is over $500

    b. any action where the amount claimed is over $500

    c. an action against a business, where the amount claimed is over $500

    d. both a and c

16. Bob, who is single and lives alone, owns a house that has a fair market value of $310,000. He still owes $250,000 on a deed of trust against the house. Joe obtained a judgment lien against Bob in the amount of $25,000. Joe can

    a. foreclose on Bob's house, but can get no more than $15,000

    b. foreclose on Bob's house, but can get no more than $10,000

    c. foreclose on Bob's house, but can get no more than $25,000

    d. none of the above

17. Sally, who is 66 years old, owns a house that has a fair market value of $300,000. Sally still owes $100,000 on a deed of trust against the house. Sally has failed to file a declaration of homestead. Bob obtains a judgment lien against Sally in the amount of $250,000. The most that Sally can receive from a foreclosure sale of her house is

    a. $50,000 less the cost of foreclosure

    b. $50,000

    c. $175,000

    d. Sally will receive nothing

18. To have a judgment lien there must be

    a. a recording of a judgment or an abstract of judgment

    b. a notice of completion

    c. a lis pendens

    d. both a and c

19. For a judgment lien, priority is determined by the date of

    a. recording the judgment

    b. entry of judgment

    c. foreclosure on the lien

    d. satisfaction of the judgment

20. Sally, who is 35, married, and has one child living at home, owns a house that has a fair market value of $400,000. She still owes $200,000 on the deed of trust against the house. Bob obtains a judgment lien in the amount of $190,000 against Sally and forecloses on the house. The total cost of the foreclosure proceedings is $10,000. Sally will likely obtain how much from the foreclosure sale?

    a. $100,000

    b. $90,000

   c. $10,000

   d. nothing

21. Unless earlier discharged, an attachment lien continues for how many years

   a. 1

   b. 2

   c. 3

   d. 4

22. Which of the following is not a specific lien?

   a. mechanics lien

   b. property tax lien

   c. special assessment lien

   d. none of the above

23. After judgment, a creditor would create a lien by filing

   a. a writ of execution

   b. a writ of attachment

   c. a lis pendens

   d. none of the above

24. After a lawsuit is begun, a court rules that a lien should be placed on certain parcel of real estate. This lien would be

   a. a lis pendens

   b. a writ of execution

   c. a mechanics lien

   d. none of the above

25. A declared homestead may provide protection against foreclosure of a

   a. deed of trust

   b. mechanics lien

   c. property tax lien

   d. none of the above

Answers to Chapter 5 Quiz

1. b. A judgment lien usually continues for 10 years from the date of entry of the judgment.

2. a. All furnishers of work or materials other than direct contractors have 30 days in which to file a mechanics lien after a notice of completion or cessation has been filed.

3. b. A direct contractor has 60 days in which to file a mechanics lien after a notice of cessation or completion has been filed.

4. b. Of the possible answers presented, only a judgment lien can arise *after* the outcome of a lawsuit.

5. b. All mechanics lien holders must file a lis pendens within 20 days of filing foreclosure action.

6. a. A notice of nonresponsibility must be posted and recorded within 10 days of discovery of the work of improvement.

7. b. In order create a judgment lien, a judgment or abstract of judgment must be recorded within 10 years of entry of judgment.

8. a. Paying the lien debt will terminate a mechanics lien.

9. a. All furnishers of work or materials including direct contractors have 90 days after the completion of the work to file a mechanics lien if the owner of the property does not file a notice of completion or cessation.

10. c. A lis pendens can only be obtained in an action that may affect the title to real property.

11. d. A wage earner does not need to file a preliminary notice.

12. d. Neither a mechanics lien, a judgment lien, nor a tax lien is a voluntarily created lien.

13. b. A notice of nonresponsibility, a mechanics lien, and a preliminary notice are terms associated with a mechanics lien, which is a specific lien.

14. d. A declared homestead does not give protection from federal income tax liens, mechanics liens, or deed of trust foreclosures.

15. d. An attachment lien can only be obtained against either a business or natural person engaged in business, where the amount claimed is over $500.

16. d. Bob's equity is only $60,000, so Joe cannot foreclose on Bob's house because of Bob's $75,000 homestead exemption.

17. c. Sally is 66 years old, so her automatic homestead exemption is $175,000, while the equity in the home is $200,000. Therefore, Bob can foreclose on the house, but the order of payment is $100,000 to the lender, and the next monies to Sally for her homestead exemption.

18. a. One need not file a lis pendens to obtain a judgment lien.

19. a. For a judgment lien, priority is determined by the date of recording the judgment.

20. a. Sally has $200,000 in her home, and she is married, so her homestead exemption is $100,000, all of which is covered by the surplus equity in a home.

21. c. An attachment lien is a prejudgment lien that continues for three years unless it is sooner terminated by discharge or by entry of judgment.

22. d. All of the listed liens are specific liens.

23. d. The creditor would record the judgment or an abstract of judgment.

24. d. This would be a prejudgment attachment lien.

25. d. A homestead exemption may provide protection against a judgment lien, but not against a deed of trust, a mechanics lien, or a property tax lien.

Chapter 6

Property Listing and Sales Contracts

CONTRACTS IN GENERAL

There probably is not a more important area of the law for real estate salespersons and brokers, and for their clients and customers, than the law of contracts. In nearly every business transaction, one or more contracts are involved.

CLASSIFICATION OF CONTRACTS

CC §1549 defines a contract as "an agreement to do or not do a certain thing."

In regard to the *manner of creation*, a contract may be **express** or **implied**. An express contract is one in which the parties declare their intention in words, whether orally or in writing. Nearly every real estate transaction must be express and, because of the statute of frauds, must be in writing (an exception is a lease for one year or less). An **implied contract** is not written or spoken; it is implied by the actions of the parties.

> **Example:** When you sit down at a restaurant and place an order, there is no written or oral agreement between you and the restaurant that you will pay for the food ordered and delivered; however, there is an implied contract to that effect — a contract ever bit as valid and, in this context, as enforceable as if it had been written. An implied contract can arise even in cases where the actions of one of the parties was not intentional — for example, if you were to fall unconscious on a sidewalk and an ambulance came and took you to a hospital, an implied contract to pay the ambulance would be enforced.

In regard to the *content of an agreement*, a contract may be **bilateral** or **unilateral**. A bilateral contract is one in which one party gives a promise in exchange for a promise from the other party. In other words, a bilateral contract contains promises on two sides; a unilateral contract, on only one.

> **Example:** If I promise to pay you $20 if you mow my lawn on Tuesday, and you promise to mow my lawn on Tuesday, we have a bilateral contract right then and there. If I promise to pay you $20 if you mow my lawn on Tuesday, and you shrug your shoulders and say, "I'll see if I have time," we have a unilateral contract — you have not promised to do anything, but I have. Unless I withdraw my offer in the meanwhile, if you go ahead and mow my lawn on Tuesday, I will owe you $20. On the other hand, if you don't mow my lawn on Tuesday, there is no penalty to you, nor is there $20 owed by me to you.

As we will see, if you have a client who gives you an exclusive authorization and right to sell listing, your client promises to pay you a commission if you find a buyer and you promise to make an effort to find a buyer for your client. In this circumstance, you and your client have exchanged promises, thereby creating a bilateral contract. But in an open listing situation, your client promises to pay you a commission if you are the first to find a buyer; you promise nothing. In this circumstance, you and your client have a unilateral contract.

In regard to the *extent of performance*, a contract may be **executory** or **executed**. An executed contract is a contract that has been fully performed. An executory contract is one in which some performance by one or both parties remains to be done.

> **Example:** If I offer to pay you $20 to mow my lawn on Tuesday and you agree to do so, our contract (bilateral) remains executory until both of us perform as agreed, at which time our contract becomes an executed contract.

Note: one must be careful to keep in mind the context in which "executed contract" is used. Because the word "executed" can mean signed, the phrase "executed contract" is also used to refer to a contract, any contract, that has been signed.

In regard to *legal effect*, a contract may be **valid**, **void**, **voidable**, or **unenforceable**. A **valid contract** is a contract that is binding and can be enforced by law. A **void contract** is not considered a contract at all and cannot be enforced by law, such as an agreement to commit a crime, or, in California, an agreement by an unemancipated minor to purchase or sell real property (although many other kinds of agreements entered into by a minor are considered voidable, not void). A **voidable contract** is a valid contract that is enforceable at the option of one party but not at the option of the other, as when the consent of one party (the party who may elect to have the contract enforced) is obtained by fraud (not forgery, which would render the contract void), coercion, misrepresentation, or undue influence.

An **_unenforceable contract_** is (or was) valid but is such that a court will not enforce it. For example, pursuant to the statute of limitations, a contract that originally was valid and fully enforceable may become unenforceable after the passage of a certain amount of time. (See Figure 6.1)

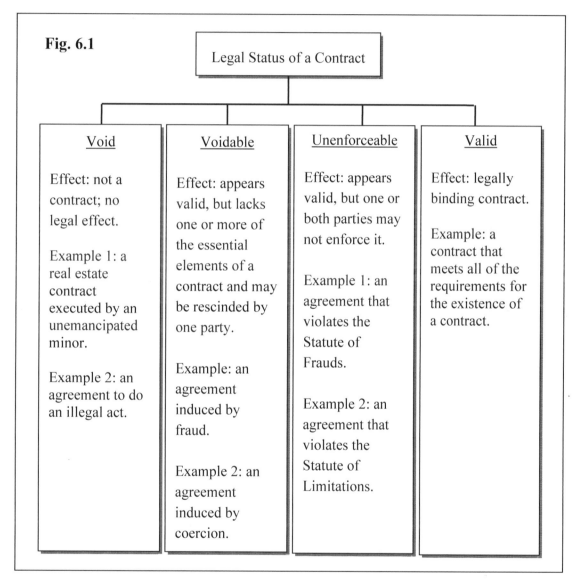

Fig. 6.1

Legal Status of a Contract

Void	Voidable	Unenforceable	Valid
Effect: not a contract; no legal effect. Example 1: a real estate contract executed by an unemancipated minor. Example 2: an agreement to do an illegal act.	Effect: appears valid, but lacks one or more of the essential elements of a contract and may be rescinded by one party. Example: an agreement induced by fraud. Example 2: an agreement induced by coercion.	Effect: appears valid, but one or both parties may not enforce it. Example 1: an agreement that violates the Statute of Frauds. Example 2: an agreement that violates the Statute of Limitations.	Effect: legally binding contract. Example: a contract that meets all of the requirements for the existence of a contract.

ESSENTIAL ELEMENTS OF A CONTRACT

CC §1550 states:

"It is essential to the existence of a contract that there should be:

1. Parties capable of contracting;
2. Their consent;

3. A lawful object; and
4. A sufficient cause or consideration."

Parties Capable of Contracting

"All persons are capable of contracting, except minors, persons of unsound mind, and persons deprived of civil rights." CC §1556.

The term "persons" includes corporations, partnerships, and other business entities, which are fully capable of entering into contracts. Pursuant to CC §671, aliens have the same rights to acquire and transfer property as citizens; however, they are subject to certain transfer reporting and tax withholding requirements. Personal representatives of decedents are capable of entering into contracts on behalf of the decedents' estates. Real estate agents often deal with such estate representatives when the latter are interested in selling real property belonging to the estates they represent.

Minors

A minor is a person under the age of 18 years; however, despite the wording of CC §1556 above, some minors have been given the right to enter into contracts. An **emancipated minor** is a minor who has been validly married (even if the marriage has been terminated), is serving in the military, or has been declared emancipated by court order. An emancipated minor may enter into any type of contract, including a contract for the purchase or sale of real property. If an unemancipated minor has a court-appointed guardian, a broker may negotiate in real property with the guardian who is acting on behalf of the minor, but the guardian needs the court's approval to carry out such negotiations. Brokers should exercise care, including seeking the advice of an attorney, before contracting with a person under 18 years of age.

Incompetents

A person who has been declared by court order to be of unsound mind does not have the capacity to enter into a contract. Similarly, if a person is entirely without understanding, even if such person has not been declared incompetent by a court, that person does not possess the power to contract. If an incompetent person enters into a contract, the contract is void. If the person is declared incompetent after a valid contract is entered into, the contract is voidable at the discretion of the incompetent person's guardian.

Persons Deprived of Civil Rights

Convicts are deprived of certain civil rights but do not forfeit their property and, except for certain classes of convicts (for example, persons sentenced to life imprisonment or the death penalty) may purchase and sell real property.

Consent

Pursuant to CC §1565, "The consent of the parties to a contract must be

1. Free;
2. Mutual; and
3. Communicated by each to the other."

Consent Freely Given

Consent that is not free, such as consent obtained by *duress*, *menace*, fraud, or undue influence, is consent that may be *rescinded*. As we have seen, a contract obtained by such consent is voidable. Duress refers to unlawful confinement of a person or physical force used against a person in order to obtain consent of that person. Menace refers to a threat of duress or of injury to person or property of a person.

Mutuality of Consent

"Consent is not mutual, unless the parties all agree upon the same thing in the same sense." CC §1580. Mutual consent (often referred to as a "meeting of the minds") is usually evidenced by an *offer* of one party that manifests contractual intention and by an *acceptance* by the other party.

An offer must not only manifest contractual intention; it must do so using terms that are clear and definite. A vague offer that does not clearly state what is being offered, even if accepted, is illusory, and an agreement based upon such an offer is unenforceable.

> **Example:** A contract that merely states that an unimproved parcel of land is to be improved with streets, but does not state where the streets should be located, how wide they should be, with what materials constructed, etc., would be unenforceable due to lack of definiteness of terms.

Note, however, that there are circumstances where clear and definite terms appear to be offered, but custom and law do not deem an offer to be made.

Example: An advertisement that lists a description of, and an asking price for, real property is not considered to be an offer; it is deemed to be merely an invitation for a buyer to make an offer.

Communication of Consent

In order for there to be the meeting of the minds that is required for mutuality of consent, both the offer and the acceptance must be communicated to the appropriate party. However, communication between the parties to a contract, especially to a real estate contract, is usually not a simple one-two process of an offer being made followed by an acceptance. Negotiations generally take the form of an offer being made by a potential buyer, rejection and counteroffer from the seller, rejection and counteroffer from the buyer, and so on (real estate agents must have patience) until the process ends — with or without a sale. (See Figure 6.2)

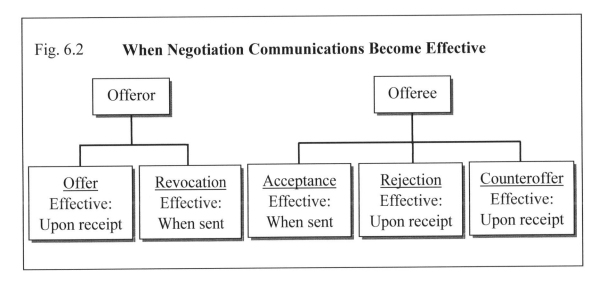

Fig. 6.2   **When Negotiation Communications Become Effective**

An offer can be terminated in several ways. (See Fig. 6.3)

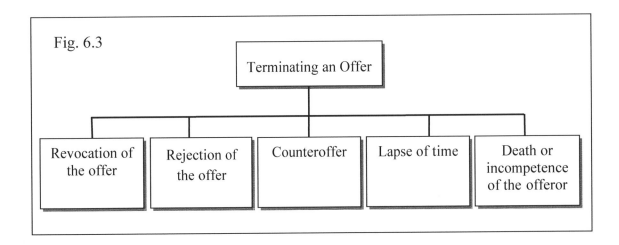

Fig. 6.3

Acceptance: acceptance is generally effective when it is sent; however, an offer can be revoked at any time before acceptance is actually received.

Revocation: an offeror can terminate (*revoke*) an offer at any time before its acceptance is received, even if the offer stated that it would remain open for a specified time (unless consideration was paid for the offer remaining open, in which case an option was created). Revocation of an offer is deemed effective when it is sent or communicated to the offeree in some manner.

> **Example:** If an offer was made to sell or purchase a property and the offeree learns that the property has in the meanwhile been purchased by someone else, revocation of the offer is deemed to have been communicated to the offeree.

Rejection: rejection of an offer by the offeree terminates the offer. Even if the offeree subsequently wants to accept the offer, the offeree may not do so unless the offer is renewed by the offeror.

Counteroffer: a counteroffer is deemed to be both a rejection of the earlier offer and the creation of a new (counter) offer.

Lapse of time: an offer is terminated if the offer states that it must be accepted by a specified time and it is not accepted within that specified time. Furthermore, even if an offer does not state a specified time in which it must be accepted, an offer is terminated after a "reasonable" time. What is a reasonable time in a certain situation is something that would be determined by a court if a dispute arises.

Death of the offeror:

An offer is terminated if the offeror dies or becomes incompetent before the offer is accepted. If the offer is accepted prior to the death, a valid contract would have been formed, and the offeror's estate would be obliged to perform according to the terms of the contract.

Lawful Object

"The object of a contract is the thing which is agreed, on the part of the party receiving the consideration, to do or not to do." CC §1595.

"The object of a contract must be lawful when the contract is made, and possible and ascertainable by the time the contract is to be performed." CC §1596.

For a contract to be valid, both its consideration and its object must be lawful. If a contract has only one object and that object is unlawful, the entire contract is void. However, if the contract has several objects, some of which are valid, the contract would normally be valid and enforced as to the lawful objects only.

Examples in the real estate field of invalid contracts due to having an unlawful object include:

- listing contracts of unlicensed brokers;
- contracts among brokers to fix commission rates; and
- contracts among brokers to sell property in their areas only to persons of a particular ethnicity.

The inability to enforce their contracts is likely to be the least negative consequence to the brokers referred to in the above examples.

Sufficient Consideration

The fourth element of a valid contract is sufficient consideration. Consideration is something of value, such as money, property, or services. It might even be an act of forbearance, such as if a grandmother promises to pay her granddaughter $10 each visit if the young woman will desist from playing a certain kind of annoying "music."

Though consideration must have some value, there is no requirement that consideration be of equal value to what is given in exchange for the consideration. The consideration may not even be adequate. One dollar given for an option to purchase a residence is sufficient consideration. However, gross inadequacy of consideration may be probative as to whether fraud was involved in a contract. Furthermore, in a court action for *specific performance*, the amount of consideration is important. Specific performance is an equitable remedy commonly sought by one party to a real estate contract seeking a court order requiring the other party to perform what was specifically stated in the contract (such as transferring the deed to the property), as an alternative to awarding damages. As a general rule, to obtain an equitable remedy (as opposed to a legal remedy of monetary damages), the fairness or adequacy of consideration will weigh heavily in the court's deliberations.

STATUTE OF FRAUDS

Modern law is more concerned with substance than with form. Therefore, as a general rule, whether the form of a contract is oral or written is immaterial unless there is a specific statutory exception that requires that the contract be in writing.

In most contracts that are required to be in writing, the statutory requirement comes from the ***Statute of Frauds***. The Statute of Frauds (CC §1624) grew out of a body of English common law, the purpose of which was to prevent perjury and dishonest conduct on the part of persons trying to prove the existence of certain kinds of contracts or the terms therein.

The California Statute of Frauds provides that certain contracts "are invalid, unless they, or some note or memorandum thereof, are in writing and subscribed by the party to be charged or by the party's agent." CC §1624(a). Contracts that are covered by the Statute of Frauds and that fail to be in writing are not void but are unenforceable. Thus, a contract covered by the Statute of Frauds that fails to be in writing is effective for all purposes until its validity is challenged. The statute is a defense only and cannot be the basis for the action of a lawsuit. Furthermore, significant partial performance of a contract is generally deemed to be sufficient evidence of the contract, thereby excusing the lack of writing. If the contract has been fully performed, the Statute of Frauds does not apply.

An agreement covered by the Statute of Frauds that fails to be committed to writing may become enforceable if a note or memorandum signed by the party against whom enforcement of the contract is sought is subsequently made that confirms the terms of the agreement.

> **Example:** An agreement to pay a real estate broker's commission is covered by the Statute of Frauds. If the agreement was oral, the broker could not enforce the agreement unless a subsequent writing signed by the person from whom the commission is sought provides sufficient evidence of the terms of the agreement, such as signed escrow instructions providing for the payment of the commission.

An exception to the Statute of Frauds of importance to real estate agents is that an agreement between brokers to share a commission is enforceable even if it is not in writing, but to be enforceable one of the brokers must have a contract with the principal and the commission must have been received.

Most contracts used in California real estate transactions are covered by the Statute of Frauds, including :

1. An agreement that by its terms is not to be performed within a year from its making;

2. An agreement for the leasing of real property for more than one year (a lease for one year or less need not be in writing, though a lease for less than one year that expires more than one year after the lease is executed

must be in writing);

3. An agreement for the sale of real property or of an interest therein;

4. An agreement that authorizes an agent or broker to purchase or sell real estate or to lease property for more than one year;

5. An agreement that authorizes an agent or broker, for a commission, to find or introduce a purchaser or seller of real property, or a lessee or lessor of real property of a lease of more than one year;

6. An agreement which by its terms is not to be performed within the lifetime of the promisor; and

7. An agreement to devise or bequeath property or make any provisions by way of a will.

Parol Evidence Rule

As a general rule, the *parol evidence rule* prohibits the introduction of extrinsic evidence of preliminary negotiations, oral or written, and of contemporaneous oral evidence, to alter the terms of a written agreement that appears to be whole. However, contracts often are long, complicated documents, and the words used therein are sometimes subject to differing interpretations, leading to agreements with ambiguous terms. In such cases, extrinsic evidence may be admitted to clarify the ambiguities. Additionally, extrinsic evidence may be introduced when necessary to prove that a contract is unenforceable because of mistake, fraud, duress, illegality, insufficiency or failure of consideration, or incapacity of a party.

STATUTE OF LIMITATIONS

The statute of limitations (CCP §§312-366) prescribes the time in which a legal action must be brought. The policy behind this statute is that the law aids the vigilant, and anyone who "slumbers upon his rights" may lose the right to bring an action. The time for filing an action varies, depending upon the type of action, and there are many different types of actions with many different limitation periods, ranging from 90 days to ten years. In general, the limitation period for an oral contract, obligation, or liability is two years; for a written contract, obligation, or liability the limitation period is four years.

REMEDIES FOR BREACHES

A breach is a failure to perform in accordance with the terms of a contract. A breach can be either material (also referred to as major) or non-material (also referred to as nominal). A material breach is often said to "reach to the heart of the contract" and deprives the non-breaching party of a substantial benefit of the bargain. A material breach may, depending on the circumstances, permit the injured party to recover damages, terminate the contract and cease performing his or her part of the bargain, rescind the contract, or seek specific performance or injunctive relief. A non-material breach allows the injured party to sue for damages (though they may be nominal or even nonexistent); however, as a general rule such an injured party must still perform his or her part of the bargain.

Rescission

Rescission extinguishes a contract and returns each party to the position that party was in immediately prior to the formation of the contract. Rescission is often sought in cases of fraud, duress, mistake, failure of consideration, or undue influence.

Damages

An injured party to a contract may sue to recover monetary damages incurred by the other party's material breach. Generally, monetary damages are limited to damages foreseeably arising from the breach, whereas damages that could not have been foreseen are not recoverable.

Liquidated Damages

Parties may agree, usually in a building contract or in a contract to purchase real estate, that if a breach occurs, a specified amount of damages, referred to as liquidated damages, will be paid in lieu of any other remedy for the breach. As long as the amount is not excessive, and provided that it would be extremely difficult to determine actual damage amounts, courts normally will enforce such liquidated damages provisions.

Specific Performance and Injunctive Relief

When monetary damages cannot provide an adequate remedy, the injured party may seek the equitable remedy of specific performance, whereby a court orders the breaching party to perform his or her part of the bargain (such as transferring the deed to a property), or injunctive relief, whereby a court orders a party to refrain from threatening to breach the contract if the breach would result in irreparable damage.

Monetary damages are often considered inadequate when the transaction involves unique items that cannot be replaced with an exchange of money. Examples include real estate (every property is unique), artwork, and family heirlooms. Personal service, though unique, cannot be compelled by specific performance.

LISTING AGREEMENTS

In order to be valid, *listing agreements* must satisfy the conditions for the validity of contracts in general, as discussed above, and they must be in writing in order to satisfy the Statute of Frauds.

A listing agreement is a contract between a real estate broker and a seller, wherein the broker (either directly or in association with salespersons or other brokers) solicits offers for the seller's property, usually in exchange for a commission, also called a *brokerage fee*. The commission is generally computed as a percentage of the price that the property is actually sold for, rather than as a percentage of the listing price. The listing itself is not an offer; it is an invitation to begin negotiations with, and for the submission of offers from, potential buyers. Therefore, a buyer cannot create a contract by accepting the terms of the listing.

Although listing agreements are often filled out and signed by salespersons, the contract is actually between the seller and the broker who employs the salesperson. As we shall see in a subsequent chapter, a real estate salesperson may not perform activities that require a real estate license unless he or she is employed by a broker.

Unlike most other real estate contracts, the listing agreement also creates a *fiduciary relationship* between the broker and the seller. This fiduciary relationship creates important duties and obligations of a real estate agent toward his or her clients over and beyond the obligations created by the contract terms of the listing agreement. The fiduciary relationship between a real estate agent and his or her client is governed by agency law — a subject we will take up in a subsequent chapter on real estate agency.

There are three basic types of listing agreements:

1. open listing;
2. exclusive agency listing; and
3. exclusive authorization and right to sell listing.

The defining characteristics of these three types of listing agreements are summarized in Figure 6.4.

Open Listings

An *open listing* agreement may be made by a seller to any number of brokers, though only one commission would be paid, going to the agent who first procurers an offer acceptable to the seller. The seller also reserves the right to sell the property to a buyer procured by the seller, without paying a commission to any broker. Furthermore, the sale of the property automatically terminates all outstanding open listing agreements for the property, without the need for notification on the part of the seller to the brokers to whom the seller gave an open listing. For these reasons, few agents are willing to spend time on open listings.

Exclusive Agency Listings

In an *exclusive agency listing*, a specific broker is employed as the seller's exclusive agent. The exclusive agent may cooperate with other brokers with whom the exclusive agent may share any commission earned. However, the seller reserves the right to sell the property to a buyer the seller personally procures, without obligation to pay a commission to the exclusive agent. If the seller procures someone who buys the property, the exclusive agency agreement automatically ends, and no notice need be given to the exclusive agent. In order to be valid, an exclusive agency agreement must contain a "definite, specified date of final and complete termination." (B&PC §10176(f)).

Exclusive Authorization and Right to Sell Listings

In an *exclusive authorization and right to sell listing*, the seller agrees to list the property with only one broker who will receive the agreed-on commission if the property sells during the term of the listing, regardless of who is responsible for procuring the buyer. Furthermore, under this type of listing, the broker is entitled to a full commission if, during the term of the listing, the seller withdraws the property from the market or makes the property unmarketable. As with an exclusive agency listing, in order to be valid, an exclusive authorization and right to sell listing agreement must have a definite, specified termination date.

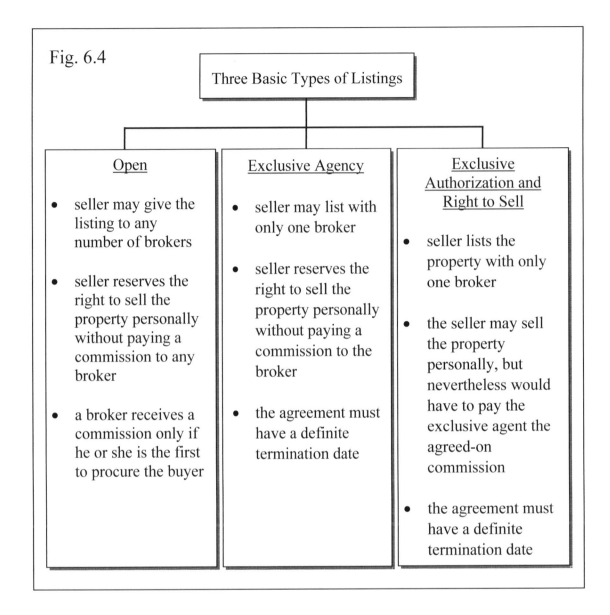

Fig. 6.4

Three Basic Types of Listings

Open

- seller may give the listing to any number of brokers

- seller reserves the right to sell the property personally without paying a commission to any broker

- a broker receives a commission only if he or she is the first to procure the buyer

Exclusive Agency

- seller may list with only one broker

- seller reserves the right to sell the property personally without paying a commission to the broker

- the agreement must have a definite termination date

Exclusive Authorization and Right to Sell

- seller lists the property with only one broker

- the seller may sell the property personally, but nevertheless would have to pay the exclusive agent the agreed-on commission

- the agreement must have a definite termination date

The exclusive authorization and right to sell listing is the most common type of listing agreement, and for good reason: because the broker is assured of a commission if the property sells during the term of the listing, the broker has incentive to put in the (often great deal of) time and effort needed to procure a buyer. However, salespersons and brokers may find some sellers reluctant to sign an exclusive authorization and right to sell listing because the sellers claim to have certain prospects of their own to whom they wish to retain the right to sell the property without paying a commission. In such cases, the salesperson or broker might suggest signing an exclusive authorization and right to sell listing with exceptions for the named prospects for a certain period of time. If such an agreement is reached with the seller, the broker should be careful to disclose the exceptions to cooperating agents or possibly face a demand for a commission from an agent (or agents) who put effort into selling the property, even though no commission is ever received by the listing agent.

Figure 6.5 reproduces an exclusive authorization and right to sell listing form. The form is reprinted with permission from the California Association of Realtors®. Endorsement is not implied.

An Analysis of an Exclusive Authorization and Right to Sell Listing Form.

The following section is an analysis of the California Association of Realtors® form RLA, revised 11/12, which is reprinted below in Figure 6.5.

Paragraph 1: Entered here should be the names of all parties selling an interest in the property and the broker receiving the listing. If a salesperson is taking the listing, the salesperson should sign at the bottom of the form (paragraph 21) but in paragraph 1 should write his or her broker's name.

After the broker's name, enter the beginning date and termination date of the listing. Remember, all exclusive listings (exclusive agency listings as well as exclusive authorization and right to sell listings) must have a definite, specific termination date. If the beginning date is left blank, the listing will be assumed to begin on the date the listing is signed. The words *"exclusive and irrevocable right to sell"* make this form an exclusive authorization and right to sell listing.

After the termination date, enter the location of the property in sufficient detail to uniquely identify it. A legal description, as is required in the deed, need not be given, unless such a description is necessary to positively identify the property.

Paragraph 2: Items of personal property (such as major appliances) that may be included in the sale are listed here. Fixtures not included in the listing should also be listed as such to avoid later disagreements as to what was, and what was not, included in the sale.

Paragraph 3: The list price and the terms of sale, such as cash or loan assumptions, are listed here.

Paragraph 4: Written in (not less than 10-point) boldface type, this paragraph informs the seller that the commission is negotiable and is not fixed by law. This statement is required on all listings of residential properties containing 1-4 residential units, or for the sale of a mobile home. The amount of the commission may not be printed on the form; it must be written in by hand. B&PC §10147.5.

Subparagraph 4A states the commission either as a percent or as a flat fee.

Subparagraph 4A(1) states that the commission is due regardless of who procurers a buyer. This subparagraph does not require the completion of the sale; it only requires that a buyer be procured who presents an offer to the seller at the listed price and terms, or an offer that is acceptable to the seller.

Subparagraph 4A(2) is known as the *safety clause*. It provides that the broker will earn the full commission if the property is sold within a specified number of days after the termination of the listing to a buyer with whom the broker has negotiated on the property and whose name was provided in writing by the broker to the seller within three calendar days of the expiration of the listing.

Typically, a safety clause states that to qualify, the buyer must have physically entered and must have been shown the property by the broker or a cooperating broker during the term of the listing, or the broker or a cooperating broker must have submitted an offer from the buyer to the seller during the term of the listing.

Subparagraph 4A(3) provides that the broker will receive the full commission if, without the broker's consent, the seller withdraws the property from the market or makes the property unmarketable during the listing period.

Subparagraph B states that if completion of the sale is prevented by the actions of any party to the transaction other than the seller (such as if the buyer defaults) and the seller collects damages, then the broker may receive either the full commission amount specified in subparagraph 4A or one-half of the net amount recovered by the seller, whichever is less.

Subparagraph C provides for any additional payments from the seller to the broker, such as for MLS fees or other advertising expenses incurred by the broker on behalf of the seller.

Fig. 6.5

CALIFORNIA
ASSOCIATION
OF REALTORS®

RESIDENTIAL LISTING AGREEMENT
(Exclusive Authorization and Right to Sell)
(C.A.R. Form RLA, Revised 11/12)

1. **EXCLUSIVE RIGHT TO SELL:** _____ ("Seller")
hereby employs and grants _____ ("Broker")
beginning (date) _____ and ending at 11:59 P.M. on (date) _____ ("Listing Period")
the exclusive and irrevocable right to sell or exchange the real property in the City of _____,
County of _____, Assessor's Parcel No. _____,
California, described as: _____ ("Property").

2. **ITEMS EXCLUDED AND INCLUDED:** Unless otherwise specified in a real estate purchase agreement, all fixtures and fittings that are attached to the Property are included, and personal property items are excluded, from the purchase price.
   ADDITIONAL ITEMS EXCLUDED: _____.
   ADDITIONAL ITEMS INCLUDED: _____.
   Seller intends that the above items be excluded or included in offering the Property for sale, but understands that: **(i)** the purchase agreement supersedes any intention expressed above and will ultimately determine which items are excluded and included in the sale; and **(ii)** Broker is not responsible for and does not guarantee that the above exclusions and/or inclusions will be in the purchase agreement.

3. **LISTING PRICE AND TERMS:**
   A. The listing price shall be: _____
      _____ Dollars ($ _____).
   B. Additional Terms: _____
      _____

4. **COMPENSATION TO BROKER:**
   Notice: The amount or rate of real estate commissions is not fixed by law. They are set by each Broker individually and may be negotiable between Seller and Broker (real estate commissions include all compensation and fees to Broker).
   A. Seller agrees to pay to Broker as compensation for services irrespective of agency relationship(s), either ☐ _____ percent of the listing price (or if a purchase agreement is entered into, of the purchase price), or ☐ $ _____,
      AND _____, as follows:
      (1) If during the Listing Period, or any extension, Broker, cooperating broker, Seller or any other person procures a buyer(s) who offers to purchase the Property on the above price and terms, or on any price or terms acceptable to Seller. (Broker is entitled to compensation whether any escrow resulting from such offer closes during or after the expiration of the Listing Period, or any extension).
      OR (2) If within _____ calendar days (a) after the end of the Listing Period or any extension; or (b) after any cancellation of this Agreement, unless otherwise agreed, Seller enters into a contract to sell, convey, lease or otherwise transfer the Property to anyone ("Prospective Buyer") or that person's related entity: (i) who physically entered and was shown the Property during the Listing Period or any extension by Broker or a cooperating broker; or (ii) for whom Broker or any cooperating broker submitted to Seller a signed, written offer to acquire, lease, exchange or obtain an option on the Property. Seller, however, shall have no obligation to Broker under paragraph 4A(2) unless, not later than **3 calendar days** after the end of the Listing Period or any extension or cancellation, Broker has given Seller a written notice of the names of such Prospective Buyers.
      (3) If, without Broker's prior written consent, the Property is withdrawn from sale, conveyed, leased, rented, otherwise transferred, or made unmarketable by a voluntary act of Seller during the Listing Period, or any extension.
   B. If completion of the sale is prevented by a party to the transaction other than Seller, then compensation due under paragraph 4A shall be payable only if and when Seller collects damages by suit, arbitration, settlement or otherwise, and then in an amount equal to the lesser of one-half of the damages recovered or the above compensation, after first deducting title and escrow expenses and the expenses of collection, if any.
   C. In addition, Seller agrees to pay Broker: _____.
   D. Seller has been advised of Broker's policy regarding cooperation with, and the amount of compensation offered to, other brokers.
      (1) Broker is authorized to cooperate with and compensate brokers participating through the multiple listing service(s) ("MLS") by offering to MLS brokers out of Broker's compensation specified in 4A, either ☐ _____ percent of the purchase price, or ☐ $ _____.
      (2) Broker is authorized to cooperate with and compensate brokers operating outside the MLS as per Broker's policy.
   E. Seller hereby irrevocably assigns to Broker the above compensation from Seller's funds and proceeds in escrow. Broker may submit this Agreement, as instructions to compensate Broker pursuant to paragraph 4A, to any escrow regarding the Property involving Seller and a buyer, Prospective Buyer or other transferee.
   F. (1) Seller represents that Seller has not previously entered into a listing agreement with another broker regarding the Property, unless specified as follows: _____.
      (2) Seller warrants that Seller has no obligation to pay compensation to any other broker regarding the Property unless the Property is transferred to any of the following individuals or entities: _____.
      (3) If the Property is sold to anyone listed above during the time Seller is obligated to compensate another broker: (i) Broker is not entitled to compensation under this Agreement; and (ii) Broker is not obligated to represent Seller in such transaction.

Seller's Initials (_____)(_____)

Reviewed by _____ Date _____

EQUAL HOUSING OPPORTUNITY

RLA REVISED 11/12 (PAGE 1 OF 4)   Print Date

RESIDENTIAL LISTING AGREEMENT - EXCLUSIVE (RLA PAGE 1 OF 4)

Property Address:_____ Date:_____

5. **OWNERSHIP, TITLE AND AUTHORITY:** Seller warrants that: **(i)** Seller is the owner of the Property; **(ii)** no other persons or entities have title to the Property; and **(iii)** Seller has the authority to both execute this Agreement and sell the Property. Exceptions to ownership, title and authority are as follows: _____
_____

6. **MULTIPLE LISTING SERVICE:** All terms of the transaction, including financing, if applicable, will be provided to the selected MLS for publication, dissemination and use by persons and entities on terms approved by the MLS. Seller acknowledges that Broker is required to comply with all applicable MLS rules as a condition of entry of the listing into the MLS and Seller authorizes Broker to comply with all applicable MLS rules. MLS rules require that the listing sales price be reported to the MLS. MLS rules allow MLS data to be made available by the MLS to additional Internet sites unless Broker gives the MLS instructions to the contrary. MLS rules generally provide that residential real property and vacant lot listings be submitted to the MLS within 48 hours or some other period of time after all necessary signatures have been obtained on the listing agreement. However, Broker will not have to submit this listing to the MLS if, within that time, Broker submits to the MLS a form signed by Seller (C.A.R. Form SEL or the locally required form). **Information that can be excluded:**
   A. **Internet Display:**
      (1) Seller can instruct Broker to have the MLS not display the Property on the Internet. Seller understands that this would mean consumers searching for listings on the Internet may not see information about the Property in response to their search; **(2)** Seller can instruct Broker to have the MLS not display the Property address on the Internet. Seller understands that this would mean consumers searching for listings on the Internet may not see the Property's address in response to their search
   B. **Features on MLS Participant and Subscriber Websites:**
      (1) Seller can instruct Broker to advise the MLS that Seller does not want visitors to MLS Participant or Subscriber Websites that display the Property listing to have **(i)** the ability to write comments or reviews about the Property on those sites; or **(ii)** the ability to hyperlink to another site containing such comments or reviews if the hyperlink is in immediate conjunction with the Property. Seller understands **(i)** that this opt-out applies only to Websites of MLS Participants and Subscribers who are real estate broker and agent members of the MLS; **(ii)** that other Internet sites may or may not have the features set forth herein; and **(iii)** that neither Broker nor the MLS may have the ability to control or block such features on other Internet sites. **(2)** Seller can instruct Broker to advise the MLS that Seller does not want MLS Participant or Subscriber Websites that display the Property listing to operate **(i)** an automated estimate of the market value of the Property; or **(ii)** have the ability to hyperlink to another site containing such automated estimate of value if the hyperlink is in immediate conjunction with the Property. Seller understands **(i)** that this opt-out applies only to Websites of MLS Participants and Subscribers who are real estate brokers and agent members of the MLS; **(ii)** that other Internet sites may or may not have the features set forth herein; and **(iii)** that neither Broker nor the MLS may have the ability to control or block such features on other Internet sites.
   Seller acknowledges that for any of the above opt-out instructions to be effective, Seller must make them on a separate instruction to Broker signed by Seller (C.A.R. Form SEL or the locally required form). Information about this listing will be provided to the MLS of Broker's selection unless a form instructing Broker to withhold the listing from the MLS is attached to this listing Agreement.

7. **SELLER REPRESENTATIONS:** Seller represents that, unless otherwise specified in writing, Seller is unaware of: **(i)** any Notice of Default recorded against the Property; **(ii)** any delinquent amounts due under any loan secured by, or other obligation affecting, the Property; **(iii)** any bankruptcy, insolvency or similar proceeding affecting the Property; **(iv)** any litigation, arbitration, administrative action, government investigation or other pending or threatened action that affects or may affect the Property or Seller's ability to transfer it; and **(v)** any current, pending or proposed special assessments affecting the Property. Seller shall promptly notify Broker in writing if Seller becomes aware of any of these items during the Listing Period or any extension thereof.

8. **BROKER'S AND SELLER'S DUTIES: (a)** Broker agrees to exercise reasonable effort and due diligence to achieve the purposes of this Agreement. Unless Seller gives Broker written instructions to the contrary, Broker is authorized to **(i)** order reports and disclosures as necessary, **(ii)** advertise and market the Property by any method and in any medium selected by Broker, including MLS and the Internet, and, to the extent permitted by these media, control the dissemination of the information submitted to any medium; and **(iii)** disclose to any real estate licensee making an inquiry the receipt of any offers on the Property and the offering price of such offers. **(b)** Seller agrees to consider offers presented by Broker, and to act in good faith to accomplish the sale of the Property by, among other things, making the Property available for showing at reasonable times and referring to Broker all inquiries of any party interested in the Property. Seller is responsible for determining at what price to list and sell the Property. **Seller further agrees to indemnify, defend and hold Broker harmless from all claims, disputes, litigation, judgments attorney fees and costs arising from any incorrect information supplied by Seller, or from any material facts that Seller knows but fails to disclose.**

9. **DEPOSIT:** Broker is authorized to accept and hold on Seller's behalf any deposits to be applied toward the purchase price.

10. **AGENCY RELATIONSHIPS:**
   A. **Disclosure:** If the Property includes residential property with one-to-four dwelling units, Seller shall receive a "Disclosure Regarding Agency Relationships" (C.A.R. Form AD) prior to entering into this Agreement.
   B. **Seller Representation:** Broker shall represent Seller in any resulting transaction, except as specified in paragraph 4F.

Seller's Initials (_____)(_____)

| Reviewed by _____ | Date _____ |

RESIDENTIAL LISTING AGREEMENT - EXCLUSIVE (RLA PAGE 2 OF 4)

Property Address:_____ Date:_____

C. **Possible Dual Agency With Buyer:** Depending upon the circumstances, it may be necessary or appropriate for Broker to act as an agent for both Seller and buyer, exchange party, or one or more additional parties ("Buyer"). Broker shall, as soon as practicable, disclose to Seller any election to act as a dual agent representing both Seller and Buyer. If a Buyer is procured directly by Broker or an associate-licensee in Broker's firm, Seller hereby consents to Broker acting as a dual agent for Seller and Buyer. In the event of an exchange, Seller hereby consents to Broker collecting compensation from additional parties for services rendered, provided there is disclosure to all parties of such agency and compensation. Seller understands and agrees that: **(i)** Broker, without the prior written consent of Seller, will not disclose to Buyer that Seller is willing to sell the Property at a price less than the listing price; **(ii)** Broker, without the prior written consent of Buyer, will not disclose to Seller that Buyer is willing to pay a price greater than the offered price; and **(iii)** except for (i) and (ii) above, a dual agent is obligated to disclose known facts materially affecting the value or desirability of the Property to both parties.

D. **Other Sellers:** Seller understands that Broker may have or obtain listings on other properties, and that potential buyers may consider, make offers on, or purchase through Broker, property the same as or similar to Seller's Property. Seller consents to Broker's representation of sellers and buyers of other properties before, during and after the end of this Agreement.

E. **Confirmation:** If the Property includes residential property with one-to-four dwelling units, Broker shall confirm the agency relationship described above, or as modified, in writing, prior to or concurrent with Seller's execution of a purchase agreement.

11. **SECURITY AND INSURANCE:** Broker is not responsible for loss of or damage to personal or real property, or person, whether attributable to use of a keysafe/lockbox, a showing of the Property, or otherwise. Third parties, including, but not limited to, appraisers, inspectors, brokers and prospective buyers, may have access to, and take videos and photographs of, the interior of the Property. Seller agrees: **(i)** to take reasonable precautions to safeguard and protect valuables that might be accessible during showings of the Property; and **(ii)** to obtain insurance to protect against these risks. Broker does not maintain insurance to protect Seller.

12. **PHOTOGRAPHS AND INTERNET ADVERTISING:**

A. In order to effectively market the Property for sale it is often necessary to provide photographs, virtual tours and other media to buyers. Seller agrees (or ☐ if checked, does not agree) that Broker may photograph or otherwise electronically capture images of the exterior and interior of the Property ("Images") for static and/or virtual tours of the Property by buyers and others on Broker's website, the MLS, and other marketing sites. Seller acknowledges that once Images are placed on the Internet neither Broker nor Seller has control over who can view such Images and what use viewers may make of the Images, or how long such Images may remain available on the Internet. Seller further agrees that such Images are the property of Broker and that Broker may use such Images for advertisement of Broker's business in the future.

B. Seller acknowledges that prospective buyers and/or other persons coming onto the property may take photographs, videos or other images of the property. Seller understands that Broker does not have the ability to control or block the taking and use of Images by any such persons. (If checked) ☐ Seller instructs Broker to publish in the MLS that taking of Images is limited to those persons preparing Appraisal or Inspection reports. Seller acknowledges that unauthorized persons may take images who do not have access to or have not read any limiting instruction in the MLS or who take images regardless of any limiting instruction in the MLS. Once Images are taken and/or put into electronic display on the Internet or otherwise, neither Broker nor Seller has control over who views such Images nor what use viewers may make of the Images.

13. **KEYSAFE/LOCKBOX:** A keysafe/lockbox is designed to hold a key to the Property to permit access to the Property by Broker, cooperating brokers, MLS participants, their authorized licensees and representatives, authorized inspectors, and accompanied prospective buyers. Broker, cooperating brokers, MLS and Associations/Boards of REALTORS® are **not** insurers against injury, theft, loss, vandalism or damage attributed to the use of a keysafe/lockbox. Seller does (or if checked ☐ does not) authorize Broker to install a keysafe/lockbox. If Seller does not occupy the Property, Seller shall be responsible for obtaining occupant(s)' written permission for use of a keysafe/lockbox (C.A.R. Form KLA).

14. **SIGN:** Seller does (or if checked ☐ does not) authorize Broker to install a FOR SALE/SOLD sign on the Property.

15. **EQUAL HOUSING OPPORTUNITY:** The Property is offered in compliance with federal, state and local anti-discrimination laws.

16. **ATTORNEY FEES:** In any action, proceeding or arbitration between Seller and Broker regarding the obligation to pay compensation under this Agreement, the prevailing Seller or Broker shall be entitled to reasonable attorney fees and costs from the non-prevailing Seller or Broker, except as provided in paragraph 20A.

17. **ADDITIONAL TERMS:** ☐ REO Advisory Listing (C.A.R. Form REOL) ☐ Short Sale Information and Advisory (C.A.R. Form SSIA)

_____

_____

_____

_____

_____

18. **MANAGEMENT APPROVAL:** If an associate-licensee in Broker's office (salesperson or broker-associate) enters into this Agreement on Broker's behalf, and Broker or Manager does not approve of its terms, Broker or Manager has the right to cancel this Agreement, in writing, within **5 Days** After its execution.

19. **SUCCESSORS AND ASSIGNS:** This Agreement shall be binding upon Seller and Seller's successors and assigns.

Seller's Initials (_____)(_____)

Copyright © 1991-2012, CALIFORNIA ASSOCIATION OF REALTORS®, INC.
RLA REVISED 11/12 (PAGE 3 OF 4)

Reviewed by _____ Date _____

RESIDENTIAL LISTING AGREEMENT - EXCLUSIVE (RLA PAGE 3 OF 4)

Property Address: _____ Date: _____

20. DISPUTE RESOLUTION:

    A. MEDIATION: Seller and Broker agree to mediate any dispute or claim arising between them out of this Agreement, or any resulting transaction, before resorting to arbitration or court action. Mediation fees, if any, shall be divided equally among the parties involved. If, for any dispute or claim to which this paragraph applies, any party (i) commences an action without first attempting to resolve the matter through mediation, or (ii) before commencement of an action, refuses to mediate after a request has been made, then that party shall not be entitled to recover attorney fees, even if they would otherwise be available to that party in any such action. THIS MEDIATION PROVISION APPLIES WHETHER OR NOT THE ARBITRATION PROVISION IS INITIALED. **Exclusions from this mediation agreement are specified in paragraph 20C.**

    B. ARBITRATION OF DISPUTES:
    Seller and Broker agree that any dispute or claim in Law or equity arising between them regarding the obligation to pay compesation under this Agreement, which is not settled through mediation, shall be decided by neutral, binding arbitration. The arbitrator shall be a retired judge or justice, or an attorney with at least 5 years of residential real estate Law experience, unless the parties mutually agree to a different arbitrator. The parties shall have the right to discovery in accordance with Code of Civil Procedure §1283.05. In all other respects, the arbitration shall be conducted in accordance with Title 9 of Part 3 of the Code of Civil Procedure. Judgment upon the award of the arbitrator(s) may be entered into any court having jurisdiction. Enforcement of this agreement to arbitrate shall be governed by the Federal Arbitration Act. **Exclusions from this arbitration agreement are specified in paragraph 20C.**

        "NOTICE: BY INITIALING IN THE SPACE BELOW YOU ARE AGREEING TO HAVE ANY DISPUTE ARISING OUT OF THE MATTERS INCLUDED IN THE 'ARBITRATION OF DISPUTES' PROVISION DECIDED BY NEUTRAL ARBITRATION AS PROVIDED BY CALIFORNIA LAW AND YOU ARE GIVING UP ANY RIGHTS YOU MIGHT POSSESS TO HAVE THE DISPUTE LITIGATED IN A COURT OR JURY TRIAL. BY INITIALING IN THE SPACE BELOW YOU ARE GIVING UP YOUR JUDICIAL RIGHTS TO DISCOVERY AND APPEAL, UNLESS THOSE RIGHTS ARE SPECIFICALLY INCLUDED IN THE 'ARBITRATION OF DISPUTES' PROVISION. IF YOU REFUSE TO SUBMIT TO ARBITRATION AFTER AGREEING TO THIS PROVISION, YOU MAY BE COMPELLED TO ARBITRATE UNDER THE AUTHORITY OF THE CALIFORNIA CODE OF CIVIL PROCEDURE. YOUR AGREEMENT TO THIS ARBITRATION PROVISION IS VOLUNTARY."

        "WE HAVE READ AND UNDERSTAND THE FOREGOING AND AGREE TO SUBMIT DISPUTES ARISING OUT OF THE MATTERS INCLUDED IN THE 'ARBITRATION OF DISPUTES' PROVISION TO NEUTRAL ARBITRATION."

Seller's Initials _____/_____	Broker's Initials _____/_____

    C. ADDITIONAL MEDIATION AND ARBITRATION TERMS: The following matters shall be excluded from mediation and arbitration: (i) a judicial or non-judicial foreclosure or other action or proceeding to enforce a deed of trust, mortgage or installment land sale contract as defined in Civil Code §2985; (ii) an unlawful detainer action; (iii) the filing or enforcement of a mechanic's lien; and (iv) any matter that is within the jurisdiction of a probate, small claims or bankruptcy court. The filing of a court action to enable the recording of a notice of pending action, for order of attachment, receivership, injunction, or other provisional remedies, shall not constitute a waiver or violation of the mediation and arbitration provisions.

21. ENTIRE AGREEMENT: All prior discussions, negotiations and agreements between the parties concerning the subject matter of this Agreement are superseded by this Agreement, which constitutes the entire contract and a complete and exclusive expression of their agreement, and may not be contradicted by evidence of any prior agreement or contemporaneous oral agreement. If any provision of this Agreement is held to be ineffective or invalid, the remaining provisions will nevertheless be given full force and effect. This Agreement and any supplement, addendum or modification, including any photocopy or facsimile, may be executed in counterparts.

By signing below, Seller acknowledges that Seller has read, understands, received a copy of and agrees to the terms of this Agreement.

Seller _____ Date _____
Address _____ City _____ State _____ Zip _____
Telephone _____ Fax _____ Email _____

Seller _____ Date _____
Address _____ City _____ State _____ Zip _____
Telephone _____ Fax _____ Email _____

Real Estate Broker (Firm) _____ DRE Lic. # _____
By (Agent) _____ DRE Lic. # _____ Date _____
Address _____ City _____ State _____ Zip _____
Telephone _____ Fax _____ Email _____

Reviewed by _____ Date _____

RLA REVISED 11/12 (PAGE 4 OF 4)

RESIDENTIAL LISTING AGREEMENT - EXCLUSIVE (RLA PAGE 4 OF 4)

Subparagraph D provides that the broker may cooperate with other brokers on the MLS. The seller may specify that such cooperating broker(s) receive a percentage of the commission or a flat fee. The broker may also cooperate with other brokers operating outside of the MLS.

Subparagraph E states that the seller irrevocably assigns to the broker the broker's compensation from the seller funds in escrow. This clause protects the broker's fee in the event that the seller later tries to order escrow to forward all of the funds to the seller rather than paying the broker the commission due from the escrow funds.

Subparagraph F requires the seller to list any other brokers to whom the seller might have an obligation to pay a commission and to list any prospective buyer with whom the seller may negotiate a sale of the property without paying the broker a commission.

Paragraph 5: In this paragraph, the seller warrants that the seller is the sole owner of the property and has authority to sell the property. Exceptions to ownership and authority must be listed. If there are none, "None" should be written in the space provided.

Paragraph 6: In this paragraph, the seller agrees that the broker may provide listing information to the MLS. A listing may not be placed on an MLS unless authorized by the seller in the listing. CC §1088. If the seller does not wish to have the property appear on the MLS, a form instructing the broker to withhold the listing from the MLS should be attached to the listing agreement. Without this authorization, the broker would not have the right to put the listing information on the MLS or to cooperate with other brokers. Subparagraph B of this paragraph provides opt-out information to the seller relating to websites of participating MLS brokers.

Paragraph 7: In this paragraph, the seller represents that, except for those stated in writing, there are no other notices of default, delinquencies, or pending litigation against the property and that the seller is not bankrupt or insolvent. If during the term of the listing the seller becomes aware of any of the above, the seller agrees to promptly notify the broker.

Paragraph 8: In this paragraph, the broker agrees to use due diligence to achieve a sale. This promise makes the contract a bilateral contract. The seller agrees to consider offers received, to act in good faith, and to hold the broker harmless from all claims that arise from any incorrect information supplied by the seller or from the seller's failure to disclose material facts to the broker. Caution: Under California law, the broker has a duty independently to discover certain defects in the property, so if the seller fails to disclose a certain defect and it is found that the broker had a duty independently to discover this certain defect and to disclose it to the buyer, this indemnification clause would have doubtful value to the broker.

Paragraph 9: In this paragraph, the seller authorizes the broker to accept a deposit on behalf of the seller. Without this clause, if the broker accepted a deposit from a prospective buyer, the broker would do so as an agent of the buyer.

Paragraph 10: In this paragraph, the broker represents that he or she is an agent of the seller. However, if the broker procurers a buyer, it may be necessary or appropriate for the broker to act in a dual agency capacity. In such cases, the broker will disclose as soon as possible that the broker is acting as a dual agent.

Paragraph 11: In this paragraph, it is acknowledged that the broker is not responsible if anyone is injured on the property during sales related activities, that the broker does not maintain insurance to protect against such losses, that the seller will obtain insurance to protect against such losses, and that the seller is responsible for protecting his or her own personal property (such as during showings of the property).

Paragraph 12: This paragraph states that to effectively market the property, photographs, virtual tours, and other media are often required. If *not* checked in the box provided, this paragraph authorizes the broker to take such photographs and virtual tours and place them on the Internet. In subparagraph B, seller acknowledges that persons coming to visit may take their own photographs, videos, or other images, and that the broker does not have the ability to control the taking or use of such images. However, a box is provided that, if checked, instructs the broker to publish on the MLS that the taking of photographs, videos, or other images is limited to persons preparing appraisals or inspection reports.

Paragraph 13: If *not* checked in the box provided, this paragraph authorizes the broker to install a lockbox that will allow cooperating agents access to show the property. This paragraph also notifies the seller that neither the broker nor cooperating agents are necessarily insured against losses resulting from showing the property.

Paragraph 14: In this paragraph, the seller indicates whether he or she permits the broker to install a FOR SALE/SOLD sign on the property.

Paragraph 15: This paragraph represents that the sale of the property is in compliance with all applicable laws. Whether stated or not, neither the seller nor the broker may discriminate on the basis of race, color, creed, or other criteria, as mandated by state or federal law.

Paragraph 16: This paragraph states that in any legal action between the parties regarding the paying of commission, the prevailing party will be entitled to reasonable attorney fees and costs from the non-prevailing party, except as provided in paragraph 20A. As a general rule, in California, attorney fees are not awarded in contract actions unless the contract so provides.

Paragraph 17: This paragraph provides space for any additional terms agreed on by the parties.

Paragraph 18: This paragraph states that if an associate-licensee of the broker enters into this agreement on behalf of the broker, the broker has the right to cancel the agreement within 5 days after its execution.

Paragraph 19: This paragraph provides that the listing agreement will be binding upon the seller and seller's successors and assigns.

Paragraph 20: Subparagraph A provides that the parties attempt to resolve any conflict between them first through nonbinding mediation before bringing any other action. If one of the parties refuses to first mediate, then that party would not be entitled to attorney fees if that party were to prevail in the action.

Subparagraph B provides that by initialing, the parties agree to resolve any issues between them through arbitration. In doing so, the parties give up their rights to litigate the matter in the courts. This paragraph also provides exceptions to arbitration and mediation for claims within probate court, small claims court, and bankruptcy court jurisdiction, and for foreclosure proceedings, unlawful detainer actions, and mechanics liens. In the spaces provided for signatures, the seller acknowledges that he or she has read, understood, and received a copy of the agreement, and agrees to the terms of the agreement. Since only brokers can contract with the seller, either the broker signs the agreement or the salesperson signs on behalf of the broker.

Paragraph 21: This paragraph provides that the parties agree that the listing agreement is the entire agreement and that the terms of the agreement may not be contradicted by any prior or contemporaneous agreement, whether written or oral.

Special Types of Listings

Net Listings

A **net listing** can take the form of any of the three basic types of listings: open, exclusive agency, or exclusive authorization and right to sell. The unique feature of a net listing is that the seller demands to receive a certain amount from the sale, regardless of the price the property is ultimately sold for. In such a listing, the broker's compensation is not based upon a percentage of the sales price; rather the compensation would be the amount left over (if anything) after subtracting from the sales price all loan balances, liens, compensation to other brokers, closing costs, etc., and the net amount demanded by the seller.

> **Example:** Suppose a broker with a net listing finds a buyer who pays $500,000 for the property; the property had a loan balance of $400,000; closing costs were $5,000; the seller's specified net was $70,000; and there were no other claims against the property or its sale. The broker would then receive compensation of $25,000: $500,000 minus the sum of $400,000 plus $5,000 plus $70,000.

Net listings are seldom used, because lurking in the background of every such listing is the potential that the broker may be subject to a charge of fraud, especially if the broker is successful in obtaining a high sales price for the property and, therefore, in obtaining what may appear to be excessive compensation. To help avoid abuses by brokers (and lawsuits by disgruntled sellers), California law requires that a broker with a net listing disclose in writing the size of the broker's compensation prior to the seller's acceptance of any offer. B&PC §10176(g). An agent who fails to comply with this notification requirement may face both a lawsuit from the seller and an action by the California real estate commissioner to suspend or revoke the broker's license.

Because real estate agents owe fiduciary duties and obligations to their principals, a broker with a net listing must present all offers to the principal, even offers below the listing price, which, if accepted by the seller, would result in the broker's receiving no commission.

Option Listings

As with the net listing, an option listing can take the form of any of the three basic types of listings: open, exclusive agency, or exclusive authorization and right to sell.

There is an obvious potential for abuse with an option listing: the agent waits until he or she arranges a sale of the property at a high price with a buyer and, rather than informing the seller of the buyer, exercises the option, thereby making a handsome (and illegal) profit. To help avoid such abuses, California law requires that the agent "prior to or coincident with election to exercise the option to purchase reveals in writing to the employer the full amount of licensee's profit and obtains the written consent of the employer approving the amount of the profit." (B&PC §10176(h)). However, an agent may, after informing the seller of everything that the agent knows about the value of the property, including the existence of any potential buyers, exercise the option and later sell the property for a profit. In this latter case, there would be no need to inform the seller of the agent's profit or to get the seller's approval.

MLS Listings

A multiple listing service (MLS) is a service provided by groups of brokers affiliated with a real estate association. Such groups pool their listings and disseminate the listings to all members of the group, usually on the Internet. The listing broker must obtain the seller's permission before submitting the listing to an MLS.

In 1976 the California Supreme Court held that "access to the multiple listing service is so essential to non-members if they are to compete effectively that such access must be granted to all licensed salesmen and brokers who choose to use the service." *Marin County Board of Realtors, Inc. v. Eugene Palsson.* Therefore, any broker, whether or not a member of the group, has the right to sell any property listed and to share in the listing broker's commission; however, the cooperating broker must obtain the listing broker's permission to advertise or promote any listed property.

An agreement between cooperating brokers to split a commission from a real estate transaction is not illegal or against public policy. Furthermore, *an oral agreement between cooperating brokers to split a commission is enforceable*, and as such is one of the few exceptions to the general rule that contracts regarding the sale of real property must be in writing, pursuant to the statute of frauds. However, because the terms of an oral agreement are often subject to dispute and difficult to prove, it is highly recommended that a commission split between brokers be in writing.

REAL ESTATE PURCHASE AGREEMENTS

A contract for the purchase of real estate must satisfy all of the elements necessary to form a valid contract and, pursuant to the statute of frauds, must be in writing. Though the use of a quality standard pre-printed form (such as the one reproduced in Figure 6.6) eliminates many of the legal problems that may befall a real estate sales transaction, several legal issues arise frequently enough to warrant special attention. In California, a real estate purchase contract is often referred to as a *deposit receipt*, in part because the agreement nearly always contains, among many other things, a receipt for the deposit given by the purchaser (see Paragraph 3A(2), Figure 6.6).

Though the agent is permitted to fill in the blanks in a pre-printed purchase contract, an agent should be very circumspect when crossing out or adding words in the pre-printed sections, because making significant changes (1) risks liability to the seller and/or buyer if the wording turns out to be ambiguous or incorrect, and (2) risks the agent's being charged with practicing law without a license to practice law. Any additions, deletions, or alterations that are made on the pre-printed form must be initialed by all parties to the contract.

LIQUIDATED DAMAGES

As a general rule, an offer to purchase is accompanied by a good-faith deposit (see Paragraph 3A, Figure 6.6), which, if the offer is accepted, is applied to the purchase price. But if the buyer defaults, an issue would arise as to whether the deposit should be returned to the buyer. To account for this situation, most purchase agreements provide that if the buyer fails to complete the purchase because of the buyer's default, the deposit will be treated as *liquidated damages* (see Paragraph 25, Figure 6.6). Civil Code §1677 requires that the liquidated damages provision be signed or initialed by each party to the contract. Furthermore, CC §1675 requires that for the purchase of a residential dwelling that contains *no more than four residential units, one of which the owner intends to occupy*, the amount retained by the seller as liquidated damages may not exceed 3% of the purchase price unless the seller establishes that the amount actually paid is reasonable as liquidated damages— the remainder of the deposit being returned to the buyer. For commercial properties and for properties consisting of more than 4 residential units, liquidated damages may be any amount that is reasonable and that reflects what possible damage might be anticipated if a breach of the contract were to occur.

CONTINGENCIES

Purchase contracts usually contain many *contingencies*, which make one party's obligation to perform dependent on the occurrence of some event. These contingencies usually relate to financing (see Paragraph 3H, Figure 6.6), appraisals (see Paragraph 3I, Figure 6.6), inspections, and the delivery of other documents (see Paragraph 14, Figure 6.6). Such contingencies can have very significant effects on the seller and/or buyer, so they should be prudently examined to be sure that they, as stated in the pre-printed form, fit the situation that exists on both the seller's and the buyer's side. Because many buyers think that having the right to cancel the contract gives them more negotiating leverage than does giving the seller the right to correct any problems found during inspections, it is not unusual that buyers want to alter the terms relating to contingencies, giving them such a right to cancel.

OPTION CONTRACTS

As we have seen, an option creates a right to purchase for a specific sum at any time during the option term without creating an obligation to do so. Because when an option is exercised it becomes a purchase agreement, an *option contract* to purchase real estate must contain all of the necessary terms of such a purchase.

Unlike an option to purchase, a **right of first refusal** does not create in the seller the obligation to sell if the holder of the right wishes to purchase — it only creates the right to purchase a property at the same price, terms, and conditions as is offered to third parties if and when the property is put up for sale. If the person holding the right of first refusal does not meet the price and terms offered, the seller is free to sell to a third party.

REAL PROPERTY SALES CONTRACTS

"A **real property sales contract** is an agreement in which one party agrees to convey title to real property to another party upon the satisfaction of specified conditions set forth in the contract and that does not require conveyance of title within one year from the date of formation of the contract." CCP §2985(a) (emphasis added).

As a general rule, a real property sales contract (also called a **land installment contract** or just a **land contract**) is a contract whereby the seller, rather than receiving the full purchase price immediately, sells the property on an installment basis, thereby becoming in essence the lender. The seller in this case is referred to as the **vendor**; the buyer as the **vendee**.

Upon the closing of a real property sales contract, the vendee takes immediate possession of the property, but the vendor does not convey legal title to the vendee until all installments are paid. During the time that the vendee is making installment payments, the vendee is said to possess **equitable title**, which is essentially the right to possess and enjoy the property. When the full purchase price is paid, the vendor conveys the deed, and therefore legal title, to the vendee.

Fig. 6.6

CALIFORNIA ASSOCIATION OF REALTORS®

**CALIFORNIA
RESIDENTIAL PURCHASE AGREEMENT
AND JOINT ESCROW INSTRUCTIONS**
For Use With Single Family Residential Property — Attached or Detached
(C.A.R. Form RPA-CA, Revised 4/13)

Date _____

1. **OFFER:**
   A. **THIS IS AN OFFER FROM** _____ ("Buyer").
   B. **THE REAL PROPERTY TO BE ACQUIRED** is described as _____
      _____, Assessor's Parcel No. _____, situated in
      _____, County of _____, California, ("Property").
   C. **THE PURCHASE PRICE** offered is _____
      _____ Dollars $ _____.
   D. **CLOSE OF ESCROW** shall occur on _____ (date)(or ☐ _____ **Days** After Acceptance).

2. **AGENCY:**
   A. **DISCLOSURE:** Buyer and Seller each acknowledge prior receipt of a "Disclosure Regarding Real Estate Agency Relationships" (C.A.R. Form AD).
   B. **POTENTIALLY COMPETING BUYERS AND SELLERS:** Buyer and Seller each acknowledge receipt of a disclosure of the possibility of multiple representation by the Broker representing that principal. This disclosure may be part of a listing agreement, buyer representation agreement or separate document (C.A.R. Form DA). Buyer understands that Broker representing Buyer may also represent other potential buyers, who may consider, make offers on or ultimately acquire the Property. Seller understands that Broker representing Seller may also represent other sellers with competing properties of interest to this Buyer.
   C. **CONFIRMATION:** The following agency relationships are hereby confirmed for this transaction:
      Listing Agent _____ (Print Firm Name) is the agent of (check one):
      ☐ the Seller exclusively; or ☐ both the Buyer and Seller.
      Selling Agent _____ (Print Firm Name) (if not the same as the Listing Agent) is the agent of (check one): ☐ the Buyer exclusively; or ☐ the Seller exclusively; or ☐ both the Buyer and Seller. Real Estate Brokers are not parties to the Agreement between Buyer and Seller.

3. **FINANCE TERMS:** Buyer represents that funds will be good when deposited with Escrow Holder.
   A. **INITIAL DEPOSIT:** Deposit shall be in the amount of ....$ _____
      (1) Buyer shall deliver deposit directly to Escrow Holder by personal check, ☐ electronic funds transfer, ☐ other _____ within 3 business days after acceptance (or ☐ Other_____);
      OR (2) (If checked) ☐ Buyer has given the deposit by personal check (or ☐ _____) to the agent submitting the offer (or to ☐ _____), made payable to _____. The deposit shall be held uncashed until Acceptance and then deposited with Escrow Holder (or ☐ into Broker's trust account) within 3 business days after Acceptance (or ☐ Other_____).
   B. **INCREASED DEPOSIT:** Buyer shall deposit with Escrow Holder an increased deposit in the amount of ....$ _____
      within _____ **Days** After Acceptance, or ☐ _____.
      If a liquidated damages clause is incorporated into this Agreement, Buyer and Seller shall sign a separate liquidated damages clause (C.A.R. Form RID) for any increased deposit at the time it is Delivered.
   C. **LOAN(S):**
      (1) **FIRST LOAN:** in the amount of ....$ _____
         This loan will be conventional financing or, if checked, ☐ FHA, ☐ VA, ☐ Seller (C.A.R. Form SFA), ☐ assumed financing (C.A.R. Form PAA), ☐ Other _____. This loan shall be at a fixed rate not to exceed _____% or, ☐ an adjustable rate loan with initial rate not to exceed _____%. Regardless of the type of loan, Buyer shall pay points not to exceed _____% of the loan amount.
      (2) ☐ **SECOND LOAN** in the amount of ....$ _____
         This loan will be conventional financing or, if checked, ☐ Seller (C.A.R. Form SFA), ☐ assumed financing (C.A.R. Form PAA), ☐ Other _____. This loan shall be at a fixed rate not to exceed _____% or, ☐ an adjustable rate loan with initial rate not to exceed _____%. Regardless of the type of loan, Buyer shall pay points not to exceed _____% of the loan amount.
      (3) **FHA/VA:** For any FHA or VA loan specified above, Buyer has **17** (or ☐ _____) **Days** After Acceptance to Deliver to Seller written notice (C.A.R. Form FVA) of any lender-required repairs or costs that Buyer requests Seller to pay for or otherwise correct. Seller has no obligation to pay or satisfy lender requirements unless otherwise agreed in writing.
   D. **ADDITIONAL FINANCING TERMS:** _____
      _____
   E. **BALANCE OF DOWN PAYMENT OR PURCHASE PRICE** in the amount of ....$ _____
      to be deposited with Escrow Holder within sufficient time to close escrow.
   F. **PURCHASE PRICE (TOTAL):** ....$ _____

Buyer's Initials (_____)(_____)   Seller's Initials (_____)(_____)

RPA-CA REVISED 4/13 (PAGE 1 OF 8) **Print Date** | Reviewed by _____ Date _____ |

CALIFORNIA RESIDENTIAL PURCHASE AGREEMENT (RPA-CA PAGE 1 OF 8)

Property Address: _____ Date: _____

G. **VERIFICATION OF DOWN PAYMENT AND CLOSING COSTS:** Buyer (or Buyer's lender or loan broker pursuant to 3H(1) shall, within **7** (or ☐ _____) **Days** After Acceptance, Deliver to Seller written verification of Buyer's down payment and closing costs. (If checked, ☐ verification attached.)

H. **LOAN TERMS:**
(1) LOAN APPLICATIONS: Within **7** (or ☐ _____) **Days** After Acceptance, Buyer shall Deliver to Seller a letter from lender or loan broker stating that, based on a review of Buyer's written application and credit report, Buyer is prequalified or preapproved for any NEW loan specified in 3C above. (If checked, ☐ letter attached.)
(2) LOAN CONTINGENCY: Buyer shall act diligently and in good faith to obtain the designated loan(s). Obtaining the loan(s) specified above **is a contingency** of this Agreement unless otherwise agreed in writing. Buyer's contractual obligations to obtain and provide deposit, balance of down payment and closing costs **are not contingencies** of this Agreement.
(3) LOAN CONTINGENCY REMOVAL:
(i) Within **17** (or ☐ _____) **Days** After Acceptance, Buyer shall, as specified in paragraph 14, in writing remove the loan contingency or cancel this Agreement;
OR **(ii)** (If checked) ☐ the loan contingency shall remain in effect until the designated loans are funded.
(4) ☐ **NO LOAN CONTINGENCY** (If checked): Obtaining any loan specified above is NOT a contingency of this Agreement. If Buyer does not obtain the loan and as a result Buyer does not purchase the Property, Seller may be entitled to Buyer's deposit or other legal remedies.

I. **APPRAISAL CONTINGENCY AND REMOVAL:** This Agreement is (or, if checked, ☐ is NOT) contingent upon a written appraisal of the Property by a licensed or certified appraiser at no less than the specified purchase price. If there is a loan contingency, Buyer's removal of the loan contingency shall be deemed removal of this appraisal contingency (or, ☐ if checked, Buyer shall, as specified in paragraph 14B(3), in writing remove the appraisal contingency or cancel this Agreement within **17** (or ____) **Days** After Acceptance). If there is no loan contingency, Buyer shall, as specified in paragraph 14B(3), in writing remove the appraisal contingency or cancel this Agreement within **17** (or ☐ ____) **Days** After Acceptance.

J. ☐ **ALL CASH OFFER** (If checked): Buyer shall, within **7** (or ☐ ____) **Days** After Acceptance, Deliver to Seller written verification of sufficient funds to close this transaction. (If checked, ☐ verification attached.)

K. **BUYER STATED FINANCING:** Seller has relied on Buyer's representation of the type of financing specified (including but not limited to, as applicable, amount of down payment, contingent or non contingent loan, or all cash). If Buyer seeks alternate financing, (i) Seller has no obligation to cooperate with Buyer's efforts to obtain such financing, and (ii) Buyer shall also pursue the financing method specified in this Agreement. Buyer's failure to secure alternate financing does not excuse Buyer from the obligation to purchase the Property and close escrow as specified in this Agreement.

4. **ALLOCATION OF COSTS** (If checked): Unless otherwise specified here, in writing, **this paragraph** only determines who is to pay for the inspection, test or service ("Report") mentioned; it **does not determine who is to pay for any work recommended or identified in the Report.**
A. **INSPECTIONS AND REPORTS:**
(1) ☐ Buyer ☐ Seller shall pay for an inspection and report for wood destroying pests and organisms ("Wood Pest Report") prepared by _____ a registered structural pest control company.
(2) ☐ Buyer ☐ Seller shall pay to have septic or private sewage disposal systems inspected _____.
(3) ☐ Buyer ☐ Seller shall pay to have domestic wells tested for water potability and productivity _____.
(4) ☐ Buyer ☐ Seller shall pay for a natural hazard zone disclosure report prepared by _____.
(5) ☐ Buyer ☐ Seller shall pay for the following inspection or report _____.
(6) ☐ Buyer ☐ Seller shall pay for the following inspection or report _____.
B. **GOVERNMENT REQUIREMENTS AND RETROFIT:**
(1) ☐ Buyer ☐ Seller shall pay for smoke detector installation and/or water heater bracing, if required by Law. Prior to Close Of Escrow, Seller shall provide Buyer written statement(s) of compliance in accordance with state and local Law, unless exempt.
(2) ☐ Buyer ☐ Seller shall pay the cost of compliance with any other minimum mandatory government retrofit standards, inspections and reports if required as a condition of closing escrow under any Law. _____.
C. **ESCROW AND TITLE:**
(1) ☐ Buyer ☐ Seller shall pay escrow fee _____.
Escrow Holder shall be _____.
(2) ☐ Buyer ☐ Seller shall pay for **owner's** title insurance policy specified in paragraph 12E _____.
Owner's title policy to be issued by _____.
(Buyer shall pay for any title insurance policy insuring Buyer's **lender**, unless otherwise agreed in writing.)
D. **OTHER COSTS:**
(1) ☐ Buyer ☐ Seller shall pay County transfer tax or fee _____.
(2) ☐ Buyer ☐ Seller shall pay City transfer tax or fee _____.
(3) ☐ Buyer ☐ Seller shall pay Homeowner's Association ("HOA") transfer fee _____.
(4) ☐ Buyer ☐ Seller shall pay HOA document preparation fees _____.
(5) ☐ Buyer ☐ Seller shall pay for any private transfer fee _____.
(6) ☐ Buyer ☐ Seller shall pay for the cost, not to exceed $ _____, of a one-year home warranty plan, issued by _____, with the following optional coverages:
☐ Air Conditioner ☐ Pool/Spa ☐ Code and Permit upgrade ☐ Other: _____
Buyer is informed that home warranty plans have many optional coverages in addition to those listed above. Buyer is advised to investigate these coverages to determine those that may be suitable for Buyer.
(7) ☐ Buyer ☐ Seller shall pay for _____.
(8) ☐ Buyer ☐ Seller shall pay for _____.

Buyer's Initials (_____)(_____)

Seller's Initials (_____)(_____)

Reviewed by _____ Date _____

RPA-CA REVISED 4/13 (PAGE 2 OF 8) Print Date

CALIFORNIA RESIDENTIAL PURCHASE AGREEMENT (RPA-CA PAGE 2 OF 8)

Property Address: _____ Date: _____

5. **CLOSING AND POSSESSION:**
   A. Buyer intends (or ☐ does not intend) to occupy the Property as Buyer's primary residence.
   B. **Seller-occupied or vacant property:** Possession shall be delivered to Buyer at 5 PM or (☐ _____ ☐ AM/☐ PM) on the date of Close Of Escrow; ☐ on _____; or ☐ no later than _____ **Days** After Close Of Escrow. If transfer of title and possession do not occur at the same time, Buyer and Seller are advised to: **(i)** enter into a written occupancy agreement (C.A.R. Form PAA, paragraph 2.); and **(ii)** consult with their insurance and legal advisors.
   C. **Tenant-occupied property: (i) Property shall be vacant** at least 5 (or ☐ _____) **Days** Prior to Close Of Escrow, unless otherwise agreed in writing. **Note to Seller: If you are unable to deliver Property vacant in accordance with rent control and other applicable Law, you may be in breach of this Agreement.**
   OR **(ii)** (if checked) ☐ **Tenant to remain in possession.** (C.A.R. Form PAA, paragraph 3.)
   D. At Close Of Escrow, **(i)** Seller assigns to Buyer any assignable warranty rights for items included in the sale, and **(ii)** Seller shall Deliver to Buyer available Copies of warranties. Brokers cannot and will not determine the assignability of any warranties.
   E. At Close Of Escrow, unless otherwise agreed in writing, Seller shall provide keys and/or means to operate all locks, mailboxes, security systems, alarms and garage door openers. If Property is a condominium or located in a common interest subdivision, Buyer may be required to pay a deposit to the Homeowners' Association ("HOA") to obtain keys to accessible HOA facilities.
6. **STATUTORY DISCLOSURES (INCLUDING LEAD-BASED PAINT HAZARD DISCLOSURES) AND CANCELLATION RIGHTS:**
   A. **(1)** Seller shall, within the time specified in paragraph 14A, Deliver to Buyer, if required by Law: **(i)** Federal Lead-Based Paint Disclosures (C.A.R. Form FLD) and pamphlet ("Lead Disclosures"); and **(ii)** disclosures or notices required by sections 1102 et. seq. and 1103 et. seq. of the Civil Code ("Statutory Disclosures"). Statutory Disclosures include, but are not limited to, a Real Estate Transfer Disclosure Statement ("TDS"), Natural Hazard Disclosure Statement ("NHD"), notice or actual knowledge of release of illegal controlled substance, notice of special tax and/or assessments (or, if allowed, substantially equivalent notice regarding the Mello-Roos Community Facilities Act and Improvement Bond Act of 1915) and, if Seller has actual knowledge, of industrial use and military ordnance location (C.A.R. Form SPQ or SSD).
   (2) Buyer shall, within the time specified in paragraph 14B(1), return Signed Copies of the Statutory and Lead Disclosures to Seller.
   (3) In the event Seller, prior to Close Of Escrow, becomes aware of adverse conditions materially affecting the Property, or any material inaccuracy in disclosures, information or representations previously provided to Buyer, Seller shall promptly provide a subsequent or amended disclosure or notice, in writing, covering those items. **However, a subsequent or amended disclosure shall not be required for conditions and material inaccuracies** of which Buyer is otherwise aware, or which are **disclosed in reports provided to or obtained by Buyer or ordered and paid for by Buyer.**
   (4) If any disclosure or notice specified in 6A(1), or subsequent or amended disclosure or notice is Delivered to Buyer after the offer is Signed, Buyer shall have the right to cancel this Agreement within **3 Days** After Delivery in person, or **5 Days** After Delivery by deposit in the mail, by giving written notice of cancellation to Seller or Seller's agent.
   (5) Note to Buyer and Seller: Waiver of Statutory and Lead Disclosures is prohibited by Law.
   B. **NATURAL AND ENVIRONMENTAL HAZARDS:** Within the time specified in paragraph 14A, Seller shall, if required by Law: **(i)** Deliver to Buyer earthquake guides (and questionnaire) and environmental hazards booklet; **(ii)** even if exempt from the obligation to provide a NHD, disclose if the Property is located in a Special Flood Hazard Area; Potential Flooding (Inundation) Area; Very High Fire Hazard Zone; State Fire Responsibility Area; Earthquake Fault Zone; Seismic Hazard Zone; and **(iii)** disclose any other zone as required by Law and provide any other information required for those zones.
   C. **WITHHOLDING TAXES:** Within the time specified in paragraph 14A, to avoid required withholding, Seller shall Deliver to Buyer or qualified substitute, an affidavit sufficient to comply with federal (FIRPTA) and California withholding Law (C.A.R. Form AS or QS).
   D. **MEGAN'S LAW DATABASE DISCLOSURE:** Notice: Pursuant to Section 290.46 of the Penal Code, information about specified registered sex offenders is made available to the public via an Internet Web site maintained by the Department of Justice at www.meganslaw.ca.gov. Depending on an offender's criminal history, this information will include either the address at which the offender resides or the community of residence and ZIP Code in which he or she resides. (Neither Seller nor Brokers are required to check this website. If Buyer wants further information, Broker recommends that Buyer obtain information from this website during Buyer's inspection contingency period. Brokers do not have expertise in this area.)
   E. **NOTICE REGARDING GAS AND HAZARDOUS LIQUID TRANSMISSION PIPELINES:** This notice is being provided simply to inform you that information about the general location of gas and hazardous liquid transmission pipelines is available to the public via the National Pipeline Mapping System (NPMS) Internet Web site maintained by the United States Department of Transportation at http://www.npms.phmsa.dot.gov/. To seek further information about possible transmission pipelines near the Property, you may contact your local gas utility or other pipeline operators in the area. Contact information for pipeline operators is searchable by ZIP Code and county on the NPMS Internet Web site.
7. **CONDOMINIUM/PLANNED DEVELOPMENT DISCLOSURES:**
   A. **SELLER HAS: 7 (or ☐ _____) Days** After Acceptance to disclose to Buyer whether the Property is a condominium, or is located in a planned development or other common interest subdivision (C.A.R. Form SPQ or SSD).
   B. If the Property is a condominium or is located in a planned development or other common interest subdivision, Seller has **3 (or ☐ _____) Days** After Acceptance to request from the HOA (C.A.R. Form HOA): **(i)** Copies of any documents required by Law; **(ii)** disclosure of any pending or anticipated claim or litigation by or against the HOA; **(iii)** a statement containing the location and number of designated parking and storage spaces; **(iv)** Copies of the most recent 12 months of HOA minutes for regular and special meetings; and **(v)** the names and contact information of all HOAs governing the Property (collectively, "CI Disclosures"). Seller shall itemize and Deliver to Buyer all CI Disclosures received from the HOA and any CI Disclosures in Seller's possession. Buyer's approval of CI Disclosures is a contingency of this Agreement as specified in paragraph 14B(3).
8. **ITEMS INCLUDED IN AND EXCLUDED FROM PURCHASE PRICE:**
   A. **NOTE TO BUYER AND SELLER:** Items listed as included or excluded in the MLS, flyers or marketing materials are **not** included in the purchase price or excluded from the sale unless specified in 8B or C.
   B. **ITEMS INCLUDED IN SALE:**
   (1) All EXISTING fixtures and fittings that are attached to the Property;
   (2) EXISTING electrical, mechanical, lighting, plumbing and heating fixtures, ceiling fans, fireplace inserts, gas logs and grates, solar systems, built-in appliances, window and door screens, awnings, shutters, window coverings, attached floor coverings, television antennas, satellite dishes, private integrated telephone systems, air coolers/conditioners, pool/spa equipment, garage door openers/remote controls, mailbox, in-ground landscaping, trees/shrubs, water softeners, water purifiers, security systems/alarms; (If checked) ☐ stove(s), ☐ refrigerator(s);

Buyer's Initials (_____)(_____)   Seller's Initials (_____)(_____)

RPA-CA REVISED 4/13 (PAGE 3 OF 8) Print Date

Reviewed by _____ Date _____

CALIFORNIA RESIDENTIAL PURCHASE AGREEMENT (RPA-CA PAGE 3 OF 8)

Property Address: _____   Date: _____

(3) The following additional items:_____.

(4) Seller represents that all items included in the purchase price, unless otherwise specified, are owned by Seller.

(5) All items included shall be transferred free of liens and without Seller warranty.

C. **ITEMS EXCLUDED FROM SALE:** Unless otherwise specified, audio and video components (such as flat screen TVs and speakers) are excluded if any such item is not itself attached to the Property, even if a bracket or other mechanism attached to the component is attached to the Property; and _____.

9. **CONDITION OF PROPERTY:** Unless otherwise agreed: **(i) the Property is sold (a) in its PRESENT physical ("as-is") condition as of the date of Acceptance and (b) subject to Buyer's Investigation rights; (ii)** the Property, including pool, spa, landscaping and grounds, is to be maintained in substantially the same condition as on the date of Acceptance; and **(iii)** all debris and personal property not included in the sale shall be removed by Close Of Escrow.

A. Seller shall, within the time specified in paragraph 14A, DISCLOSE KNOWN MATERIAL FACTS AND DEFECTS affecting the Property, including known insurance claims within the past five years, and make any and all other disclosures required by law.

B. Buyer has the right to inspect the Property and, as specified in paragraph 14B, based upon information discovered in those inspections: (i) cancel this Agreement; or (ii) request that Seller make Repairs or take other action.

C. **Buyer is strongly advised to conduct investigations of the entire Property in order to determine its present condition. Seller may not be aware of all defects affecting the Property or other factors that Buyer considers important. Property improvements may not be built according to code, in compliance with current Law, or have had permits issued.**

10. **BUYER'S INVESTIGATION OF PROPERTY AND MATTERS AFFECTING PROPERTY:**

A. Buyer's acceptance of the condition of, and any other matter affecting the Property, is a contingency of this Agreement as specified in this paragraph and paragraph 14B. Within the time specified in paragraph 14B(1), Buyer shall have the right, at Buyer's expense unless otherwise agreed, to conduct inspections, investigations, tests, surveys and other studies ("Buyer Investigations"), including, but not limited to the right to: **(i)** inspect for lead-based paint and other lead-based paint hazards; **(ii)** inspect for wood destroying pests and organisms; **(iii)** review the registered sex offender database; **(iv)** confirm the insurability of Buyer and the Property; and **(v)** satisfy Buyer as to any matter specified in the attached Buyer's Inspection Advisory (C.A.R. Form BIA). Without Seller's prior written consent, Buyer shall neither make nor cause to be made: **(i)** invasive or destructive Buyer Investigations; or **(ii)** inspections by any governmental building or zoning inspector or government employee, unless required by Law.

B. Seller shall make the Property available for all Buyer Investigations. Buyer shall **(i)** as specified in paragraph 14B, complete Buyer Investigations and, either remove the contingency or cancel this Agreement, and **(ii)** give Seller, at no cost, complete Copies of all Investigation reports obtained by Buyer, which obligation shall survive the termination of this Agreement.

C. Seller shall have water, gas, electricity and all operable pilot lights on for Buyer's Investigations and through the date possession is made available to Buyer.

D. **Buyer indemnity and seller protection for entry upon property:** Buyer shall: **(i)** keep the Property free and clear of liens; **(ii)** repair all damage arising from Buyer Investigations; and **(iii)** indemnify and hold Seller harmless from all resulting liability, claims, demands, damages and costs. Buyer shall carry, or Buyer shall require anyone acting on Buyer's behalf to carry, policies of liability, workers' compensation and other applicable insurance, defending and protecting Seller from liability for any injuries to persons or property occurring during any Buyer Investigations or work done on the Property at Buyer's direction prior to Close Of Escrow. Seller is advised that certain protections may be afforded Seller by recording a "Notice of Non-responsibility" (C.A.R. Form NNR) for Buyer Investigations and work done on the Property at Buyer's direction. Buyer's obligations under this paragraph shall survive the termination of this Agreement.

11. **SELLER DISCLOSURES; ADDENDA; ADVISORIES; OTHER TERMS:**

A. **Seller Disclosures (if checked):** Seller shall, within the time specified in paragraph 14A, complete and provide Buyer with a:

☐Seller Property Questionnaire (C.A.R. Form SPQ)   **OR**   ☐Supplemental Contractual and Statutory Disclosure (C.A.R. Form SSD)

B. **Addenda (if checked):**   ☐Addendum #_____ (C.A.R. Form ADM)

☐Wood Destroying Pest Inspection and Allocation of Cost Addendum (C.A.R. Form WPA)

☐Purchase Agreement Addendum (C.A.R. Form PAA)   ☐Septic, Well and Property Monument Addendum (C.A.R. Form SWPI)

☐Short Sale Addendum (C.A.R. Form SSA)   ☐Other

C. **Advisories (if checked):**   ☐Buyer's Inspection advisory (C.A.R. Form BIA)

☐Probate Advisory (C.A.R. Form PAK)   ☐Statewide Buyer and Seller Advisory (C.A.R.Form SBSA)

☐Trust Advisory (C.A.R. Form TA)   ☐REO Advisory (C.A.R. Form REO)

D. **Other Terms:**_____

12. **TITLE AND VESTING:**

A. Within the time specified in paragraph 14, Buyer shall be provided a current preliminary title report, which shall include a search of the General Index, Seller shall within 7 Days After Acceptance, give Escrow Holder a completed Statement of Information. The preliminary report is only an offer by the title insurer to issue a policy of title insurance and may not contain every item affecting title. Buyer's review of the preliminary report and any other matters which may affect title are a contingency of this Agreement as specified in paragraph 14B.

B. Title is taken in its present condition subject to all encumbrances, easements, covenants, conditions, restrictions, rights and other matters, whether of record or not, as of the date of Acceptance except: **(i)** monetary liens of record unless Buyer is assuming those obligations or taking the Property subject to those obligations; and **(ii)** those matters which Seller has agreed to remove in writing.

C. Within the time specified in paragraph 14A, Seller has a duty to disclose to Buyer all matters known to Seller affecting title, whether of record or not.

D. At Close Of Escrow, Buyer shall receive a grant deed conveying title (or, for stock cooperative or long-term lease, an assignment of stock certificate or of Seller's leasehold interest), including oil, mineral and water rights if currently owned by Seller. Title shall vest as designated in Buyer's supplemental escrow instructions. THE MANNER OF TAKING TITLE MAY HAVE SIGNIFICANT LEGAL AND TAX CONSEQUENCES. CONSULT AN APPROPRIATE PROFESSIONAL.

E. Buyer shall receive a CLTA/ALTA Homeowner's Policy of Title Insurance. A title company, at Buyer's request, can provide information about the availability, desirability, coverage, and cost of various title insurance coverages and endorsements. If Buyer desires title coverage other than that required by this paragraph, Buyer shall instruct Escrow Holder in writing and pay any increase in cost.

Buyer's Initials (_____)(_____)   Seller's Initials (_____)(_____)

Property Address: _____   Date: _____

13. SALE OF BUYER'S PROPERTY:
    A. This Agreement is NOT contingent upon the sale of any property owned by Buyer.
OR B. ☐ (If checked): The attached addendum (C.A.R. Form COP) regarding the contingency for the sale of property owned by Buyer is incorporated into this Agreement.

14. TIME PERIODS; REMOVAL OF CONTINGENCIES; CANCELLATION RIGHTS: The following time periods may only be extended, altered, modified or changed by mutual written agreement. Any removal of contingencies or cancellation under this paragraph by either Buyer or Seller must be exercised in good faith and in writing (C.A.R. Form CR or CC).
    A. **SELLER HAS: 7 (or ☐ _____) Days** After Acceptance to Deliver to Buyer all Reports, disclosures and information for which Seller is responsible under paragraphs 4, 6A, B and C, 7A, 9A, 11A and B and 12A. Buyer may give Seller a Notice to Seller to Perform (C.A.R. Form NSP) if Seller has not Delivered the items within the time specified.
    B. **(1) BUYER HAS: 17 (or ☐ _____) Days** After Acceptance, unless otherwise agreed in writing, to:
        (i) complete all Buyer Investigations; approve all disclosures, reports and other applicable information, which Buyer receives from Seller; and approve all matters affecting the Property; and
        (ii) Deliver to Seller Signed Copies of Statutory and Lead Disclosures Delivered by Seller in accordance with paragraph 6A.
      (2) Within the time specified in 14B(1), Buyer may request that Seller make repairs or take any other action regarding the Property (C.A.R. Form RR). Seller has no obligation to agree to or respond to Buyer's requests.
      (3) By the end of the time specified in 14B(1) (or as otherwise specified in this Agreement), Buyer shall, Deliver to Seller a removal of the applicable contingency or cancellation (C.A.R. Form CR or CC) of this Agreement. However, if any report, disclosure or information for which Seller is responsible is not Delivered within the time specified in 14A, then Buyer has **5 (or ☐ _____) Days** After Delivery of any such items, or the time specified in 14B(1), whichever is later, to Deliver to Seller a removal of the applicable contingency or cancellation of this Agreement.
      (4) Continuation of Contingency: Even after the end of the time specified in 14B(1) and before Seller cancels, if at all, pursuant to 14C, Buyer retains the right to either (i) in writing remove remaining contingencies, or (ii) cancel this Agreement based on a remaining contingency. Once Buyer's written removal of all contingencies is Delivered to Seller, Seller may not cancel this Agreement pursuant to 14C(1).
    C. **SELLER RIGHT TO CANCEL:**
      (1) Seller right to Cancel; Buyer Contingencies: If, by the time specified in this Agreement, Buyer does not Deliver to Seller a removal of the applicable contingency or cancellation of this Agreement then Seller, after first Delivering to Buyer a Notice to Buyer to Perform (C.A.R. Form NBP) may cancel this Agreement. In such event, Seller shall authorize return of Buyer's deposit.
      (2) Seller right to Cancel; Buyer Contract Obligations: Seller, after first Delivering to Buyer a NBP may cancel this Agreement for any of the following reasons: **(i)** if Buyer fails to deposit funds as required by 3A or 3B; **(ii)** if the funds deposited pursuant to 3A or 3B are not good when deposited; **(iii)** if Buyer fails to Deliver a notice of FHA or VA costs or terms as required by 3C(3) (C.A.R. Form FVA); **(iv)** if Buyer fails to Deliver a letter as required by 3H; **(v)** if Buyer fails to Deliver verification as required by 3G or 3J; **(vi)** if Seller reasonably disapproves of the verification provided by 3G or 3J; **(vii)** if Buyer fails to return Statutory and Lead Disclosures as required by paragraph 6A(2); or **(viii)** if Buyer fails to sign or initial a separate liquidated damages form for an increased deposit as required by paragraphs 3B and 25. In such event, Seller shall authorize return of Buyer's deposit.
      (3) Notice To Buyer To Perform: The NBP shall: **(i)** be in writing; **(ii)** be signed by Seller; and **(iii)** give Buyer at least **2 (or ☐ _____) Days** After Delivery (or until the time specified in the applicable paragraph, whichever occurs last) to take the applicable action. A NBP may not be Delivered any earlier than **2 Days** Prior to the expiration of the applicable time for Buyer to remove a contingency or cancel this Agreement or meet an obligation specified in 14C (2).
    D. **EFFECT OF BUYER'S REMOVAL OF CONTINGENCIES:** If Buyer removes, in writing, any contingency or cancellation rights, unless otherwise specified in a separate written agreement between Buyer and Seller, Buyer shall conclusively be deemed to have: **(i)** completed all Buyer Investigations, and review of reports and other applicable information and disclosures pertaining to that contingency or cancellation right; **(ii)** elected to proceed with the transaction; and **(iii)** assumed all liability, responsibility and expense for Repairs or corrections pertaining to that contingency or cancellation right, or for inability to obtain financing.
    E. **CLOSE OF ESCROW:** Before Seller or Buyer may cancel this Agreement for failure of the other party to close escrow pursuant to this Agreement, Seller or Buyer must first Deliver to the other a demand to close escrow (C.A.R. Form DCE).
    F. **EFFECT OF CANCELLATION ON DEPOSITS:** If Buyer or Seller gives written notice of cancellation pursuant to rights duly exercised under the terms of this Agreement, Buyer and Seller agree to Sign mutual instructions to cancel the sale and escrow and release deposits, if any, to the party entitled to the funds, less fees and costs incurred by that party. Fees and costs may be payable to service providers and vendors for services and products provided during escrow. **Release of funds will require mutual Signed release instructions from Buyer and Seller, judicial decision or arbitration award. A Buyer or Seller may be subject to a civil penalty of up to $1,000 for refusal to sign such instructions if no good faith dispute exists as to who is entitled to the deposited funds (Civil Code §1057.3).**

15. REPAIRS: Repairs shall be completed prior to final verification of condition unless otherwise agreed in writing. Repairs to be performed at Seller's expense may be performed by Seller or through others, provided that the work complies with applicable Law, including governmental permit, inspection and approval requirements. Repairs shall be performed in a good, skillful manner with materials of quality and appearance comparable to existing materials. It is understood that exact restoration of appearance or cosmetic items following all Repairs may not be possible. Seller shall: **(i)** obtain receipts for Repairs performed by others; **(ii)** prepare a written statement indicating the Repairs performed by Seller and the date of such Repairs; and **(iii)** provide Copies of receipts and statements to Buyer prior to final verification of condition.

16. FINAL VERIFICATION OF CONDITION: Buyer shall have the right to make a final inspection of the Property within **5 (or _____) Days** Prior to Close Of Escrow, NOT AS A CONTINGENCY OF THE SALE, but solely to confirm: **(i)** the Property is maintained pursuant to paragraph 9; **(ii)** Repairs have been completed as agreed; and **(iii)** Seller has complied with Seller's other obligations under this Agreement (C.A.R. Form VP).

17. PRORATIONS OF PROPERTY TAXES AND OTHER ITEMS: Unless otherwise agreed in writing, the following items shall be PAID CURRENT and prorated between Buyer and Seller as of Close Of Escrow: real property taxes and assessments, interest, rents, HOA regular, special, and emergency dues and assessments imposed prior to Close Of Escrow, premiums on insurance assumed by Buyer, payments on bonds and assessments assumed by Buyer, and payments on Mello-Roos and other Special Assessment District bonds and assessments that are now a lien. The following items shall be assumed by Buyer WITHOUT CREDIT toward the purchase price: prorated payments on Mello-Roos and other Special Assessment District bonds and assessments and HOA special assessments that are now a lien but not yet due. Property will be reassessed upon change of ownership. Any supplemental tax bills shall be paid as follows: **(i)** for periods after Close Of Escrow, by Buyer; and **(ii)** for periods prior to Close Of Escrow, by Seller (see C.A.R. Form SPT or SBSA for further information). TAX BILLS ISSUED AFTER CLOSE OF ESCROW SHALL BE HANDLED DIRECTLY BETWEEN BUYER AND SELLER. Prorations shall be made based on a 30-day month.

Buyer's Initials (_____)(_____)   Seller's Initials (_____)(_____)

Property Address: _____ Date: _____

18. **SELECTION OF SERVICE PROVIDERS:** Brokers do not guarantee the performance of any vendors, service or product providers ("Providers"), whether referred by Broker or selected by Buyer, Seller or other person. Buyer and Seller may select ANY Providers of their own choosing.

19. **MULTIPLE LISTING SERVICE ("MLS"):** Brokers are authorized to report to the MLS a pending sale and, upon Close Of Escrow, the sales price and other terms of this transaction shall be provided to the MLS to be published and disseminated to persons and entities authorized to use the information on terms approved by the MLS.

20. **EQUAL HOUSING OPPORTUNITY:** The Property is sold in compliance with federal, state and local anti-discrimination Laws.

21. **ATTORNEY FEES:** In any action, proceeding, or arbitration between Buyer and Seller arising out of this Agreement, the prevailing Buyer or Seller shall be entitled to reasonable attorney fees and costs from the non-prevailing Buyer or Seller, except as provided in paragraph 26A.

22. **DEFINITIONS:** As used in this Agreement:
    A. **"Acceptance"** means the time the offer or final counter offer is accepted in writing by a party and is delivered to and personally received by the other party or that party's authorized agent in accordance with the terms of this offer or a final counter offer.
    B. **"C.A.R. Form"** means the specific form referenced or another comparable form agreed to by the parties.
    C. **"Close Of Escrow"** means the date the grant deed, or other evidence of transfer of title, is recorded.
    D. **"Copy"** means copy by any means including photocopy, NCR, facsimile and electronic.
    E. **"Days"** means calendar days. However, after Acceptance, the last **Day** for performance of any act required by this Agreement (including Close Of Escrow) shall not include any Saturday, Sunday, or legal holiday and shall instead be the next Day.
    F. **"Days After"** means the specified number of calendar days after the occurrence of the event specified, not counting the calendar date on which the specified event occurs, and ending at 11:59PM on the final day.
    G. **"Days Prior"** means the specified number of calendar days before the occurrence of the event specified, not counting the calendar date on which the specified event is scheduled to occur.
    H. **"Deliver", "Delivered"** or **"Delivery"** means and shall be effective upon (i) personal receipt by Buyer or Seller or the individual Real Estate Licensee for that principal as specified in paragraph D of the section titled Real Estate Brokers on page 8, regardless of the method used (i.e. messenger, maill, email, fax, other); OR (ii) if checked, ☐ per the attached addendum (C.A.R. Form RDN).
    I. **"Electronic Copy"** or **"Electronic Signature"** means, as applicable, an electronic copy or signature complying with California Law. Buyer and Seller agree that electronic means will not be used by either party to modify or alter the content or integrity of this Agreement without the knowledge and consent of the other.
    J. **"Law"** means any law, code, statute, ordinance, regulation, rule or order, which is adopted by a controlling city, county, state or federal legislative, judicial or executive body or agency.
    K. **"Repairs"** means any repairs (including pest control), alterations, replacements, modifications or retrofitting of the Property provided for under this Agreement.
    L. **"Signed"** means either a handwritten or electronic signature on an original document, Copy or any counterpart.

23. **BROKER COMPENSATION:** Seller or Buyer, or both, as applicable, agrees to pay compensation to Broker as specified in a separate written agreement between Broker and that Seller or Buyer. Compensation is payable upon Close Of Escrow, or if escrow does not close, as otherwise specified in the agreement between Broker and that Seller or Buyer.

24. **JOINT ESCROW INSTRUCTIONS TO ESCROW HOLDER:**
    A. **The following paragraphs, or applicable portions thereof, of this Agreement constitute the joint escrow instructions of Buyer and Seller to Escrow Holder,** which Escrow Holder is to use along with any related counter offers and addenda, and any additional mutual instructions to close the escrow: 1, 3, 4, 6C, 11B and D, 12, 13B, 14F, 17, 22, 23, 24, 28, 30 and paragraph D of the section titled Real Estate Brokers on page 8. If a Copy of the separate compensation agreement(s) provided for in paragraph 23, or paragraph D of the section titled Real Estate Brokers on page 8 is deposited with Escrow Holder by Broker, Escrow Holder shall accept such agreement(s) and pay out from Buyer's or Seller's funds, or both, as applicable, the Broker's compensation provided for in such agreement(s). The terms and conditions of this Agreement not set forth in the specified paragraphs are additional matters for the information of Escrow Holder, but about which Escrow Holder need not be concerned. Buyer and Seller will receive Escrow Holder's general provisions directly from Escrow Holder and will execute such provisions upon Escrow Holder's request. To the extent the general provisions are inconsistent or conflict with this Agreement, the general provisions will control as to the duties and obligations of Escrow Holder only. Buyer and Seller will execute additional instructions, documents and forms provided by Escrow Holder that are reasonably necessary to close the escrow.
    B. A Copy of this Agreement shall be delivered to Escrow Holder within **3** business days after Acceptance (or ☐ _____). Escrow Holder shall provide Seller's Statement of Information to Title company when received from Seller. Buyer and Seller authorize Escrow Holder to accept and rely on Copies and Signatures as defined in this Agreement as originals, to open escrow and for other purposes of escrow. The validity of this Agreement as between Buyer and Seller is not affected by whether or when Escrow Holder Signs this Agreement.
    C. Brokers are a party to the escrow for the sole purpose of compensation pursuant to paragraph 23 and paragraph D of the section titled Real Estate Brokers on page 8. Buyer and Seller irrevocably assign to Brokers compensation specified in paragraph 23, respectively, and irrevocably instruct Escrow Holder to disburse those funds to Brokers at Close Of Escrow or pursuant to any other mutually executed cancellation agreement. Compensation instructions can be amended or revoked only with the written consent of Brokers. Buyer and Seller shall release and hold harmless Escrow Holder from any liability resulting from Escrow Holder's payment to Broker(s) of compensation pursuant to this Agreement. Escrow Holder shall immediately notify Brokers: **(i)** if Buyer's initial or any additional deposit is not made pursuant to this Agreement, or is not good at time of deposit with Escrow Holder; or **(ii)** if Buyer and Seller instruct Escrow Holder to cancel escrow.
    D. A Copy of any amendment that affects any paragraph of this Agreement for which Escrow Holder is responsible shall be delivered to Escrow Holder within **2** business days after mutual execution of the amendment.

Buyer's Initials (_____)(_____)   Seller's Initials (_____)(_____)

RPA-CA REVISED 4/13 (PAGE 6 OF 8) Print Date | Reviewed by _____ Date _____ |

CALIFORNIA RESIDENTIAL PURCHASE AGREEMENT (RPA-CA PAGE 6 OF 8)

Property Address: _____ Date: _____

25. **LIQUIDATED DAMAGES: If Buyer fails to complete this purchase because of Buyer's default, Seller shall retain, as liquidated damages, the deposit actually paid. If the Property is a dwelling with no more than four units, one of which Buyer intends to occupy, then the amount retained shall be no more than 3% of the purchase price. Any excess shall be returned to Buyer. Release of funds will require mutual, Signed release instructions from both Buyer and Seller, judicial decision or arbitration award. AT TIME OF THE INCREASED DEPOSIT BUYER AND SELLER SHALL SIGN A SEPARATE LIQUIDATED DAMAGES PROVISION FOR ANY INCREASED DEPOSIT (C.A.R. FORM RID)**

Buyer's Initials _____ / _____	Seller's Initials _____ / _____

26. **DISPUTE RESOLUTION:**
   A. **MEDIATION:** Buyer and Seller agree to mediate any dispute or claim arising between them out of this Agreement, or any resulting transaction, before resorting to arbitration or court action. **Buyer and Seller also agree to mediate any disputes or claims with Broker(s), who, in writing, agree to such mediation prior to, or within a reasonable time after, the dispute or claim is presented to the Broker.** Mediation fees, if any, shall be divided equally among the parties involved. If, for any dispute or claim to which this paragraph applies, any party (i) commences an action without first attempting to resolve the matter through mediation, or (ii) before commencement of an action, refuses to mediate after a request has been made, then that party shall not be entitled to recover attorney fees, even if they would otherwise be available to that party in any such action. THIS MEDIATION PROVISION APPLIES WHETHER OR NOT THE ARBITRATION PROVISION IS INITIALED. Exclusions from this mediation agreement are specified in paragraph 26C.
   B. **ARBITRATION OF DISPUTES:**
   Buyer and Seller agree that any dispute or claim in Law or equity arising between them out of this Agreement or any resulting transaction, which is not settled through mediation, shall be decided by neutral, binding arbitration. Buyer and Seller also agree to arbitrate any disputes or claims with Broker(s), who, in writing, agree to such arbitration prior to, or within a reasonable time after, the dispute or claim is presented to the Broker. The arbitrator shall be a retired judge or justice, or an attorney with at least 5 years of residential real estate Law experience, unless the parties mutually agree to a different arbitrator. The parties shall have the right to discovery in accordance with Code of Civil Procedure §1283.05. In all other respects, the arbitration shall be conducted in accordance with Title 9 of Part 3 of the Code of Civil Procedure. Judgment upon the award of the arbitrator(s) may be entered into any court having jurisdiction. Enforcement of this agreement to arbitrate shall be governed by the Federal Arbitration Act. Exclusions from this arbitration agreement are specified in paragraph 26C.
   "NOTICE: BY INITIALING IN THE SPACE BELOW YOU ARE AGREEING TO HAVE ANY DISPUTE ARISING OUT OF THE MATTERS INCLUDED IN THE 'ARBITRATION OF DISPUTES' PROVISION DECIDED BY NEUTRAL ARBITRATION AS PROVIDED BY CALIFORNIA LAW AND YOU ARE GIVING UP ANY RIGHTS YOU MIGHT POSSESS TO HAVE THE DISPUTE LITIGATED IN A COURT OR JURY TRIAL. BY INITIALING IN THE SPACE BELOW YOU ARE GIVING UP YOUR JUDICIAL RIGHTS TO DISCOVERY AND APPEAL, UNLESS THOSE RIGHTS ARE SPECIFICALLY INCLUDED IN THE 'ARBITRATION OF DISPUTES' PROVISION. IF YOU REFUSE TO SUBMIT TO ARBITRATION AFTER AGREEING TO THIS PROVISION, YOU MAY BE COMPELLED TO ARBITRATE UNDER THE AUTHORITY OF THE CALIFORNIA CODE OF CIVIL PROCEDURE. YOUR AGREEMENT TO THIS ARBITRATION PROVISION IS VOLUNTARY."
   "WE HAVE READ AND UNDERSTAND THE FOREGOING AND AGREE TO SUBMIT DISPUTES ARISING OUT OF THE MATTERS INCLUDED IN THE 'ARBITRATION OF DISPUTES' PROVISION TO NEUTRAL ARBITRATION."

Buyer's Initials _____ / _____	Seller's Initials _____ / _____

   C. **ADDITIONAL MEDIATION AND ARBITRATION TERMS:**
   (1) EXCLUSIONS: The following matters are excluded from mediation and arbitration: (i) a judicial or non-judicial foreclosure or other action or proceeding to enforce a deed of trust, mortgage or installment land sale contract as defined in Civil Code §2985; (ii) an unlawful detainer action; (iii) the filing or enforcement of a mechanic's lien; and (iv) any matter that is within the jurisdiction of a probate, small claims or bankruptcy court. The filing of a court action to enable the recording of a notice of pending action, for order of attachment, receivership, injunction, or other provisional remedies, shall not constitute a waiver nor violation of the mediation and arbitration provisions.
   (2) BROKERS: Brokers shall not be obligated nor compelled to mediate or arbitrate unless they agree to do so in writing. Any Broker(s) participating in mediation or arbitration shall not be deemed a party to the Agreement.

27. **TERMS AND CONDITIONS OF OFFER:**
   This is an offer to purchase the Property on the above terms and conditions. The liquidated damages paragraph or the arbitration of disputes paragraph is incorporated in this Agreement if initialed by all parties or if incorporated by mutual agreement in a counter offer or addendum. If at least one but not all parties initial, a counter offer is required until agreement is reached. Seller has the right to continue to offer the Property for sale and to accept any other offer at any time prior to notification of Acceptance. Buyer has read and acknowledges receipt of a Copy of the offer and agrees to the above confirmation of agency relationships. If this offer is accepted and Buyer subsequently defaults, Buyer may be responsible for payment of Brokers' compensation. This Agreement and any supplement, addendum or modification, including any Copy, may be Signed in two or more counterparts, all of which shall constitute one and the same writing.

28. **TIME OF ESSENCE; ENTIRE CONTRACT; CHANGES:** Time is of the essence. All understandings between the parties are incorporated in this Agreement. Its terms are intended by the parties as a final, complete and exclusive expression of their Agreement with respect to its subject matter, and may not be contradicted by evidence of any prior agreement or contemporaneous oral agreement. If any provision of this Agreement is held to be ineffective or invalid, the remaining provisions will nevertheless be given full force and effect. Except as otherwise specified, this Agreement shall be interpreted and disputes shall be resolved in accordance with the laws of the State of California. **Neither this Agreement nor any provision in it may be extended, amended, modified, altered or changed, except in writing Signed by Buyer and Seller.**

Buyer's Initials (_____)(_____)   Seller's Initials (_____)(_____)

Reviewed by _____ Date _____

Property Address: _____   Date: _____

29. EXPIRATION OF OFFER: This offer shall be deemed revoked and the deposit shall be returned unless the offer is Signed by Seller and a Copy of the Signed offer is personally received by Buyer, or by _____,
who is authorized to receive it, by 5:00 PM on the third Day after this offer is signed by Buyer (or, if checked,
☐ by _____ ☐AM/☐PM, on _____(date))

Date _____   Date _____

BUYER _____   BUYER _____

_____   _____
(Print name)   **(Print name)**

_____
(Address)

30. ACCEPTANCE OF OFFER: Seller warrants that Seller is the owner of the Property, or has the authority to execute this Agreement. Seller accepts the above offer, agrees to sell the Property on the above terms and conditions, and agrees to the above confirmation of agency relationships. Seller has read and acknowledges receipt of a Copy of this Agreement, and authorizes Broker to Deliver a Signed Copy to Buyer.
☐ (If checked) **SUBJECT TO ATTACHED COUNTER OFFER (C.A.R. Form CO) DATED:** _____,

Date _____   Date _____

SELLER _____   SELLER _____

_____   _____
(Print name)   **(Print name)**

_____
(Address)

(___/___) **CONFIRMATION OF ACCEPTANCE:** A Copy of Signed Acceptance was personally received by Buyer or Buyer's authorized
(Initials) agent on (date) _____ at _____ ☐AM/☐PM. **A binding Agreement is created when a Copy of Signed Acceptance is personally received by Buyer or Buyer's authorized agent whether or not confirmed in this document. Completion of this confirmation is not legally required in order to create a binding Agreement; it is solely intended to evidence the date that Confirmation of Acceptance has occurred.**

REAL ESTATE BROKERS:
A. Real Estate Brokers are not parties to the Agreement between Buyer and Seller.
B. Agency relationships are confirmed as stated in paragraph 2.
C. If specified in paragraph 3A, Agent who submitted the offer for Buyer acknowledges receipt of deposit.
D. COOPERATING BROKER COMPENSATION: Listing Broker agrees to pay Cooperating Broker (**Selling Firm**) and Cooperating Broker agrees to accept, out of Listing Broker's proceeds in escrow: **(i)** the amount specified in the MLS, provided Cooperating Broker is a Participant of the MLS in which the Property is offered for sale or a reciprocal MLS; or **(ii)** ☐ (if checked) the amount specified in a separate written agreement (C.A.R. Form CBC) between Listing Broker and Cooperating Broker. Declaration of License and Tax (C.A.R. Form DLT) may be used to document that tax reporting will be required or that an exemption exists.

Real Estate Broker (Selling Firm) _____   DRE Lic. # _____
By _____ DRE Lic. # _____   Date _____
Address _____ City _____   State _____ Zip _____
Telephone _____ Fax _____   E-mail _____
Real Estate Broker (Listing Firm) _____   DRE Lic. # _____
By _____ DRE Lic. # _____   Date _____
Address _____ City _____   State _____ Zip _____
Telephone _____ Fax _____   E-mail _____

ESCROW HOLDER ACKNOWLEDGMENT:
Escrow Holder acknowledges receipt of a Copy of this Agreement, (if checked, ☐ a deposit in the amount of $ _____),
counter offer numbers _____ ☐ Seller's Statement of Information and _____
_____, and agrees to act as Escrow Holder subject to paragraph 24 of this Agreement, any
supplemental escrow instructions and the terms of Escrow Holder's general provisions.

Escrow Holder is advised that the date of Confirmation of Acceptance of the Agreement as between Buyer and Seller is _____

Escrow Holder _____   Escrow # _____
By _____   Date _____
Address _____
Phone/Fax/E-mail _____
Escrow Holder is licensed by the California Department of ☐ Corporations, ☐ Insurance, ☐ Real Estate. License # _____

PRESENTATION OF OFFER: (_____ **)** Listing Broker presented this offer to Seller on _____ (date).
                                 Broker or Designee Initials

REJECTION OF OFFER: (_____ **)(** _____ **)** No counter offer is being made. This offer was rejected by Seller on _____ (date).
                    Seller's Initials

REBS Published and Distributed by:
REAL ESTATE BUSINESS SERVICES, INC.
a subsidiary of the CALIFORNIA ASSOCIATION OF REALTORS®
525 South Virgil Avenue, Los Angeles, California 90020

REVISION DATE 4/13   Print Date

Reviewed by _____
Broker or Designee _____ Date _____

CALIFORNIA RESIDENTIAL PURCHASE AGREEMENT   (RPA-CA PAGE 8 OF 8)

Key Terms for Chapter 6

acceptance — consent (by an offeree) to an offer made (by an offeror) to enter into and be bound by a contract.

bilateral contract — a contract in which a promise given by one party is exchanged for a promise given by the other party.

commission — an agent's compensation for performance of his or her duties as an agent; in real estate, it is usually a percent of the selling price of the property or, in the case of leases, of rentals.

consideration — anything of value given or promised, such as money, property, services, or a forbearance, to induce another to enter into a contract.

contingency — an event that may, but is not certain to, happen, the occurrence upon which the happening of another event is dependent.

counteroffer — a new offer by an offeree that acts as a rejection of an offer by an offeror.

deposit receipt — a written document indicating that a good-faith deposit has been received as part of an offer to purchase real property; also called a purchase and sale agreement.

duress — unlawful force or confinement used to compel a person to enter into a contract against his or her will.

emancipated minor — a minor who, because of marriage, military service, or court order, is allowed to contract for the sale or purchase of real property.

equitable title — the right to possess and enjoy a property while the property is being paid for.

exclusive agency listing — a listing agreement that gives a broker the right to sell property and receive compensation (usually a commission) if the property is sold by anyone other than the owner of the property during the term of the listing.

exclusive authorization and right to sell listing — a listing agreement that gives a broker the exclusive right to sell property and receive compensation (usually a commission) if the property is sold by anyone, including the owner of the property, during the term of the listing.

executed contract— a contract that has been fully performed; may also refer to a contract that has been signed by all of the parties to the contract.

executory contract — a contract that has not yet been fully performed by one or both parties.

express contract — a contract stated in words, written or oral.

fiduciary relationship — a relationship in which one owes a duty of utmost care, integrity, honesty, loyalty, trust, and confidence to another.

implied contract— a contract not expressed in words, but, through action or inaction, understood by the parties.

land installment contract — a real property sales contract.

land contract — a real property sales contract.

liquidated damages — a sum of money that the parties agree, usually at the formation of a contract, will serve as the exact amount of damages that will be paid upon a breach of the contract.

listing agreement — a written contract between a real estate broker and a property owner (the principal) stipulating that in exchange for the real estate broker's procuring a buyer for the principal's property, the principal will compensate the broker, usually with a percentage of the selling price.

menace — a threat to commit duress or to commit injury to person or property.

minor — in California, a person who is under 18 years of age.

multiple listing service — an organization (MLS) of real estate brokers who share their listings with other members of the organization.

mutual consent — refers to the situation in which all parties to a contract freely agree to the terms of the contract; sometimes referred to as a "meeting of the minds."

net listing — a listing agreement providing the broker with all proceeds received from the sale over a specified amount.

offer — a proposal by one person (the offeror) to enter into a contract with another (the offeree).

offeree — one to whom an offer to enter into a contract is made.

offeror — one who makes an offer to enter into a contract.

open listing — a listing agreement that gives a broker the nonexclusive right to sell property and receive compensation (usually a commission) if, but only if, the broker is the first to procure a buyer for the property.

option listing — a listing agreement in which the broker is given the right to sell the subject property or to purchase it at a specified price for a specified time.

option contract — a contract that gives the purchaser of the option the right to buy or lease a certain property at a set price any time during the option term.

parol evidence rule — a rule that prohibits the introduction of extrinsic evidence of preliminary negotiations, oral or written, and of contemporaneous oral evidence, to alter the terms of a written agreement that appears to be whole.

real property sales contract — an agreement in which one party agrees to convey title to real property to another party upon the satisfaction of specified conditions set forth in the contract and that does not require conveyance of title within one year from the date of formation of the contract.

rejection — the act of an offeree that terminates an offer. An offer may be rejected (1) by submitting a new offer, (2) by submitting what purports to be an acceptance but is not because it contains a variance of a material term of the original offer, or (3) by express terms of rejection.

rescission — the cancellation of a contract and the restoration of each party to the same position held before the contract was entered into.

revocation — the withdrawal of an offer by the person who made the offer.

right of first refusal — the right to be given the first chance to purchase a property at the same price, terms, and conditions as is offered to third parties if and when the property is put up for sale.

safety clause — a clause in a listing agreement that protects the broker's commission for a sale that is consummated after the termination of the broker's listing agreement to a buyer who is found by the broker during the term of the listing agreement.

specific performance — a court order that requires a person to perform according to the terms of a contract.

statute of frauds — a law that requires certain types of contracts, including most real estate contracts, to be in writing and signed by the party to be bound in order for the contract to be enforceable.

statute of limitations — a law that requires particular types of lawsuits to be brought within a specified time after the occurrence of the event giving rise to the lawsuit.

unenforceable contract — a contract that a court would not enforce.

unilateral contract — a contract in which one party gives a promise that is to be accepted not by another promise but by performance.

valid contract — a contract that is binding and enforceable in a court of law.

vendee — the purchaser in a real property sales agreement

vendor — the seller in a real property sales agreement.

void contract — a purported contract that has no legal effect.

voidable contract — a contract that, at the request of one party only, may be declared unenforceable, but is valid until it is so declared.

Quiz for Chapter 6

1. An executed contract is one that has been
   a. breached
   b. canceled
   c. fully performed
   d. torn up by one or both of the parties
2. Joe entered into a written contract to sell his house to Susan, but Joe now refuses to go through with the sale. If Susan wants a court to order Joe to complete the sale, she should seek
   a. damages
   b. rescission and restitution of her deposit money
   c. the liquidated damages provided for in the sales contract
   d. specific performance
3. Joe submits an offer to Bob to purchase Bob's house. Bob writes back, "I accept your offer, but you'll need to paint the house at your expense."
   a. Joe and Bob have a valid, binding contract
   b. Joe's offer has been rejected
   c. Joe and Bob have a voidable contract
   d. Joe and Bob have a void contract
4. Susan is able to absolutely and positively prove the existence of an oral contract with Joe to sell her house to Joe. Joe refuses to complete to the purchase. In a court of law, the contract will be
   a. enforced
   b. not enforced
   c. not enforced unless Susan wants it enforced
   d. enforced if the contract selling price was the fair market value of the house
5. The four essential elements of a valid contract are
   a. capable parties, mutual consent, lawful object, consideration
   b. mutual consent, written, capable parties, consideration
   c. valid purpose, mutual consent, consideration, lawful object
   d. capable parties, lawful object, written, consideration
6. The Statute of Frauds
   a. states that if there is a fraud the contract is voidable
   b. states that a contract cannot be enforced after a certain lapse of time
   c. states that certain types of contracts must be in writing to be enforced

    d. states that if fraud was involved in the formation of the contract, the one who committed the fraud may not enforce the contract

7. Susan enters into an oral contract with Jane to rent Jane Susan's apartment for one year. The contract is
    a. voidable
    b. valid
    c. void
    d. illegal

8. Susan's offer to buy Joe's house states that the offer is irrevocable
    a. Susan may not revoke the offer
    b. Susan may revoke the offer only until Joe receives the offer
    c. Susan may not revoke the offer unless Joe rejects it
    d. Susan may revoke the offer until Joe accepts it, unless Joe gave consideration for the offer

9. In California, the Statute of Limitations for oral contracts is
    a. one year
    b. two years
    c. four years
    d. ten years

10. Susan agrees in writing to sell Jane her house, and Jane agrees in writing to buy the house for a specific price in the future. Their contract is
    a. executed, unilateral, and enforceable
    b. executory, bilateral, and express
    c. bilateral, implied, and executory
    d. express, executory, and voidable

11. Janet offers to buy Bob's house for $200,000. Bob replies that he won't take a penny less than $250,000. Janet says, "Forget it." Bob then says that he has thought it over and will accept the $200,000. Janet replies, "Now, I'll give you only $190,000." Janet and Bob have
    a. no contract
    b. a contract for $190,000
    c. Bob has an offer to sell his house for $190,000
    d. both a and c

12. A contract cannot be valid and binding unless
    a. it is in writing
    b. there is sufficient consideration
    c. the parties are compatible
    d. both b and c

13. To be legally capable of contracting for real property, a person must
    a. be an emancipated minor
    b. have at least an eighth grade education
    c. have been declared incompetent by a court of law
    d. none of the above

14. All of the following are covered by the Statute of Frauds except for
    a. a listing agreement
    b. a three-year lease
    c. an agreement to will property to a relative
    d. none of the above

15. Joe offers to buy Bob's house for $300,000. Bob replies that he would take $325,000. Within this scenario can be found
    a. an offer
    b. a rejection
    c. a counteroffer
    d. all of the above

16. Susan signed a listing agreement with Bob and with Joe and retains the right to sell the property herself without paying a commission to anyone. This probably is an example of
    a. an unenforceable listing
    b. an open listing
    c. an exclusive agency listings
    d. an exclusive authorization and right to sell listing

17. Joe threatens to burn down Bob's ugly guesthouse if Bob doesn't agree to paint it. This is an example of
    a. duress
    b. menace
    c. what homeowners associations are all about
    d. an illegal contract

18. Which of the following is generally not unessential to the validity of a contract?
    a. mutual consent
    b. lawful objects
    c. a disinterested witness
    d. both a and b

19. A valid contract requires
    a. a capable witness
    b. consideration of value approximately equal to what is given for
    c. a written document
    d. none of the above

20. Consideration for a contract can be in the form of
    a. services
    b. a forbearance
    c. neither a nor b
    d. either a or b

21. An offer cannot be revoked if
    a. the seller has not received the offer
    b. the seller has received the offer

    c. the time stated in the offer that it would be irrevocable has not expired

    d. none of the above

22. Which of the following is true?

    a. revocation is effective upon mailing

    b. acceptance is effective upon mailing unless the offer had been revoked

    c. acceptance is effective only upon receipt

    d. both a and b

23. A voidable contract is

    a. void unless the injured party brings an action to declare it unenforceable

    b. not enforceable

    c. enforceable by either party

    d. none of the above

24. The Statute of Frauds requires that

    a. all contracts have sufficient consideration

    b. all contracts have a legal purpose

    c. all contracts be between capable parties

    d. none of the above

25. A listing agreement creates what type of relationship between the seller and the broker?

    a. contractual

    b. voidable

    c. fiduciary

    d. both a and c

26. The type of listing agreement that provides that the broker will receive a commission only if he or she procures the buyer is

    a. a net listing

    b. an exclusive authorization and right to sell listing

    c. an exclusive agency list

    d. none of the above

27. The type of listing agreement providing the broker with all proceeds received from the sale over a specified amount is

    a. an exclusive agency list

    b. a net listing

    c. an option listing

    d. none of the above

28. Jane has an Exclusive Authorization and Right to Sell listing agreement with broker Bob. Bob procures a buyer ready, willing, and able to meet Jane's terms as stated in the listing agreement. Which of the following is true?

    a. Jane must accept the buyer's offer and pay Bob a commission

b. if Jane refuses to sell, the buyer probably can get specific performance and Bob can get the commission
c. Jane need not accept the offer, but she owes Bob the commission
d. none of the above

29. A safety clause
a. provides that to be a valid contract the object of the contract must be safe to use
b. provides that if something necessary to form a valid contract is absent, a court will provide the missing essential element
c. provides that an action to enforce the contract must be brought within a certain time
d. none of the above

30. Joe contracted with Bob to provide Bob with narcotics in exchange for Bob's fixing Joe's car. Joe and Bob have
a. a voidable contract
b. a void contract
c. an executory contract
d. a bilateral contract

31. Liquidated damages cannot exceed how much if the property purchased consists of no more than 4 residential units and the purchaser intends to reside in one of the dwelling units at the close of the sale?
a. any reasonable and fair amount that is explicitly stated in the contract
b. 2% of the purchase price
c. 3% of the purchase price
d. none of the above

32. A deposit receipt is
a. a receipt for a good-faith deposit for the purchase of real estate
b. a receipt for an advance fee the seller gives to his or her agent
c. an offer to purchase real estate
d. both a and c

33. A certain deposit receipt contains a term that states that the contract will not be binding if the property fails a pest inspection. This contract term is called a
a. safety clause
b. liquidated damages clause
c. contingency clause
d. right of refusal clause

34. Bob purchases a residence from Jane under a real property sales contract. Bob will receive legal title to the residence
a. at the close of escrow
b. as soon as Jane receives the down payment
c. as soon as the title insurance company issues title insurance on the property
d. none of the above

35. A term in Jane's lease gives her the right to purchase the property if the landlord puts the property up for sale and she matches the price and other terms offered by any other potential buyer. Jane probably has
    a. an option to purchase
    b. a land contract
    c. a right of first refusal
    d. a contingency agreement

Answers to Chapter 6 Quiz

1. c. Depending on the context, an executed contract can refer either to a contract that has been fully performed or to a contract that has been signed by all parties.
2. d. Susan is asking the court to order Joe to complete the sale, not to give her damages; therefore, Susan should seek an order for specific performance.
3. b. Bob's "acceptance" is actually a counteroffer because it is at variance to Joe's offer with respect to a material term (the painting of the house).
4. b. Unless Susan's proof included some memo or other writing evidencing the sale and signed by Joe, the statute of frauds as it applies to real estate transactions would prevent the enforcement of the oral contract between Susan and Joe.
5. a. The four essential elements of a valid contract are that the contract be between parties capable of contracting who have given their mutual consent and consideration to an agreement about a lawful object.
6. c. The Statute of Frauds states that for certain types of contracts there must be some writing evidencing the terms of the contract for the contract to be enforceable.
7. b. The Statute of Frauds states that a lease for *more than* one year must be in writing.
8. d. Even though an offer includes a statement that it is irrevocable, it is nevertheless revocable at any time until it is accepted, unless consideration was given to the offeror to make the offer irrevocable.
9. b. As a general rule, the Statute of Limitations for oral contracts is two years; it is four years for written contracts.
10. b. The contract is bilateral because a promise was given for another promise; express because it is in writing; and executory because neither side has completed performance of the promise given.
11. d. Because both a and c are correct, d is the best answer.
12. b. A contract must be supported by sufficient consideration between *capable* parties.
13. d. An emancipated minor is capable of contracting, but one need not be an emancipated minor to be capable of contracting.
14. d. Each of a, b, and c is an agreement that must be in writing.
15. d. Joe made an offer, and Bob rejected the offer with a counteroffer.

16. b. Because Susan signed a listing agreement with more than one broker, the listing was not (or should not have been) exclusive in any sense.

17. b. Duress is the use of force; menace is the threat to use force.

18. d. Be careful with questions that contain a double negative. Not unessential means essential.

19. d. Though certain contracts must be in writing or signed by a capable witness, other contracts require neither; and, as a general rule, unless specific performance is requested, there need be no showing of consideration that was fair as between the parties.

20. d. Consideration for a contract may consist of anything of value to the parties, including services rendered or forbearance.

21. d. The offer can be revoked in a, b, and c, unless consideration was given to have the offer irrevocable for the stated period.

22. d. While revocation of an offer by the offeror is effective upon mailing, acceptance of an offer is effective upon mailing unless the offer was revoked before the acceptance was received.

23. d. A voidable contract is valid unless and until the injured party brings an action to declare it unenforceable.

24. d. The Statute of Frauds requires that certain contracts be in writing and signed.

25. d. A listing agreement is a contract that creates an agency relationship in which the agent owes a fiduciary duty to the principal.

26. d. This would be an open listing. In an exclusive agency listing, the listing broker would receive a commission even if another broker procured the buyer.

27. b. A net listing is an agreement that provides the broker with all proceeds received from the sale over a specified amount.

28. c. Jane need not accept any offer; however, Bob fully performed the contract so Jane owes him the commission.

29. d. A safety clause protects the broker's commission for a sale that is consummated after the termination of the broker's listing agreement to a buyer who is found by the broker during the term of the listing agreement.

30. b. The illegal consideration makes this agreement void.

31. c. In the situation as stated in the question, 3% is the maximum amount of liquidated damages allowed.

32. d. In addition to being both a and c, if the seller signs the deposit receipt, it becomes a binding contract for the sale of the property.

33. c. This clause is a contingency clause because it makes the binding effect of the contract dependent on the outcome of a future event.

34. d. Under a real property sales contract, the vendee receives legal title to the property after the final installment payment is made.

35. c. Because she has the right to purchase the property if she matches any offer by another buyer, she has a right of first refusal.

Chapter 7

Real Estate Agency

"An *agent* is one who represents another, called the *principal*, in dealings with third persons. Such representation is called *agency*." CC §2295 (emphasis added).

"An agent for a particular act or transaction is called a *special agent*. All others are called *general agents*." CC §2297 (emphasis added).

Most general agents are an integral part of an ongoing business enterprise, such as a branch manager who is authorized to conduct business on an ongoing basis for the branch on behalf of a company. A special agent, on the other hand, is employed by a principal for a specific transaction or limited number of specific transactions. A real estate broker nearly always is a special agent because he or she is employed by a principal (also referred to as a *client*) only to negotiate the sale or purchase of a property or properties — not to conduct other business affairs of the principal.

An agent occupies a special legal relationship, referred to as a *fiduciary relationship*, of loyalty to his or her principal. As we shall see, a real estate broker who represents a seller (or a buyer) also owes certain legal responsibilities to the buyer (or to the seller, as the case may be); but to his or her principal, the real estate broker owes this special relationship known as a fiduciary relationship, which imposes on real estate agents many strict legal obligations of "utmost care, integrity, honesty, and loyalty." CC §2079.16.

CREATING AN AGENCY RELATIONSHIP

California recognizes two basic types of agency: "An agency is either *actual* or *ostensible*." CC §2298 (emphasis added).

"An agency is actual when the agent is really employed by the principal." CC §2299.

"Agency is ostensible when the principal intentionally, or by want of ordinary care, causes a third person to believe another to be his agent who is not really employed by him." CC §2300.

Actual agency can be created in three ways: by **express agreement**, by **ratification**, or by **implication**. Ostensible agency is created by **estoppel**. (See Figure 7.1).

Fig. 7.1	Types of Agency
<u>Actual Agency</u>	<u>Ostensible Agency</u>
• <u>Express Agreement</u>: created by oral or written contract between principal and agent • <u>Ratification</u>: created by a principal's accepting or retaining the benefit of an act made by an unauthorized agent • <u>Implication</u>: created by an unauthorized agent who acts as if he or she is the agent of a principal, and this principal reasonably believes that the unauthorized agent is acting as his or her actual agent	• <u>Estoppel</u>: created when a principal and an unauthorized agent act in a manner toward a third party that leads the third party to rely on the actions of the unauthorized agent, believing that the actions are authorized by the principal

ACTUAL AGENCY BY EXPRESS AGREEMENT

Usually, an agency relationship is created by express agreement between the principal and the agent. We analyzed an example of the most common type of written express agreement in Chapter 6 — the Exclusive Authorization and Right to Sell agreement.

Unless the statute of frauds requires that the agreement be in writing, an express agency agreement can be oral. However, under a principle of agency law known as the **equal dignities rule**, the authorization of an agent requires the same formality as is required for the act(s) the agent is hired to perform. CC §2390.

The equal dignities rule is essentially a corollary of the statute of frauds, which, as regards real estate brokers' agreements to buy or sell real estate, states in relevant part: "The following contracts are invalid, unless they, or some note or memorandum thereof, are in writing and subscribed by the party to be charged…: An agreement authorizing or employing an agent, broker, or any other person to purchase or sell real estate… for compensation or commission." CC §1624(a). In short, unless a real estate broker can produce some writing subscribed to by the broker's principal to the effect that the broker is in fact the principal's agent for the purpose of selling or buying a specific parcel of real estate, the broker cannot enforce the collection of a commission from the principal for the sale or purchase of that specific parcel of real estate.

However, even though a broker cannot enforce the payment of a commission, an actual agency relationship between the broker and the principal can be created — thereby possibly creating liability of the broker to the principal, and liability of the principal and/or the broker to third parties — by ratification or implication.

ACTUAL AGENCY BY RATIFICATION

By accepting or retaining the benefit of an act made by an unauthorized agent or by an agent who has exceeded his or her authority, a principal can create an agency by ratification. CC §2310. The ratification is not valid unless, at the time of ratifying the act, the principal has the power to confer authority to the agent for such an act. CC §2312. Therefore, for example, an unemancipated minor could not ratify the purchase of real property by an agent.

Furthermore, ratification cannot be for merely part of a transaction conducted by an agent; ratification of a part of a transaction is ratification of the whole. CC §2311. In other words, a principal who has ratified a transaction cannot split the transaction into separate parts, taking the beneficial parts and disavowing the rest.

ACTUAL AGENCY BY IMPLICATION

Agency by implication may be created if someone reasonably believes that someone else is acting as his or her agent, and the supposed agent fails to correct the impression. In such a case, the supposed agent may in fact owe the other person the duties of an agent.

OSTENSIBLE AGENCY

There is a rule of equity known as **estoppel** that holds that one who causes another to rely on his or her words or actions shall be **estopped** (prohibited) from later taking a contrary position detrimental to the person who so relied. Ostensible agency is agency created by estoppel in a situation where (1) an unauthorized person performs actions as if he or she were the agent of a principal, (2) the principal is aware of this conduct, and (3) the agent's actions and the principal's actions (or inactions) cause a third party to rely on the supposed agent's actions, believing that the actions are authorized by the principal.

Though agency by implication and ostensible agency appear to be much the same, the crucial difference is that in agency by implication the supposed agent is found to owe agency duties to the principal, whereas in ostensible agency, the agent and the principal are found to be liable for their actions to a third party.

REAL ESTATE AGENTS, INDEPENDENT CONTRACTORS, AND EMPLOYEES

An **employee** works for another person (the **employer**) who directs and controls the services rendered by the employee. An **independent contractor** is a person who performs work for someone, but does so independently in a private trade, business, or profession, with little or no supervision from the person for whom the work is performed. An agent also works for another person (sometimes referred to as the employer, but more often as the principal), but usually acts for and represents that principal in negotiating and/or creating narrowly defined, specific legal relationships with third parties.

REAL ESTATE BROKERS AND SALESPERSONS

"It is unlawful for any person to engage in the business, act in the capacity of, advertise or assume to act as a real estate broker or a real estate salesman within this state without first obtaining a real estate license from the department." B&PC §10130.

The "department" referred to above is the California Bureau of Real Estate (the "CalBRE"), which recognizes two categories of real estate licensees: **brokers** and **salespersons**.

"A real estate broker... is a person who, for a compensation or an expectation of a compensation..." represents another in the transfer of an interest in real property, which may include the sale, purchase or exchange of real property, the negotiation of loans and leases, the management of certain properties, and various other transactions involving real estate. B&PC §10131.

"A real estate salesman... is a natural person who, for a compensation or an expectation of a compensation, is employed by a licensed real estate broker..." B&PC §10132. In this book we will use the term "salesperson" rather than "salesman."

A real estate broker must pass the CalBRE's broker exam and be licensed as a real estate broker. A person who is licensed as a broker may choose to work for another broker as a salesperson (often referred to as an associate broker). All other persons employed as salespersons must pass the CalBRE's salesperson exam and be licensed as a salesperson.

Not all persons dealing with real property need to be real estate licensees. There are many exceptions (set out mainly in B&PC §10133), a few of which are: a person holding a power of attorney from the owner of the real property with respect to which the acts are performed, an attorney at law rendering legal services to a client, and resident managers of apartment buildings. A *power of attorney* is a special written instrument that gives authority to an agent to conduct certain business on behalf of the principal. The agent acting under such a grant is sometimes called an *attorney in fact*. A real estate broker with a listing agreement or a buyer's agent agreement does *not* thereby have a power of attorney to sign a purchase agreement to sell the property on behalf of the principal. **Note:** A real estate licensee may *not* negotiate, arrange for, or otherwise perform loan modifications or other loan forbearance for a fee or other compensation *or take any power of attorney from the borrower for any purpose*.

Also exempted are so-called finders. A *finder* is someone who merely introduces a buyer to the seller, but does nothing else to facilitate a transaction between the buyer and seller, such as rendering assistance in negotiating terms.

Real estate licensees are categorized by different regulatory agencies differently: sometimes as an agent, sometimes as an independent contractor, sometimes as an employee — depending upon the context of with whom and under what circumstances the licensee is performing. Not surprisingly, the CalBRE *Real Estate Reference Book* states that the "subject of agency and the fiduciary relationships between real estate brokers and their principals are among the most difficult concepts for real estate licensees to understand and apply when engaged in real property or real property secured transactions."

Because real estate law requires the employing broker to supervise the activities of the salespersons employed by the broker, the Real Estate Commissioner (the person who holds the top spot at the CalBRE) regulates the relationship between the broker and his or her employed licensees as *an employer-employee relationship*. As an employee of the broker, a salesperson receives compensation from the broker and may not accept compensation from any other person, such as from a seller or a buyer, for any act that requires a real estate license. A salesperson may accept a finder's fee for an *introduction only*, such as a fee from a builder for the introduction of a prospective purchaser, because such activity does not require a real estate license.

However, as a practical matter, a licensee who works for a broker works quite independently — for example, the employing broker does not, as a general rule, tell the licensee when to take lunch, how many hours to work, and so on. Therefore, a licensee for the most part appears to be an independent contractor vis-à-vis the employing broker — and the state and federal taxing authorities recognize a salesperson *as an independent contractor* by not requiring the employing broker to withhold from the salesperson's paychecks for items such as federal or state income taxes, Medicare, Social Security, or unemployment insurance, as long as there is a written contract between the broker and the salesperson that clearly states that the employment relationship between the broker and the salesperson is one between an employer and an independent contractor (see Figure 7.2).

On the other hand, the California Labor and Workforce Development Agency insists that the broker-salesperson relationship is *an employer-employee relationship* for the purposes of workers' compensation and commands that workers' compensation insurance be paid by the employing broker on all employed salespersons (see Paragraph 3G of Figure 7.2.).

Finally, the salesperson is seen *as being an agent* of his or her employing broker, representing the broker vis-à-vis third parties; namely, with the buyers or sellers with whom the broker has an agency relationship. Though, as a general rule, both salespersons and brokers are referred to as real estate agents, only brokers are authorized by law to be the actual agents in a contractual relationship with sellers and/or buyers. Nevertheless, as agents for their employing brokers, *salespersons owe the same fiduciary obligations to the sellers and/or buyers with whom they work as do the brokers who technically are representing the sellers and/or buyers*. Therefore, going forward in this book, we will speak, as most do, of salespersons and brokers as being real estate agents, distinguishing between brokers and the salespersons only when necessary. We will also refer to a salesperson as the seller's agent (or the buyer's agent, as the case may be) even though the seller's (or buyer's) agent technically is the broker who employs the salesperson.

AUTHORITY OF AGENT

An agent has authority to do everything necessary, proper, or usual in the ordinary course of business, for effectuating the purpose that his or her agency was created to do. CC §2319. As in the creation of the agency itself, the authority that the agent has can be express, ratified, implied, or ostensible. Though a principal is liable to third parties for the actions of an agent who acts within his or her authority, no liability is incurred by a principal for the acts of an agent beyond the scope of the agent's actual or ostensible authority. A third party who is aware that he or she is dealing with an authorized agent has the duty to ascertain the purpose and scope of the agency.

An agent who is given the power to sell real property does not have the authority to modify or cancel a contract of sale after it has been made, nor does the agent have the authority to enter into a contract to transfer title to the property on behalf of the principal.

TRUST FUNDS

A real estate licensee is presumed to know the law relating to trust fund handling and accounting, and ignorance of the law is not a defense against a finding of trust fund violations. How seriously the Real Estate Commissioner considers trust fund violations, even violations supposedly committed through ignorance, can be seen in the 1966 case *Brown v. Gordon*, where the court upheld the Commissioner's decision to revoke the license of a broker who received a $1,000 deposit for the purchase of real estate, deposited the $1,000 into his personal account, and withdrew $420 for his personal expenses. The court held that the "fact that he [the broker] may have been unaware of his obligations as a trustee of the $1,000 and that he may have thought that he was justified in using this money for his personal expenses does not furnish an excuse for his conduct…"

The CalBRE's *Reference Book* defines trust funds as: "money or other things of value that are received by a broker or salesperson on behalf of a principal or any other person, and which are held for the benefit of others in the performance of any acts for which a real estate license is required. Trust funds may be cash or non-cash items. Some examples are: cash; a check used as a purchase deposit (whether made payable to the broker or to an escrow or title company); a personal note made payable to the seller; or even an automobile's 'pink slip' given as a deposit."

Fig. 7.2

CALIFORNIA
ASSOCIATION
OF REALTORS®

INDEPENDENT CONTRACTOR AGREEMENT
(Between Broker and Associate-Licensee)
(C.A.R. Form ICA, Revised 6/11)

This Agreement, dated _____, is made between _____
_____ ("Broker")
and_____("Associate-Licensee").
In consideration of the covenants and representations contained in this Agreement, Broker and Associate-Licensee agree as follows:

1. BROKER: Broker represents that Broker is duly licensed as a real estate broker by the State of California,
☐ doing business as _____(firm name), ☐ a sole proprietorship, ☐ a partnership, or
☐ a corporation. Broker is a member of the _____
Association(s) of REALTORS®, and a subscriber to the _____
Multiple Listing Service(s). Broker shall keep Broker's license current during the term of this Agreement.

2. ASSOCIATE-LICENSEE: Associate-Licensee represents that: **(i)** he/she is duly licensed by the State of California as a ☐ real estate broker, ☐ real estate salesperson, and **(ii)** he/she has not used any other names within the past five years, except _____.
Associate-Licensee shall keep his/her license current during the term of this Agreement, including satisfying all applicable continuing education and provisional license requirements.

3. INDEPENDENT CONTRACTOR RELATIONSHIP:
   A. Broker and Associate-Licensee intend that, to the maximum extent permissible by law: **(i)** This Agreement does not constitute an employment agreement by either party; **(ii)** Broker and Associate-Licensee are independent contracting parties with respect to all services rendered under this Agreement; and **(iii)** This Agreement shall not be construed as a partnership.
   B. Broker shall not: **(i)** restrict Associate-Licensee's activities to particular geographical areas, or **(ii)** dictate Associate-Licensee's activities with regard to hours, leads, open houses, opportunity or floor time, production, prospects, sales meetings, schedule, inventory, time off, vacation, or similar activities, except to the extent required by law.
   C. Associate-Licensee shall not be required to accept an assignment by Broker to service any particular current or prospective listing or parties.
   D. Except as required by law: **(i)** Associate-Licensee retains sole and absolute discretion and judgment in the methods, techniques, and procedures to be used in soliciting and obtaining listings, sales, exchanges, leases, rentals, or other transactions, and in carrying out Associate-Licensee's selling and soliciting activities; **(ii)** Associate-Licensee is under the control of Broker as to the results of Associate-Licensee's work only, and not as to the means by which those results are accomplished; **(iii)** Associate-Licensee has no authority to bind Broker by any promise or representation; and **(iv)** Broker shall not be liable for any obligation or liability incurred by Associate-Licensee.
   E. Associate-Licensee's only remuneration shall be the compensation specified in paragraph 8.
   F. Associate-Licensee who only performs as a real estate sales agent, shall not be treated as an employee for state and federal tax purposes. However, an Associate-Licensee who performs loan activity shall be treated as an employee for state and federal tax purposes unless the activity satisfies the legal requirements to establish an independent contractor relationship.
   G. The fact the Broker may carry workers' compensation insurance for Broker's own benefit and for the mutual benefit of Broker and licensees associated with Broker, including Associate-Licensee, shall not create an inference of employment.
   (Workers' Compensation Advisory: Even though a Real Estate sales person may be treated as independent contractors for tax and other purposes, the California Labor and Workforce Development Agency considers them to be employees for workers' compensation purposes. According to that Agency: **(i)** Broker must obtain workers' compensation insurance for a Real Estate sales person and **(ii)** Broker, not a Real Estate sales person, must bear the cost of workers' compensation insurance. Penalties for failure to carry workers' compensation include, among others, the issuance of stop-work orders and fines of up to $1,000 per agent, not to exceed $100,000 per company.)

4. LICENSED ACTIVITY:
   A. All listings of property, and all agreements, acts or actions for performance of licensed acts, which are taken or performed in connection with this Agreement, shall be taken and performed in the name of Broker. Associate-Licensee agrees to and does hereby contribute all right and title to such listings to Broker for the benefit and use of Broker, Associate-Licensee, and other licensees associated with Broker.

Broker's Initials (_____)(_____)   Associate-Licensee's Initials (_____)(_____)

ICA REVISED 6/11 (PAGE 1 OF 4)

Reviewed by _____ Date _____

INDEPENDENT CONTRACTOR AGREEMENT (ICA PAGE 1 OF 4)

B. Broker shall make available to Associate-Licensee, equally with other licensees associated with Broker, all current listings in Broker's office, except any listing which Broker may choose to place in the exclusive servicing of Associate-Licensee or one or more other specific licensees associated with Broker.

C. Associate-Licensee shall provide and pay for all professional licenses, supplies, services, and other items required in connection with Associate-Licensee's activities under this Agreement, or any listing or transaction, without reimbursement from Broker except as required by law.

D. Associate-Licensee shall work diligently and with his/her best efforts to: **(i)** sell, exchange, lease, or rent properties listed with Broker or other cooperating Brokers; **(ii)** solicit additional listings, clients, and customers; and **(iii)** otherwise promote the business of serving the public in real estate transactions to the end that Broker and Associate-Licensee may derive the greatest benefit possible, in accordance with law.

E. Associate-Licensee shall not commit any unlawful act under federal, state or local law or regulation while conducting licensed activity. Associate-Licensee shall at all times be familiar, and comply, with all applicable federal, state and local laws, including, but not limited to, anti-discrimination laws and restrictions against the giving or accepting a fee, or other thing of value, for the referral of business to title companies, escrow companies, home inspection companies, pest control companies and other settlement service providers pursuant to the California Business and Professions Code and the Real Estate Settlement Procedures Acts (RESPA).

F. Broker shall make available for Associate-Licensee's use, along with other licensees associated with Broker, the facilities of the real estate office operated by Broker at _____ and the facilities of any other office locations made available by Broker pursuant to this Agreement.

G. PROHIBITED ACTIVITIES: Associate-Licensee agrees not to engage in any of the following Real Estate licensed activities without the express written consent of Broker:
- ☐ Property Management;
- ☐ Loan Brokerage
- ☐ _____ ;
- ☐ _____

However, if Associate-Licensee has a Real Estate Broker's License, Associate-Licensee may nonetheless engage in the following prohibited activity(ies) only: provided that **(1)** such prohibited activities are not done under the Broker's License, **(2)** no facilities of Broker (including but not limited to phones, fax, computers, and office space) are used for any such prohibited activities, **(3)** Associate-Licensee shall not use any marketing, solicitation or contact information that include Broker's name (including business cards) for such prohibited activities, **(4)** Associate-Licensee informs any actual or intended Principal for whom Associate-Licensee performs or intends to perform such prohibited activities the name of the broker under whose license the prohibited activities are performed, and **(5)** if Associate-Licensee is performing other permitted licensed activity for that Principal under Broker's license, then Associate-Licensee shall inform any actual or intended Principal for whom the prohibited activities are performed that the prohibited activities are not performed under Broker's license.

5. PROPRIETARY INFORMATION AND FILES:
A. All files and documents pertaining to listings, leads and transactions are the property of Broker and shall be delivered to Broker by Associate-Licensee immediately upon request or termination of this Agreement.
B. Associate-Licensee acknowledges that Broker's method of conducting business is a protected trade secret.
C. Associate-Licensee shall not use to his/her own advantage, or the advantage of any other person, business, or entity, except as specifically agreed in writing, either during Associate-Licensee's association with Broker, or thereafter, any information gained for or from the business, or files of Broker.

6. SUPERVISION: Associate-Licensee, within 24 hours (or ☐ _____) after preparing, signing, or receiving same, shall submit to Broker, or Broker's designated licensee: **(i)** all documents which may have a material effect upon the rights and duties of principals in a transaction; **(ii)** any documents or other items connected with a transaction pursuant to this Agreement in the possession of or available to Associate-Licensee; and **(iii)** all documents associated with any real estate transaction in which Associate-Licensee is a principal.

7. TRUST FUNDS: All trust funds shall be handled in compliance with the Business and Professions Code, and other applicable laws.

8. COMPENSATION:
A. TO BROKER: Compensation shall be charged to parties who enter into listing or other agreements for services requiring a real estate license:
- ☐ as shown in "Exhibit A" attached, which is incorporated as a part of this Agreement by reference, or
- ☐ as follows: _____

_____

_____

Any deviation which is not approved in writing in advance by Broker, shall be: **(1)** deducted from Associate-Licensee's compensation, if lower than the amount or rate approved above; and, **(2)** subject to Broker approval, if higher than the amount approved above. Any permanent change in commission schedule shall be disseminated by Broker to Associate-Licensee.

Broker's Initials (_____)(_____)   Associate-Licensee's Initials (_____)(_____)

Reviewed by _____ Date _____

INDEPENDENT CONTRACTOR AGREEMENT (ICA PAGE 2 OF 4)

B. TO ASSOCIATE-LICENSEE: Associate-Licensee shall receive a share of compensation actually collected by Broker, on listings or other agreements for services requiring a real estate license, which are solicited and obtained by Associate-Licensee, and on transactions of which Associate-Licensee's activities are the procuring cause, as follows:

☐ as shown in "Exhibit B" attached, which is incorporated as a part of this Agreement by reference, or
☐ other: _____
_____
_____
_____

C. PARTNERS, TEAMS, AND AGREEMENTS WITH OTHER ASSOCIATE-LICENSEES IN OFFICE: If Associate-Licensee and one or more other Associate-Licensees affiliated with Broker participate on the same side (either listing or selling) of a transaction, the commission allocated to their combined activities shall be divided by Broker and paid to them according to their written agreement. Broker shall have the right to withhold total compensation if there is a dispute between associate-licensees, or if there is no written agreement, or if no written agreement has been provided to Broker.

D. EXPENSES AND OFFSETS: If Broker elects to advance funds to pay expenses or liabilities of Associate-Licensee, or for an advance payment of, or draw upon, future compensation, Broker may deduct the full amount advanced from compensation payable to Associate-Licensee on any transaction without notice. If Associate-Licensee's compensation is subject to a lien, garnishment or other restriction on payment, Broker shall charge Associate-Licensee a fee for complying with such restriction.

E. PAYMENT: (i) All compensation collected by Broker and due to Associate-Licensee shall be paid to Associate-Licensee, after deduction of expenses and offsets, immediately or as soon thereafter as practicable, except as otherwise provided in this Agreement or a separate written agreement between Broker and Associate-Licensee. **(ii)** Compensation shall not be paid to Associate-Licensee until both the transaction and file are complete. **(iii)** Broker is under no obligation to pursue collection of compensation from any person or entity responsible for payment. Associate-Licensee does not have the independent right to pursue collection of compensation for activities which require a real estate license which were done in the name of Broker. **(iv)** Expenses which are incurred in the attempt to collect compensation shall be paid by Broker and Associate-Licensee in the same proportion as set forth for the division of compensation (paragraph 8(B)). **(v)** If there is a known or pending claim against Broker or Associate-Licensee on transactions for which Associate-Licensee has not yet been paid, Broker may withhold from compensation due Associate-Licensee on that transaction amounts for which Associate-Licensee could be responsible under paragraph 14, until such claim is resolved. **(vi)** Associate-Licensee shall not be entitled to any advance payment from Broker upon future compensation.

F. UPON OR AFTER TERMINATION: If this Agreement is terminated while Associate-Licensee has listings or pending transactions that require further work normally rendered by Associate-Licensee, Broker shall make arrangements with another associate-licensee to perform the required work, or Broker shall perform the work him/herself. The licensee performing the work shall be reasonably compensated for completing work on those listings or transactions, and such reasonable compensation shall be deducted from Associate-Licensee's share of compensation. Except for such offset, Associate-Licensee shall receive the compensation due as specified above.

9. TERMINATION OF RELATIONSHIP: Broker or Associate-Licensee may terminate their relationship under this Agreement at any time, with or without cause. After termination, Associate-Licensee shall not solicit: **(i)** prospective or existing clients or customers based upon company-generated leads obtained during the time Associate-Licensee was affiliated with Broker; **(ii)** any principal with existing contractual obligations to Broker; or **(iii)** any principal with a contractual transactional obligation for which Broker is entitled to be compensated. Even after termination, this Agreement shall govern all disputes and claims between Broker and Associate-Licensee connected with their relationship under this Agreement, including obligations and liabilities arising from existing and completed listings, transactions, and services.

10. DISPUTE RESOLUTION:
Broker and Associate-Licensee agree to mediate all disputes and claims between them arising from or connected in any way with this Agreement before resorting to court action. If any dispute or claim is not resolved through mediation, or otherwise, instead of resolving the matter in court, Broker and Associate-Licensee may mutually agree to submit the dispute to arbitration at, and pursuant to the rules and bylaws of, the Association of REALTORS® to which both parties belong.

11. AUTOMOBILE: Associate-Licensee shall maintain automobile insurance coverage for liability and property damage in the following amounts $_____/$_____. Broker shall be named as an additional insured party on Associate-Licensee's policies. A copy of the endorsement showing Broker as an additional insured shall be provided to Broker.

Broker's Initials (_____)(_____)   Associate-Licensee's Initials (_____)(_____)

Reviewed by _____ Date _____

12. **PERSONAL ASSISTANTS:** Associate-Licensee may make use of a personal assistant, provided the following requirements are satisfied. Associate-Licensee shall have a written agreement with the personal assistant which establishes the terms and responsibilities of the parties to the employment agreement, including, but not limited to, compensation, supervision and compliance with applicable law. The agreement shall be subject to Broker's review and approval. Unless otherwise agreed, if the personal assistant has a real estate license, that license must be provided to the Broker. Both Associate-Licensee and personal assistant must sign any agreement that Broker has established for such purposes.

13. **OFFICE POLICY MANUAL:** If Broker's office policy manual, now or as modified in the future, conflicts with or differs from the terms of this Agreement, the terms of the office policy manual shall govern the relationship between Broker and Associate-Licensee.

14. **INDEMNITY AND HOLD HARMLESS; NOTICE OF CLAIMS:**
    A. Regarding any action taken or omitted by Associate-Licensee, or others working through, or on behalf of Associate-Licensee in connection with services rendered or to be rendered pursuant to this Agreement or Real Estate licensed activity prohibited by this agreement: (i) Associate-Licensee agrees to indemnify, defend and hold Broker harmless from all claims, disputes, litigation, judgments, awards, costs and attorney's fees, arising therefrom and (ii) Associate-Licensee shall immediately notify Broker if Associate-Licensee is served with or becomes aware of a lawsuit or claim regarding any such action.
    B. Any such claims or costs payable pursuant to this Agreement, are due as follows:
    ☐ Paid in full by Associate-Licensee, who hereby agrees to indemnify and hold harmless Broker for all such sums, or
    ☐ In the same ratio as the compensation split as it existed at the time the compensation was earned by Associate-Licensee ☐ Other: _____

    Payment from Associate-Licensee is due at the time Broker makes such payment and can be offset from any compensation due Associate-Licensee as above. Broker retains the authority to settle claims or disputes, whether or not Associate-Licensee consents to such settlement.

15. **ADDITIONAL PROVISIONS:** _____
    _____

16. **DEFINITIONS:** As used in this Agreement, the following terms have the meanings indicated:
    A. "Listing" means an agreement with a property owner or other party to locate a buyer, exchange party, lessee, or other party to a transaction involving real property, a mobile home, or other property or transaction which may be brokered by a real estate licensee, or an agreement with a party to locate or negotiate for any such property or transaction.
    B. "Compensation" means compensation for acts requiring a real estate license, regardless of whether calculated as a percentage of transaction price, flat fee, hourly rate, or in any other manner.
    C. "Transaction" means a sale, exchange, lease, or rental of real property, a business opportunity, or a manufactured home, which may lawfully be brokered by a real estate licensee.

17. **ATTORNEY FEES:** In any action, proceeding, or arbitration between Broker and Associate-Licensee arising from or related to this Agreement, the prevailing Broker or Associate-Licensee shall be entitled to reasonable attorney fees and costs.

18. **ENTIRE AGREEMENT:** All prior agreements between the parties concerning their relationship as Broker and Associate-Licensee are incorporated in this Agreement, which constitutes the entire contract. Its terms are intended by the parties as a final and complete expression of their agreement with respect to its subject matter, and may not be contradicted by evidence of any prior agreement or contemporaneous oral agreement. This Agreement may not be amended, modified, altered, or changed except by a further agreement in writing executed by Broker and Associate-Licensee.

Broker: **Associate-Licensee:**

_____   _____
(Brokerage firm name)   (Signature)

By _____
Its Broker/Office manager (circle one)   _____
                                                     (Print name)

_____
(Print name)   _____
                                                     (Address)

_____
(Address)   _____
                                                     (City, State, Zip)

_____
(City, State, Zip)   _____ _____
                                                     (Telephone)   (Fax)

_____ _____
(Telephone)   (Fax)

R E B S | I N C
Published and Distributed by:
REAL ESTATE BUSINESS SERVICES, INC.
a subsidiary of the California Association of REALTORS®
525 South Virgil Avenue, Los Angeles, California 90020

ICA REVISED 6/11 (PAGE 4 OF 4) | Reviewed by _____ Date _____ | EQUAL HOUSING OPPORTUNITY

Common sources of trust funds are the ***earnest money deposits*** that buyers give to agents along with offers to purchase, and the ***advance fees*** that sellers may pay in advance to agents to cover expected cash outlays, such as advertising expenses. Most disciplinary actions against licensees are caused by licensees' misuse or mishandling of such funds; therefore, it is imperative that licensees thoroughly acquaint themselves with the proper handling of such funds.

Note regarding advance fee agreements: An advance fee agreement and all other materials used in advertising, promoting, soliciting, and negotiating the advance fee agreement must be submitted to the Bureau of Real state not less than 10 calendar days before publication or other use. An advance fee agreement and corresponding materials cannot be used and advance fees cannot be collected until the Bureau of Real Estate informs the broker that it has no objection to the use of the advance fee agreement and materials by the broker.

Commingling results from the failure to properly segregate the funds belonging to the agent from the funds received and held on behalf of the seller or buyer. Commingling of funds is strictly prohibited and, pursuant to B&PC §10176(e), is grounds for suspension or revocation of a real estate license. ***Conversion*** is the unauthorized misappropriation and use of another's funds or other property. Such misappropriation is a crime and can result in jail time as well as revocation of a license.

As in the agreement (at Paragraph 9) that we analyzed in Chapter 6, nearly all listing agreements provide that real estate agents may collect earnest money deposits on behalf of the seller. This authority also applies to cooperating brokers. If a buyer gives a deposit to an agent who was not given authority by the seller to accept a deposit, then the agent accepts the deposit as an agent for the buyer, and the risk of loss is on buyer. In any case, the agent may not endorse a negotiable instrument received unless specifically granted such authority by the principal.

Except in the case where the buyer gives a check as an earnest money deposit to an agent and (1) the check is not negotiable by the broker or (2) the buyer has given written instructions to hold the check until acceptance of the offer, the agent must, *no later than 3 business days after receipt*, place such earnest money deposits

1. into the hands of the seller,
2. into a neutral escrow depository, or
3. into a trust fund account in the name of the broker, or in a fictitious name of the broker if the broker's license bears a fictitious name, as trustee.

In those cases where deposit money is not put into escrow, title to the money vests in the seller when the seller accepts the offer. If the deposit money is to become part of the down payment, title to the money vests in the seller at the time the deed is put into escrow.

An agent must be careful not to accept a ***post-dated check*** as a deposit without so informing the seller. This is because California law holds that a check dated the date it is made is an assurance by the check writer that sufficient funds currently exist in the writer's account to cover the check, and it is a criminal offense to write a non-sufficient (NSF) funds check. However, a post-dated check is deemed to be merely a promise to pay in the future, and unless the check was written with fraudulent intent, it is not illegal for the account subsequently to be closed or to have insufficient funds in it to clear the post-dated check on the future date printed on the check.

If the buyer gives the agent a check not negotiable by the agent or gives the agent written instructions to hold the check until acceptance of the offer, the agent must abide by the buyer's instructions; however,

- the agent must see to it that a record of receipt of the deposit is recorded in the broker's trust fund records;
- must, at or before the time that the offer is presented to the seller, inform the seller that the deposit is being held and not negotiated; and
- upon acceptance of the offer by the seller, the broker must, *no later than 3 business days after the acceptance*, place the earnest money deposit in the hands of the seller, into a neutral escrow depository, or into a trust fund account in the name of the broker as trustee (for further clarification of this point, see the next section, Identifying the Owner of the Trust Funds).

Trust funds not forwarded directly to the seller or placed into an escrow account must be placed into the broker's trust fund bank account. The broker's trust fund bank account must meet the following criteria:

- designated in the broker's name as trustee;
- maintained in an account insured by the Federal Deposit Insurance Corporation with a bank, savings and loan association, credit union, or industrial loan company located in California; and
- not an interest-bearing account for which prior notice can be required as a condition of withdrawal. (This last requirement can be waived if done so in writing by the principal and if certain other requirements set out in B&PC §10145(d) are met.)

The primary reason for maintaining a trust fund bank account is to avoid commingling. There are two exceptions to the rule against commingling funds in a broker's trust account:

1. the broker *may keep no more than $200* of his personal funds in the account to pay service charges on the account; and

2. the broker *must, within 25 days* of receiving a commission into the trust account, withdraw the amount of the commission from the account.

Identifying the Owner of the Trust Funds

It is important for the broker to be able to identify who owns the earnest money deposit and who is entitled to receive it, because trust funds can only be deposited by authority of that person. Furthermore, ownership of the funds may change as the real estate transaction progresses from offer to acceptance.

Prior to acceptance of the offer, the funds belong to the offeror and must be handled according to his or her instructions. *After acceptance of the offer,* the funds must be handled as follows:

- A check held uncashed by the broker before acceptance of the offer may continue to be held uncashed after acceptance of the offer only on written authorization from the seller.

- The check may be given to the seller only if the seller and the buyer expressly so provide in writing.

- No part of the deposit may be refunded by an agent or a subagent of the seller without the express written permission of the seller.

Interpleader

If the transaction falls apart, the broker might be placed in the unenviable position of having to defend against a lawsuit brought by both the buyer and the seller to obtain the deposit or down payment funds held in the broker's trust account. In such a situation, the broker can get out of having to defend against the lawsuits by filing an ***interpleader*** action with the court and depositing with the clerk of the court the funds in contention.

In fact, if two or more parties are having a dispute over who owns the funds held in a broker's trust account, the broker need not wait to become a defendant in a lawsuit brought by one or both of those parties. The broker may preemptively file an interpleader action and deposit the trust funds in contention with the clerk of the court, thereby leaving the other parties to litigate among themselves.

Shortages and Overages

Funds on deposit in a broker's trust account must always equal the amount of funds received from or for the benefit of a principal. The process of comparing what is in the account with what should be in the account is called **reconciliation**. Commissioner's Regulations 2831.2 requires that this reconciliation process be performed monthly except in those months when there is no activity in the trust fund account, and that a record of each reconciliation be maintained.

An excellent visual walk-through (PowerPoint) of the bank account reconciliation process and the trust account reconciliation process can be found on the CalBRE website at:

www.dre.ca.gov/files/ppt/TrustAccountReconciliation.ppsx.

If, after reconciliation, it is found that the account balance is less than it should be, there is a **trust fund shortage**. Having a trust fund shortage is a violation of CalBRE regulations. If the trust fund account balance is greater than it should be, there is a **trust fund overage**. Because of the rule against commingling, a trust fund overage is also a violation of CalBRE regulations.

In addition to rigorously keeping proper trust fund account records, one way a broker can avoid having a trust fund shortage is to be sure that any check deposited into the account clears before dispersing funds from the account against that check.

Trust Fund Accounting Records

There are two types of accounting systems the broker may use to keep track of trust funds:

- a columnar system; or
- an alternative system deemed compatible with accepted accounting practices.

Regardless of which method of record-keeping is chosen, the accounting system must provide the following information:

1. all trust fund receipts and disbursements, with pertinent details presented in chronological order;
2. the balance of each trust fund account;
3. all receipts and disbursements affecting each beneficiary's balance presented in chronological order; and
4. the balance owing to each beneficiary.

Columnar Records

If a broker decides to use the columnar system of accounting, three types of records must be kept:

1. *A columnar record of all trust funds received and paid out.* This record is used to record all trust funds deposited to and disbursed from the trust fund account and must show the following:
   a) the date the funds were received;
   b) the name of the person from whom the funds were received;
   c) the amount received;
   d) the date the funds were deposited;
   e) the amount paid out and to whom;
   f) the check number and date
   g) the daily balance of the trust account.

2. *A separate record for each beneficiary or transaction.* This record lists the funds received from or for each client or customer, and must show the following in chronological order:
   a) the date of the deposit;
   b) the amount of the deposit;
   c) the name of the payee or payor;
   d) the check number;
   e) the date and amount received; and
   f) the daily balance of the individual account.

3. *A record of all trust funds received but not placed in the broker's trust account,* such as earnest money deposits forwarded to escrow. This record must show the following:
   a) the date the funds were received;
   b) the form of payment;
   c) the amount received;
   d) a description of any property received (such as an automobile pink slip);
   e) the identity of the person to whom the funds were forwarded; and
   f) the date of disposition.

Other Accounting Systems

If a broker uses trust fund records not in a columnar form, the broker must use a record-keeping system that complies with generally accepted accounting principles. Such an alternative record-keeping system must include:

1. *Journal.* A journal is a daily chronological record of trust fund receipts and disbursements that must:

a) record all trust fund transactions in chronological order;
b) show enough information to identify the date, the amount received or disbursed, the name of the payee or payor, the check number, and the identification of the beneficiary; and
c) the total of the receipts and disbursements at least once a month.

2. *Cash Ledger*. The cash ledger shows, usually in summary form, the increases and decreases in the trust fund account and the resulting account balance.

3. *Beneficiary Ledger*. A separate ledger must be kept for each beneficiary or for each transaction or series of transactions. This ledger must show in chronological order the details of all receipts and disbursements and the resulting account balance.

Audits and Examinations

Because of the importance of trust fund handling, the CalBRE Commissioner has an ongoing program of examining brokers' records. If any trust fund shortages or overages are found, disciplinary actions may be initiated. Trust fund records must be kept for a minimum of 3 years from either (1) the date of the closing of the transaction, or (2) if the transaction is not consummated, from the date of the listing.

AGENCY DISCLOSURE

A *seller's agent* is a real estate broker appointed by the seller to represent the seller. The seller's agent does not represent the buyer, but nevertheless must deal with the buyer honestly and in good faith, disclosing known defects in the property.

A *buyer's agent* is a real estate broker appointed by a buyer to find property for the buyer. A buyer's agent owes fiduciary duties to the buyer, not to the seller; however, a buyer's agent must inform the seller that he or she is representing the buyer, not the seller, and also must deal with the seller honestly and in good faith.

A broker may also be a *dual agent*, representing both the seller and the buyer, but only with the knowledge and written consent of both parties (B&PC §10176 (d)). Dual agency can arise if the listing broker, who is the agent of the seller, also becomes the agent (actual or ostensible) of the buyer. By contrast, a *single agency* is an agency in which a broker represents the seller or the buyer, but not both. An agent who represents both the seller and the buyer without obtaining the consent of both is guilty of a **divided agency**, which is in violation of B&PC §10176(d).

> **Example:** Dual agency can also arise in a case where one salesperson of a broker represents the seller and another salesperson of the same broker represents the buyer. In such a case, the broker becomes a dual agent and, consequently, owes fiduciary duties to both principals.

In any dual agency, conflicts of loyalty and confidentiality can arise, such as when, for example, the buyer wants to know whether the seller is willing to take a lower price. Civil Code, Section 2079.21, addresses this issue: "A dual agent shall not disclose to the buyer that the seller is willing to sell the property at a price less than the listing price, without the express written consent of the seller. A dual agent shall not disclose to the seller that the buyer is willing to pay a price greater than the offering price, without the express written consent of the buyer. This section does not alter in any way the duty or responsibility of a dual agent to any principal with respect to confidential information other than price."

As we saw when analyzing the Exclusive Authorization and Right to Sell listing agreement in Chapter 6, a principal in a real property transaction often agrees to allow the listing broker to delegate some of his or her authority to a **cooperating broker**. The cooperating broker becomes the **subagent** of the principal, and, as such, the acts (negligent or otherwise) of the cooperating broker may be imputed to the principal. On the other hand, if the listing broker appoints another broker without the consent of the principal, the appointed broker becomes an agent of the listing broker, and the acts (negligent or otherwise) may be imputed to the listing broker.

A **selling agent** is the agent who in fact sells or finds and obtains a buyer for the property. As such, a selling agent may be the seller's agent, the buyer's agent, a dual agent, a subagent, or a cooperating agent.

Because a broker can act as an agent for the seller, the buyer, or both, it is important that a broker involved in a real estate transaction inform both the buyer and the seller precisely for whom the broker is acting as an agent. The California Civil Code, Sections 2079.13-24, provides the format for a disclosure informing buyers and sellers of certain duties and obligations that a licensee owes to a principal and whether the broker is acting as the seller's agent, the buyer's agent, or a dual agent. A disclosure form created by the California Association of Realtors® to conform to these statutory agency disclosure requirements is displayed in Figure 7.3.

The *listing broker* (or a salesperson or associate broker of the listing broker) must deliver the agency disclosure form to the seller *before entering into the listing agreement.*

The *selling broker* (or a salesperson or associate broker of the selling broker) must deliver the agency disclosure form *to the seller before presenting the offer to the seller,* or, if the selling broker does not deal face to face with the seller, have the agency disclosure form delivered by the listing broker or delivered by certified mail.

The *selling broker* must deliver the form *to the buyer before the buyer signs the offer to buy.* If the offer is not prepared by the selling broker, the form must be delivered to the buyer by the next business day after the selling broker receives the offer from the buyer.

Fig. 7.3

DISCLOSURE REGARDING
REAL ESTATE AGENCY RELATIONSHIP
(As required by the Civil Code)
(C.A.R. Form AD, Revised 11/12)

❑ (If checked) This form is being provided in connection with a transaction for a leasehold interest in a dwelling exceeding one year as per Civil Code section 2079.13(j) and (l).

When you enter into a discussion with a real estate agent regarding a real estate transaction, you should from the outset understand what type of agency relationship or representation you wish to have with the agent in the transaction.

SELLER'S AGENT

A Seller's agent under a listing agreement with the Seller acts as the agent for the Seller only. A Seller's agent or a subagent of that agent has the following affirmative obligations:

To the Seller: A Fiduciary duty of utmost care, integrity, honesty and loyalty in dealings with the Seller.

To the Buyer and the Seller:

   (a) Diligent exercise of reasonable skill and care in performance of the agent's duties.

   (b) A duty of honest and fair dealing and good faith.

   (c) A duty to disclose all facts known to the agent materially affecting the value or desirability of the property that are not known to, or within the diligent attention and observation of, the parties. An agent is not obligated to reveal to either party any confidential information obtained from the other party that does not involve the affirmative duties set forth above.

BUYER'S AGENT

A selling agent can, with a Buyer's consent, agree to act as agent for the Buyer only. In these situations, the agent is not the Seller's agent, even if by agreement the agent may receive compensation for services rendered, either in full or in part from the Seller. An agent acting only for a Buyer has the following affirmative obligations:

To the Buyer: A fiduciary duty of utmost care, integrity, honesty and loyalty in dealings with the Buyer.

To the Buyer and the Seller:

   (a) Diligent exercise of reasonable skill and care in performance of the agent's duties.

   (b) A duty of honest and fair dealing and good faith.

   (c) A duty to disclose all facts known to the agent materially affecting the value or desirability of the property that are not known to, or within the diligent attention and observation of, the parties.

An agent is not obligated to reveal to either party any confidential information obtained from the other party that does not involve the affirmative duties set forth above.

AGENT REPRESENTING BOTH SELLER AND BUYER

A real estate agent, either acting directly or through one or more associate licensees, can legally be the agent of both the Seller and the Buyer in a transaction, but only with the knowledge and consent of both the Seller and the Buyer.

In a dual agency situation, the agent has the following affirmative obligations to both the Seller and the Buyer:

   (a) A fiduciary duty of utmost care, integrity, honesty and loyalty in the dealings with either the Seller or the Buyer.

   (b) Other duties to the Seller and the Buyer as stated above in their respective sections.

In representing both Seller and Buyer, the agent may not, without the express permission of the respective party, disclose to the other party that the

Seller will accept a price less than the listing price or that the Buyer will pay a price greater than the price offered.

The above duties of the agent in a real estate transaction do not relieve a Seller or Buyer from the responsibility to protect his or her own interests. You should carefully read all agreements to assure that they adequately express your understanding of the transaction. A real estate agent is a person qualified to advise about real estate. If legal or tax advice is desired, consult a competent professional. Throughout your real property transaction you may receive more than one disclosure form, depending upon the number of agents assisting in the transaction. The law requires each agent with whom you have more than a casual relationship to present you with this disclosure form. You should read its contents each time it is presented to you, considering the relationship between you and the real estate agent in your specific transaction. **This disclosure form includes the provisions of Sections 2079.13 to 2079.24, inclusive, of the Civil Code set forth on page 2. Read it carefully. I/WE ACKNOWLEDGE RECEIPT OF A COPY OF THIS DISCLOSURE AND THE PORTIONS OF THE CIVIL CODE PRINTED ON THE BACK (OR A SEPARATE PAGE).**

Buyer/Seller/Landlord/Tenant _____   Date _____

Buyer/Seller/Landlord/Tenant _____   Date _____

Agent _____   DRE Lic. # _____

             Real Estate Broker (Firm)

By _____   DRE Lic. # _____   Date _____

       (Salesperson or Broker-Associate)

Agency Disclosure Compliance (Civil Code §2079.14):

• When the listing brokerage company also represents Buyer/Tenant: The Listing Agent shall have one AD form signed by Seller/Landlord and a different AD form signed by Buyer/Tenant.

• When Seller/Landlord and Buyer/Tenant are represented by different brokerage companies: (i) the Listing Agent shall have one AD form signed by Seller/Landlord and (ii) the Buyer's/Tenant's Agent shall have one AD form signed by Buyer/Tenant and either that same or a different AD form presented to Seller/Landlord for signature prior to presentation of the offer. If the same form is used, Seller may sign here:

_____   _____   _____   _____
   Seller/Landlord   Date   Seller/Landlord   Date

Reviewed by _____ Date _____

AD REVISED 11/12 (PAGE 1 OF 2) Print Date

DISCLOSURE REGARDING REAL ESTATE AGENCY RELATIONSHIP (AD PAGE 1 OF 2)

Reprinted with permission, CALIFORNIA ASSOCIATION OF REALTORS®. Endorsement not implied.

CIVIL CODE SECTIONS 2079.24 (2079.16 APPEARS ON THE FRONT)

2079.13 As used in Sections 2079.14 to 2079.24, inclusive, the following terms have the following meanings:
(a) "Agent" means a person acting under provisions of title 9 (commencing with Section 2295) in a real property transaction, and includes a person who is licensed as a real estate broker under Chapter 3 (commencing with Section 10130) of Part 1 of Division 4 of the Business and Professions Code, and under whose license a listing is executed or an offer to purchase is obtained. **(b)** "Associate licensee" means a person who is licensed as a real estate broker or salesperson under Chapter 3 (commencing with Section 10130) of Part 1 of Division 4 of the Business and Professions Code and who is either licensed under a broker or has entered into a written contract with a broker to act as the broker's agent in connection with acts requiring a real estate license and to function under the broker's supervision in the capacity of an associate licensee. The agent in the real property transaction bears responsibility for his or her associate licensees who perform as agents of the agent. When an associate licensee owes a duty to any principal, or to any buyer or seller who is not a principal, in a real property transaction, that duty is equivalent to the duty owed to that party by the broker for whom the associate licensee functions. **(c)** "Buyer" means a transferee in a real property transaction, and includes a person who executes an offer to purchase real property from a seller through an agent, or who seeks the services of an agent in more than a casual, transitory, or preliminary manner, with the object of entering into a real property transaction. "Buyer" includes vendee or lessee. **(d)** "Dual agent" means an agent acting, either directly or through an associate licensee, as agent for both the seller and the buyer in a real property transaction. **(e)** "Listing agreement" means a contract between an owner of real property and an agent, by which the agent has been authorized to sell the real property or to find or obtain a buyer. **(f)** "Listing agent" means a person who has obtained a listing of real property to act as an agent for compensation. **(g)** "Listing price" is the amount expressed in dollars specified in the listing for which the seller is willing to sell the real property through the listing agent. **(h)** "Offering price" is the amount expressed in dollars specified in an offer to purchase for which the buyer is willing to buy the real property. **(i)** "Offer to purchase" means a written contract executed by a buyer acting through a selling agent which becomes the contract for the sale of the real property upon acceptance by the seller. **(j)** "Real property" means any estate specified by subdivision (1) or (2) of Section 761 in property which constitutes or is improved with one to four dwelling units, any leasehold in this type of property exceeding one year's duration, and mobile homes, when offered for sale or sold through an agent pursuant to the authority contained in Section 10131.6 of the Business and Professions Code. **(k)** "Real property transaction" means a transaction for the sale of real property in which an agent is employed by one or more of the principals to act in that transaction, and includes a listing or an offer to purchase. **(l)** "Sell," "sale," or "sold" refers to a transaction for the transfer of real property from the seller to the buyer, and includes exchanges of real property between the seller and buyer, transactions for the creation of a real property sales contract within the meaning of Section 2985, and transactions for the creation of a leasehold exceeding one year's duration. **(m)** "Seller" means the transferor in a real property transaction, and includes an owner who lists real property with an agent, whether or not a transfer results, or who receives an offer to purchase real property of which he or she is the owner from an agent on behalf of another. "Seller" includes both a vendor and a lessor. **(n)** "Selling agent" means a listing agent who acts alone, or an agent who acts in cooperation with a listing agent, and who sells or finds and obtains a buyer for the real property, or an agent who locates property for a buyer or who finds a buyer for a property for which no listing exists and presents an offer to purchase to the seller. **(o)** "Subagent" means a person to whom an agent delegates agency powers as provided in Article 5 (commencing with Section 2349) of Chapter 1 of Title 9. However, "subagent" does not include an associate licensee who is acting under the supervision of an agent in a real property transaction

2079.14 Listing agents and selling agents shall provide the seller and buyer in a real property transaction with a copy of the disclosure form specified in Section 2079.16, and, except as provided in subdivision (c), shall obtain a signed acknowledgement of receipt from that seller or buyer, except as provided in this section or Section 2079.15, as follows: **(a)** The listing agent, if any, shall provide the disclosure form to the seller prior to entering into the listing agreement. **(b)** The selling agent shall provide the disclosure form to the seller as soon as practicable prior to presenting the seller with an offer to purchase, unless the selling agent previously provided the seller with a copy of the disclosure form pursuant to subdivision (a). **(c)** Where the selling agent does not deal on a face-to-face basis with the seller, the disclosure form prepared by the selling agent may be furnished to the seller (and acknowledgement of receipt obtained for the selling agent from the seller) by the listing agent, or the selling agent may deliver the disclosure form by certified mail addressed to the seller at his or her last known address, in which case no signed acknowledgement of receipt is required. **(d)** The selling agent shall provide the disclosure form to the buyer as soon as practicable prior to execution of the buyer's offer to purchase, except that if the offer to purchase is not prepared by the selling agent, the selling agent shall present the disclosure form to the buyer not later than the next business day after the selling agent receives the offer to purchase from the buyer.

2079.15 In any circumstance in which the seller or buyer refuses to sign an acknowledgement of receipt pursuant to Section 2079.14, the agent, or an associate licensee acting for an agent, shall set forth, sign, and date a written declaration of the facts of the refusal.

2079.16 Reproduced on Page 1 of this AD form.

2079.17(a) As soon as practicable, the selling agent shall disclose to the buyer and seller whether the selling agent is acting in the real property transaction exclusively as the buyer's agent, exclusively as the seller's agent, or as a dual agent representing both the buyer and the seller. This relationship shall be confirmed in the contract to purchase and sell real property or in a separate writing executed or acknowledged by the seller, the buyer, and the selling agent prior to or coincident with execution of that contract by the buyer and the seller, respectively. **(b)** As soon as practicable, the listing agent shall disclose to the seller whether the listing agent is acting in the real property transaction exclusively as the seller's agent, or as a dual agent representing both the buyer and seller. This relationship shall be confirmed in the contract to purchase and sell real property or in a separate writing executed or acknowledged by the seller and the listing agent prior to or coincident with the execution of that contract by the seller.
(c) The confirmation required by subdivisions (a) and (b) shall be in the following form.

_____(DO NOT COMPLETE. SAMPLE ONLY)_____ is the agent of (check one): ❏ the seller exclusively; or ❏ both the buyer and seller.
(Name of Listing Agent)

_____(DO NOT COMPLETE. SAMPLE ONLY)_____ is the agent of (check one): ❏ the buyer exclusively; or ❏ the seller exclusively; or
(Name of Selling Agent if not the same as the Listing Agent)   ❏ both the buyer and seller.

(d) The disclosures and confirmation required by this section shall be in addition to the disclosure required by Section 2079.14.

2079.18 No selling agent in a real property transaction may act as an agent for the buyer only, when the selling agent is also acting as the listing agent in the transaction.

2079.19 The payment of compensation or the obligation to pay compensation to an agent by the seller or buyer is not necessarily determinative of a particular agency relationship between an agent and the seller or buyer. A listing agent and a selling agent may agree to share any compensation or commission paid, or any right to any compensation or commission for which an obligation arises as the result of a real estate transaction, and the terms of any such agreement shall not necessarily be determinative of a particular relationship.

2079.20 Nothing in this article prevents an agent from selecting, as a condition of the agent's employment, a specific form of agency relationship not specifically prohibited by this article if the requirements of Section 2079.14 and Section 2079.17 are complied with.

2079.21 A dual agent shall not disclose to the buyer that the seller is willing to sell the property at a price less than the listing price, without the express written consent of the seller. A dual agent shall not disclose to the seller that the buyer is willing to pay a price greater than the offering price, without the express written consent of the buyer. This section does not alter in any way the duty or responsibility of a dual agent to any principal with respect to confidential information other than price.

2079.22 Nothing in this article precludes a listing agent from also being a selling agent, and the combination of these functions in one agent does not, of itself, make that agent a dual agent.

2079.23 A contract between the principal and agent may be modified or altered to change the agency relationship at any time before the performance of the act which is the object of the agency with the written consent of the parties to the agency relationship.

2079.24 Nothing in this article shall be construed to either diminish the duty of disclosure owed buyers and sellers by agents and their associate licensees, subagents, and employees or to relieve agents and their associate licensees, subagents, and employees from liability for their conduct in connection with acts governed by this article or for any breach of a fiduciary duty or a duty of disclosure.

Reviewed by _____ Date _____

AD REVISED 11/12 (PAGE 2 OF 2)

DISCLOSURE REGARDING REAL ESTATE AGENCY RELATIONSHIP (AD PAGE 2 OF 2)

PERSONAL ASSISTANTS

A broker is responsible for supervising his or her salespersons, including any unlicensed personal assistants who work for salespersons. The broker must take great care to ensure that such unlicensed personal assistants do not perform acts that the law restricts to licensees. Activities that an *unlicensed* personal assistant may perform are:

- Cold Calling: may make outgoing calls to canvass for interest in using the services of a real estate broker. If the recipient of the call answers affirmatively, the call must immediately be put through to a licensee — the personal assistant may *not* discuss properties available or attempt to induce the person called to use the services of the broker. Care must be taken when making cold calls to comply with the Federal Trade Commission's telemarketing rules, which, among other things, makes it illegal to call a phone number that appears on the **National "DO NOT CALL" Registry**.

- Open House: with the principal's consent, may place signs, greet the public, hand out factual information, or arrange appointments with a licensee — but the personal assistant may *not* show the property, discuss terms, or even discuss other features of the property, such as benefits of the location or neighborhood schools.

- Comparative Analysis: may prepare a comparative market analysis of a property for use by a licensee.

- Advertising: may prepare advertising for a property if the advertising is reviewed and approved by the broker prior to its publication.

- Preparation of Documents: may prepare and complete documents related to a transaction if the documents are reviewed and approved by the broker.

- Delivery of Documents: may mail, deliver, or pickup documents related to the transaction, including obtaining signatures to the documents from relevant parties — but may *not* discuss the content, relevance, or significance of any portion of the documents.

- Trust Funds: may accept, account for, or provide a receipt for trust funds received.

- <u>Communication with Principals</u>: may communicate as to when reports or documents are to be completed, or services performed.

SECRET PROFIT

B&PC §10176(g) addresses a potential abuse by real estate licensees, referred to as **secret profit**, which typically arises when an agent arranges with a "dummy" purchaser to purchase a property at a lower price than has already been offered to the agent. Agents must always disclose any interest that they, their relatives, or anyone with whom they have a special relationship (such as a business partner) have in a transaction and obtain their principals' written consent.

ADVERTISING REGULATIONS

In addition to ensuring that no advertisement is submitted that is deceptive or discriminatory, a broker must not run a **blind ad**, which is an advertisement that fails to reveal that the advertiser is an agent, not a principal. "A real estate licensee shall not publish, circulate, distribute, or cause to be published, circulated, or distributed in any newspaper or periodical, or by mail, any matter pertaining to any activity for which a real estate license is required that does not contain a designation disclosing that he or she is performing acts for which a real estate license is required." B&PC §10140.6(a).

In addition, "a real estate licensee shall disclose his or her license identification number… on all solicitation materials intended to be the first point of contact with consumers and on real property purchase agreements when acting as an agent for those transactions.… For purposes of this section, 'solicitation materials intended to be the first point of contact with consumers' includes business cards, stationery, advertising flyers, and other materials designed to solicit the creation of a professional relationship between the licensee and a consumer, and excludes an advertisement in print or electronic media and 'for sale' signs." B&PC §10140.6(b)(1)-(b)(2).

> **Example:** A licensee's business card must contain both a designation that the licensee is a real estate agent and his or her license identification number, whereas a newspaper print ad need only have a designation that the ad is being published by a real estate licensee.

Advertisements by a broker who is also a mortgage loan originator are even more strictly regulated. These regulations will be discussed in the subsequent chapter on Real Estate Financing.

DUTIES OWED TO A PRINCIPAL

As we have already seen, an agent has a fiduciary relationship with the principal, which imposes on the agent many strictly enforced duties, including loyalty, confidentiality, the exercise of utmost care, disclosure of all material facts, the obligation to act fairly and honestly, and the duty to explain and counsel about the real estate transaction in order to help the principal make informed decisions (taking care not to step over the line into the practice of law).

The fiduciary duty to disclose all material facts includes the duty to inform the principal that the buyer with whom the agent is negotiating is related to the agent by blood, or has another relationship with the agent, such as a marital relationship or business relationship, that would possibly entail the agent's acquiring an indirect interest in the property.

The duty to disclose also requires that an agent submit *all* offers to the principal within a reasonable time. Unless the principal has instructed otherwise, even if an offer is so low that the agent is certain that the offer would be rejected, the offer must still be presented to the principal.

There are, however, at least two types of disclosure that an agent should not disclose to a principal:

1. as we have seen in our discussion of dual agency, an agent who represents both the buyer and the seller must not inform the buyer that the seller is willing to take a lower price, or, conversely, that the buyer is willing to pay a higher price; and
2. according to the California Attorney General's opinion (Op. 69/263), an agent should not, even if asked by the principal, disclose the race, creed, or color of a potential buyer (or seller, if the agent represents the buyer).

DISCLOSURES TO PURCHASERS OF RESIDENTIAL PROPERTIES

Beginning with the *Easton v. Strassburger* decision in 1984, California real estate agents have, as the *Easton* court held, an "affirmative duty to conduct a reasonably competent and diligent inspection of the residential property listed for sale and to disclose to prospective purchasers all facts materially affecting the value of the property that such an investigation would reveal."

The *Easton* court suggested that its decision did not apply to commercial transactions, and the California Civil Code subsequently codified an agent's duties to inspect and disclose in Section 2079, summarized as follows:

1. The seller's agent and each cooperating agent has the duty to the buyer of *residential real property of 1 to 4 units* (including manufactured homes) to make a reasonably competent visual inspection of the property and to disclose to the buyer all material facts that affect the value, desirability, or intended use of the property.

2. This duty also applies to leases of such residential property with an option to buy.

3. The standard of care owed by the agent to the buyer is the degree of care that a reasonably prudent real estate agent would exercise (as measured by the degree of knowledge that should be acquired through the education and experience required to obtain a real estate license).

4. The inspection to be performed does not include areas that are reasonably and normally not accessible.

5. The code establishes a statute of limitations of 2 years that runs from the date of recordation, close of escrow, or occupancy, whichever comes first.

6. The inspection to be performed does not extend to areas off the site, to public records, or to common areas of condominiums, planned developments, and stock cooperatives.

TRANSFER DISCLOSURE STATEMENT

The *seller of a residential real estate property of 1 to 4 units (or a manufactured home)* must, pursuant to CC §1102.3, disclose known property defects to the buyer on a ***Real Estate Transfer Disclosure Statement*** ("TDS"). Figure 7.4 displays the TDS form created by the California Association of Realtors® to comply with CC §1102.3 and with the agent's inspection and disclosure acquirements, discussed above, pursuant to CC §2079.

The TDS must be signed by the sellers, buyers, seller's agent, and selling agent, and should be given to the buyers at the time they sign the purchase agreement. If the TDS is provided later, the buyers have 3 days after delivery of the TDS to cancel the sale. Some sellers and even some agents erroneously believe that if the property is sold "as is" they are relieved of all liability. However, in California, selling a property "as is" only relieves the seller from liability for not disclosing defects that are observable on reasonable inspection. Furthermore, selling the property "as is" does not diminish in any way the agent's duty to inspect and disclose.

OTHER REQUIRED DISCLOSURE STATEMENTS

In addition to the Disclosure Regarding Real Estate Agency Relationship (Figure 7.3) and the Real Estate Transfer Disclosure Statement (Figure 7.4), there are many other disclosures mandated for transactions involving the sale of residential real property of 1 to 4 units.

Smoke Detector and Water Heater Bracing Statement Compliance: This is a written statement of compliance regarding the installation of smoke detectors and water heater bracing. If an agent uses the TDS form created by the California Association of Realtors® ("C.A.R.") (Figure 7.4), this statement need no longer be given to the buyer, as the new TDS form incorporates a seller's certificate that, by close of escrow, the seller will be in compliance with requirements for smoke detectors and water heater bracing (see Paragraph D of Figure 7.4). The current C.A.R. TDS form also includes the required disclosure as to whether the seller has installed **carbon monoxide detectors**. This carbon monoxide disclosure addresses a law requiring California homeowners to have installed carbon monoxide detectors in single-family homes by July 1, 2011, in hotel and motel dwelling units intended for human occupancy by January 1, 2016, and in all other existing dwelling units (such as apartments and condos) by January 1, 2013. The carbon monoxide installation requirement applies to dwellings with a fossil fuel burning heater or appliance, a fireplace, or an attached garage.

Disclosure Regarding Lead-Based Paint Hazards: Pursuant to the federal Real Estate Disclosure and Notification rule, a seller (or lessor) of a residential dwelling unit built before 1978 must notify a buyer (or tenant) in writing about required disclosures for lead-based paint. The seller must disclose any knowledge he or she has about whether lead-based paint was used in the dwelling unit and must provide the buyer with an EPA pamphlet titled *"Protect Your Family From Lead In Your Home,"* which describes ways to recognize and reduce lead hazards. The seller must deliver this pamphlet to a prospective buyer before the contract is completed. The seller must also offer a prospective buyer 10 days to inspect for lead-based paint and lead-based paint hazards. The seller is not required to pay for this inspection.

Fig. 7.4

REAL ESTATE TRANSFER DISCLOSURE STATEMENT
(CALIFORNIA CIVIL CODE §1102, ET SEQ.)
(C.A.R. Form TDS, Revised 11/11)

THIS DISCLOSURE STATEMENT CONCERNS THE REAL PROPERTY SITUATED IN THE CITY OF _____
_____, COUNTY OF _____, STATE OF CALIFORNIA,
DESCRIBED AS _____.

THIS STATEMENT IS A DISCLOSURE OF THE CONDITION OF THE ABOVE DESCRIBED PROPERTY IN COMPLIANCE
WITH SECTION 1102 OF THE CIVIL CODE AS OF (date) _____. IT IS NOT A WARRANTY OF ANY
KIND BY THE SELLER(S) OR ANY AGENT(S) REPRESENTING ANY PRINCIPAL(S) IN THIS TRANSACTION, AND IS
NOT A SUBSTITUTE FOR ANY INSPECTIONS OR WARRANTIES THE PRINCIPAL(S) MAY WISH TO OBTAIN.

I. COORDINATION WITH OTHER DISCLOSURE FORMS

This Real Estate Transfer Disclosure Statement is made pursuant to Section 1102 of the Civil Code. Other statutes require disclosures, depending upon the details of the particular real estate transaction (for example: special study zone and purchase-money liens on residential property).

Substituted Disclosures: The following disclosures and other disclosures required by law, including the Natural Hazard Disclosure Report/Statement that may include airport annoyances, earthquake, fire, flood, or special assessment information, have or will be made in connection with this real estate transfer, and are intended to satisfy the disclosure obligations on this form, where the subject matter is the same:

☐ Inspection reports completed pursuant to the contract of sale or receipt for deposit.
☐ Additional inspection reports or disclosures: _____
_____

II. SELLER'S INFORMATION

The Seller discloses the following information with the knowledge that even though this is not a warranty, prospective Buyers may rely on this information in deciding whether and on what terms to purchase the subject property. Seller hereby authorizes any agent(s) representing any principal(s) in this transaction to provide a copy of this statement to any person or entity in connection with any actual or anticipated sale of the property.

THE FOLLOWING ARE REPRESENTATIONS MADE BY THE SELLER(S) AND ARE NOT THE REPRESENTATIONS OF THE AGENT(S), IF ANY. THIS INFORMATION IS A DISCLOSURE AND IS NOT INTENDED TO BE PART OF ANY CONTRACT BETWEEN THE BUYER AND SELLER.

Seller ☐ is ☐ is not occupying the property.

A. The subject property has the items checked below:*

☐ Range	☐ Wall/Window Air Conditioning	☐ Pool:
☐ Oven	☐ Sprinklers	☐ Child Resistant Barrier
☐ Microwave	☐ Public Sewer System	☐ Pool/Spa Heater:
☐ Dishwasher	☐ Septic Tank	☐ Gas ☐ Solar ☐ Electric
☐ Trash Compactor	☐ Sump Pump	☐ Water Heater:
☐ Garbage Disposal	☐ Water Softener	☐ Gas ☐ Solar ☐ Electric
☐ Washer/Dryer Hookups	☐ Patio/Decking	☐ Water Supply:
☐ Rain Gutters	☐ Built-in Barbecue	☐ City ☐ Well
☐ Burglar Alarms	☐ Gazebo	☐ Private Utility or
☐ Carbon Monoxide Device(s)	☐ Security Gate(s)	Other_____
☐ Smoke Detector(s)	☐ Garage:	☐ Gas Supply:
☐ Fire Alarm	☐ Attached ☐ Not Attached	☐ Utility ☐ Bottled (Tank)
☐ TV Antenna	☐ Carport	☐ Window Screens
☐ Satellite Dish	☐ Automatic Garage Door Opener(s)	☐ Window Security Bars
☐ Intercom	☐ Number Remote Controls ____	☐ Quick Release Mechanism on
☐ Central Heating	☐ Sauna	Bedroom Windows
☐ Central Air Conditioning	☐ Hot Tub/Spa:	☐ Water-Conserving Plumbing Fixtures
☐ Evaporator Cooler(s)	☐ Locking Safety Cover	

Exhaust Fan(s) in _____ 220 Volt Wiring in _____ Fireplace(s) in _____
☐ Gas Starter _____ ☐ Roof(s): Type: _____ Age: _____ (approx.)
☐ Other: _____

Are there, to the best of your (Seller's) knowledge, any of the above that are not in operating condition? ☐ Yes ☐ No. If yes, then describe. (Attach additional sheets if necessary):_____
_____

(*see note on page 2)

Buyer's Initials (_____)(_____)   Seller's Initials (_____)(_____)

TDS REVISED 11/11 (PAGE 1 OF 3) Print Date

Reviewed by _____ Date _____

REAL ESTATE TRANSFER DISCLOSURE STATEMENT (TDS PAGE 1 OF 3)

Property Address: _____ Date: _____

B. Are you (Seller) aware of any significant defects/malfunctions in any of the following? ☐ Yes ☐ No. If yes, check appropriate space(s) below.

☐ Interior Walls ☐ Ceilings ☐ Floors ☐ Exterior Walls ☐ Insulation ☐ Roof(s) ☐ Windows ☐ Doors ☐ Foundation ☐ Slab(s) ☐ Driveways ☐ Sidewalks ☐ Walls/Fences ☐ Electrical Systems ☐ Plumbing/Sewers/Septics ☐ Other Structural Components (Describe: _____

_____

_____)

If any of the above is checked, explain. (Attach additional sheets if necessary.): _____

_____

_____

_____

*Installation of a listed appliance, device, or amenity is not a precondition of sale or transfer of the dwelling. The carbon monoxide device, garage door opener, or child-resistant pool barrier may not be in compliance with the safety standards relating to, respectively, carbon monoxide device standards of Chapter 8 (commencing with Section 13260) of Part 2 of Division 12 of, automatic reversing device standards of Chapter 12.5 (commencing with Section 19890) of Part 3 of Division 13 of, or the pool safety standards of Article 2.5 (commencing with Section 115920) of Chapter 5 of Part 10 of Division 104 of, the Health and Safety Code. Window security bars may not have quick-release mechanisms in compliance with the 1995 edition of the California Building Standards Code. Section 1101.4 of the Civil Code requires all single-family residences built on or before January 1, 1994, to be equipped with water-conserving plumbing fixtures after January 1, 2017. Additionally, on and after January 1, 2014, a single-family residence built on or before January 1, 1994, that is altered or improved is required to be equipped with water-conserving plumbing fixtures as a condition of final approval. Fixtures in this dwelling may not comply with section 1101.4 of the Civil Code.

C. Are you (Seller) aware of any of the following:

1. Substances, materials, or products which may be an environmental hazard such as, but not limited to, asbestos, formaldehyde, radon gas, lead-based paint, mold, fuel or chemical storage tanks, and contaminated soil or water on the subject property . . . . ☐ Yes ☐ No

2. Features of the property shared in common with adjoining landowners, such as walls, fences, and driveways, whose use or responsibility for maintenance may have an effect on the subject property . . . . ☐ Yes ☐ No

3. Any encroachments, easements or similar matters that may affect your interest in the subject property . . . . ☐ Yes ☐ No

4. Room additions, structural modifications, or other alterations or repairs made without necessary permits . . . . ☐ Yes ☐ No

5. Room additions, structural modifications, or other alterations or repairs not in compliance with building codes . . . . ☐ Yes ☐ No

6. Fill (compacted or otherwise) on the property or any portion thereof . . . . ☐ Yes ☐ No

7. Any settling from any cause, or slippage, sliding, or other soil problems . . . . ☐ Yes ☐ No

8. Flooding, drainage or grading problems . . . . ☐ Yes ☐ No

9. Major damage to the property or any of the structures from fire, earthquake, floods, or landslides . . . . ☐ Yes ☐ No

10. Any zoning violations, nonconforming uses, violations of "setback" requirements . . . . ☐ Yes ☐ No

11. Neighborhood noise problems or other nuisances . . . . ☐ Yes ☐ No

12. CC&R's or other deed restrictions or obligations . . . . ☐ Yes ☐ No

13. Homeowners' Association which has any authority over the subject property . . . . ☐ Yes ☐ No

14. Any "common area" (facilities such as pools, tennis courts, walkways, or other areas co-owned in undivided interest with others) . . . . ☐ Yes ☐ No

15. Any notices of abatement or citations against the property . . . . ☐ Yes ☐ No

16. Any lawsuits by or against the Seller threatening to or affecting this real property, including any lawsuits alleging a defect or deficiency in this real property or "common areas" (facilities such as pools, tennis courts, walkways, or other areas co-owned in undivided interest with others) . . . . ☐ Yes ☐ No

If the answer to any of these is yes, explain. (Attach additional sheets if necessary.): _____

_____

_____

D. 1. The Seller certifies that the property, as of the close of escrow, will be in compliance with Section 13113.8 of the Health and Safety Code by having operable smoke detector(s) which are approved, listed, and installed in accordance with the State Fire Marshal's regulations and applicable local standards.

2. The Seller certifies that the property, as of the close of escrow, will be in compliance with Section 19211 of the Health and Safety Code by having the water heater tank(s) braced, anchored, or strapped in place in accordance with applicable law.

Seller certifies that the information herein is true and correct to the best of the Seller's knowledge as of the date signed by the Seller.

Buyer's Initials (_____)(_____)

TDS REVISED 11/11 (PAGE 2 OF 3)

Reviewed by _____ Date _____

REAL ESTATE TRANSFER DISCLOSURE STATEMENT (TDS PAGE 2 OF 3)

Property Address: _____ Date _____

Seller _____ Date _____

Seller _____ Date _____

III. AGENT'S INSPECTION DISCLOSURE

(To be completed only if the Seller is represented by an agent in this transaction.)

THE UNDERSIGNED, BASED ON THE ABOVE INQUIRY OF THE SELLER(S) AS TO THE CONDITION OF THE PROPERTY AND BASED ON A REASONABLY COMPETENT AND DILIGENT VISUAL INSPECTION OF THE ACCESSIBLE AREAS OF THE PROPERTY IN CONJUNCTION WITH THAT INQUIRY, STATES THE FOLLOWING:

☐ See attached Agent Visual Inspection Disclosure (AVID Form)

☐ Agent notes no items for disclosure.

☐ Agent notes the following items: _____

_____

_____

Agent (Broker Representing Seller) _____ By _____ Date _____
                                     (Please Print)   (Associate Licensee or Broker Signature)

IV. AGENT'S INSPECTION DISCLOSURE

(To be completed only if the agent who has obtained the offer is other than the agent above.)

THE UNDERSIGNED, BASED ON A REASONABLY COMPETENT AND DILIGENT VISUAL INSPECTION OF THE ACCESSIBLE AREAS OF THE PROPERTY, STATES THE FOLLOWING:

☐ See attached Agent Visual Inspection Disclosure (AVID Form)

☐ Agent notes no items for disclosure.

☐ Agent notes the following items: _____

_____

_____

Agent (Broker Obtaining the Offer) _____ By _____ Date _____
                                     (Please Print)   (Associate Licensee or Broker Signature)

V. BUYER(S) AND SELLER(S) MAY WISH TO OBTAIN PROFESSIONAL ADVICE AND/OR INSPECTIONS OF THE PROPERTY AND TO PROVIDE FOR APPROPRIATE PROVISIONS IN A CONTRACT BETWEEN BUYER AND SELLER(S) WITH RESPECT TO ANY ADVICE/INSPECTIONS/DEFECTS.

I/WE ACKNOWLEDGE RECEIPT OF A COPY OF THIS STATEMENT.

Seller _____ Date _____ Buyer _____ Date _____

Seller _____ Date _____ Buyer _____ Date _____

Agent (Broker Representing Seller) _____ By _____ Date _____
                                     (Please Print)   (Associate Licensee or Broker Signature)

Agent (Broker Obtaining the Offer) _____ By _____ Date _____
                                     (Please Print)   (Associate Licensee or Broker Signature)

SECTION 1102.3 OF THE CIVIL CODE PROVIDES A BUYER WITH THE RIGHT TO RESCIND A PURCHASE CONTRACT FOR AT LEAST THREE DAYS AFTER THE DELIVERY OF THIS DISCLOSURE IF DELIVERY OCCURS AFTER THE SIGNING OF AN OFFER TO PURCHASE. IF YOU WISH TO RESCIND THE CONTRACT, YOU MUST ACT WITHIN THE PRESCRIBED PERIOD.

A REAL ESTATE BROKER IS QUALIFIED TO ADVISE ON REAL ESTATE. IF YOU DESIRE LEGAL ADVICE, CONSULT YOUR ATTORNEY.

Published and Distributed by:
REAL ESTATE BUSINESS SERVICES, INC.
a subsidiary of the California Association of REALTORS®
525 South Virgil Avenue, Los Angeles, California 90020

TDS REVISED 11/11 (PAGE 3 OF 3)

Reviewed by _____ Date _____

REAL ESTATE TRANSFER DISCLOSURE STATEMENT (TDS PAGE 3 OF 3)

Natural Hazard Disclosure: Sellers and their agents must certify in a separate disclosure report titled *Natural Hazard Disclosure Statement* (see Figure 7.6) whether the property lies in one or more of the following special hazards zones:

- a special flood hazard area
- an area of potential flooding
- a very high fire hazard severity zone
- a wildland area that may contain substantial fire risk
- an earthquake fault zone
- a seismic hazard zone

Many other disclosures typically provided in a residential real estate transaction include:

Disclosure of Ordnance Location. This disclosure must be provided by the seller of residential property located within 1 mile of an area once used for military training where potentially explosive munitions may still exist.

Mold Disclosure. The TDS asks whether the owner is aware of any mold. Because mold has become such a litigious issue in California real estate (lawyers have a saying "Asbestos is old, mold is gold"), in addition to relying on the TDS mold disclosure, real estate agents would be wise, as part of their duty to inspect, to use their noses to sniff for signs of mold, and to strongly suggest that a professional mold inspection be performed on the property.

Environmental Hazard Disclosure Booklet. The pamphlet titled *"Environmental Hazards: A Guide for Homeowners, Buyers, Landlords, and Tenants,"* which identifies various earthquake issues and also discusses asbestos, mold, radon, lead, and formaldehyde, should be provided to every prospective buyer (or tenant) of residential real property.

Mello-Roos Disclosure. A prospective purchaser of real property that is subject to a continuing lien securing the levy of special taxes pursuant to the Mello-Roos Community Facilities Act or pursuant to the Improvement Bond Act of 1915 must be given a disclosure so stating.

Megan's Law. The prospective buyer of real estate must be given notice that a website (currently active at www.meganslaw.ca.gov) is available for information on registered sex offenders.

Seller Financing Disclosure Statement. If the sale involves a seller's assisting in the financing of the sale by extending credit to the buyer in the form of a seller "carry-back" loan, a statement clearly outlining the financing terms of the carry-back loan must be signed by the buyer, seller, and real estate agent, if one is involved, before the buyer signs the promissory note.

Gas and Hazardous Liquid Transmission Pipelines

Every contract for the sale of residential real estate entered into on or after July 1, 2013, must contain a notice of the availability of the National Pipeline Mapping System Internet Web site, which contains information about possible transmission pipelines near the property. CC §2079.10.5.

RETENTION OF DOCUMENTS

In addition to the requirement that trust fund records must be retained by the broker for at least 3 years, all other documents connected with a real estate transaction (with the exceptions discussed in the following sentence) must also be retained for at least *3 years from the date of closing, or, if the transaction does not close, from the date of listing.* Disclosure statements given to individual (non-institutional) lenders or trust deed purchasers and real property security statements must be retained for 4 years.

DUTIES TO THIRD PARTIES

In addition to the duties to disclose discussed above, an agent has certain obligations of fair dealing and honesty to third parties, even though the agent does not have a fiduciary relationship with such parties.

Secret Profits

We have already discussed an agent's obligation to inform principals of an interest that the agent or the agent's relatives have in a real estate transaction. Likewise, because the agent has a duty to be fair to everyone involved in a real estate transaction, not just to the principal, courts hold that agents must also inform buyers of any agent interest in the transaction; otherwise, the buyer may force the agent to return any secret profit made on the transaction.

Conflict of Interest

A **conflict of interest** is a situation in which an individual or organization is involved in several *potentially* competing interests, creating a risk that one interest *might* unduly influence another interest.

As discussed above, secret profits involve a conflict of interest, generally in the form of surreptitious self-dealing by a real estate licensee, either directly or indirectly as the seller, or directly or indirectly as the buyer, to gain an undisclosed profit for the licensee in a real estate transaction in which the licensee is performing acts that require a real estate license.

However, a conflict of interest can exist:

- regardless of any pecuniary gain;

- regardless of any actual undue influence; and

- regardless of any evidence of wrongdoing or impropriety.

Furthermore, not all conflicts of interest are considered unethical or illegal. For example, the conflict of interest known as dual agency in which the agent owes fiduciary duties to both the buyer and seller is perfectly legal in California (but not in all states) as long as the appropriate disclosures are made and agreed upon by all parties to the transaction. However, dual agency must be handled with utmost care (some would say super-human care) to avoid stumbling into impropriety, thereby risking suspension or revocation of the licensee's license, as well as civil actions against the licensee.

A Licensee Acting Solely As a Principal

Real estate law does not require that a licensee who is acting *solely* as a principal in a real estate transaction reveal his or her status as a licensee. However, the practical risk in not revealing the existence of his or her license almost surely outweighs any potential benefit to be gained from secrecy. If after closing the buyer (or seller, as the case may be) feels that something had been done wrong in the transaction and sues, it is almost certain that the attorney handling the case will try to sway the jury by pointing out that the real estate licensee possessed much greater knowledge of real estate in general, and the subject property in particular, and "clearly took unfair advantage of my client!"

Making Any Substantial Misrepresentation

Misrepresentations can be either intentional or negligent. However, in real estate law even negligent misrepresentation is often characterized as fraudulent. Normally, to find fraudulent misrepresentation there must be a finding of an intention to deceive; however, even without bad intention and even believing his or her assertions to be true, a real estate agent may be guilty of fraudulent misrepresentation if the assertions are made in a manner not warranted by the information available to the agent.

Nondisclosures

As we have seen, a real estate agent has a duty to disclose any known defect in the property or any defect that could have been discovered upon reasonable visual inspection. Civil liability for misrepresentation, as well as disciplinary action from the CalBRE Commissioner, can result from an agent's failure to make these required disclosures. Nondisclosure can also result from an affirmative act of hiding defects in the property to prevent the buyer from discovering the defects. Such acts are referred to as **concealment**, and sometimes as **negative fraud.**

Stigmatized Properties

A stigmatized property is a property having a condition that certain persons may find materially negative in a way that does not relate to the property's actual physical condition. An agent has no duty to disclose to the buyer that a death occurred on the property more than three years before the buyer's offer; nor need the agent voluntarily provide information as to whether a current or former owner or resident has AIDS or is HIV-positive. *"No cause of action arises against an owner of real property or his or her agent, or any agent of a transferee of real property, for the failure to disclose to the transferee the occurrence of an occupant's death upon the real property or the manner of death where the death has occurred more than three years prior to the date the transferee offers to purchase, lease, or rent the real property, or that an occupant of that property was afflicted with, or died from, Human T-Lymphotropic Virus Type III/Lymphadenopathy-Associated Virus."* CC §1710.2

CC §1710.2(a) does not *"immunize an owner or his or her agent from making an intentional misrepresentation in response to a direct inquiry from a transferee or a prospective transferee of real property, concerning deaths on the real property."* CC §1710.2(d). In other words, although neither the transferor of real property nor any real estate agent involved in the transaction needs to *voluntarily* disclose the facts referred to in CC §1710.2(a)(1), when specifically asked about death on the property, no intentional misrepresentation may be made in response.

Note, however, that most stigmatized properties should be disclosed as such to prospective purchasers.

> **Example:** If in a particular community a house is widely believed to be haunted, regardless of whether such a belief is utter nonsense, what is important with respect to real estate agency disclosure is whether such a belief materially affects the value of the property.

Puffing

Somewhat overblown "sales talk" or "**puffing**" can also result in a finding of misrepresentation.

Example: In *Wood v. Kalbaugh*, 39 Cal. App. 3d 926 (1974), the court found that a licensee's statement "that with the exception of the dishwasher everything was in perfect shape" was, in fact, an actionable misrepresentation, *even though the agent had no knowledge of the defect that was eventually found.* The court stated: "according to early concepts [such a representation] would have been treated as commendatory language known as 'sales talk' or 'puffing.' Under the modern trend, such statements, particularly when made by builders and real estate agents, are considered representations of a material fact because they tend to induce reasonable men to purchase the property which is up for sale."

While in certain circumstances a statement such as "this property is the best buy in town" likely is acceptable sales talk (until some court finds otherwise), a real estate agent should always maintain keen awareness that if, *for any reason,* a buyer comes to be unhappy with his or her purchase, such unhappiness is fertile breeding ground for lawsuits against the seller, real estate agents, and anyone else, such as builders, inspectors, or appraisers, who were involved in the transaction. Therefore, the more rigorously honest an agent is, even to the point of eliminating "mere sales talk," the less risk the agent will run in our increasingly litigious society.

False Promise

A *false promise* is "a promise made without any intention of performing it," (CC §1710) and is a deceit for which liability to anyone damaged thereby can arise. A false promise differs from a misrepresentation in that a false promise involves making a promise to do something, rather than making a statement of fact.

Example: An agent who promises to paint the fence with no intention of doing so would be guilty of this type of fraud.

ANTITRUST

Antitrust laws, which are intended to safeguard competitive free enterprise, impose restrictions on a real estate agents' conduct toward competitors, clients, and customers. Having a firm grasp of the basics of how antitrust laws impact a real estate agent's behavior is very important because

- it is easy to unintentionally violate antitrust laws; and
- the penalties, both criminal and civil, can be severe, very severe — treble damages, astronomical fines, and long jail times.

The basic federal antitrust law is the **Sherman Act** passed in 1890, which prohibits agreements, verbal or written, that have the effect of restraining free trade, including conspiracies. An antitrust **conspiracy** occurs when

1. two or more persons agree to act (referred to as "**group action**"); and
2. the agreed-upon action has the effect of restraining trade.

California has its own antitrust laws based upon the **Cartwright Act** (B&PC §§16700-16770), which closely parallels federal law.

ANTITRUST VIOLATIONS AND HOW TO AVOID THEM

The prohibited activities that a real estate agent must be aware of can be grouped into four main categories:

1. price fixing;
2. group boycotts;
3. tying arrangements; and
4. market allocation.

Price Fixing

Price fixing is an agreement between competitors to set prices or price ranges. It is immaterial whether the price fixed is a maximum price, a minimum price, a fair price, or a reasonable price — *all* agreements to fix prices between competitors are criminal acts according to federal law. As we saw in our discussion of the Exclusive Authorization and Right to Sell listing agreement in Chapter 6 (see Figure 6.5, Paragraph 4), California emphasizes that commissions may not be fixed by requiring that printed listing agreements must contain certain language in bold face 10 point type:

> **"NOTICE: The amount or rate of commission is not fixed by law. They are set by each Broker individually and may be negotiable between Seller and Broker (real estate commissions include all compensation and fees to Broker)."**

To avoid price fixing, real estate agents should avoid discussing prices (commission rates or referral fees) or pricing strategy with a competitor. The only exceptions to this rule are that a broker can offer a competing broker a referral fee and discuss the amount of that fee or may discuss with a cooperating broker how to split a commission or referral fee when negotiating regarding a particular transaction.

Group Boycotts

A *group boycott* occurs when two or more brokers agree not to deal with another broker or brokers. It is important when thinking about group boycotts to understand the distinction between individual action and group action. A broker may choose not to do business with another broker if he or she so wishes (e.g., if the broker feels that the other broker is dishonest), but the broker may not encourage other brokers to do likewise.

Tying Arrangements

A *tying arrangement* (also referred to as a tied-in arrangement) occurs when a seller conditions the sale of one product on the purchase of another (the tied) product. Not all tying arrangements are illegal, but the analysis of what is permissible and what is impermissible tying involves a complex analysis of whether the seller has such an advantage as to coerce the buyer to purchase the tied product. In real estate agency, a typical case of an *impermissible* tying arrangement occurs when the sale of a property is conditioned upon the agent's obtaining the listing for future sales.

Market Allocation

Market allocation occurs when competitors agree to divide up geographic areas or types of products or services they offer to customers. Market allocations are actually a form of price fixing, in that they reduce competition and therefore tend to raise prices. However, it should be noted that because a real estate office is usually considered to be an individual entity for antitrust purposes, a real estate office may assign salespersons to work specific areas — a practice called "farming."

RECOVERY ACCOUNT

All real estate license fees go to a *Real Estate Fund* at the State Treasury. Some of the money in the Real Estate Fund is credited to the *Recovery Account*, which is used to reimburse members of the public who have obtained a civil judgment or criminal restitution order against a real estate licensee but have not been able to collect fully from the licensee through normal collection efforts. The Recovery Account will pay up to a statutory maximum of *$50,000 per transaction*, with a total aggregate *maximum of $250,000 per licensee*. Once payment is made from the Recovery Account, the licensee is automatically suspended until he or she has repaid the Recovery Account in full, plus interest.

TERMINATION OF AGENCY

An agency relationship can be terminated by

- actions of the parties, and
- operation of law.

TERMINATION BY ACTION OF THE PARTIES

An agency relationship can be terminated by *mutual agreement*. Also, because agency is a personal relationship based on trust and confidence, either party may *unilaterally terminate* the agency at any time (*unless, as discussed below, the agency is coupled with an interest*). However, though the principal may revoke and the agent may renounce the agency at any time, doing so may result in liability for breach of contract, such as if the principal revokes the agency prior to the termination of an exclusive authorization and right to sell listing and then sells the property him or herself.

An agency is **coupled with an interest** if the agent has a financial interest *in the subject of the agency* (as distinct from the compensation that may result for the agent from his or her performance as an agent).

> **Example:** If an agent is a co-owner of a property and the other owners authorize the agent to represent the property for sale, then the other owners may not revoke the agency.

TERMINATION BY OPERATION OF LAW

Several events may terminate the agency relationship automatically by operation of law:

Expiration of the Agency Term: The agency relationship automatically terminates when its term ends. If the agency agreement did not include a termination date (which it must if it is an exclusive agency), then the agency would expire after a reasonable time. Without a stated termination date, either party may terminate the agency at any time without liability, although the agent might be able to demand reimbursement for expenses incurred before the termination.

Death or Incapacity: Because agency is a personal relationship, death or incapacity of either the principal or the agent would terminate the agency. Thus, if an agent loses his or her license, the agency relationship would end due to incapacity. Note, however, that since a corporation is considered a separate entity, the death of corporate officers of either the principal or the agent would not terminate the agency.

Fulfillment of Purpose: When the purpose of the agent's job is accomplished — such as by the sale of a property if the agent is a listing agent, or the purchase of a property if the agent is a buyer's agent — the agency ends.

Bankruptcy: The trustee in a bankruptcy may choose either to terminate or to continue the agency. If the bankruptcy impairs the agent's performance, the principal may revoke the agency.

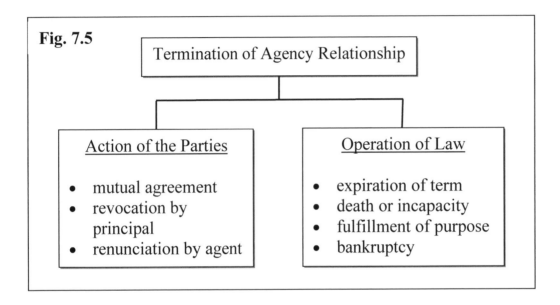

Fig. 7.5

Termination of Agency Relationship

Action of the Parties	Operation of Law
• mutual agreement • revocation by principal • renunciation by agent	• expiration of term • death or incapacity • fulfillment of purpose • bankruptcy

TRADE ASSOCIATIONS

The largest real estate trade association in the United States is the **National Association of Realtors®** (N.A.R.), which was established in 1908. The **California Association of Realtors®**, which has been kind enough to permit reproduction of several of their forms in this text, is the state organization of N.A.R. Membership in a local board of Realtors® automatically includes membership in the N.A.R. and the C.A.R.

Another large trade association called the **National Association of Real Estate Brokers** was established in 1947. Members of this organization are called **Realtists®**.

Fig. 7.6

 CALIFORNIA
ASSOCIATION
OF REALTORS®

NATURAL HAZARD DISCLOSURE STATEMENT
(C.A.R. Form NHD, Revised 10/04)

This statement applies to the following property: _____

The transferor and his or her agent(s) or a third-party consultant disclose the following information with the knowledge that even though this is not a warranty, prospective transferees may rely on this information in deciding whether and on what terms to purchase the subject property. Transferor hereby authorizes any agent(s) representing any principal(s) in this action to provide a copy of this statement to any person or entity in connection with any actual or anticipated sale of the property.

The following are representations made by the transferor and his or her agent(s) based on their knowledge and maps drawn by the state and federal governments. This information is a disclosure and is not intended to be part of any contract between the transferee and transferor.

THIS REAL PROPERTY LIES WITHIN THE FOLLOWING HAZARDOUS AREA(S):

A SPECIAL FLOOD HAZARD AREA (Any type Zone "A" or "V") designated by the Federal Emergency Management Agency.

Yes _____   No _____   Do not know and information not available from local jurisdiction _____

AN AREA OF POTENTIAL FLOODING shown on a dam failure inundation map pursuant to Section 8589.5 of the Government Code.

Yes _____   No _____   Do not know and information not available from local jurisdiction _____

A VERY HIGH FIRE HAZARD SEVERITY ZONE pursuant to Section 51178 or 51179 of the Government Code. The owner of this property is subject to the maintenance requirements of Section 51182 of the Government Code.

Yes _____   No _____

A WILDLAND AREA THAT MAY CONTAIN SUBSTANTIAL FOREST FIRE RISKS AND HAZARDS pursuant to Section 4125 of the Public Resources Code. The owner of this property is subject to the maintenance requirements of Section 4291 of the Public Resources Code. Additionally, it is not the state's responsibility to provide fire protection services to any building or structure located within the wildlands unless the Department of Forestry and Fire Protection has entered into a cooperative agreement with a local agency for those purposes pursuant to Section 4142 of the Public Resources Code.

Yes _____   No _____

AN EARTHQUAKE FAULT ZONE pursuant to Section 2622 of the Public Resources Code.

Yes _____   No _____

A SEISMIC HAZARD ZONE pursuant to Section 2696 of the Public Resources Code.

Yes (Landslide Zone) _____   Yes (Liquefaction Zone) _____

No _____   Map not yet released by state _____

Buyer's Initials (_____)(_____)
Seller's Initials (_____)(_____)

Reviewed by _____ Date _____

NHD REVISED 10/04 (PAGE 1 OF 2) Print Date

NATURAL HAZARD DISCLOSURE STATEMENT (NHD PAGE 1 OF 2)

Reprinted with permission, CALIFORNIA ASSOCIATION OF REALTORS®. Endorsement not implied.

Property Address: _____ Date: _____

THESE HAZARDS MAY LIMIT YOUR ABILITY TO DEVELOP THE REAL PROPERTY, TO OBTAIN INSURANCE, OR TO RECEIVE ASSISTANCE AFTER A DISASTER.

THE MAPS ON WHICH THESE DISCLOSURES ARE BASED ESTIMATE WHERE NATURAL HAZARDS EXIST. THEY ARE NOT DEFINITIVE INDICATORS OF WHETHER OR NOT A PROPERTY WILL BE AFFECTED BY A NATURAL DISASTER. TRANSFEREE(S) AND TRANSFEROR(S) MAY WISH TO OBTAIN PROFESSIONAL ADVICE REGARDING THOSE HAZARDS AND OTHER HAZARDS THAT MAY AFFECT THE PROPERTY

Signature of Transferor(s) _____ Date _____

Signature of Transferor(s) _____ Date _____

Agent(s) _____ Date _____

Agent(s) _____ Date _____

Check only one of the following:

☐ Transferor(s) and their agent(s) represent that the information herein is true and correct to the best of their knowledge as of the date signed by the transferor(s) and agent(s).

☐ Transferor(s) and their agent(s) acknowledge that they have exercised good faith in the selection of a third-party report provider as required in Civil Code Section 1103.7, and that the representations made in this Natural Hazard Disclosure Statement are based upon information provided by the independent third-party disclosure provider as a substituted disclosure pursuant to Civil Code Section 1103.4. Neither transferor(s) nor their agent(s) (1) has independently verified the information contained in this statement and report or (2) is personally aware of any errors or inaccuracies in the information contained on the statement. This statement was prepared by the provider below:

Third-Party Disclosure Provider(s)_____ Date _____

Transferee represents that he or she has read and understands this document. Pursuant to Civil Code Section 1103.8, the representations made in this Natural Hazard Disclosure Statement do not constitute all of the transferor's or agent's disclosure obligations in this transaction.

Signature of Transferee(s) _____ Date _____

Signature of Transferee(s) _____ Date _____

Published and Distributed by:
REAL ESTATE BUSINESS SERVICES, INC.
a subsidiary of the California Association of REALTORS®
525 South Virgil Avenue, Los Angeles, California 90020

Reviewed by _____ Date _____

NHD REVISED 10/04 (PAGE 2 OF 2) Print Date

NATURAL HAZARD DISCLOSURE STATEMENT (NHD PAGE 2 OF 2)

Key Terms for Chapter 7

actual agency — an agency in which the agent is employed by the principal, either by express agreement, ratification, or implication.

advance fee — a fee paid by a seller to an agent to cover expected cash outlays of the agent, such as advertising expenses.

agency — the representation of a principal by an agent.

agent — a person who represents another.

associate broker — a person with a real estate broker license who is employed as a salesperson by another broker.

attorney in fact — a holder of a power of attorney.

blind ad — an advertisement that does not disclose that the person submitting the ad is doing so in the capacity of a real estate licensee.

broker — a person who, for a compensation or an expectation of compensation, represents another in the transfer of an interest in real property. A real estate broker must pass the CalBRE's broker exam and be licensed as a real estate broker.

buyer's agent — a real estate broker appointed by a buyer to find property for the buyer.

California Association of Realtors® — the state organization of the National Association of Realtors®.

carbon monoxide (CO) detector — a CO detector/alarm or a CO alarm combined with a smoke detector.

Cartwright Act — the California legislative act that is the basis for California's antitrust laws.

client — an agent's principal

commingling — regarding trust fund accounts, the act of improperly segregating the funds belonging to the agent from the funds received and held on behalf of another.

concealment — the act of preventing disclosure of something.

conflict of interest —a situation in which an individual or organization is involved in several *potentially* competing interests, creating a risk that one interest *might* unduly influence another interest.

conspiracy — in antitrust law, occurs when two or more persons agree to act and the agreed-upon action has the effect of restraining trade.

conversion — the unauthorized misappropriation and use of another's funds or other property.

cooperating broker — a broker who attempts to find a buyer for a property listed by another broker.

coupled with an interest — an aspect of an agency that refers to the agent's having a financial interest in the subject of the agency.

dual agent — a real estate broker who represents both the seller and the buyer in a real estate transaction.

earnest money deposit — a deposit that accompanies an offer by a buyer and is generally held in the broker's trust account.

Easton v. Strassburger — the 1984 landmark California court case that held that real estate agents have an "affirmative duty to conduct a reasonably competent and diligent inspection of the residential property listed for sale and to disclose to prospective purchasers all facts materially affecting the value of the property that such an investigation would reveal."

employee — a person who works for another who directs and controls the services rendered by the person.

employer — a person who directs and controls the services rendered by an employee.

equal dignities rule — a principle of agency law that requires the same formality to create the agency as is required for the act(s) the agent is hired to perform.

estoppel — a legal principle that bars one from alleging or denying a fact because of one's own previous actions or words to the contrary. Ostensible agency can be created by estoppel when a principal and an unauthorized agent act in a manner toward a third-party that leads the third party to rely on the actions of the unauthorized agent, believing that the actions are authorized by the principal.

false promise — a promise made without any intention of performing it.

fiduciary relationship — a special relationship wherein one person owes another an obligation of utmost care, integrity, honesty, trust, confidence, and loyalty.

finder — a person who merely introduces a buyer to a seller, but does nothing else to facilitate a transaction between the buyer and seller, such as rendering assistance in negotiating terms.

general agent — an agent who is authorized by a principal to act for more than a particular act or transaction. General agents are usually an integral part of an ongoing business enterprise.

group action — in antitrust law, two or more persons agreeing to act in a certain way.

group boycott — in antitrust law, the action of two or more brokers agreeing not to deal with another broker or brokers.

implication — the act of creating an agency relationship by an unauthorized agent who acts as if he or she is the agent of a principal, and this principal reasonably believes that the unauthorized agent is acting as his or her actual agent.

independent contractor — a person who performs work for someone, but does so independently in a private trade, business, or profession, with little or no supervision from the person for whom the work is performed.

interpleader — an action that allows for a neutral third party (such as a real estate agent) to avoid liability to two or more claimants (such as a seller and buyer) to the same money or property (such as an earnest money deposit) by forcing the claimants to litigate among themselves, letting the court determine who deserves what while not enmeshing the neutral third party in the litigation.

market allocation — in antitrust law, the process of competitors agreeing to divide up geographic areas or types of products or services they offer to customers.

National "Do Not Call" Registry — a registry established by the Federal Trade Commission to protect consumers from unwanted commercial telephone solicitations.

National Association of Real Estate Brokers — a real estate trade association whose members are called Realtists®.

National Association of Realtors® — the largest real estate trade association in the United States, founded in 1908, whose members are called Realtors®.

negative fraud — the act of not disclosing a material fact which induces someone to enter into a contractual relationship and that causes that person damage or loss.

ostensible agency — an agency in which the principal intentionally, or by want of ordinary care, causes a third person to believe another to be his agent who was not actually employed by him.

post-dated check — a check dated with a date after the date the check is written and signed.

power of attorney — a special written instrument that gives authority to an agent to conduct certain business on behalf of the principal. The agent acting under such a grant is sometimes called an attorney in fact.

price fixing — an agreement between competitors to set prices or price ranges.

principal — the one whom an agent represents.

puffing — the act of expressing a positive opinion about something to induce someone to become a party to a contract.

ratification —the act of creating an agency relationship by a principal who accepts or retains the benefit of an act made by an unauthorized agent.

Real Estate Transfer Disclosure Statement"("TDS") — a form that a seller of a residential real estate property of 1 to 4 units must complete, sign, and have delivered to a buyer. The TDS must also be completed in part by the agent representing the seller, stating whatever defects are discovered or known by the agent.

Real Estate Fund — a special account controlled by the California State Treasury into which real estate license fees are deposited.

Real Estate Recovery Account — a special account into which is credited some of the funds from the Real Estate Fund, which funds are used to reimburse members of the public who have obtained a civil judgment or criminal restitution order against a real estate licensee but have not been able to collect fully from the licensee through normal collection efforts.

Realtist® — a member of the National Association of Real Estate Brokers.

Realtor® — a member of the National Association of Realtors®.

reconciliation — the process of comparing what is in a trust fund account with what should be in the account.

salesperson — a natural person who is employed by a licensed real estate broker to perform acts that require having a real estate license.

secret profit — any compensation or beneficial gain realized by an agent not disclosed to the principal. Real estate agents must always disclose any interest that they or their relatives have in a transaction and obtain their principals' consent.

seller's agent — a real estate broker appointed by the seller to represent the seller.

selling agent — the real estate agent who sells or finds and obtains a buyer for the property in a real estate transaction.

Sherman Act — the federal law passed in 1890 that prohibits agreements, verbal or written, that have the effect of restraining free trade.

special agent — an agent for a particular act or transaction.

stigmatized property — a property having a condition that certain persons may find materially negative in a way that does not relate to the property's actual physical condition.

subagent — an agent of an agent.

trust fund overage — a situation in which a trust fund account balance is greater than it should be.

trust fund shortage — a situation in which a trust fund account balance is less than it should be.

tying arrangement — occurs in antitrust law when the seller conditions the sale of one product or service on the purchase of another product or service.

Quiz for Chapter 7

1. Seemingly incompatible duties of a dual agent are
   a. loyalty and trust
   b. full disclosure and confidentiality
   c. trust and confidentiality
   d. accountability and disclosure

2. What is the principle of agency law that requires the authorization of an agent to have the same formality as is required for the act(s) the agent is hired to perform?
   a. equal dignities rule
   b. ratification
   c. estoppel
   d. implication

3. An agent for a particular act or transaction is called _____. All others are called _____.
   a. a special agent, general agents
   b. a general agent, special agents
   c. a principal, customers
   d. a customer, principles

4. When a principal and an unauthorized agent act in a manner toward a third party that leads the third party to rely on the actions of the unauthorized agent, believing that the actions are authorized by the principal, which type of agency is created?
   a. express agency
   b. ostensible agency
   c. single agency
   d. general agency

5. A principal may give authority to an agent
   a. by accepting or retaining the benefit of an act made by the agent
   b. by signing a written agency agreement with the agent
   c. by entering into an oral agreement with the agent
   d. all of the above

6. A real estate agent generally is a(n)
   a. special agent
   b. specific agent
   c. express agent
   d. both a and c

7. ABC Realty's listing agreement truthfully states, among other things, that the "going rate" for commissions is 5%. ABC's listing agreement is
   a. legal because it is truthful
   b. legal because it doesn't insist on a 5% commission
   c. not an antitrust violation
   d. none of the above

8. Broker Jane and broker Bob orally agree to share commissions on the sale of a house. This oral agreement is
   a. enforceable
   b. invalid due to the statute of frauds
   c. against CalBRE regulations
   d. both b and c

9. Bob and Sally are brokers who own separate realty companies. They meet at a C.A.R. convention, where Bob tells Sally that Joe, a broker they both know, is dishonest and an embarrassment to the profession. Bob says that he has stopped doing business with Joe and thinks that Sally should, too. Sally simply nods, but after the convention she stops dealing with Joe.
   a. Bob could be found guilty of group boycott.
   b. Bob but not Sally could be found guilty of group boycott.
   c. Sally could be found guilty of group boycott.
   d. both a and c

10. Which of the following persons owes a fiduciary duty to clients?
   a. a salesperson
   b. a broker
   c. neither a nor b
   d. both a and b

11. To find an action a violation of antitrust law, the act must
   a. ensure that prices are not as low as possible
   b. increase prices
   c. maximize profits
   d. none of the above

12. Which of the following words least belongs with the others?
   a. ratification
   b. ostensible
   c. implication
   d. express agreement

13. A real estate salesperson may accept payment from
   a. the broker who employs the salesperson
   b. the seller
   c. the buyer
   d. both a and b

14. An agent's authority can arise from
   a. a listing agreement

    b. what is considered usual in the ordinary course of business

    c. what is considered necessary to perform the agency duties

    d. all of the above

15. The equal dignities rule refers to

    a. an agent's duty to treat both the seller and the buyer fairly

    b. an agent's obligation to always act with skill and dignity

    c. an agent's obligation to be sure that the seller approves of the agent's actions

    d. none of the above

16. A real estate agent is required to exercise

    a. skill

    b. good faith

    c. fair dealing

    d. all of the above

17. Joe is a developer. Janet, a builder, wants to buy a lot from Joe and build a house on it. Joe agrees to Janet's offer on condition that when Janet sells the house, she do so through Joe's familiar broker, Bob. This is an example of

    a. a tying arrangement

    b. a group boycott

    c. price fixing,

    d. market allocation

18. Which of the following terms least belongs with the others?

    a. reconciliation

    b. trust fund ratification

    c. trust fund shortage

    d. trust fund overage

19. A blind ad is an advertisement that

    a. states no price for the offered property

    b. states that neither blind persons nor any other persons with a disability are discriminated against by the agent or by the seller of the property

    c. does not state that the broker is incapable of performing the required visual inspection of the property

    d. none of the above

20. An agent's business card must contain

    a. the designation that the agent is a real estate agent

    b. the number of years the agent has been a licensee

    c. the agent's license identification number

    d. both a and c

21. A dual agent owes a fiduciary duty to the buyer as well as to the seller. Therefore, the agent must

    a. disclose to the seller that the buyer is willing to pay more

    b. refuse to represent the buyer

    c. disclose that the seller is willing to take less

    d. none of the above

22. The *Easton v. Strassburger* decision

    a. held that an agent has a duty to make a visual inspection of the property

    b. suggested that the decision would apply to sales of commercial real estate

    c. held that an agent must disclose to prospective purchasers all facts materially affecting the value of the property

    d. both a and c

23. Bob is a broker who represents the seller, Jane. Joe, a prospective buyer, asks Bob: "Do you think that Jane would entertain a somewhat lower price?" Bob answers: "If you make a reasonable and fair offer." Bob has violated

    a. his duty of full disclosure

    b. his duty of utmost care

    c. his duty to refrain from price-fixing

    d. no law

24. A broker is always the agent of

    a. the seller

    b. the buyer

    c. whoever pays the commission

    d. none of the above

25. Janet is a broker who owns a real estate company that employs 5 salespersons. At a company meeting, Janet announces that she is raising the commission rate charged to clients from 6% to 7% and that all her salespersons should do likewise, which they all do.

    a. Janet could be guilty of price-fixing, but her salespersons could not

    b. Janet and all of her salespersons could be guilty of price-fixing

    c. Janet could be guilty of group boycott

    d. none of the above

26. A real estate agent most likely is

    a. an ostensible agent

    b. a special agent

    c. a general agent

    d. none of the above

27. Which of the following persons must have a real estate license?

    a. a finder

    b. a person who holds a power of attorney to sell a house

    c. a resident manager of an apartment building

    d. none of the above

28. What are the two types of California agency?

    a. fiduciary and express

    b. express and ostensible

    c. ostensible and actual

    d. none of the above

29. Joe is an agent who represents Jane. Joe receives two offers: one for $250,000 from a person with excellent credit and one for $250,000 from someone who just came out of bankruptcy a year ago and, Joe's been told, is often late paying his rent. Joe should

    a. present Jane with the offer from the person with excellent credit and wait to see if she accepts it before presenting her with the other offer

    b. throw away the offer that Joe thinks is worthless

    c. present Jane with both offers

    d. either a or c

30. Which of the following concepts least belongs with the others?

    a. expiration of term

    b. death or incapacity

    c. revocation by a principal

    d. fulfillment of purpose

31. If a purchase agreement contains an "as is" clause

    a. the listing agent need not perform a visual inspection

    b. the selling agent need not disclose material facts

    c. the seller is relieved from disclosing defects that are observable on reasonable inspection

    d. none of the above

32. It is not true that an agent's personal assistant may

    a. make outgoing calls to canvass for interest in using the services of a real estate agent

    b. place "FOR SALE" signs on the property without the principal's consent

    c. accept trust funds from customers

    d. do any of the above

33. Broker Bob tells broker Jane, who works in a different realty company, that he will split his commission with her if she finds a buyer for a particular property that he has listed. Janet agrees. This is an example of

    a. price-fixing

    b. market allocation

    c. tying arrangement

    d. none of the above

34. Broker Joe is a co-owner of a house with Bob, who signed a listing agreement with Joe to sell the house. The agency created by the listing agreement can be terminated by

    a. the death of Joe

    b. Bob's revoking the agency

    c. neither a nor b

    d. both a and b

35. Jane is a client of Joe, who is an attorney. Joe helps Jane sell her house and receives compensation for his services in selling the house. Joe
    a. must have a real estate license to receive compensation for selling the house
    b. must deal fairly with the buyer
    c. must split his compensation with the buyer's agent
    d. none of the above

36. Jason is 16 years of age. Broker Sally thought that Jason was older, signed a listing agreement with him, and closed the purchase of a house on his behalf. A month later, Jason wrote a letter to Sally, stating how much he loved the house and how grateful he was for her services. Even though Jason is a minor
    a. he ratified the agency relationship
    b. he would be estopped from an action to void the agency and the purchase
    c. he and Sally had a valid agency relationship by implication
    d. none of the above

37. Which of the following items may be trust funds?
    a. a check made payable to the agent
    b. a pearl necklace
    c. both a and b
    d. neither a nor b

38. Unless the buyer gives the agent instructions that an earnest money deposit should be held by the agent and not negotiated until the seller accepts the offer, the agent must no later than how many business days place the earnest money deposit in the hands of the seller, into a neutral escrow depository, or into a trust fund account in the name of the broker as trustee?
    a. 2
    b. 3
    c. 5
    d. 10

39. A broker must within how many days of receiving a commission into a trust funds account withdraw the amount of the commission from the account?
    a. The broker cannot withdraw any funds without the principal's written consent.
    b. 10 days
    c. 25 days
    d. 30 days

40. The listing agent must deliver the agency disclosure form to the seller before
    a. entering into the listing agreement
    b. presenting an offer to the seller

c. accepting an offer from a prospective buyer

d. none of the above

Answers to Chapter 7 Quiz

1. b. A dual agent owes fiduciary duties to both the seller and the buyer — duties that generally include full disclosure and confidentiality. However, a dual agent may not, without express approval from the buyer, disclose to the seller that the buyer is willing to pay a higher price than offered, nor may a dual agent, without express approval from the seller, disclose to the buyer that the seller is willing to take a lower price than the listing price.

2. a. Under a principle of agency law known as the equal dignities rule, the authorization of an agent requires the same formality as is required for the act(s) the agent is hired to perform. CC §2309.

3. a. California Civil Code §2297 states: "An agent for a particular act or transaction is called a special agent. All others are called general agents."

4. b. When a principal and an unauthorized agent act in a manner toward a third party that leads the third party to rely on the actions of the unauthorized agent, believing that the actions are authorized by the principal, an ostensible agency is created by estoppel.

5. d. Agency can be created in numerous ways, including ratification (answer a) or by oral or written express agreement.

6. d. Real estate agents are nearly always agents of a principal for a specific transaction, and the agreement between the principal and the agent nearly always is (and definitely should be) in writing.

7. d. Stating what is the "going rate" and stating a specific commission rate are likely to be antitrust violations, as they both give the impression that the commission rate is fixed. The truthfulness of the statements is immaterial.

8. a. An oral agreement between brokers to split the commission on a real estate transaction is contrary neither to the statute of frauds nor to antitrust laws. However, because the terms of an oral agreement are often subject to dispute and difficult to prove, it is highly recommended that a commission split between brokers be in writing.

9. d. The appearance of an implied agreement to exclude another broker from their business dealings is enough for finding a group boycott.

10. d. A broker owes fiduciary duties to his or her clients and the salesperson owes the same duties to the employing broker's clients as does the broker.

11. d. Price fixing can result from fixing prices low, high, reasonable, or fair. No finding that that profits are maximized or prices increased need be found.

12. b. Actual agency can be created by ratification, implication, or express agreement.

13. a. All compensation to a salesperson for services that require a real estate license must come only from the employing broker.

14. d. An agent's authority can arise in any of the three ways listed.

15. d. The equal dignity's rule states that an authorization of the agency requires the same formality as is required for the acts the agent is hired to perform.

16. d. A real estate agent is required to exercise the three attributes listed and to perform all duties required of a fiduciary relationship with the principal.

17. a. A tying arrangement occurs in antitrust law when the seller conditions the sale of one product or service on the purchase of another product or service.

18. b. Reconciliation, trust fund shortage, and trust fund overage all relate to the proper handling of trust fund accounts.

19. d. A blind ad is an advertisement that does not disclose the identity of the agent submitting the advertisement for publication.

20. d. An agent's business card must contain both the designation that the person is a real estate agent and the agent's license identification number.

21. d. By law, a dual agent may not inform the seller that the buyer is willing to pay more; nor may the agent inform the buyer that the seller is willing to take less.

22. d. The *Easton v. Strassburger* decision held that an agent has a duty to make a visual inspection of the property and disclose all facts materially affecting the value of the property to prospective buyers.

23. b. Bob owes Jane a duty of good faith and utmost care — both violated by suggesting that she might accept a lower price.

24. d. Be careful of the word "always." A broker can represent the seller, the buyer, or both. If the broker represents the buyer, and the seller pays the entire commission, the broker did not represent the person who paid the commission.

25. d. A real estate company is generally considered to be a single entity for antitrust purposes, and one of the requirements to find an antitrust violation is that there existed an agreement between two or more parties.

26. b. Nearly all real estate agents represent principals for a specific transaction and are, therefore, special agents.

27. d. A real estate license is not required to perform any of the three listed activities.

28. c. The California Civil Code specifically states that the two types of California agency are actual and ostensible.

29. c. Joe must present Jane with *all* offers as soon as he reasonably can.

30. c. Though all three of these concepts relate to the termination of agency, a, b, and d result in termination by operation of law, whereas c results in termination by action of the parties.

31. c. An "as is" clause in a real estate purchase agreement does not relieve the agents involved from the usual duties to inspect and disclose; however, it does relieve the seller from disclosing those defects that are observable on reasonable investigation.

32. b. It is permissible for a real estate assistant to place a FOR SALE sign on the principal's property, but only with the principal's consent.

33. d. A broker's agreement with a cooperating broker on a commission split on a particular property is permissible.

34. a. Because Joe's agency was coupled with an interest, Bob may not revoke the agency.

35. b. An attorney who represents a client need not have a real estate license or split any compensation received with the buyer's agent unless there was an agreement otherwise. The buyer's agent would look to the buyer for compensation.

36. d. In order to ratify an agency, the principal must have the power to authorize the act that the agent was hired to perform. A minor has no power to authorize the purchase of real estate.

37. c. Anything of value received by an agent on behalf of a client or customer must be included in the broker's trust funds.

38. b. Unless the buyer gives the agent instructions that an earnest money deposit should be held by the agent and not negotiated until the seller accepts the offer, the agent must within 3 business days perform one of the acts listed.

39. c. In order not to violate the rule against commingling personal funds with trust funds, a broker must withdraw any commission earned from a transaction within 25 days of receiving such commission.

40. a. The listing agent must deliver the agency disclosure form to the seller before the seller signs the listing agreement.

Chapter

8

Real Estate Math

It is best while reading this chapter and working through the questions presented to have a basic calculator handy (one that simply adds, subtracts, multiplies and divides — not a "scientific" or a "financial" calculator). Currently, the centers where real estate license exams are given supply a basic calculator to each examinee (you are not permitted to bring your own), so getting used to solving math problems on such a calculator is highly recommended.

There is no indication from past exams that you need to be familiar with math concepts beyond what is taught in grade school, so even if math was never your favorite subject, you should not fear the types of questions that appear on real estate license exams. Remember, you will be taking an exam on real estate principles, not a math exam. The only math you are expected to know is the basic math that will help you solve practical, everyday real estate problems like the problems presented in this chapter. Memorize the few measurement correspondences that we have already seen in Chapter 1, become familiar with a few simple equations and how they apply to practical real estate problems, and you will do just fine.

Here are the measurement correspondences that you should memorize:

- 1 mile = 5,280 feet or 320 rods
- 1 rod = 16½ ft.
- 1 township = 6 mi. x 6 mi. = 36 sections
- 1 section = 1 mi. x 1 mi. = 640 acres
- 1 acre = 43,560 square feet
- 1 square acre ≈ 208.7 ft. x 208.7 ft. (i.e., a "square acre" has 208.7 ft. on each side.)

Also, remember that a *commercial acre* = the buildable part of an acre that remains after subtracting land needed for streets, sidewalks, alleys, curbs, etc.

CONVERTING DECIMALS, PERCENTAGES, AND FRACTIONS

To convert a percentage to a decimal, simply remove the % sign and move the decimal point two places to the left:

$15\% \rightarrow .15$

$74.6\% \rightarrow .746$

To convert a decimal to a percent, move the decimal point two places to the right and add the % sign:

$.75 \rightarrow 75\%$

$1.12 \rightarrow 112\%$

To convert a fraction to a decimal, divide the numerator (the number on top) by the denominator (the number on the bottom):

$^1/_5 \rightarrow 1 \div 5 \rightarrow .20$

$^3/_4 \rightarrow 3 \div 4 \rightarrow .75$

To convert a decimal to a fraction first write down the number like this: **decimal/1**. Then multiply both the top number and the bottom number by 10 for every number after the decimal point, and then reduce the resulting fraction, if possible, by dividing both the top number and the bottom number by the same number:

$$.75 \rightarrow \frac{.75}{1} \rightarrow \frac{.75 \times 100}{1 \times 100} \rightarrow \frac{75}{100} \rightarrow \frac{75/25}{100/25} \rightarrow {}^3/_4$$

$$.125 \rightarrow \frac{.125}{1} \rightarrow \frac{.125 \times 1000}{1 \times 1000} \rightarrow \frac{125}{1000} \rightarrow \frac{125/25}{1000/25} \rightarrow \frac{5}{40} \rightarrow \frac{5/5}{40/5} \rightarrow {}^1/_8$$

Many everyday real estate issues involve percentages: commissions, rate of return on investments, depreciation, and proration. We will discuss examples of each of these kinds of issues and how percentages apply to each.

Commission Problems:

Because nearly every real estate agent expects to receive commissions (many, hopefully!), it is not unlikely that a question or two relating to commissions might appear on an exam.

Example 1: *Jessica is a real estate salesperson who found a buyer for a home that sold for $800,000. Jessica's employing broker received a 5% commission for the sale. The agreement between the broker and Jessica provides that she receive 40% of the broker's commission on every sale she procures. What is Jessica's commission on this transaction?*

Here the solution is to first find the broker's commission:

5% of $800,000 = .05 × $800,000 = $40,000. Jessica is to receive 40% of $40,000 = .40 × $40,000 = $16,000.

Another way to think about such a problem is to note that Jessica receives 40% of 5% = .40 × .05 = .02 = 2% of the sales price. Using this 2% figure, we find that 2% of $800,000 = .02 × $800,000 = $16,000.

Example 2: A somewhat more interesting problem (writers of textbooks are fond of using the word "interesting" rather than "difficult") is as follows:

Bob is a salesperson who works for broker Janet. Bob's agreement with Janet is that he gets a commission of 40% of whatever commission Janet receives on sales made by Bob. Bob procures a sale of a house that was listed by broker Susan, who had a cooperating agent agreement with Janet to split the commission on the sale 50-50. Susan's listing agreement with the owner called for a 6% commission. Bob's commission on the sale was $6,000. How much did the house sell for?

Because they tend to be long-winded, these types of problems *appear* to involve much more thought than they actually do — they simply need to be approached methodically, step-by-simple-step, until the answer falls out:

The problem tells us that:
$6,000 = 40% of 50% of 6% of Sales Price
      = (.4 × .5 × .06) × Sales Price
      = .012 × Sales Price (i.e., 1.2% of Sales Price)
Therefore, dividing each side of the equation by .012, we get
$500,000 = Sales Price

Example 3: *Ernesto sold his house, receiving for $423,000 after paying a 6% commission. For how much did Ernesto sell his house?*
We are told that the price the house sold for — its "Sales Price" — minus the commission paid was $423,000. Therefore,
Sales Price - Commission = $423,000
Sales Price - (6% of Sales Price) = $423,000

Sales price - (.06 × Sales Price) = $423,000
.94 × Sales Price = $423,000
Finally, dividing both sides of the equation by .94, we get
Sales Price = $450,000

Investment Problems:

Investment problems involve four concepts:

1. Investment — the amount of dollars invested
2. Income — the amount of dollars earned (or lost) from the investment
3. Rate — the rate of return on the investment (often referred to as the "ROI")
4. Time — the amount of time the Investment is earning the Rate

Investment problems involve the following relationships (formula):
Income = Investment × Rate × Time
When dealing with investment problems (as well as with other problems, such as profit and loss, interest, and depreciation problems), it is ***crucially important*** to carefully pay close attention to the time periods provided, and asked for, in the question. If there are different time periods presented, the first thing you should do is convert all the periods to the same value measured in years, quarters, months or days.

Example 4: *Joe wants to make $750 per month from an investment that will earn 5% per year. How much must Joe invest to obtain his desired monthly investment income?*

Here we are told that Joe wants to earn $750 *per month*, which is
12 × $750 = $9,000 *per year*. Therefore, the problem has given us
Income = $9,000 (per year)
Rate = 5% (per year)
Putting these given bits of information into our formula, we have:
$9,000 = 5% (*per year*) of Investment for 1 year
        = .05 (per year) × Investment × 1 year
By dividing both sides of this equation by .05, we get

$$\frac{\$9,000}{.05} = \text{Investment}$$

$180,000 = Investment

The question in Example 4 involved the rate of return on Joe's investment where the investment Joe made (the principal) was not yet converted back into dollars. Such a situation usually involves investing money in some kind of interest-bearing account. Other investment problems involve situations where the principal amount invested (the Investment) is eventually sold (the Sales Price). In such problems Income = Sales Price - Investment.
Therefore, the investment formula

$$\text{Income} = \text{Investment} \times \text{Rate} \times \text{Time}$$

becomes:

$$\text{Sales Price} - \text{Investment} = \text{Investment} \times \text{Rate} \times \text{Time}$$

Example 5: *Sarah bought her house for $300,000 and sold it for $375,000 five years later. What was the rate of return on her investment?*

The problem tells us that Sarah's Income (Sales Price - Investment) is $75,000. Therefore,

$75,000 = $ Investment $\times$ Rate (*per year*) $\times$ Time (in *years*)

$75,000 = $300,000 \times$ Rate (*per year*) $\times$ 5 (*years*)

[Remember to keep the time periods consistent throughout the formula!]

Therefore, by dividing both sides of the equation by $300,000 $\times$ 5 (years) we get:

$$\frac{\$75,000}{\$300,000 \times 5 \, (years)} = \text{Rate (per } year)$$

.05 (per year) = Rate (per year)

5% (per year) = Rate (per year)

Note that if the question asked for the rate per month, the answer would be $\frac{.05}{12}$ = .00417 (rounded off) or .417% per month.

Investors in property are often concerned with what is called the **capitalization rate** (the "cap rate"), which is simply what we have been calling Rate calculated on an annual basis and where the Income is the net annual income of the property.

Example 6: *Susan is interested in a building that she has learned produces $100,000 net income per year. The capitalization rate that she wants to earn is 8%. What is the maximum price she should pay for this building?*

The maximum price she should pay would be the amount of Investment that would yield Income of $100,000 each year at the Rate of 8% per year. Using our formula

Income = Investment × Rate × Time, we get
$100,000 = Investment × 8% × 1 year
$100,000 = Investment × .08
$1,250,000 = Investment

Investors also sometimes purchase promissory notes at a discount, as in the following example:

Example 7: *Susan owns a promissory note for $10,000 payable in 12 months at a rate of 6% interest, which is also payable at the end of the note term. Wanting to convert the note into cash, Susan sells the note to her friend Bob at a 5% discount. Assuming that the note and interest are paid in full at the end of the note term, what rate of return will Bob receive?*

Here the question asks for a Rate, so we must figure out the amount of Income Bob will earn and the amount of his Investment. His Investment is $10,000 - (5% of $10,000) = $10,000 - $500 = $9,500. His income is 6% of $10,000 + $500 which is $600 + $500 = $1,100. Therefore, Bob's Rate = Income ÷ Investment which is $1,100 ÷ $9,500 = 11.58% (rounded off).

Depreciation Problems:

Although many different ways to calculate depreciation are allowed by law (depending on what law one has to satisfy), the only method of depreciation that appears to be tested on real estate license exams is **straight-line depreciation**, which assumes that the property depreciates by an *equal amount* each year.

Depreciation is based on what is considered the **useful life** (also referred to as the **economic life**) of the property and on the estimated **residual value** (also referred to as **salvage value** or **scrap value**) of the property at the end of the property's useful life. Some things, such as computers, have a much shorter useful life than do buildings, so it is always important when considering depreciation to know what the useful life of the item being depreciated is. The straight-line depreciation is defined as:

$$\text{Annual Depreciation} = \frac{\text{Cost of Property} - \text{Residual Value}}{\text{useful life of the property in years}}$$

Thus, if the property has a 5-year useful life and no residual value, the rate of (straight-line) depreciation is:

$$\frac{100\%}{5 \text{ years}} = 20\% \text{ per year}$$

Example 8: *Evan purchases a building for $3,000,000 that has a useful life of 30 years and salvage value of $0. After 10 years, what is the value of the building, if by "value" we mean the original cost less accumulated straight-line depreciation?*

Here the depreciation rate is:

$$\frac{100\%}{30 \text{ years}} = 3 \text{ 1/3 \% per year}$$

$3^1/_3$ % per year × 10 years = 33 1/3% depreciation

33 1/3% of the initial value = 33 1/3% × $3 million = $1,000,000
Therefore, value = cost - depreciation = $2,000,000

Interest Problems: Interest is the "rent" we pay to possess, use, and enjoy someone else's money. The yearly rent for each dollar we use (borrow) is called the interest rate — if we pay 8¢ each year for each dollar, the interest rate is 8% per year.

Interest problems generally involve four simple concepts:

1. *Interest Rate* (which, to avoid wordiness, we will call Rate);
2. *Principal* (the amount of money borrowed);
3. *Time* (the number of years or fraction of years the principal is borrowed);
4. *Interest Due and Owing* (which we will call Interest).

Because the interest due and owing (Interest) is equal to the interest rate (Rate) times the amount of money borrowed (Principal) times the amount of time the money is borrowed (Time),

Interest = Rate × Principal × Time

The above formula is known as **simple interest**, which considers interest to be generated only on the principal invested. A more rapid method of generating interest earnings is referred to as compounding. **Compound interest** is generated when accumulated interest is reinvested to generate interest earnings from previous interest earnings. Though the amount of interest generated can be revved up by compounding yearly, semiannually, quarterly, daily, or even continuously, real estate exams stick with simple interest, as do most real estate loans on which interest is paid monthly. There is a story — perhaps apocryphal — that Albert Einstein once said that the power of compounding is the eighth wonder of the world.

When calculating interest, it is also important to know what **day count convention** to use. An exact interest calculation would take into account the precise number of days money is loaned: 30 days for some months, 31 or 28 or 29 for other months; 365 days for some years, 366 for leap years. In the days before computers, such calculations would have been quite burdensome, so the **30/360 day count convention** was adopted to simplify interest calculations. When using the 30/360 day count convention, each month is considered to have 30 days, and each year is considered to have 360 days. A year consisting of 360 days with 12 months of 30 days each is often referred to as a **statutory year**, or a banker's year. The 30/360 day count convention for calculating interest is standard in the real estate market, is the method used on real estate exams, and is the method that will be used throughout this text. Interest calculated by the 30/360 day count convention is referred to as **ordinary interest**.

Example 9: *What is the interest on a $400,000 loan for 1 year, 2 months, and 10 days at 6% interest (using a statutory year)?*

The time elapsed is 360 days + 60 days +10 days = 430 days.
430 ÷ 360 = 1.19444 years. Therefore, applying our formula
Interest = Rate x Principal x Time, we get
Interest = .06 x $400,000 x 1.19444 = $28,666.56

Example 10: *Jessica borrows $12,000 from her friend Susan. The terms of the loan are that principal will be paid back in equal monthly installments over a five-year period along with the interest that was generated at the annual rate of 6% during the month on the outstanding balance of principal owing. What is Jessica's payment to Susan at the end of the second month?*

To answer this question, we first have to answer another question; namely, how much principal does Jessica pay Susan at the end of the first month? This is due to the fact that Susan's first month payment will reduce the principal amount on which the second month payment must be calculated.

Because there are 60 months in 5 years, the amount of Susan's monthly payment attributable to principal is $12,000 ÷ 60 = $200. Therefore, the amount of principal owed after the first-month payment is made is $12,000 - $200 = $11,800. Consequently, the second month payment will be $200 + the interest due on $11,800 *for one month*. Because the interest rate is 6%

annually, the monthly rate is 1/2%. Thus, the second-month payment is $200 + 1/2% of $11,800 = $259.

Amortization Charts

Although interest and principal payments for loans are now calculated on financial calculators or on calculation software freely available on the Internet, we will look briefly at a simplified amortization chart to get a feel for how such a chart was used (in the old days) to calculate the monthly payments for fixed-rate loans at various interest rates. (See Figure 8.1).

The chart displays in the left column the interest rate, and in columns to the right, the term in years of a fixed-rate, fully amortized loan. To find the monthly payment *per $1,000* principal borrowed, simply find the intersection of the rate and term of the loan.

Fig. 8.1

Monthly Payment Per $1,000 on Fixed-Rate, Fully Amortized Loans				
Rate	10-year term	15-year term	30-year term	40-year term
4%	10.125	7.397	4.775	4.180
5%	10.607	7.908	5.369	4.822
6%	11.102	8.439	5.996	5.503
7%	11.611	8.989	6.653	6.215
8%	12.133	9.557	7.338	6.954

Example 11: *Susan makes payments of $936 per month, including 6% interest on a fixed-rate, fully amortized 30-year loan. What was the initial amount of her loan?*

Finding where 6% and a 30-year term intersect in the chart, we obtain the number 5.996 which is the dollar amount per month per $1,000 of initial loan. $936 ÷ 5.996 = $156.104 per $1,000. $156.104 x 1000 = $156,104

Proration Problems:

As a general rule, at the close of escrow in a real estate transaction certain allocations of expenses incurred in the ordinary course of property ownership must be made. For example, if the escrow closes midyear or midmonth, the seller may have prepaid taxes, insurance, or association dues, in which case credit to the seller's account should be made. Conversely, if the seller is behind on paying taxes or insurance, etc., the seller's account should be debited. Such an adjustment of expenses that either have been paid or are in arrears in proportion to actual time of ownership as of the closing or other agreed-upon date is called **proration**. Proration, like ordinary interest, is generally calculated according to the 30/360 day count convention (statutory year).

To compute proration, follow these steps:

1. determine which, if any, expenses are to be prorated;
2. determine to whom the expenses should be credited or debited;
3. determine how many days the expenses are to be prorated;
4. calculate the per day proration amount; and
5. multiply the number of days by the per day proration amount.

Example 12: *Susan purchased a condo that had been rented from Bob at $1,500 a month. Escrow closed on September 16. Who pays whom in regard to proration of the rent?*

Rent is normally collected *in advance* on the first day of the month, so unless stated otherwise one should make this assumption in proration of rent problems. Under this assumption, Bob received $1,500 on or about September 1, but only deserved to keep half of the month's rent because Susan acquired ownership of the condo on September 16. Therefore, Susan should be credited $750 at the close of escrow.

Example 13: *Emily purchased a home from Bob on which Bob had an outstanding loan balance of $385,000 on April 20, the day that escrow closed. The interest rate on the loan was 5% and was payable with the loan payment on the first of each month. If Emily assumed Bob's loan, who should have paid whom in regard to proration of the interest?*

Interest on home loans is normally paid *after* it has accrued, and we will make that assumption here. Therefore, the seller, Bob, owned the home for 19 days before closing — 19 days for which he had not paid the interest on the loan as of the closing of escrow. Emily should, therefore, have been credited for 19 day's interest.

The annual interest on the loan was 5%, and $385,000 was the loan balance on which interest would be paid by Emily (who assumed the loan) on May 1. Figured on an *annual* basis, interest of 5% on $385,000 = $19,250, so to obtain the *daily* interest amount for each day of April we divide $19,250 by 360 (using a statutory year) to get $53.4722. [Note that in proration problems it is best to use at least four numbers after the decimal point until you get to the final answer, which can be rounded off.] Because Emily should have been credited for 19 days, her credit should have been 19 × $53.4722 = $1,015.97.

Length and Square Footage Problems

When calculating the square footage of something, remember that the area of a rectangle is base × height and the area of a triangle is ½ × base × height.

Example 14: *Kevin is going to purchase the lot shown in Figure 8.2 and build on it a house and garage, also shown in Figure 8.2. He has been quoted the following:*

- *$150 per square foot for the house*
- *$40 per square foot for the garage*
- *$10 per square foot for the land*

What is the total amount that Evan will pay for this lot, house, and garage?

First we calculate the square footage of each item:

house area = 60' × 30' = 1,800 ft.²
garage area = 25' × 18' = 450 ft.²
lot area = ½ × 100 × 150 = 7,500 ft.²

cost of house = 1800 ft.² × $150 per ft.² = $270,000
cost of garage = 450 ft.² × $40 per ft.² = $18,000
cost of the lot = 7500 ft.² × $10 per ft.² = $75,000
                              Total = $363,000

Fig. 8.2

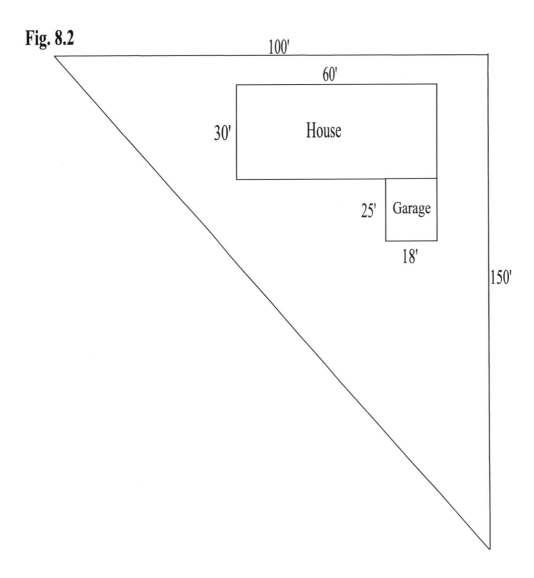

Key Terms for Chapter 8

30/360 day count convention — a convention for calculating interest or allocating expenses in which each month is considered to have 30 days, and each year is considered to have 360 days.

capitalization rate — the annual net income of a property divided by the initial investment in, or value of, the property.

compound interest — the type of interest that is generated when accumulated interest is reinvested to generate interest earnings from previous interest earnings.

economic life — the useful life of a property.

ordinary interest — interest calculated by the 30/360 day count convention.

proration — an adjustment of expenses that either have been paid or are in arrears in proportion to actual time of ownership as of the closing of escrow or other agreed-upon date.

simple interest — the type of interest that is generated only on the principal invested.

residual value — an estimate of the reasonable fair market value of a property at the end of its useful life.

salvage value — residual value.

scrap value — residual value.

statutory year — contrasted with a calendar year, a "year" period consisting of 360 days, with 12 months of 30 days (also referred to as a banker's year).

straight-line depreciation — the expensing of a property by equal amounts over the useful life of the property, determined by subtracting from the cost of the property the estimated residual value of the property and dividing that amount by the useful life of the property measured in years.

useful life — the estimated period during which a property generates revenue (if the property is an income property) or usefulness (if the property, such as a private residence, has value other than income value).

Quiz for Chapter 8

1. Ernesto owns a 300 yd.² rectangular lot with frontage of 50 feet. What is the depth of Ernesto's lot?
   a. 6 yards
   b. 54 feet
   c. 9 yards
   d. 18 feet

2. Jessica gets a 30-year, 6% level-payment loan (i.e., a loan whereby periodic payments are equal and the loan is fully paid off at the end of the term) of $400,000 to purchase a house. Her monthly payments are $2,400. What is her interest charge for the second month?
   a. $2,000
   b. $1,998
   c. $1,996
   d. $2,400

3. Jessica bought her house for $200,000. Five years later she sold the house for $230,000. What percentage gross profit did she make on the sale of the house?
   a. 3%
   b. 5%
   c. 15%
   d. 20%

4. If Oliver wishes to deposit enough money into a savings account that pays 3% annual interest to earn $1,000 each month, how much does he need to deposit into this account?
   a. $33,333
   b. $99,999
   c. $400,000
   d. none of the above

5. Adrienne owns an office building worth $1,450,000 on which she earns 12% gross income annually. What is her annual gross income from this investment?
   a. $175,000
   b. $168,000
   c. $162,000
   d. none of the above

6. A 15,000 ft.² lot costs $21 per square foot. The 2,700 ft.² house on the lot costs $125 per square foot, and the 430 ft.² garage costs $35 per square foot. How much does this property cost?
   a. $652,550
   b. $667,550
   c. $654,050
   d. none of the above

7. After owning a building for nine years, Kevin sold it for $1,750,000. His initial cost for the building was $2,150,000. What was the average annual rate of depreciation (loss in value) of the building?
   a. 2.07%
   b. 2.54%
   c. 2.33%
   d. 2.86%

8. Sam is a salesperson who receives 50% of the commission on all sales commissions that his employing broker, Bob, receives due to Sam's effort. Sam receives a commission of $8,450 due to his procurement of the sale of a house for which Bob had a 6% commission listing agreement. How much did the house sell for?
   a. $140,833
   b. $422,500
   c. $280,000
   d. none of the above

9. Susan owns a 2-acre rectangular lot and wishes to divide it into 4 lots of equal size, each having a depth of 200 feet. What would be the width of each of these lots?
   a. 108.9 feet
   b. 217.8 feet
   c. 54.45 feet
   d. none of the above

10. A building depreciates by 2% each year. How many years will it take for the building to be worth only 70% of its initial value?
   a. 20 years
   b. 18 years
   c. 16 years
   d. none of the above

11. An office building rents for $14,500 per month. If the building cost $2 million, what is the annual gross rental income rate of this property?
   a. 8.7%
   b. 0.725%
   c. 1.25%
   d. 8.33%

12. Susan is a salesperson who sold a 1/4 acre lot for $17 per square foot. The commission rate her broker received was 8%, and Susan split the

commission with her broker 50-50. How much did Susan earn on the sale?

a. $29,620.80

b. $14,810.40

c. $7,405.20

d. none of the above

13. Emily, Susan, and Janet are partners who own a building that produces rent of $17,000 per month. Susan owns a 41% interest in the building. How much rental income from the building does Susan earn each year?

a. $6,970

b. $68,000

c. $8,500

d. none of the above

14. Jon financed his home with an 85% loan at a fixed annual rate of 5½%. Jon paid $3,895.83 interest the first month. How much did Jon pay for the house (rounded to the nearest dollar)?

a. $849,999

b. $722,499

c. $70,833

d. $999,999

15. A rectangular lot contains 4.7 acres and is 220 feet wide. What is the depth of the lot?

a. 1023.66 feet

b. 930.60 feet

c. 969.05 feet

d. 974.6 feet

16. A square lot of 200 feet on each side has a building setback of 25 feet from each side. What is the maximum square footage of a three-story office building that can be built on this lot?

a. 30,625 ft.^{2}

b. 90,000 ft.^{2}

c. 67,500 ft.^{2}

d. 91,875 ft.^{2}

17. Jennifer owns a rectangular lot that is 175 feet deep and 105 feet wide. She has contracted to have a 4 1/2 foot high fence built around the lot. Materials cost will be $.55 per square foot and the labor cost will be $2.15 per linear foot. What will the fence cost Jennifer?

a. $2,590.00

b. $46,682.12

c. $1,980.00

d. $1,295.00

18. A road runs along the west side of the S½ of the NW¼ of a section. If the road is 45 feet wide how many acres does the road contain?

a. 2.727 acres

b. .682 acres

c. 1.364 acres

d. .341 acres

19. A triangular lot with height 105 feet and width 95 feet sold for $12 per square foot. What did the lot sell for?

a. $119,700

b. $29,925

c. $55,775

d. $59,850

20. Julio sold a house for $475,000 and received $11,875 in commission. What commission rate did Julio receive on the sale?

a. 3%

b. 3.5%

c. 2%

d. none of the above

Answers to Chapter 8 Quiz

1. b. A square yard is 3' x 3' = 9 ft.², so the lot is 300 yd.² x 9 ft.²/yd.² = 2,700 ft.². Since the frontage is 50 feet the depth is 2,700 feet ÷ 50 feet = 54 feet.

2. b. Jessica's per month interest rate is 6% ÷ 12 equals 1/2%. Therefore, the interest payment during the first month is 1/2% of $400,000 = $2,000. Since she paid $2,400 for the first month, $400 went to paying down the principal. Therefore, for the second month, her interest charge would be 1/2% of $399,600 = $1,198.

3. c. She made $30,000 gross profit. $30,000 ÷ $200,000 = 15%. Note that the question does not ask for a *rate* of profit.

4. c. Oliver wants to earn interest at the rate of $12,000 per year. $12,000 ÷ 3% = $400,000.

5. d. $1,450,000 at 12% = $174,000.

6. b. Lot: 15,000 ft.² x $21/ft.² = $315,000
   House: 2,700 ft.² x 125/ft.² = $337,500
   Garage: 430 ft.² x 35/ft.² = $15,050
   Total = $667,550

7. a. Loss = $2,150,000 $-1,750,000 = $400,000.
   Average annual loss = $400,000 ÷ 9 years = $44,444.4444/yr.
   $44,444.4444/yr. ÷ $2,150,000 = 2.07% per year.

8. d. Sam effectively receives 3% of the sales he makes from Bob's listing. (Note that there would be no cooperating agent involved in such cases this.) Therefore, $8,450 = 3% of Sales Price.
   $8,450 ÷ .03 = $281,667.

9. a. Susan's 2-acre lot has 2 x 43,560 ft.² = 87,120 ft.². Therefore, each of the equal-size lots would be 87,120 ft.² ÷ 4 = 21,780 ft.². 21,700 ft.² ÷ 200 ft. = 108.9 ft. width.

10. d. The answer can be rephrased as: How long does it take to depreciate by 30%. Since the building depreciates 2%/yr., it takes 30% ÷ 2%/yr. =

15 years.

11. a. $14,500/ mo. x 12 mo./yr. = $174,000 rent per year.
$174,000/yr. ÷ $2,000,000 = 8.7% per year.

12. c. ¼ acre is 43,560 ft.² ÷ 4 = 10,890 ft.².
10,890 ft.² x $17/ ft.² = $185,130. Susan's commission was
4% of $185,130 = $7,405.20

13. d. The annual rental income is $17,000/mo. x 12 mo./yr. = $204,000/yr.
41% of $204,000/yr. = $83,640/yr..

14. d. ($3,895.83 x 12) ÷ 5 1/2% = $849,999.27, which
represents 85% of the cost of the house. Therefore, the cost
of the house is $849,999.27 ÷ 85% = $999,999 (rounded).

15. b. There are 4.7 acres x 43,560 ft.²/acre = 204,732 ft.².
204,732 ft.² ÷ 220 ft. = 930.6 ft.

16. c. Because of the 25 ft. setback on each side, the maximum footprint of
the building would be 150 ft. x 150 ft. =
22,500 ft.².   22,500 ft.² x 3 = $67,500.

17. a. 175 ft. X 4.5 ft. = 1,575 ft.²
105 ft. x 4.5 ft. = 945 ft.²
Total = 2,520 ft.²
2,520 ft.² x $.55 = $1,386

175 ft. x 2 + 105 ft. x 2 = 560 linear feet
560 ft. x $2.15/ ft. = $1,204

$1,386 + $1,204 = $2,590

18. c. The road is 5,280 ÷ 4 = 1,320 ft. long.
1,320 ft. x 45 ft. = 59,400 ft.².
59,400 ft.² ÷ 43,560 ft.²/acre = 1.364 acres.

19. d. ½ x 105 x 95 = 49,875 ft.²
49,875 ft.² x $12/ ft.² = $59,800

20. d. $11,875 ÷ $475,000 = 2.5%

Real Estate Financing

A buyer's having access to financing is critical to nearly all real estate transactions. Even the few buyers who accumulate enough cash to make an all-cash purchase of real property often choose to **leverage** their money by financing the bulk of the purchase with borrowed funds.

USURY LAWS

"**Interest** is the compensation allowed by law or fixed by the parties for the use, or forbearance, or detention of money." CC §1915 (emphasis added) **Usury** is the charging of interest in excess of that allowed by law.

Usury laws contained in Article XV Section 1 of the California Constitution and codified in numerous code sections (including the Civil Code, Corporations Code, Financial Code, and Government Code) make California usury law very complex. However, except for the (many) exempt lenders, the general rule is that the maximum interest charged shall be (1) 10% per year on a loan primarily for personal, family, or household purposes or (2) for loans that are not primarily for personal, family, or household purposes, the greater of 10% per year or 5% over the amount charged by the Federal Reserve Bank of San Francisco on advances to member banks on the 25th day of the month before the loan was made.

Real estate brokers and lenders can take comfort in the fact that loans "made or arranged by any person licensed as a real estate broker by the State of California and secured in whole or in part by liens on real property..." (California Constitution, Article XV Section 1) are free from the constitutional restriction on interest rates. The language "made or arranged by," as explicated in CC §1916.1, makes the level of participation necessary for a broker to qualify as exempt for a particular transaction not very high; however, to qualify, the real estate broker must do more than simply perform escrow services on a loan that has already been negotiated and signed by the borrower and lender (*Gibbo v. Berger* 123 Cal.App.4th 396 (2004).

A seller of real estate who finances the purchase for the buyer with a note secured by a deed of trust is also exempt from California usury laws, even if the loan was not negotiated by real estate broker. Such loans (or "sales on credit," as courts see it) by sellers of real property are referred to as **seller carry back loans**.

Additionally, loans made by most banks, savings and loans, credit unions, agricultural cooperatives, industrial loan companies, personal finance companies, and pawnbrokers are exempt from California usury laws. Therefore, as a practical matter, California's usury laws apply only to private lenders, other than private lenders who make seller carry back loans or make loans that are secured by real estate and that are negotiated by real estate brokers.

During times of tight money, the federal government frequently preempts state usury laws.

PROMISSORY NOTES

A real estate transaction usually involves two documents: a promissory note and a security instrument.

A **promissory note** (often referred to simply as a note) is a contract whereby one person (the **maker**) unconditionally promises to pay another (the **payee**) a certain sum of money, either at a fixed or determinable future date or on demand of the payee. For real estate loans, promissory notes typically include specific terms dealing with the principal amount loaned, interest rate, maturity date, prepayment, acceleration, due-on-sale, attorneys' fees, and the security (the the real property against which a mortgage or deed of trust is recorded).

Promissory notes are classified according to the schedule by which the principal and interest are paid. **Straight notes** are notes under which periodic payments consist of interest only — the full amount of the principal being due at the end of the loan term in one lump sum.

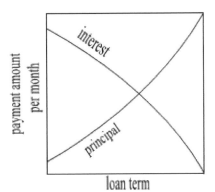

Installment notes require periodic payments that include some repayment of principal as well as interest. Installment notes are the most common type of promissory note used to finance real estate, and the most frequently used installment note is the **level payment note** — a note under which all periodic installment payments are equal, though the amount allocated to principal and interest may vary over the term of the loan. A loan wherein the payments are sufficient to pay off the entire loan by the end of the loan term is referred to as a ***fully amortized loan***. The above diagram shows that with a level payment, fully amortized loan, during the first years of the loan term most of each month's payment goes to interest, but during the final years of the loan term most of each month's payment goes to reducing the principal. For a 30-year loan, the breakeven point occurs at 222 months (18.5 years) into the loan term.

There are many variations in installment notes. One such variation is to have the monthly payments pay all of the interest due but not enough of the principal to fully pay off the loan at the end of the loan term. In such a case, a ***balloon payment*** (generally considered to be any payment, most likely the final payment, that is more than twice the lowest installment payment) would be due at the end of the loan term.

Another type of loan, referred to as a ***negative amortized loan*** (or a "NegAm" loan), has been used by some borrowers. Under a negative amortized loan, the monthly installment payments do not cover all of the interest due — the unpaid part of the interest due being tacked onto the principal, thereby causing the principal to grow and grow as each month goes by. During housing booms, such loans may look appealing, but if housing prices do not continue to rise as fast as the outstanding principal rises under negative amortized loans, the buyers will eventually be stuck with loan balances greater than the value of their property — they will, in other words, be "underwater."

Interest rates on certain loans, referred to as ***adjustable-rate loans*** or ***adjustable-rate mortgages (ARMs),*** vary over the term of the loan. Under an adjustable-rate loan, the interest rate remains fixed during certain time intervals, referred to as the ***adjustment periods***, such as 3 months or 6 months, and then at the end of each adjustment period the rate increases or decreases according to some set ***index*** beyond the control of the lender. The most common indexes used are Treasury securities (T-bills), the 11th District cost of funds of the Federal Home Loan Bank Board, and the London inter-bank offered rate (LIBOR).

The ***fully indexed rate*** on an ARM is the index plus a ***margin*** (also referred to as a *spread*), which is a predetermined number of percentage points. In other words,

$$\text{ARM fully indexed rate} = \text{index} + \text{margin}.$$

The margin is negotiated between each borrower and lender and, though the index varies over the term of the loan, the margin usually remains fixed over the loan term. Sometimes a lender will give a few months initial interest rate on an ARM that is less than the fully indexed rate. Such an initial rate is called a ***discounted rate*** (also referred to as a *teaser rate*). Discounted rates are usually accompanied by higher initial loan fees, called *points*, and with higher rates after the initial discounted rate expires. Therefore, though the loan payments may remain low for a short time, any savings during the discount period may (and likely will) be offset by higher cumulative payments over the remaining life of the loan.

Many lenders place *interest-rate caps* on ARMs. The most common two types of interest rate caps are:

1. a periodic adjustment cap, which limits the rate increase or decrease from one adjustment period to the next; and
2. a lifetime cap, which limits the interest rate increase over the entire loan term.

It is important to note that with some ARMs that have interest-rate caps, the cap may hold the interest rate below the fully indexed rate. Any increase in the interest rate not imposed because of the interest-rate cap might carry over to later rate adjustments. This increase in future rate adjustments is called a *carryover.* In a situation where there is a carryover, future monthly payments may actually increase even though actual interest rates remain the same or decline.

In addition to interest-rate caps, some ARMs limit the amount of installment payment increases. Under ARMs with *payment caps*, any interest not paid because of the payment cap will be added to the balance of the loan, thereby resulting in negative amortization.

There are many other types of ARMs with creative loan terms, so it is always important to have your customer carefully examine the loan terms and payment schedules to be sure that future loan payments can be made given the realistically anticipated future income and lifestyle of your customer.

SECURITY INSTRUMENTS

As we have already discussed, the purchase of real estate involves a *security instrument* as well as a promissory note. The promissory note is a promise to repay the loan. The security interest, which can be either a *mortgage* or a *deed of trust*, makes the real property collateral for the loan, securing the loan by creating a lien on the property. The lien allows the lender to foreclose on the property if the note is not paid as agreed.

Mortgages Compared with Deeds of Trust

In Chapter 3, we found that deeds of trust are three-party instruments, involving the trustor (the borrower), the beneficiary (the lender), and a neutral third party (the trustee). [See the discussion of Figure 3.5] Under a deed of trust, the borrower retains equitable title to the property, but legal title is held by the trustee.

A mortgage, on the other hand, typically is a two-party instrument, by which the legal title remains with the borrower. Because legal title remains with the borrower, a foreclosure by the lender requires the lender to wrest legal title from the borrower, which, as we will see below in our discussion of foreclosures, involves a cumbersome, time-consuming court action — a court action that is not necessary to pursue when foreclosing on a deed of trust. Hence, mortgages are seldom used in California.

Provisions Generally Found in Security Instruments and/or Deeds of Trust

While there is no standard form used for all mortgages or deeds of trust, most contain certain important provisions either in the promissory note, in the security instrument, or in both.

Acceleration Clause

An *acceleration clause* states that, upon default (such as failure to make payments as agreed) or a violation of other conditions (such as failure to maintain proper insurance), the lender has the option of declaring the entire balance of outstanding principal and interest due and payable immediately.

Due-On-Sale Clause

A *due-on-sale clause* (also referred to as an *alienation clause*) states that the lender has the right to accelerate the loan — declare the entire outstanding principal and interest due and payable immediately — if the secured property is sold or some other interest in the property is transferred. Without an alienation clause in the loan, the property would be freely transferable. With an alienation clause, the property can still be sold, but only if the existing loan is paid off in full.

Until 1982, enforceability of due-on-sale clauses was a matter of state law. But the *Garn-St. Germain Act* (12 USC §1701J-3) made the enforceability of due-on-sale provisions a federal issue. This act provides that due-on-sale provisions are enforceable except for certain transfers, such as transfers:

1. by devise, descent, or operation of law on the death of a joint tenant
2. granting a leasehold interest of three years or less not containing an option to purchase
3. to a relative resulting from the death of the borrower

4. where the spouse or a child of the borrower becomes an owner of the property
5. resulting from a decree of dissolution of marriage or legal separation
6. to a family trust

Regardless of whether the loan contains a due-on-sale clause, the sale of the secured property does not extinguish the lien that the lender obtained through the loan's security instrument. In such a case, if the loan is not paid off in full when the property is sold, the new owner can either assume the outstanding mortgage or deed of trust, or take title subject to the mortgage or deed of trust.

In an **assumption**, the purchaser agrees to be primarily liable on the loan, but the original borrower remains secondarily liable in case the purchaser defaults, unless there is a complete novation, in which case the seller would be relieved of all responsibility. If, on the other hand, the purchaser takes title **subject to** an existing loan, the original borrower remains fully liable for the debt, not the purchaser, but in the event of a default, the property can be foreclosed on.

The distinction between a buyer's assuming a loan versus taking the property subject to a loan becomes important in a case where the proceeds of a foreclosure sale of the property are insufficient to satisfy the amount due on the mortgage or deed of trust, in which case the lender might seek to recover the deficiency from whoever is liable for the loan payments. Such a recovery, if permitted by law, is called a **deficiency judgment**. Under an assumption, the buyer commits to being personally liable for the loan payments, so any deficiency judgment obtained would be a judgment against the buyer. If, on the other hand, the buyer purchased the property subject to the underlying loan, the seller remained personally liable, and the deficiency action would be brought against the seller. Because of strict antideficiency laws, few deficiency judgments are rendered in California against borrowers who obtained loans for the purchase of residential property. Foreclosure procedures will be discussed in greater detail later in this chapter.

Late Payment Clause

When a conventional loan is secured by a mortgage or deed of trust on a single-family, owner-occupied residence, a charge for a late payment shall not exceed 6% of the installment or $5, whichever is greater, and no late charge can be imposed on any installment that is paid in full within 10 days after its scheduled due date. CC §2954.4(a) and (b). Furthermore, no late charge can be imposed until (1) the borrower has been notified in writing and given at least 10 days from mailing of the notice in which to cure the delinquency, or (2) the borrower has been notified in the billing statement that the fee will be imposed after 10 days. CC §2954.5(a).

For FHA and VA loans, if the loan is not paid within 15 days of the due date, the late charge would be 4% of the monthly payment. For Cal-Vet loans, the late charge is $4 if the monthly payment is made after the 10th day of the month.

Prepayment Clause

A prepayment clause states the terms by which a loan may be paid off faster than the agreed-upon schedule of payments without incurring a *prepayment penalty*. Without a prepayment clause, where the loan is secured by a residential property of 4 units or fewer, the borrower may prepay the whole or any part of the balance due, together with accrued interest, at any time without penalty. CC §2954.9 (a) (1).

Many loans secured by an owner-occupied residential real property containing 4 units or fewer contain a "5-year, 20% prepayment penalty" clause. Within the first 5 years of the life of such a loan, up to 20% of the original principal amount may be paid without penalty in any 12-month period. For any amount prepaid in excess of 20% of the original principal amount of the loan, the prepayment penalty cannot exceed an amount equal to the payment of 6 months' advance interest on the excess amount prepaid. California law prohibits prepayment penalties on owner-occupied residential properties consisting of 4 or fewer dwelling units if, after 5 years from the date of execution of the mortgage or deed of trust, a payment pays off the loan in whole or in part. CC §2954.9 (b).

The federal government has prohibited prepayment penalties from being imposed on loans secured by owner-occupied dwellings if the loan has been accelerated by a due-on-sale clause. 12 USC §1701J-3.

Most federal government loans contain prepayment penalty provisions that preempt California law. As we shall see in the next chapter, FHA-insured, VA-guaranteed, and Cal-Vet home loans do not have prepayment penalties of any kind.

Subordination Clause

A *subordination clause* states that the mortgage or deed of trust will have lower priority than a mortgage or deed of trust recorded later. This clause is common in deeds of trust securing unimproved land, making it far easier for the borrower to obtain a construction loan to improve the property. Because lien priority is usually determined by recording date, a subordination clause allows a construction lender to take a first lien position even though the construction lender's lien is recorded later.

Defeasance Clause

A **defeasance clause** states that when the loan debt has been fully paid, the lender must release the property from the lien so that legal title free from the lien will be owned by the borrower. As we saw in Chapter 3, under a deed of trust, the formal process of transferring legal title is by way of having the trustee sign a deed of reconveyance (see Figure 3.9). The lender is required to submit to the trustee a **request for reconveyance** within 30 days after the loan is paid off. Within 21 days after receiving the request for reconveyance, the trustee must execute and record the deed of reconveyance. In the case of a mortgage (under which legal title has remained with the borrower), a **certificate of discharge** is used to release the lien. The certificate of discharge must be recorded by the mortgagee within 30 days after the loan is paid off.

VARIOUS TYPES OF SECURED LOANS

Though a two-party mortgage and a three-party deed of trust are two very different security instruments, the terms "mortgage" and "deed of trust" are generally not used in a strict sense — not by the public, not by real estate agents, and not even by textbook writers. Therefore, unless the distinction is crucial, throughout the remainder of this text we will follow the well-trod path of using the term "mortgage" rather than the more cumbersome "mortgage or deed of trust" to refer to either a mortgage or a deed of trust. Despite this apparent abuse of terminology, the reader should keep in mind that, for reasons already discussed, true two-party mortgages are rare in California — the usual security instrument being a deed of trust.

A few of the most common mortgage types are discussed below. Mortgages that refer to specific government lenders, such as *conforming loans*, *nonconforming loans*, *conventional loans* and *jumbo loans*, will be discussed in the next chapter.

First Mortgage

A **first mortgage** (often referred to simply as a "first") is a security instrument that holds a first-priority claim against the secured property in the event of a default. A first mortgage is referred to as **primary financing**. Primary financing usually carries a lower interest rate than other loans on the property because a first mortgage has a lower risk of nonpayment.

A **second mortgage** (a "second") is a security instrument that holds a second-priority claim against the secured property in the event of a default. The term "**junior mortgage**" is used to refer to any mortgage that, relative to another "**senior mortgage**," has a lower lien-priority position. Thus, a second mortgage is a junior mortgage relative to a first mortgage, but a second mortgage would be a senior mortgage relative to a mortgage in third-priority position. Second mortgages and other junior mortgages are referred to as **secondary financing**, and usually carry a higher interest rate than first mortgages because of greater risk.

> **Example:** If a borrower defaults on a property with outstanding principal and interest balances on the first and second mortgages of $200,000 and $50,000, respectively, and if the property, net of sale costs, garners $225,000 in foreclosure, the holder of the first would receive $200,000 plus any lender-foreclosure costs; the holder of the second would receive what is left over; the holder of a mortgage junior to the second would receive nothing.

Bridge Loan

A **bridge loan** (also referred to as a swing loan) is often used when a buyer of a new residence has not yet sold his or her former home and needs money to pay the down payment and closing costs on the new residence. A bridge loan would use the equity that the buyer has in the buyer's former residence as security for the loan, which would be paid off when the sale of the former residence closes.

Blanket Mortgage

A **blanket mortgage** is a mortgage used to finance two or more parcels of real estate. Blanket loans are used by borrowers in case one property does not provide sufficient equity to obtain the amount of funds the borrower needs, in which case the borrower may offer another property in which she or he has equity as additional collateral.

Blanket mortgages are also commonly used by developers who buy large tracts of land with the intention of subdividing them into many individual parcels to be sold individually over a period of time. Such a blanket mortgage would probably contain a **partial release clause**, which would allow the developer to sell off individual parcels and pay back, according to a release schedule, only a proportionate amount of the blanket loan. Note that with a normal due-on-sale clause, the sale of any interest in a property would require a repayment of the entire loan.

Construction Mortgage

A **construction mortgage** is a security instrument used to secure a loan to finance improvements to a property. A typical construction loan is a short-term loan that provides for a schedule of obligatory advances made by the lender according to a schedule based on stages of construction. The lender will usually hold back around 10% of the loan amount until the period for filing mechanics liens has expired. Once construction is completed, the construction loan would be replaced by permanent financing, referred to as a **take-out loan**. A **standby loan commitment** is an agreement by a lender (perhaps the same lender that made the construction loan) to make a take-out loan after construction is completed.

Reverse Mortgage

A **reverse mortgage** is a security instrument for a loan for homeowners over the age of 62 who have a large amount of equity in their homes. The reverse loan is usually designed to provide such homeowners with monthly payments, often over the lifetime of the last surviving homeowner or until such person either permanently leaves the home or dies, at which time the outstanding balance must be repaid or the house sold. The estate is not liable for any deficiency should the house sell for less than the outstanding balance of the loan.

If the reverse mortgage is insured by the FHA, it is called a **Home Equity Conversion Mortgage (HECM)**. For an HECM, the definition of "permanently leaves the home" is 365 days of continuous absence. Under an HECM, homeowners can receive a percentage of the value of their equity in one lump sum, as monthly payments (either for a fixed term or for life), or as a line of credit.

A homeowner with a reverse mortgage continues to be responsible for the following:

- paying property taxes;
- paying homeowners insurance premiums;
- paying any homeowners association assessment fees; and
- maintaining the home in good repair.

The decision as to whether to enter into a reverse mortgage, and, if so, which one and on what terms, involves many complex issues. Accordingly the California Legislature has passed a law (CC §1923.2) that requires a lender to provide a prospective borrower with a list of not fewer than 10 housing counseling agencies approved by the United States Department of Housing and Community Development to engage in reverse mortgage counseling. Additionally, this law prohibits a lender from accepting a final and complete application for a reverse mortgage or assessing any fees upon a prospective borrower without receiving certification from the applicant that the applicant has received this counseling from an approved counseling agency.

Home Equity Mortgage

A *home equity mortgage* is a security instrument used to provide the borrower with a revolving line of credit based on the amount of equity in the borrower's home. Compared to a usual second mortgage, which provides the borrower with a lump sum payment, a *home equity line of credit* (referred to as a *HELOC*) allows borrowers to borrow only what they need as they need it (for example, to purchase a refrigerator or to remodel the kitchen).

Typically, lenders set the credit limit on a HELOC as a percentage of the appraised value of the home minus any balance owed on existing liens against the home.

> **Example:** If the appraised value of the home is $700,000, the only lien against the home is a first mortgage with balance outstanding of $300,000, and the percentage the lender is willing to lend on the appraised value of the home is 80%, then the lender would establish a HELOC with credit limit equal to $260,000 (($700,000 x .8) - $300,000).

FORECLOSURES

Foreclosure is a legal process by which a lender, in an attempt to recover the balance of a loan from a borrower who has defaulted on the loan, forces the sale of the collateral that secured the loan. The two primary purposes of a security instrument, be it a mortgage or a deed of trust, are (1) to create the legal groundwork for the lender's right to foreclose and (2) to establish the lender's priority among creditors. Unless timely cured, defaults leading to foreclosure can result from a variety of breaches of loan agreements, such as failure to make installment payments, to maintain fire insurance, or to pay property taxes.

California has a "one-action" foreclosure rule, in which the lender who wishes to foreclose on a mortgage or deed of trust must choose one action only against a defaulting borrower: either a judicial foreclosure in which a deficiency judgment may, in certain cases, be sought, or a non-judicial foreclosure in which a lender may not seek to recover a deficiency.

Judicial Foreclosure

A *judicial foreclosure* is a foreclosure carried out not by way of a power-of-sale clause in a security instrument, but under the supervision of a court. A holder of a mortgage or deed of trust with a power-of-sale clause may, if so desired, use judicial foreclosure, but, pursuant to the one-action rule, a choice of either judicial or non-judicial foreclosure must be made. Because judicial foreclosures are seldom used in California to foreclose on residential real estate, our discussion of judicial foreclosure will be very brief.

In California, judicial foreclosures on residential properties containing 4 or fewer dwelling units are much less used than non-judicial foreclosures because:

(1) nearly all deeds of trust and mortgages contain power-of-sale clauses;

(2) deficiency judgments can rarely be obtained (see below);

(3) judicial foreclosures are much more expensive to pursue (requiring court action rather than a private sale);

(4) judicial foreclosures typically take much longer to finalize (again because of the court proceeding, which can often take a year or more to be resolved); and

(5) even after a lender successfully obtains a court order for a *sheriff's sale* (as opposed to a *trustee's sale*), the borrower may redeem his or her property by paying off the entire debt plus costs. The *redemption period* is 3 months after the sheriff's sale if the proceeds of the sale were enough to pay off the debt and all costs of foreclosure; it is 1 year if the proceeds of the sale were not enough to pay off the debt *and* the lender pursues a deficiency judgment. If the lender elects not to pursue a deficiency judgment, there is no right of redemption.

Dispersal of proceeds from a sheriff's sale is made in the following order:

(1) to the costs of the lawsuit and attorney fees;

(2) to the costs of the sale;

(3) to the amount due to the beneficiary/mortgagee of the security instrument that was foreclosed;

(4) to the amount due to junior lien holders in order of priority; and finally

(5) any excess to the borrower.

A lender who wishes to seek a deficiency judgment must file an application in the court case within 3 months of the sheriff's sale.

Deficiency Judgments

New California law effective January 1, 2013, redefined a "*purchase money loan*" to be *"a deed of trust or mortgage on a dwelling for not more than four families given to a lender to secure repayment of a loan which was in fact used to pay all or part of the purchase price of that dwelling, occupied entirely or in part by the purchaser."* CCP §580b. Therefore, the borrower who obtains a second mortgage, as well as a first, entered into after January 1, 2013, that is a "wrap" and therefore used to pay part of the purchase price of an owner-occupied dwelling of not more than 4 residential units is protected from a **deficiency judgment** on that second mortgage.

Furthermore, no deficiency judgment may be obtained on any loan, refinance, or other credit transaction that is used to refinance a purchase money loan, or subsequent refinances of a purchase money loan, except to the extent that in such credit transaction the lender or creditor advances new principal (cash-out) that is not applied to any obligation owed or to be owed under the purchase money loan, or to fees, costs, or related expenses of the credit transaction. Any new credit transaction is deemed to be a purchase money loan except as to the principal amount of any new advance. CCP §580b(c). Under CCP §580b(c), any payment of principal will be deemed to be applied first to the principal balance of the purchase money loan, and then to the principal balance of any new advance, and interest payments will be applied to any interest due and owing.

The provisions of CCP §580b(c) only apply to credit transactions entered into on or after January 1, 2013. Therefore, if a borrower refinanced before January 1, 2013, and refinanced again after January 1, 2013, the second refinance, even though entered into after January 1, 2013, would not be protected from a deficiency judgment because the funds obtained from the second refinance would have been used to pay off the first refinance, which was not a "purchase money loan" as it was entered into prior to January 1, 2013.

Non-judicial Foreclosure

Most foreclosures in California use the **non-judicial foreclosure** process. The right to pursue a non-judicial foreclosure is contained in the power-of-sale clause of a mortgage or deed of trust, which, upon borrower default and the beneficiary's request, empowers the trustee to sell the secured property at a public auction.

Foreclosure Prevention Alternative

Effective January 1, 2013, California law mandates that *"as part of the non-judicial foreclosure process, borrowers are considered for, and have a meaningful opportunity to obtain, available loss mitigation options, if any, offered by or through the borrower's mortgage servicer, such as loan modifications or other alternatives to foreclosure."* CC 2923.4(a). [Note: Several alternatives to foreclosure are discussed in the section below entitled A Borrower's Alternatives to Foreclosure.]

Accordingly, a mortgage servicer, mortgagee, trustee, beneficiary, or authorized agent may not record a notice of default (see below) until all of the following:

(1) The mortgage servicer has sent the following information in writing to the borrower: A statement that the borrower may request the following:

(i) a copy of the borrower's promissory note or other evidence of indebtedness;

(ii) a copy of the borrower's deed of trust or mortgage; and

(iii) a copy of any assignment, if applicable, of the borrower's mortgage or deed of trust required to demonstrate the right of the mortgage servicer to foreclose.

(2) Thirty days have elapsed after the mortgage servicer contacts the borrower to assess the borrower's financial situation and explores options for the borrower to avoid foreclosure, or 30 days have elapsed after the mortgage servicer has failed to contact the borrower despite performing "due diligence" to do so pursuant to CC §2923.5 (e).

(3) If the borrower requests a foreclosure prevention alternative, the mortgage servicer must promptly establish a *single point of contact (SPOC)* to assess the viability of providing the borrower with some form of loan loss mitigation and must provide to the borrower a direct means of communication with the single point of contact pursuant to CC §2923.7. A "single point of contact" is defined as an individual or team of personnel employed by a mortgage loan servicer, each of whom has the ability and authority to assist a borrower in assessing whether the borrower may be able to take advantage of a foreclosure prevention alternative offered by, or through, the mortgage servicer. CCP §2923.7(e). A *foreclosure prevention alternative* is defined as a first lien loan modification or another available loss mitigation option. CC §2920.5 (d).

(4) If the borrower provides an application for a loan modification or other foreclosure prevention alternative, then the application must be considered (assuming the mortgage servicer has a loan modification program) and approved or rejected pursuant to CC §2924.18. This means that while a foreclosure prevention alternative is being considered, a foreclosure may not proceed; in other words, the so-called "*dual tracking*" of foreclosure proceedings and loan modification or other foreclosure prevention alternative is forbidden.

[Note: In January 2013, the federal Consumer Financial Protection Bureau (CFPB) issued rules that provide for a "continuity of contact" (comparable to California's "single point of contact") for the homeowner with the mortgage servicer, and that prohibit dual tracking of foreclosure procedures with foreclosure prevention alternatives, such as loan modification. However, unlike California's mandated 30-day wait period from the date of first contacting the borrower about a loan default until filing a notice of default, the CFPB rules mandate a 120-day wait period from the date that the loan goes delinquent until filing a notice of default. In certain cases, this 120 day wait rule is likely to preempt the California 30-day wait rule — a determination ultimately to be made the courts. The CFPB rules do not apply to small banks and credit unions.]

Notice of Default

Non-judicial foreclosure proceedings are begun with the mortgagee, the trustee, or an authorized person filing a *notice of default (NOD)* in the office of the recorder of each county in which the property or a part thereof is located. The notice of default must contain the following (CC §2924 (1)):

a. identification of the trustor (the borrower) and a description of the property in sufficient detail to identify the property;

b. a statement that a default of the loan obligation has occurred; and

c. a statement setting forth the nature of the default(s) and the beneficiary's election to foreclose.

Within 10 business days after the filing of the notice of default, copies of the recorded notice of default with an attached summary document of the notice of default must be mailed to the trustor, pursuant to CC §2923.3. A copy of the recorded notice of default must also be sent within 10 days after the filing of the notice of default to anyone who had requested special notice in accordance with CC §2924b.

Additionally, within 1 month following the recordation of the notice of default, a copy of the notice of default must be sent to all persons with recorded interests in the subject property (such as junior liens), and to others as provided for in CC §2924b(c)(2).

Notice of Sale

The trustee, mortgagee, or other authorized person shall give *notice of sale*, stating the date and time thereof, after the lapse of 3 months from the recording of the notice of default. The sale may not occur until 3 months and 20 days after the recording of the notice of default. (CC §2924 (A)).

At least 20 days prior to the sale date, pursuant to CC §2924b(b)(2), a notice of the sale must be sent to the trustor and to any person who requested a notice thereof. Additionally, pursuant to CC §2924f, all of the following procedures must be followed:

(1) Notice of the sale must begin being published in a newspaper of general circulation in the city in which the property is located (or county if the property is not in a city). The publication must appear at least once a week for three weeks prior to the sale.

(2) A written notice must be posted — stating the time of sale and the street address and the specific place at the street address where the sale will be held, and describing the property to be sold — in one public place in the city where the property is to be sold, if the property is to be sold in a city, or, if not, then in one public place in the judicial district in which the property is to be sold.

(3) A copy of the notice of sale must also be posted in a conspicuous place on the property to be sold, where possible and where not restricted for any reason. If the property is a single-family residence the posting must be on a door of the residence, but, if not possible or restricted, then the notice must be posted in a conspicuous place on the property; however, if access is denied because a common entrance to the property is restricted by a guard gate or similar impediment, the property may be posted at that guard gate or similar impediment to any development community.

(4) The notice of sale must be recorded with the county recorder of the county in which the property or some part thereof is situated at least 20 days prior to the date of sale.

Additionally, at least 20 days before the date of sale, a copy of the notice of sale must be sent to any state taxing agency that has recorded, subsequent to the deed of trust or mortgage being foreclosed, a notice of tax lien prior to the recording date of the notice of default against the real property to which the notice of default applies. CC §2924b (c)(2)(F)(3). At least 25 days prior to the sale, a copy of the notice of sale should be sent to the IRS pursuant to Section 7425 of the Internal Revenue Code. CC §2924b (c)(2)(F)(4).

Trustee Sale Procedures

Any bid made by a bidder at a trustee's sale is deemed to be an irrevocable offer by the bidder to purchase the property being sold for the amount of the bid. The trustee has the right to require every bidder at the auction sale to show evidence of the bidder's ability to deposit with the trustee the full amount of his or her final bid in cash, check, cashier's check, or other cash equivalent that has been designated in the notice of sale as acceptable to the trustee. The beneficiary of the deed of trust under foreclosure has the right to offset his or her bid or bids to the extent of the total amount due the beneficiary, including the trustee's fees and expenses, which are generally paid by the beneficiary prior to the sale. A **credit bid** is a bid at a foreclosure sale made by the beneficiary up to the amount owed to the beneficiary. The trustee's sale is deemed to be final upon the acceptance of the last and highest bid.

Priority of Payment

Pursuant to CC §2924k, proceeds of the trustee's sale are to be distributed in the following order of priority:

(1) to the costs and expenses of exercising the power of sale and of sale, including the payment of the trustee's fees and attorney's fees;

(2) to the payment of the obligations secured by the deed of trust or mortgage that is the subject of the trustee's sale;

(3) to satisfy the outstanding balance of obligations secured by any junior liens or encumbrances in the order of their priority; and finally

(4) to the trustor or the trustor's successor in interest, or if the property had been sold or transferred to another, to the vested owner of record at the time of the trustee's sale.

Reinstatement Period

At any time within the period from the date of recordation of the notice of default until 5 business days prior to the date of sale, the trustor (or any beneficiary of a subordinate lien or encumbrance) may exercise the **right of reinstatement** of the mortgage being foreclosed by paying all delinquent loan installments, foreclosure costs, and trustee's fees. CC §2924c. No right of reinstatement exists after the trustee's sale, when the purchaser immediately acquires all rights held by the former owner, subject to the rights of holders of rights superior to the mortgage that was foreclosed.

CONDITION OF THE TITLE CONVEYED

The title conveyed to the successful bidder at a trustee's sale is without covenant or warranty that no title defects exist. Furthermore, certain liens against the title remain:

- federal tax liens that were filed more than 30 days prior to the date of the trustee's sale, unless the proper 25-day notice of sale was given to the IRS;

- real property taxes and assessments;

- liens that are senior to the foreclosed security instrument; and

- valid mechanics liens.

Though mortgages, deeds of trust, judgment liens, and easements that do not have priority over the security instrument that was foreclosed are extinguished from the record of title to the property, tenants who entered into a lease of the property prior to the foreclosure retain certain rights, such as possibly being able to remain in possession of the premises until the end of the lease term, pursuant to CCP §1161b.

Summary of Non-judicial Foreclosure Process Timeline	
Timeline	**Process**
Prior to filing Notice of Default (NOD)	Lender must contact the trustor at least 30 days prior to filing NOD to determine whether trustor wishes to pursue a foreclosure prevention alternative.
Day 1: Foreclosure process begins	NOD filed in county recorder's office.
Within 10 business days	Copy and summary of NOD mailed to trustor. Copy of NOD mailed to anyone who requested notice thereof.
Within 1 month	Copy of NOD mailed to junior lien holders and others pursuant to CC §2924b(c)(2).
After 3 months	Unless bankruptcy has been filed or other event holds the timeline (such as ongoing foreclosure alternative procedures), sale date and place is set.
25 days prior to sale date	Notice of sale sent to IRS.
20 days prior to sale date	Notice of sale sent to trustor, junior lien holders, and others pursuant to CC §2924. Notice of sale recorded in county recorder's office.
5 business days prior to sale date	Trustor's right of reinstatement expires.
Sale date	Property sold to highest bidder, which is usually the lender who submits a credit bid.

Rights of Junior Lien Holders

If the holder of a junior lien forecloses, there is no effect on senior liens. However, if a senior lien is foreclosed, all junior liens are extinguished. The rationale for this is that when the beneficiary of the senior lien acquired the lien, the property was free from these junior liens, and the beneficiary should therefore be able to obtain all the value of the property through foreclosure that they would have without the existence of these junior liens.

As stated above, a junior lien holder may gain protection from such an extinguishment of the junior lien by paying the amount due to the holder of the senior lien to reinstate the mortgage pursuant to CC §2924c. The junior lien holder may then add the amounts paid to the senior lien holder to the balance of the junior lien, demand payment from the borrower, and if payment is not forthcoming, foreclose on the property. The successful bidder at this foreclosure of the junior lien (which likely will be the junior lien holder) will acquire the property, subject to rights of the senior lien holder.

Blight on Foreclosed Properties

One of the negative effects of the upsurge in foreclosures in recent years has been a downward spiral of home values in neighborhoods caused in part by the unkept, deteriorating condition of many foreclosed properties, which leads to decreased desirability and value of neighboring properties and to increased crime. To help break this vicious cycle, the California legislature has mandated that the legal owner of vacant residential property purchased at a foreclosure sale or acquired by that owner through foreclosure under a mortgage or deed of trust maintain that property, pursuant to CC §2929.3. This law authorizes a local governmental entity to impose civil fines and penalties for failure to maintain that property of up to $1,000 per day for a violation. The governmental entity that seeks to impose those fines and penalties must give notice of the claimed violation and an opportunity to correct the violation to the owner at least 14 days prior to imposing the fines and penalties, and to allow a hearing for contesting those fines and penalties.

Additionally, the State Housing Law (Health and Safety Code §17980) permits the appropriate local enforcement agency to bring an action to prevent, restrain, correct, or abate blight or nuisance. Such enforcement agency may also go to court to seek receivership of the property; however, such enforcement action may not proceed if the owner of the property is in the process of abating a violation, unless a specific condition of the property threatens public health or safety.

Of course, the sale of most foreclosed properties results in no bids other than the secured creditor's bid, because if there had been enough equity in the property to fully satisfy the loan, the owner likely would have sold the property and prevented foreclosure. Such bank-owned properties acquired through foreclosure are called **Real Estate Owned (REO)** properties. The laws discussed above prohibiting blight on foreclosed properties were designed in part to force lenders to maintain their REOs.

ALTERNATIVES TO FORECLOSURE

If a borrower cannot make payments on his or her loan, or, if because of a steep decline in property values the borrower simply wants to stop making payments on a property in which the borrower has negative equity, the borrower has several possible alternatives to foreclosure, including:

- loan modification;
- short sale;
- surrender the deed in lieu of foreclosure; or
- bankruptcy.

FORECLOSURE CONSULTANTS

Civil Code §2945 (a) states that the California Legislature finds and declares that homeowners whose residences are in foreclosure are subject to fraud, deception, harassment, and unfair dealing by foreclosure consultants from the time a notice of default is recorded until the time surplus funds from any foreclosure sale are distributed to the homeowner or his or her successor. Foreclosure consultants represent that they can assist homeowners who have defaulted on obligations secured by their residences. These foreclosure consultants, however, often charge high fees, the payment of which is often secured by a deed of trust on the residence to be saved, and perform no service or essentially a worthless service. Homeowners, relying on the foreclosure consultants' promises of help, take no other action, are diverted from lawful businesses that could render beneficial services, and often lose their homes, sometimes to the foreclosure consultants who purchase homes at a fraction of their value before the sale. Vulnerable homeowners are increasingly relying on the services of foreclosure consultants who advise the homeowner that the foreclosure consultant can obtain the remaining funds from the foreclosure sale if the homeowner executes an assignment of the surplus, a deed, or a power of attorney in favor of the foreclosure consultant. This results in the homeowner paying an exorbitant fee for a service when the homeowner could have obtained the remaining funds from the trustee's sale from the trustee directly for minimal cost if the homeowner had consulted legal counsel or had sufficient time to receive notices from the trustee of the mortgage or deed of trust regarding how and where to make a claim for excess proceeds.

Civil Code §2945.1 defines *foreclosure consultant* as any person who makes any solicitation, representation, or offer to any owner to perform for compensation or who, for compensation, performs any service that the person in any manner represents will in any manner do any of the following:

(1) stop or postpone the foreclosure sale;

(2) obtain any forbearance from any beneficiary or mortgagee;

(3) assist the owner to exercise the right of reinstatement;

(4) obtain any extension of the period within which the owner may reinstate his or her obligation;

(5) obtain any waiver of an acceleration clause contained in any promissory note or contract secured by a deed of trust or mortgage on a residence in foreclosure or contained that deed of trust or mortgage;

(6) assist the owner to obtain a loan or advance of funds;

(7) avoid or ameliorate the impairment of the owner's credit resulting from the recording of a notice of default or the conduct of a foreclosure sale;

(8) save the owner's residence from foreclosure; or

(9) assist the owner in obtaining from the beneficiary, mortgagee, trustee under a power of sale, or counsel for the beneficiary, mortgagee, or trustee, the remaining proceeds from the foreclosure sale of the owner's residence.

Foreclosure consultants must now submit a completed registration form, along with applicable fees and a surety bond in the amount of $100,000 to the California Department of Justice. CCP §2945.1 contains several exemptions from the definition of foreclosure consultant, including licensed attorneys who render foreclosure consultant services to clients in the course of their law practice, licensed real estate brokers, and licensed real estate salespersons who work under the supervision of their employing broker.

However, CC §2944.7(a) and B&PC §10085.6(a) provide that any person, including attorneys and real estate agents, may not collect advance fees for loan modification services related to mortgages or deeds of trust secured by a residential property containing four or fewer dwelling units. Specifically, these sections provide that it is unlawful for any person who negotiates, attempts to negotiate, arranges, attempts to arrange, or otherwise offers to perform a mortgage loan modification or other form of mortgage loan forbearance for a fee or other compensation paid by the borrower, to do any of the following:

(1) claim, demand, charge, collect, or receive any compensation until after the person has fully performed each and every service the person contracted to perform or represented that he or she would perform;

(2) take any wage assignment, any lien of any type on real or personal property, or other security to secure the payment of compensation; or

(3) take any power of attorney from the borrower for any purpose.

A violation of these sections by a natural person is punishable by a fine not exceeding $10,000 and/or imprisonment in the county jail for up to one year. A violation of this section by a business entity is punishable by a fine not exceeding $50,000.

LOAN MODIFICATION

Loan modification is a restructuring or modification of a mortgage or deed of trust on terms more favorable to the buyer's ability (or desire) to continue making loan payments.

Until recently, because a refinance loan was not considered a purchase money loan, if the borrower defaulted on a loan refinance, the lender would have had a right to seek a deficiency judgment for the full amount of the refinance loan through judicial foreclosure. However, as discussed above in the section entitled Deficiency Judgments, a refinance loan entered into after January 1, 2013, is protected from a deficiency judgment except to the extent that the lender advances new principal (cash-out) that exceeds the original purchase money loan balance.

Though lenders need not approve a loan modification, loan modification often is a viable option for many homeowners who are facing financial hardship. As discussed above, state law makes it mandatory that at least 30 days before lenders file a notice of default to begin the process of non-judicial foreclosure, they must contact the borrower to let the borrower know that various foreclosure prevention alternatives, including loan modification, may be available. Additionally, lenders have a significant economic interest in working with borrowers to prevent foreclosure because the foreclosure process is expensive, time-consuming, and REO properties often sell for an amount much less than the outstanding loan balance and even significantly less than fair market value.

In order to obtain a loan modification, homeowners should be able to substantiate sufficient and consistent income to cover the new monthly payments being sought under the loan modification. In order to be a viable loan modification, the new monthly payments, including property taxes and insurance, should be no more than about 30% of monthly income. Furthermore, a homeowner who is in bankruptcy, whose property is not his or her principal residence, or whose foreclosure sale is coming soon, is likely not to qualify for a loan modification.

Additionally, real estate agents and homeowners (who often seek help and advice from real estate agents) should be aware that the real estate crisis, which has caused so much financial hardship for so many, has also spawned numerous fraudulent schemes that seek to take advantage of people in desperate financial condition — and, as the saying goes, "desperate people do desperate things," including sometimes placing themselves into the jaws of fraudsters.

SHORT SALE

A *short sale* is a pre-foreclosure sale made by the borrower (usually with the help of a real estate agent) with lender approval of real estate for less than the balance due on the mortgage loan. A lender may collect no deficiency upon a note secured solely by a deed of trust or mortgage for a dwelling of not more than four units, in any case in which the trustor or mortgagor sells the dwelling for a sale price less than the remaining amount of the indebtedness outstanding at the time of sale, in accordance with the written consent of the holder of the deed of trust or mortgage, provided that:

- title has been voluntarily transferred to a buyer by grant deed or by other document of conveyance that has been recorded in the county where all or part of the real property is located; and
- the proceeds of the sale have been tendered to the mortgagee, beneficiary, or the agent of the mortgagee or beneficiary, in accordance with the parties' agreement. CCP §580e (a) (1).

A short sale may be welcomed by a lender for several reasons, including:

- the amount the lender receives from the short sale may be greater than the amount likely to be received at a foreclosure sale;
- a short sale eliminates the risk of vandalism of REO properties left vacant after a foreclosure sale; and
- a short sale eliminates the costs of maintenance of, and property taxes on, the property while owned by the lender.

Short Sale Debt Cancellation in California Is Not Subject to State or Federal Income Tax.

Ordinarily, debt cancellation results in both the IRS and the California Franchise Tax Board (FTB) treating the amount of debt canceled as income and taxed accordingly. However, in a September 19, 2013 letter to Senator Barbara Boxer, the IRS stated: "We believe that a homeowner's obligation under the anti-deficiency provision of section 580e of the CCP would be a nonrecourse obligation to the extent that, for federal income tax purposes, the homeowner will not have cancellation of indebtedness income."

Shortly after the IRS issued this letter, the FTB also issued a letter stating that short sales made pursuant to CCP §580e would not be subject to state income taxation.

These clarifications came as a welcome relief to distressed California homeowners who now have a better chance of avoiding foreclosure or bankruptcy by opting for a short sale without incurring federal or state income taxation of the debt cancellation, even after the expiration of the Mortgage Forgiveness Debt Relief Act of 2007 on December 31, 2013.

Note, however, that both the IRS and the FTB letters state that even though there will be no income taxation of the short sale debt cancellation, the taxpayer may have capital gain to the extent that the outstanding debt or the fair market value of the property, whichever is greater, exceeds their basis in the property. However, pursuant to 26 U.S.C. §121, gain on a principal residence is generally excluded from capital gains up to $250,000 for single taxpayers and $500,000 for married couples filing joint returns (see Income Tax Ramifications of Homeownership in Chapter 15 below).

DEED IN LIEU OF FORECLOSURE

Surrendering a *deed in lieu of foreclosure* is a method of avoiding foreclosure by conveying to a lender title to a property lieu of the lender's foreclosing on the property. This is a quick way out from under a mortgage and is likely to be less damaging to the borrower's credit than a foreclosure. The lender need not accept a deed in lieu of foreclosure, but it is less expensive than a foreclosure proceeding and it permits the lender to take over the property immediately rather than letting the borrower live rent free for months on end during a foreclosure proceeding.

A borrower with other liens on his or her home is unlikely to qualify for a deed in lieu of foreclosure because, as we have discussed, a foreclosure usually results in the lender's receiving a "clean" title, whereas accepting a deed in lieu of foreclosure would not. A borrower may be able to remain in his or her home if a tenant relationship with the lender can be established as part of a deed in lieu of foreclosure agreement.

BANKRUPTCY

Bankruptcy is a legal process conducted in a United States Bankruptcy Court, in which a person declares his or her inability to pay debts. In general, the purpose of a bankruptcy proceeding is to discharge or restructure most of the debts of the debtor. Individuals have three forms of bankruptcy available to them: Chapter 7, Chapter 11, and Chapter 13.

Chapter 11 is mainly used by businesses for reorganization, but it can also be used by individuals who own large amounts of non-exempt properties.

In a Chapter 7 bankruptcy filing, most of the debtor's assets are liquidated and debts discharged. Chapter 7 is the fastest and least expensive form of bankruptcy and is the form chosen by the majority of personal bankruptcy filings. Assets that are not liquidated in Chapter 7 include exempt property such as clothes, household goods, cars, pensions, and public benefits. There is also the homestead exemption that we discussed in Chapter 5 that protects some of the debtor's equity in his or her home. Debts that are not discharged include child support, alimony, and some taxes. Following amendments to the Bankruptcy Code in 2005, Chapter 7 is not available to individuals who pass a "means test," which analyzes whether the individual earns enough money to be able to fund a Chapter 13 bankruptcy proceeding.

In a Chapter 13 bankruptcy filing, the individual must work with the court to come up with a debt repayment plan. To qualify for Chapter 13, an individual must not have debts that exceed certain limits, which are reset every 3 years. As of 2012, these limits were $1,081,450 for secured debt and $360,475 for unsecured debt.

One of the powerful features of a Chapter 13 filing available to eligible debtors who have more than one lien on their home is called "*lien stripping*," which in certain cases can eliminate junior liens on the debtor's home and is an alternative to foreclosure that should be considered with advice of counsel. Also to be considered before foreclosure is the possibility that the Chapter 13 debtor may be allowed to put past-due payments on secured loans into the debt repayment plan and pay them off over a period of years — a very limited form of loan modification that applies only to past-due payments, not to future payments on a secured loan.

REGULATION OF REAL ESTATE FINANCING

Financing for home loans is a process that has greatly increased in complexity in recent years due to extensive federal and state legislation that attempts to address lending practices that are considered to be unfair, deceptive, or fraudulent.

Truth-in-Lending Act

The **Truth-in-Lending Act (TILA)** is a federal consumer protection law that was enacted in 1968 with the intention of helping borrowers understand the costs of borrowing money by requiring certain disclosures about loan terms and costs and to standardize the way in which certain costs related to the loan are calculated and disclosed. The set of regulations that implemented TILA is known as **Regulation Z**.

One of the most important aspects of Regulation Z is that the **annual percentage rate (APR)**, the terms of the loan, and the total costs to the borrower must be disclosed before the loan is consummated. The APR expresses the effective annual rate of the cost of borrowing, which includes all finance charges, such as interest, prepaid finance charges, prepaid interest, and service fees A disclosure of the APR is helpful in providing consumer information and protection because simply looking at interest rate quotes for a loan can be deceptive, as other costs incurred in closing a loan can vary significantly from lender to lender. The APR, by contrast, gives the prospective borrower a way to compare "apples to apples."

Regulation Z also provides for a 3-day right of rescission for certain types of refinancing loans and junior deeds of trust, but not for seller carry back loans or first trust deeds. Additionally, prepayment penalties, if any, and late charges must be disclosed.

Another important mandate of Regulation Z is that any advertising that contains a **triggering term** must disclose a number of other credit terms, including the APR. A Regulation Z triggering term is any specific term that states the amount or percentage of any down payment (such as" no money down"), the number of payments to be made or the period of repayment, the amount of any payment (such as "$900 per month"), or the amount of any finance charge. Stating only the APR in an advertisement does not trigger the requirement for additional financial term disclosures.

TILA's advertising rules apply to any advertisement that promotes consumer credit for either real or personal property, and to consumer leases. All advertisers, including real estate brokers and developers, as well as lenders and lessors, must comply with TILA's advertising rules.

TILA has been amended numerous times since its inception in 1968 when the power to issue implementing regulations was given to the Federal Reserve Board. In July 2011, TILA's regulatory making authority was transferred to the Consumer Financial Protection Bureau (CFBP).

ATR/QM RULES

One of recent important amendments to Regulation Z is the CFPB's Ability-to-Repay and Qualified Mortgage Rules (**ATR/QM Rules**), which are effective for applications for loans taken on or after January 10, 2014. The ATR/QM Rules require lenders to demonstrate a good-faith effort to determine a borrower's ability to repay loans secured by a residential structure containing 1 to 4 dwelling units, including condominium units, cooperative units, mobile homes, and trailers, if used as a residence. Exceptions include home-equity lines of credit, timeshares, and certain reverse mortgages and bridge loans.

The minimum requirements that creditors must consider under the ATR/QM Rules are:

1. current or reasonably expected income or assets;

2. current employment status;

3. the monthly payment on the covered transaction;

4. the monthly payment on any simultaneous loan that the creditor knows or has reason to know will be made;

5. the monthly payment for mortgage-related obligations;

6. current debt obligations, alimony, and child support;

7. the monthly debt-to-income ratio or residual income (the amount of income remaining after all personal debts, including mortgage payments, have been paid); and

8. credit history.

Also effective January 10, 2014, Fannie Mae and Freddie Mac will no longer purchase a loan that is subject to the ATM/QM rules if the loan:

- is not fully amortizing;

- has a term of longer than 30 years; or

- includes points and fees in excess of 3% of the total loan amount, or such other limits for loan balances as set forth in the Ability-to-Repay rule.

Equal Credit Opportunity Act

Enacted in 1974, the ***Equal Credit Opportunity Act (ECOA)*** is a federal law that prohibits a lender from discriminating against any applicant for credit on the basis of race, color, religion, national origin, sex, marital status, age (unless a minor), or on the grounds that some of the applicant's income derives from a public assistance program. The law applies to all persons who regularly participate in decisions involving the extending of credit, including retailers, credit card companies, banks and other mortgage lenders. As of July 2011, the

Consumer Financial Protection Bureau became the authority for promulgating regulations to implement and enforce ECOA.

Some of the most important provisions of ECOA are that lenders may not:

- ask if the applicant is divorced or widowed; but may ask if the applicant is married, unmarried (meaning single, divorced, or widowed), or separated;
- ask about birth-control practices, child-bearing capacity or expectations, or whether a woman of child-bearing age will stop working to raise children;
- ask about the applicant's receipt of alimony or child support unless the applicant is first notified that such information need not be given; however, such questions may be asked if the applicant requests that income from such sources be used to qualify for a loan. Lenders may ask whether the applicant has any obligations to pay alimony or child support; or
- discount income based on sex or marital status.

Under ECOA, an applicant has the right to receive notification from the lender within 30 days as to what action the lender has taken on a loan application. If an adverse action was taken, the lender must send the applicant an ECOA notice about prohibitions against lending discrimination, the name of the federal agency that enforces compliance with ECOA, and the specific reasons for the denial of credit.

From its inception in 1974, ECOA has been particularly instrumental in helping women obtain credit on an equal footing with men. Failure to comply with the provisions of ECOA can result in punitive damages up to $10,000 for an individual action and up to the lesser of $500,000 or 1% of the creditor's net worth in class actions.

Real Estate Settlement Procedures Act

Enacted in 1974, the **Real Estate Settlement Procedures Act (RESPA)** is a federal law designed to prevent lenders, real estate agents, developers, title insurance companies, and other agents (such as appraisers and inspectors) who service the real estate settlement process from providing kickbacks or referral fees to each other, and from facilitating bait-and-switch tactics. RESPA applies to all purchases of owner-occupied residences of 4 or fewer dwelling units that use funds from institutional lenders regulated by the federal government.

RESPA requires lenders to provide an applicant within *3 business days* of receiving a loan application the following information:

1. a good-faith estimate (GFE) of all costs related to a loan;

2. an information booklet entitled *Shopping for Your Home Loan: HUD's Settlement Cost Booklet*, which summarizes RESPA, closing costs, and the settlement statement; and

3. a mortgage servicing statement that discloses whether the lender will service the loan or transfer the servicing of the loan to another entity.

Violation of RESPA's prohibitions on kickbacks and referral fees can result in criminal penalties up to $10,000 and a 1-year prison sentence.

CALIFORNIA'S REAL PROPERTY LOANS ACT

Found in B&PC §10240, et seq., the **Real Property Loans Act** (also referred to as the Mortgage Loan Broker Law) addresses abuses and loan charges on small loans secured by real property. The law applies only to mortgages or deeds of trust secured by California residential property consisting of a unit in a condominium or cooperative or a residential building where the number of units is 4 or fewer, and where the principal amount of the loan secured by a first lien is less than $30,000 or to loans secured by junior liens, where the principal is less than $20,000. This law requires that real estate brokers who help negotiate a loan must act pursuant to laws regulating mortgage loan originators (which we will discuss briefly in the next chapter), providing borrowers with a loan disclosure statement and, for loans secured by residential property, limits the size of the fees, charges, and commissions paid by the borrower or received by the broker.

Maximum Charges for Costs and Expenses

B&PC §10242 limits the maximum amount of costs and expenses in making the loan that are paid by the borrower, exclusive of actual title charges and recording fees, to 5% of the principal amount of the loan or $390, whichever is greater, but in no event to exceed $700.

Maximum Commissions

Additionally, the Real Property Loans Act limits the total amount of commissions borrowers can be charged on loans secured by a *first trust deed* to 5% of the principal amount of the loan if the loan term is less than three years and 10% if the term is three years or more. For loans that are secured by *junior trust deeds*, the commission may not exceed 5% of the principal amount of the loan where the loan term is less than two years, 10% where the term is at least two years but less than three years, and 15% where the term is three years or more (see Figure 9.1).

Fig. 9.1   **Real Property Loan Law Maximum Commissions**

	Less than 2 years	2 years but less than 3 years	More than 3 years	For loans less than:
First trust deeds	5%	5%	10%	$30,000
Junior trust deeds	5%	10%	15%	$20,000

Balloon Payments

Balloon payments are prohibited if the term of a loan is 6 years or less and the loan is secured by a single dwelling unit in a condominium or cooperative or a residential building of fewer than 3 separate dwelling units. CC §10244.1. This provision does not apply to seller carry back loans.

Charges for Late Payments

A charge for a late payment on an installment due on a loan secured by a mortgage or deed of trust on real property may not exceed $5 or 10% of the installment due, whichever is greater. B&PC §10242.5(a).

Prepayment

A prepayment penalty may not be assessed if the loan is secured by a mortgage or deed of trust on a single-family, owner-occupied dwelling and the loan term is more than 7 years. However, during the first 7 years an amount not exceeding 20% of the unpaid balance may be prepaid in any 12-month period without penalty. A prepayment charge, not to exceed an amount equal to the payment of 6 month's advance interest, may be imposed on any amount prepaid in any 12-month period in excess of 20% of the unpaid balance. B&PC §10242.6(a).

Retention of Loan Documents

The mortgage loan broker must retain copies of loan documents for at least 4 years (most other real estate documents must be retained for at least 3 years). B&PC §10231.2(b).

CALIFORNIA'S SELLER FINANCING DISCLOSURE LAW

Many of the borrower protection laws we have examined exempt seller financing; however, under California's *Seller Financing Disclosure Law* (also referred to as the *Residential Purchase Money Loan Disclosure Law*) if a seller carries back a purchase money loan on residential property consisting of 1-4 dwelling units and an arranger of credit is involved, then the borrower is entitled to receive loan disclosures similar to the disclosures required in conventional loans. A real estate broker who is involved in negotiating the credit, preparing the loan documents, or who is in any way compensated for arranging the credit is considered an arranger of credit under this law. Under this law, an arranger of credit is responsible for providing the required disclosures. CC §§2956-2967. These code protections do not apply if the transaction is already covered by other disclosure laws, such as TILA, RESPA, or the Real Property Loan Law. CC §2958.

Key Terms for Chapter 9

acceleration clause — a clause in either a promissory note, a security instrument, or both that states that upon default the lender has the option of declaring the entire balance of outstanding principal and interest due and payable immediately.

adjustable-rate mortgage (ARM) — a mortgage under which interest rates applicable to the loan vary over the term of the loan.

adjustment period — the time intervals in an adjustable-rate mortgage during which interest rates are not adjusted.

alienation clause — a due-on-sale clause

annual percentage rate (APR) — expresses the effective annual rate of the cost of borrowing, which includes all finance charges, such as interest, prepaid finance charges, prepaid interest, and service fees.

assumption — an agreement by a purchaser to be primarily liable on a loan taken out by the seller.

balloon payment — a payment, usually the final payment, of an installment loan that is significantly greater than prior payments — "significantly greater" generally being considered as being more than twice the lowest installment payment paid over the loan term.

bankruptcy — a legal process conducted in a United States Bankruptcy court, in which a person declares his or her inability to pay debts.

blanket mortgage — a mortgage used to finance two or more parcels of real estate.

bridge loan — a short-term loan (often referred to as a swing loan) that is used by a borrower until permanent financing becomes available.

carryover —under an adjustable-rate loan, an increase in the interest rate not imposed because of an interest-rate cap that is carried over to later rate adjustments.

certificate of discharge — a written instrument used to release a lien created by a mortgage.

construction mortgage — a security instrument used to secure a short-term loan to finance improvements to a property.

credit bid — a bid at a foreclosure sale made by the beneficiary up to the amount owed to the beneficiary.

deed in lieu of foreclosure — a method of avoiding foreclosure by conveying to a lender title to a property lieu of the lender's foreclosing on the property.

defeasance clause — a provision in a loan that states that when the loan debt has been fully paid, the lender must release the property from the lien so that legal title free from the lien will be owned by the borrower.

deficiency judgment — a judgment given to a lender in an amount equal to the balance of the loan minus the net proceeds the lender receives after a judicial foreclosure.

discounted rate — a rate (also called a teaser rate) on an adjustable-rate mortgage that is less than the fully indexed rate.

dual tracking —pursuing foreclosure proceedings and loan modification or other foreclosure prevention alternatives at the same time.

due-on-sale clause — a clause in the promissory note, the security instrument, or both that states that the lender has the right to accelerate the loan if the secured property is sold or some other interest in the property is transferred.

Equal Credit Opportunity Act (ECOA) — a federal law that prohibits a lender from discriminating against any applicant for credit on the basis of race, color, religion, national origin, sex, marital status, or age (unless a minor), or on the grounds that some of the applicant's income derives from a public assistance program.

first mortgage — a security instrument that holds first-priority claim against certain property identified in the instrument.

foreclosure — a legal process by which a lender, in an attempt to recover the balance of a loan from a borrower who has defaulted on the loan, forces the sale of the collateral that secured the loan.

foreclosure consultant — any person who makes any solicitation, representation, or offer to any owner to perform for compensation or who, for compensation, performs any service which the person in any manner represents will in any manner stop or postpone the foreclosure sale; obtain any forbearance from any beneficiary or mortgagee; assist the owner to exercise the right of reinstatement; obtain any extension of the period within which the owner may reinstate his or her obligation; obtain any waiver of an acceleration clause contained in any promissory note or contract secured by a deed of trust or mortgage on a residence in foreclosure or contained that deed of trust or mortgage; assist the owner to obtain a loan or advance of funds; avoid or ameliorate the impairment of the owner's credit resulting from the recording of a notice of default or the conduct of a foreclosure sale; save the owner's residence from foreclosure; or assist the owner in obtaining from the beneficiary, mortgagee, trustee under a power of sale, or counsel for the beneficiary, mortgagee, or trustee, the remaining proceeds from the foreclosure sale of the owner's residence. Exempted from the definition of foreclosure consultant are licensed attorneys who render foreclosure consultant services to clients in the course of his or her practice as an attorney, licensed real estate brokers, and licensed real estate salespersons who work under the supervision of their employing broker.

foreclosure prevention alternative — a first lien loan modification or another available loss mitigation option.

fully amortized loan — a loan whereby the installment payments are sufficient to pay off the entire loan by the end of the loan term.

fully indexed rate — on an adjustable-rate mortgage, the index plus the margin.

Garn-St. Germain Act — a federal law that made enforceability of due-on-sale provisions a federal issue.

home equity line of credit (HELOC) — a revolving line of credit provided by a home equity mortgage.

home equity mortgage — a security instrument used to provide the borrower with a revolving line of credit based on the amount of equity in the borrower's home.

index — under an adjustable-rate mortgage, a benchmark rate of interest that is adjusted periodically according to the going rate of T-bills, LIBOR, or the like.

installment note — a promissory note in which periodic payments are made, usually consisting of interest due and some repayment of principal.

interest — the compensation allowed by law or fixed by the parties for the use, or forbearance, or detention of money.

interest-rate cap —under an adjustable-rate mortgage, the maximum that the interest rate can increase from one adjustment period to the next or over the life of the entire loan.

judicial foreclosure — a foreclosure carried out not by way of a power-of-sale clause in a security instrument, but under the supervision of a court.

junior mortgage — a mortgage that, relative to another mortgage, has a lower lien-priority position.

level payment note — a promissory note under which all periodic installment payments are equal.

leverage — a method of multiplying gains or losses on investments, usually by using borrowed money to acquire the investments.

lien stripping — a method sometimes used in Chapter 13 bankruptcies to eliminate junior liens on the debtor's home.

loan modification — a restructuring or modification of a mortgage or deed of trust on terms more favorable to the buyer's ability (or desire) to continue making loan payments.

maker — the person who makes a promissory note.

margin — a number of percentage points, usually fixed over the life of the loan, that is added to the index of an adjustable-rate mortgage to arrive at the fully indexed rate.

Mortgage Forgiveness Debt Relief Act of 2007 — a federal law that allowed taxpayers to exclude from income debt that was canceled on their principal residence (not on a second home) through foreclosure, loan modification, or other form of debt cancellation. The amount of canceled debt that could be excluded from income was $2 million for a married couple filing jointly, or $1 million for individuals or married persons filing separately. After being extended several times, this Act expired at the end of 2013.

negative amortization — a loan repayment scheme in which the outstanding principal balance of the loan increases because the installment payments do not cover the full interest due.

negative amortized loan (NegAm loan) — a loan by which the installment payments do not cover all of the interest due — the unpaid part of the interest due being tacked onto the principal, thereby causing the principal to grow as each month goes by.

non-judicial foreclosure — a foreclosure process culminating in a privately conducted, publicly held trustee's sale. The right to pursue a non-judicial foreclosure is contained in the power-of-sale clause of a mortgage or deed of trust, which, upon borrower default and the beneficiary's request, empowers the trustee to sell the secured property at a public auction.

notice of default (NOD) — a document prepared by a trustee at the direction of a lender to begin a non-judicial foreclosure proceeding.

notice of sale — a document prepared by a trustee at the direction of a lender that gives notice of the time and place of sale of an identified foreclosed property.

one-action rule — California's foreclosure rule that states that a lender who wishes to foreclose on a mortgage or deed of trust must choose one action only against a defaulting borrower: either a judicial foreclosure in which a deficiency judgment may, in certain cases, be sought, or a non-judicial foreclosure in which a lender may not seek to recover a deficiency.

partial release clause — a clause in a blanket mortgage that allows a developer to sell off individual parcels and pay back, according to a release schedule, only a proportionate amount of the blanket loan.

payee — the person to whom a promissory note is made out.

payment cap —under an adjustable-rate mortgage, the maximum amount that installment payments may increase from one adjustment period to the next or over the life of the loan.

period of redemption — a period of time after a sheriff's sale in a judicial foreclosure proceeding during which the borrower may redeem his or her property by paying off the entire debt plus costs.

power-of-sale clause — a clause contained in most trust deeds that permits the trustee to foreclose on, and sell, the secured property without going to court.

prepayment penalty — a fee charged to a borrower for paying off the loan faster than scheduled payments call for.

primary financing — first mortgage property financing.

promissory note — a contract whereby one person unconditionally promises to pay another a certain sum of money, either at a fixed or determinable future date or on demand of the payee.

purchase money loan — a deed of trust or mortgage on a dwelling for not more than four families given to a lender to secure repayment of a loan which was in fact used to pay all or part of the purchase price of that dwelling, occupied entirely or in part by the purchaser.

real estate owned (REO) — property acquired by a lender through a foreclosure sale.

Real Estate Settlement Procedures Act (RESPA) — a federal law designed to prevent lenders, real estate agents, developers, title insurance companies, and other agents (such as appraisers and inspectors) who service the real estate settlement process from providing kickbacks or referral fees to each other, and from facilitating bait-and-switch tactics.

Real Property Loans Act — a California law that addresses abuses and loan charges on small loans secured by real property.

redemption period — a period of time extending for 3 months after a sheriff's sale if the proceeds of the sale are enough to pay off the debt and all costs of foreclosure; it is 1 year if the proceeds of the sale are not enough to pay off the debt *and* the lender pursues a deficiency judgment. If the lender elects not to pursue a deficiency judgment, there is no right of redemption.

Regulation Z — the set of regulations that implement the Truth-in-Lending Act (TILA).

request for a reconveyance — an instrument that a lender sends to a trustee requesting that the trustee execute and record a deed of reconveyance that is then sent to the borrower.

reverse mortgage — a security instrument for a loan for homeowners over the age of 62 who have a large amount of equity in their homes, usually designed to provide such homeowners with monthly payments, often over the lifetime of the last surviving homeowner who either moves out of the house or dies.

right of reinstatement —at any time within the period from the date of recordation of the notice of default until 5 business days prior to the date of sale, a borrower's right to have his or her loan reinstated by paying all delinquent loan installments, foreclosure costs, and trustee's fees. No right of reinstatement exists after a trustee's sale, when the purchaser immediately acquires all rights held by the former owner, subject to the rights of holders of rights superior to the mortgage that was foreclosed.

second mortgage — a security instrument that holds second-priority claim against certain property identified in the instrument.

secondary financing — second mortgage and junior mortgage property financing

security instrument — the written instrument by which a debtor pledges property as collateral to secure a loan.

seller carry back loan — a loan or credit given by a seller of real property to the purchaser of that property.

Seller Financing Disclosure Law — a California law that requires the seller of real property who carries back a loan to give the purchaser loan disclosures similar to the disclosures required in conventional loans.

senior mortgage — a mortgage that, relative to another mortgage, has a higher lien-priority position.

sheriff's sale — a sale of property following a judicial foreclosure.

short sale — *Error! Bookmark not defined.*a pre-foreclosure sale made by the borrower (usually with the help of a real estate agent) with lender approval of real estate for less than the balance due on the mortgage loan.

single point of contact — an individual or team of personnel employed by a mortgage loan servicer, each of whom has the ability and authority to assist a borrower in assessing whether the borrower may be able to take advantage of a foreclosure prevention alternative offered by, or through, the mortgage servicer.

standby loan commitment — a commitment by a lender to make a take-out loan after construction on a property is completed

straight note — a promissory note under which periodic payments consist of interest only.

subject to — acquiring real property that is burdened by a mortgage without becoming personally liable for the mortgage debt.

subordination clause — a provision in a mortgage or deed of trust that states that the mortgage or deed of trust will have lower priority than a mortgage or deed of trust recorded later.

take-out loan — a loan that provides long-term financing for a property on which a construction loan had been made.

triggering term — any of a number of specific finance terms stated in an advertisement for a loan that triggers Regulation Z disclosure requirements in the advertisement.

Truth-in-Lending Act (TILA) — a federal consumer protection law that was enacted in 1968 with the intention of helping borrowers understand the costs of borrowing money by requiring disclosures about loan terms and costs (in particular, the APR) and to standardize the way in which certain costs related to the loan are calculated and disclosed.

usury — the charging of interest in excess of that allowed by law.

Quiz for Chapter 9

1. As a general rule, a deed of trust has how many parties?
   a. 4
   b. 3
   c. 2
   d. 1

2. Which of the following is a purchase money loan?
   a. a loan to purchase an owner-occupied house
   b. a loan to refinance an owner-occupied house that was previously refinanced before January 1, 2013
   c. both a and b
   d. neither a nor b

3. California's Real Property Loans Act applies to first deeds of trust secured by residential property consisting of 4 or fewer dwelling units where the principal amount of the loan is
   a. less than $20,000
   b. less than $30,000
   c. greater than $50,000
   d. any amount

4. One of the most important aspects of the Truth-in-Lending Act is
   a. to standardize the way in which certain costs of a loan are calculated and disclosed
   b. to prevent lenders and others who service real estate loan transactions from providing kickbacks to each other
   c. to prevent charges and recording fees from exceeding a maximum of $700
   d. none of the above

5. Which of the following terms least belongs with the others?
   a. "no money down"
   b. "low interest rates"
   c. "only 36 payments"
   d. $350,000 asking price

6. A method of multiplying gains or losses on investments, usually by using borrowed money to acquire the investments, is called
   a. indexing
   b. risk stripping

    c. discount rating

    d. none of the above

7. A promissory note under which periodic payments consist of interest only is referred to as a

    a. straight note

    b. fully amortized note

    c. negative amortized note

    d. none of the above

8. Under a deed of trust, who holds legal title as security for a loan?

    a. trustee

    b. beneficiary

    c. trustor

    d. none of the above

9. Which of the following terms least belongs with the others?

    a. trustee

    b. promissory note

    c. payee

    d. maker

10. A method of avoiding foreclosure by having the borrower give possession and title to a property to the lender is called

    a. loan modification

    b. bankruptcy

    c. lien stripping

    d. none of the above

11. A clause in a deed of trust that makes it junior to a later recorded deed of trust is called

    a. a defeasance clause

    b. an alienation clause

    c. a subordination clause

    d. an acceleration clause

12. Under a level payment note

    a. periodic installment payments are equal

    b. there is an initial discount rate

    c. the size of the installment payments vary over the life of the loan

    d. none of the above

13. A judgment given to a lender in an amount equal to the balance of the loan minus the net proceeds the lender receives after a judicial foreclosure is called a

    a. discounted judgment

    b. discharge judgment

    c. deficiency judgment

    d. foreclosure judgment

14. A mortgage that the purchaser gives the seller is called a

    a. seller carry back loan

b. purchase money mortgage
c. reverse mortgage
d. blanket mortgage

15. A developer owns three parcels of real property. He wants to get a mortgage for which he plans to offer all three parcels as security. What type of mortgage will he try to obtain?
    a. bridge mortgage
    b. blanket mortgage
    c. purchase money mortgage
    d. none of the above

16. A fully amortized loan is one in which
    a. the periodic payments pay all of the interest but not enough principal to fully pay off the loan by the end of the loan term
    b. there is a balloon payment
    c. there is an initial discount rate
    d. none of the above

17. Under California's Real Property Loans Act the maximum amount of costs and expenses in making any covered loan that are paid by the borrower, exclusive of actual title charges and recording fees is
    a. $700
    b. $390
    c. 5% of the loan amount
    d. 10% of the loan amount

18. A clause in a mortgage that states that when the loan debt has been paid in full the lender must release the property from the lien is called a
    a. subordination clause
    b. defeasance clause
    c. reconveyance clause
    d. none of the above

19. Under a deed of trust, within how many days after a loan is paid off does a lender have to submit to the trustee a request for reconveyance?
    a. 10 days
    b. 20 days
    c. 30 days
    d. 45 days

20. A clause in a promissory note that, in the event of a default, gives the payee the right to declare the entire amount due and payable immediately is called
    a. an acceleration clause
    b. a due-and-payable clause
    c. a defeasance clause
    d. an alienation clause

21. A mortgage that, relative to another mortgage, has a lower lien-priority position is called a

a. second mortgage
b. subordinated mortgage
c. nonconforming mortgage
d. none of the above

22. A sale of property following a judicial foreclosure of a mortgage loan is called a
    a. mortgage sale
    b. trustee's sale
    c. judicial sale
    d. none of the above

23. Which of the following terms least belongs with the others?
    a. nonjudicial foreclosure
    b. deficiency judgment
    c. right of reinstatement
    d. trustee's sale

24. A deed of reconveyance is
    a. an instrument used by a seller to convey title to a purchaser
    b. an instrument used to eliminate a deed of trust from the records
    c. an instrument used by a beneficiary to place legal title with a trustee
    d. none of the above

25. Bank-owned properties acquired through foreclosure are called
    a. blighted properties
    b. reinstated properties
    c. take-out properties
    d. none of the above

26. The most important difference between a typical mortgage and a typical deed of trust is the
    a. length of the loan term
    b. interest rate on the loan
    c. foreclosure process
    d. loan modification

27. Under a deed of trust, the party who has the right to possess, use, and enjoy the property is called the
    a. beneficiary
    b. trustee
    c. trustor
    d. mortgagee

28. The Truth-in-Lending Act is implemented by
    a. Regulation X
    b. Regulation Y
    c. Regulation Z
    d. Regulation A

29. Under California usury laws, in which of the following loans can a lender charge any amount of interest that the market will bear?

   a. seller carry back loans
   b. loans made by a California state bank
   c. loans negotiated by a real estate broker
   d. all of the above

30. Even if a deed of trust contains a due-on-sale clause, the clause cannot be enforced if the transfer of an interest in the secured property
   a. is made to the seller's spouse
   b. is made to the seller's children
   c. is by devise
   d. all of the above

31. The typical mortgage that most likely would contain a partial release clause is a
   a. bridge mortgage
   b. purchase money mortgage
   c. blanket mortgage
   d. junior mortgage

32. A type of mortgage that allows borrowers to borrow only what they need as they need it is a
   a. purchase money mortgage
   b. standby mortgage
   c. home equity mortgage
   d. blanket mortgage

33. A type of mortgage for homeowners over the age of 62 who have large amounts of equity in their home would most likely be a
   a. reverse mortgage
   b. blanket mortgage
   c. retirement mortgage
   d. purchase money mortgage

34. Who is entitled to receive any proceeds from the trustee's sale that are left over after all liens and foreclosure costs are paid?
   a. the beneficiary
   b. the trustor
   c. the sheriff
   d. the trustee

35. If after a sheriff's sale the lender pursues a deficiency judgment, the borrower has how long in which to redeem the property?
   a. 20 days
   b. 3 months
   c. 1 year
   d. there is no redemption period after a sheriff's sale

Answers for Chapter 9 Quiz

1. b. A deed of trust is a three-party agreement involving a trustor, the beneficiary, and a trustee.

2. a. A purchase money loan is currently defined as "a deed of trust or mortgage on a dwelling for not more than four families given to a lender to secure repayment of a loan which was in fact used to pay all or part of the purchase price of that dwelling, occupied entirely or in part by the purchaser." CCP §580b. Therefore, a refinance prior to January 1, 2013 is not a purchase money loan and a refinance of a loan that is not a purchase money loan is itself not a purchase money loan.

3. b. In the hypothesized situation, the Real Property Loans Act applies only to loans under $30,000.

4. a. The Truth-in Lending Act is a federal consumer protection law that was enacted in 1968 with the intention of helping borrowers understand the costs of borrowing money by requiring disclosures about loan terms and costs (in particular, the APR) and to standardize the way in which certain costs related to the loan are calculated and disclosed.

5. d. "No money down," "low interest rates," and "only 36 payments" are TILA triggering terms; price is not.

6. d. Leverage is a method of multiplying gains or losses on investments, usually by using borrowed money to acquire the investments.

7. a. A straight note is a promissory note under which periodic payments consist of interest only.

8. a. Under a deed of trust, the beneficiary receives a promissory note; the trustee holds legal title.

9. a. A promissory note is a contract whereby a maker unconditionally promises to pay a payee a certain sum of money at a future date.

10. d. Deed in lieu of foreclosure is a method of a borrower to avoid foreclosure of a loan secured by property by giving legal title to the property to the lender.

11. c. A subordination clause is a provision in a mortgage or deed of trust that states that the mortgage or deed of trust will have lower priority than a mortgage or deed of trust recorded later.

12. a. A level payment note is a promissory note under which all periodic installment payments are equal.

13. c. A deficiency judgment is a judgment given to a lender in an amount equal to the balance of the loan minus the net proceeds the lender receives after a judicial foreclosure.

14. a. A seller carry back loan is a loan or credit given by a seller of real property to the purchaser of that property.

15. b. A blanket mortgage is a mortgage used to finance two or more parcels of real estate.

16. d. A fully amortized loan is a loan whereby the installment payments are sufficient to pay off the entire loan by the end of the loan term.

17. a. The operative word here is "any," so the formula "5% of the principal amount of the loan or $390 whichever is greater, but in no event to exceed $700" gives us $700 as the maximum for *any* possible covered loan.

18. b. A defeasance clause is a provision in the loan that states that when the loan debt has been fully paid, the lender must release the property from the lien so that legal title free from the lien will be owned by the borrower.

19. c. The lender is required to submit to the trustee a request for reconveyance within 30 days after the loan is paid off.

20. a. An acceleration clause is a clause in either a promissory, a security instrument, or both that states that upon default the lender has the option of declaring the entire balance of outstanding principal and interest due and payable immediately.

21. d. A junior lien secures a mortgage that, relative to another mortgage, has a lower lien-priority position. Though a second mortgage is junior to a first, it is senior to a third.

22. d. A sheriff's sale is a sale of property following a judicial foreclosure on a mortgage loan.

23. b. The trustee's sale is a nonjudicial sale in which the borrower has a right of reinstatement up until 5 business days prior to the sale.

24. b. A deed of reconveyance is an instrument that a trustee signs that transfers legal title to a borrower after the borrower has paid the loan in full.

25. d. Bank-owned properties acquired through foreclosure are called real estate owned properties.

26. c. If a default occurs, a typical true mortgage uses a judicial foreclosure proceeding while a deed of trust will generally use a nonjudicial foreclosure proceeding.

27. c. Under a deed of trust, the borrower (the trustor) has possession of the secured property.

28. c. Regulation Z is the set of regulations that implement the Truth-in-Lending Act (TILA).

29. d. California usury laws exempt seller carry back loans, loans made by a California state bank, and loans negotiated by real estate brokers.

30. d. A transfer by devise or to a spouse or child does not permit the enforcement of due-on-sale clauses.

31. c. A partial release clause is a clause in a blanket mortgage that allows a developer to sell off individual parcels and pay back, according to a release schedule, only a proportionate amount of the blanket loan.

32. c. A home equity mortgage is a security instrument used to provide the borrower with a revolving line of credit based on the amount of equity in the borrower's home.

33. a. A reverse mortgage is a security instrument for a loan for homeowners over the age of 62 who have a large amount of equity in their homes, usually designed to provide such homeowners with monthly payments, often over the lifetime of the last surviving homeowner who either moves out of the house or dies.

34. b. If after the sale there are any proceeds remaining after all liens and foreclosure expenses have been paid, such remaining proceeds would belong to the borrower (trustor).

35. c. The period of redemption is 3 months after the sheriff's sale if the proceeds of the sale were enough to pay off the debt and all costs of foreclosure; it is 1 year if the proceeds of the sale were not enough to pay off the debt *and* the lender pursues a deficiency judgment. If the lender elects not to pursue a deficiency judgment, there is no right of redemption.

Chapter 10

The Primary & Secondary Mortgage Markets

In this chapter we will discuss the primary and secondary mortgage markets, with an emphasis on residential loans. The ***primary mortgage market*** consists of the market wherein mortgage loans are originated. Lenders that create these mortgages include institutional lenders such as commercial banks, savings and loan associations, and life insurance companies, as well as noninstitutional lenders, such as credit unions, pension funds, mortgage companies, private individuals, and real estate investment trusts (REITs). We will also discuss the loan process, the originators and lenders of loans, and the federal programs that either purchase many of these loans or guarantee them, thereby creating a flourishing secondary mortgage market.

The ***secondary mortgage market*** is the market wherein mortgages are sold by primary mortgage lenders to investors, such as pension funds and insurance companies.

THE LOAN PROCESS

The ***residential loan*** process consists of:

1. application;
2. loan processing;
3. underwriting analysis; and
4. loan approval, funding and closing.

By "residential loan" we mean (as defined by the ***Secure and Fair Enforcement for Mortgage Licensing Act of 2008*** ("***SAFE Act***")) a loan primarily for personal, family, or household use secured by a residential structure that contains 1 to 4 dwelling units. The term "residential structure that contains 1 to 4 dwelling units" includes an individual condominium unit, cooperative unit, mobile home, manufactured home, and trailer, if it is used as a residence.

Another term intimately connected with the SAFE Act is "***mortgage loan originator***" (MLO). A mortgage loan originator is anyone who takes, or offers to take a residential mortgage loan application or offers or negotiates terms of a residential mortgage application for compensation or gain or in expectation of compensation or gain. Thus, a licensed real estate broker would be subject to the strict regulations governing an MLO (regulations that we examine briefly later in this chapter) if he or she received or expected to receive something of value from the lender, another MLO, or any agent of a lender or another MLO, for taking, offering, or negotiating the terms of a residential loan. A seller who finances the purchaser of a residential property through a seller carry back loan is not considered an MLO.

APPLICATION

In the years leading up to the mortgage loan crisis that began in 2007, getting a mortgage was relatively easy — in many cases, too easy. During those heady years, a prospective purchaser could call up a real estate agent, hop into the agent's car, go looking for the purchaser's dream house, and, when found, apply for a loan on the house, being reasonably confident that the loan would be approved. But after the loan crisis began, prospective purchasers and real estate agents quickly became aware that the first step in shopping for a house is shopping for a loan.

There are two approaches to beginning the loan process: *loan prequalification* and *loan preapproval*. To obtain a prequalification letter, a prospective purchaser simply has to call an MLO, provide some information on income, assets, debts, and potential down payment. The MLO will probably get back to the prospect by fax or e-mail within a few minutes with a prequalification letter that gives an estimate of the amount of loan for which the prospect might be able to qualify. There is no cost, no verification, and no commitment involved. Today, all of this can even be done on various websites, with an instant response generated by a computer program. The only value of obtaining a prequalification letter is that (assuming the information provided was accurate) it gives the prospective purchaser an idea as to the price range of a house for which the purchaser might be able to obtain a loan.

Obtaining a preapproval letter, on the other hand, involves verification of the information provided and may require an application fee. Citing B&PC §§10176(a),(b),(c) and (k) and 10177 (g) and (j), the CalBRE takes the position that, unless authorized by a creditor/lender to do so, an MLO who is not a creditor/lender may not give a preapproval letter — only creditors/lenders may give a preapproval letters.

Though obtaining a preapproval letter is not a guarantee that a loan will be approved (approval would only come after appraisal of the property, title search, and other verifications not performed during the preapproval stage), having a preapproval letter in hand gives the prospective purchaser legitimacy in the eyes of sellers (who may not wish to negotiate at all with anyone who is not preapproved) and in the eyes of real estate agents who probably will work harder, knowing that the prospect is a well-qualified, serious potential purchaser of a home.

Advance fees paid upfront by the prospective borrower to cover costs of services performed in arranging and originating the loan are subject to strict regulations. An MLO must obtain approval from the CalBRE before charging advance loan fees. Additionally, all advance fees must be placed into the broker's trust account and withdrawn only after the services charged for are paid by the broker.

LOAN PROCESSING

As discussed in the immediately preceding chapter, once a prospective borrower has submitted a completed application with the supporting documentation required to make a credit decision, the lender must make numerous disclosures required by RESPA, ECOA, TILA, and other federal and state laws. The application form that has become standard for residential loans is often referred to as *Form 1003*.

Loan processing consists of assembling all of the information necessary for a lender to assess the risk of the proposed loan. There are two broad categories of information to be assembled to determine a borrower's ability and willingness to repay the debt: borrower information and property information. Investigation and analysis of borrower information and property information, in turn, exposes what is often spoken of as the *three Cs of credit*: capacity, character, and collateral.

Borrower Information

The loan processor gathers information and verifies that information to help the lender assess the borrower's *character* and *capacity*.

Character

In loan processing, character refers to a borrower's willingness/desire to make payments and fulfill other obligations under a mortgage loan.

Purpose of the Loan

The borrower's intended purpose for using the loan funds is important for assessing risk. There are five common categories of loan purpose:

1. to purchase an owner-occupied residence — considered to be the loan purpose with the lowest risk — or second home;
2. to purchase investment property;
3. to obtain a loan with a better interest rate or more favorable terms;
4. to obtain an equity loan to finance home improvements or other financial need, such as tuition for college; or
5. for the purpose of "cashing out," where the new loan is large enough to pay off an old loan in full plus give the borrower extra cash. Cash-out refinances are considered to have a higher risk than other loans and usually carry a .25% to .50% increase in the interest rate.

Credit History

Lenders place considerable emphasis on the borrower's ability/willingness to fulfill financial obligations as evidenced by the borrower's track record of repaying past debt obligations in a timely manner. To help make this assessment, lenders rely on credit scores and reports by the large credit reporting agencies and on a **FICO (Fair Isaac Corporation) score**, which ranges from 300 to 850 (median≈720), where a higher score indicates less risk. Probably the second most significant credit report qualifier is the borrower's history of making timely payments on an existing mortgage or, if renting, on lease payments. Delinquencies during the past couple of years are usually considered unacceptable.

Capacity to Repay

Capacity refers to the borrower's ability to repay the loan in accordance with loan terms. The main components of capacity are

1. source of income;
2. assets; and
3. liabilities.

Source of Income

Data on the borrower's historical income, length of employment, future trends of such employment, investment income, and income from other sources are important for proper analysis of future ability to make mortgage payments. W-2 statements for wage earners, tax returns for self-employed persons, and eligibility to receive pension or Social Security income for retired persons are generally required.

Assets

The amount of assets owned by a borrower and the liquidity of those assets are important determinants as to whether the borrower has the ability to make the down payment as well as to overcome interruptions in income. Having equity in assets, such as other real estate, stocks, or insurance policies, also demonstrates the owner's overall financial substance.

Liabilities

A loan processor must also obtain information on monthly housing expenses, which the underwriter will use to establish a ratio of monthly housing expenses to monthly gross income (referred to as the ***front-end ratio***), and information on total monthly recurring debt obligations, which the underwriter will use to establish a ratio of total monthly expenses to monthly gross income (referred to as the ***back-end ratio***). Monthly housing expenses include home-loan payments, property taxes, private mortgage insurance (PMI), hazard insurance, and dues and assessments of homeowner's associations. Total monthly expenses include housing expenses plus additional long-term monthly debt service, such as for car payments, credit card payments, child support, and alimony. In this context, "long-term debt" typically refers to debt that is not scheduled to be retired within 9 months.

> **Example:** Suppose that
>
> - monthly gross income = $4,000;
> - monthly housing expenses = $1,000; and
> - additional long-term monthly debt expenses = $400.
>
> In this case,
>
> - front-end ratio = $1,000 ÷ $4,000 = 25%
> - back-end ratio = $1,400 ÷ $4,000 = 35%

As we will see later in this lesson, a front-end ratio of 25% and a back-end ratio of 35% will qualify for most loans, assuming that other elements of the borrower's loan application are within loan guidelines.

Property Information

After a lender has granted a loan on a property, the lender has to rely for many years or decades on the value of the property — the ***collateral*** — as security for the loan. Therefore, the lender will want from the loan processor information sufficient to qualify the property as well as the borrower. To obtain this information the loan processor will order the following reports:

1. *Preliminary Title Report*: A preliminary title report
   a) identifies the property with an assessor's parcel number, street address, and legal description;
   b) identifies the current owner of the residence; and
   c) reveals title policy exceptions, such as property taxes, assessments, encumbrances, liens, and easements.
2. *Appraisal*: To determine the value of a property an appraiser will be engaged to inspect the property to ascertain such things as current market value, conditions of the land and of property improvements, the appeal and amenities of the neighborhood, and market conditions, such as sales of similar homes of neighboring properties. We will discuss real estate appraisal in greater depth in the next chapter
3. *Property Due Diligence*: The loan processor should also determine whether there is an occupant of the residence (such as a long-term guest) who is asserting a claim, whether there are any assessments against the property not disclosed on the preliminary title report, and whether there has been any work done on the property within the last 90 days that might result in mechanics' liens against the property.

UNDERWRITING ANALYSIS

When the loan processor has completed assembling and verifying the borrower and the property information, all of this data is sent to a **loan underwriter** who analyzes the risk of, and recommends whether to approve, the proposed loan. Today, the process of underwriting a mortgage loan is increasingly being performed by computerized underwriting systems such as Desktop Underwriter® rather than by the traditional manual system. Such automated underwriting increases objectivity and reduces underwriting time from weeks to minutes.

Borrower's Capacity

In analyzing the borrower's capacity for repaying the loan, the underwriter calculates the front-end and back-end ratios and compares them to the underwriting guidelines established for the type of loan the borrower is applying for. For **conventional loans** (loans that are not FHA insured or VA guaranteed) the current Federal National Mortgage Association ("Fannie Mae") guideline is that the back-end ratio (referred to by Fannie Mae as "maximum DTI" (debt-to-income ratio)) should be no greater than 36%, with allowable ratios up to 45% if specific criteria of Fannie Mae's Eligibility Matrix are met. FHA-insured and VA-guaranteed loans have their own debt-to-income ratio guidelines, which are discussed below.

Security of the Property

In analyzing the amount of security the lender should have in the property used to secure the loan, the underwriter will consider the property appraisal and other property information, as described above, the type of property, the loan-to-value ratio, and private mortgage insurance (PMI).

Type of Property

Owner-occupied homes are considered to have the least risk. Duplexes, townhouses, condominiums, and investment properties have higher rates of default.

Loan-to-Value Ratio

The *loan-to-value ratio (LTV)* is an important risk factor lenders use to assess the viability of a proposed loan. LTV is defined as the amount of a first mortgage divided by the lesser of (1) the appraised value of the property or (2) the purchase price of the property. As a general rule, a high LTV (usually seen as over 80%) will either cause:

- the loan to be denied;
- the lender to increase the cost of the loan to the borrower; or
- the lender to require that the borrower pay for private mortgage insurance.

Private Mortgage Insurance

Private mortgage insurance (PMI) is insurance that lenders often require for loans with an LTV more than 80%. PMI covers the top amount of the loan in case of default.

> **Example:** For a property with an appraised value of $100,000 and a loan of $90,000, the LTV would be 90%. If the lender required PMI to cover the top 20% of the loan, the PMI coverage for the lender would be 20% of $90,000 = $18,000.

In the past, lenders usually honored a borrower's request to cancel PMI once the borrower's equity in the home reached 80% of the value of the property and the borrower had a good payment history. However, many homeowners did not know, or did not remember, that they could make this request, so they continued paying unnecessary PMI premiums. The *Homeowner's Protection Act (HPA)* of 1998 requires lenders to provide borrowers with certain disclosures, including when the balance of the loan is scheduled to reach 80% of the property value, as does CC §2954.6. [Note: neither HPA nor CC §2954.6

applies to FHA-insured or VA-guaranteed loans.] HPA also requires that PMI be canceled when the mortgage balance reaches 78% of the property value (77% for "high risk loans") and the borrower is current on the loan.

LOAN APPROVAL, FUNDING, AND CLOSING

Once the residential loan processing and underwriting analysis has been completed, a lender's loan committee will approve or disapprove the loan. If the loan is approved, the borrower will receive and sign a final Uniform Settlement Statement (HUD-1); the closing agent (usually an escrow or title company) will record the mortgage or deed of trust at the county recorder's office; a title company will issue a title insurance policy; and the loan funds will be dispersed.

LOAN ORIGINATORS AND LENDERS

A residential loan typically begins with the potential borrower contacting an MLO, who may be a real estate broker who has an MLO endorsement. Effective January 1, 2011, all real estate licensed salespersons, brokers, and companies must obtain an MLO license endorsement before soliciting, offering, or participating in negotiations for residential loans. The SAFE Act, which established the **Nationwide Mortgage Licensing System and Registry (NMLS)**, requires state-licensed MLOs to complete 20 hours of pre-license education, pass both a National and a California MLO examination, and submit fingerprints and an authorization to obtain a credit report. Yearly renewal of the MLO license endorsement is required. To obtain the annual renewal, the MLO must complete 8 hours of continuing education. MLOs employed by an insured depository institution (such as a bank or savings and loan) must register with the NMLS but do not need to be licensed under California state law.

Many different kinds of lenders operate in the primary mortgage market. While institutional lenders such as state banks, national banks, and savings and loans create many residential loans, life insurance companies operating in the primary mortgage market create mortgages mainly for large commercial and industrial properties.

Many noninstitutional lender mortgages are created by mortgage companies, which can be either **mortgage bankers** (who lend their own money, either selling the loan to another lender or keeping the loan as an investment) or **mortgage brokers**, who find borrowers and match them with lenders for a fee.

A **real estate investment trust (REIT)** is a company that invests in and, in most cases, operates income-producing real estate. REITs typically combine the capital of individual investors with the mortgage skills of a sponsor, who specializes in properties such as large apartment buildings and shopping centers, the purchase of which requires financing that could not be handled by a signal purchaser. Because of their involvement in real estate transactions, real estate licensees have for many years been involved in the syndication of REITs.

One of the advantages of a REIT is that it can qualify for the pass-through of U.S. corporate income tax (i.e., distributed income would not be subject to federal corporate tax) if it satisfies numerous criteria, including:

- be jointly owned by at least 100 persons;
- distribute annually at least 90% of its taxable income;
- have no more than 50% of its shares held by five or fewer individuals during the last half of each taxable year (the 5/50 rule);
- have at least 75% of its assets invested in real estate; and
- derive at least 75% of its gross income from rents on real property or from mortgage interest.

FHA, VA, DVA, AND CALHFA

In this section we will discuss the influences that the Federal Housing Administration (FHA), the Department of Veterans Affairs (VA), the California Housing Finance Agency (CalHFA), and the California Department of Veterans Affairs (DVA) have on the primary mortgage market.

FHA-INSURED LOANS

The FHA was created by the National Housing Act of 1934 in order to make housing more affordable by increasing home construction, reducing unemployment, and making home mortgages more available and affordable. The FHA does not make loans; it insures loans that approved lenders make for residential properties of 1 to 4 dwelling units. The availability of FHA-insured loans is particularly helpful for people who cannot afford a conventional down payment or do not qualify for PMI.

The benefits of FHA-insured loans include:

- relatively high LTVs, with down payments as little as 3.5%;
- down payments can be gifted by a relative;
- the loans cannot have a prepayment penalty;
- lower FICO scores are required than are required by conventional loans;
- the loans are assumable upon approval by the FHA; and
- relatively lenient front-end debt-to-income ratios (the standard guideline is 29%; 31% max) and back-end debt-to-income ratios (the standard guideline is 41%; 43% max).

The disadvantages of FHA-insured loans include:

- relatively low loan amounts: FHA-insured loans have caps that the FHA will insure of varying amounts depending upon the relative value of homes in various areas. As of 2014, the maximum loan amount the FHA will insure for California single-family homes is $625,500;
- upfront mortgage insurance premium (upfront MIP) and annual MIP premiums;
- requires that properties meet certain minimum standards as determined by an FHA-approved appraiser.

VA-GUARANTEED LOANS

The VA-guaranteed loan program is designed to help veterans obtain affordable loans. Like the FHA, the VA does not make loans — approved lenders make the loans. The VA guarantee works much like PMI in that the VA will reimburse the lender for part of the lender's loss in case of default and foreclosure.

Eligibility

Eligibility for a VA-guaranteed loan depends upon the length of active service in the United States armed forces. Periods are longer for peacetime service (181 days) than for wartime service (90 days). Persons who served in the National Guard or Selected Services are also eligible, usually with six years service. Persons dishonorably discharged are not eligible

Application

Eligible persons must apply to the VA for a *Certificate of Eligibility* (can be done online), which the applicant must present to the lender. The property must be appraised pursuant to VA guidelines. The appraisal value is presented in a *Certificate of Reasonable Value (CRV)*.

Advantages of a VA-Guaranteed Loan

Reasons why VA-guaranteed loans are attractive include:

- do not require a down payment (so long as the loan does not exceed certain limits, see example below), so LTV can be 100%;
- underwriting standards are less stringent than for FHA or conventional loans;
- no mortgage insurance required; and
- loans are assumable if approved by the VA.

Other VA-Guaranteed Loan Features

Although the VA loan guarantee program does not set a maximum amount that an eligible veteran may borrow using a VA-guaranteed loan, the maximum amount of the guarantee for a veteran with full entitlement is 25% of the VA-determined county loan limit (which in California ranges up to a maximum of $987,500 for 2013) or the appraised value, whichever is less. For example, if the county loan limit is $625,000 and the appraised value is $500,000, the maximum guarantee would be 25% of $500,000 = $125,000. If the appraised value and the loan amount are greater than the county limit, the lender may require a down payment.

The VA does not dictate the interest rate charged by the lender. However, if the rate the lender requires is not acceptable to the borrower, a motivated seller may sweeten the deal by paying a **discount fee** to the lender. Such discount fees are generally determined as follows: 1 per cent of discount (1 point) = 1/6 of 1% interest on the loan. Therefore, for a lender to reduce the interest rate on the loan by 1%, the lender would likely require that six discount points, or 6% of the loan amount, be deducted from the seller's net proceeds of the sale.

CALVET LOANS

The California Department of Veterans Affairs, Farm and Home Loan Division, provides **CalVet loans** to eligible military veterans in California. Calvet loans are direct loans to the veteran, not insured or guaranteed loans, as is the case for FHA and VA programs, respectively.

Eligibility

A military veteran is eligible for a CalVet loan when certain criteria are met, including:

- he or she is currently serving or has been honorably discharged;
- seeks a loan to buy a California farm or home;
- has served a minimum of 90 days active duty, or (1) is a member of the California National Guard or the US Military Reserves, (2) has served at least one year of a six-year obligation, and (3) is seeking to purchase property in a "Targeted Area."

Characteristics of a CalVet Loan

- loans up to a maximum of $521,250 in 2013;
- term of loan is 30 years;
- no prepayment penalty;
- variable interest rates depending on market conditions;

- the loan is not assumable;
- low down payment of 0% to 3% of the purchase price or the appraised value, whichever is the lesser;
- inexpensive life and home hazard insurance;
- the property must be occupied by the veteran;
- title to the property is held by the Department of Veteran Affairs, which first purchases the property, then sells the property to the veteran under a Contract of Sale. When the loan is paid off, a grant deed is issued that transfers the legal title to the veteran.

THE SECONDARY MORTGAGE MARKET

Mortgages created by primary lenders often are sold into the secondary market, thereby creating a source of capital that the primary lenders can use to fund still more loans. Many of these mortgages are packaged into mortgage-backed securities and sold to investors such as pension funds, insurance companies, and hedge funds.

In this section we will discuss four government-related entities, one California and three federal, that purchase mortgages and trust deeds created by primary lenders.

CALHFA PROGRAM

The **California Housing Finance Agency (CalHFA)** was established in 1975 as the state's affordable housing bank to help make low interest loans available to "first-time homebuyers." CalHFA obtains its funds through the sale of tax-exempt bonds. CalHFA uses these funds to purchase mortgages and trust deeds from approved primary lenders. The mortgages that CalHFA-approved lenders write for subsequent CalHFA purchase are fixed-rate, 30-year term mortgages. Mortgage insurance is required.

Eligibility of the purchaser

- must be a U.S. citizen, permanent resident, or qualified alien;
- must satisfy the underwriting requirements of the CalHFA-approved lender and mortgage insurer;
- must live in the home during the entire loan term;
- must complete a CalHFA homebuyer education counseling course; and
- must be a "first-time home buyer," which is defined as someone who has not owned and occupied a home in the past 3 years (there is an exception to this rule for veterans or persons who wish to purchase a home in a **federally designated targeted area**, defined as an area where 70% of

the families who live there earn an income that is less than or equal to 80% of the statewide median income).

Eligibility of the Property

- the home must be located in California;
- the home must be the purchaser's primary residence;
- the sales price of the home must be less than the allowable sales price limit, which varies county by county;
- the area of property must be 5 acres or less; and
- the home must be a detached single-family residence, a condominium, or an attached unit in a planned unit development (PUD).

CalHFA has numerous programs to help California homeowners. For example, in August 2013, CalHFA launched a new CalPLUS loan to address the problem that down payments are one of today's biggest obstacles for first-time homebuyers. CalPLUS is an FHA-insured, 30-year fixed mortgage that can be combined with a zero-interest junior loan up to 3.5% of the first mortgage loan amount for down payment assistance.

FANNIE MAE, FREDDIE MAC, AND GINNIE MAE

As we have seen, the FHA was established in 1934 to help alleviate the housing crisis caused by the 1930's economic depression. The FHA did this by insuring certain loans. The continuing depression demonstrated the need for still more government assistance, and in 1938 the *Federal National Mortgage Association (Fannie Mae)* was established to purchase mortgages from primary lenders, thereby (1) transferring the risks of these loans from the primary lenders to Fannie Mae, and (2) freeing up funds for the lenders to make more loans.

In 1968 Fannie Mae was effectively split into two entities: a privately held corporation that retained the name Fannie Mae and a wholly owned a government corporation within the Department of Housing and Urban Development (HUD) called the *Government National Mortgage Association (Ginnie Mae)*. Whereas Fannie Mae continued to purchase mortgages, Ginnie Mae's role was to guarantee pools of eligible loans that primary lenders issued as Ginnie Mae mortgage-backed securities. Also in 1968, the *Federal Home Loan Mortgage Corporation (Freddie Mac)* was created, also as a privately held corporation, essentially to compete with Fannie Mae in the purchasing of eligible loans.

Though both Fannie Mae and Freddie Mac were private corporations, there was widespread belief that they were impliedly government backed, which helped to drive down their borrowing costs, drive up their stock prices, and lower concern about the extent of risks they were incurring in many of the loans they purchased. And, of course, the more questionable loans Fannie Mae and Freddie Mac were willing to purchase at a profit to the primary lenders, the more questionable loans the primary lenders were willing to make.

As the housing crisis that began in late 2007 worsened, concern mounted that Fannie Mae and Freddie Mac might go bankrupt, and their stock plummeted. Fearing that Fannie Mae and Freddie Mac might take the entire financial system down with them, Secretary of the Treasury, Henry M. Paulson, Jr., decided that a swift, surprise government takeover was required. In his book *On the Brink: Inside the Race to Stop the Collapse of the Global Financial System*, Mr. Paulson states that on Thursday morning, September 4, 2008, he told President Bush: "The first sound they'll hear is their heads hitting the floor." On Sunday, September 7, 2008, the announcement came: Fannie Mae and Freddie Mac were being put into government conservatorship under the **Federal Housing Finance Agency (FHFA)**.

As government conservatorships, Fannie Mae and Freddie Mac still play a major role in the secondary market, purchasing FHA-insured, VA-guaranteed, and conventional loans on residential properties of 1 to 4 dwelling units, condominiums, and PUDs that have been created in conformance with FHFA guidelines. The maximum conforming loan limit for loans originated in 2014 for one-unit properties is $417,000 for most of the country. In the District of Columbia and all of the U.S. states except Alaska and Hawaii, the highest-possible local area loan limit for one-unit properties is $625,500. Loans that exceed these FHFA guidelines are called **jumbo loans**.

Loans created in conformance with FHFA guidelines are called **conforming loans**. **Nonconforming loans** are more difficult to sell into the secondary market, and these loans usually cost borrowers 1/4% to 1/2% more. Loans that primary lenders retain in their own investment portfolios rather than sell into the secondary market are referred to as **portfolio loans**.

Key Terms for Chapter 10

advance fee — a fee charged in advance of services rendered.

back-end ratio — the ratio of total monthly expenses, including housing expenses and long-term monthly debt payments, to monthly gross income.

California Housing Finance Agency (CalHFA) — a California state agency that makes low-interest loans to "first-time homebuyers" from funds derived from the sale of tax-exempt bonds.

CalVet loan — a loan made by the Farm and Home Loan Division of the DVA to eligible military veterans for the purchase of a home or farm in California.

Certificate of Eligibility — a certificate issued by the VA, certifying that the applicant is eligible for a VA-guaranteed loan of a certain amount.

Certificate of Reasonable Value (CRV) — a certificate issued by a VA-approved appraiser that certifies, pursuant to VA guidelines, the reasonable value of a property that is to be used as security for a VA-guaranteed loan.

conforming loan — a loan in conformance with FHFA guidelines.

conventional loan — a mortgage loan that is not FHA insured or VA guaranteed.

discount points — a form of prepaid interest on a mortgage, or a fee paid to a lender to cover cost the making of a loan. The fee for one discount point is equal to 1% of the loan amount.

DVA — the California Department of Veterans Affairs is a California state agency whose mission is to promote and deliver benefits to military veterans and their families who live in California.

Fannie Mae — a U.S. government conservatorship originally created as the Federal National Mortgage Association in 1938 to purchase mortgages from primary lenders.

federally designated targeted area — federally designated locations where homeownership is encouraged and incentivized.

FHA — the Federal Housing Administration is a federal agency that was created by the National Housing Act of 1934 in order to make housing more affordable by increasing home construction, reducing unemployment, and making home mortgages more available and affordable.

FHFA — the Federal Housing Finance Agency is a U.S. government agency created by the Housing and Economic Recovery Act of 2008 to oversee the activities of Fannie Mae and Freddie Mac in order to strengthen the secondary mortgage market.

FICO score — a credit score created by the Fair Isaac Corporation that ranges from 300 to 850 and is used by lenders to help evaluate the creditworthiness of a potential borrower.

Freddie Mac — a U.S. government conservatorship originally created as the Federal Home Loan Mortgage Corporation in 1968 to purchase mortgages from primary lenders.

front-end ratio — the ratio of monthly housing expenses to monthly gross income.

Ginnie Mae — the Government National Mortgage Association is a wholly owned U.S. government corporation within HUD to guarantee pools of eligible loans that primary lenders issue as Ginnie Mae mortgage-backed securities.

Homeowner's Protection Act (HPA) — a federal law that requires lenders to disclose to borrowers when the borrowers' mortgages no longer require PMI.

jumbo loan — a mortgage loan the amount of which exceeds conforming loan limits set by the FHFA on an annual basis.

loan-to-value ratio (LTV) — the amount of a first mortgage divided by the lesser of (1) the appraised value of the property or (2) the purchase price of the property.

mortgage banker — a primary lender that uses its own money in creating a mortgage loan.

mortgage broker — an individual or company that finds borrowers and matches them with lenders for a fee.

mortgage loan originator (MLO) — a person who takes, or offers to take, a residential mortgage loan application or offers or negotiates terms of a residential mortgage application for compensation or gain or in expectation of compensation or gain.

NMLS — the Nationwide Mortgage Licensing System and Registry is a mortgage licensing system developed and maintained by the Conference of State Bank Supervisors and the American Association of Residential Mortgage Regulators for the state licensing and registration of state-licensed loan originators.

nonconforming loan — a loan not in conformance with FHFA guidelines.

points — see discount points.

portfolio loans — loans that primary lenders retain in their own investment portfolios rather than sell into the secondary market.

preapproval —an evaluation of a potential borrower's ability to qualify for a loan that involves a credit check and verification of income and debt of the potential borrower.

prequalification — an initial unverified evaluation of a potential borrower's ability to qualify for a mortgage loan.

primary lender — lenders who originate mortgage loans.

primary mortgage market — the market where mortgage loans are originated.

private mortgage insurance (PMI) — mortgage insurance that lenders often require for loans with an LTV more than 80%.

real estate investment trust (REIT) — a company that invests in and, in most cases operates, income-producing real estate and that meets numerous criteria, such as the necessity of being jointly owned by at least 100 persons.

residential loan — a loan primarily for personal, family, or household use secured by a residential structure that contains 1 to 4 dwelling units. The term also includes a loan for an individual condominium unit, cooperative unit, mobile home, manufactured home, and trailer, if it is used as a residence.

SAFE Act — the Safe and Fair Enforcement for Mortgage Licensing Act of 2008 was designed to improve consumer protection and reduce mortgage fraud by setting minimum standards for the licensing and registration of mortgage loan originators.

secondary mortgage market — the market where mortgages are sold by primary mortgage lenders to investors.

underwriter — one who analyzes the risk of, and recommends whether to approve, a proposed mortgage loan.

VA — the Department of Veterans Affairs is a federal agency designed to benefit veterans and members of their families.

Quiz for Chapter 10

1. A mortgage loan originator may be someone who
   a. creates residential loans
   b. negotiates residential loans
   c. is a licensed real estate broker who takes a residential mortgage application
   d. all of the above

2. Preapproval typically involves
   a. verification of income
   b. appraisal of the property securing the loan
   c. a guarantee that a loan will be approved
   d. both a and b

3. FHA stands for
   a. Federal Housing Association
   b. Federal Housing Assistance
   c. Federal Housing Agency
   d. none of the above

4. Which of the following terms least belongs with the others?
   a. source of income
   b. assets
   c. appraised value
   d. liabilities

5. Monthly car payments are likely to be included in
   a. front-end ratio
   b. back-end ratio
   c. PMI
   d. LTV

6. The secondary mortgage market refers to
   a. the making of second loans
   b. the making of junior loans
   c. neither a nor b
   d. both a and b

7. One of the primary concerns of the SAFE Act is with
   a. ensuring that new homes are built to the latest safety standards as set by the FHFA
   b. reducing mortgage fraud
   c. both a and b
   d. neither a nor b

8. Which of the following terms least belongs with the others?
   a. source of income
   b. property due diligence
   c. appraisal
   d. preliminary title report

9. PMI stands for
   a. primary mortgage insurance
   b. property mortgage insurance
   c. primary mortgage investment
   d. none of the above

10. The law requires lenders to provide borrowers with disclosures as to when PMI is no longer required on the borrowers' loans is referred to as
    a. Nationwide Mortgage Licensing Act
    b. Homeowner's Protection Act
    c. Federal Home Loan Protection Act
    d. none of the above

11. Conventional loans typically require PMI if
    a. the sales price is less than the appraised value
    b. the appraised value is less than the sales price
    c. the LTV is over 80%
    d. the LTV is over 75%

12. The SAFE Act requires how many hours of pre-license education for state-licensed MLOs?
    a. 10
    b. 15
    c. 20
    d. 25

13. Life insurance companies operating in the primary mortgage market primarily fund
    a. residential loans
    b. REIT loans
    c. loans for commercial and industrial properties
    d. FHA loans

14. If it qualifies, one of the advantages of a REIT is
    a. that it only needs 10 persons to get started
    b. that it only needs 50 persons to get started
    c. pass-through of corporate income
    d. none of the above

15. Which of the following terms least belongs with the others?
    a. tax returns for self-employed persons
    b. FICO scores
    c. eligibility to receive pension or Social Security income for retired persons
    d. W-2 statements for wage earners

16. A house that is being purchased for $600,000 has an appraised value of $610,000. If the LTV is 85%, what is the loan amount?
    a. $480,000
    b. $510,000
    c. $518,500
    d. none of the above

17. FHA loans
    a. are always assumable
    b. are assumable only with FHA approval
    c. are never assumable
    d. none of the above

18. VA loans
    a. are always assumable
    b. are assumable only with VA approval
    c. are never assumable
    d. none of the above

19. The SAFE Act does not apply to
    a. individual condominium units
    b. mobile homes
    c. manufactured homes
    d. none of the above

20. Monthly house mortgage payments would be included in
    a. front-end ratio
    b. back-end ratio
    c. DVA
    d. both a and b

21. An FHA loan will have
    a. MIP
    b. PMI
    c. DTI
    d. none of the above

22. Which of the following terms least belongs with the others?
    a. FHA
    b. VA
    c. certificate of eligibility
    d. certificate of reasonable value

23. Conventional loans are never
    a. jumbo loans
    b. portfolio loans
    c. residential loans
    d. none of the above

24. Emily purchased a home for $500,000 for which she obtained a loan of $450,000. The appraised value of the house was $520,000. If the lender

required PMI to cover the top 20% of the loan, the PMI coverage for the lender would be

a. $90,000
b. $100,000
c. $104,000
d. none of the above

25. The California Housing Finance Agency
    a. guarantees loans to veterans
    b. insures loans to veterans
    c. makes loans to veterans
    d. none of the above

26. The SAFE Act requires state licensed MLOs to complete how many hours of continuing education annually?
    a. 5
    b. 8
    c. 10
    d. 12

27. Loans that primary lenders retain rather than sell into the secondary market are referred to as
    a. primary loans
    b. investment loans
    c. portfolio loans
    d. none of the above

28. FHA loans can be
    a. made for any amount
    b. can never exceed $500,000
    c. can never exceed $1 million
    d. none of the above

29. Fannie Mae is
    a. a private corporation
    b. a government conservatorship
    c. no longer operating
    d. none of the above

30. Ginnie Mae is
    a. a private corporation
    b. a government conservatorship
    c. a government corporation
    d. none of the above

Answers for Chapter 10 Quiz

1. d. An MLO is a person who takes, or offers to take, a residential mortgage loan application or offers or negotiates terms of a residential mortgage application for compensation or gain or in expectation of compensation or gain.

2. a. A preapproval typically involves verifying the potential borrower's income and credit but not an appraisal of the property.

3. d. FHA is an acronym for Federal Housing Administration.

4. c. Source of income, assets, and liabilities are the main determinants of a borrower's capacity to pay.

5. b. Back-end ratio is the ratio of total monthly expenses, including housing expenses and long-term monthly debt payments (including such items as car payments), to monthly gross income.

6. c. The secondary mortgage market is the market where mortgages are sold by primary mortgage lenders to investors.

7. b. The SAFE Act was designed to improve consumer protection and reduce mortgage fraud by setting minimum standards for the licensing and registration of mortgage loan originators.

8. a. Property due diligence, appraisals, and preliminary title reports are components of property information that a loan processor assembles.

9. d. PMI is an acronym for private mortgage insurance.

10. b. The Homeowner's Protection Act requires lenders disclose to borrowers when the borrowers' mortgages no longer require PMI.

11. c. As a general rule, conventional loans with LTV over 80% require PMI.

12. c. The SAFE Act requires 20 hours of pre-license education for state-licensed MLOs.

13. c. While institutional lenders such as state banks, national banks, and savings and loans create many residential loans, life insurance companies operating in the primary mortgage market create mortgages mainly for large commercial and industrial properties.

14. c. If it is able to satisfy certain criteria, a REIT may pass-through income for U.S. corporate tax purposes.

15. b. W-2 statements for wage earners, tax returns for self-employed persons, and eligibility to receive pension or Social Security income for retired persons are considered components of a potential borrower's capacity to repay a loan.

16.b. The LTV is the loan amount divided by the lesser of the appraised value and the sales price.

17.b. FHA-insured loans are assumable with FHA approval.

18.b. VA-guaranteed loans are assumable with VA approval.

19.d. The SAFE Act applies to loans primarily for personal, family, or household use secured by residential structures that contains 1 to 4 dwelling units. The term "residential structures" includes individual condominium units, cooperative units, mobile homes, manufactured homes, and trailers, if they are used as residences.

20.d. Everything included in front-end ratios is also included in back-end ratios.

21.a. All FHA-insured loans require that mortgage insurance premiums be paid.

22.a. To obtain a VA-guaranteed loan, a veteran must obtain a certificate of eligibility for himself or herself and a certificate of reasonable value for the property.

23.d. Conventional loans are loans that are not FHA insured or VA guaranteed. They can be jumbo, portfolio, or residential loans.

24.a. 20% of $450,000 = $90,000.

25.d. CalHFA purchases mortgages from approved lenders. The borrower need not be a veteran.

26.b. The SAFE Act requires 8 hours of continuing education annually for state-licensed MLOs.

27.c. Portfolio loans are loans that primary lenders retain in their own investment portfolios rather than sell into the secondary market.

28.a. An FHA loan can be made for any amount, but the FHA will only insure loans up to a maximum that varies from area to area.

29.b. Fannie Mae is a government conservatorship that still purchases huge amounts of eligible mortgages.

30.c. Ginnie Mae was established as, and remains, a wholly-owned government corporation.

Real Estate Valuation and Appraisal

One of the most important characteristics of property, real or personal, is its value. Value has many forms: monetary, sentimental, cultural, educational, etc. In this chapter, we will consider the monetary value of real property and the appraisal process as one method of determining that value.

Because the value of property lies at the heart of the real estate business, real estate agents should have a good grasp of the theoretical concepts of value and of the appraisal process. As a real estate agent, you will constantly be asked by clients what you think is the sales value or rental value of their property.

TWO MAIN TYPES OF VALUE

Though there are many definitions of value, for appraisal purposes they may be divided into two main classifications: subjective value and market value:

Subjective value (also referred to as *value in use*) is value placed on the amenities of a property by a specific person.

> **Example:** If an owner builds a house for his or her specific needs and desires without due concern for resale value (such as a large house with only one bedroom), such a house would likely have more subjective value to the original owner than for most other potential future owners.

Market value is defined for appraisal purposes by HUD/FHA as: *"The most probable price which a property should bring in a competitive and open market under all conditions requisite to a fair sale, the buyer and seller each acting prudently, knowledgeably and assuming the price is not affected by undue stimulus."*

Market value is a distinct concept from market price. ***Market price*** is the price actually paid for a particular property, which might not have been the "most probable price" that the property "should bring" in a competitive and open market with buyers and sellers acting "knowledgeably" and "prudently."

THE FOUR ELEMENTS OF VALUE

For our discussion, we will accept the CalBRE Reference Book definition of the **value** of property: *"value is the present worth of all rights to future benefits, arising out of property ownership, to typical users or investors."* Stated more succinctly, *value is the present worth of future benefits*.

Value is not something intrinsic to property; rather, it is a creation in the minds of people based on certain external circumstances, generally accepted as being the **four elements of value**:

1. **Utility** (also referred to as *functional utility*) refers to the usefulness of property — its ability to satisfy a potential buyer's need or desire, such as to provide shelter or income.
2. **Scarcity** refers to a lack of abundance and is a key component of the theory that supply and demand drive market prices.
3. **Demand** refers to the level of desire for a product. *Effective demand* refers to demand coupled with purchasing power sufficient to acquire the property from a willing seller in a free market.
4. **Transferability** refers to the ability to transfer (such as by sale, gift, or lease) some interest in property to another.

If the property is to have monetary value, it must possess all four of the elements of value to some degree.

> **Example:** An item might be scarce, but with no demand, in which case the scarce item would be essentially worthless (except perhaps in a nonmonetary sense). Or, if an item is not transferable, it will command no market price even if there is high demand for the item.

THE FOUR FORCES THAT CHANGE VALUE

Once established, value can be increased, decreased, or even destroyed by the interplay of four main types of external forces:

1. **environmental and physical characteristics**, such as climate, earthquakes, typography, the availability of shopping centers and other amenities, and the quality of nearby schools and transportation systems;
2. **social forces, ideals, and standards**, such as population growth, divorce rates, and attitudes toward education, recreation or ideal family size;

3. *economic influences*, such as unemployment rates, interest rates, availability of credit, and rental costs; and

4. *political forces and governmental regulations*, such as zoning laws, which affect use and demand for property, rent controls, environmental legislation controlling development, governmental fiscal policy, government guaranteed loans, and government housing.

These four forces constantly interweave to affect, positively or negatively, the value of property. Together, they largely determine the advantages or disadvantages of a particular location — "location, location, location," which are popularly thought of as being the three most important determinants of real property value.

PRINCIPLES OF VALUATION

As we shall see later in this chapter, there are several methods of appraisal (sales comparison approach, cost approach, and income approach); however, regardless of the appraisal method being used, the appraiser takes into account numerous principles of valuation that have been developed by appraisers over the years:

Principle of supply and demand — states that the value of property in a competitive market is influenced by the relative levels of supply and demand: the greater level of demand in relation to the level of supply, the greater the value.

Principle of the highest and best use — states that the best use of a property in terms of value is the use most likely to produce the greatest net return (in terms of money or other valued items, such as amenities) over a given period of time.

Principle of conformity — states that the maximum value of land is achieved when there is a reasonable degree of social, economic, and architectural conformity in the area. For a particular property, however, nonconformity may benefit or reduce the property's value.

> **Example:** If a smaller, lower-quality home is in a neighborhood of larger, higher-quality homes, the value of the lesser home will be raised simply due to its proximity to more valuable properties. This rise in value is referred to as the *principle of progression*. Conversely, the value of a large, high quality home will be lessened by proximity to smaller, lower quality homes by the *principle of regression.*

Principle of change — states that property values are in a constant state of flux due to economic, environmental, political, social, and physical forces in the area.

Principle of four-stage life cycle — states that property goes through a process of development, stability, and eventual wearing out. Property is often seen as being in one of four phases of change:

- *growth* (also referred to as *integration)* is the development stage of the property;
- *stability* (also referred to as *equilibrium)* is the period of stability when the property changes very little;
- *decline* (also referred to as *disintegration)* is the phase when the property's usefulness is in decline and constant upkeep is necessary;
- *revitalization* (also referred to as *rejuvenation)* is the phase when the property is rebuilt, remodeled, or otherwise revitalized to a new highest and best use

Closely associated with the principle of change are the concepts of the *economic life* and *physical life* of a property. A property's economic life (also referred to as *useful life*) is the period of time that the property is useful or profitable to the average owner or investor. The physical life of the property is the period of time that the property lasts with normal maintenance. The economic life of a property almost always ends before its physical life ends.

Principle of substitution — states that the value of a property will tend toward the cost of a comparable, or of an equally desirable, substitute property.

Principle of contribution — states that improvements made to a property will contribute to its value or that, conversely, the lack of a needed improvement will detract from the value of the property. Of course, to maximize net return, the cost of the improvement should be less than the improvement's increase in value to the property as a whole.

Principle of anticipation — states that value is derived from a calculation of anticipated future benefits to be derived from the property, not from past benefits, though past benefits may inform as to what might be expected in the future.

Principle of competition — states that increased competition results in increased supply in relation to demand, and thereby to lower profit margins. Furthermore, where substantial profits are being made, competition likely will follow, reducing the margin of profits and thereby reducing the value of (especially income) properties.

Principle of balance — states that the maximum value of property, its highest and best use, is created and maintained when land use by interacting elements of production are in equilibrium or balance.

> **Example:** If a property is over-improved, too much has been invested in relation to the value of the property, and the property's

return on investment will be lower than — out of equilibrium with — the return on investment of other properties in the area.

LOSS IN VALUE: DEPRECIATION

For appraisal purposes, **depreciation** is defined as the loss in value due to any cause. **Appreciation**, on the other hand, is an increase in value due to any cause (such as inflation or increased demand). The appraisal concept of depreciation ("*actual depreciation*") is distinct from the income tax concept of depreciation ("*book depreciation*" or "*cost recovery*"), which is a mathematical calculation used by tax authorities and accountants to determine a depreciation deduction from gross income. In this chapter, we will only consider depreciation as applied in the appraisal process.

There are three main causes of depreciation:

1. **Physical deterioration** results from wear and tear of use and from natural causes such as water damage or termites. A closely related concept, referred to as **deferred maintenance**, is any type of depreciation that has not been corrected by diligent maintenance.
2. **Functional obsolescence** results (1) from deficiencies arising from poor architectural design, out-dated style or equipment, and changes in utility demand, such as for larger houses with more garage space, or (2) from over-improvements, where the cost of the improvements was more than the addition to market value.
3. **External obsolescence** (also referred to as **economic obsolescence**) results from things such as (1) changes in zoning laws or other government restrictions, (2) proximity to undesirable influences such as traffic, airport flight patterns, or power lines, and (3) general neighborhood deterioration, as might result from increased crime.

Depreciation can be either curable or incurable. **Curable depreciation** is physical deterioration or functional obsolescence that can be repaired or replaced by a prudent property owner at a cost that is less than or equal to the value added to the property. **Incurable depreciation** is (1) physical deterioration or functional obsolescence that cannot be repaired at a cost that is less than or equal to the value added to the property and (2) economic obsolescence (which is beyond the control of the property owner).

PURPOSE AND USES OF APPRAISALS

The basic **purpose of an appraisal** is to estimate the value of a property for a particular use. Appraisals are used for many reasons, including:

1. *Transfer of ownership.*

a) to help sellers determine an asking price;

b) to help buyers determine an offering price;

c) to help listing agents decide whether to accept a listing from an owner (who may have unrealistic expectations) and to help listing agents assist their clients in arriving at realistic expectations regarding the sales price of their clients' properties; and

d) to determine valuation for distribution of estate properties to heirs.

2. *Financing, credit, and insurance.*

a) To help lenders decide whether a property provides sufficient security for a loan or for an extension of credit;

b) to help evaluate the amount of insurance coverage for a property; and

c) to help evaluate the cost of replacement and the settling of claims.

3. *Taxation.*

a) to establish value of improvements for real estate taxes;

b) to help ascertain estate and gift taxes; and

c) to help ascertain the basis for depreciation in regard to income-producing properties.

4. *Miscellaneous appraisal purposes.*

a) to help establish a price the government must pay in eminent domain proceedings;

b) to help establish rents; and

c) to help establish the value of traded properties.

LICENSING OF REAL ESTATE APPRAISERS

The California Real Estate Appraisers' Licensing and Certification Law (B&PC §11300, et. seq.) regulates California real estate appraisers through licensing and investigation of complaints against licensed appraisers. There are four levels of appraiser licenses:

1. Trainee License

a) Education requirement: 150 Hours of education covering 7 modules including the 15 Hour National Uniform Standards of Professional Appraisal Practice (USPAP) Course module. The education may not be more than 5 years old. The applicant must also have successfully completed the Uniform State Residential Licensed Real Property Appraiser Examination.

b) Experience requirement: Once licensed, must be supervised by a certified residential or general licensee in good standing.

c) Scope of permitted practice: Any property that the supervising appraiser is permitted to appraise.

2. Residential License

    a) Education requirement: 150 Hours of education covering 7 modules including the 15 Hour National USPAP Course module.

    b) Experience requirement: A minimum of 2,000 hours encompassing 12 months of acceptable experience.

    c) Scope of permitted practice: Any non-complex 1-4 unit residential property with a transaction value up to $1 million; and non-residential property with a transaction value up to $250,000.

3. Certified Residential License

    a) Education requirement: 200 Hours of education covering 10 modules, including the 15 Hour National USPAP Course and an Associate Degree. In lieu of a Degree, 21 semester credits in specific subject matters may be substituted.

    b) Experience requirement: A minimum 2,500 hours encompassing at least 30 months of acceptable experience.

    c) Scope of permitted practice: Any 1-4 unit residential property without regard to transaction value or complexity; and non-residential property with a transaction value up to $250,000.

4. Certified General License

    a) Education requirement: 300 Hours of education covering 10 modules, including the 15 Hour National USPAP Course and a Bachelors Degree. In lieu of a Degree, semester credits in specific subject matters may be substituted.

    b) Experience requirement: A minimum 3,000 hours encompassing at least 30 months of acceptable experience. At least 1,500 hours of the experienced must be non-residential.

    c) Scope of permitted practice: All real estate without regard to transaction value or complexity.

APPRAISER INDEPENDENCE REQUIREMENTS

Fannie Mae and Freddie Mac will not purchase loans from lenders who do not prohibit sellers, lenders, borrowers and their agents from influencing an appraisal report with respect to mortgages on single-family homes by doing any of the following:

1. withholding or threatening to withhold payment for an appraisal report;
2. withholding or threatening to withhold doing future business with an appraiser;
3. promising future business or increased compensation for an appraiser;
4. conditioning the ordering of an appraisal or payment for an appraisal on the valuation reached by the appraisal or on a preliminary estimation of value reached by an appraiser;

5. requesting that an appraiser provide an estimated or desired valuation prior to the appraiser's completion of an appraisal report;

6. providing an appraiser with an estimated or desired value for the subject property, except that a copy of the sales contract for the purchase transaction may be provided; and

7. any other act that attempts to impair an appraiser's independence, objectivity, or impartiality, or that violates any law or regulation, including the Truth-in-Lending Act (TILA) and Regulation Z, or the Uniform Standards of Professional Appraisal Practice.

Additionally, lenders must ensure that each borrower is provided with a copy of any appraisal report concerning the subject property promptly — in any event, no less than 3 days prior to the closing of the mortgage.

The CalBRE Commissioner has also issued regulations concerning the improper influence of real property appraisers by real estate licensees as follows:

Article 11. Licensee Ethics

2785. Improper Influence of Real Property Appraisers.

(a) In conformance with Civil Code section 1090.5, real estate licensees engaged in a real estate transaction involving an appraisal shall not improperly influence or attempt to improperly influence the development, reporting, result, or review of a real estate appraisal sought in connection with a mortgage loan. For the purposes of the Real Estate Law, "improper influence" as the term is used in Civil Code section 1090.5, includes but is not limited to:

(1) withholding or threatening to withhold timely payment or partial payment for a completed appraisal report, regardless of whether a sale or financing transaction closes;

(2) withholding or threatening to withhold future business from an appraiser, or demoting or terminating or threatening to demote or terminate an appraiser;

(3) expressly or impliedly promising future business, promotions, or increased compensation for an appraiser;

(4) conditioning the ordering of an appraisal report or the payment of an appraisal fee or salary or bonus on the opinion, conclusion, or valuation to be reached, or on a preliminary value estimate requested from an appraiser;

(5) requesting that an appraiser provide an estimated, predetermined, or desired valuation in an appraisal report prior to the completion of the

appraisal report, or requesting that an appraiser provide estimated values or comparable sales at any time prior to the appraiser's completion of an appraisal report;

(6) providing to an appraiser an anticipated, estimated, encouraged, or desired value for a subject property or a proposed or target amount to be loaned to the borrower, except that a copy of the sales contract for purchase transactions may be provided;

(7) requesting the removal of language related to observed physical, functional or economic obsolescence, or adverse property conditions noted in an appraisal report;

(8) providing to an appraiser, appraisal company, or appraisal management company, stock or other financial or non-financial benefits.

(b) Subdivision (a) does not prohibit a person with an interest in a real estate transaction from asking an appraiser to do any of the following:

(1) Consider additional, appropriate property information.

(2) Provide further detail, substantiation, or explanation for the appraiser's value conclusion.

(3) Correct errors in the appraisal report.

(c) Nothing in this section shall be construed to authorize communications that are otherwise prohibited under existing law.

ADDITIONAL REGULATIONS CONCERNING APPRAISALS

Real estate brokers who engage in mortgage loan activities must be careful to remain in compliance with CalBRE requirements concerning appraisals, including the following:

- advance fees for appraisals must be treated as trust funds;
- brokers may not markup fees paid for an appraisal; and
- brokers must provide a copy of all appraisals to prospective purchasers. [Note: effective January 1, 2014, a new rule of the federal Consumer Financial Protection Bureau (CFPB) requires that creditors/lenders of first-lien mortgages must provide notice to loan applicants that they have the right to receive a copy of all appraisals promptly, or three days before closing, whichever is earlier.)

THE APPRAISAL PROCESS

While there is no official order in which the appraisal process is carried out, the following are steps that appraisers typically follow in the process of developing an appraisal report:

Step 1: Define the appraisal problem.

a) Identify the client and the intended users of the appraisal.
b) Identify the intended use of the appraisal. Clients have different appraisal problems they want to solve, such as determining the value for sale, the value for insurance, etc.
c) Identify the relevant characteristics of the property, such as land, improvements, and rights.

Step 2: Determine the scope of work necessary to achieve the purpose of the appraisal.

a) What data specific to the property are needed?
b) What data concerning the neighborhood are needed?
c) Where is this data to be found?

Step 3: Collect, verify, and analyze the data.

Step 4: Apply the pertinent approaches to value: cost, sales comparison, and/or income.

Step 5 Reconciliation: perform a reconciliation of value indications and determine a final opinion of value.

Step 6: Issue the appraisal report.

THE THREE APPRAISAL APPROACHES

There are three appraisal approaches that may be considered, and if necessary reconciled, in making a market valuation of a property:

1. **Sales comparison approach** — compares recent sales of similar properties in the area to evaluate the market value of the subject property.
2. **Cost approach** — obtains the market value of the subject property by adding the value of the land (unimproved) of the subject property to the depreciated value of the cost (if purchased at current prices) of the improvements on the subject property.
3. **Income approach** — determines the market value of the subject property by capitalizing the estimated future income of the property.

Sales Comparison Approach

The sales comparison approach is the best method for appraising land, residences, and other properties for which there is a ready market of similar properties. It is based on what is referred to as the **principle of substitution**, which holds that buyers are generally unwilling to pay more for a property than for a substitute property in the area. Using this method, the appraiser gathers data on recent sales (if sold at fair market value) of comparable properties in the area and makes comparisons of each of the features of the comparable properties to arrive at an estimate of the current market value of the subject property.

Once these data are collected, the appraiser adjusts the sales price of the comparable properties by *estimating what these properties would have sold for if they had had the same features as the subject property*. A **comparable property** is a property similar to the subject property that recently sold at arm's length, where neither the buyer nor the seller was acting under significant financial pressure. Note that it is the value of the similar features of the comparable properties that are adjusted, not the value of the features of the subject property. If a feature of a comparable property is superior to the same type of feature of the subject property, then an adjustment equal to the estimated difference in value of the feature of the comparable property to the feature of the subject property is subtracted from the comparable. If, on the other hand, the feature of the comparable property is inferior to the same type of feature of the subject property, then the estimated difference between the value of that feature of the subject property and the feature of the comparable is added to the comparable.

Cost Approach

The cost approach calculates the value of a subject property by:

1. estimating the value of the land as if vacant;

2. adding the estimated cost of replacing (or reproducing) the improvements at current prices; and then

3. subtracting the accrued depreciation of the improvements.

Fig. 11.1   **Example of Sales Comparison Approach**

Assume that the subject property is a 2,200 ft.², 10-year-old, single-family home in good condition, with a good view, 3 bedrooms, 3 baths, and a 2-car garage. Assume also that there has been no appreciation in home values since the dates of the sales of the three comparables.

	Comparable 1	Comparable 2	Comparable 3	Subject
sales price	$850,000	$920,000	$880,000	?
condition	equal	equal	equal	good
view adjustment	inferior* + $5,000	superior* - $2,000	equal	good
age	equal	equal	equal	10 years old
square footage adjustment	equal	superior*(2,250) - $50,000	equal	2,200
bedrooms	equal	equal	equal	3
baths adjustment	inferior*(2 ½) + $5,000	equal	superior*(3½) - $5,000	3
garage	equal	equal	equal	2
Net adjustment	+ $10,000	- $52,000	- $5,000	
Adjusted sale price	$860,000	$868,000	$875,000	
Indicated value				$870,000

*Inferior means that the comparable's feature is inferior to the same feature of the subject property. Superior means the opposite. A subtraction of value is estimated if the comparable feature is superior; an addition of value if inferior.

Reconciliation: Comparable 3 is the most similar to the subject property, so its adjusted value is given slightly more weight. Indicated value: $870,000.

1. Estimating the value of the land as if vacant: this step is usually performed using the sales comparison approach.

2. Estimating the cost of replacing (or reproducing) the improvements: this step involves first deciding whether to use replacement cost or reproduction cost. **Reproduction cost** is the cost of replacing the improvements with exact replicas at current prices. **Replacement cost** is the cost of replacing the improvements with those having equivalent utility, but constructed with modern materials, designs, and workmanship. If a building is quite old, it likely was built with materials that are now quite expensive and that were installed with detailed hand-labor. In such a case, reproduction cost would not, in general, represent the current market value of the building, so the appraiser would use replacement cost in the appraisal.

3. Calculating the accrued depreciation of the improvements: **Accrued depreciation** is depreciation that has happened prior to the date of valuation.

By contrast, *remainder depreciation* is depreciation that will occur after the date of valuation. The two most used methods of calculating accrued depreciation are the straight-line method and the cost-to-cure method.

The *straight-line method* (also referred to as the *age-life method*) calculates the amount of annual depreciation by dividing the cost of the improvement by the estimated *useful life* (*economic life*) of a typical such improvement. Once the cost and the useful life of an improvement have been determined, calculating the straight-line depreciation is easy, as illustrated in the following example..

> **Example:** If an improvement had a cost of $1,000,000 and a typical such improvement had a useful life of 50 years (with no residual value), the straight-line method would determine the annual depreciation to be $1,000,000 ÷ 50 = $20,000, which is a depreciation rate of 2% per year. Next, the appraiser would estimate the *effective age* of the improvement, which is defined as the age that is indicated by the condition of the structure, as distinct from its chronological age. If in this example, the appraiser determined that the effective age of the improvement was 10 years rather than its chronological age of 20 years (perhaps because of greater than average care and upkeep) then the accrued depreciation would be $20,000 x 10 = $200,000 (rather than $20,000 x 20).

The *cost-to-cure method* calculates depreciation by estimating the cost of curing the curable depreciation and adding to it the value of the incurable depreciation.

The cost approach is the approach of choice if (1) there are few if any comparables in the area (thus eliminating the sales-comparison approach) and the income approach is inappropriate, or (2) the improvements are quite new so that data on precise current costs can be gathered. The older the improvement, the less likely it is that an estimate of replacement cost can be made with precision. Furthermore, replacement cost would not take into consideration changes in the neighborhood, zoning laws, etc. that would have occurred in the meanwhile. Therefore, appraising a 50-year old house using the cost method would likely result in an unrealistic appraisal.

Fig. 11.2   **Example of Cost Approach**

Assume that the subject property is a 50 ft. x 40 ft. rectangular single-story house with an attached 20 ft. x 20 ft. garage. Suppose also that
- the land value is $200,000,
- the replacement cost of the house is $150 per square foot,
- the replacement cost of the garage is $40 per square foot,
- the estimated useful life of similar houses and garages is 50 years, and
- the effective age of this house and garage is 20 years.

Problem: What is the estimated value of the subject property?

Cost Approach Solution:

Subject value = land value + replacement cost - accrued depreciation.

Replacement cost of the house = 50 ft. x 40 ft. x $150/ ft.² = $300,000
Replacement cost of the garage = 20 ft. x 20 ft. x $40/ ft.² = $16,000
Total replacement cost = $300,000 + $16,000 = $316,000

Because the useful life is 50 years, using the straight-line method the rate of depreciation is 100% ÷ 50 years = 2% per year.
The effective age is 20 years, so the accrued depreciation percent in this case would be 20 years x 2% per year = 40%
40% of $316,000 = $126,400 = the accrued depreciation.

  $316,000 replacement cost
- $126,400 accrued depreciation
  $189,600 present value of the house and garage
+$200,000 land value
  $389,600 estimated of value of subject property

Income Approach

The **income approach** (also referred to as the **capitalization approach**) estimates the value of an income-producing property as being an investment (like stocks or bonds) worth the present value of the future income of the property through a three-step process:

1. determine the net annual income,
2. determine an appropriate capitalization rate, and
3. divide the net income by the capitalization rate to obtain the estimate of value; i.e., value = net income ÷ capitalization rate.

Net income is determined as follows:

a) estimate the annual gross income the property;
b) deduct from the gross income an annual allowance for vacancies and uncollectible rents to arrive at the ***effective gross income***; and
c) deduct from the effective gross income the estimate of annual operating expenses, including fixed expenses (such as hazard insurance and real estate taxes), maintenance, and reserves for replacements of building components.

Not all expenses are deducted from effective gross income to obtain net income. Examples of such expenses include mortgage payments and taxes on income.

The ***capitalization rate*** (also referred to as the ***cap rate***) is the rate that an appraiser estimates is the yield rate expected by investors from comparable properties in current market conditions. To estimate the capitalization rate of a certain property, an appraiser will collect data on the market value of comparable properties, on the vacancies and uncollectible rents of these comparable properties, and on the operating expenses these comparable properties. Then, because value = net income ÷ capitalization rate, the capitalization rate can be calculated for these comparable properties as net income ÷ market value.

> **Example:** If the net annual income of a property is $20,000 and the capitalization rate is 8.5% per year, then the income approach valuation of the property would be $20,000 ÷ 8.5% = $235,294 (rounded).

The above example might also take the following form: if an investor purchased a property for $235,294 and derives an annual net income from the property of $20,000, what is the property's capitalization rate? Answer: $20,000 ÷ $235,294 = 8.5%.

A finance concept closely related to the capitalization rate is ***return on investment (ROI)***, which is the investor's cash flow (net income minus financing charges) divided by the investor's actual cash investment (as distinct from the purchase price). Note that the capitalization rate and the ROI would be the same if the investor had paid all cash for the property because in such a case there would be no finance charges and the initial investment would be equal to the sale price.

Though the income approach attempts to measure value through the eyes of an investor, real estate agents should keep in mind that the income approach valuation of property likely will differ significantly from many investors' views of the value of property. This is because investors often value income property for reasons additional to income, such as to obtain deductions from income tax or to obtain the value of anticipated property price appreciation.

Fig.11.3　　　　　**Example of Income Approach**

Assume that an apartment building has the following:
- 10 rental units each having fair market rent of $2,000 per month
- estimated loss for vacancies and uncollectible rents is 10%
- annual fixed expenses (property tax, insurance, etc.) are $30,000
- annual maintenance expense is $45,000
- annual reserve for replacements is $20,000
- the appraiser's capitalization rate is 8%

Problem: What is the value of the apartment building?

Solution

gross income ($2,000/unit x 10 units x 12 months)	$240,000
less vacancies & collection loss (10% of $240,000):	- $24,000
effective gross income :	$216,000
less annual expenses and replacement reserves:	- $95,000
net operating income:	$121,000

value = $121,000 ÷ 8% = $1,512,500

Gross Rent and Gross Income Multipliers

As we have seen, the income approach uses capitalization of *net* income to arrive at the valuation of a property. However, some investors, especially of single-family homes, use a simpler method of determining value: capitalization of *gross* income. If only gross rents are capitalized, this approach to value is called the **gross rent multiplier (GRM)** approach; if additional income is involved (such as from parking fees), the method is called the **gross income multiplier (GIM)** approach.

> **Example:** Using the gross rent multiplier approach, suppose the sales price of a house is $500,000 and the monthly rent is $2,000. In this case the sales price is $500,000 ÷ $2,000 = 250 times the monthly rental; i.e., the monthly gross rent multiplier is 250.
>
> Suppose now that other comparable homes in the area have a monthly gross rent multiplier similar to the home in the prior example. Further, suppose that a comparable home in the area

with a fair market value of $800,000 is to be rented. Using the gross rent multiplier approach, we can simply determine the monthly rent for this subject property by dividing the value ($800,000) by the monthly gross rent multiplier (250) to get a rent of $3,200 per month.

RECONCILIATION

Some properties lend themselves only to one of the above three approaches to valuation.

> **Example:** If the subject property is an older single-family home that has never been rented and is located in an area where few if any homes are being rented, then the only reasonable approach to value is the sales comparison approach. But suppose instead that the subject property is a relatively new single-family home in an area where a significant number of comparable homes are being rented. In this case, all three approaches (sales comparison, cost, and income) may contribute insight into the value of the property, and all three approaches likely would be investigated by an appraiser. Of course, the three approaches probably would give different valuations, in which case the appraiser must use his or her expert experience and judgment to arrive at a final estimate of value. This process of ascertaining value by comparing and evaluating values obtained from different valuation approaches is called *reconciliation*. Note that the reconciliation of estimated values is *not* simply an averaging of those values.

TYPES OF APPRAISAL REPORTS

An appraiser presents his or her final estimate of value in appraisal report, of which there are three types:

Restricted Use Report. This type of report is sometimes used when the client is familiar with the area and a report summarizing the data that supports the final estimate of value is not necessary. The Restricted Use Report must contain a notice that it is to be used only by the client for one particular purpose, not by potential buyers, lenders, or others.

Summary Report. This type of report (also referred to as a *Form Report*) typically consists of several pages of forms to be filled out by an appraiser that contain pertinent data about the subject property, along with photos, maps, and plans. This type of report is most often used by lending institutions, insurance companies, and government agencies.

Self-Contained Report. This type of report (also referred to as a **Narrative Report**) contains a complete description of the data relied on, including data about the neighborhood as well as the property; the reasons the appraiser used for his or her interpretation of the estimate of value; and pertinent maps, photographs, charts, and the plot plans. This type of report is the most complete (and expensive) type of appraisal report and is used for court cases and for clients who are unfamiliar with the area and are, therefore, in need of all the factual data available.

Key Terms for Chapter 11

accrued depreciation — depreciation that has happened prior to the date of valuation.

age-life method — *see*, straight-line method.

appraisal — an estimate of the value of property resulting from an analysis and evaluation made by an appraiser of facts and data regarding the property.

appreciation — an increase in value due to any cause.

book depreciation — a mathematical calculation used by tax authorities and accountants to determine a depreciation deduction from gross income.

capitalization approach — *see*, income approach

capitalization rate — the rate that an appraiser estimates is the yield rate expected by investors from comparable properties in current market conditions.

comparable property — a property similar to the subject property being appraised that recently sold at arm's length, where neither the buyer nor the seller was acting under significant financial pressure.

cost approach — an appraisal approach that obtains the market value of the subject property by adding the value of the land (unimproved) of the subject property to the depreciated value of the cost (if currently purchased new) of the improvements on subject property.

cost recovery — the recoupment of the purchase price of a property through book depreciation.

cost-to-cure method — a method of calculating depreciation by estimating the cost of curing the curable depreciation and adding it to the value of the incurable depreciation.

curable depreciation — depreciation that results from physical deterioration or functional obsolescence that can be repaired or replaced at a cost that is less than or equal to the value added to the property.

deferred maintenance — any type of depreciation that has not been corrected by diligent maintenance.

demand — the level of desire for a product.

depreciation — the loss in value due to any cause.

disintegration — the phase when a property's usefulness is in decline and constant upkeep is necessary.

economic life — the period of time that the property is useful or profitable to the average owner or investor.

economic obsolescence — *see*, external obsolescence.

effective age — the age of an improvement that is indicated by the condition of the improvement, as distinct from its chronological age.

effective demand — demand coupled with purchasing power sufficient to acquire the property from a willing seller in a free market.

effective gross income — income from a property after an allowance for vacancies and uncollectible rents is deducted from gross income.

equilibrium — the period of stability when the property changes very little.

external obsolescence — depreciation that results from things such as (1) changes in zoning laws or other government restrictions, (2) proximity to undesirable influences such as traffic, airport flight patterns, or power lines, and (3) general neighborhood deterioration, as might result from increased crime.

Form Report — *see*, Summary Report.

functional obsolescence — depreciation that results (1) from deficiencies arising from poor architectural design, out-dated style or equipment, and changes in utility demand, such as for larger houses with more garage space, or (2) from over-improvements, where the cost of the improvements was more than the addition to market value.

gross income — total income from a property before any expenses are deducted.

gross income multiplier (GIM) — a number equal to the estimated value of a property divided by the gross income of the property.

gross rent multiplier (GRM) — a number equal to the estimated value of a property divided by the gross rental income of the property.

income approach — an appraisal approach that estimates the value of an income-producing property as being worth the present value of the future income of the property through a three-step process: (1) determine the net annual income, (2) determine an appropriate capitalization rate, and (3) divide the net income by the capitalization rate to obtain the estimate of value.

incurable depreciation — depreciation that results from (1) physical deterioration or functional obsolescence that cannot be repaired at a cost that is less than or equal to the value added to the property and (2) economic obsolescence (which is beyond the control of the property owner).

integration — the growth and development stage of property.

market price — the price actually paid for a particular property.

market value — as defined for appraisal purposes by HUD/FHA is: "The most probable price which a property should bring in a competitive and open market under all conditions requisite to a fair sale, the buyer and seller, each acting prudently, knowledgeably and assuming the price is not affected by undue stimulus."

Narrative Report — *see*, Self-Contained Report.

net income — income from a property remaining after expenses are deducted from gross income.

physical deterioration — depreciation that results from wear and tear of use and from natural causes.

physical life — the period of time that the property lasts with normal maintenance.

principle of anticipation — principle that value is derived from a calculation of anticipated future benefits to be derived from the property, not from past benefits, though past benefits may inform as to what might be expected in the future.

principle of balance — principle that the maximum value of property, its highest and best use, is created and maintained when land use by interacting elements of production are in equilibrium or balance.

principle of change — principle that property values are in a constant state of flux due to economic, environmental, political, social, and physical forces in the area.

principle of competition — principle that increased competition results in increased supply in relation to demand, and thereby to lower profit margins.

principle of conformity — principle that the maximum value of land is achieved when there is a reasonable degree of social, economic, and architectural conformity in the area.

principle of contribution — principle that improvements made to a property will contribute to its value or that, conversely, the lack of a needed improvement will detract from the value of the property.

principle of four-stage life cycle — principle that property goes through a process of growth, stability, decline, and revitalization.

principle of progression — principle that the value of a residence of less value tends to be enhanced by proximity to residences of higher value.

principle of regression — principle that the value of a residence of higher value tends to be degraded by the proximity to residences of lower value.

principle of substitution — principle that the value of a property will tend toward the cost of an equally desirable substitute property.

principle of supply and demand — principle that the value of property in a competitive market is influenced by the relative levels of supply and demand: the greater level of demand in relation to the level of supply, the greater the value.

principle of the highest and best use — principle that the best use of a property in terms of value is the use most likely to produce the greatest net return (in terms of money or other valued items).

reconciliation — the process of ascertaining value by comparing and evaluating values obtained from comparables or from different valuation approaches.

rejuvenation — the phase when a property is rebuilt, remodeled, or otherwise revitalized to a new highest and best use.

remainder depreciation — depreciation that will occur after the date of valuation.

replacement cost — the cost of replacing improvements with those having equivalent utility, but constructed with modern materials, designs, and workmanship.

reproduction cost — the cost of replacing improvements with exact replicas at current prices.

Restricted Use Report — a type of appraisal report that is sometimes used when the client is familiar with the area and a report summarizing the data that supports the final estimate of value is not necessary. The Restricted Use Report must contain a notice that it is to be used only by the client for one particular purpose, not by potential buyers or lenders or others.

return on investment (ROI) — an investor's cash flow (net income minus financing charges) divided by the investor's actual cash investment (as distinct from the purchase price).

sales comparison approach — an appraisal approach that compares recent sales of similar properties in the area to evaluate the market value of the subject property.

scarcity — a lack of abundance.

Self-Contained Report — a type of appraisal report that contains a complete description of the data relied on, including data about the neighborhood as well as the property; the reasons the appraiser used for his or her interpretation of the estimate of value; and pertinent maps, photographs, charts, and the plot plans.

straight-line method — a method of calculating annual depreciation of an improvement by dividing the cost of the improvement by the estimated useful life of a typical such improvement.

subjective value — (also referred to as *value in use*) is value placed on the amenities of a property by a specific person.

Summary Report — a type of appraisal report that typically consists of several pages of forms to be filled out by an appraiser that contain pertinent data about the subject property, along with photos, maps, and plans. This type of appraisal report is most often used by lending institutions, insurance companies, and government agencies.

transferability — the ability to transfer some interest in property to another.

useful life — *see*, economic life.

utility — the usefulness of property; its ability to satisfy a potential buyer's need or desire, such as to provide shelter or income.

value — the present worth of all rights to future benefits, arising out of property ownership, to typical users or investors.

Quiz for Chapter 11

1. Which of the following words least belongs with the others?
   a. utility
   b. price
   c. scarcity
   d. demand
2. Effective gross income is
   a. the rate that an appraiser estimates is the yield rate expected by investors
   b. the income from a property that remains after expenses are deducted from gross income
   c. the total income from a property before expenses are deducted
   d. none of the above
3. The principal of contribution states that
   a. the value of a property will tend toward the cost of a comparable, or of an equally desirable, substitute property
   b. increased competition results in increased supply in relation to demand, and thereby to lower profit margins
   c. the maximum value of land is achieved when there is a reasonable degree of social, economic, and architectural conformity in the area
   d. none of the above
4. If the subject property has an appraised value of $2 million, land value of $500,000, and accrued depreciation on the structure of $200,000, what is the structure's replacement cost?
   a. $1,700,000
   b. $1,800,000
   c. $1,500,000
   d. none of the above
5. Market value is
   a. the price actually paid for a property
   b. the most probable price a property should bring in a competitive market
   c. the value placed on amenities of a property by a specific person
   d. the value of economic influences
6. As a general rule, curable depreciation is
   a. economic obsolescence
   b. functional obsolescence that cannot be repaired at a cost that is less than or equal to the value added to the property
   c. physical deterioration that cannot be repaired at a cost that is less than or equal to the value added to the property

   d. none of the above

7. A Summary Report is also referred to as a
   a. Self-Contained Report
   b. Restricted Use Report
   c. Form Report
   d. none of the above

8. An appraiser is analyzing a property that is comparable to the subject property for which she has been hired to give an appraisal. The comparable has a more valuable swimming pool than does the subject property. The appraiser will do which of the following to find the adjusted value of the comparable?
   a. subtract an amount from the sales price of the comparable
   b. add an amount to the sales price of the comparable
   c. make no adjustment due to the pool's value
   d. none of the above

9. One of the purposes of an appraisal is not to help
   a. decide whether a property provides sufficient security for a loan
   b. establish the price the government must pay in eminent domain proceedings
   c. establish rents
   d. none of the above

10. A house rents for $2,000 per month. What would be the value of the property as calculated using a monthly gross rent multiplier of 150 if the upkeep on the property averaged $100 per month?
   a. $285,000
   b. $300,000
   c. $165,000
   d. none of the above

11. The four elements of value are
   a. utility, scarcity, demand, highest and best use
   b. conformity, transferability, demand, utility
   c. demand, scarcity, transferability, utility
   d. utility, scarcity, demand, conformity

12. A concept closely related to ROI is the
   a. effective gross rate
   b. GRM
   c. cap rate
   d. GIM

13. A Residential License permits the licensee to
   a. appraised any residential property and any non-residential property with a transaction value up to $250,000
   b. appraise any residential and non-residential properties
   c. appraise residential properties with a transaction value up to $2 million

    d. none of the above

14. A property nearing the end of its useful life is likely in which stage of its lifecycle?
    a. equilibrium
    b. revitalization
    c. integration
    d. none of the above

15. Barbara's house is currently valued at $450,000. Since she bought the house five years ago, it has appreciated by 15%. What did she pay for the house?
    a. $382,500
    b. $391,304
    c. $517,500
    d. none of the above

16. Four forces that change value are
    a. environmental characteristics, social standards, economic influences, government regulations
    b. highest and best use, supply and demand, principal of change, principal of regression
    c. highest and best use, supply and demand, principal of change, principal of progression
    d. none of the above

17. Lenders must ensure that a borrower on a loan for a single-family house receive any appraisal report concerning the subject property no less than how many days prior to the closing of the mortgage
    a. 2 days
    b. 4 days
    c. 6 days
    d. none of the above

18. An appraiser calculated depreciation on the subject property by estimating the curable depreciation and adding to it the value of the incurable depreciation. This appraiser used what method of calculating depreciation?
    a. economic life method
    b. straight-life method
    c. cost-to-cure method
    d. age-life method

19. Which of the following terms least belongs with the others?
    a. contribution
    b. integration
    c. equilibrium
    d. rejuvenation

20. A property with value of $700,000 has a structure with replacement cost of $525,000 and accrued depreciation of $75,000. What is the value of the land?
    a. $175,000
    b. $475,000
    c. $100,000
    d. none of the above

21. Which of the following terms least belongs with the others?
    a. physical deterioration
    b. functional obsolescence
    c. depreciable obsolescence
    d. external obsolescence

22. The economic life of a property
    a. is the phase of revitalization
    b. is the phase of stability
    c. is the phase of integration
    d. none of the above

23. An appraiser capitalized the rents and parking fees of a building to arrive at its value. This appraiser used what approach to value?
    a. cost approach
    b. gross rent multiplier
    c. cost-to-cure approach
    d. none of the above

24. Bob owns an apartment building having 20 rental units, each with a fair market rent of $1,500 per month. Estimated loss for vacancies and uncollectible rents is 10%; annual fixed expenses are $40,000; annual maintenance expenses are $50,000; annual reserve for replacements is $25,000; and the capitalization rate is 7%. What is the annual gross income from Bob's apartment building?
    a. $30,000
    b. $320,000
    c. $324,000
    d. $360,000

25. Bob owns an apartment building having 20 rental units, each with a fair market rent of $1,500 per month. Estimated loss for vacancies and uncollectible rents is 10%; annual fixed expenses are $40,000; annual maintenance expenses are $50,000; annual reserve for replacements is $25,000; and the capitalization rate is 7%. What is the effective gross income from Bob's apartment building?
    a. $360,000
    b. $284,000
    c. $259,000
    d. none of the above

26. Bob owns an apartment building having 20 rental units, each with a fair market rent of $1,500 per month. Estimated loss for vacancies and uncollectible rents is 10%; annual fixed expenses are $40,000; annual maintenance expenses are $50,000; annual reserve for replacements is $25,000; and the capitalization rate is 7%. What is the net income from Bob's apartment building?
   a. $209,000
   b. $234,000
   c. $284,000
   d. $324,000

27. Bob owns an apartment building having 20 rental units, each with a fair market rent of $1,500 per month. Estimated loss for vacancies and uncollectible rents is 10%; annual fixed expenses are $40,000; annual maintenance expenses are $50,000; annual reserve for replacements is $25,000; and the capitalization rate is 7%. Using the income approach, what is the value Bob's apartment building?
   a. $4,628,571
   b. $4,057,143
   c. $3,342,857
   d. $2,985,714

28. The order in which the appraisal process is most likely to be conducted is
   a. define the appraisal problem; determine the scope of work necessary to achieve the purpose of the appraisal; collect, verify, and analyze the data; apply the pertinent approaches to value
   b. determine the scope of work necessary to achieve the purpose of the appraisal; collect, verify, and analyze the data; perform a reconciliation of the value indications; apply the pertinent approaches to value
   c. define the appraisal problem; apply the pertinent approaches to value; determine the scope of work necessary to achieve the purpose of the appraisal; collect, verify, and analyze the data
   d. determine the scope of work necessary to achieve the purpose of the appraisal; apply the pertinent approaches to value; collect, verify, and analyze the data; perform a reconciliation of the value indications

29. Replacement cost of an improvement is
   a. the cost of curing the curable depreciation and adding to it the cost of the incurable depreciation
   b. the cost of replacing the improvement with an exact replica
   c. the cost of adding the accrued depreciation to the remainder depreciation
   d. none of the above

30. The principle of conformity states that

a. property values are in a constant state of flux due to economic, environmental, political, social, and physical forces in the area

b. the value of a property will tend toward the cost of an equally desirable substitute property

c. the maximum value of property, its highest and best use, is created and maintained when land use by interacting elements of production are in equilibrium or balance

d. none of the above

31. Adjacent to a vacant lot that Sally owns, developers have begun constructing a large, upscale shopping center. Sally's lot probably will go up in value due to

a. the principle of balance

b. the principle of change

c. the principle of anticipation

d. the principle of contribution

32. If an appraiser applies the income approach to value, which of the following would not be deducted from effective gross income to arrive at net income?

a. maintenance expenses

b. mortgage payments

c. uncollectible rents

d. both b and c

33. If an appraiser wishes to use the sales comparison approach to value a subject property, which of the following homes would he or she not use as a comparable?

a. a nearby home that sold nine months ago

b. a home next door that was sold in foreclosure

c. a house that is 6 blocks away

d. a larger home that is much closer to the beach and has a better view

34. Emily built a high-quality house for $1 million in a neighborhood where other houses were valued at about $500,000. As soon as her house was completed, Emily had it appraised. The appraisal value was $700,000. This is an example of the principle of

a. regression

b. curable depreciation

c. capitalization

d. progression

35. For a house that has a poor floor plan, loss in value is at least partially due to

a. external obsolescence

b. physical deterioration

c. functional obsolescence

d. economic obsolescence

Answers for Chapter 11 Quiz

1. b. Utility, scarcity, and demand are three of the four elements of value.
2. d. Effective gross income is income from a property after an allowance for vacancies and uncollectible rents is deducted from gross income.
3. d. The principle of contribution states that improvements made to a property will contribute to its value or that, conversely, the lack of a needed improvement will detract from the value of the property.
4. a. Here we are clearly dealing with the cost approach to value, where the estimate of value = land value + replacement cost - accrued depreciation. Therefore, here replacement value = $2,000,000 - $500,000 + $200,000 = $1,700,000.
5. b. Market value is the most probable price which a property should bring in a competitive and open market under all conditions requisite to a fair sale, the buyer and seller, each acting prudently, knowledgeably and assuming the price is not affected by undue stimulus. Note that even though answer b isn't a complete answer, it is the *best* answer offered.
6. d. Curable depreciation is depreciation that results from physical deterioration or functional obsolescence that can be repaired or replaced at a cost that is less than or equal to the value added to the property.
7. c. A Summary Report is also referred to as a Form Report.
8. a. In the sales comparison approach, the appraiser compares recent sales of similar properties in the area to evaluate the market value of the subject property. Therefore, because the subject property had a pool of lesser value, the sale price of the comparable would be adjusted down.
9. d. Answers a, b, and c are all potential purposes of an appraisal.
10. b. $2,000 x 150 = $300,000. The GRM approach does not take into consideration expenses.
11. c. The four elements of value are demand, scarcity, transferability, and utility.
12. c. A finance concept closely related to the capitalization rate is ROI.
13. d. The scope of a Residential License is any non-complex 1-4 unit residential property with a transaction value up to $1 million; and non-residential property with a transaction value up to $250,000.
14. d. Disintegration is the phase when a property's usefulness is in decline and constant upkeep is necessary.
15. b. $450,000 ÷ 1.15 = $391,304.
16. a. Four forces that change value are environmental characteristics, social standards, economic influences, and government regulations.

17.d. Lenders must ensure that a borrower on a loan for a single-family home receive any appraisal report concerning the subject property no less than 3 days prior to the closing of the mortgage.

18.c. Cost-to-cure is a method of calculating depreciation by estimating the cost of curing the curable depreciation and adding it to the value of the incurable depreciation.

19.a. Answer is b, c, and d are stages in the four-stage lifecycle of property.

20.d. Property value = land value + replacement cost - accrued depreciation. $700,000 = land value + $525,000 - $75,000. $250,000 = land value.

21.c. Answers a, b and d are the three main causes of depreciation.

22.d. The economic life of a property is the period of time that the property is useful or profitable to the average owner or investor.

23.d. Because income in addition to rents was capitalized, this appraiser used the gross income multiplier approach.

24.d. Gross income = $1,500 x 20 x 12 = $360,000.

25.d. Gross income = $1,500 x 20 x 12 = $360,000.
Effective gross income = $360,000 - $36,000 = $324,000.

26.a. Gross income = $1,500 x 20 x 12 = $360,000.
Effective gross income = $360,000 - $36,000 = $324,000.
Net income = $324,000 - ($40,000 + $50,000 + $25,000) = $209,000

27.d. Gross income = $1,500 x 20 x 12 = $360,000.
Effective gross income = $360,000 - $36,000 = $324,000.
Net income = $324,000 - ($40,000 + $50,000 + $25,000) = $209,000
Property value = $209,000 ÷ 7% = $2,985,714.

28.a. Define the appraisal problem; determine the scope of work necessary to achieve the purpose of the appraisal; collect, verify, and analyze the data; apply the pertinent approaches to value; and perform a reconciliation of the value indications.

29.d. Replacement cost is the cost of replacing improvements with those having equivalent utility, but constructed with modern materials, designs, and workmanship.

30.d. The principle of conformity states that the maximum value of land is achieved when there is a reasonable degree of social, economic, and architectural conformity in the area.

31.c. The principle of anticipation states that value is derived from a calculation of anticipated future benefits to be derived from the property, not from past benefits, though past benefits may inform as to what might be expected in the future.

32.d. Uncollectible rents and vacancies are deducted to obtain effective gross income. Mortgage payments are not deducted to obtain net income in the income approach.

33.b. Foreclosure sales, short sales, and other forced sales are never comparables. Comparables are properties similar to the subject property being appraised that recently sold at arm's length, where neither the buyers nor the sellers were acting under significant financial pressures.

34.a. The principle of regression states that the value of a residence of higher value tends to be degraded by proximity to residences of lower value.

35.c. Functional obsolescence is depreciation that results (1) from deficiencies arising from poor architectural design, out-dated style or equipment, and changes in utility demand, such as for larger houses with more garage space, or (2) from over-improvements, where the cost of the improvements was more than the addition to market value.

Chapter 12

Escrow and Closing

As we have discussed thus far, there are many considerations that go into a real estate transaction, probably the most prominent being the listing agreement, the purchase agreement, the financing, and, finally, the closing — the main subject of this chapter.

A real estate **closing** (also referred to as a **settlement**) is a process leading up to, and concluding with, a buyer's receiving the deed to the property and the seller's receiving the purchase money (or other consideration, pursuant to the terms of the sale agreement). In California this process is usually conducted by a neutral party (referred to as an **escrow agent**) who acts as an agent for both the buyer and the seller — an agent with whom:

1. the buyer can feel safe depositing all of or part of the purchase price before receiving the deed;
2. the seller can feel safe depositing the deed before receiving the purchase price; and
3. the lender can feel secure that none of its loan funds will be disbursed until the promissory note and the deed of trust (or mortgage) are signed by the buyer.

DEFINITION OF ESCROW

California Financial Code Section 17003(a) defines **escrow** as:

> "any transaction in which one person, for the purpose of effecting the sale, transfer, encumbering, or leasing of real or personal property to another person, delivers any written instrument, money, evidence of title to real or personal property, or other thing of value to a third person to be held by that third person until the happening of a specified event or the performance of a prescribed condition, when it is then to be delivered by that third person to a grantee, grantor, promisee, promisor, obligee, obligor, bailee, bailor, or any agent or employee of any of the latter."

California Civil Code Section 1057 further elucidates what an escrow is:

"A grant may be deposited by the grantor with a third person, to be delivered on performance of a condition, and, on delivery by the depositary, it will take effect. While in the possession of the third person, and subject to condition, it is called an escrow."

ESSENTIAL ELEMENTS OF AN ESCROW

For a real estate transaction, every valid escrow must have four basic elements:

1. a binding contract between buyer and seller;
2. an escrow agent;
3. irrevocable delivery of transfer instruments and deposits called for in the contract; and
4. instructions to the escrow agent that impose conditions as to the delivery of instruments and funds on the performance of the stipulated conditions.

Binding Contract

No escrow can be opened until there exists a binding contract between buyer and the seller, which can be in any legal form, including a deposit receipt, a sale agreement, an option, or the escrow instructions of the buyer and seller. Because of the statute of frauds, these documents must be in writing to constitute an enforceable contract for the purchase of real estate.

Escrow Agent

An **escrow agent** (also referred to as an **escrow holder**) is an impartial agent who holds possession of written instruments and deposits until all of the conditions of escrow have been fully performed. An escrow agent is a special agent whose only authority is to see to it that all of the escrow instructions are fully performed. Who will serve as escrow agent and which party or parties will pay the escrow fees are matters to be negotiated between the buyer and the seller; neither the real estate broker nor the lender may dictate either of these matters.

Many lenders and title companies have escrow departments to close real estate transactions in which they are involved. Division 6 of the California Financial Code provides that, with numerous exceptions, escrow agents must be licensed by the California Department of Corporations. Only corporations may be licensed, not individuals. However, banks, title companies, insurance companies, attorneys, and real estate brokers— entities and individuals supervised by other government agencies — are exempt from the escrow licensing law and may serve as escrow agents, sometimes in only limited circumstances.

Section 17006(a)(4) provides the exemption for licensed real estate brokers:

> "Any broker licensed by the Real Estate Commissioner while performing acts in the course of or incidental to a real estate transaction in which the broker is an agent or a party to the transaction and in which the broker is performing an act for which a real estate license is required."

Note that even though a broker is a party to a real estate transaction, the broker is *not* exempt under §17006(a)(4) unless the broker is also "performing an act for which a real estate license is required," i.e., acting as an agent on his or her own behalf or on behalf of the other party.

The Department of Corporations has interpreted the Section 17006 (a)(4) exemption for real estate brokers to mean, among other things, that a broker may not state in any advertisement that he or she serves as an escrow agent without specifying that such services are only in connection with real estate transactions in which the broker is involved.

Escrow Activity Reporting

Effective July 1, 2012, B&PC §10141.6 requires real estate brokers who are exempt under §17006(a)(4) and who engage in escrow activities of 5 or more transactions in a calendar year or for whose escrow activities equal or exceed $1 million in a calendar year to file with the CalBRE an **Escrow Activity Report**, detailing the number of escrows conducted by the broker and the dollar volume escrowed by the broker during the calendar year in which the threshold was met. The Escrow Activity Report must be filed within 60 days after the end of the calendar year in which the broker met the escrow threshold.

Irrevocable Delivery of Transfer Instruments and Deposits

The delivery of the deposits and transfer instruments must be irrevocable. The escrow agent may not return an item deposited by one of the parties without the consent of the other party. Though the seller deposits an executed deed into escrow and may not revoke or withdraw the deed during escrow, this deposit is not viewed as being a delivery of the deed. The seller retains legal title and may collect rents and otherwise use the property. If during escrow the property is lost or damaged, the loss is borne by the seller. Likewise, if during escrow there is any loss or embezzlement of funds or property deposited by the buyer, the loss is borne by the buyer. When all of the conditions of the escrow are fully performed, however, legal title passes to the buyer and any damage or loss to the property is borne by the buyer, while any loss of the purchase consideration is borne by the seller.

Escrow Instructions

Escrow instructions are the written instructions signed by all of the principals to the escrow (buyers, sellers, and lenders) that specify all of the conditions that must be met before the escrow agent may release whatever was deposited into escrow to the rightful parties. No party may unilaterally change the instructions. The instructions signed by the principals are often identical, but if not, must be conforming.

Escrow instructions constitute a binding contract, and if there are conflicts between the terms of the instructions and the terms of the purchase agreement, the escrow instructions, being the later contract, control. In case a controversy arises between the buyer and seller as to what certain escrow instructions mean, the escrow agent may petition a court to decide the issue through interpleader.

A real estate broker who acts as an escrow agent for a real estate transaction must be careful to avoid acts that are prohibited by the Real Estate Commissioner's Regulation 2950, including

- accepting escrow instructions that contain one or more blanks to be filled in after the signing of the instructions;
- failing to deliver at the time of signing any instruction a copy thereof to all persons signing the instruction; and
- failing upon closing of escrow to deliver to each principal a written statement of all receipts and disbursements of the escrow.

HUD-1 UNIFORM SETTLEMENT STATEMENT

As we discussed in Chapter 9 ("Real Estate Financing"), RESPA applies to all purchases of owner-occupied residences of 1-4 dwelling units that use funds from institutional lenders regulated by the federal government — in other words, to the vast majority of non-commercial real estate transactions with which nearly all real estate agents will become involved. In this section we will focus on RESPA's requirements regarding the **HUD-1 Uniform Settlement Statement** (hereinafter, "settlement statement") (see Figure 12.1) and the closing of escrow.

Preparing the settlement statement involves determining what **credits** (items payable *to* a party) and **debits** (items payable *by* a party) apply to the transaction and taking care that each is allocated to the correct party. In making this allocation, the escrow agent acts pursuant to the escrow instructions. [Note: these definitions of credits and debits as used for escrow accounts do not conform to the definition of these terms as used in double-entry bookkeeping or accounting.] As we saw in Chapter 8 ("Real Estate Math"), some items (such as prepaid rents or prepaid taxes) typically are allocated partially to one party and partially to the other — a process called proration.

If the borrower so requests, the escrow agent must provide the borrower with a copy of the settlement statement one business day before closing. Even if the borrower does not request to see a copy of the statement prior to closing, the escrow agent must deliver or mail a copy of the statement to both the borrower and seller at or before the closing.

CLOSING

Closing is the final set of acts performed by the escrow agent that complete escrow, including:

- recording the deed and the deed of trust at the recorder's office, confirming the recordation, and informing the principals of the recordation;
- delivering or mailing the settlement statement to the borrower and seller;
- delivering all other deposits and funds allocated pursuant to the settlement statement; and
- verifying that the title policy is in place and sending the original policy to the borrower.

TERMINATION OF ESCROW

There are three ways in which escrow can terminate:

1. *Closing* — automatically terminates escrow with the full performance of all conditions and the disbursement of all deposits.
2. *Mutual Agreement* — of both the borrower and the seller terminates closing. However, the listing agreement is a separate agreement, and a commission may be owed to the real estate agent. Furthermore, the purchase agreement is also a separate agreement, so in the case of a termination of escrow due to mutual agreement, the escrow agent and/or broker should see to it that a cancellation agreement is prepared that cancels both the escrow and the purchase agreement.
3. *Default* —a material breach by one party would allow the other party to terminate the escrow. As a general rule, escrow instructions include a "time is of the essence" clause, and failure to close on time likely would be seen (by many courts) as being a default sufficient to terminate the escrow. Therefore, to ensure that escrow remains valid in such a case, if the parties wish to continue with the transaction the escrow agent should obtain new signed escrow instructions.

TAX-RELATED ASPECTS OF ESCROW

Nearly all transactions involving items of value have tax implications; the handling of escrow is no exception.

1099-S Reporting

The IRS requires escrow agents to report every sale of real estate on Form 1099-S, giving the seller's name, Social Security number, and the gross sale proceeds. If the escrow agent fails to perform this reporting duty, the obligation becomes the lender's. If the lender also fails to report the sale, the obligation becomes the broker's.

Foreign Investment in Real Property Tax Act (FIRPTA)

After becoming concerned that foreign investors may have been evading their income tax liabilities, Congress passed FIRPTA, which requires the *buyer* to determine whether the seller is a non-resident alien; and if so, the buyer has the responsibility of withholding 10% of the amount realized from the sale and sending that 10% to the IRS. In practice, the obligation to check the seller's residency status and, if appropriate, withhold the 10% and send it to the IRS is given to the escrow agent in the escrow instructions. As not all real estate transactions are subject to FIRPTA, current IRS regulations should be consulted in any real estate transaction involving a non-resident alien.

California Withholding Law

Similar in purpose to FIRPTA, California's withholding law for sales of California real estate requires the buyer to withhold 3⅓% of the gross sales price from any individual seller (regardless of whether the seller is a non-resident alien, a U.S. citizen, or a California resident) and to send the withholding amount to the Franchise Tax Board by the 20th day of the month after the month of closing. As with FIRPTA, these withholding requirements are usually assumed by the escrow agent pursuant to the escrow instructions. There are certain exemptions to this withholding law, including individual sellers selling property that is their principal residence and transactions in which the sale price is $100,000 or less.

LOAN SERVICING

Loan servicing is the administration of a loan from the time the loan proceeds are dispersed to the time the loan is paid off in full. This loan administration typically includes sending monthly statements, collecting loan payments, and maintaining records of payments and balances due. Loan servicing is either performed by the lender or by a subservicer to whom loan servicing obligations are transferred. Loan servicers are usually compensated by receiving a percentage of the balance due on the loan being serviced.

To ensure that certain property related expenses are paid on time, a lender may require the borrower to fund a new escrow account at the closing of the escrow for the sales transaction. Under this new escrow (also referred to as a *reserve* or *impound* account) the loan servicer typically pays, on behalf of the borrower, property taxes, hazard insurance, and any other charges (such as mortgage insurance) with respect to the loan.

Certain duties and obligations of the loan servicer with respect to such reserve account escrows are mandated by RESPA, including:

- must within 45 days of the closing of escrow for the sale transaction give the borrower an initial reserve account statement detailing all of the payments to be deposited to, and all disbursements to be made from, the account during the first year;
- may require the borrower to make monthly payments to the reserve account of 1/12 of the total amount of payments to be made from the escrow during the following year;
- may require an additional escrow payment cushion of no more than 1/6 the estimated total annual payments to be made from the escrow account to cover unanticipated disbursements from the account;
- must deliver to the borrower an annual escrow statement that summarizes all deposits to, and all payments from, the escrow during the prior year; and
- must recompute the monthly reserve amounts to be deposited into the escrow and the maximum cushion at least once each 12 months.

Fig.12.1   HUD - 1 UNIFORM SETTLEMENT STATEMENT   OMB Approval No. 2502-0265

A. U.S. DEPARTMENT OF HOUSING AND URBAN DEVELOPMENT	SETTLEMENT STATEMENT

B. TYPE OF LOAN 1. X FHA 2. FmHA 3. Cony.Unins. 4. VA 5. Conv. Ins.	6. File Number: 7. Loan Number: 8. Mortgage Insurance Case Number

C. NOTE: This form is furnished to give you a statement of actual settlement costs. Amounts paid to and by the settlement agent are shown. Items marked "(p.o.c.)" were paid outside the closing; they are shown here for informational purposes and are not included in the totals.
NOTE: TIN = Taxpayers Identification Number

D. NAME AND ADDRESS OF BORROWER:	E. NAME, ADDRESS AND TIN OF SELLER:	F. NAME AND ADDRESS OF LENDER:
G. PROPERTY LOCATION:	H. SETTLEMENT AGENT NAME, ADDRESS AND TIN	
	PLACE OF SETTLEMENT	I. SETTLEMENT DATE

J. SUMMARY OF BORROWERS TRANSACTION		K. SUMMARY OF SELLER'S TRANSACTION	
100. GROSS AMOUNT DUE FROM BORROWER:		400. GROSS AMOUNT DUE TO SELLER:	
101. Contract sales price		401. Contract sales price	
102. Personal property		402. Personal property	
103. Settlement charges to borrower (Line 1400)		403.	
104.		404.	
105.		405.	
Adjustments for items paid by seller in advance		Adjustments for items paid by seller in advance	
106. City/town taxes		406. City/town taxes	
107. County taxes		407. County taxes	
108. Assessments		408. Assessments	
109.		409.	
110.		410.	
111.		411.	
112.		412.	
120. GROSS AMOUNT DUE FROM BORROWER		420. GROSS AMOUNT DUE TO SELLER	

200. AMOUNTS PAID BY OR IN BEHALF OF BORROWER:		500. REDUCTIONS IN AMOUNT DUE TO SELLER:	
201. Deposit or earnest money		501. Excess deposit	
202. Principal amount of new loan(s)		502. Settlement charges to seller (Line 1400)	
203. Existing loan(s) taken subject to		503. Existing loan(s) taken subject to	
204.		504. Payoff of first mortgage loan	
205.		505. Payoff of second mortgage loan	
206.		506.	
207.		507.	
208.		508.	
209.		509.	
Adjustments for items unpaid by seller		Adjustments for items unpaid by seller	
210. City/town taxes		510. City/town taxes	
211. County taxes		511. County taxes	
212. Assessments		512. Assessments	
213.		513.	
214.		514.	
215.		515.	
216.		516.	
217.		517.	
218.		518.	
219.		519.	
220. TOTAL PAID BY/FOR BORROWER		520. TOTAL REDUCTION AMOUNT DUE SELLER	

300. CASH AT SETTLEMENT FROM/TO BORROWER		600. CASH AT SETTLEMENT FROM/TO SELLER	
301. Gross amount due from borrower (Line 120)		601. Gross amount due to seller (Line 420)	
302. Less amount paid by/for borrower (Line 220)		602. Less reduction in amount due seller (Line 520)	
303. CASH FROM BORROWER		603. CASH TO SELLER	

SELLERS STATEMENT

The information contained in Blocks E, G, H, and I and on line 401 (or, if line 401 is asterisked, line 403 and 404) is important tax information and is being furnished to the Internal Revenue Service (see Seller Certification). If you are required to file a return, a negligence penalty or other sanction will be imposed on you if this item is required to be reported and the IRS determines that it has not been reported. You are required to provide the Settlement Agent with your correct taxpayer identification number. If you do not provide the Settlement Agent with your correct taxpayer identification number you may be subject to civil or criminal penalties imposed by law. Under penalties of perjury, I certify that the number shown on this statement is my correct taxpayer identification number.

_____   _____
(Seller's Signature)   (Seller's Signature)

L. SETTLEMENT CHARGES

700. TOTAL SALES/BROKER's COMMISSION based on price $ @	PAID FROM BORROWER'S FUNDS AT SETTLEMENT	PAID FROM SELLER'S FUNDS AT SETTLEMENT
Division of Commission (line 700) as follows:		
701. $		
702. $		
703. Commission paid at Settlement		
704.		
800. ITEMS PAYABLE IN CONNECTION WITH LOAN		
801. Loan Origination Fee $		
802. Loan Discount $		
803. Appraisal Fee to		
804. Credit report to		
805. Lender's Inspection Fee		
806. Mortgage insurance Application Fee to		
807. Assumption Fee		
808.		
809.		
810.		
811.		
900. ITEMS REQUIRED BY LENDER TO BE PAID IN ADVANCE		
901. Interest from		
902. Mortgage Insurance Premium for		
903. Hazard insurance Premium for		
904.		
905.		
1000. RESERVES DEPOSITED WITH LENDER		
1001. Hazard insurance		
1002. Mortgage insurance		
1003. City Property Taxes		
1004. County Property Taxes		
1005. Annual assessments		
1006.		
1007.		
1008. Aggregate Accounting Adjustment		
1100. TITLE CHARGES		
1101. Settlement or closing fee to		
1102. Abstract or title search to		
1103. Title Examination to		
1104. Title insurance binder to		
1105. Document preparation to		
1106. Notary fees to		
1107. Attorney's fees to		
(includes line numbers:		
1108. Title Insurance to		
(includes line numbers		
1109 Lenders coverage $		
1110. Owner's coverage $		
1111.		
1112.		
1113.		
1200. GOVERNMENT RECORDING AND TRANSFER CHARGES		
1201. Recording fees: Deed $ Mortgage $ Release $		
1202. City/enty tax/stamps: Deed $ Mortgage $		
1203. State tax/stamps: Deed $ Mortgage $		
1204.		
1205.		
1300. ADDITIONAL SETTLEMENT CHARGES		
1301. Survey to		
1302. Pest inspection to		
1303.		
1304.		
1305.		
1306.		
1307.		
1308.		
1400. TOTAL SETTLEMENT CHARGES (enter on lines 103, Section J and 502, Section K)		

CERTIFICATION: I have carefully reviewed the HUD-1 Settlement Statement and to the best of my knowledge and belief it is a true and accurate statement of all receipts and disbursements made on my account or by me in this transaction. I further certi~ that I received a copy of the HUD-1 Settlement Statement

Seller   Borrower

Seller   Borrower

The HUD-1 Settlement Statement which I have prepared is a true and accurate account of the funds disbursed or to be disbursed by the undersigned as part of the settlement of this transaction.

Settlement Agent   Date

WARNING: It is a crime to knowingly make false statements to the United States on this or any other similar form. Penalties upon conviction can include a fine and imprisonment. For details see: Title 18 U.S. Code Section 1001 and Section 1010.

Key Terms for Chapter 12

1099-S Reporting — a report to be submitted on IRS Form 1099-S by escrow agents to report the sale of real estate, giving the seller's name, Social Security number, and the gross sale proceeds.

California Withholding Law — a California law that, with certain exceptions, requires the buyer of California real estate to withhold 3⅓% of the gross sales price from any individual seller.

closing — in reference to an escrow, a process leading up to, and concluding with, a buyer's receiving the deed to the property and the seller's receiving the purchase money.

credits — in reference to an escrow account, items payable to a party. This definition of a debit does not conform to its use in double-entry bookkeeping or accounting.

debits — in reference to an escrow account, items payable by a party. This definition of a debit does not conform to its use in double-entry bookkeeping or accounting.

escrow — a neutral depository in which something of value is held by an impartial third party (called the escrow agent) until all conditions specified in the escrow instructions have been fully performed.

escrow activity report — a report that certain real estate brokers must file with the CalBRE if their escrow activities exceed a certain threshold.

escrow agent — an impartial agent who holds possession of written instruments and deposits until all of the conditions of escrow have been fully performed.

escrow holder — an escrow agent

escrow instructions — the written instructions signed by all of the principals to the escrow (buyers, sellers, and lenders) that specify all of the conditions that must be met before the escrow agent may release whatever was deposited into escrow to the rightful parties.

Foreign Investment in Real Property Tax Act (FIRPTA) — a federal act that, with certain exceptions, requires the buyer in a real estate transaction to determine whether the seller is a non-resident alien; and if so, the buyer has the responsibility of withholding 10% of the amount realized from the sale and sending that 10% of the IRS.

HUD-1 Uniform Settlement Statement — an escrow settlement form mandated by RESPA for use in all escrows pertaining to the purchase of owner-occupied residences of 1-4 dwelling units that use funds from institutional lenders regulated by the federal government.

impound account — *see*, reserve account

loan servicing — the administration of a loan from the time the loan proceeds are dispersed to the time the loan is paid off in full.

reserve account — in reference to loan servicing, the escrow account from which the loan servicer typically pays, on behalf of the borrower, property taxes, hazard insurance, and any other charges (such as mortgage insurance) with respect to the loan.

settlement — *see*, closing

Quiz for Chapter 12

1. Closing is also referred to as
   a. escrow
   b. credits and debits
   c. reserve
   d. none of the above

2. An escrow agent should be someone with whom the
   a. buyer can feel safe depositing the purchase price before receiving the deed
   b. seller can feel safe depositing the deed before receiving the purchase price
   c. both a and b
   d. neither a nor b

3. A real estate broker who is not licensed as an escrow agent may always conduct an escrow
   a. if the broker represents the seller
   b. if the broker is a party to the transaction
   c. neither a nor b
   d. both a and b

4. An escrow agent is also referred to as an escrow
   a. owner
   b. holder
   c. principal
   d. beneficiary

5. The HUD-1 Uniform Settlement Statement is
   a. mandated for use by RESPA in all commercial real estate transactions
   b. only needs to be used for purchases of single-family homes if the loan does not come from a lender regulated by the federal government
   c. is only used for seller carry back loans
   d. none of the above

6. If the terms of agreed-upon written escrow instructions conflict with the terms of the purchase agreement
   a. the terms of the purchase agreement control
   b. the terms of the listing agreement control
   c. the terms of the escrow instructions control
   d. it depends upon which agreement was printed using the larger font size

7. As the term is used in reference to escrow accounting, a debit is

    a. any item payable to a party

    b. any item deposited into escrow

    c. any escrow instruction relating to deposits of funds

    d. none of the above

8. A real estate broker who acts as an escrow agent for a real estate transaction

    a. may accept escrow instructions that contain one or more blanks to be filled in after the signing of the instructions

    b. need not deliver at the time of the signing of any escrow instruction a copy thereof to all persons signing the instruction

    c. both a and b

    d. neither a nor b

9. An escrow is

    a. a settlement form mandated by RESPA for use in all purchases of owner-occupied residences of 1-4 dwelling units that use funds from institutional lenders regulated by the federal government

    b. a report to be submitted to the IRS to report the sale of real estate, giving the seller's name, Social Security number, and the gross sale proceeds

    c. the written instructions that specify all of the conditions that must be met before the escrow agent may release whatever was deposited to the rightful parties

    d. none of the above

10. A real estate broker must file a threshold report with the CalBRE if he or she engages in how many escrow activities in a calendar year?

    a. 5

    b. 4

    c. 3

    d. 2

11. A seller who signs a grant deed and deposits it into escrow

    a. may collect rents from the property during escrow

    b. may not collect rents from the property during escrow

    c. bears any loss to the property until all conditions of the escrow are fully performed

    d. both a and c

12. If a real estate broker advertises that he or she serves as an escrow agent, the broker must state that

    a. such services are only in connection with real estate transactions in which the broker is involved

    b. such services are available for any real estate transaction regardless of the ethnicity of the parties

    c. such services are available for any real estate transaction regardless of the religion of the parties

    d. all of the above

13. Ways in which an escrow can terminate include
   a. closing
   b. default
   c. issuance of a preliminary title report
   d. either a or b

14. The California Financial Code provides that, unless exempted, an escrow agent
   a. must be a corporation
   b. must be licensed by the Bureau of Real Estate
   c. must be a party to the real estate transaction
   d. both a and b

15. The proper delivery to escrow of deposits and transfer instruments
   a. can be revoked by either party within three days of delivery
   b. can be revoked by either party within two days of delivery
   c. can be revoked by either party within one day of delivery
   d. none of the above

16. Closing acts performed by the escrow agent include
   a. recording the deed and the deed of trust at the recorder's office, confirming the recordation, and informing the principles of the recordation
   b. delivering or mailing the settlement statement to the borrower and the seller
   c. verifying that the title policy is in place and sending the original policy to the borrower
   d. all of the above

17. A 1099-S report is
   a. required by California law for all sales of California real estate
   b. a settlement statement required by HUD for certain real estate transactions
   c. only required if the seller is a non-resident alien
   d. none of the above

18. Loan servicing is
   a. the administration of escrow involving the deposit of transfer instruments and purchase money for a real estate transaction
   b. the withholding of a certain amount realized from the sale of real property and sending that amount the IRS
   c. the administration of a loan from the time the loan proceeds are dispersed to the time the loan is paid off in full
   d. none of the above

19. If a real estate transaction involves a seller who is a non-resident alien
   a. the seller has the responsibility to determine whether the buyer is a non-resident alien; and if so, the seller has the responsibility of withholding 10% of the amount realized from the sale and sending that 10% of the IRS

b. the lender has the responsibility to determine whether the seller is a non-resident alien; and if so, the lender has the responsibility of withholding 10% of the amount realized from the sale and sending that 10% of the IRS

c. the buyer has the responsibility to determine whether the seller is a non-resident alien; and if so, the buyer has the responsibility of withholding 10% of the amount realized from the sale and sending that 10% of the IRS

d. none of the above

20. For some real estate transactions, FIRPTA requires the withholding of what percentage of the amount realized from the sale?

a. 3⅓

b. 5

c. 10

d. none of the above

Answers for Chapter 12 Quiz

1. d. Closing is also referred to as settlement.
2. c. An escrow agent is someone with whom buyer can feel safe depositing the purchase price before receiving the deed, the seller can feel safe depositing the deed before receiving the purchase price, and the lender can feel secure that none of its loan funds will be disbursed until the promissory note and the deed of trust (or mortgage) are signed by the buyer.
3. a. A broker may conduct an escrow if the broker represents the seller or buyer, or the broker is a party to the transaction *and* performs an act for which a real estate license is required.
4. b. An escrow agent is also referred to as an escrow holder.
5. d. RESPA requires the use of the HUD-1 Uniform Settlement Statement for all purchases of owner-occupied residences of 1-4 dwelling units that use funds from institutional lenders regulated by the federal government.
6. c. If the terms of agreed-upon written escrow instructions conflict with the terms of the purchase agreement, the terms of the escrow instructions control, unless the escrow instructions specify that in case of conflict the terms of the purchase agreement control.
7. d. As the term is used in reference to escrow accounting, a debit is an item payable by a party.
8. d. A real estate broker who acts as an escrow agent for a real estate transaction must not accept escrow instructions that contain one or more blanks to be filled in after the signing of the instructions and must not fail to deliver, at the time of the signing any escrow instruction, a copy thereof to all persons signing the instruction.
9. d. An escrow is a neutral depository in which something of value is held by an impartial third party (called the escrow agent) until all conditions specified in the escrow instructions have been fully performed.
10. a. A real estate broker who engages in 5 or more escrow activities in a calendar year must file a threshold report with the CalBRE.
11. d. A seller who signs the grant deed and deposits it into escrow may collect rents from the property during escrow and bears any loss due to damage to the property until all conditions of escrow fully performed.
12. a. A broker may not state in any advertisement that he or she serves as an escrow agent without specifying that such services are only in connection with real estate transactions in which the broker is involved.
13. d. There are three ways in which an escrow can terminate: closing, mutual agreement, or default.

14.a. The California Financial Code provides that, unless exempted, an escrow agent must be a corporation.

15.d. The proper delivery to escrow of the deposits and transfer instruments must be irrevocable.

16.d. Closing acts performed by the escrow agent include (1) recording the deed and the deed of trust at the recorder's office, confirming the recordation, and informing the principles of the recordation; (2) delivering or mailing the settlement statement to the borrower and seller; (3) delivering all of the deposits and funds allocated pursuant to the settlement statement; and (4) verifying that the title policy is in place and sending the original policy to the borrower.

17.d. A 1099-S report is a report to be submitted on IRS Form 1099-S by escrow agents to report the sale of real estate, giving the seller's name, Social Security number, and the gross sale proceeds.

18.c. Loan servicing is the administration of a loan from the time the loan proceeds are dispersed to the time the loan is paid off in full.

19.c. FIRPTA states that, with certain exceptions, the buyer must determine whether the seller is a nonresident alien; and if so, the buyer has the responsibility of withholding 10% of the amount realized from the sale and sending that 10% of the IRS.

20.c. Foreign Investment in Real Property Tax Act (FIRPTA) is a federal act that, with certain exceptions, requires the buyer in a real estate transaction to determine whether the seller is a non-resident alien; and if so, the buyer has the responsibility of withholding 10% of the amount realized from the sale and sending that 10% of the IRS.

Chapter 13

Landlord/Tenant Relations and Property Management

As we discussed in Chapter 2, "Estates in Land," a leasehold interest temporarily provides the tenant with exclusive possession and use of the leased property. During the period of tenancy, the landlord holds title and a reversionary interest in the property. The four types of leasehold estates we briefly examined were:

1. estate for years;
2. estate from period to period (periodic tenancy);
3. estate at will; and
4. estate at sufferance.

Figure 2.4 shows the characteristics, creation, duration, limitation on term, and termination of these four leasehold interests.

DUAL NATURE OF A LEASE

Whether written or oral, a lease has two distinct characteristics:

1. As discussed in Chapter 2, a lease transfers an estate in the real property leased. This transfer of a real property interest creates **privity of estate** between the landlord and tenant.
2. A lease also constitutes an executory contract between landlord and tenant that governs such matters as the landlord's maintenance of the property and the tenant's duty to make lease payments. This contract aspect of a lease creates **privity of contract** between landlord and tenant, which makes a leasehold estate a **chattel real** — an interest in land that is less than a freehold estate and is also a form of personal property governed by laws applicable to personal property.

TYPES OF LEASES

There are five major types of leases:

1. ***Gross Lease***. Under a gross lease (also referred to as a ***fixed lease***), the tenant pays a fixed rental amount, and the landlord pays all of the operating expenses for the premises.

2. ***Net Lease***. Under a net lease, the tenant pays a fixed rental amount plus some of the landlord's operating expenses (such as a percent of property taxes). A common variation on the net lease is the ***triple net lease***, under which the tenant pays a fixed rent plus the landlord's property taxes, hazard insurance, and all maintenance costs not specifically reserved for the landlord's maintenance (such as repairs to the roof).

3. ***Graduated Lease***. A graduated lease (also referred to as a ***step-up lease***) is similar to a gross lease except that it provides (in a lease provision referred to as an ***escalator clause***) for periodic increases in the rent, often based on the Consumer Price Index.

4. ***Percentage Lease***. Under a percentage lease, which is often used in shopping centers, the tenant typically pays a base rent amount plus a percentage of the gross receipts of the tenant's business. The percentage of gross charged is usually dependent on the percent markup used in the tenant's business. Thus, under a percentage lease the percentage of gross paid by a grocery store is likely to be much less than the percentage of gross paid by a parking lot.

5. ***Ground Lease***. Under a ground lease, a tenant leases land and agrees to construct a building or to make other significant improvement on the land. At the end of the lease term, the improvement becomes the property of the landlord. These leases tend to be for long periods in order to make it economically viable for the tenant to incur the large expense of the construction.

SPECIFIC ASPECTS OF A LEASE

In this chapter we will primarily be examining the law relating to residential leases — a body of law that evolved primarily to address the perceived lesser power of tenants in relation to the power of landlords. Commercial tenants are perceived as being more capable of protecting their own interests, and thus tenants with commercial leases have been provided with fewer legal protections.

VALID CONTRACT

Because a lease is a contract, it must possess all of the requisites of a valid contract: offer and acceptance, competent parties, lawful object, and sufficient consideration. Additionally, pursuant to the statute of frauds, a lease must be in writing if it either (1) has a term of longer than one year, or (2) has a term of one year or less that expires more than one year after the execution of the lease.

A lease signed and delivered by the landlord is enforceable by the tenant even if the tenant fails to sign the lease. If the tenant takes possession of the premises or begins to pay rent, the lease becomes enforceable against the tenant; however, to enforce special contractual provisions of the lease against the tenant (such as recovery of attorney fees) the lease must be fully executed.

Note: Even though the statute of frauds does not require a lease for one year or less to be in writing, CC §1962 requires that a landlord must provide a tenant with certain information in writing even for an oral lease agreement; namely:

1. the name, telephone number, and the street address at which personal service can be effected on (a) each person who is authorized to manage the premises, and (b) the owner of the premises or a person authorized to act on behalf of the owner for the purpose of service of process;
2. the name, telephone number, and street address of the person or entity to whom rental payments are to be made; and
3. the form or forms in which rental payments are to be made.

These three statutory written disclosures may either (a) be furnished to the tenant within 15 days of the agreement, or (b) by posting such information in every elevator (if the building has an elevator) and one other conspicuous place or (if the premises does not have an elevator) and at least two conspicuous places. CC §1962.5.

Recording

A lease may be recorded in the county the property is situated if it is acknowledged by the lessor.

ESSENTIAL TERMS OF A RESIDENTIAL LEASE

Though no standard pre-printed form or specific words are required, the terms of a valid, enforceable lease must:

1. establish a term for the lease, whether periodic or fixed;

2. identify the parties;

3. evidence the parties' intent to form a landlord-tenant relationship (e.g., by using such words as "lease" or "rent";

4. properly describe the leased property; and

5. specify the amount of rent, when due, and the manner in which the payments should be made.

THE CALIFORNIA ASSOCIATION OF REALTORS® RESIDENTIAL LEASE FORM AND RELATED LAW

In this section we will examine in detail a few of the terms of the CAR residential lease form (Figure 13.1), commenting on related landlord-tenant law as we go.

Term: The CAR lease, paragraph 2, provides for a lease term that commences on a specific date and continues either month to month or until a specified termination date. The term of a lease is an essential element of a lease; but if a lease fails to specify a term, a specified period of time will be implied pursuant to CC §1943-44 as follows:

- for lodgings, dwelling-houses, and residential properties the lease term will be presumed to be the time period adopted for rent payment. If the lease does not state a period of time adopted for rent payments, the lease term is presumed to be one month.
- for agricultural land, one year.
- for other properties where there is no custom or usage on the subject, tenancy is presumed to be month to month.

Periodic tenancy and fixed-term (estate-for-years) tenancy can be continued through ***lease renewal*** or ***lease extension***. Lease renewal creates a new lease distinct from the first, and the parties should execute a new lease instrument. A lease extension is a continuation of tenancy under the original lease.

If a tenant remains in possession of the leased property after the expiration of the lease and the landlord accepts rent from the tenant, the lease is presumed to have been extended (or renewed) on the same terms and for the same time, not exceeding one month if the rent under the original lease is payable monthly, or in any case not exceeding one year.

A lease that provides for a contractual right on the part of the tenant to renew or extend is an irrevocable offer by the landlord to lease the property to the tenant on the specified terms. A lease for residential property that provides for an automatic extension of the lease if the tenant remains in possession after the expiration of the lease, or if the tenant fails to give notice of the tenant's intention not to renew or extend, is voidable by the party who did not prepare the lease, unless the renewal or extension clause is printed in at least 8-point boldface type and a recital of such clause is printed in at least 8-point boldface type above the tenant's signature line (CC §1945.5).

Rent: The CAR lease, paragraph 3, provides for the tenant's consideration for entering into the lease; namely, rent. Though the CAR form provides (as most leases do) that rent is payable *in advance* for each calendar month, in the absence of such a provision or course of dealing between the parties, CC §1947 provides that payment of rent is due at the termination of the successive lease periods (e.g., at the end of the day, week, month, quarter, or year).

In general, if rent is payable in advance, it is not apportionable (i.e., it does not accrue on a basis, such as daily, less than the time period of rent payments), and, therefore, should the tenant vacate the premises before the end of the term, the tenant would not be entitled to a refund of rent. However, if the lease is terminated due to a fault of the landlord, or if the lease specifically provides for apportionment, then the rent for that period may be apportioned. If rent is not payable in advance and the lease is terminated prior to the expiration of the term, then rent would be due for the time that the tenant had the right to possess the property.

For a fixed-term tenancy, and absent a specific provision in the lease to the contrary, there can be no rent increases during the term. However, for a periodic tenancy, and absent rent-control restrictions (see below), the landlord may raise the amount of rent as frequently and by any amount that the landlord wishes. To do so, however, would be to modify the lease agreement, and, as a general rule, the landlord would have to give at least a 30-day notice of the rent increase. In all residential leases, from week to week, month to month, or any period less than a month, if the rent increase is greater than 10% of the rental amount charged to that tenant at any time during the 12 months prior to the effective date of the increase, the notice of increase must be given at least 60 days prior to the effective date of the increase (CC §827(b)).

Local ordinances in some cities restrict the amount and frequency of rent increases. Enacted in 1995, the **Costa-Hawkins Rental Housing Act** (CC §1954.50 *et seq.*) places restrictions on such local rent control ordinances as they pertain to rent, though not as they pertain to evictions:

- localities are prohibited from enacting new rent control ordinances;
- for leases on single-family homes or single condominium units entered into after January 1, 1996, there can be no control of rents;
- there can be no rent restrictions on rental units issued a certificate of occupancy after February 1, 1995; and
- if a tenant in a rent-controlled unit vacates voluntarily or is evicted for nonpayment of rent, the landlord may raise the initial rent to the new tenant by any amount.

Note: As with the withholding of a certain percent of the sale price of real property by foreign investors that we discussed in Chapter 12, both the federal government and California require the withholding of a percent of rents paid to non-resident aliens (or, in the case of California, to non-resident persons). Under FIRPTA, the renter who makes payments to a non-resident alien must withhold a flat rate of 30% of the rents, unless a tax treaty provides for a lower rate. If the renter does not make the required payment to the IRS, the manager of the rental property must make the withholding and payment. Under California law (California Revenue and Taxation Code Section 18662), the renter who makes rent payments to a non-resident person must withhold 7% of the amount that exceeds $1,500 in a calendar year and send it to the Franchise Tax Board (FTB). If the renter does not make the required payment to the FTB, the manager of the rental property must make the withholding and the payment.

Security Deposit: Paragraph 4 of the CAR lease provides for a security deposit, which is intended to secure performance of the tenant's lease obligations. In a residential lease, the deposit, regardless of what it is called ("cleaning fee," "advance payment," etc.), is refundable, less debits for the tenant's defaults as specified in the lease — for example, for unpaid rent, repair of damages, cleaning fees, etc. No lease or rental agreement may contain any provision characterizing any security as "nonrefundable." CC §1950.5(m).

The security deposit (not including the first month's rent) may not exceed a maximum of:

- two month's rent for an unfurnished residential property, or, pursuant to CC §1940.5(g), two and one-half of one months' rent if the tenant has a waterbed;

- three month's rent for a furnished residential property, or, pursuant to CC §1940.5(g), three and one-half of one months' rent if the tenant has a waterbed.

Fig. 13.1

CALIFORNIA
ASSOCIATION
OF REALTORS ®

**RESIDENTIAL LEASE OR
MONTH-TO-MONTH RENTAL AGREEMENT**
(C.A.R. Form LR, Revised 11/12)

Date _____ , _____ ("Landlord") and
_____ ("Tenant") agree as follows:

1. PROPERTY:
   A. Landlord rents to Tenant and Tenant rents from Landlord, the real property and improvements described as: _____
   _____ ("Premises").
   B. The Premises are for the sole use as a personal residence by the following named person(s) **only**: _____
   _____
   C. The following personal property, maintained pursuant to paragraph 11, is included: _____
   _____ or ☐ (if checked) the personal property on the attached addendum.
   D. The Premises may be subject to a local rent control ordinance _____.
2. TERM: The term begins on (date)_____ ("Commencement Date"), **(Check A or B):**
   ☐ **A. Month-to-Month:** and continues as a month-to-month tenancy. Tenant may terminate the tenancy by giving written notice at
       least 30 days prior to the intended termination date. Landlord may terminate the tenancy by giving written notice as provided
       by law. Such notices may be given on any date.
   ☐ **B. Lease:** and shall terminate on (date)_____ at _____ ☐ AM/ ☐ PM. Tenant
       shall vacate the Premises upon termination of the Agreement, unless: **(i)** Landlord and Tenant have extended this Agreement
       in writing or signed a new agreement; **(ii)** mandated by local rent control law; or **(iii)** Landlord accepts Rent from Tenant (other
       than past due Rent), in which case a month-to-month tenancy shall be created which either party may terminate as specified
       in paragraph 2A. Rent shall be at a rate agreed to by Landlord and Tenant, or as allowed by law. All other terms and conditions
       of this Agreement shall remain in full force and effect.
3. RENT: "Rent" shall mean all monetary obligations of Tenant to Landlord under the terms of the Agreement, except security deposit.
   A. Tenant agrees to pay $_____ per month for the term of the Agreement.
   B. Rent is payable in advance on the **1st (or ☐ _____) day** of each calendar month, and is delinquent on the next day.
   C. If Commencement Date falls on any day other than the day Rent is payable under paragraph 3B, and Tenant has paid one full
       month's Rent in advance of Commencement Date, Rent for the second calendar month shall be prorated based on a 30-day period.
   D. PAYMENT: Rent shall be paid by ☐ personal check, ☐ money order, ☐ cashier's check, or ☐ other _____, to
       (name) _____ (phone) _____ at (address)
       _____, (or at any other location
       subsequently specified by Landlord in writing to Tenant) (and ☐ if checked, rent may be paid personally, between the hours of
       _____ and _____ on the following days _____). If any payment is
       returned for non-sufficient funds ("NSF") or because tenant stops payment, then, after that: (i) Landlord may, in writing, require
       Tenant to pay Rent in cash for three months and (ii) all future Rent shall be paid by ☐ money order, or ☐ cashier's check.
4. SECURITY DEPOSIT:
   A. Tenant agrees to pay $_____ as a security deposit. Security deposit will be
       ☐ transferred to and held by the Owner of the Premises, or ☐ held in Owner's Broker's trust account.
   B. All or any portion of the security deposit may be used, as reasonably necessary, to: **(i)** cure Tenant's default in payment of Rent (which
       includes Late Charges, NSF fees or other sums due); **(ii)** repair damage, excluding ordinary wear and tear, caused by Tenant or by a guest
       or licensee of Tenant; **(iii)** clean Premises, if necessary, upon termination of the tenancy; and **(iv)** replace or return personal property or
       appurtenances. **SECURITY DEPOSIT SHALL NOT BE USED BY TENANT IN LIEU OF PAYMENT OF LAST MONTH'S RENT.** If
       all or any portion of the security deposit is used during the tenancy, Tenant agrees to reinstate the total security deposit within five days
       after written notice is delivered to Tenant. Within 21 days after Tenant vacates the Premises, Landlord shall: **(1)** furnish Tenant an
       itemized statement indicating the amount of any security deposit received and the basis for its disposition and supporting
       documentation as required by California Civil Code § 1950.5(g); and **(2)** return any remaining portion of the security deposit to Tenant.
   **C. Security deposit will not be returned until all Tenants have vacated the Premises and all keys returned. Any security
       deposit returned by check shall be made out to all Tenants named on this Agreement, or as subsequently modified.**
   D. No interest will be paid on security deposit unless required by local law.
   E. If the security deposit is held by Owner, Tenant agrees not to hold Broker responsible for its return. If the security deposit is held
       in Owner's Broker's trust account, **and** Broker's authority is terminated before expiration of this Agreement, **and** security deposit
       is released to someone other than Tenant, **then** Broker shall notify Tenant, in writing, where and to whom security deposit has been
       released. Once Tenant has been provided such notice, Tenant agrees not to hold Broker responsible for the security deposit.
5. MOVE-IN COSTS RECEIVED/DUE: Move-in funds made payable to _____ shall
   be paid by ☐ personal check, ☐ money order, or ☐ cashier's check.

Category	Total Due	Payment Received	Balance Due	Date Due
Rent from _____ to _____ (date)				
*Security Deposit				
Other _____				
Other _____				
Total				

*The maximum amount Landlord may receive as security deposit, however designated, cannot exceed two months' Rent for
unfurnished premises, or three months' Rent for furnished premises.

Tenant's Initials (_____)(_____)   Landlord's Initials (_____)(_____)

LR REVISED 11/12 (PAGE 1 OF 6) Print Date

Reviewed by _____ Date _____

EQUAL HOUSING OPPORTUNITY

RESIDENTIAL LEASE OR MONTH-TO-MONTH RENTAL AGREEMENT (LR PAGE 1 OF 6)

Premises: _____ Date: _____

6. **LATE CHARGE; RETURNED CHECKS:**
   A. Tenant acknowledges either late payment of Rent or issuance of a returned check may cause Landlord to incur costs and expenses, the exact amounts of which are extremely difficult and impractical to determine. These costs may include, but are not limited to, processing, enforcement and accounting expenses, and late charges imposed on Landlord. If any installment of Rent due from Tenant is not received by Landlord within **5 (or ☐ _____) calendar days** after the date due, or if a check is returned, Tenant shall pay to Landlord, respectively, an additional sum of $ _____ or _____ % of the Rent due as a Late Charge and $25.00 as a NSF fee for the first returned check and $35.00 as a NSF fee for each additional returned check, either or both of which shall be deemed additional Rent.
   B. Landlord and Tenant agree that these charges represent a fair and reasonable estimate of the costs Landlord may incur by reason of Tenant's late or NSF payment. Any Late Charge or NSF fee due shall be paid with the current installment of Rent. Landlord's acceptance of any Late Charge or NSF fee shall not constitute a waiver as to any default of Tenant. Landlord's right to collect a Late Charge or NSF fee shall not be deemed an extension of the date Rent is due under paragraph 3 or prevent Landlord from exercising any other rights and remedies under this Agreement and as provided by law.
7. **PARKING: (Check A or B)**
   ☐ A. Parking is permitted as follows: _____

   The right to parking ☐ is ☐ is not included in the Rent charged pursuant to paragraph 3. If not included in the Rent, the parking rental fee shall be an additional $ _____ per month. Parking space(s) are to be used for parking properly licensed and operable motor vehicles, except for trailers, boats, campers, buses or trucks (other than pick-up trucks). Tenant shall park in assigned space(s) only. Parking space(s) are to be kept clean. Vehicles leaking oil, gas or other motor vehicle fluids shall not be parked on the Premises. Mechanical work or storage of inoperable vehicles is not permitted in parking space(s) or elsewhere on the Premises.
   OR ☐ B. Parking is not permitted on the Premises.
8. **STORAGE: (Check A or B)**
   ☐ A. Storage is permitted as follows: _____
   The right to separate storage space ☐ is, ☐ is not, included in the Rent charged pursuant to paragraph 3. If not included in the Rent, storage space fee shall be an additional $ _____ per month. Tenant shall store only personal property Tenant owns, and shall not store property claimed by another or in which another has any right, title or interest. Tenant shall not store any improperly packaged food or perishable goods, flammable materials, explosives, hazardous waste or other inherently dangerous material, or illegal substances.
   OR ☐ B. Except for Tenant's personal property, contained entirely within the Premises, storage is not permitted on the Premises.
9. **UTILITIES:** Tenant agrees to pay for all utilities and services, and the following charges: _____ except _____, which shall be paid for by Landlord. If any utilities are not separately metered, Tenant shall pay Tenant's proportional share, as reasonably determined and directed by Landlord. If utilities are separately metered, Tenant shall place utilities in Tenant's name as of the Commencement Date. Landlord is only responsible for installing and maintaining one usable telephone jack and one telephone line to the Premises. Tenant shall pay any cost for conversion from existing utilities service provider.
10. **CONDITION OF PREMISES:** Tenant has examined Premises and, if any, all furniture, furnishings, appliances, landscaping and fixtures, including smoke detector(s).
    (Check all that apply:)
    ☐ A. Tenant acknowledges these items are clean and in operable condition, with the following exceptions: _____
    _____
    ☐ B. Tenant's acknowledgment of the condition of these items is contained in an attached statement of condition (C.A.R. Form MIMO).
    ☐ C. (i) Landlord will Deliver to Tenant a statement of condition (C.A.R. Form MIMO) ☐ within **3 days** after execution of this Agreement; ☐ prior to the Commencement Date; ☐ within **3 days** after the Commencement Date.
    (ii) Tenant shall complete and return the MIMO to Landlord within **3 (or ☐ _____) days** after Delivery. Tenant's failure to return the MIMO within that time shall conclusively be deemed Tenant's Acknowledgement of the condition as stated in the MIMO.
    ☐ D. Tenant will provide Landlord a list of items that are damaged or not in operable condition within **3 (or ☐ _____) days** after Commencement Date, not as a contingency of this Agreement but rather as an acknowledgment of the condition of the Premises.
    ☐ E. Other: _____.
11. **MAINTENANCE:**
    A. Tenant shall properly use, operate and safeguard Premises, including if applicable, any landscaping, furniture, furnishings and appliances, and all mechanical, electrical, gas and plumbing fixtures, and keep them and the Premises clean, sanitary and well ventilated. Tenant shall be responsible for checking and maintaining all carbon monoxide and smoke detectors and any additional phone lines beyond the one line and jack that Landlord shall provide and maintain. Tenant shall immediately notify Landlord, in writing, of any problem, malfunction or damage. Tenant shall be charged for all repairs or replacements caused by Tenant, pets, guests or licensees of Tenant, excluding ordinary wear and tear. Tenant shall be charged for all damage to Premises as a result of failure to report a problem in a timely manner. Tenant shall be charged for repair of drain blockages or stoppages, unless caused by defective plumbing parts or tree roots invading sewer lines.
    B. ☐ Landlord ☐ Tenant shall water the garden, landscaping, trees and shrubs, except _____
    _____.
    C. ☐ Landlord ☐ Tenant shall maintain the garden, landscaping, trees and shrubs, except _____
    _____.
    D. ☐ Landlord ☐ Tenant shall maintain _____.
    E. Tenant's failure to maintain any item for which Tenant is responsible shall give Landlord the right to hire someone to perform such maintenance and charge Tenant to cover the cost of such maintenance.
    F. The following items of personal property are included in the Premises without warranty and Landlord will not maintain, repair or replace them: _____.

Tenant's Initials (_____)(_____)   Landlord's Initials (_____)(_____)

LR REVISED 11/12 (PAGE 2 OF 6)

Reviewed by _____ Date _____

Premises: _____ Date: _____

12. **NEIGHBORHOOD CONDITIONS:** Tenant is advised to satisfy him or herself as to neighborhood or area conditions, including schools, proximity and adequacy of law enforcement, crime statistics, proximity of registered felons or offenders, fire protection, other governmental services, availability, adequacy and cost of any wired, wireless internet connections or other telecommunications or other technology services and installations, proximity to commercial, industrial or agricultural activities, existing and proposed transportation, construction and development that may affect noise, view, or traffic, airport noise, noise or odor from any source, wild and domestic animals, other nuisances, hazards, or circumstances, cemeteries, facilities and condition of common areas, conditions and influences of significance to certain cultures and/or religions, and personal needs, requirements and preferences of Tenant.

13. **PETS:** Unless otherwise provided in California Civil Code § 54.2, no animal or pet shall be kept on or about the Premises without Landlord's prior written consent, except: _____.

14. ☐ **(If checked) NO SMOKING:** No smoking of any substance is allowed on the Premises or common areas. If smoking does occur on the Premises or common areas, (i) Tenant is responsible for all damage caused by the smoking including, but not limited to stains, burns, odors and removal of debris; (ii) Tenant is in breach of this Agreement; (iii) Tenant, guests, and all others may be required to leave the Premises; and (iv) Tenant acknowledges that in order to remove odor caused by smoking, Landlord may need to replace carpet and drapes and paint the entire premises regardless of when these items were last cleaned, replaced. or repainted. Such actions and other necessary steps will impact the return of any security deposit. The Premises or common areas may be subject to a local non-smoking ordinance.

15. **RULES/REGULATIONS:**
    A. Tenant agrees to comply with all Landlord rules and regulations that are at any time posted on the Premises or delivered to Tenant. Tenant shall not, and shall ensure that guests and licensees of Tenant shall not, disturb, annoy, endanger or interfere with other tenants of the building or neighbors, or use the Premises for any unlawful purposes, including, but not limited to, using, manufacturing, selling, storing or transporting illicit drugs or other contraband, or violate any law or ordinance, or commit a waste or nuisance on or about the Premises.
    B. **(If applicable, check one)**
       ☐ 1. Landlord shall provide Tenant with a copy of the rules and regulations within _____ days
           or _____.
       OR ☐ 2. Tenant has been provided with, and acknowledges receipt of, a copy of the rules and regulations.

16. ☐ **(If checked) CONDOMINIUM; PLANNED UNIT DEVELOPMENT:**
    A. The Premises are a unit in a condominium, planned unit development, common interest subdivision or other development governed by a homeowners' association ("HOA"). The name of the HOA is _____. Tenant agrees to comply with all HOA covenants, conditions and restrictions, bylaws, rules and regulations and decisions ("HOA Rules"). Landlord shall provide Tenant copies of HOA Rules, if any. Tenant shall reimburse Landlord for any fines or charges imposed by HOA or other authorities, due to any violation by Tenant, or the guests or licensees of Tenant.
    B. **(Check one)**
       ☐ 1. Landlord shall provide Tenant with a copy of the HOA Rules within _____ days
           or _____.
       OR ☐ 2. Tenant has been provided with, and acknowledges receipt of, a copy of the HOA Rules.

17. **ALTERATIONS; REPAIRS:** Unless otherwise specified by law or paragraph 29C, without Landlord's prior written consent, (i) Tenant shall not make any repairs, alterations or improvements in or about the Premises including: painting, wallpapering, adding or changing locks, installing antenna or satellite dish(es), placing signs, displays or exhibits, or using screws, fastening devices, large nails or adhesive materials; (ii) Landlord shall not be responsible for the costs of alterations or repairs made by Tenant; (iii) Tenant shall not deduct from Rent the costs of any repairs, alterations or improvements; and (iv) any deduction made by Tenant shall be considered unpaid Rent.

18. **KEYS; LOCKS:**
    A. Tenant acknowledges receipt of (or Tenant will receive ☐ prior to the Commencement Date, or ☐ _____):
       ☐ _____ key(s) to Premises,   ☐ _____ remote control device(s) for garage door/gate opener(s),
       ☐ _____ key(s) to mailbox,   ☐ _____,
       ☐ _____ key(s) to common area(s),   ☐ _____.
    B. Tenant acknowledges that locks to the Premises ☐ have, ☐ have not, been re-keyed.
    C. If Tenant re-keys existing locks or opening devices, Tenant shall immediately deliver copies of all keys to Landlord. Tenant shall pay all costs and charges related to loss of any keys or opening devices. Tenant may not remove locks, even if installed by Tenant.

19. **ENTRY:**
    A. Tenant shall make Premises available to Landlord or Landlord's representative for the purpose of entering to make necessary or agreed repairs (including, but not limited to, installing, repairing, testing, and maintaining smoke detectors and carbon monoxide devices, and bracing, anchoring or strapping water heaters), decorations, alterations, or improvements, or to supply necessary or agreed services, or to show Premises to prospective or actual purchasers, tenants, mortgagees, lenders, appraisers, or contractors.
    B. Landlord and Tenant agree that 24-hour written notice shall be reasonable and sufficient notice, except as follows. 48-hour written notice is required to conduct an inspection of the Premises prior to the Tenant moving out, unless the Tenant waives the right to such notice. Notice may be given orally to show the Premises to actual or prospective purchasers provided Tenant has been notified in writing within 120 days preceding the oral notice, that the Premises are for sale and that oral notice may be given to show the Premises. No notice is required: (i) to enter in case of an emergency; (ii) if the Tenant is present and consents at the time of entry; or (iii) if the Tenant has abandoned or surrendered the Premises. No written notice is required if Landlord and Tenant orally agree to an entry for agreed services or repairs if the date and time of entry are within one week of the oral agreement.
    C. ☐ (If checked) Tenant authorizes the use of a keysafe/lockbox to allow entry into the Premises and agrees to sign a keysafe/lockbox addendum (C.A.R. Form KLA).

20. **SIGNS:** Tenant authorizes Landlord to place FOR SALE/LEASE signs on the Premises.

21. **ASSIGNMENT; SUBLETTING:** Tenant shall not sublet all or any part of Premises, or assign or transfer this Agreement or any interest in it, without Landlord's prior written consent. Unless such consent is obtained, any assignment, transfer or subletting of Premises or this Agreement or tenancy, by voluntary act of Tenant, operation of law or otherwise, shall, at the option of Landlord, terminate this Agreement. Any proposed assignee, transferee or sublessee shall submit to Landlord an application and credit information for Landlord's approval and, if approved, sign a separate written agreement with Landlord and Tenant. Landlord's consent to any one assignment, transfer or sublease, shall not be construed as consent to any subsequent assignment, transfer or sublease and does not release Tenant of Tenant's obligations under this Agreement.

Tenant's Initials (_____)(_____)   Landlord's Initials (_____)(_____)

LR REVISED 11/12 (PAGE 3 OF 6)

Reviewed by _____ Date _____

RESIDENTIAL LEASE OR MONTH-TO-MONTH RENTAL AGREEMENT (LR PAGE 3 OF 6)

Premises: _____   Date: _____

22. **JOINT AND INDIVIDUAL OBLIGATIONS:** If there is more than one Tenant, each one shall be individually and completely responsible for the performance of all obligations of Tenant under this Agreement, jointly with every other Tenant, and individually, whether or not in possession.

23. ☐ **LEAD-BASED PAINT (If checked):** Premises were constructed prior to 1978. In accordance with federal law, Landlord gives and Tenant acknowledges receipt of the disclosures on the attached form (C.A.R. Form FLD) and a federally approved lead pamphlet.

24. ☐ **MILITARY ORDNANCE DISCLOSURE:** (If applicable and known to Landlord) Premises are located within one mile of an area once used for military training, and may contain potentially explosive munitions.

25. ☐ **PERIODIC PEST CONTROL:** Landlord has entered into a contract for periodic pest control treatment of the Premises and shall give Tenant a copy of the notice originally given to Landlord by the pest control company.

26. ☐ **METHAMPHETAMINE CONTAMINATION:** Prior to signing this Agreement, Landlord has given Tenant a notice that a health official has issued an order prohibiting occupancy of the property because of methamphetamine contamination. A copy of the notice and order are attached.

27. **MEGAN'S LAW DATABASE DISCLOSURE:** Notice: Pursuant to Section 290.46 of the Penal Code, information about specified registered sex offenders is made available to the public via an Internet Web site maintained by the Department of Justice at www.meganslaw.ca.gov. Depending on an offender's criminal history, this information will include either the address at which the offender resides or the community of residence and ZIP Code in which he or she resides. (Neither Landlord nor Brokers, if any, are required to check this website. If Tenant wants further information, Tenant should obtain information directly from this website.)

28. **POSSESSION:**
    A. Tenant is not in possession of the Premises. If Landlord is unable to deliver possession of Premises on Commencement Date, such Date shall be extended to the date on which possession is made available to Tenant. If Landlord is unable to deliver possession within 5 (or ☐ _____) calendar days after agreed Commencement Date, Tenant may terminate this Agreement by giving written notice to Landlord, and shall be refunded all Rent and security deposit paid. Possession is deemed terminated when Tenant has returned all keys to the Premises to Landlord.
    B. ☐ Tenant is already in possession of the Premises.

29. **TENANT'S OBLIGATIONS UPON VACATING PREMISES:**
    A. Upon termination of this Agreement, Tenant shall: **(i)** give Landlord all copies of all keys or opening devices to Premises, including any common areas; **(ii)** vacate and surrender Premises to Landlord, empty of all persons; **(iii)** vacate any/all parking and/or storage space; **(iv)** clean and deliver Premises, as specified in paragraph C below, to Landlord in the same condition as referenced in paragraph 10; **(v)** remove all debris; **(vi)** give written notice to Landlord of Tenant's forwarding address; and **(vii)** _____
    B. All alterations/improvements made by or caused to be made by Tenant, with or without Landlord's consent, become the property of Landlord upon termination. Landlord may charge Tenant for restoration of the Premises to the condition it was in prior to any alterations/improvements.
    C. **Right to Pre-Move-Out Inspection and Repairs: (i)** After giving or receiving notice of termination of a tenancy (C.A.R. Form NTT), or before the end of a lease, Tenant has the right to request that an inspection of the Premises take place prior to termination of the lease or rental (C.A.R. Form NRI). If Tenant requests such an inspection, Tenant shall be given an opportunity to remedy identified deficiencies prior to termination, consistent with the terms of this Agreement. **(ii)** Any repairs or alterations made to the Premises as a result of this inspection (collectively, "Repairs") shall be made at Tenant's expense. Repairs may be performed by Tenant or through others, who have adequate insurance and licenses and are approved by Landlord. The work shall comply with applicable law, including governmental permit, inspection and approval requirements. Repairs shall be performed in a good, skillful manner with materials of quality and appearance comparable to existing materials. It is understood that exact restoration of appearance or cosmetic items following all Repairs may not be possible. **(iii)** Tenant shall: **(a)** obtain receipts for Repairs performed by others; **(b)** prepare a written statement indicating the Repairs performed by Tenant and the date of such Repairs; and **(c)** provide copies of receipts and statements to Landlord prior to termination. Paragraph 29C does not apply when the tenancy is terminated pursuant to California Code of Civil Procedure § 1161(2), (3) or (4).

30. **BREACH OF CONTRACT; EARLY TERMINATION:** In addition to any obligations established by paragraph 29, in the event of termination by Tenant prior to completion of the original term of the Agreement, Tenant shall also be responsible for lost Rent, rental commissions, advertising expenses and painting costs necessary to ready Premises for re-rental. Landlord may withhold any such amounts from Tenant's security deposit.

31. **TEMPORARY RELOCATION:** Subject to local law, Tenant agrees, upon demand of Landlord, to temporarily vacate Premises for a reasonable period, to allow for fumigation (or other methods) to control wood destroying pests or organisms, or other repairs to Premises. Tenant agrees to comply with all instructions and requirements necessary to prepare Premises to accommodate pest control, fumigation or other work, including bagging or storage of food and medicine, and removal of perishables and valuables. Tenant shall only be entitled to a credit of Rent equal to the per diem Rent for the period of time Tenant is required to vacate Premises.

32. **DAMAGE TO PREMISES:** If, by no fault of Tenant, Premises are totally or partially damaged or destroyed by fire, earthquake, accident or other casualty that render Premises totally or partially uninhabitable, either Landlord or Tenant may terminate this Agreement by giving the other written notice. Rent shall be abated as of the date Premises become totally or partially uninhabitable. The abated amount shall be the current monthly Rent prorated on a 30-day period. If the Agreement is not terminated, Landlord shall promptly repair the damage, and Rent shall be reduced based on the extent to which the damage interferes with Tenant's reasonable use of Premises. If damage occurs as a result of an act of Tenant or Tenant's guests, only Landlord shall have the right of termination, and no reduction in Rent shall be made.

33. **INSURANCE:** Tenant's or guest's personal property and vehicles are not insured by Landlord, manager or, if applicable, HOA, against loss or damage due to fire, theft, vandalism, rain, water, criminal or negligent acts of others, or any other cause. **Tenant is advised to carry Tenant's own insurance (renter's insurance) to protect Tenant from any such loss or damage.** Tenant shall comply with any requirement imposed on Tenant by Landlord's insurer to avoid: **(i)** an increase in Landlord's insurance premium (or Tenant shall pay for the increase in premium); or **(ii)** loss of insurance.

34. **WATERBEDS:** Tenant shall not use or have waterbeds on the Premises unless: **(i)** Tenant obtains a valid waterbed insurance policy; **(ii)** Tenant increases the security deposit in an amount equal to one-half of one month's Rent; and **(iii)** the bed conforms to the floor load capacity of Premises.

Tenant's Initials (_____)(_____)   Landlord's Initials (_____)(_____)

Reviewed by _____ Date _____

RESIDENTIAL LEASE OR MONTH-TO-MONTH RENTAL AGREEMENT (LR PAGE 4 OF 6)

Premises: _____ Date: _____

35. WAIVER: The waiver of any breach shall not be construed as a continuing waiver of the same or any subsequent breach.

36. NOTICE: Notices may be served at the following address, or at any other location subsequently designated:
Landlord: _____   Tenant: _____
_____   _____
_____   _____

37. TENANT ESTOPPEL CERTIFICATE: Tenant shall execute and return a tenant estoppel certificate delivered to Tenant by Landlord or Landlord's agent within **3 days** after its receipt. Failure to comply with this requirement shall be deemed Tenant's acknowledgment that the tenant estoppel certificate is true and correct, and may be relied upon by a lender or purchaser.

38. REPRESENTATIONS:
  A. TENANT REPRESENTATION; OBLIGATIONS REGARDING OCCUPANTS; CREDIT: Tenant warrants that all statements in Tenant's rental application are accurate. Landlord requires all occupants 18 years of age or older and all emancipated minors to complete a lease rental application. Tenant acknowledges this requirement and agrees to notify Landlord when any occupant of the Premises reaches the age of 18 or becomes an emancipated minor. Tenant authorizes Landlord and Broker(s) to obtain Tenant's credit report periodically during the tenancy in connection with the modification or enforcement of this Agreement. Landlord may cancel this Agreement: **(i)** before occupancy begins; **(ii)** upon disapproval of the credit report(s); or **(iii)** at any time, upon discovering that information in Tenant's application is false. A negative credit report reflecting on Tenant's record may be submitted to a credit reporting agency if Tenant fails to fulfill the terms of payment and other obligations under this Agreement.
  B. LANDLORD REPRESENTATIONS: Landlord warrants that, unless otherwise specified in writing, Landlord is unaware of **(i)** any recorded Notices of Default affecting the Premise; **(ii)** any deliquent amounts due under any loan secured by the Premises; and **(iii)** any bankruptcy proceeding affecting the Premises.

39. MEDIATION:
  A. Consistent with paragraphs B and C below, Landlord and Tenant agree to mediate any dispute or claim arising between them out of this Agreement, or any resulting transaction, before resorting to court action. Mediation fees, if any, shall be divided equally among the parties involved. If, for any dispute or claim to which this paragraph applies, any party commences an action without first attempting to resolve the matter through mediation, or refuses to mediate after a request has been made, then that party shall not be entitled to recover attorney fees, even if they would otherwise be available to that party in any such action.
  B. The following matters are excluded from mediation: **(i)** an unlawful detainer action; **(ii)** the filing or enforcement of a mechanic's lien; and **(iii)** any matter within the jurisdiction of a probate, small claims or bankruptcy court. The filing of a court action to enable the recording of a notice of pending action, for order of attachment, receivership, injunction, or other provisional remedies, shall not constitute a waiver of the mediation provision.
  C. Landlord and Tenant agree to mediate disputes or claims involving Listing Agent, Leasing Agent or property manager ("Broker"), provided Broker shall have agreed to such mediation prior to, or within a reasonable time after, the dispute or claim is presented to such Broker. Any election by Broker to participate in mediation shall not result in Broker being deemed a party to this Agreement.

40. ATTORNEY FEES: In any action or proceeding arising out of this Agreement, the prevailing party between Landlord and Tenant shall be entitled to reasonable attorney fees and costs, except as provided in paragraph 39A.

41. C.A.R. FORM: C.A.R. Form means the specific form referenced or another comparable form agreed to by the parties.

42. OTHER TERMS AND CONDITIONS;SUPPLEMENTS: ☐ Interpreter/Translator Agreement (C.A.R. Form ITA);
☐ Keysafe/Lockbox Addendum (C.A.R. Form KLA); ☐ Lead-Based Paint and Lead-Based Paint Hazards Disclosure (C.A.R. Form FLD);
☐ Landlord in Default Addendum (C.A.R. For LID)
_____
The following ATTACHED supplements are incorporated in this Agreement: _____
_____

43. TIME OF ESSENCE; ENTIRE CONTRACT; CHANGES: Time is of the essence. All understandings between the parties are incorporated in this Agreement. Its terms are intended by the parties as a final, complete and exclusive expression of their Agreement with respect to its subject matter, and may not be contradicted by evidence of any prior agreement or contemporaneous oral agreement. If any provision of this Agreement is held to be ineffective or invalid, the remaining provisions will nevertheless be given full force and effect. Neither this Agreement nor any provision in it may be extended, amended, modified, altered or changed except in writing. This Agreement is subject to California landlord-tenant law and shall incorporate all changes required by amendment or successors to such law. This Agreement and any supplement, addendum or modification, including any copy, may be signed in two or more counterparts, all of which shall constitute one and the same writing.

44. AGENCY:
  A. CONFIRMATION: The following agency relationship(s) are hereby confirmed for this transaction:
Listing Agent: (Print firm name) _____ is the agent of
(check one): ☐ the Landlord exclusively; or ☐ both the Landlord and Tenant.
Leasing Agent: (Print firm name) _____ (if not same as Listing Agent) is
the agent of (check one): ☐ the Tenant exclusively; or ☐ the Landlord exclusively; or ☐ both the Tenant and Landlord.
  B. DISCLOSURE: ☐ (If checked): The term of this lease exceeds one year. A disclosure regarding real estate agency relationships (C.A.R. Form AD) has been provided to Landlord and Tenant, who each acknowledge its receipt.

45. ☐ **TENANT COMPENSATION TO BROKER:** Upon execution of this Agreement, Tenant agrees to pay compensation to Broker as specified in a separate written agreement between Tenant and Broker.

Tenant's Initials (_____)(_____)   Landlord's Initials (_____)(_____)

Reviewed by _____ Date _____

RESIDENTIAL LEASE OR MONTH-TO-MONTH RENTAL AGREEMENT (LR PAGE 5 OF 6)

Premises: _____ Date: _____

46. ☐ **INTERPRETER/TRANSLATOR:** The terms of this Agreement have been interpreted for Tenant into the following language: _____. Landlord and Tenant acknowledge receipt of the attached interpreter/translator agreement (C.A.R. Form ITA).

47. FOREIGN LANGUAGE NEGOTIATION: If this Agreement has been negotiated by Landlord and Tenant primarily in Spanish, Chinese, Tagalog, Korean or Vietnamese, pursuant to the California Civil Code, Tenant shall be provided a translation of this Agreement in the language used for the negotiation.

48. OWNER COMPENSATION TO BROKER: Upon execution of this Agreement, Owner agrees to pay compensation to Broker as specified in a separate written agreement between Owner and Broker (C.A.R. Form LCA).

49. RECEIPT: If specified in paragraph 5, Landlord or Broker, acknowledges receipt of move-in funds.

> Landlord and Tenant acknowledge and agree Brokers: **(a)** do not guarantee the condition of the Premises; **(b)** cannot verify representations made by others; **(c)** cannot provide legal or tax advice; **(d)** will not provide other advice or information that exceeds the knowledge, education or experience required to obtain a real estate license. Furthermore, if Brokers are not also acting as Landlord in this Agreement, Brokers: **(e)** do not decide what rental rate a Tenant should pay or Landlord should accept; and **(f)** do not decide upon the length or other terms of tenancy. Landlord and Tenant agree that they will seek legal, tax, insurance and other desired assistance from appropriate professionals.

Tenant agrees to rent the Premises on the above terms and conditions.

Tenant _____ Date _____
Address _____ City _____ State _____ Zip _____
Telephone_____ Fax _____ E-mail _____
Tenant _____ Date _____
Address _____ City _____ State _____ Zip _____
Telephone_____ Fax _____ E-mail _____

☐ **GUARANTEE:** In consideration of the execution of this Agreement by and between Landlord and Tenant and for valuable consideration, receipt of which is hereby acknowledged, the undersigned ("Guarantor") does hereby: **(i)** guarantee unconditionally to Landlord and Landlord's agents, successors and assigns, the prompt payment of Rent or other sums that become due pursuant to this Agreement, including any and all court costs and attorney fees included in enforcing the Agreement; **(ii)** consent to any changes, modifications or alterations of any term in this Agreement agreed to by Landlord and Tenant; and **(iii)** waive any right to require Landlord and/or Landlord's agents to proceed against Tenant for any default occurring under this Agreement before seeking to enforce this Guarantee.

Guarantor (Print Name) _____
Guarantor _____ Date _____
Address _____ City _____ State _____ Zip _____
Telephone _____ Fax _____ E-mail _____

Landlord agrees to rent the Premises on the above terms and conditions.

Landlord _____ Landlord _____
Address _____
Telephone_____ Fax _____ E-mail _____

> **REAL ESTATE BROKERS:**
> **A.** Real estate brokers who are not also Landlord under this Agreement are not parties to the Agreement between Landlord and Tenant.
> **B.** Agency relationships are confirmed in paragraph 44.
> **C. COOPERATING BROKER COMPENSATION:** Listing Broker agrees to pay Cooperating Broker (Leasing Firm) and Cooperating Broker agrees to accept: **(i)** the amount specified in the MLS, provided Cooperating Broker is a Participant of the MLS in which the Property is offered for sale or a reciprocal MLS; or **(ii)** ☐ (if checked) the amount specified in a separate written agreement between Listing Broker and Cooperating Broker.

Real Estate Broker (Listing Firm) _____ DRE Lic. # _____
By (Agent) _____ DRE Lic. # _____ Date _____
Address _____ City _____ State _____ Zip _____
Telephone _____ Fax _____ E-mail _____

Real Estate Broker (Leasing Firm) _____ DRE Lic. # _____
By (Agent) _____ DRE Lic. # _____ Date _____
Address _____ City _____ State _____ Zip _____
Telephone _____ Fax _____ E-mail _____

R I
E N
B S
S C ®
Published and Distributed by:
REAL ESTATE BUSINESS SERVICES, INC.
a subsidiary of the California Association of REALTORS®
525 South Virgil Avenue, Los Angeles, California 90020

Reviewed by _____ Date _____

However, CC §1950.5(c) provides that if the term of the lease is 6 months or longer, then there is no prohibition against the landlord's charging an *advance fee* of 6 months *or more* rent. Curiously, this means, for example, that in a one-year lease, the landlord could require a 7-month advance payment but not a 5-month advance payment. Furthermore, at the request of the tenant, the landlord and tenant may agree that the landlord will make structural, decorative, furnishing, or other similar alterations and charge such alterations to the tenant as long as the alterations are for other than cleaning or repairs that the landlord could have charged the previous tenant.

No later than 21 calendar days after the tenant vacates the premises, but not earlier than the time that either the landlord or the tenant gives a notice to terminate the tenancy or not earlier than 60 calendar days prior to the expiration of a fixed-term lease, the landlord must furnish the tenant, by personal delivery or first-class mail, a copy of an itemized statement indicating the amount of any security received, copies of documents showing charges incurred and deducted to repair or clean the premises, and the landlord must return any remaining portion of the security to the tenant.

Another exception to the amount of charges that a tenant may be required to pay the landlord is an application fee to cover such items as a credit report and a verification of references. The application fee cannot be more than the landlord's actual costs, and, pursuant to CC §1950.6, may not exceed a certain specified amount, which started at $30 and may be increased commensurate with the Consumer Price Index, beginning on January 1, 1998, making the maximum amount of the fee $44.51 in 2012.

Any security must be held by the landlord for the benefit of the tenant, and any claim of the tenant to the security is given priority over the claim of any other creditor of the landlord. The landlord need not pay the tenant interest on the security unless the lease provides otherwise or there is a local ordinance that requires the landlord to do so.

Late Charge and Returned Checks: Paragraph 6 of the CAR lease provides that the landlord may require the tenant to pay a late charge and a charge for any returned check. Such charges are enforceable if the amount specified in the lease is reasonably related to the anticipated administrative costs and loss of interest caused by the late payment or returned check. The CAR lease states that the acceptance of any late charge or returned check charge does not prevent the landlord from exercising any of the rights and remedies provided for in the lease; however, because courts consider forfeiture of a lease to be a drastic remedy, if the lease provides for a late charge, the landlord may lose the right to terminate the lease solely because of a late rental payment.

Utilities: Paragraph 9 of the CAR lease provides for the tenant's responsibility to pay utility charges. In residential leases, the landlord is responsible for providing the availability of basic utilities, but the landlord is not obligated to pay for these utilities unless so specified in the lease. Utilities can be either metered for multiple dwelling units or separately metered for each dwelling unit. If the utilities are master metered, the landlord pays the utilities and requires the tenants to make reasonably apportioned payments to the landlord for the utilities. If utilities are separately metered, the tenant is generally responsible for putting the utilities in the tenant's name, in which case the utilities provider may not charge either the property owner or future tenants for unpaid utility bills (Public Utilities Code §10009.6).

Condition of Premises: Although paragraph 10 of the CAR lease provides that the tenant acknowledge a statement of condition of the premises, and that the tenant will provide to the landlord, as further acknowledgment of the condition of the premises, a list of items that are damaged or not in operable condition within a specified number of days of commencement of the lease, California law does not require that the landlord and tenant inspect the premises and fill out a document describing the condition of the property before the commencement of tenancy. This type of inspection is, however, an excellent practice as it prevents either party from making false or exaggerated claims when the tenancy terminates.

Maintenance: Paragraph 11 of the CAR lease provides that the tenant must properly use, operate, and safeguard the premises and must immediately notify the landlord in writing of any problem, malfunction, or damage.

On the other hand, California law imposes strict duties on the landlord of a *residential* building to keep the dwelling in a habitable condition. A breach by a landlord of its duty to maintain the dwelling in a habitable condition, or of its duty to provide tenants with quiet enjoyment of the premises, is called **constructive eviction**.

Civil Code §1941.1 enumerates the following criteria of habitability:

- provide effective waterproofing and weather protection of the roof and exterior walls, including unbroken windows and doors;
- install and maintain plumbing and gas facilities that conform to applicable law;
- provide hot and cold running water furnished to appropriate fixtures and connected to a sewage disposal system approved under applicable law;
- provide and maintain heating facilities that conform to applicable law;
- provide and maintain electrical lighting that conforms to applicable law;
- provide that the building, grounds, appurtenances, and all areas under the control of the landlord be kept clean, sanitary, and free from all accumulations of debris, filth, rubbish, garbage, rodents, and vermin;

- provide and maintain an adequate number of appropriate receptacles for garbage and rubbish; and
- provide and maintain floors, stairways, and railings in good repair.

In addition, CC §1941.3 provides that the landlord of a residential building:

- install and maintain an operable deadbolt lock on each main swinging entry door of a dwelling unit;
- for doors that cannot be equipped with deadbolt locks, the landlord must equip the door with a metal strap affixed across the midsection of the door with a deadbolt that protrudes into the doorjamb;
- install and maintain operable window security or locking devices for windows that are designed to be opened; and
- install locking mechanisms that comply with applicable fire and safety codes on the exterior doors that provide ingress or egress to common areas with access to dwelling units in multifamily developments

Other statutory provisions require that every dwelling unit have an operable smoke detector at the time the tenant takes possession. After taking possession, the tenant then has the duty to notify the landlord if the detector becomes inoperable (Health and Safety Code §13113.7(d)). Additionally, the **Carbon Monoxide Poisoning Prevention Act** requires that every owner of a dwelling unit intended for human occupancy must install a carbon monoxide device, approved and listed by the State Fire Marshall, in each existing dwelling unit having a fossil fuel burning heater or appliance, fireplace, or an attached garage, within the earliest applicable time period as follows:

1) For all existing single-family dwelling units intended for human occupancy, on or before July 1, 2011.

2) For all existing hotel and motel dwelling units intended for human occupancy, on or before January 1, 2016.

3) For all other existing dwelling units intended for human occupancy, on or before January 1, 2013. HSC §17926(a).

If the landlord of a residential property fails to provide habitable premises, the tenant may give the landlord notice to repair the premises. If after receiving notice the landlord fails within a reasonable time (usually considered to be 30 days) to remedy the problem, the tenant may either:

- "repair and deduct" by spending up to one month's rent in repairs and deducting the amount spent from the rent due (this remedy may be used only twice in any 12-month period); or
- vacate the premises, in which case the tenant shall be discharged from further payment of rent or performance of other conditions as of the date of vacating the premises. CC §1942.

In addition to the above statutory duties of habitability for residential buildings, there is a nonwaivable common-law *implied warranty of habitability* to meet bare living requirements, and that if the landlord breaches this implied warranty the tenant will remain liable for the reasonable rental value of the property in its existing condition as long as the tenant remains in possession of the premises.

If the tenant breaches the lease, the landlord may sue for damages or injunctive relief. However, because of the severity of the remedy of termination, courts are unlikely to allow the landlord to terminate the lease for cause unless the breach is material and substantial. Such material and substantial breaches include failure to pay rent, material damage to the property, interference with other tenants' right to quiet enjoyment, breach of a covenant not to assign or sublease the premises, and illegal use of the premises. Even the occasional illegal use of the premises is not sufficient grounds for termination unless the lease specifically so provides or the illegality specifically relates to the use of the premises.

According to the *doctrine of dependent covenants*, if the tenant fails to pay rent, the landlord must continue to honor its lease obligations, and conversely, if the landlord fails to honor lease obligations, the tenant must continue to pay rent. However, if the landlord breaches the implied warranty of habitability, the tenant may withhold all but the reasonable rental value of the premises until the landlord satisfies its maintenance and repair obligations.

For a non-residential lease, the landlord has no legal duty to make repairs or to provide the premises in a condition suitable for the tenant's intended purpose; except that (1) the landlord must maintain and repair those parts of the premises for which the landlord has contractually assumed such obligation pursuant to the terms of the lease, and (2) the landlord must ensure that building codes and other government ordinances are satisfied if the tenant has not assumed those obligations in the lease.

Neighborhood Conditions: Paragraph 12 of the CAR lease attempts to shift the responsibility of becoming aware of neighborhood conditions to the tenant. However, landlords should be cognizant of the fact that courts tend to favor tenants, especially in situations that appear particularly egregious. If, for example, a landlord were aware that a serial rapist was on the loose in the immediate vicinity, it probably would be unwise for the landlord to rely on this paragraph 12 provision to insulate the landlord from responsibility to notify a prospective tenant of the problem.

Entry: The essence of every leasehold interest is exclusive possession of the leased premises. Accordingly, in every lease, the law implies a covenant that the landlord will provide the tenant with possession and "quiet enjoyment" of the premises. Though this implied covenant protects the tenant from disturbances to a tenant's right to possession and quiet enjoyment from the landlord, it does not protect the tenant from acts of third parties over whom the landlord has no control.

Addressing one aspect of a tenant's right to quiet enjoyment, paragraph 19 of the CAR lease provides conditions for the landlord's entry to the premises subsequent to the commencement of a residential lease. The provisions of this paragraph of the lease are based primarily on the statutory requirements in CC §1954, which states that a landlord may enter a dwelling unit *only* in the following cases:

- in case of emergency;
- to make necessary or agreed repairs;
- to supply necessary or agreed services;
- to exhibit the dwelling unit to prospective or actual purchasers, mortgagees, tenants, workers, or contractors, or to make an initial inspection before the end of the tenancy, as provided for in CC §1950.5 (f);
- when the tenant has abandoned or surrendered the premises;
- pursuant to court order; or
- if the tenant has a waterbed, to inspect the bedding installation upon completion, and periodically thereafter, to ensure its conformity with applicable law, as provided for in CC §1940.5(f).

Additionally, except in cases of emergency or when the tenant has abandoned or surrendered the premises, entry may only be made during normal business hours unless the tenant consents to an entry during other than normal business hours at the time of entry. Furthermore, unless it is impractical to do so (such as in an emergency), the landlord must give the tenant reasonable notice in writing of his or her intent to enter — 24 hours being the presumed reasonable period absent evidence to the contrary.

The provisions of CC §1954 may not be modified or waived by any provision in a lease. CC §1953(b).

Assignment; Subletting: Though a landlord may freely transfer its interest in the leased property to a third party unless the terms of the lease provide otherwise, paragraph 21 of the CAR lease provides that the tenant may not sublet all or any part of the leased premises, or assign or transfer the lease or any interest in it, without the landlord's prior written consent. Courts typically interpret lease provisions that prohibit the tenant from transferring any interest in the premises without with the landlord's consent as implying that the landlord will not unreasonably withhold consent.

Unless, as in the CAR lease, a lease expressly prohibits the tenant from transferring its interest in the premises, the tenant may ***assign*** (i.e., transfer the tenant's entire interest in the premises) or **sublease** (i.e., transfer the tenant's right to a portion of the premises or to the entire premises for less than the entire remaining lease term) its interest in the premises to any third party.

In an **assignment**, the original tenant remains secondarily liable under the lease through the lease term. The successor tenant (the **assignee**) becomes primarily liable to the landlord through the remainder of the lease term. If the assignee expressly assumed all obligations of the **assignor**, then the assignee will be fully liable under the lease. If, instead, the assignment was less than an express **assumption**, the assignee will be liable only for obligations that derive from its "privity of estate" or its occupancy of the premises, such as rent and duty to maintain, but will not be liable for certain other *purely contractual* obligations, such as an obligation to pay attorney fees in certain litigation outcomes with the landlord.

In a **sublease** the original tenant remains liable under the lease through the end of the lease term. However, because there is neither "privity of estate" nor "privity of contract" between the **subtenant** and the landlord, the subtenant has no direct lease obligations to the landlord. In a sublease situation, the subtenant is liable for the rent to the original tenant, and the original tenant is liable for the rent to the landlord. It is for this reason that a sublease is sometimes referred to as a **sandwich lease**, the original tenant being sandwiched between the subtenant and the landlord.

The landlord has no right to enforce the lease obligations against the subtenant but can enforce the obligations against the original tenant, regardless of whether it was the tenant or subtenant who performed an act or omission leading to a default. If, thereby, the original tenant's rights are extinguished, the subtenant's rights, which derive entirely from the original tenant, would also be extinguished. Nevertheless, if the landlord consents to a sublease, or a subtenant assumes certain obligations of the tenant, a sufficiently direct relationship may be found to enable the parties to enforce the terms of the lease against each other.

In addition to assignment and sublease, interests in the lease can be transferred through a **novation**, which occurs when the lease is replaced with a new one, or one party is replaced by another party. If a novation replaces the original tenant with another, then the liability of the original tenant under the lease would be terminated.

Notices to Tenant: Paragraphs 23-27 provide certain required landlord disclosures:

- **Lead-Based Paint**. If the property was built before 1978, Federal law requires that the landlord (1) provide the tenant with notice that the dwelling was built before 1978, (2) disclose the presence of known lead-based paint and lead-based paint hazards, and (3) give the prospective tenant a pamphlet titled "Disclosure of Information on Lead-Based Paint and/or Lead Based Paint Hazards."

The landlord is not required to conduct an evaluation of the lead-based paint or to remove it.

- **Military Ordnance Disclosure**. If a landlord knows that a rental unit is within 1 mile of a closed military ordnance in which ammunition or explosives were used, the landlord must, prior to the tenant's signing the lease, disclose this fact to the prospective tenant.
- **Periodic Pest Control**. Pest control companies must give to landlords and tenants of residential properties a written notice of the pesticides that will be used as part of an ongoing pest-control service. The landlord must give a copy of this notice to every new tenant who will occupy a dwelling unit that will be serviced under the pest-control service contract.
- **Methamphetamine Contamination**. If a local health official inspects rental property and finds that it is contaminated with a hazardous chemical related to methamphetamine production, the official must issue an order that prohibits the use or occupancy of the property and must serve the order on the landlord and all occupants. The landlord and all occupants must then vacate the affected units and not return until the official sends the owner notice that the property requires no further action. A landlord who receives such health official's notice of contamination must, until receiving notice that no further action is required, give a copy of the notice of contamination to all potential tenants who complete an application to rent the contaminated property.
- **Megan's Law Database Disclosure**. Pursuant to CC §2074.10a, every lease for residential property entered into after April 1, 2006 must contain, in not less than 8-point type, the specific wording contained in paragraph 27 of the CAR lease.

Landlords should also check to see whether they are required to give any notice under rent control laws in the area in which their rental properties lies.

Tenant's Obligations Upon Vacating Premises. Paragraph 29 of the CAR lease provides for acts that the tenant must perform before or upon vacating the leased premises. This paragraph also provides for the statutorily required written notice that landlords must give, informing the tenant that the tenant has the right to request an initial inspection of the premises before the tenant moves out. If the tenant requests the inspection, then the landlord must perform the inspection at a reasonable time but no earlier than two weeks before the termination of the lease. The tenant may be present at the inspection if the tenant so wishes. Based on the initial inspection, the landlord must give the tenant an itemized statement specifying repairs or cleaning that are proposed to be the basis of any deductions from the security deposit the landlord intends to make. The tenant then has an opportunity during the period following the inspection until the termination of the tendency to remedy identified deficiencies in order to avoid deductions from the security. CC §1950.5(f).

EVICTION

Eviction of a tenant is a three-step process, involving:

1. termination of the lease;

2. filing, serving, and succeeding in an **unlawful detainer** action; and

3. if the tenant has not already vacated, physical removal of the tenant by the sheriff.

Termination

A breach of a lease by a tenant, even nonpayment of rent, does not terminate the lease — the tenancy continues until the landlord gives proper notice, which typically is a 3-day, 30-day, 60-day, or 90-day notice, depending on the reason for termination and the type of tenancy involved.

Both tenants and landlords should be aware that because the law (1) frowns on the forfeiture of leases, and (2) provides landlords with expedited eviction procedures, if the landlord makes even a small mistake in drafting or serving the required notice, the court may deny the eviction, thereby returning the landlord to step one: the drafting and serving of a new termination notice.

IMPORTANT: In rent-controlled cities, landlords may not be able to evict tenants, even with notice, except for special reasons, as specified in each city's rent-control/eviction ordinances. Also, if the property is under foreclosure, tenants may have special statutory rights to remain through the duration of their leases, and different rules and notice requirements may apply. *See*, Rights of Tenants During a Foreclosure below.

3-Day Notice

Coincidentally, there are three different three-day notices provided for by the Code of Civil Procedure, depending on the nature of the breach:

1. Three-day notice to pay or quit (CCP §1161.2): Landlords can use this notice when the tenant has failed to pay rent on time.

2. Three-day notice to perform covenants or quit (CCP §1161.3): Landlords can use this notice when the tenant has neglected or failed to perform other conditions or covenants and the problem can be fixed, thereby saving the lease from termination.

3. Three-day notice to quit (CCP §1161.4): Landlords can use this notice if the tenant (a) assigns or sublets the premises contrary to the terms of the lease, (b) commits waste upon (materially damages) the premises, (c) commits a nuisance on the property, or (d) uses the premises for an unlawful purpose.

How the Three Days Are Counted

A tenant has 3 full days to comply with a three-day notice, counting day 1, even a holiday, as the first day after notice is served. The next day, day 2, is any calendar day. Finally, if the next calendar day falls on a Saturday, Sunday, or holiday, the 3-day period does not expire until midnight of the following Monday or nonholiday. CCP §12, 12a; GOV §6806.

> **Example:** Suppose that tenant Joe is handed a 3-day "pay or quit" notice on a Thursday. Day 1 is Friday. Day 2 is Saturday. Because the next day is Sunday, it does not count as the third day. If Monday is not a holiday, Joe may hand the overdue rent to his landlord as late as 11:59 PM Monday to satisfy the notice demand and continue his tenancy.

Proper Service of Notices

Service of a 3-day notice: A 3-day notice can be served on a tenant in one of 3 ways: by personal service, by substituted service, or by posting and mailing.

- **Personal service**: A tenant may be served personally by handing the tenant the notice or, if the tenant refuses to take it, by simply leaving it with the tenant. CCP §1162(a)(1).

- **Substituted service**: If the tenant is absent from his or her place of residence, and from his or her usual place of business, by leaving a copy with some person of suitable age and discretion at either place, and sending a copy through the mail addressed to the tenant at his or her place of residence. CCP §1162(a)(2).

- **Posting and mailing**: If the tenant's residence and place of business cannot be ascertained, or a person of suitable age and discretion there cannot be found, then service can be made by affixing a copy in a conspicuous place on the property, and also delivering a copy to a person there residing, if such person can be found; and also sending a copy through the mail addressed to the tenant at the place where the property is situated. CCP §1162(a)(3).

For the purpose of serving notice, a person of "suitable age and discretion" normally would be an adult at the tenant's home or workplace, or a teenage member of the tenant's household.

30- or 60-Day Notice

To terminate a month-to-month tenancy (other than for non-payment of rent or other breach of the rental or lease agreement), a landlord may use a 30-day notice if the tenant has resided in the rental unit for less than a year. If the tenant has resided in the rental unit for a year or more, at least a 60-day notice is required. If no notice to terminate is given, a month-to-month tenancy (or any other periodic tenancy) automatically renews at the end of each period. CC §1946.

Note: If the rental unit is in a rent-control/eviction-control city, the landlord may only terminate a month-to-month tenancy for a limited number of reasons.

Service of a 30- or 60-day notice: A 30- or 60-day notice can be served on a tenant by any of the above methods used for a three-day notice (CCP §1162), or by sending a copy by certified or registered mail addressed to the tenant (CC §1946). Days are counted for a 30- or 60-day notice in the same manner as are days for a 3-day notice.

For a month-to-month tenancy, the 30-or 60-day notice may be served on any day of the month, and the rent will be due and payable to and including the date of termination.

> **Example:** If a landlord gives a tenant a 60-day notice on August 10, the tenant is supposed to vacate on October 10, unless October 10 is a Saturday, Sunday, or holiday, in which case the tenant is supposed to vacate on the next business day.

> **Example:** In a month-to-month tenancy, the tenant may give notice on the 15th of the month and move out on the 15th of the following month, owing rent only for the first 15 days of the following month.

90-Day Notice to Quit

For a tenant residing in government-subsidized housing, the landlord must give 90 day's notice and must have good reasons ("just cause") for terminating the tenancy. A 90-day notice to quit can be served in the same manner as a 30- or 60-day notice.

When Notice is not Required

- **Fixed-term leases**: At the expiration of a fixed-term lease, the lease automatically terminates, and the landlord who does not wish to extend the lease may file an unlawful detainer action (except in some rent-control/eviction-control cities) without giving notice if the tenant holds over. However, if the landlord accepts rent after the expiration of the lease, a month-to-month lease is created.

- **Tenant gives notice**: If a tenant gives notice that he or she intends to vacate on a certain date but then does not, the landlord may file an unlawful detainer action without giving notice.

- **The tenant is an employee of the landlord**: If the tenant is an employee of the landlord (such as a resident manager) and refuses to leave when ordered to do so, the landlord may file an unlawful detainer action without giving notice.

RIGHTS OF TENANTS DURING A FORECLOSURE

A tenant or subtenant in possession of a rental housing unit under a month-to-month lease or periodic tenancy at the time the property is sold in foreclosure must be given at least 90 days' written notice to quit before an unlawful detainer action may be filed. CCP §1161b(a).

Tenants or subtenants holding possession of a rental housing unit under a fixed-term residential lease entered into before transfer of title at the foreclosure sale have the right to remain in possession until the end of the lease term, and all rights and obligations under the lease will survive foreclosure, except that the tenancy may be terminated upon 90 days' written notice to quit if any of the following conditions apply:

(1) The purchaser or successor in interest will occupy the housing unit as a primary residence.

(2) The lessee is the mortgagor or the child, spouse, or parent of the mortgagor.

(3) The lease was not the result of an arms' length transaction.

(4) The lease requires the receipt of rent that is substantially less than fair market rent for the property, except when rent is reduced or subsidized due to a federal, state, or local subsidy or law. CCP §1161b(b).

Note, however, that rent-control/eviction-control cities may prohibit new owners from using foreclosure as a reason for evicting tenants.

TERMINATION OF MOBILE HOME PARK TENANCY

A *mobile home park* is an area of land where two or more mobile home sites are rented, or held out for rent, to accommodate mobile homes used for human habitation. In a mobile home park, the tenant typically owns the mobile home and rents the site on which the mobile home sits. Because of the high cost of mobile homes, of moving and installing mobile homes, and of landscaping and lot preparation, special laws that differ from typical landlord-tenant laws apply to mobile home park tenancy.

Owners or managers of mobile home parks may not terminate or refuse to renew a tenancy unless the tenant is given at least a 60-day notice (CC §798.55) and at least one of the following reasons apply (CC §798.56):

1. Failure to comply with local or state law within a reasonable time after being notified of noncompliance from the appropriate governmental agency.

2. Conduct that constitutes substantial annoyance to other tenants.

3. Conviction of prostitution or a felony controlled substance offense if the act resulting in conviction occurred within the mobile home park.

4. Failure to comply with a reasonable rule or regulation of the park that is part of the rental agreement.

5. Nonpayment of rent or other charges.

6. Condemnation of the park.

7. Change of use of the park.

Mobile homes are discussed more extensively in a subsequent chapter.

FILING AND SERVING AN UNLAWFUL DETAINER ACTION

If the tenant receives a notice to "pay or quit" or to "perform covenants or quit" and neither pays nor performs prior to the expiration of the notice, or if the tenant receives a notice to quit and does not vacate by the end of the notice period, the landlord may begin eviction proceedings by filing an unlawful detainer complaint in Superior Court.

As with a 3-day notice, service of the complaint on the tenant may be performed by personal service, substituted service, or posting and mailing.

THE "SUMMARY" NATURE OF AN UNLAWFUL DETAINER ACTION

An unlawful detainer action is a "summary" proceeding that differs from other court actions in several ways, primarily in that an unlawful detainer court action typically moves much more quickly. Once the action is filed, the landlord serves the tenant with the complaint; and thereafter, the tenant has only 5 days to respond, including Saturdays and Sundays but excluding all other judicial holidays. If the last day for filing the response falls on a Saturday or Sunday, the response period is extended to the next court day. If the tenant fails to respond within the 5 days, a default judgment is obtained. CCP §1167.

If the tenant files a response, the unlawful detainer action will be given docket preference over most other civil actions. CCP §1179a. In fact, the court will normally hear and decide the matter within 20 days after either the landlord or tenant requests that a time for trial be set. CCP §1170.5(a).

Another aspect of this summary proceeding that tends to move it along expeditiously is that the tenant may not assert a cross-complaint or file a counterclaim, though an affirmative defense (such as retaliatory eviction (see the discussion below) or breach of the warranty of habitability) may be raised in residential leases to defeat the landlord's unlawful detainer action. A tenant who has a complaint against the landlord that is extrinsic to the issue of possession of the rental unit may bring such action in a separate lawsuit through a normal court proceeding.

ILLEGAL RETALIATORY EVICTION

A typical affirmative defense that a tenant might state in a written answer to an unlawful detainer complaint is that the landlord filed the eviction action in retaliation for the tenant's having exercised one of the tenant's rights, such as complaining to a governmental agency about the habitability of the premises. This defense, and others that a tenant might have, must be asserted in writing in the tenant's answer and filed with the Clerk of Court by the end of the fifth day after notice or the defense will be waived.

If a landlord files an unlawful detainer action within 180 days of certain actions taken by a tenant, the landlord would be deemed guilty of *retaliatory eviction*. Such actions by a tenant include:

- complaining to the landlord or to a governmental agency regarding a condition of habitability

- filing a lawsuit or beginning an arbitration proceeding involving an issue of habitability

- using the "repair and deduct" remedy

- opposing practices of, or informing law enforcement officials about, a landlord's discriminatory practices

- exercising any other of the tenant's rights.

Any landlord who is found guilty of retaliatory eviction will be liable to the tenant in a civil action for the following (CC §1942.5(f)):

- actual damages sustained by the lessee.

- punitive damages in an amount of not less than $100 nor more than $2,000 for each retaliatory act where the landlord has been guilty of fraud, oppression, or malice with respect to the retaliatory act.

- reasonable attorney fees and court costs

In addition to using retaliatory eviction as a defense to an unlawful detainer action, a tenant who feels that a landlord has begun an unlawful detainer action as a means of retaliation should also consider contacting the California Department of Consumer Affairs or an attorney.

EVICTION BY A SHERIFF

If in an unlawful detainer action the court finds for the landlord, the court will issue a *writ of possession*, which the landlord may then deliver to the sheriff. CCP §715.010. The sheriff will serve the tenant with a copy of the writ of possession, which instructs the tenant to vacate the premises within 5 days, and that if the tenant remains in the premises thereafter, the sheriff will physically remove the tenant. CCP §715.020. If the tenant's personal belongings remain on the premises, the sheriff may either remove them or have them stored by the landlord.

If the landlord stores the property, the landlord must give written notice to the tenant and to any other person the landlord reasonably believes to be the owner of the property, describing the property and stating that reasonable storage costs may be charged before the property is returned. The date specified in the notice must be a date not less than 15 days after the notice is personally delivered or, if mailed, not less than 18 days after the notice is deposited in the mail. CC §1983. The notice must also contain one of the following statements:

(1) "If you fail to reclaim the property, it will be sold at a public sale after notice of the sale has been given by publication. You have the right to bid on the property at this sale. After the property is sold and the cost of storage, advertising, and sale is deducted, the remaining money will be paid over to the

county. You may claim the remaining money at any time within one year after the county receives the money."

(2) "Because this property is believed to be worth less than $700, it may be kept, sold, or destroyed without further notice if you fail to reclaim it within the time indicated above." CC §1984.

If neither the tenant nor a person reasonably believed by the landlord to be the owner of the property reclaims the property by paying a reasonable cost of storage, the property will be sold at public sale by competitive bidding. However, if the landlord reasonably believes that the total resale value of the property not reclaimed is less than $700, the landlord may retain the property for his or her own use or dispose of it in any manner. After deduction of the costs of storage, advertising, and sale, any balance of the proceeds of the sale that is not claimed by the former tenant or an owner other than such tenant will be paid into the treasury of the county in which the sale took place not later than 30 days after the date of sale. The former tenant or other owner may claim the balance within one year from the date of payment to the county by making application to the county treasurer or other official designated by the county.CC §1988.

ABANDONMENT

Abandonment by a tenant occurs whenever the tenant moves out of the premises before a fixed term expires or moves out without giving proper notice. A tenant who abandons leased property without good cause is liable (1) for rent unpaid at the time of termination and (2) for unpaid rent that would have been earned after termination that could not have been reasonably avoided by the landlord's legal duty to mitigate damages by re-renting the premises as soon as possible.

Tenants who abandon leased premises without leaving notice of where to contact them present landlords with the problem of establishing the fact of abandonment (as opposed to temporary absence). In such a case, the landlord may statutorily prove abandonment if:

1. the tenant is at least 14 days delinquent on rent payments;

2. the landlord reasonably believes that the tenant abandoned the premises;

3. the landlord personally delivers or mails to the tenant's last known address a Notice of Belief of Abandonment substantiality in the form specified in CC §1951.3(d); and

4. the tenant does not then pay any portion of the rent due or respond in writing of his or her intent not to abandon the premises.

If all four of the above conditions obtain, then after 15 days after the Notice of Belief of Abandonment is served personally or, if mailed, 18 days after the notice is mailed, there is legal abandonment, and the landlord can regain possession of the premises. This procedure for proving abandonment and regaining possession of the property is faster and less expensive than bringing an unlawful detainer action.

If the landlord finds that the tenant abandoned the premises leaving personal property behind, the landlord must handle and a dispose of such personal property in the same manner as was discussed in the section Eviction by a Sheriff above.

ILLEGAL SELF-HELP EVICTIONS

It is illegal for a landlord to evict a tenant by any means other than by way of the unlawful detainer process described above. Even if the tenant is behind on rent, the landlord may not:

- physically remove the tenant (which may result in a civil action of forcible detainer (CC §1160), and criminal charges of assault, battery, and kidnapping);

- change the locks or otherwise prevent the tenant from occupying the premises;

- remove any of the tenant's personal property;

- cut off the utilities, even if the landlord is paying for the utilities; or

- remove any outside doors or windows.

Pursuant to CC §798.3(c), a landlord guilty of *self-help eviction* will be liable to the tenant in a civil action for all of the following:

- actual damages;

- an amount not to exceed $100 for each day or part thereof that the landlord remains in violation of laws against self-help eviction (such as by keeping the tenant from occupying the premises);

- at least $250 for each separate act of self-help eviction;

- appropriate injunctive relief to prevent continuing or further acts of self-help eviction; and

- reasonable attorney fees.

LIABILITY OF LANDLORD OR TENANT FOR INJURIES RESULTING FROM CONDITION OF PREMISES

As a general rule (applicable to both residential and commercial leases), liability for injuries to a tenant or to a third party that result from a condition of the premises rests with the one who is in control of the premises; i.e., the tenant for parts of the premises under the tenant's control, the landlord for parts (if any) of the premises under the landlord's control or duty to maintain (for example, hallways, stairs, and other common areas).

There are, however, exceptions to the above general rule. A residential landlord can be found liable for negligence for injuries that result from hazards or defects that existed prior to leasing the premises if such conditions could have been discovered by reasonable inspection of the premises. Additionally, if a defect in the premises occurs after the commencement of a lease, the residential landlord has a duty to repair the defect after receiving notice of the defect from the tenant. Failure to make such repairs would subject the landlord to liability for injuries resulting from such uncorrected defects. Furthermore, if the landlord repairs the defects but does so in a negligent manner, the landlord would be liable for injuries resulting from such negligence.

PROPERTY MANAGEMENT

Property managers represent owners in advertising rental properties, screening tenants, negotiating lease agreements, hiring persons to maintain and repair properties, and hiring on-site resident managers. Though neither managers of hotels, motels, auto and trailer parks, nor resident managers of apartment buildings or their employees need a real estate license, all nonresident property managers who are not owners of the properties managed must have a real estate broker license. B&PC §10131.01.

Property management is a specialty for real estate brokers who, in addition to having knowledge of agency, contracts, leases, etc., must also acquire knowledge in such matters as business administration, marketing, purchasing, extensions of credit, and repairs and maintenance. The Institute of Real Estate Management (IREM), which is associated with the National Association of REALTORS®, and the National Association of Residential Property Managers (NARPM) are professional associations dedicated to fostering professionalism and ethical standards among their members. IREM issues the designation Accredited Residential Manager (ARM) for residential managers and Certified Property Manager (CMP) to certify individuals meeting a high degree of educational and experience requirements. NARPM also offers firms and individuals designations, including Master Property Manager (MPM).

Although not official designations, the following are three generally recognized designations held by persons who manage properties:

1. **Individual Property Manager**. An individual property manager is a real estate broker who manages properties for one or more property owners. An individual property manager could be a member of a property management firm, own his or her own firm, or be one among many property management specialists in a large real estate organization.

2. **Individual Building Manager**. An individual building manager may be employed directly by the owner or by a property manager, and usually manages a single large property.

3. **Resident Manager**. A resident manager lives on the premises and may be employed by the owner or by a property manager. Under California law (California Code of Regulations, Article 5, Section 42), every apartment building in which there are 16 or more apartments must have a resident manager who must be a "responsible" person who has "charge" of the apartment building, but who need not have a real estate license. Mobile home parks in which there are 50 or more units must have a resident manager.

Key Terms for Chapter 13

advance fee — a fee paid in advance of any services rendered, such as money advanced by a tenant to the landlord to pay future rent.

assignment — a transfer of a tenant's entire interest in the tenant's leased premises.

assumption — an adoption of an obligation that primarily rests upon another person.

Carbon Monoxide Poisoning Prevention Act — a California law that requires the installation of carbon monoxide alarms in most residential units.

chattel real — personal property that contains some interest in real property, the most common example being a lease.

constructive eviction — a breach by the landlord of the covenant of habitability or quiet enjoyment.

Costa-Hawkins Rental Housing Act — a state law that places restrictions on local rent control laws.

escalator clause — a provision in a lease that provides for periodic increases in rent, often based on the Consumer Price Index.

fixed lease — a gross lease

graduated lease — a lease that is similar to a gross lease except that it provides for periodic increases in rent, often based on the Consumer Price Index.

gross lease — a lease under which the tenant pays a fixed rental amount, and the landlord pays all of the operating expenses for the premises.

ground lease — a lease under which a tenant leases land and agrees to construct a building or to make other significant improvements on the land.

individual building manager — a property manager who usually manages just a single large property.

individual property manager — a real estate broker who manages properties for one or more property owners.

lease extension — a continuation of tenancy under the original lease.

lease renewal — a continuation of tenancy under a new lease.

Megan's Law — a law that provides for the registration of sex offenders and for the making available to the public information regarding the location of these offenders.

mobile home park — an area of land where two or more mobile home sites are rented, or held out for rent, to accommodate mobile homes used for human habitation.

net lease — a lease under which the tenant pays a fixed rental amount plus some of the landlord's operating expenses.

novation — a substitution of a new obligation or contract for an old one, or the substitution of one party to a contract by another, relieving the original party of liability under the contract.

percentage lease — a lease, often used in shopping centers, under which the tenant typically pays a base rent amount plus a percentage of the gross receipts of the tenant's business.

privity of contract — a legal doctrine that states that a legally enforceable relationship exists between the persons who are parties to a contract.

privity of estate — a legal doctrine that states that a legally enforceable relationship exists between the parties who hold interests in the same real property.

resident manager — an individual who resides on the premises, is a "responsible" person, and has "charge" of the apartment building.

retaliatory eviction — an eviction action brought to retaliate against a tenant for making a habitability complaint or for asserting other of the tenant's legal rights.

sandwich lease — a leasehold interest that lies between a primary lease and a sublease.

self-help eviction — a landlord's denial of possession of leased premises to a tenant without complying with the legal process of eviction.

step-up lease — a graduated lease

sublease — a transfer of a tenant's right to a portion of the leased premises or to the entire premises for less than the entire remaining lease term.

triple net lease — a lease under which the tenant pays a fixed rent plus the landlord's property taxes, hazard insurance, and all maintenance costs.

unlawful detainer — a legal action to regain possession of real property.

warranty of habitability — mandated by both statutes and by common law, an implied warranty in any residential lease that the premises are suitable for human habitation.

writ of possession — a court order that authorizes the sheriff or other eviction authority to remove a tenant and the tenant's possessions from leased premises.

Quiz for Chapter 13

1. A landlord's denial of possession of leased premises to a tenant without complying with the legal process of eviction is called
    a. unlawful detainer
    b. rescission
    c. self-help eviction
    d. restitution

2. If a tenant is behind on rent, the landlord may
    a. change the locks
    b. cut the utilities
    c. physically remove the tenant
    d. none of the above

3. The substitution of a new obligation or contract or an old one, or the substitution of one party to a contract by another, relieving the original party of liability under the contract, is
    a. an assignment
    b. a novation
    c. a sandwich lease
    d. a lease renewal

4. A provision in a lease that provides for periodic increases in rent, often based on the Consumer Price Index, is
    a. an escalator clause
    b. a novation clause
    c. an assumption clause
    d. a chattel clause

5. A lease under which the tenant pays a fixed rent plus the landlord's property taxes, hazard insurance, and all maintenance costs is a
    a. graduated lease
    b. triple-net lease
    c. gross lease
    d. ground lease

6. A lease creates between landlord and tenant
    a. an estate for years
    b. privity of estate
    c. both a and b
    d. neither a nor b

7. The landlord may enter a leased residential unit

   a. at any time in case of an emergency
   b. during normal business hours after giving at least a 24-hour written notice to the tenant
   c. both a and b
   d. neither a nor b

8. A lease that provides that the tenant will pay as part of the rent a certain portion of the tenant's gross sales most likely is a
   a. graduated lease
   b. percentage lease
   c. gross lease
   d. net lease

9. John may legally be a property manager who manages several different apartment buildings
   a. if he is licensed as either a real estate salesperson or as a broker
   b. if he is not licensed, but is a resident manager of one of the apartment buildings
   c. if he is not licensed, but none of the apartment buildings have more than 10 residential units
   d. none of the above

10. A residential tenant may assign his or her interest in the premises
   a. only if the lease so provides
   b. only if the tenant gives the landlord at least a 60-day notice of the assignment
   c. only if the assignment is to a financially responsible person
   d. none of the above

11. Jane's lease provides that she pay her landlord a fixed amount of rent each month and that the landlord pay all operating expenses for the premises. Jane has a
   a. net lease
   b. triple net lease
   c. graduated lease
   d. none of the above

12. A lease can be continued through
   a. renewal
   b. extension
   c. either a or b
   d. neither a nor b

13. An apartment building must have a resident manager if it has
   a. 10 or more residential units
   b. 12 or more residential units
   c. 14 or more residential units
   d. none of the above

14. In all residential leases with terms of one month or less, if the rent increase is greater than 10% of the rental amount charged to the tenant at

any time during the 12 months prior to the effective date of the increase, the notice of increase must be given at least how many days prior to the effective date of the increase?

a. 60
b. 45
c. 30
d. 15

15. The state law that places restrictions on local rent control ordinances is known as the
a. California Rent Quality Act
b. Fair Rent Protection Act
c. Mello-Roos Community Facilities Act
d. none of the above

16. The landlord need not pay the tenant interest on a security fee unless
a. the lease provides otherwise
b. there is a local ordinance that requires the landlord to do so
c. either a or b
d. neither a nor b

17. A landlord may require a tenant to pay a charge for late payment of rent if the amount specified in the lease
a. does not exceed $10
b. does not exceed $25
c. is reasonably related to the administrative costs and loss of interest caused by the late payment
d. none of the above

18. A California renter who makes rent payments to a non-resident person
a. must withhold 7% of the rent and send it to the Franchise Tax Board
b. must withhold 10% of the rent and send it to the Franchise Tax Board
c. must withhold 3 1/3% of the rent and send it to the Franchise Tax Board
d. none of the above

19. For a residential building, California law requires that the landlord
a. provide hot and cold running water
b. install and maintain operable window security or locking devices for all windows that are designed to be opened
c. both a and b
d. neither a nor b

20. A leasehold estate is a
a. freehold estate
b. chattel real
c. neither a nor b
d. both a and b

21. The Carbon Monoxide Poisoning Prevention Act requires that a carbon monoxide device be installed

a. in every single-family residential unit by July 1, 2011
b. in every other residential unit by January 1, 2013
c. neither a nor b
d. both a and b

22. The security deposit (not including the first month's rent) may not exceed
a. 3 month's rent for an unfurnished residential property
b. 4 month's rent for a furnished residential property
c. neither a nor b
d. both a and b

23. If the landlord of a residential property fails to provide habitable premises and the tenant chooses to" repair and deduct," how many times during any 12 month period may the tenant spend up to one month's rent and deduct the amount spent from rent due?
a. 1
b. 2
c. 3
d. 4

24. A landlord's interest in leased property is a
a. remainder interest
b. reversionary interest
c. possessory interest
d. detainer interest

25. A lease signed by the landlord but not by the tenant
a. can never be valid and enforceable against the tenant
b. can always be enforceable against both the landlord and the tenant
c. neither a nor b
d. both a and b

26. In an assignment
a. the assignor remains primarily liable under the lease
b. the assignee is secondarily liable under the lease
c. neither a nor b
d. both a and b

27. Joe wishes to assign his lease to Sally. Sally is college educated, has no criminal record, but has a poor credit report. Joe's lease states that he may assign his lease only with the landlord's consent.
a. The landlord owns the property so he can withhold his consent for any reason other than for a reason based upon prohibited discrimination
b. Sally's poor credit report may provide the landlord with a sufficient reason to withhold his consent
c. California law does not permit restrictions on the assignment of leases
d. none of the above

28. If a lease for a residential unit does not establish a term, the lease term will be presumed to be
    a. one month
    b. one week
    c. the period of time adopted for rent payment
    d. none of the above

29. Bob leases a commercial property that provides for his paying a fixed monthly rent and all of the property taxes, hazard insurance, and maintenance costs related to the property. Bob has a
    a. gross lease
    b. graduated lease
    c. ground lease
    d. none of the above

30. A tenant who subleases to another is said to have a
    a. lease extension
    b. fixed lease
    c. sandwich lease
    d. none of the above

31. Disclosures that a landlord must give to a new tenant include
    a. the Megan's Law Database Disclosure
    b. whether the premises is in a high-crime area
    c. both a and b
    d. neither a nor b

32. A periodic tenancy may be terminated by either party giving the other party 30 day's notice in writing, unless the tenant has lived on the premises for a year or more, in which case the landlord must give at least how many day's notice?
    a. 45
    b. 60
    c. 90
    d. none of the above

33. Robert is 25 years of age, single, and has rented space for his mobile home in a mobile home park for just 3 months. Under the terms of the lease, rent is due on the first of each month. Robert is now 45 days late in paying rent to the park. If the park wants to terminate Bob's lease, how many day's notice must be given to Bob?
    a. 60
    b. 45
    c. 7
    d. 3

34. Before the end of the lease term, the landlord of a residential property must give the tenant notice of the tenant's right to request an initial inspection
    a. only if the lease provides for such notice

b. only if the landlord believes that some deduction will be made from the tenant's security deposit

c. in all cases

d. none of the above

35. Sally rents under a month-to-month lease in which rent is due in advance on the first day of each month. On April 10, she gives the landlord a 30-day notice of termination, and she vacates the premises on May 10. Sally owes the landlord for

a. 10 days in May

b. 15 days in May

c. the entire month of May

d. none of the above

Answers for Chapter 13 Quiz

1. c. Self-help eviction is a landlord's denial of possession of leased premises to a tenant without complying with the legal process of eviction.

2. d. Even if a tenant stops paying rent, a landlord may not do any of the actions listed in answers a-c, which would be considered self-help eviction.

3. b. A novation is the substitution of a new obligation or contract for an old one, or the substitution of one party to a contract by another, relieving the original party of liability.

4. a. An escalator clause is a provision in a lease that provides for periodic increases in rent, often based on the Consumer Price Index.

5. b. A triple-net lease is a lease under which the tenant pays a fixed rent plus the landlord's property taxes, hazard insurance, and all maintenance costs.

6. b. A lease creates both privity of estate and privity of contract between a landlord and a tenant.

7. a. In order to enter, the landlord must have an acceptable reason, as defined by statute. This requirement is nonwaivable by the tenant. Merely giving a 24-hour written notice is not enough.

8. b. A percentage lease is a lease, often used in shopping centers, under which the tenant typically pays a base rent amount plus a percentage of the gross receipts of the tenant's business.

9. d. John must be licensed as a real estate broker.

10. d. Unless the lease expressly prohibits the tenant from transferring its interest in the premises, the tenant may assign or sublease its interest to any third party.

11. d. Jane has a gross lease.

12. c. A lease can be continued either through lease renewal or lease extension.

13. d. An apartment building with 16 or more residential units must have a resident manager.

14. a. In all residential leases with terms of one month or less, if the rent increase is greater than 10% of the rental amount charged to the tenant at any time during the 12 months prior to the effective date of the increase, the notice of increase must be given at least 60 days prior to the effective date of the increase.

15. d. The Costa-Hawkins Rental Housing Act places restrictions on local rent control ordinances.

16.c. Unless the lease provides for the payment of interest on a security fee or there is a local ordinance that requires the landlord to pay interest on a security fee, the landlord need not pay interest on a security fee.

17.c. A late charge is enforceable if the amount specified in the lease is reasonably related to the anticipated administrative costs and loss of interest caused by the late payment.

18.d. Under California law, the renter who makes rent payments to a non-resident person must withhold 7% of the amount that exceeds $1,500 in a calendar year and send it to the Franchise Tax Board.

19.c. California law requires that the landlord of residential property provide numerous amenities, including providing hot and cold running water and installing and maintaining operable window security or locking devices on all windows that are designed to be opened.

20.b. A leasehold estate is a less-than-freehold estate and is a chattel real.

21.c. The Carbon Monoxide Poisoning Prevention Act requires a carbon monoxide device be installed in all residential units with an attached garage or a fossil fuel source.

22.c. A security deposit (not including the first month's rent) may not exceed two month's rent for an unfurnished residential property or three month's rent for a furnished residential property.

23.b. If the landlord of a residential property fails to provide habitable premises, the tenant may give the landlord notice to repair the problem. If after receiving notice, the landlord fails within a reasonable time to remedy the problem, the tenant may either "repair and deduct" by spending up to one month's rent in repairs and deducting the amount spent from the rent due (this remedy may be used only twice in any 12-month period) or vacate the premises.

24.b. A landlord holds title to, and has a reversionary interest in, the property.

25.c. A lease signed by the landlord but not by the tenant nevertheless becomes valid and enforceable against both parties if the tenant accepts delivery of the lease and moves in or begins paying rent.

26.c. In an assignment, the assignor remains secondarily liable under the lease; the assignee becomes primarily liable.

27.b. The landlord must allow the assignment unless the assignee is not a reasonable substitute tenant. Sally's poor credit rating may provide the landlord with a sufficient reason to withhold his consent.

28.c. If a lease for a residential unit does not establish a term, the lease term will be presumed to be the period of time adopted in the lease for rent payment.

29.d. Bob has a triple net lease.

30.c. A tenant who subleases to another is said to have a sandwich lease.

31.a. The Megan's Law disclosure is required; whether the neighborhood is a high-crime area is not.

32.b. A periodic tenancy may be terminated by either party by giving the other party proper advance notice in writing equal to the lesser of the term of the tenancy or 30 days, unless the tenant has lived in the premises for a year or more, in which case the landlord must give at least a 60-day notice.

33.a. Nonpayment of rent is a sufficient reason to terminate a mobile home park tenant's lease. The notice to terminate must be given at least 60 days in advance of termination.

34.c. The requirement to give written notice to the tenant of the tenant's right to an initial inspection is a statutory requirement.

35.a. In a month-to-month tenancy, the tenant's notice of termination may correspond to a date different from the date rent is due.

Chapter

Public Limitations on Use of Real Estate

Limitations on the use of real estate fall into two main categories: private restrictions and public restrictions. Private restrictions, which are restrictions voluntarily imposed on real estate by landowners or by private organizations such as homeowners associations, include covenants and conditions and were discussed in Chapter 1. Public restrictions, the subject of this chapter, grow out of the authority of federal, state, and local governments to use police power to enact laws to protect the health, safety, and welfare of the public. To be validly used (i.e., constitutional), police power in the real estate context must:

1. be reasonably related to protecting the health, safety, or general welfare of the public;
2. apply similarly to all property similarly situated; and
3. not reduce the value of the real estate to such an extent as to amount to confiscation (in which case eminent domain must be used and compensation paid to the property owner).

GENERAL PLANS

In the early years of the Industrial Revolution, most people had to live within walking distance of their places of work, which resulted in overcrowding and a deterioration of living conditions in city centers. With the coming first of electric trolleys and then of automobiles, a mass movement to the cleaner and less congested suburbs ensued, which brought on its own problems of land speculation and unregulated urban sprawl. As these latter problems became more severe, civic leaders came to see the need for comprehensive, area-wide plans that expressed and enforced community goals of preserving and enhancing public health, safety, and welfare.

California state law mandates that the legislative body of every city and county must adopt a "comprehensive, long-term *general plan* for the physical development of the county or city, and of any land outside its boundaries which in the planning agency's judgment bears relation to its planning." Government Code §65300. These general plans are required to address transportation, housing, conservation, open spaces, noise, and safety. The general plan for each city and county is proposed by a *planning commission* (also referred to as a planning agency), whose members are appointed by the city council or county board of supervisors. The planning commission makes recommendations to the relevant legislative body (city council or board of supervisors), which renders the final decision on the plan.

Preparation of a General Plan

Typically, general plans are prepared as follows:

1. data on the local economy, characteristics of the community, environmental conditions, and the capacity of public facilities and services are collected and analyzed;
2. a formulation of community goals and development policies based on the analysis of the above data is drafted;
3. diagrams that reflect and support the formulated development policies are prepared;
4. measures to implement the proposed general plan are prepared; and
5. once a proposed general plan is completed, the planning commission holds at least one public hearing after which the proposed plan is forwarded to the relevant local legislative body, which holds at least one additional public hearing before adopting, amending, or rejecting the proposed plan.

After a general plan is adopted, the local government implements the plan by use of police power, eminent domain, taxation, and fiscal control.

ZONING

Zoning laws split the jurisdiction into distinct land-use zones — residential, commercial, industrial, and rural being the basic zone-use categories. These main categories are often further refined into subcategories. For example, the residential category can be split into zones for single-family homes (often referred to as R-1 zones), duplexes (R-2 zones), and condominiums and apartment buildings (R-3 zones). Zoning laws also regulate many aspects of development, such as height, size, setback and side-yard requirements to control population density and promote the aesthetic appeal of the community. *Inclusionary zoning* refers to the highly controversial city and county zoning ordinances that require builders to set aside a given portion of new construction for people of low to moderate incomes. A 2009 California Court of Appeal case invalidated the Los Angeles inclusionary zoning ordinance for rental housing because it conflicted with the Costa-Hawkins Rental Housing Act's prohibition on local ordinances that restrict the right of landlord's to set the initial rental rate for new housing units.

Zoning Exceptions and Amendments

There are four ways in which property owners may request relief from zoning ordinances:

Nonconforming use — refers to an exception for areas that are zoned for the first time or that are rezoned and where established property uses that previously were permitted to not conform to the new zoning requirements. As a general rule, such existing properties are "grandfathered in," allowing them to continue the old use but not to extend the old use to additional properties or to continue the old use after rebuilding or abandonment.

Conditional use — refers to an exception for special uses such as churches, schools, and hospitals that wish to locate to areas zoned exclusively for residential use. In these cases, the zoning authority may issue a *conditional use permit* to a limited number of such community service uses provided that they meet certain requirements for parking and security to minimize any negative impact on the neighborhood.

Variance — refers to an exception that may be granted in cases where damage to the value of a property from the strict enforcement of zoning ordinances would far outweigh any benefit to be derived from enforcement. As a general rule, variances are given only for rather minor departures from zoning requirements, relating to such things as setbacks, building height, and parking.

Rezoning amendment — refers to an amendment to a zoning ordinance that property owners may request if they feel that their area has been improperly zoned. Rezoning for a particular property that would not apply to neighboring properties is called *spot zoning* and is a violation of the requirement that police power apply similarly to all property similarly situated, which in turn arises from the constitutional guarantee of equal protection under the law.

BUILDING CODES

Building codes are federal, state, and local laws that govern all aspects of building construction, such as design, materials, electrical wiring, and plumbing. FHA, VA, and Cal-Vet requirements regulate construction of housing that participate in their programs. Additionally, the **State Housing Law** provides for minimum construction and occupancy requirements. The California **Factory Built Housing Law** provides for regulations of factory built housing. The California **Constructors' State License Law** provides that, with the exception of public entities, public utilities, gas operations, certain agricultural construction, minor work not exceeding $500, and an owner's work on his or her own property (unless the property is offered for sale within one year of the work's completion), every contractor must be licensed by the **Contractors' State License Board**.

REDEVELOPMENT

The California **Community Redevelopment Law** (Health and Safety Code §§33000, et seq.) provides local governments with the authority to correct blighted conditions in areas within their jurisdictions. This law is intended to expand the availability of low to moderate income housing, create opportunities for the jobless, and, in general, to promote the improvement and safety of neighborhoods. Local community redevelopment agencies have the authority to replace, or cause to be replaced, low and moderate income housing that is lost due to destruction, removal, rehabilitation, or development of a residential unit.

ENVIRONMENTAL CONTROLS

The environmental laws of federal, state, and local governments can have a significant impact on how property owners may use their properties.

The preamble to the **National Environmental Policy Act** (**NEPA**) states:

> *The purposes of this Act are: To declare a national policy which will encourage productive and enjoyable harmony between man and his environment; to promote efforts which will prevent or eliminate damage to the environment and biosphere and stimulate the health and welfare of man; to enrich the understanding of the ecological systems and natural resources important to the Nation; and to establish a Council on Environmental Quality.*

The NEPA requires that federal agencies prepare an **Environmental Impact Statement** (**EIS**) for any development project that a federal agency could prohibit or regulate, and any development project for which any portion is federally financed.

The **California Environmental Quality Act** (**CEQA**) requires state and local agencies to consider and respond to the environmental effects of private and public development projects. One of the first steps in analyzing a project is the preparation of an *initial study* that addresses the project's potential for significant adverse effects on the environment. If the public agency determines that the project will not have a significant adverse impact, the agency issues a *negative declaration* prior to making a final decision on the project. However, if the project is determined to have a possible negative environmental impact, the agency must prepare a draft **environmental impact report** (**EIR**) to be circulated and commented on. In response to a final EIR, the responsible agencies must attempt to mitigate any significant negative environmental impact by incorporating feasible changes into the project.

The **California Coastal Zone Conservation Act** is intended to promote the preservation and protection of California's diverse coastal zone. All land development within the designated coastal zone must obtain either a permit or exemption from the provisions of this act.

The federal **Endangered Species Act** states as its purpose:

> *"to provide a means whereby the ecosystems upon which endangered species and threatened species depend may be conserved, to provide a program for the conservation of such endangered species and threatened species..."*

This act can result in burdensome restrictions being placed on property on which an endangered owl, minnow, plant, or other living thing is found.

SUBDIVISION LAWS

State and local governments also control land use by regulating how improved or unimproved land is divided for the purpose of sale, lease, or financing. In California, there are two basic subdivision laws:

- **Subdivision Map Act** (Government Code §§66410, et seq.), which is administered by local officials and sets forth the conditions and procedures for obtaining a subdivision map; and
- **Subdivided Lands Law** (B&PC §§11000-11200), which is a consumer protection law administered by the Real Estate Commissioner to protect purchasers from fraud, misrepresentation, or deceit in the *initial* sale of subdivided property.

TYPES OF SUBDIVISIONS

There are several types of subdivisions in California:

<u>Standard</u>. A **standard subdivision** is a subdivision with no common areas of ownership or use among the owners of the subdivision parcels. The prime example of a standard subdivision is a typical housing development in which each parcel is owned separately and there are no common areas.

Common Interest. A *common interest development* (*CID*) is a subdivision in which purchasers own or lease a separate lot, unit, or interest, and have an undivided interest or membership in a portion of the common area of the subdivision. There are four types of common interest developments (CC §1351):

- *Condominiums*. A condominium consists of a residential unit owned in severalty, the boundaries of which are usually walls, floors, and ceilings, and an undivided interest in portions of the real property, such as halls, elevators, and recreational facilities. Condominiums have homeowners' associations that are responsible for levying assessments and providing for management, maintenance, and control of the common areas.
- *Stock cooperatives*. A stock cooperative is a corporation formed or availed of primarily for the purpose of holding title to improved real property either in fee simple or for a term of years. In a stock cooperative, all or substantially all of the shareholders of the corporation receive a right of exclusive occupancy in a portion of the real property, title to which is held by the corporation. Most stock cooperatives are of the apartment house type that include community recreational facilities and are governed by a homeowners' association.
- *Community apartment projects*. A community apartment project is a development in which an undivided interest in the land is coupled with the right of exclusive occupancy of an apartment located thereon. The owners elect a governing board that manages and maintains the project.
- *Planned developments*. A planned development (PD) is a development (other than a condominium, community apartment project, or stock cooperative) consisting of lots or parcels owned separately and areas owned in common and reserved for the use of some or all the owners of the separate interests. Generally, as with condominiums, a PD has an owner's association that is responsible for levying assessments and providing for management, maintenance, and control of the common areas. Townhouses are typical structures in a PD.

Undivided Interest. In an *undivided interest subdivision*, owners own a partial or fractional interest in an entire parcel of land. The land in an undivided interest subdivision is not divided; its ownership is divided. An example of an undivided interest subdivision is a recreational vehicle development.

Time-Share Interests. The CalBRE has jurisdiction over two basic types of time-share interests:

- *time-share estate*, which refers to an estate in real property coupled with the right of occupancy for certain periods of time (such as one month per year). Time-share estate interests are typically transferred by a grant deed.

- ***time-share use***, which refers to a purchase of a right to occupancy for certain periods time, not coupled to an estate in real property. Time-share use is typically transferred by license or membership agreement, not by grant deed.

The California ***Vacation Ownership and Time-Share Act of 2004*** (B&PC §11210 et seq.) is a consumer protection law that regulates disclosures and representations made by time-share salespersons. This Act specifically requires that in space immediately above the signature of the purchaser of a time-share interest a notice of cancellation be printed, stating that the purchaser has 7 days to cancel after receipt of the public report (see discussion of public reports in the section on Subdivided Lands Law below) or after the date of signing the purchase agreement, whichever is later.

SUBDIVISION MAP ACT

The general purpose of the Subdivision Map Act is to ensure that any proposed subdivision is in compliance with the local general plan and that adequate services, such as streets, water supply, sewage disposal, telephone, gas, and electricity, are provided for the subdivision. For the purposes of this act, a subdivision is any division of contiguous land into 2 or more lots, units, or parcels for the purpose of sale, lease, or financing, but its most significant provisions are for subdivisions that contain 5 or more lots, units, or parcels.

With certain exceptions, the Subdivision Map Act requires tentative and final maps for subdivisions that create 5 or more parcels, 5 or more condominiums, a community apartment project containing 5 or more interests, or the conversion of a dwelling into a stock cooperative of 5 or more dwelling units. The ***tentative map***, which is to be filed with the local planning commission, must include a legal description of the property; the location and description of all adjoining highways, streets, and waterways; the location and description of easements for roads, drainage, sewers, and other public utilities; proposed public areas; and proposed provisions for floods and other natural hazards.

The planning commission sends copies of the tentative map to other government agencies, such as health, transportation, and parks departments, and to school districts and utilities companies for their comments and recommendations. Once all of the comments and recommendations have been received, the planning commission can approve or reject the tentative map, or give approval conditioned upon changes to the development plan.

After the planning commission approves a tentative map, the subdivider must prepare a ***final map***. Prior to approval of the final map, the subdivider must improve or agree to improve portions of the land to be used for streets, highways, and easements, and must secure with bond or cash deposit the funds to make these improvements. No contract for the sale or lease of a subdivided property is valid until a final map is approved and recorded.

SUBDIVIDED LANDS LAW

The Subdivided Lands Law is intended to protect purchasers from fraud, misrepresentation, and deceit (1) by making it illegal to commence sales until the Real Estate Commissioner has determined that the offering meets certain standards and has issued a *final public report*, and (2) by disclosing in the public report terms of the offering and pertinent facts about the property. The Subdivided Lands Law defines a subdivision as any division of land into 5 or more lots, units, or parcels for the purpose of sale, lease, or financing, whether now or in the future. This law does not require that the land to be subdivided is contiguous. This law also does not apply to land or lands sold by lots or parcels of not less than 160 acres, unless the land or lands are divided or proposed to be divided for the purpose of sale for oil and gas purposes.

The final public report will not be issued unless the proposed subdivision:

- is suitable for the use proposed by the subdivider; and
- will give the purchaser what he or she bargains for.

To help ensure that the purchaser will receive what he or she bargains for, the subdivider must demonstrate that

- the buyer's security deposit will be protected;
- arrangements have been made to clear mechanic's liens;
- arrangements have been made to release the interest from any blanket mortgage lien; and
- proper title will be conveyed to the buyer.

Fig. 14.1

Subdivided Land Law	Subdivision Map Act
5 or more lots, units, or parcels	2 or more lots, units, or parcels
no contiguity requirement	land must be contiguous units
160 acre and larger parcels are exempt unless they are divided for the purpose of sale for oil and gas purposes	no exemption for 160 acre and larger parcels
condominiums included	same
stock cooperatives included	not included unless 5 or more existing dwelling units are converted
requires a final public report	requires tentative and final maps for certain subdivisions
administered by the California Real Estate Commissioner	administered by local officials

A subdivider who wishes to begin a marketing effort before a final public report is issued may request that a *preliminary public report* be issued. A preliminary public report requires fewer disclosures than does a final public report and only allows the subdivider to accept reservations from potential purchasers. The funds received from these reservations must be kept in an escrow account and must be fully refundable until the buyer receives a final public report. The term of a preliminary public report is one year but may be extended through renewal.

A final public report is valid for 5 years; however, if the subdivision undergoes "material change" (such as change of ownership or use, the sale of 5 or more parcels to one party, or new conditions arise that affect the value of the parcels) the subdivider must apply for an *amended public report*. If at the end of the final public report's life all of the parcels have not been sold, the subdivider may apply for a renewal of the final public report for another five years. Sales of subdivision parcels after the initial sale do not require that the buyer receive a copy of the final public report.

OUT-OF-STATE SUBDIVISIONS

In general, if property in a subdivision located outside of California but within the United States is offered in California, the offeror must register the project with the CalBRE and include certain disclaimers in advertising and sales contracts. If the subdivision is located outside of the United States, the offeror need not register with the CalBRE, but sales contracts and advertising must contain certain disclosures. These disclosures for both domestic and foreign out-of-state subdivisions must be made in sales contracts and in advertising and must state (1) that the CalBRE has not examined the offering and (2) urge the prospective buyer to seek competent legal advice in the jurisdiction where the subdivision is located.

INTERSTATE LAND SALES FULL DISCLOSURE ACT

The federal ***Interstate Land Sales Full Disclosure Act*** requires that certain land developers register with the Bureau of Consumer Financial Protection if they offer across state lines parcels in subdivisions containing 100 or more lots. A regulated developer must provide each prospective buyer with a **Property Report** that contains pertinent information about the subdivision and that discloses to the prospective buyer that he or she has a minimum of 7 days in which to cancel a purchase agreement.

FAIR HOUSING

There are numerous federal and state laws designed to promote fair housing and anti-discriminatory practices. These laws effectively make it against public policy in California to discriminate in real estate practice on the basis of race, color, national origin, religion, sex, sexual orientation, mental or physical handicap, familial status, or marital or registered partner status.

Federal Legislation

Dred Scott and the Thirteenth Amendment

In the 1857 case ***Dred Scott v. Stanford***, the United States Supreme Court ruled that "Persons of African descent cannot be, nor were ever intended to be, citizens under the U.S. Constitution," that persons of African descent (both slaves and freed) had no right to sue in federal court, and that the federal government had no power to "ban slavery in the territories" (at issue was the constitutionality of the Missouri Compromise). This decision stirred up anger in the North, divided the nation, helped propel Abraham Lincoln to the presidency, and was a significant cause of the Civil War.

Immediately following the Civil War, the ***Thirteenth Amendment*** to the Constitution (ratified in 1865) effectively nullified certain aspects of the *Dred Scott* decision:

Section 1

Neither slavery nor involuntary servitude, except as a punishment for crime whereof the party shall have been duly convicted, shall exist within the United States, or any place subject to their jurisdiction.

Section 2

Congress shall have power to enforce this article by appropriate legislation.

One of the most significant differences between the Thirteenth Amendment and subsequent post-Civil War antidiscrimination legislation (such as the Fourteenth Amendment) is that the Thirteenth Amendment prohibits certain actions by private persons (such as enslaving another person) as well as what came to be called "state action."

Civil Rights Act of 1866. The *Civil Rights Act of 1866* was the first law that protected persons against discrimination in the lease or purchase of real property. This Act states in part that:

"citizens, of every race and color, without regard to any previous condition of slavery or involuntary servitude, except as a punishment for crime whereof the party shall have been duly convicted, shall have the same right, in every State and Territory in the United States, to make and enforce contracts, to sue, be parties, and give evidence, to inherit, purchase, lease, sell, hold, and convey real and personal property, and to full and equal benefit of all laws and proceedings for the security of person and property, as is enjoyed by white citizens…"

The protections under this Act, while stated broadly, apply only to race (though Native Americans living on reservations were excluded from its protections) and, unfortunately, were flaunted by many private citizens, real estate agents, and financial institutions, as well as by certain state and local governments, until the civil rights movement of the mid-20th century.

Note that the Civil Rights Act of 1866 does not prohibit discrimination only as to certain residential properties (as, we shall see, many later laws do); it applies to all real property, commercial and residential, and to personal property.

In 1968, the United States Supreme Court held in the landmark case, *Jones v. Mayer*, that the Civil Rights Act of 1866 was constitutional (based on the Thirteenth Amendment) and that it prohibited all racial discrimination, whether private or public, in the sale or rental of property.

The Fourteenth Amendment.

In response to the Civil Rights Act of 1866, many former Confederate states passed laws to limit the rights of former slaves. This led Congress to propose a new amendment to provide protection in the Constitution for rights granted in the 1866 Act. Section 1 of the *Fourteenth Amendment* (ratified in 1868) states:

All persons born or naturalized in the United States, and subject to the jurisdiction thereof, are citizens of the United States and of the State wherein they reside. No State shall make or enforce any law which shall abridge the privileges or immunities of citizens of the United States; nor shall any State deprive any person of life, liberty, or property, without due process of law; nor deny to any person within its jurisdiction the equal protection of the laws.

The hidebound forces of racial (and other forms of) repression clung tightly to the words "no State shall" to argue, in general successfully, that though the Fourteenth Amendment prohibits state and local governments from committing discriminatory acts, it could not be used by federal courts to prohibit private discriminatory conduct. A notable exception finally came in the 1948 Supreme Court case of **Shelley v. Kraemer**, 34 U.S. 1, which held that private racially-based restrictive covenants (the one in *Shelley* being that the property could not be transferred to "people of the Negro or Mongolian Race") are invalid under the Fourteenth Amendment. The Court's reasoning was that to enforce such a covenant, the courts would have to be used, and actions of courts are actions of state or federal governments, and hence constitute "state action."

Federal Fair Housing Act (FFHA). The **Civil Rights Act of 1968** prohibited discrimination in housing based on *race, color, religion,* or *national origin.* The **Housing and Community Development Act of 1974** expanded the scope of protected classes to include *sex.* The **Fair Housing Amendment Act of 1988** further expanded the scope of protected classes to include persons with *disabilities* and to *familial status.* Taken together, the Civil Rights Act of 1968 and its subsequent amendments constitute what is called the **Federal Fair Housing Act (FFHA)**, which prohibits discrimination in the sale, rental, and advertising of residential housing.

Real estate salespersons and brokers should be particularly aware that the FFHA prohibits the following:

- directing people of protected classes away from, or toward, particular areas (a practice called **steering**);

- refusal to loan in particular areas (a practice called **redlining**);

- representing that prices will decline, or crime increase, or other negative effects will occur because of the entrance of minorities into particular areas (a practice called **blockbusting** or **panic selling**);

- discriminatory advertising, sales, or loan terms;

- discriminatory access to multiple listing services; and

- retaliation against, or intimidation of, anyone making a fair-housing complaint.

The Fair Housing Act does not cover all types of housing. In particular, the Act does not:

"(1) Prohibit a religious organization, association, or society, or any nonprofit institution or organization operated, supervised or controlled by or in conjunction with a religious organization, association, or society, from limiting the sale, rental or occupancy of dwellings which it owns or operates for other than a commercial purpose to persons of the same religion, or from giving preference to such persons, unless membership in such religion is restricted because of race, color, or national origin;

(2) Prohibit a private club, not in fact open to the public, which, incident to its primary purpose or purposes, provides lodgings which it owns or operates for other than a commercial purpose, from limiting the rental or occupancy of such lodgings to its members or from giving preference to its members;

(3) Limit the applicability of any reasonable local, State or Federal restrictions regarding the maximum number of occupants permitted to occupy a dwelling; or

(4) Prohibit conduct against a person because such person has been convicted by any court of competent jurisdiction of the illegal manufacture or distribution of a controlled substance as defined in section 102 of the Controlled Substances Act (21 U.S.C. 802).

(b) Nothing in this part regarding discrimination based on familial status applies with respect to housing for older persons as defined in subpart E of this part.

(c) Nothing in this part, other than the prohibitions against discriminatory advertising, applies to:

(1) The sale or rental of any single family house by an owner, provided the following conditions are met:

(i) The owner does not own or have any interest in more than three single family houses at any one time.

(ii) The house is sold or rented without the use of a real estate broker, agent or salesperson or the facilities of any person in the business of selling or renting dwellings. If the owner selling the house does not reside in it at the time of the sale or was not the most recent resident of the house prior to such sale, the exemption in this paragraph (c)(1) of this section applies to only one such sale in any 24-month period.

(2) Rooms or units in dwellings containing living quarters occupied or intended to be occupied by no more than four families living independently of each other, if the owner actually maintains and occupies one of such living quarters as his or her residence."

Familial Status Exemptions

While the prohibition against discrimination based on familial status means that it is illegal to discrimination against pregnant women or persons with children, and that it is illegal to have "adults only" apartment buildings or condominium complexes, or to divide such buildings or complexes into "adult" or "family" areas, federal law provides an exception to allow children to be excluded from properties:

- occupied solely by persons 62 years of age or older; or

- where at least 80% of the dwelling units are occupied by at least one person who is 55 years of age or older.

The above exceptions apply to occupancy, not to ownership. Thus, a couple both 50 years of age may, for example, purchase a dwelling in a condominium complex that only persons 62 years of age or older may occupy, but this couple would not be able to move in for 12 years (though they may rent the dwelling to qualified persons in the meanwhile).

Discriminatory Advertising

Care must be taken not to include in advertising for residential properties words, phrases, symbols, or visual aids that might convey either overt or tacit discriminatory *limitations* or *preferences*. What constitutes discriminatory advertising is of particular concern to real estate agents because they are often involved in advertising properties, and are often encouraged by their clients to make certain statements in the advertising, such as that their property is close to certain facilities. If identifying those facilities indicated, for example, a preference for a particular protected group (e.g., "close to Mid-City Korean Recreation Center" or "just two blocks from a popular Jewish deli"), the advertising very likely would be considered impermissibly discriminatory. For guidance in this area, HUD publishes a list of words, phrases, symbols and visual aids that it considers impermissible in advertising (see HUD's PART 109--FAIR HOUSING ADVERTISING below). But there are a lot of words in the English language that have subtle connotations, which means that there is a broad gray area in this subject of discriminatory advertising. This author's suggestion is when in doubt, leave it out.

The following is from HUD's PART 109--FAIR HOUSING ADVERTISING

§ 109.20 Use of words, phrases, symbols, and visual aids.

The following words, phrases, symbols, and forms typify those most often used in residential real estate advertising to convey either overt or tacit discriminatory preferences or limitations. In considering a complaint under the Fair Housing Act, the Department will normally consider the use of these and comparable words, phrases, symbols, and forms to indicate a possible violation of the act and to establish a need for further proceedings on the complaint, if it is apparent from the context of the usage that discrimination within the meaning of the act is likely to result.

a) Words descriptive of dwelling, landlord, and tenants. White private home, Colored home, Jewish home, Hispanic residence, adult building.

b) Words indicative of race, color, religion, sex, handicap, familial status, or national origin-

1)   Race--Negro, Black, Caucasian, Oriental, American Indian.

*2)   Color--*White, Black, Colored.

*3)   Religion--*Protestant, Christian, Catholic, Jew.

*4)   National origin--*Mexican American, Puerto Rican, Philippine, Polish, Hungarian, Irish, Italian, Chicano, African, Hispanic, Chinese, Indian, Latino.

*5)   Sex--*the exclusive use of words in advertisements, including those involving the rental of separate units in a single or multi-family dwelling, stating or tending to imply that the housing being advertised is available to persons of only one sex and not the other, except where the sharing of living areas is involved. Nothing in this part restricts advertisements of dwellings used exclusively for dormitory facilities by educational institutions.

*6)   Handicap--*crippled, blind, deaf, mentally ill, retarded, impaired, handicapped, physically fit. Nothing in this part restricts the inclusion of information about the availability of accessible housing in advertising of dwellings.

*7)   Familial status--*adults, children, singles, mature persons. Nothing in this part restricts advertisements of dwellings which are intended and operated for occupancy by older persons and which constitute *housing for older persons* as defined in Part 100 of this title.

*8)   Catch words--*Words and phrases used in a discriminatory context should be avoided, e.g., *restricted, exclusive, private, integrated, traditional, board approval or membership approval.*

c)   Symbols or logotypes. Symbols or logotypes which imply or suggest race, color, religion, sex, handicap, familial status, or national origin.

d)   *Colloquialisms.* Words or phrases used regionally or locally which imply or suggest race, color, religion, sex, handicap, familial status, or national origin.

e)   *Directions to real estate for sale or rent (use of maps or written instructions).* Directions can imply a discriminatory preference, limitation, or exclusion. For example, references to real estate location made in terms of racial or national origin significant landmarks, such as an existing black development (signal to blacks) or an existing development known for its exclusion of minorities (signal to whites). Specific directions which make reference to a racial or national origin significant area may indicate a preference. References to a synagogue, congregation or parish may also indicate a religious preference.

f)   *Area (location) description.* Names of facilities which cater to a particular racial, national origin or religious group, such as country club or private school designations, or names of facilities which are used exclusively by one sex may indicate a preference.

Americans with Disabilities Act. The *Americans with Disabilities Act (ADA)* is a civil rights act enacted by Congress in 1990 and amended effective as of January 1, 2009. This Act prohibits discrimination against persons with disabilities, where "disability" is defined as "a physical or mental impairment that substantially limits a major life activity." Impairment due to substance abuse is not covered.

The Act applies to providers of public transportation and accommodations, which must make their facilities accessible to an extent that can be accomplished without unreasonable expense. As used in ADA, the term "public accommodation" includes hotels, motels, stores, care givers, property management firms, and places of dining, recreation, and education.

The Act also applies to employers engaging in interstate commerce and having 15 or more employees. Such employers must alter areas of their workplaces (e.g., entrances, waiting areas, and restrooms) in a manner to accommodate handicapped employees, unless such alterations would place an undue hardship on the business.

ADA allows private individuals to receive back pay and injunctive relief for violations of its employment requirements and injunctive relief for violation of its public accommodation requirements, but does not provide for monetary damages (unlike California state law).

State Laws

There are numerous state laws that duplicate or extend federal laws that prohibit discrimination in housing.

Unruh Civil Rights Act. The *Unruh Civil Rights Act*, CC §51 et seq., was enacted in 1959 and received its name from its principal author, Jesse M. Unruh, and provides that:

> All persons within the jurisdiction of this state are free and equal, and no matter what their sex, race, color, religion, ancestry, national origin, disability, medical condition, genetic information, marital status, or sexual orientation are entitled to the full and equal accommodations, advantages, facilities, privileges, or services in all business establishments of every kind whatsoever. CC §51 (b).

Additionally, a "violation of the right of any individual under the federal Americans with Disabilities Act of 1990" also violates the Unruh Act. CC §51 (f).

The Unruh Act applies to real estate salespersons and brokers because they must work for a brokerage firm, which is a business establishment. The protections afforded by the Unruh Civil Rights Act include prohibitions against the practices of steering and blockbusting.

The remedies afforded by the Unruh Act are quite severe. Violators of the Act are "liable for each and every offense for the actual damages, and any amount that may be determined by a jury, or a court sitting without a jury, up to a maximum of three times the amount of actual damage but in no case less than four thousand dollars ($4,000), and any attorney's fees that may be determined by the court in addition thereto..." CC §52 (a). Because California attorneys often maintain hourly fees in the $300-$500 per hour range, in cases brought under the Unruh Act, it is not uncommon for attorneys fees to vastly exceed actual plus exemplary damages, thus giving a tremendous incentive to defendants to settle rather than go to court.

Fair Employment and Housing Act. The *California Fair Employment and Housing Act*, GOV 12900 et seq., (also known as the *Rumford Act*) prohibits discrimination in the sale, leasing, or financing of nearly all types of housing, except the rental to one boarder in a single-family, owner-occupied home or to accommodations operated by charitable, fraternal, or religious organizations.

The Rumford Act states that:

"the practice of discrimination because of race, color, religion, sex, gender, gender identity, gender expression, sexual orientation, marital status, national origin, ancestry, familial status, source of income, disability, or genetic information in housing accommodations is declared to be against public policy.

It is the purpose of this part to provide effective remedies that will eliminate these discriminatory practices.

This part shall be deemed an exercise of the police power of the state for the protection of the welfare, health, and peace of the people of this state." Gov 12920.

The Rumford Act specifically prohibits landlords from discriminating or harassing "any person because of the race, color, religion, sex, gender, gender identity, gender expression, sexual orientation, marital status, national origin, ancestry, familial status, source of income, disability, or genetic information of that person." GOV 12955(a).

Furthermore, the Act declares it to be unlawful for "the owner of any housing accommodation to make or to cause to be made any written or oral inquiry concerning the race, color, religion, sex, gender, gender identity, gender expression, sexual orientation, marital status, national origin, ancestry, familial status, disability, or genetic information of any person seeking to purchase, rent, or lease any housing accommodation." GOV 12955(b)

Between them the Unruh Civil Rights Act and the Rumford Act prohibit discrimination against 16 protected classes (see Table below).

16 Classes Protected by the Unruh and Rumford Acts	
race	marital status
color	national origin
religion	ancestry
sex	familial status
gender	source of income
gender identity	disability
gender expression	genetic information
sexual orientation	medical condition

<u>Housing Financial Discrimination Act of 1977</u>. The *Housing Financial Discrimination Act of 1977* , HSC §3500 et seq., (also referred to as the *Holden Act*) prohibits redlining by making it illegal for financial institutions such as banks, savings and loan associations, mortgage loan brokers, and mortgage bankers to consider the racial, ethnic, national origin, or religious composition of a neighborhood when determining whether to make loans or to provide financial assistance for housing in that neighborhood.

Fair Lending Notice

The Holding Act requires such financial institutions to notify all applicants for financial assistance of the prohibitions contained in the Act. This notice, referred to as the Fair Lending Notice, states:

The Housing Financial Discrimination Act of 1977 Fair Lending Notice

It is illegal to discriminate in the provision of or in the availability of financial assistance because of the considerations of:

1. Trends, characteristics or conditions in the neighborhood or geographic area surrounding a housing accommodation unless the financial institution can demonstrate in the particular case that such consideration is required to avoid an unsafe and unsound business practice, or

2. Race, color, religion, sex, marital status, national origin or ancestry.

It is illegal to consider the racial, ethnic, religious or national origin composition of a neighborhood or geographic area surrounding a housing accommodation or whether or not such composition is undergoing change or is expected to undergo change, in appraising a housing accommodation or in determining whether or not, or under what terms and conditions, to provide financial assistance.

These provisions govern financial assistance for the purpose of the purchase, construction, rehabilitation or refinancing of one-to-four unit family residences occupied by the owner and for the purpose of the home improvement of any one-to-four unit family residence.

If you have questions about your rights, or if you wish to file a complaint, contact the management of this financial institution or:

Department of Financial Institutions

Consumer Information Desk 1810 13th Street

Sacramento, CA 95814

(800) 622-0620

Regulations of the Real Estate Commissioner §§ 2780-2781: Discrimination and Panic Selling. The California Real Estate Commissioner has issued regulations that prohibit discriminatory practices by licensees. Violations of these regulations are the basis for disciplinary actions, including license suspension or revocation. Real estate brokers have the duty to supervise their salespersons and broker associates to prevent violations of federal or state laws or of the Regulations of the Real Estate Commissioner.

The following are sections 2780-271 of the Regulations of the Real Estate Commissioner, which give examples and exceptions of what constitutes discriminatory conduct on the part of real estate licensees.

2780. Discriminatory Conduct as the Basis for Disciplinary Action.

Prohibited discriminatory conduct by a real estate licensee based upon race, color, sex, religion, ancestry, physical handicap, marital status or national origin includes, but is not limited to, the following:

(a) Refusing to negotiate for the sale, rental or financing of the purchase of real property or otherwise making unavailable or denying real property to any person because of such person's race, color, sex, religion, ancestry, physical handicap, marital status or national origin.

(b) Refusing or failing to show, rent, sell or finance the purchase of real property to any person or refusing or failing to provide or volunteer information to any person about real property, or channeling or steering any person away from real property, because of that person's race, color, sex, religion, ancestry, physical handicap, marital status or national origin or because of the racial, religious, or ethnic composition of any occupants of the area in which the real property is located.

It shall not constitute discrimination under this subdivision for a real estate licensee to refuse or fail to show, rent, sell or finance the purchase of real property to any person having a physical handicap because of the presence of hazardous conditions or architectural barriers to the physically handicapped which conform to applicable state or local building codes and regulations.

(c) Discriminating because of race, color, sex, religion, ancestry, physical handicap, marital status or national origin against any person in the sale or purchase or negotiation or solicitation of the sale or purchase or the collection of payment or the performance of services in connection with contracts for the sale of real property or in connection with loans secured directly or collaterally by liens on real property or on a business opportunity.

Prohibited discriminatory conduct by a real estate licensee under this subdivision does not include acts based on a person's marital status which are reasonably taken in recognition of the community property laws of this state as to the acquiring, financing, holding or transferring of real property.

(d) Discriminating because of race, color, sex, religion, ancestry, physical handicap, marital status or national origin against any person in the terms, conditions or privileges of sale, rental or financing of the purchase of real property.

This subdivision does not prohibit the sale price, rent or terms of a housing accommodation containing facilities for the physically handicapped to differ reasonably from a housing accommodation not containing such facilities.

(e) Discriminating because of race, color, sex, religion, ancestry, physical handicap, marital status or national origin against any person in providing services or facilities in connection with the sale, rental or financing of the purchase of real property, including but not limited to: processing applications differently, referring prospects to other licensees because of the prospects' race, color, sex, religion, ancestry, physical handicap, marital status or national origin, using with discriminatory intent or effect, codes or other means of identifying minority prospects, or assigning real estate licensees on the basis of a prospective client's race, color, sex, religion, ancestry, physical handicap, marital status or national origin.

Prohibited discriminatory conduct by a real estate licensee under this subdivision does not include acts based on a person's marital status which are reasonably taken in recognition of the community property laws of this state as to the acquiring, financing, holding or transferring of real property.

 (f) Representing to any person because of his or her race, color, sex, religion, ancestry, physical handicap, marital status or national origin that real property is not available for inspection, sale or rental when such real property is in fact available.

(g) Processing an application more slowly or otherwise acting to delay, hinder or avoid the sale, rental or financing of the purchase of real property on account of the race, color, sex, religion, ancestry, physical handicap, marital status or national origin of a potential owner or occupant.

(h) Making any effort to encourage discrimination against persons because of their race, color, sex, religion, ancestry, physical handicap, marital status or national origin in the showing, sale, lease or financing of the purchase of real property.

(i) Refusing or failing to cooperate with or refusing or failing to assist another real estate licensee in negotiating the sale, rental or financing of the purchase of real property because of the race, color, sex, religion, ancestry, physical handicap, marital status or national origin of any prospective purchaser or tenant.

(j) Making any effort to obstruct, retard or discourage the purchase, lease or financing of the purchase of real property by persons whose race, color, sex, religion, ancestry, physical handicap, marital status or national origin differs from that of the majority of persons presently residing in a structural improvement to real property or in an area in which the real property is located.

(k) Performing any acts, making any notation, asking any questions or making or circulating any written or oral statement which when taken in context, expresses or implies a limitation, preference or discrimination based upon race, color, sex, religion, ancestry, physical handicap, marital status or national origin; provided, however, that nothing herein shall limit the administering of forms or the making of a notation required by a federal, state or local agency for data collection or civil rights enforcement purposes; or in the case of a physically handicapped person, making notation, asking questions or circulating any written or oral statement in order to serve the needs of such a person.

(l) Making any effort to coerce, intimidate, threaten or interfere with any person in the exercise or enjoyment of, or on account of such person's having exercised or enjoyed, or on account of such person's having aided or encouraged any other person in the exercise or enjoyment of any right granted or protected by a federal or state law, including but not limited to: assisting in any effort to coerce any person because of his or her race, color, sex, religion, ancestry, physical handicap, marital status or national origin to move from, or to not move into, a particular area; punishing or penalizing real estate licensees for their refusal to discriminate in the sale or rental of housing because of the race, color, sex, religion, ancestry, physical handicap, marital status or national origin of a prospective purchaser or lessee; or evicting or taking other retaliatory action against any person for having filed a fair housing complaint or for having undertaken other lawful efforts to promote fair housing.

(m) Soliciting of sales, rentals or listings of real estate from any person, but not from another person within the same area because of differences in the race, color, sex, religion, ancestry, physical handicap, marital status or national origin of such persons.

(n) Discriminating because of race, color, sex, religion, ancestry, physical handicap, marital status or national origin in informing persons of the existence of waiting lists or other procedures with respect to the future availability of real property for purchase or lease.

(o) Making any effort to discourage or prevent the rental, sale or financing of the purchase of real property because of the presence or absence of occupants of a particular race, color, sex, religion, ancestry, physical handicap, marital status or national origin, or on the basis of the future presence or absence of a particular race, color, sex, religion, ancestry, physical handicap, marital status or national origin, whether actual, alleged or implied.

(p) Making any effort to discourage or prevent any person from renting, purchasing or financing the purchase of real property through any representations of actual or alleged community opposition based upon race, color, sex, religion, ancestry, physical handicap, marital status or national origin.

(q) Providing information or advice to any person concerning the desirability of particular real property or a particular residential area(s) which is different from information or advice given to any other person with respect to the same property or area because of differences in the race, color, sex, religion, ancestry, physical handicap, marital status or national origin of such persons.

This subdivision does not limit the giving of information or advice to physically handicapped persons for the purpose of calling to the attention of such persons the existence or absence of housing accommodation services or housing accommodations for the physically handicapped.

(r) Refusing to accept a rental or sales listing or application for financing of the purchase of real property because of the owner's race, color, sex, religion, ancestry, physical handicap, marital status or national origin or because of the race, color, sex, religion, ancestry, physical handicap, marital status or national origin of any of the occupants in the area in which the real property is located.

(s) Entering into an agreement, or carrying out any instructions of another, explicit or understood, not to show, lease, sell or finance the purchase of real property because of race, color, sex, religion, ancestry, physical handicap, marital status or national origin.

(t) Making, printing or publishing, or causing to be made, printed or published, any notice, statement or advertisement concerning the sale, rental or financing of the purchase of real property that indicates any preference, limitation or discrimination because of race, color, sex, religion, ancestry, physical handicap, marital status or national origin, or any intention to make such preference, limitation or discrimination.

This subdivision does not prohibit advertising directed to physically handicapped persons for the purpose of calling to the attention of such persons the existence or absence of housing accommodation services or housing accommodations for the physically handicapped.

(u) Using any words, phrases, sentences, descriptions or visual aids in any notice, statement or advertisement describing real property or the area in which real property is located which indicates any preference, limitation or discrimination because of race, color, sex, religion, ancestry, physical handicap, marital status or national origin.

This subdivision does not prohibit advertising directed to physically handicapped persons for the purpose of calling to the attention of such persons the existence or absence of housing accommodation services or housing accommodations for the physically handicapped.

(v) Selectively using, placing or designing any notice, statement or advertisement having to do with the sale, rental or financing of the purchase of real property in such a manner as to cause or increase discrimination by restricting or enhancing the exposure or appeal to persons of a particular race, color, sex, ancestry, physical handicap, marital status or national origin.

This subdivision does not limit in any way the use of an affirmative marketing program designed to attract persons of a particular race, color, sex, religion, ancestry, physical handicap, marital status or national origin who would not otherwise be attracted to the real property or to the area.

(w) Quoting or charging a price, rent or cleaning or security deposit for a particular real property to any person which is different from the price, rent or security deposit quoted or charged to any other person because of differences in the race, color, sex, religion, ancestry, physical handicap, marital status or national origin of such persons.

This subdivision does not prohibit the quoting or charging of a price, rent or cleaning or security deposit for a housing accommodation containing facilities for the physically handicapped to differ reasonably from a housing accommodation not containing such facilities.

(x) Discriminating against any person because of race, color, sex, religion, ancestry, physical handicap, marital status or national origin in performing any acts in connection with the making of any determination of financial ability or in the processing of any application for the financing or refinancing of real property.

Nothing herein shall limit the administering of forms or the making of a notation required by a federal, state or local agency for data collection or civil rights enforcement purposes. In any evaluation or determination as to whether, and under what terms and conditions, a particular lender or lenders would be likely to grant a loan, licensees shall proceed as though the lender or lenders are in compliance with Sections 35800 through 35833 of the California Health and Safety Code (The Housing Financial Discrimination Act of 1977).

Prohibited discriminatory conduct by a real estate licensee under this subdivision does not include acts based on a person's marital status which are reasonably taken in recognition of the community property laws of this state as to the acquiring, financing, holding or transferring of real property.

(y) Advising a person of the price or value of real property on the basis of factors related to the race, color, sex, religion, ancestry, physical handicap, marital status or national origin of residents of an area or of residents or potential residents of the area in which the property is located.

(z) Discriminating in the treatment of, or services provided to, occupants of any real property in the course of providing management services for the real property because of the race, color, sex, religion, ancestry, physical handicap, marital status or national origin of said occupants.

This subdivision does not prohibit differing treatment or services to a physically handicapped person because of the physical handicap in the course of providing management services for a housing accommodation.

(aa) Discriminating against the owners or occupants of real property because of the race, color, sex, religion, ancestry, physical, handicap, marital status or national origin of their guests, visitors or invitees.

(bb) Making any effort to instruct or encourage, expressly or impliedly, by either words or acts, licensees or their employees or other agents to engage in any discriminatory act in violation of a federal or state fair housing law.

(cc) Establishing or implementing rules that have the effect of limiting the opportunity for any person because of his or her race, color, sex, religion, ancestry, physical handicap, marital status or national origin to secure real property through a multiple listing or other real estate service.

(dd) Assisting or aiding in any way, any person in the sale, rental or financing of the purchase of real property where there are reasonable grounds to believe that such person intends to discriminate because of race, color, sex, religion, ancestry, physical handicap, marital status or national origin.

2781. Panic Selling as the Basis for Disciplinary Action.

Prohibited discriminatory conduct includes, but is not limited to, soliciting sales or rental listings, making written or oral statements creating fear or alarm, transmitting written or oral warnings or threats, or acting in any other manner so as to induce or attempt to induce the sale or lease of real property through any representation, express or implied, regarding the present or prospective entry of one or more persons of another race, color, sex, religion, ancestry, marital status or national origin into an area or neighborhood.

amended public report — a report that a subdivider must apply for if, after the issuance of a final public report, new conditions arise that affect the value of the subdivision parcels.

Americans with Disabilities Act — a federal act that prohibits discrimination against persons with disabilities, where "disability" is defined as "a physical or mental impairment that substantially limits a major life activity."

blockbusting — the illegal practice of representing that prices will decline, or crime increase, or other negative effects will occur because of the entrance of minorities into particular areas.

California Coastal Zone Conservation Act — a California state law that is intended to promote the preservation and protection of California's diverse coastal zone.

California Environmental Quality Act (CEQA) — a California state law that requires state and local agencies to consider and respond to the environmental effects of private and public development projects.

Civil Rights Act of 1866 — a federal law enacted during Reconstruction that stated that people of any race may enjoy the right to enforce contracts, to sue, be parties, and give evidence, to inherit, purchase, lease, sell, hold, and convey real and personal property, and to full and equal benefit of all laws.

Civil Rights Act of 1968 — a federal law (often referred to as the Federal Fair Housing Act) that prohibited discrimination in housing based on race, creed, or national origin. An amendment to this Act in 1974 added prohibition against discrimination based on gender, and an amendment in 1988 added prohibition against discrimination based on a person's disabilities or familial status.

common interest development (CID) — a subdivision in which purchasers own or lease a separate lot, unit, or interest, and have an undivided interest or membership in a portion of the common area of the subdivision.

community apartment project — a development in which an undivided interest in the land is coupled with the right of exclusive occupancy of an apartment located thereon.

Community Redevelopment Law — a California state law that provides local governments with the authority to correct blighted conditions in areas within their jurisdictions.

conditional use — a zoning exception for special uses such as churches, schools, and hospitals that wish to locate to areas zoned exclusively for residential use.

condominium — a residential unit owned in severalty, the boundaries of which are usually walls, floors, and ceilings, and an undivided interest in portions of the real property, such as halls, elevators, and recreational facilities.

Constructors' State License Law — a California state law that, with certain exceptions, requires that every building contractor must be licensed by the Contractors' State License Board.

Endangered Species Act — a federal law that is intended to provide a means whereby the ecosystems upon which endangered species and threatened species depend may be conserved, and to provide a program for the conservation of such endangered species and threatened species.

environmental impact report (EIR) — a report that the agency investigating the feasibility of a development project pursuant to the California Environmental Quality Act is required to make if it is determined that there is substantial evidence of the project would have a significant adverse environmental impact.

environmental impact statement (EIS) — a statement that certain agencies are required to make pursuant to the National Environmental Policy Act regarding development that might significantly impact the quality of the environment.

Factory Built Housing Law — a California state law that regulates factory built housing.

Fair Employment and Housing Act — a California state law (also known as the Rumford Act) that prohibits discrimination in the sale, leasing, or financing of nearly all types of housing, except the rental to one boarder in a single-family, owner-occupied home or to accommodations operated by charitable, fraternal, or religious organizations. The Rumford Act specifically prohibits landlords from asking prospective buyers or tenants about race, color, religion, gender, sexual orientation, marital status, familial status, national origin, ancestry, or disability.

Federal Fair Housing Act — *see*, Civil Rights Act of 1968

final map —a final map that a planning commission must approve after consideration of a tentative map before regulated subdivided property may be sold.

final public report — a report that the Real Estate Commissioner issues after determining that a subdivision offering meets certain consumer protection standards.

general plan — a comprehensive, long-term plan for the physical development of a city or county that is implemented by zoning, building codes, and other laws or actions of the local governments.

Holden Act — *see*, Housing Financial Discrimination Act.

Housing Financial Discrimination Act — a California state law (also referred to as the Holden Act) that prohibits redlining by making it illegal for financial institutions to consider the racial, ethnic, national origin, or religious composition of a neighborhood when determining whether to make loans or to provide financial assistance for housing in that neighborhood.

inclusionary zoning — a zoning law that requires builders to set aside a specific portion of new construction for people of low to moderate incomes.

Interstate Land Sales Full Disclosure Act — a federal consumer protection act that requires that certain land developers register with the Bureau of Consumer Financial Protection if they offer across state lines parcels in subdivisions containing 100 or more lots. A regulated developer must provide each prospective buyer with a Property Report that contains pertinent information about the subdivision and that discloses to the prospective buyer that he or she has a minimum of 7 days in which to cancel a purchase agreement.

Jones v. Mayer — a landmark 1968 United States Supreme Court case that held that the Civil Rights Act of 1866 was constitutional and that the Act prohibited all racial discrimination, whether private or public, in the sale or rental of property.

National Environmental Policy Act (NEPA) — a federal law intended to protect, and to promote the enhancement of, the environment.

negative declaration — a report issued by a state or local agency acting pursuant to the California Environmental Quality Act if the agency determines that a development project will not have a significant adverse environmental impact.

nonconforming use — a zoning exception for areas that are zoned for the first time or that are rezoned and where established property uses that previously were permitted to not conform to the new zoning requirements. As a general rule, such existing properties are "grandfathered in," allowing them to continue the old use but not to extend the old use to additional properties or to continue the old use after rebuilding or abandonment.

planned development (PD) — a development (other than a condominium, community apartment project, or stock cooperative) consisting of lots or parcels owned separately and areas owned in common and reserved for the use of some or all the owners of the separate interests.

planning commission — the city or county agency responsible for proposing a general plan for the city or county.

preliminary public report — a report that a subdivider may request that requires fewer disclosures than does a final public report and that only allows the subdivider to accept reservations from potential purchasers.

redlining — the illegal practice of refusing to make loans for real property in particular areas.

rezoning amendment — an amendment to a zoning ordinance that property owners may request if they feel that their area has been improperly zoned.

Rumford Act — *see*, Fair Employment and Housing Act

spot zoning — an improper use of zoning whereby a particular property is zoned differently from similar property similarly situated in the neighborhood.

standard subdivision — is a subdivision with no common areas of ownership or use among the owners of the subdivision parcels.

State Housing Law — a California state law that provides for minimum construction and occupancy requirements for housing.

steering — the illegal practice of directing people of protected classes away from, or toward, housing in particular areas.

stock cooperative — a corporation formed or availed of primarily for the purpose of holding title to improved real property either in fee simple or for a term of years.

Subdivided Lands Law — a California state law that requires subdividers to disclose certain pertinent information to the initial purchasers of parcels in subdivisions.

Subdivision Map Act — a California state law that gives local officials the authority to regulate subdivisions to ensure that they conform to local general plans.

tentative map — a map required pursuant to the Subdivision Map Act for subdivisions that create five or more parcels, five or more condominiums, a community apartment project containing 5 or more interests, or the conversion of a dwelling into a stock cooperative of 5 or more dwelling units. The tentative map, which is to be filed with the local planning commission, must include a legal description of the property; the location and description of all adjoining highways, streets, and waterways; the location and description of easements for roads, drainage, sewers, and other public utilities; proposed public areas; and proposed provisions for floods and other natural hazards.

time-share estate — an estate in real property coupled with the right of occupancy for certain periods of time.

time-share use — a right to occupancy during certain periods of time, not coupled to an estate in real property.

undivided interest subdivision — a subdivision in which owners own a partial or fractional interest in an entire parcel of land. The land in an undivided interest subdivision is not divided; its ownership is divided.

Unruh Civil Rights Act — a California state law that prohibits persons engaged in business from discriminating on the basis of race, color, religion, ancestry, national origin, gender, disability, medical condition, or age when providing products or services in California. In housing related activities, businesses are also prohibited from discriminating on the basis of marital status, familial status, sexual orientation, or source of income. This law applies to all real estate salespersons and brokers.

Vacation Ownership and Time-Share Act of 2004 — a California state consumer protection law that regulates disclosures and representations made by time-share salespersons.

variance — an exception that may be granted in cases where damage to the value of a property from the strict enforcement of zoning ordinances would far outweigh any benefit to be derived from enforcement.

zoning — laws of a city or county that specify the type of land-use that is acceptable in certain areas.

Quiz for Chapter 14

1. The Federal Fair Housing Act (FFHA) prohibits discrimination in the sale, rental, and advertisement of
   a. most commercial properties
   b. most residential properties
   c. both a and b
   d. neither a nor b

2. The Federal Fair Housing Act (FFHA) also prohibits
   a. discriminatory access to multiple listing services
   b. retaliation against, or intimidation of, anyone making a fair-housing complaint
   c. both a and b
   d. neither a nor b

3. The federal Interstate Land Sales Disclosure Act requires that certain land developers register with the Bureau of Consumer Financial Protection if they offer across state lines parcels in subdivisions containing ___ or more lots.
   a. 10
   b. 100
   c. 500
   d. 1,000

4. The Americans with Disabilities Act (ADA) prohibits
   a. discrimination against persons with a physical or mental impairment that substantially limits a major life activity
   b. impairment due to substance abuse
   c. both a and b
   d. neither a nor b

5. The Housing Financial Discrimination Act of 1977 prohibits
   a. smoking in restaurants
   b. redlining
   c. discrimination in college or university admissions
   d. all of the above

6. A law that provides local governments with the authority to correct blighted conditions in areas within their jurisdictions is
   a. California Environmental Quality Act
   b. Holden Act
   c. Housing Financial Discrimination Act
   d. none of the above

7. The National Environmental Policy Act (NEPA) requires federal agencies to prepare what for any development project that a federal agency could prohibit or regulate, and any development project for which any portion is federally financed?
   a. environmental quality report
   b. environmental impact report
   c. environmental impact statement
   d. none of the above

8. In an undivided interest subdivision
   a. the land is not divided
   b. ownership of title to the land is divided
   c. both a and b
   d. neither a nor b

9. After a general plan is adopted, the local government implements the plan by use of
   a. eminent domain
   b. police power
   c. both a and b
   d. neither a nor b

10. A subdivision with no common areas of ownership or use among the owners of the subdivision parcels is called
    a. an undivided interest subdivision
    b. a standard subdivision
    c. a planned developments subdivision
    d. a stock cooperative subdivision

11. The Civil Rights Act of 1866 applied to what type of discrimination?
    a. race
    b. religion
    c. both a and b
    d. neither a nor b

12. A condominium complex is
    a. a standard subdivision
    b. a common interest development
    c. an undivided interest subdivision
    d. none of the above

13. The general plan of a city or county is proposed by
    a. a zoning commission
    b. a planning commission
    c. the subdivision map agency
    d. none of the above

14. A community apartment project is
    a. a common interest development
    b. a development in which an undivided interest in the land is coupled with the right of exclusive occupancy of an apartment located thereon

    c. both a and b

    d. neither a nor b

15. A final public report will not be issued unless the proposed subdivision

    a. is suitable for the use proposed by the subdivider

    b. will give the purchaser what he or she bargains for

    c. both a and b

    d. neither a nor b

16. Under the Civil Rights Act of 1968, which of the following phrases would likely be found to be discriminatory?

    a. "prefer African-American couple"

    b. "just two blocks from the Rose St. Mormon Tabernacle"

    c. both a and b

    d. neither a nor b

17. Inclusionary zoning refers to

    a. zoning for condominiums and apartment buildings

    b. zoning for setback and side-yard requirements

    c. zoning to promote aesthetic appeal of the community

    d. none of the above

18. For the purposes of the Subdivision Map Act, a subdivision is any division of contiguous land into how many lots, units, or parcels for the purpose of sale, lease, or financing?

    a. 2 or more

    b. 3 or more

    c. 4 or more

    d. 5 or more

19. A final public report for a subdivision is valid for how many years?

    a. 5

    b. 4

    c. 3

    d. 2

20. A real estate broker installed a ramp to the office's entrance to accommodate persons in wheelchairs. The broker likely did this to comply with the

    a. Holden Act

    b. California Environmental Quality Act

    c. Subdivision Map Act

    d. none of the above

21. A zoning exception for special uses such as churches, schools, and hospitals that wish to locate to areas zoned exclusively for residential use is referred to as

    a. nonconforming use

    b. conditional use

    c. variance

    d. none of the above

22. Under the Subdivided Lands Law it is illegal to commence sales of regulated subdivision parcels until the Real Estate Commissioner has issued a
    a. tentative map
    b. final map
    c. negative declaration
    d. none of the above

23. As a general rule, if property in a subdivision located outside of California but within the United States is offered in California, the offeror
    a. must register the property with the CalBRE
    b. include certain disclaimers in advertising and sales contracts
    c. both a and b
    d. neither a nor b

24. A real estate agent's client requested that the agent show his house only to other African-Americans because the client wanted to keep the neighborhood integrated. If the agent complies, the agent's actions would be considered
    a. steering
    b. illegal
    c. both a and b
    d. neither a nor b

25. Most building contractors in California must be licensed by the
    a. California Community Development Agency
    b. California Environmental Quality Board
    c. California Zoning Oversight Board
    d. none of the above

26. John, age 56, and Susan, age 58, wish to purchase a condominium in a complex that restricts occupancy solely to persons 62 years of age or older.
    a. they cannot purchase the condo because they are not both 62 years of age
    b. they may purchase the condo but cannot move in together until Susan reaches the age of 62
    c. they may purchase the condo but cannot move in together until John reaches the age of 62
    d. none of the above

27. Which state law specifically prohibits businesses from certain discriminatory practices?
    a. Civil Rights Act of 1968
    b. Unruh Civil Rights Act
    c. Civil Rights Act of 1866
    d. none of the above

28. Representing that prices will decline, or crime increase, or other negative effects will occur because of the entrance of minorities into particular areas is called
    a. steering
    b. blockbusting
    c. redlining
    d. none of the above
29. The Fair Employment and Housing Act is also known as the
    a. Holden Act
    b. Rumford Act
    c. Unruh Act
    d. none of the above
30. The Housing Financial Discrimination Act is also known as the
    a. Holden Act
    b. Rumford Act
    c. Unruh Act
    d. none of the above

Answers for Chapter 14 Quiz

1. b. The Federal Fair Housing Act prohibits discrimination in the sale, rental, and advertisement of most residential properties.

2. c. Each of the answers a and b is correct.

3. b. The federal Interstate Land Sales Full Disclosure Act requires that certain land developers register with the Bureau of Consumer Financial Protection if they offer across state lines parcels in subdivisions containing 100 or more lots.

4. a. The Americans with Disabilities Act (ADA) prohibits discrimination against persons with disabilities, where" disability" is defined as "a physical or mental impairment that substantially limits a major life activity." Impairment due to substance abuse is not covered.

5. b. The Housing Financial Discrimination Act of 1977, HSC §3500 et seq., (also referred to as the Holden Act) prohibits redlining by making it illegal for financial institutions such as banks, savings and loan associations, mortgage loan brokers, and mortgage bankers to consider the racial, ethnic, national origin, or religious composition of a neighborhood when determining whether to make loans or to provide financial assistance for housing in that neighborhood.

6. d. The California Community Redevelopment Law provides local governments with the authority to correct blighted conditions in areas within their jurisdictions.

7. c. Certain agencies are required to issue an environmental impact statement pursuant to the National Environmental Policy Act regarding development that might significantly impact the quality of the environment.

8. c. An undivided interest subdivision is a subdivision in which owners own a partial or fractional interest in an entire parcel of land. The land in an undivided interest subdivision is not divided; its ownership is divided.

9. c. After a general plan is adopted, the local government implements the plan by using police power, eminent domain, taxation, and fiscal control.

10. b. A standard subdivision is a subdivision with no common areas of ownership or use among the owners of the subdivision parcels.

11. a. The protections under this Act, while stated broadly, apply only to race (though Native Americans living on reservations were excluded from its protections).

12.b. A common interest subdivision is a subdivision in which purchasers own or lease a separate lot, unit, or interest, and have an undivided interest or membership in a portion of the common area of the subdivision, of which a condominium complex is a particular type.

13.b. The general plan for each city and county is proposed by a planning commission (also referred to as a planning agency), whose members are appointed by the city council or county board of supervisors.

14.c. A common interest subdivision is a subdivision in which purchasers own or lease a separate lot, unit, or interest, and have an undivided interest or membership in a portion of the common area of the subdivision, of which a community apartment project is a type.

15.c. The final public report will not be issued unless the proposed subdivision is suitable for the use proposed by the subdivider and will give the purchaser what he or she bargains for.

16.c. Both answers a and b demonstrate prohibited preferences for particular ethnic, racial, or religious groups.

17.d. Inclusionary zoning refers to a zoning law that requires builders to set aside a specific portion of new construction for people of low to moderate incomes.

18.a. For the purposes of the Subdivision Map Act, a subdivision is any division of contiguous land into 2 or more lots, units, or parcels for the purpose of sale, lease, or financing.

19.a. A final public report for a subdivision is valid for five years, but if at the end of the final public report's life all of the parcels have not been sold, the subdivider may apply for a renewal of the final public report for another five years.

20.d. The Americans with Disabilities Act prohibits discrimination against persons with disabilities, where "disability" is defined as "a physical or mental impairment that substantially limits a major life activity."

21.b. Conditional use is a zoning exception for special uses such as churches, schools, and hospitals that wish to locate to areas zoned exclusively for residential use.

22.d. Under the Subdivided Lands Law it is illegal to commence sales of regulated subdivision parcels until the Real Estate Commissioner has issued a final public report.

23.c. In general, if property in a subdivision located outside of California but within the United States is offered in California, the offeror must register the project with the CalBRE and include certain disclaimers in advertising and sales contracts.

24.c. Steering is the illegal practice of directing people of protected classes away from, or toward, housing in particular areas.

25.d. Most building contractors in California must be licensed by the Contractors' State License Board.

26.c. Federal law permits properties to exclude everyone less than 62 years of age; therefore, both John and Susan must be 62 years of age before they can move into the condo together.

27.b. The Unruh Civil Rights Act specifically prohibits businesses from certain discriminatory practices. The other two mentioned acts are not California acts.

28.b. Blockbusting is the illegal practice of representing that prices will decline, or crime increase, or other negative effects will occur because of the entrance of minorities into particular areas.

29.b. The Fair Employment and Housing Act is also known as the Rumford Act.

30.a. The Housing Financial Discrimination Act is also known as the Holden Act.

Taxation and Real Estate

A *tax* is a levy by a government authority on persons or property to finance government expenditures. Because taxation is a burden and, therefore, a significant limiting factor on the value of property, real estate agents should become familiar with the various taxes that may affect property and the transfer of property: real property taxes, transfer taxes, special assessments, income taxes, personal property taxes, estate taxes, and gift taxes.

REAL PROPERTY TAXES

Real property taxes are the main source of revenue for local governments. Real property taxes are levied on an *ad valorem* (according to value) basis, modified by laws such as Proposition 13.

Exemptions

All property in the state is taxable unless it is exempt. Such exemptions include:

- **Government lands**. Approximately half of California is owned by governments and is, therefore, exempt from property taxation.
- **Homeowner's exemption**. Every residential property that is owner-occupied as of January 1 qualifies for a *homeowner's exemption* of $7,000 from the assessed value for the next the fiscal tax year, which begins on July 1. Application for this exemption must be filed by February 15. Renters of residential property do not qualify for this exemption.
- **Veteran's exemption**. The *veteran's exemption* provides an exemption of up to $4,000 from the assessed value of a qualified veteran's property. To qualify, the veteran:
  1. may not own real or personal property worth more in the aggregate than $5,000 if the veteran is single, or $10,000 if married;
  2. must have lived in California on January 1 prior to the relevant fiscal year; and

3. must be serving in, or has served in and has been honorably discharged from, the armed services *and* satisfies any of the following criteria:
   a) served in time of war
   b) served in time of peace and has been issued a medal by Congress
   c) served in time of peace and was released from active duty because of a service-connected disability.

The veteran's exemption and homeowner's exemption may not be applied to the same property, but if the veteran owned property in addition to the home he or she owns and occupies, the veteran's exemption may be applied to that other property. Upon the death of the veteran, the veteran's spouse, registered domestic partner, or parent may acquire this exemption. Application for the exemption should be filed before February 15.

- **Disabled Veteran's Exemption**. The *Disabled Veteran's Exemption* can reduce the tax liability of a qualified veteran on property that is the principal place of residence of the veteran or the unmarried surviving spouse of a qualified veteran. No other property tax exemption may be granted to a residence that receives a Disabled Veteran's Exemption. The Disabled Veteran's Exemption may be claimed as follows:
   a) an exemption from property taxation on that part of the assessed value of the residence that does not exceed $100,000; or
   b) an exemption from property taxation on that part of the assessed value of the residence that does not exceed $150,000 if the household income of the veteran does not exceed 40,000.

The amounts of this exemption and the income threshold are increased annually due to inflation, so a qualified veteran should contact either a tax consultant or a veteran's official to determine the amount of exemption that the disabled veteran qualifies for.

A veteran is qualified as "disabled" for the purposes of the Disabled Veteran's Exemption if any one of the following criteria applies:

   a) blind in both eyes;
   b) has lost the use of two or more limbs; or
   c) was totally disabled as a result of injury or disease incurred while in military service.

Application for this exemption should be filed before February 15.

- **Other Exemptions**. There are many other property tax exemptions provided for by the Revenue and Taxation Code, including exemptions that may be claimed by churches, colleges, libraries, public schools, vessels, and works of art.

Property Tax Postponement Programs

Until recently California had a property tax postponement program that gave seniors (defined as 62 years of age or older) and blind or disabled persons the option of having the state pay all or part of the real property tax on his or her residence until he or she moved, sold the property, died, or transferred title to the property. To qualify, there were household income thresholds that could not be exceeded, and there was an equity interest threshold that had to be met. Repayment of all postponed taxes had to be made when the property was sold or title transferred.

In February 2009, the State Legislature indefinitely suspended this program. However, in September 2011, a bill was signed by the Governor that permits each county to implement a property tax postponement program for property located in their county. These voluntary county-administered property tax postponement programs became effective January 1, 2012; therefore, California residents should now inquire with their county to determine whether they qualify for a tax postponement program.

Collection Process

County budgets are established and property tax rates for the county are set by the county board of supervisors; county tax rolls are maintained by the county *tax auditor*; county property appraisals are performed by the county *tax assessor*; and collection of the county property taxes is the responsibility of the county *tax collector*.

The California *fiscal year* begins on July 1 and ends on June 30 of the following calendar year. The tax on real property becomes a lien on the property on January 1 of the year during which the fiscal year begins. For example, for the fiscal year that begins July 1, 2014, the real property tax for that fiscal year becomes a lien against the property on January 1, 2014.

Real property taxes are payable in two equal installments:

- November 1 — first installment due
- December 10 — first installment becomes delinquent
- February 1 — second installment due
- April 10 — second installment becomes delinquent

To remember these dates, it may be helpful to use the mnemonic "No Darn Fooling Around."

Fig. 15.1	Real Property Tax Calendar
January 1	Tax for the next fiscal year becomes a lien
February 1	Second installment of taxes is due
February 15	Homeowner's, veteran's, disabled veteran's, and most other exemption applications become due
April 10	Second installment of taxes becomes delinquent
June 30	Fiscal year ends
July 1	Fiscal year begins
November 1	First installment of taxes is due
December 10	First installment of taxes becomes delinquent

Tax-Defaulted Property

If delinquent real property taxes remain unpaid until June 30, the county tax collector publishes an "intent to sell" the property. The "sale" referred to here is not an actual sale, but what is referred to as a **book sale,** which does not entail an actual transfer property. A 5-year redemption period follows, during which the taxpayer may (1) possess and use the property and (2) redeem the property by paying all delinquent taxes and penalties. The taxpayer's right of redemption terminates at the end of the 5-year redemption period, giving the county the right to sell the property. However, the tax payer may still redeem the property by paying all delinquent taxes and penalties until the close of business on the last day prior to the date that the property actually sells. Furthermore, there is a one-year period of time after the date the **tax deed** (the deed that the successful bidder at a tax auction receives) has been executed that a proceeding based on alleged invalidity or irregularity can be commenced to challenge the validity of the tax sale (Revenue and Taxation Code §3725).

All county tax sales are for cash (no financing), and because state taxes (such as property taxes) that become liens on real property "have priority over all other liens on the property, regardless of the time of their creation..." (Revenue and Taxation Code §2192.1), a tax deed **conveys title free and clear from all private liens** (*including judgment liens and deeds of trust in favor of lenders — even those liens that were recorded before the tax lien attached*). However, a tax deed will not convey title free from **certain other tax liens or special assessment liens, or from easements and recorded restrictions.**

Proposition 13

Proposition 13 was approved by California voters in 1978 as an amendment to the State Constitution. Basically, this amendment places a maximum ad valorem tax on real property equal to 1% of the "full cash value" plus a maximum increase of the assessed value of up to 2% per year, as long as the annual increase does not exceed the Consumer Price Index (CPI). Note that

Proposition 13 applies only to ad valorem real estate taxes, not to special taxes or assessments that impose a tax not based on the value of the real estate (see, for example, the discussion on Mello-Roos assessments below).

There are a few exceptions to Proposition 13 that may result in real property being burdened by a greater than a 1% ad valorem tax. These exceptions include Proposition 39 school bonds (which require a 55% majority vote and are limited to $60 per $100,000 of assessed value), voter-approved assessments (which require approval by a two thirds supermajority vote and are, therefore, rare), and bonds that were approved before 1978.

Under Proposition 13, the value shown on the county assessor's tax rolls for fiscal year 1975-1976 serves as the basis for assessment of real property. If after March 1, 1975, the property is transferred (such as by sale, gift, or inheritance), the assessed value of the property becomes either the sale price or the market value of the property as of the date transfer.

If improvements are made to a property, the property retains its current adjusted base value, and the improvements are valued separately as of the date of completion. The tax bills going forward would reflect the sum of the tax on the property taxed at its adjusted base value plus the tax on the value of the improvements (which value would also increase annually by up to 2%, but not more than the CPI for the given fiscal tax year).

> **Example:** Alice purchases a home on July 1, 2012, for its fair market value of $500,000. Because the home is newly purchased, the adjusted base value will be $500,000 and her property tax (assuming no bond or assessments issues other than the basic 1% levy) would be $500,000 x 0.01 = $5,000. For the next fiscal year, July 1, 2013-June 30, 2014, the adjusted value of Alice's home would be increased by 2% or the CPI, whichever is less. Assuming the 2% figure, her 2013-2014 adjusted base value would be $500,000 x 1.02 = $510,000. Therefore, assuming the tax rate remained 1%, her property tax for 2013-2014 would be $510,000 x 0.01 = $5,100.

Proposition 8

Proposition 8 requires the county assessor to assess real property either at the property's Proposition 13 adjusted value or its current market value, whichever is less. Proposition 8 can, therefore, reduce the assessed value of property in times of decreasing property values.

Propositions 58 and 193

Proposition 58 provides for an exclusion from reassessment when property is transferred between spouses. It also provides for an exclusion from reassessment of a transfer of a principal residence and transfers of the first $1 million of other real property between parent and child. **Proposition 193** extends this tax relief to certain transfers from grandparents to their grandchildren, but not transfers from grandchildren to their grandparents.

Propositions 60 and 90

Proposition 60 allows certain older persons to transfer the adjusted basis of their present principal residence to a replacement if the replacement is in the same county and is of equal or lesser value than the prior residence. To qualify, the transferor or the transferor's spouse must be 55 years of age or older at the time of the transfer. **Proposition 90** extended Proposition 60 to allow the purchase of a new residence in a different California county, but only if the county in which the new residence lies adopts Proposition 90. Currently, the only counties that have adopted Proposition 90 are Alameda, El Dorado, Los Angeles, Orange, San Diego, San Mateo, Santa Clara, and Ventura.

Special Assessments

As discussed above, Proposition 13 only addresses limits on ad valorem taxes, which are, in general, used to pay for general government expenses that benefit essentially all persons and property in the county or city. Examples of such general government expenses include police and fire protection. Certain laws lay the groundwork for significant increases in taxes on property by permitting local governments to tax property for "special benefits" conferred on properties in particular limited areas. There are many such special assessments for such items as streets, sewers, lighting, water service, parks, playgrounds, tree planting, landscaping, parking facilities, geologic hazard abatement, and so on.

The **Vrooman Street Act of 1885** provides local governments with authority to construct streets, sewers, and other improvements. Funds for these improvements are secured by the issuance of bonds, which are redeemed by assessing the properties benefited.

The **Street Improvement Act of 1911** provides local governments with the authority to issue bonds to improve streets and make other improvements to specific areas. Assessments on properties are due in equal installments during the term of the bonds, which can run for decades.

The ***Improvement Bond Act of 1915*** permits local governments to issue bonds to finance subdivision street improvements. Owners of the subdivisions bear the cost of redeeming the bonds.

The ***Community Facilities Act of 1982*** (commonly known as the ***Mello-Roos Community Facilities Act***, so named after its co-authors) provides for the construction or improvement of a wide variety of facilities and services. This act has no requirement that the facilities or improvements confer "special benefits" to individual properties. Mello-Roos districts are created for which bonds are sold to finance improvements in the district, and properties in the district are assessed to redeem the bonds. Because the property tax burden in Mello-Roos districts can be quite high (the Mello-Roos act is often considered an end run around Proposition 13), Civil Code §1102.6b requires the seller of a residential structure consisting of 4 or fewer dwellings that is subject to a lien of a Mello-Roos district to make a good-faith effort to obtain from the district a disclosure notice concerning the special assessment and give notice of the disclosure to prospective purchasers.

INCOME TAXES

Transfers of real estate can have significant federal and state income tax consequences. Income taxes are ***progressive***, meaning that the greater an individual's income, the higher the tax rate on that individual's income. Rental income is taxed at the individual's regular income tax rate, but gains on the sale of ***capital assets*** are taxed at a ***capital gain rate***. What constitutes a capital asset is a technical question often hinging on how the asset is used or held. In very general terms, capital assets are non-inventory assets held by individuals or businesses for personal or investment purposes, and include homeowners' homes, household furnishings, stocks, bonds, land, buildings, and machinery.

Capital gain rates vary depending on whether the gain is a ***short-term capital gain*** or a ***long-term capital gain***. Short-term rates are typically applicable to investments held for one year or less and have often been equal to the individual's regular income tax rate; long-term rates are typically applicable to investments held for more than 12 months and are usually lower than short-term rates. Income tax rules and rates for both regular income and capital gain income are constantly changing; therefore, *before* entering into a real estate transaction, it is prudent to seek the advice of an attorney or accountant who is an income tax specialist.

Income Tax Ramifications of Home Ownership

Homeowners are eligible for certain income tax benefits, including:

1. Interest paid on a mortgage secured by a principal residence or by a second home is deductible from personal income. There is a limit on how much interest can be deducted, which limit currently is the interest on the portion of a loan that does not exceed $1 million. The mortgage interest deduction can only be taken on a principal residence and one second home.

2. Property taxes paid on a homeowner's residence are also deductible from personal income.

3. Pursuant to 26 U.S.C. §121, an individual of any age who sells a property that has been his or her principal place of residence for at least 2 out of the 5 years prior to the sale may exclude $250,000 from capital gains on the sale. For married couples who have both lived in the residence for the requisite 2-year period, the exclusion is $500,000. These exclusions can only be taken once every two years. If the home was not the principal residence for the requisite 2-year period, individuals and married couples can still obtain a partial exclusion if the sale was necessitated by a change of employment, health problems, or other unforeseen circumstances, such as divorce or a death in the family. In such cases, an exclusion based on the portion of the requisite 2-year period can be taken. For example, if because of a change of employment a married couple moves and sells their home, having lived there only one year, the exclusion would be ½ of $500,000, or $250,000.

Compared to ownership of investment properties (see below), there are a few negative tax consequences of home ownership. For example, loss on the sale of a taxpayer's personal residence is not tax deductible. Repairs, maintenance, and other operating expenses of owning a principal place of residence are also not tax deductible.

TAX ISSUES REGARDING INVESTMENT PROPERTY

Though property taxes and interest on real estate loans are in general deductible, there are numerous regulations limiting such deductions.

Passive income. As a general rule, passive losses are deductible only to the extent of passive income. There are only two sources of *passive income*: (1) rental activity and (2) a business in which the taxpayer does not materially participate. Salaries, wages, interest, dividends, royalties, annuities, and gains on stocks and bonds are not considered passive income and, therefore, income from such sources may not be used to offset passive losses.

An exception to the passive loss limitation rules exists for an active investor. An *active investor* is someone who actively participates in the activities of a business invested in (for example, an individual who manages his or her own rental properties), as distinguished from a *passive investor*, who is someone who does not actively participate in the activities of a business invested in. Under this exception, an active investor who has adjusted gross income of $100,000 or less may deduct up to $25,000 of losses from passive rental real estate activities from personal income. If the taxpayer's adjusted gross income is between $100,000 and $150,000, the taxpayer loses $1 of their $25,000 maximum for every $2 above the $100,000. Passive losses that are unused in one tax year may be carried forward for possible use in subsequent years.

Investors who qualify as "real estate professionals" can benefit even further than the $25,000 exception discussed above. A **real estate professional** for this purpose is a real estate investor who (1) materially participates for at least 750 hours during the tax year in the real estate business and (2) spends more than 50% of his or her personal services performed in all businesses during the tax year in the real estate business that he or she materially participates in. An individual who so qualifies as a real estate professional would not have their rental income automatically treated as passive income, so the full amount of losses from rental income could be deducted from personal income.

Depreciation. Depreciation in the tax context (as distinguished from the appraisal context, which we discussed in Chapter 11) is a method of book accounting that in some sense reflects anticipated wear resulting from the use of improvements to property. Because depreciation is an accounting vehicle for reflecting replacement cost, it is technically referred to as **cost recovery**. Depreciation can only be used to benefit the improvements to investment or income property; it cannot be taken on owner-occupied residences or on the value of the portion of property attributable to land.

A **depreciation deduction** is an annual allowance for the depreciation of property. As a general rule, real property is depreciated in equal annual amounts over the depreciable life of the property, which for residential properties is 27½ years, and for nonresidential properties is 39 years. As an alternative, both residential and nonresidential properties may elect to use 40 years as their depreciable lives. The depreciation deduction can be used to reduce a taxpayer's ordinary income. However, numerous tax regulations (which we will not pursue here) place restrictions on how much depreciation can be taken to shelter non-rent income.

1031 exchanges. An owner of a property that has appreciated significantly in value may be reluctant to sell the property and have to pay the taxes associated with the gain from the sale. However, if properly structured, a property may be exchanged rather than sold and the tax liability deferred pursuant to Internal Revenue Code section 1031 (California has a similar code section).

To qualify as a **1031 exchange** (which is a tax-deferred exchange, though it is often misleadingly called a tax-free exchange), the property must be of "like kind" and held for productive use. In general, this means that any property held for business use or investment can be exchanged for any other like-kind property held for business use or investment (for example, a farm can be exchanged for an apartment building), though rules for exchanges of personal property (such as office furniture) are a bit more involved than are exchanges of real property. *A personal residence does not qualify for a 1031 exchange, nor do vacation or second homes, unless they are held as rentals for sufficient periods of time pursuant to IRS Rev Proc 2008-16.*

If a 1031 exchange has been properly structured, neither gain nor loss is recognized at the time of the exchange. If, on the other hand, a like-kind property is received in exchange along with **boot** (cash and/or unlike property), gain is recognized on the value of the boot, but losses are still excluded from recognition.

> **Example:** If an apartment building with a adjusted cost basis of $2 million is exchanged for an office building worth $2.3 million plus $100,000 cash (resulting in a $400,000 gain to the apartment building owner), the boot is $100,000 and will be recognized as taxable income at the time of the exchange. The $300,000 additional gain the apartment owner received due to the greater value of the like-kind property received will not be recognized at the time of the exchange, but the cost basis of the $2.3 million office building will be lowered to $2 million, so that the additional $300,000 gain will be recognized when the newly acquired property is eventually sold.

Many additional tax regulations can affect a 1031 exchange; therefore, a taxpayer considering making such an exchange should consult a tax specialist.

INSTALLMENT SALES

An installment sale is a sale in which the seller receives at least one payment in a later tax period and may report part of the gain from the sale (as well as any interest received) for the year in which a payment is received. An installment sale can confer tax benefits on the seller by spreading tax on the gain from the sale out over a number of years. This may be particularly beneficial to a seller who anticipates being in a lower tax bracket in the year or years subsequent to the sale.

The installment sales method cannot be used for the regular sale of inventory of personal property, sales of stock or securities traded on established securities markets, or dealer sales (sales of real property held for sale to customers in the ordinary course of a trade or business, or regular sales of the same type of personal property) even if the sale is made in installments. IRS Pub. 537.

STATE INCOME TAX

While there are a number of differences between California income tax rules and federal income tax rules, the two tax systems are generally in conformity.

ESTATE TAXES

Though California does not tax inheritances, the federal government taxes some decedents' estates. Individuals of relatively high net worth should consider seeking the advice of estate planners or tax specialists because there are ways reduce estate taxes.

GIFT TAXES

The federal government (but not California) taxes gifts of real and personal property when the value of the gifts exceeds a certain amount, which varies from year to year. In 2014, the first $14,000 of gifts by an individual to any other individual during the year period is not subject to gift tax. There is also a lifetime exemption that has varied considerably from year to year. In 2014, the first $5.34 million of lifetime gifts (including estates of decedents who die in 2014) above and beyond the annual exclusions are exempt from gift taxes. There is an unlimited exemption for gifts to a spouse who is a U.S. citizen.

DOCUMENTARY TRANSFER TAXES

When there is a transfer of real property, the deed must be recorded in the recorder's office of the county where the property is located. At the time of recordation, the county recorder collects a documentary transfer fee, which is a tax imposed by the county and/or city. The county transfer tax is $0.55 per $500 (or fraction thereof) of the transfer price and is uniform throughout the state. Cities may also impose a documentary transfer tax, which vary among the cities and can be much higher than the county transfer tax. San Francisco, being both a county and the city, has a combined county/city documentary transfer tax that varies from $5.00 per $1,000 to $25.00 per $1,000, depending on the sales price of the property.

The documentary transfer tax does not apply to the amount of a loan or other liens the seller had on the property that the buyer assumes responsibility for paying.

> **Example:** Suppose that a home sells for $750,000. The buyer pays $200,000 cash and assumes a $550,000 loan that the seller has on the property. In this case, the documentary transfer tax would be applied only to the $200,000. If only the county in

which the property lay had a documentary transfer tax of $1.10 per $1,000 (i.e., there was no city documentary transfer tax), the total documentary transfer bill would be $1.10 x 200 = $220. As a general rule, however, the documentary transfer tax is applied to the full sales price because loans and liens are usually paid off in escrow at the time of the sale.

Whether the buyer or seller pays the documentary transfer tax is negotiable between the buyer and seller. However, the general practice in Southern California is that the seller pays the documentary transfer tax; in Northern California, the buyer generally pays.

SUPPLEMENTAL PROPERTY TAX

A *supplemental tax assessment* is an event that occurs upon the sale of real property or completion of new construction on real property when the county assessor determines the current market value of the transferred property or the newly constructed real property and subtracts the prior assessed value from the current assessed value to obtain the net supplemental value that will be enrolled as a supplemental assessment. The increase (or decrease) in assessed value is then reflected in a prorated supplemental tax bill that covers the period from the first day of the month following the transfer or completion of construction to the end of the fiscal year, which runs from July 1 to June 30.

It is the responsibility of the seller of any residential property consisting of 4 or fewer dwelling units to deliver to a prospective purchaser a disclosure notice regarding supplemental tax assessments. CC §1102.6c.

Key Terms for Chapter 15

1031 exchange — under Internal Revenue Code section 1031, a tax-deferred exchange of "like kind" properties.

1031 exchange boot — cash and/or unlike property received in a 1031 exchange.

active investor — an investor who actively contributes to the management of the business invested in.

ad valorem — a Latin phrase meaning "according to value." The term is usually used regarding property taxation.

book sale — a "sale" for accounting purposes regarding tax-delinquent property; this "sale" does not entail an actual transfer property.

capital asset — permanent, non-inventory assets held for personal or investment purposes, such as householders' homes, household furnishings, stocks, bonds, land, buildings, and machinery.

capital gain — the amount by which the net sale proceeds from the sale of a capital asset exceeds the adjusted cost value of the asset.

cost recovery — a phrase referring to the tax concept of depreciation.

depreciation deduction — an annual tax allowance for the depreciation of property.

disabled veteran's exemption — and exemption that can reduce the tax liability of a qualified veteran's principal place of residence.

documentary transfer tax — a tax imposed by counties and cities on the transfer of real property within their jurisdictions.

fiscal year — in California, the fiscal year begins on July 1 and ends on June 30 of the following calendar year.

homeowner's exemption — and exemption of $7,000 from the assessed value of a homeowner's residence.

Improvement Bond Act of 1915 — this act permits local governments to issue bonds to finance subdivision street improvements. Owners of the subdivisions bear the cost of redeeming the bonds.

installment sale — a sale in which the seller receives at least one payment in a later tax period and may report part of the gain from the sale for the year in which a payment is received.

long-term capital gain — the capital gain on the sale of a capital asset that was held for a relatively long period of time, usually more than one year.

Mello-Roos Community Facilities Act — this act provides for the construction or improvement of a wide variety of facilities and services. Because the property tax burden on Mello-Roos districts can be quite high, a seller of a residential structure consisting of 4 or fewer dwellings that is subject to a lien of a Mello-Roos district must make a good-faith effort to obtain from the district a disclosure notice concerning the special assessment and give notice of the disclosure to prospective purchasers.

Mortgage Forgiveness Debt Relief Act of 2007 — this act allowed taxpayers to exclude from income debt that is canceled due to foreclosure, a short sale, or mortgage modification of their principal residence (not on a second home). After being extended several times, this Act expired at the end of 2013.

passive income — in general, income from either rental activity or from a business in which the taxpayer does not materially participate.

passive investor — an investor who does not actively contribute to the management of the business invested in.

property tax postponement program — a program in which the state pays all or part of the real property tax on a qualified senior's residence until he or she moves, sells the property, dies, or transfers title to the property. Repayment of all postponed taxes must be paid when the property is sold or title transferred.

Proposition 13 — an amendment to the California state Constitution that places a maximum ad valorem tax on real property equal to 1% of the "full cash value" plus a maximum increase of the assessed value of up to 2% per year, as long as the annual increase does not exceed the Consumer Price Index for that year.

Proposition 193 — this law extends Proposition 58 tax relief to certain transfers from grandparents to their grandchildren, but not transfers from grandchildren to their grandparents.

Proposition 58 — this law provides for an exclusion from reassessment when property is transferred between spouses. It also provides for an exclusion from reassessment of a transfer of a principal residence and transfers of the first $1 million of other real property between parent and child.

Proposition 60 — this law allows certain older persons to transfer the adjusted basis of their present principal residence to a replacement if the replacement is in the same county and is of equal or lesser value than the prior residence.

Proposition 8 — this law requires the county assessor to assess real property either at the property's Proposition 13 adjusted value or its current market value, whichever is less.

Proposition 90 — this law extends Proposition 60 to allow the purchase of a new residence in a different California county, but only if the county in which the new residence lies adopts Proposition 90.

real estate professional — a real estate investor who (1) materially participates for at least 750 hours during the tax year in the real estate business and (2) spends more than 50% of his or her personal services performed in all businesses during the tax year in the real estate business that he or she materially participates in.

short-term capital gain — the capital gain on the sale of a capital asset that was held for a relatively short period of time, usually one year or less.

Street Improvement Act of 1911 — this act provides local governments with the authority to issue bonds to improve streets and make other improvements to specific areas. Assessments on properties are due in equal installments during the term of the bonds, which can run for decades.

supplemental tax assessment — an event that occurs upon the sale of real property or completion of new construction on real property when the county assessor determines the current market value of the transferred property or the newly constructed real property and subtracts the prior assessed value from the current assessed value to obtain the net supplemental value that will be enrolled as a supplemental assessment. The increase (or decrease) in assessed value is then reflected in a prorated supplemental tax bill that covers the period from the first day of the month following the transfer or completion of construction to the end of the fiscal year, which runs from July 1 to June 30.

tax assessor — the county or city official who is responsible for appraising property.

tax auditor — the county or city official who maintains the county tax rolls.

tax collector — the county or city official who is responsible for collecting taxes.

tax deed — the deed given to the successful buyer at a tax sale. A tax deed conveys title free and clear from private liens, but not from certain tax liens or special assessment liens, or from easements and recorded restrictions.

veteran's exemption — and exemption of up to $4,000 from the assessed value of a qualified veteran's property.

Vrooman Street Act of 1885 — this act provides local governments with authority to construct streets, sewers, and other improvements. Funds for these improvements are secured by the issuance of bonds, which are redeemed by assessing the properties benefited.

Quiz for Chapter 15

1. As a general rule, for tax purposes the depreciable life of a residential property is considered to be
   a. 27 years
   b. 27½ years
   c. 39 years
   d. 39½ years

2. County budgets are established and property taxes for the county are set by
   a. the Franchise Tax Board
   b. the county board of assessors
   c. the state legislature
   d. none of the above

3. An installment sale can confer tax benefits on the seller by
   a. recognizing all of the gain in the tax year the sale was made
   b. allowing the buyer to use 40 years as the depreciable life of the property
   c. allowing the seller to utilize what the seller believes to be the lower tax rates in the year of the sale than will be available in subsequent years
   d. none of the above

4. A residential property that is owner-occupied as of the lien date qualifies for a homeowner's exemption of how much from the assessed value of the property for the current fiscal tax year?
   a. $4,000
   b. $7,000
   c. $10,000
   d. none of the above

5. Except in San Francisco, the county documentary transfer tax is
   a. $0.50 per $500 (or fraction thereof) of the transfer price
   b. $0.60 per $500 (or fraction thereof) of the transfer price
   c. $0.75 per $500 (or fraction thereof) of the transfer price
   d. none of the above

6. A tax deed
   a. conveys title free and clear from all liens and other encumbrances
   b. is the deed the buyer at a public auction of tax-defaulted property receives
   c. both a and b
   d. neither a nor b

7. As a general rule, passive losses are
   a. deductible only to the extent of passive income
   b. generated by rental activity
   c. both a and b
   d. neither a nor b

8. A disabled veteran's exemption can apply to what kind of property?
   a. a principal place of residence
   b. any real property
   c. any real or personal property
   d. none of the above

9. To qualify as a 1031 exchange, the properties must be
   a. depreciated over a period of 40 years
   b. of like kind
   c. real property not for personal use
   d. real property for personal use

10. Pursuant to Proposition 13, the assessed value of real property for property tax purposes may be
    a. increased by 2% per year
    b. increased by up to be CPI for the relevant fiscal year
    c. may be decreased if property values decrease
    d. none of the above

11. If an office building with a adjusted cost basis of $10 million is traded in a 1031 exchange for an apartment building worth $10.5 million plus $300,000 cash, how much will the original owner of the office building recognize as taxable income due to the exchange at the time of the exchange?
    a. $300,000
    b. $500,000
    c. $800,000
    d. $0

12. A condo is purchased for $720,100 cash. How much is the documentary transfer tax on this purchase if only the county (not the city) in which the property lies has a documentary transfer tax?
    a. $792
    b. $793
    c. $1,440
    d. none of the above

13. Which of the following least belongs with the others?
    a. Mello-Roos Community Facilities Act of 1982
    b. Proposition 13
    c. Street Improvement Act of 1911
    d. Improvement Bond Act of 1915

14. Federal income taxes
    a. tax property "according to value"

b. provide an exemption of $7,000 from the assessed value of a homeowner's residence

c. provide that passive income can, in general, be deducted from ordinary income

d. none of the above

15. Tom, single and 35 years of age, has lived in his owner-occupied personal residence for the past three years and has just sold his home. He may exclude how much from capital gains on the sale?
    a. $0
    b. $250,000
    c. $500,000
    d. none of the above

16. The second installment of real property taxes becomes delinquent
    a. January 1
    b. February 1
    c. December 10
    d. none of the above

17. Which of the following provides for an exclusion from reassessment when property is transferred between spouses?
    a. Proposition 58
    b. Proposition 193
    c. Proposition 60
    d. Proposition 90

18. José actively participates in the management of an apartment building that he owns. His adjusted gross income for the current fiscal year is $120,000. Under the exemption to the passive loss limitation rules that exists for active investors, José may deduct up to how much of his losses from passive rental income from the apartment building?
    a. $15,000
    b. $5,000
    c. $25,000
    d. none of the above

19. The documentary transfer tax is
    a. usually applicable to the full sales price
    b. usually not applicable to the full sales price
    c. not applied to the amount of a loan the buyer assumes
    d. both a and c

20. Tax on real property for the fiscal year that begins July 1, 2013, becomes a lien on
    a. July 1, 2013
    b. November 1, 2013
    c. January 1, 2014
    d. none of the above

21. Which of the following allows certain older persons to transfer the adjusted basis of their present principal residence to a replacement if the replacement is in the same county and is of equal or lesser value than the prior residence?
    a. Proposition 8
    b. Proposition 60
    c. Proposition 58
    d. Proposition 193

22. An active investor with adjusted gross income of $150,000 may deduct from personal income what amount of passive losses from passive rental real estate activities?
    a. $0
    b. $25,000
    c. $50,000
    d. none of the above

23. Which of the following are incorrect?
    a. the veteran's exemption provides an exemption of up to $4,000
    b. the second installment of property taxes is due February 10
    c. both a and b
    d. neither a nor b

24. For income tax purposes, a homeowner may deduct which of the following?
    a. homeowner's association dues
    b. property taxes
    c. roof repairs
    d. all of the above

25. Because of a change of employment, a married couple moves and sells their personal residence after having lived there for only 18 months. Assuming that they have never before sold a personal residence, they can obtain an exclusion from capital gains tax of how much?
    a. $0
    b. $250,000
    c. $500,000
    d. none of the above

Answers for Chapter 15 Quiz

1. b. As a general rule, for tax purposes the depreciable life of residential property is considered to be 27½ years.

2. d. County budgets are established and property taxes for the county are set by the county board of supervisors.

3. d. An installment sale can confer tax benefits on the seller by spreading tax on the gain from the sale out over a number of years. This may be particularly beneficial to a seller who anticipates being in a lower tax bracket in the year or years subsequent to the sale.

4. b. Every residential property that is owner-occupied as of January 1 qualifies for a homeowner's exemption of $7,000 from the assessed value for the next the fiscal tax year.

5. d. The county documentary transfer tax is $0.55 per $500 (or fraction thereof) of the transfer price.

6. b. A tax deed conveys title free and clear from private liens, but not from certain tax liens or special assessment liens, or from easements and recorded restrictions.

7. c. As a general rule, passive losses are deductible only to the extent of passive income. There are only two sources of passive income: (1) rental activity and (2) a business in which the taxpayer does not materially participate. Salaries, wages, interest, dividends, royalties, annuities, and gains on stocks and bonds are not considered passive income and, therefore, income from such sources may not be used to offset passive losses.

8. a. The Disabled Veteran's Exemption can reduce the tax liability of a qualified veteran on property that is the principal place of residence of the veteran or the unmarried surviving spouse of a qualified veteran.

9. b. To qualify as a 1031 exchange, the property must be of like kind. In general, this means that any property held for business use or investment can be exchanged for any other like-kind property held for business use or investment (for example, a farm can be exchanged for an apartment building).

10. d. Proposition 13 allows for a maximum increase of the assessed value of up to 2% per year, as long as the annual increase does not exceed the Consumer Price Index (CPI).

11.a. The $300,000 boot in this exchange will be recognized immediately as taxable income, but the other $500,000 gain will not be recognized until the new owner of the office building sells it.

12.d. The documentary transfer tax would be $0.55 per $500 (or fraction thereof). $720,100 ÷ $500 = 1,440.2, so the documentary transfer tax would be 1441 x $0.55 = $792.55.

13.b. Answers a, c, and d are all laws relating to special assessments that can raise the tax burden on property over the ad valorem property tax limited by Proposition 13.

14.d. Federal income taxes do none of the things stated in answers a, b, or c.

15.b. An individual of any age who sells a property that has been his or her principal place of residence for at least 2 out of the 5 years prior to the sale may exclude $250,000 from capital gains on the sale.

16.d. The second installment of real property taxes becomes delinquent on April 10.

17.a. Proposition 58 provides for an exclusion from reassessment when property is transferred between spouses.

18.a. If an active investor's adjusted gross income is between $100,000 and $150,000, the taxpayer loses $1 of their $25,000 maximum for every $2 above the $100,000.

19.d. As a general rule, the documentary transfer tax is applied to the full sales price because loans and liens are usually paid off in escrow at the time of the sale.

20.d. Tax on real property for the fiscal year that begins July 1, 2013, becomes a lien on January 1, 2013.

21.b. Proposition 60 allows certain older persons to transfer the adjusted basis of their present principal residence to a replacement if the replacement is in the same county and is of equal or lesser value than the prior residence. To qualify, the transferor or the transferor's spouse must be 55 years of age or older at the time of the transfer.

22.a. An active investor who has adjusted gross income of $100,000 or less may deduct up to $25,000 of losses from passive rental real estate activities from personal income. If the taxpayer's adjusted gross income is between $100,000 and $150,000, the taxpayer loses $1 of their $25,000 maximum for every $2 above the $100,000.

23.b. The second installment of property taxes is due February 1.

24.b. Repairs, maintenance, and other operating expenses of owning a principal place of residence are not tax deductible.

25.d. If a personal residence was not the principal residence for the requisite 2-year period, individuals and married couples can still obtain a partial exclusion if the sale was necessitated by a change of employment, health problems, or other unforeseen circumstances, such as divorce or a death in the family. In such cases, an exclusion based on the portion of the requisite 2-year period can be taken. Therefore, the exclusion for this married couple would be 3/4 of $500,000 = $375,000.

Home Styles and Benefits of Investment vs. Renting

As we discussed in Chapter 11, Real Estate Valuation and Appraisal, one of the most important aspects of a home's market value is determined by its functional utility — its ability to provide adequate living conditions. Functional obsolescence, on the other hand, results (1) from deficiencies arising from poor architectural designs, out-dated style or equipment, and changes in utility demand, such as for larger houses with more garage space, and (2) from over-improvements, where the cost of the improvements was more than the addition to market value.

Both of these concepts — functional utility and functional obsolescence — in large part result from the architectural design as well as from the construction materials and workmanship that go into a finished, marketable house, condo, or mobile home. It is for these reasons that not only appraisers, but also real estate agents should have a working knowledge of home design and construction.

Pluses of home design and construction include:

- use of quality materials;
- rooms of proper proportions;
- all of the bedrooms having their own bathrooms and closets;
- bedrooms that do not open to entertainment or guest areas;
- having the master bedroom on the first floor if the home is in a retirement community;
- a half bath for guests near the foyer;
- kitchen with a dining area separate from the dining room; and so on.

Additionally, it is a plus for a house to be of approximately the same size and style as others in the immediate neighborhood — an "odd duck" may run into resistance when it comes time to sell. Also, architectural styles can lose their appeal because of changing tastes of homeowners. Thus, real estate agents should be familiar with home architectural styles and be knowledgeable as to how styles in their areas affect market price.

Fig. 16.1

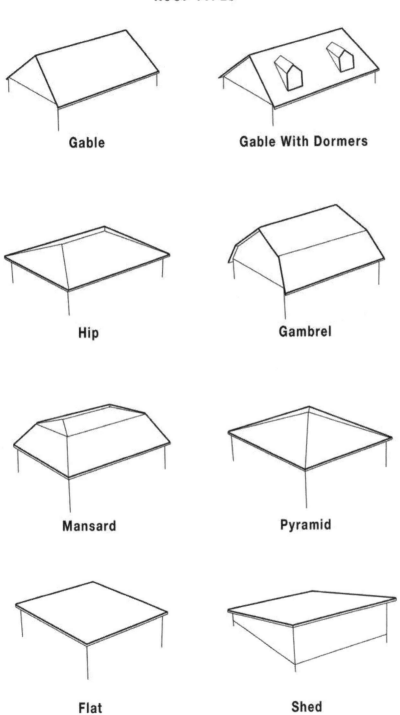

ROOF TYPES

Gable

Gable With Dormers

Hip

Gambrel

Mansard

Pyramid

Flat

Shed

ONE-STORY, ONE AND ONE-HALF STORY, TWO-STORY, AND SPLIT-LEVEL HOUSES: A COMPARISON

One-story. A one-story house has all of its living area on the ground floor, and may or may not have a basement. A one-story home is the simplest to construct and maintain, and is generally the preferred construction for families with young children or elderly parents or grandparents, as falls on stairs are a significant source of in-home injuries. However, one-story homes have a larger footprint per square foot of living space than two-story homes, so are likely to cost more per square foot, especially in areas with high land prices.

One and one-half story. A one and one-half story house typically has a steeply pitched roof, usually with dormers, that allows for the attic to be used for extra living space.

Two-story. Because up to twice as much living space can be obtained from one foundation, one roof, and the same amount of land area, two-story construction can result in lower per square foot cost. Two-story houses can also be "greener" due to the lower surface-area-to-volume ratio that makes heating and air-conditioning more efficient. However, the inconvenience and possible danger of stairs, as well as the wasted space taken up by stairs, present significant disadvantages of a two-story house.

Split-level. Split-level houses usually have two to four levels, each level being separated from the next by a short flight of stairs. Split-level homes offer some of the advantages of a two-story house (such as privacy that is appreciated by middle or high-school children and families with live in parents or in-laws), but with far fewer steps to negotiate. This style of home construction is also well-suited for the sloping topographies that characterize so much of California land area.

HOUSE ARCHITECTURAL STYLES

The following are brief descriptions of several house style archetypes. Many houses are hybrid, however, the architect having borrowed and/or modified features from several archetypes.

Cape Cod and Cape Ann Colonial. Typically a fairly small house with steeply pitched gable or gambrel wood-shingled roof with little overhang; usually one-story or one and one-half stories with dormers; central front door with multi-paned windows symmetrically balanced on each side.

New England Colonial. Rectangular or square, box-shaped giving maximum usable space; one and one-half or two stories; wood-shingled gable roof; multi-paned windows placed in a balanced, symmetrical fashion on both sides of the central front door.

Dutch Colonial. Gambrel roof, often with flared eaves; symmetrical front with central front door; one-story or one and one-half story with dormers, or two-story, also with dormers.

Georgian Colonial. Simple, usually two-story house; strict symmetrical arrangements; central front door with flattened columns on each side; chimneys on both sides of the house.

Southern Colonial. Large two-or-three-story house with a row of colonnades across the front; roof overhangs the colonnades and portico; strict symmetry with central front door.

French Normandy. Typically has stone exterior with asymmetrical plan; round tower with conical roof; steeply pitched roof.

French Provincial. Has no tower (unlike French Normandy); tall second-story windows, often rising above the eaves; steeply pitched roof; central front door with windows symmetrically balanced on each side; windows usually have shutters.

True Spanish. Red-tile roof; enclosed patios; stucco walls; and wrought-iron ornamentation around doors and windows.

Monterey Spanish. Two-story; stucco; low-pitched, red-tile gable roof; cantilevered second-story balconies; wrought-iron ornamental railings.

Modern and Contemporary. Flat or low-pitched roof; clean lines; avoids superfluous ornamentation; a lot of glass; emphasis on openness conducive to indoor/outdoor living.

California Bungalow. Often one or one and one-half stories; low sloping roof; typically has a porch covered overhead with a roof supported by solid beams.

California Ranch. One-story; low roofline; often L-shaped; attached garage; generally stucco with wood trim; vaulted ceilings with exposed beams.

GLOSSARY OF CONSTRUCTION TERMS

The following is a brief glossary of terms relating to house construction that real estate agents should be familiar with.

anchor bolt — a bolt inserted into concrete that secures structural members to the foundation.

beam — a horizontal member of a building attached to framing, rafters, etc., that transversely supports a load.

bearing wall — a wall that supports structures (such as the roof or upper floors) above it. In condominiums, non-bearing walls are owned by the individual condominium owners, whereas bearing walls usually are property owned in common.

board foot — a unit of measure of the volume of lumber, equivalent to the volume of lumber of 1 square foot and 1 inch thick; 144 cubic inches.

BTU (British Thermal Unit) — A measure of heating (or cooling) capacity equivalent to the amount of heat required to raise the temperature of 1 pound of water 1° Fahrenheit (from 39°F to 40°F).

caulking — a putty-like material used to seal cracks and joints to make tight against leakage of air or water, as in making windows watertight.

collar beam — a beam connecting pairs of opposite rafters well above the attic floor.

column — a circular or rectangular vertical structural member that supports the weight of the structure above it.

conduit — a (usually) metal pipe in which electrical wiring is installed.

crawlspace — the space between the ground and the first floor that permits access beneath the building.

dormer — a projecting structure built out from a sloping roof that is used to provide windows and additional headroom for the upper floor.

drywall — prefabricated sheets or panels nailed to studs to form an interior wall or partition.

eaves — the overhang of a roof that projects over an exterior wall of a house.

EER and SEER — Air-conditioners have an efficiency rating that states the ratio of the cooling capacity (how many BTUs per hour) to the power drawn (in watts). For room air conditioners the ratio is the EER (energy efficiency ratio); for central air conditioners the rating is the SEER (seasonal energy efficiency ratio). The higher the EER or SEER, the greater the efficiency of the air-conditioning unit. Significant savings in electricity costs can be obtained by installing more efficient air-conditioning units.

fire stop — a block or board placed horizontally between studs to form a tight closure of a concealed space, thereby decreasing drafts and retarding the spread of fire and smoke.

flashing — sheet metal or other material used in roof and wall construction to prevent water from entering.

flue — a channel in a chimney through which flame and smoke passes upward to the outer air.

footing — concrete poured on solid ground that provides support for the foundation, chimney, or support columns. Footing should be placed below the frost line to prevent movement.

gable roof — a roof with two sloping sides but not sloping ends.

gambrel roof — a roof sloped on two sides, each side having a steep lower slope and a flatter upper slope.

hip roof — a sloping roof that rises from all four sides of the house.

jamb — the vertical sides of a door or window that contact the door or sash.

joist — one of a series of parallel heavy horizontal timbers used to support floor or ceiling loads.

moldings — patterned strips, usually of wood, used to provide ornamental finish to cornices, bases, windows, and door jambs.

mudsill — for houses built on a concrete slab, the wood sills that are bolted to all sides of the slab, providing a means of attaching portions of the framing for the house to the foundation.

pitch — the degree of inclination or slope of a roof.

plaster — a mixture of lime or gypsum, sand, water, and fiber that is applied to walls and ceilings and that hardens into a smooth coating.

pyramid roof — a hip roof that has no ridge.

rafter — one of a series of parallel sloping timbers that extend from the ridgeboard to the exterior walls, providing support for the roof.

reinforced concrete — concrete poured around steel bars or metal netting to increase its ability to withstand tensile, shear, and compression stresses.

ridgeboard — a horizontal board placed on edge at the apex of a roof to which the upper ends of the rafters are attached.

R-value — a measure of the resistance of insulation to heat transfer. The FTC requires sellers of new homes to disclose the R-value of each home's insulation. The higher the R-value, the greater is the effectiveness of the insulation.

sash — frames that contain one or more windowpanes.

SEER — (see EER)

sill — the board or metal forming the lower side of the frame for a window or door; the lowest part of the frame of a house, resting on the foundation and providing the base for the studs.

studs — vertical wood or metal members in wall or partition framing that serve as the main support for upper floors or roof. Studs are usually placed 16 to 24 inches apart.

CONDOMINIUMS

As we discussed in Chapter 14, a condominium is a residential unit owned in severalty, the boundaries of which are usually walls, floors, and ceilings, and an undivided interest in portions of the real property, such as halls, elevators, and recreational facilities.

Advantages of Condominium Ownership

Ease of maintenance. An owner need not worry about mowing the lawn, shoveling snow, weeding, landscaping, cleaning the pool, taking care of the roof, etc. The burden of accomplishing these tasks is the responsibility of the condominium homeowner's association or management board.

Tax benefits. Condominium owners receive the same tax benefits (mortgage interest and property tax deductions, homeowner's exemption, homeowner's exclusion, etc.) as do owners of single-family residences.

Appreciation. Historically, homeowners, including condominium owners, have enjoyed significant long-term appreciation in their investments in their primary places of residence. Whether this long-term upward trend will continue is a matter of conjecture.

Disadvantages of Condominium Ownership

Homeowner's association fees. All of that maintenance (mowing the lawn, cleaning the pool, etc.) that a condominium owner is free from performing must to be paid for — through homeowner's association fees. These fees must be high enough to also pay for electricity and insurance for common areas, professional management of the property, legal and audit fees, contributions to a reserve for maintenance and/or replacement of expensive property items such as elevators, roof, balconies, heating and air-conditioning systems, and so on.

Restrictions. Condominium projects are managed by homeowner's associations or management boards that place restrictions (CC&Rs) on the use of the property. Some of these restrictions might prohibit pets, renting or subletting, or limit the kinds of improvements owners can make to their units. Prospective buyers should make a point of becoming acquainted with such restrictions that pertain to any condominium complex in which they are considering investing.

Less privacy. As compared to a single-family house, there is less privacy in the communal living of a condominium complex. Such close proximity to others often also comes with increased noise.

<u>Proximity to renters</u>. Most condominiums permit renting and some condominium projects have a high renter/owner ratio. As renters may not exercise the same degree of care of the property as do owners, prospective buyers should inquire as to the renter/owner ratio of any condominium complex in which they are considering investing.

MOBILE AND MANUFACTURED HOMES

Though the California Health and Safety Code (HSC) makes a distinction between "manufactured home" and "mobile home," the term "mobile home" is generally used for both. Technically, a **manufactured home** *"means a structure that was constructed on or after June 15, 1976, is transportable in one or more sections, is eight body feet or more in width, or 40 body feet or more in length, in the traveling mode, or, when erected on site, is 320 or more square feet, is built on a permanent chassis and designed to be used as a single-family dwelling with or without a foundation when connected to the required utilities..."* HSC §18007(a). A **mobile home** is essentially the same except that it was constructed prior to June 15, 1976. Probably the most important distinction is that manufactured homes are factory-built on or after June 15, 1976 to HUD standards, whereas mobile homes are "pre-HUD Code" homes.

Tax on Mobile and Manufactured Homes

Manufactured and mobile homes are subject either to vehicle "in-lieu" license fees or to local property taxes. Before July 1, 1980, manufactured and mobile homes not secured to permanent foundations were treated as motor vehicles and charged an in-lieu fee. In 1980, California Adopted the Mobilehome Property Tax Law, which provides that all new and most used manufactured and mobile homes purchased on or after July 1, 1980 be subject to property tax like conventional homes. Additionally, manufactured homes come out of the factory as personal property and must be registered with the Department of Housing and Community Development (HCD) before being sold in California. When first sold, a manufactured home is subject to sales tax. Manufactured homes become real property once they are fixed to a permanent foundation.

Sales of Manufactured Homes by Real Estate Brokers

A person who sells manufactured homes must possess a valid HCD Occupational License. An exception to this requirement is that real estate brokers licensed by the CalBRE may sell manufactured homes that have been registered with the HCD or have been installed on a permanent foundation pursuant to Health and Safety Code §18551. However, a real estate broker who maintains a place of business where two or more manufactured homes or mobile homes are displayed and offered for sale by the broker must obtain the HCD Occupational License

Escrows for Manufactured or Mobile Homes

Before a manufactured or mobile home becomes real property by being affixed to the land, they are escrowed as personal property, which is quite different from the escrow process for standard residences and is usually handled by an escrow officer who specializes in manufactured and mobile home transfers. Once manufactured or mobile homes become real property, they are sold and escrowed like other standard homes.

FACTORY-BUILT HOUSING

The primary distinction between a manufactured home and a factory-built home is that a manufactured home is manufactured as a vehicle on a permanent chassis, whereas a *factory-built home* is specifically manufactured to conform to the local building codes of the site, transported on flatbed trucks, and assembled on the site, affixing it to a permanent foundation. However, like manufactured homes, factory-built homes are personal property until they become affixed to a permanent foundation, and, therefore, having a real estate license does not authorize an agent to sell them from the factory or off a sales lot. If a real estate agent wishes to sell factory-built homes while the homes are still personal property, the agent must obtain the HCD Occupational License.

SECOND HOMES

As with other investments, there are advantages and disadvantages to consider before investing in a second home.

Advantages of Owning a Second Home

- In the right location, a second home can be used as a vacation home — a summer cottage near a lake or ocean beach, a winter chalet near a ski area, a cabin near a favorite hunting area. Trips to such vacation homes can become a family tradition, the properties being handed down generation to generation.
- Like a principal place of residence, the second home can become an appreciating asset.
- Second homes can become primary residences if after retirement the former primary residence is sold.
- Though there is potential to obtain rental income from a second home, the tax accounting for such rental income is quite complicated (probably requiring the expense of a tax accountant). Many people overestimate

the amount of income they will receive from renting their second home, so it is advisable to think twice (and probably consult an investment advisor) before relying on such income to pay the many expenses of owning a second home.

Disadvantages of Owning a Second Home

- Property taxes are often higher in or near resort areas than in residential areas.
- As we have seen since the housing crisis began in 2008, homes of all kinds can be a depreciating — not an appreciating — asset.
- Insurance rates are usually higher for second homes. Homes that are often vacant are more subject to loss due to break-ins and to such causes as leaking roofs or burst water pipes, which can cause significant damage if not caught and remedied quickly.
- Likewise, mortgage interest rates are nearly always higher for second homes. Lenders know that a borrower who gets into financial trouble is much more likely to protect his or her principal residence than a second home. Therefore, the interest on a mortgage for second home is often a half point to a full point above the rate for primary residences, the percentage down payment is likely to be higher for a second home, and the mortgage insurance is also likely to be higher.
- A second home too far away for the owner to manage can incur substantial management fees.

BUY OR RENT?

Benefits of Owning a Home

- **Pride of ownership**. This is probably the single greatest factor that motivates people to purchase their own home.
- **Appreciation**. Traditionally, homes have been a safe investment and appreciate at a rate slightly greater than the rate of inflation.
- **Favorable tax treatment**. As we have discussed in prior chapters, homeowners enjoy several tax advantages: mortgage interest deduction, property tax deduction, capital gains treatment, capital gains exclusion, and homeowner's and other possible exemptions.
- **Equity use and protection**. As the equity in one's home increases over time, that equity can be used as a source of obtaining a home equity loan. There is also the homestead exemption for homeowners who run into financial trouble and have judgment liens placed against their properties.
- **Stability**. Homeowners generally have long-term loans that permit them to plan quite accurately what their non-maintenance expenses will be

years into the future. Renters, on the other hand, usually have short-term leases, leaving them subject to unpredictable rent increases as well as to the possibility of being forced to move when the lease term expires.

Benefits of Renting

- **<u>Low maintenance cost</u>**. Residential leases typically provide that most repairs and maintenance to the property are the responsibility of the landlord.
- **<u>Flexibility</u>**. It is easier and less expensive for a renter than for homeowner to move, whether for financial, job, or other reasons (such as objectionable neighbors). As we have discussed, there are substantial transaction costs associated with buying and selling a home, and often it takes a considerable period of time to consummate a transfer.
- **<u>No market risk</u>**. Home prices can go up — and they can go down. Renters are never forced into foreclosure.
- **<u>Low cash outlay</u>**. Closing on a house purchase usually requires a much greater cash outlay than does a first-and-last month deposit for a lease.

The bottom line is that unless you plan on staying in a home for at least 5 years, unless your job is secure, unless you have enough cash for a significant down payment, and unless you are reasonably confident that the home and the neighborhood will be suitable for your family long-term, it is probably better to rent.

Key Terms for Chapter 16

factory-built home — a home specifically manufactured to conform to the local building codes of the site, transported on flatbed trucks rather than being built on a permanent chassis, and assembled on the site where it is affixed it to a permanent foundation.

manufactured home — a structure that was constructed on or after June 15, 1976 and built to HUD standards; transportable in one or more sections; eight body feet or more in width, or 40 body feet or more in length, in the traveling mode, or, when erected on site, is 320 or more square feet; built on a permanent chassis.

mobile home — a structure that was constructed before June 15, 1976; transportable in one or more sections; eight body feet or more in width, or 40 body feet or more in length, in the traveling mode, or, when erected on site, is 320 or more square feet; built on a permanent chassis.

Quiz for Chapter 16

1. Functional utility refers to
   a. a determination of value based on sales of comparable properties
   b. a home's ability to provide adequate living conditions
   c. supply and demand
   d. the percentage return on investment

2. A house having two to four levels, each level being separated from the next by a short flight of stairs, is a
   a. one and one-half story house
   b. two-story house
   c. factory-built home
   d. none of the above

3. EER (energy efficiency ratio) refers to
   a. a measure of heating capacity
   b. the measure of the resistance of insulation to heat transfer
   c. compression stresses
   d. none of the above

4. A sloping roof that rises from all four sides of a house is a
   a. gambrel roof
   b. hip roof
   c. gable roof
   d. shed roof

5. One board foot is
   a. 144 in.³ of lumber
   b. 24 in.³ of lumber
   c. 12 in.³ of lumber
   d. none of the above

6. Drywall consists of
   a. a mixture of lime, sand, water, and fiber that is applied to walls and ceilings
   b. one of a series of timbers that extends from the ridgeboard to the exterior walls
   c. the vertical sides of a door or window that contact the door or sash
   d. none of the above

7. A projecting structure built out from a sloping roof that is used to provide windows and additional headroom for the upper floor is called
   a. flashing
   b. eaves
   c. dormer

    d. ridgeboard

8. The horizontal board placed on edge at the apex of a roof to which the upper ends of the rafters are attached is the
    a. collar beam
    b. dormer
    c. flue
    d. none of the above

9. A newly built manufactured home
    a. must be registered with the Department of Housing and Community Development before it can be sold in California
    b. comes out of the factory as personal property
    c. both a and b
    d. neither a nor b

10. A real estate broker may sell a manufactured home that
    a. has been installed on a permanent foundation
    b. has been registered with the Department of Housing and Community Development
    c. either a or b
    d. neither a nor b

Answers for Chapter 16 Quiz

1. b. Functional utility refers to a home's ability to provide adequate living conditions.
2. d. A house having two to four levels, each level being separated from the next by a short flight of stairs, is a split-level house.
3. d. Energy efficiency ratio (EER) refers to the ratio of the cooling capacity to power consumption of a room air conditioner.
4. b. A hip roof is a sloping roof that rises from all four sides of the house.
5. a. One board foot is 144 in.^{3} of lumber.
6. d. Drywall consists of prefabricated sheets or panels nailed to studs to form an interior wall or partition.
7. c. A dormer is a projecting structure built out from a sloping roof that is used to provide windows and additional headroom for the upper floor.
8. d. A ridgeboard is the horizontal board placed on edge at the apex of a roof to which the upper ends of the rafters are attached.
9. c. A newly built manufactured home comes out of the factory as personal property and must be registered with the Department of Housing and Community Development before it can be sold in California.
10. c. A person who sells manufactured homes must possess a valid Department of Housing and Community Development (HCD) Occupational License. An exception to this requirement is that real estate brokers licensed by the CalBRE may sell manufactured homes that have been registered with the HCD or have been installed on a permanent foundation pursuant to Health and Safety Code §18551.

Obtaining and Maintaining a Real Estate License

Having a real estate license can open doors to many opportunities. You can help people acquire their dream home, which will probably be the largest purchase they make in their lives. You can set your own work schedule, build your own base of clients, and decide how best to market your services.

You can choose your own specialty. If you want to sell, buy, or lease real estate, you can specialize in residential, commercial, or industrial real estate. Additionally, as we have discussed throughout this text, being a real estate licensee also opens up other opportunities, such as becoming a mortgage loan broker or a property manager. There is one more opportunity available to real estate licensees that we will briefly explore: selling and buying business opportunities.

BUSINESS OPPORTUNITIES

A ***business opportunity*** involves the sale or lease of the assets of an existing business enterprise or opportunity, including the goodwill of the business or opportunity, enabling the purchaser or lessee to begin a business. B&PC §10030. ***Goodwill*** is an intangible asset derived from the expectation of continued public patronage. Since 1966 when the merger of real estate and business opportunity licenses occurred, a real estate license has been required to negotiation to buy, sell, or lease a business opportunity or to negotiate a loan secured directly or collaterally by liens on a business opportunity. As a general rule, if real estate is involved as part of a transfer of a business opportunity, a bill of sale is prepared for the transfer of all personal property, a deed is prepared for the transfer of the real estate, and the separate and concurrent transactions are processed by separate and concurrent escrows. Unlike a deed, a bill of sale is not usually recorded; therefore, public records may not disclose the condition of title to personal property.

The transfer of a business opportunity requires certain documentation additional to the documentation necessary to transfer only real estate: a balance sheet showing the assets, liabilities, and net worth of the business; and a profit and loss statement showing the gross income, expenses, and net worth (total assets minus total liabilities) of the business during some period of time.

Bulk Sales and the Uniform Commercial Code

Article 6 of the **Uniform Commercial Code (UCC)** pertains to bulk sales of a business. A **bulk sale** is a sale, not in the ordinary course of the seller's business, of more than half of the value of the seller's inventory as of the date of the bulk sale agreement (UCC §6-102). In a bulk sale situation, the *buyer* (not the seller) must give notice to the public of the proposed transaction at least 12 business days before the sale is completed by recordation of a notice of intent to sell in bulk in each county recorder's office where any of the merchandise is located. Additionally, this notice must be published at least once and at least 12 days before the bulk sale is consummated in a newspaper of general circulation in the judicial district in which the property is located.

This notice of intent to sell in bulk is intended to give creditors of the business an opportunity to file claims before the seller can sell the assets and vanish with the proceeds. In the event of noncompliance with this notice requirement, the *buyer* is liable to creditors who had valid claims against the business before the bulk transfer occurred. The statute of limitations period for such creditor claims against the buyer is one year from the date of the bulk sale or, if the transfer was concealed, one year from the date of discovery of the transfer by the creditor.

California Sales and Use Tax

The buyer of a business must withhold from the seller enough of the sales price to cover any outstanding sales and use tax liability (which results from the sale or purchase of tangible personal property) of the seller (or any former owner) of the business due to the business's activities. The purchaser of the business will be released from the obligation to withhold part of the sales price only upon receiving from the Board of Equalization a certificate (known as a **certificate of clearance**) stating that no taxes, interest, or penalties are due from the seller or from any previous owner of the business.

Alcoholic Beverage Control Act

Pursuant to the Alcoholic Beverage Control Act, any person engaged in the business of manufacturing, selling, or distributing alcoholic beverages must have a state license to do so from the Department of Alcoholic Beverage Control. Consequently, any sale of a business that has alcoholic beverages as part of its inventory must include the transfer of a valid liquor license. A prospective purchaser of a business that involves alcoholic beverages should not make any investment in the business until the prospective purchaser has applied for, and received, approval for the assumption of the alcoholic beverage license.

OBTAINING A REAL ESTATE SALESPERSON LICENSE

Anyone wishing to obtain a real estate salespersons license must qualify for and pass an examination consisting of 150 multiple-choice questions. After passing the examination, the prospective licensee must submit a license application to, and be approved by, the CalBRE. The qualifications for an original salesperson license are:

1. **Age**. Must be 18 years of age or older.
2. **Residence**. Though California residency is not required, proof of legal presence in the United States is required.
3. **Honesty**. Failure to disclose any criminal violation or disciplinary action by a governmental authority in the applicant's entire life history may result in the denial (or revocation) of a license. Conviction of a crime may also result the denial (or revocation) of a license.
4. **Education**. Successful completion of three college-level courses:
   a) **Real Estate Principles;**
   b) **Real Estate Practice;** and
   c) one of the following:
      - Real Estate Appraisal
      - Property Management
      - Real Estate Finance
      - Real Estate Economics
      - Legal Aspects of Real Estate
      - Real Estate Office Administration
      - General Accounting
      - Business Law
      - Escrows
      - Mortgage Loan Brokering and Lending
      - Computer Applications in Real Estate
      - Common Interest Developments
5. **Experience**. There is no experience requirement.

Note. Members of the California State Bar are exempt from the above education requirements. Attorneys licensed in other states as well as individuals with an LL.B. or J.D. degree may submit evidence of the license or degree for evaluation by the CalBRE and are generally found to qualify on the basis of the college-level course requirements.

Evidence of satisfaction of the above requirements must be submitted to the CalBRE on your application to take the examination, which application must be approved before your examination will be scheduled. Once you pass the examination, you must complete and submit an application for your license. The application must include the applicable (nonrefundable) fee, your Social Security number, fingerprints, and proof of legal presence in the United States.

OBTAINING A REAL ESTATE BROKER LICENSE

Anyone wishing to obtain a real estate broker license must qualify for and pass an examination consisting of 200 multiple-choice questions. After passing the examination, the prospective licensee must submit a license application to, and be approved by, the CalBRE.

On August 27, 2012, the Governor signed a bill that amends B&PC §10150.6, changing the work experience qualification requirement to obtain a real estate broker license. Effective January 1, 2013, the qualifications for original broker examination applicants are:

1. **Age.** Must be 18 years of age or older.
2. **Residence**. Though California residency is not required, proof of legal presence in the United States is required.
3. **Honesty**. Failure to disclose any criminal violation or disciplinary action by a governmental authority in the applicant's entire life history may result in the denial (or revocation) of a license. Conviction of a crime may also result the denial (or revocation) of a license.
4. **Education**. The education requirement consists of successful completion of 8 college-level courses as follows:
   a) **Real Estate Practice**
   b) **Legal Aspects of Real Estate**
   c) **Real Estate Finance**
   d) **Real Estate Appraisal**
   e) **Real Estate Economics or General Accounting***
   f) And three* courses from the following group:
      - Real Estate Principles
      - Business Law
      - Property Management
      - Escrows
      - Real Estate Office Administration

- Mortgage Loan Brokering and Lending
- Advanced Legal Aspects of Real Estate
- Advanced Real Estate Finance
- Advanced Real Estate Appraisal
- Computer Applications in Real Estate
- Common Interest Developments

*If you complete both Real Estate Economics and General Accounting, you need to complete only two courses from the "**f**" group.

5. **Experience**. A minimum of two years full-time licensed salesperson experience, or the equivalent, within the five years immediately preceding the date of your broker examination application is required. Equivalence can be met by working as a salesperson on a part-time basis. Such part-time activity will be given credit on a prorated basis. Equivalence can also be met by:

a) experience as an escrow or title officer or as a loan officer handling financing or the conveying of real property;

b) experience as a subcontractor, contractor, or speculative builder, which experience included the purchase, finance, development, and sale or lease of real property;

c) experience as a real property appraiser;

d) other equivalent experience that, in the opinion of the CalBRE, qualifies as the applicant for the broker examination; or

e) prior to January 1, 2013, any four-year degree from an accredited college or university could have been used in lieu of the requirement of two-years experience as a salesperson. Effective January 1, 2013, the two-year experience requirement may be waived for applicants submitting evidence of a four-year degree from an accredited college or university, *provided* the course of study to obtain their degree includes a *major* or *minor* in real estate.

Note. Members of the California State Bar are exempt from both the 8 college-level course requirements and the two-year experience requirement; however, effective January 1, 2013, merely holding a J.D. degree from an accredited law school will not in itself satisfy the education and experience requirements of the new law.

LICENSE RENEWAL

Both salesperson and broker licenses are issued for a four-year period. Renewal should be made prior to the expiration date listed on the license. Renewal applications may be submitted no earlier than 90 days prior to the expiration of the license. The CalBRE offers a secure *eLicensing* online system that makes the renewal process easy to accomplish once the continuing education requirements have been met.

CONTINUING EDUCATION REQUIREMENTS

Brokers renewing a license for the first time and real estate salespersons who qualified by passing the examination and/or submitted a license application on or after 10/1/2007, and are renewing an original license for the first time, must complete 45 clock hours of CalBRE-approved continuing education consisting of:

- Five separate three-hour courses in the following subjects: Ethics, Agency, Trust Fund Handling, Fair Housing, and Risk Management;

- A minimum of 18 clock hours of consumer protection courses; and

- The remaining clock hours required to complete the 45 hours of continuing education may be related to either consumer service or consumer protection courses.

For subsequent renewals, all real estate brokers and salespersons must complete 45 clock hours of CalBRE-approved continuing education consisting of:

- **Either** 15 hours of continuing education courses in the following subjects: Ethics, Agency, Trust Fund Handling, Fair Housing, and Risk Management **OR** one eight-hour survey course that covers the five mandatory subjects (Ethics, Agency, Trust Fund Handling, Fair Housing, and Risk Management);

- At least 18 clock hours of consumer protection courses; and

- The remaining clock hours required to complete the 45 hours of continuing education may be related to either consumer service or consumer protection courses

THE 70/30 CONTINUING EDUCATION EXEMPTION

Real estate licensees who are 70 years of age or older and have been "licensees in good standing" for 30 continuous years in California are exempt from the continuing education requirements for license renewal.

THE CALBRE: AN OVERVIEW

The *Bureau of Real Estate (CalBRE)* is a consumer-focused department that monitors and regulates real estate industry practice, promotes public awareness, and provides timely and efficient services to licensees, subdividers, and consumers. The *Real Estate Commissioner* is appointed by the governor and is the chief executive officer of the CalBRE. The Commissioner's responsibility is to oversee and enforce the Real Estate Law and the Subdivided Lands Law and to issue regulations, known as the Regulations of the Real Estate Commissioner, that have the full force and effect of law.

CALBRE DISCIPLINARY ACTIVITIES

The CalBRE is empowered to discipline licensees who violate real estate law or CalBRE regulations. Once instituted, a disciplinary action can result in the suspension, revocation, or restriction of an existing license. According to the CalBRE, the following are the 6 most common enforcement violations:

1. **Trust Fund Record Keeping Violations**The keeping of poor trust fund records most often results from a lack of knowledge of proper trust fund accounting and insufficient bookkeeping and accounting skills. The CalBRE warns that just because a broker license permits the broker to handle large amounts of trust funds for clients does not mean that the broker should do so. Until the broker possesses the knowledge and skills necessary to satisfy the numerous strict regulations relating to proper trust fund accounting, the broker should hire a properly trained bookkeeper or accountant to do so. Brokers also run into trust fund record-keeping problems through a lack of supervision over office personnel to whom the broker delegates trust fund record-keeping functions. Brokers must be ever vigilant in overseeing their trust fund operations.

2. **Trust Fund Shortages**. Trust fund shortages can result from poor record-keeping, as discussed above. A more serious offense, however, is a trust fund shortage that results from the conversion of trust funds for personal use either by the broker or by an employee of the broker. Conversion can result in criminal prosecution in addition to disciplinary action against the offender's license.

3. **Failure to Supervise**. Brokers are responsible for, and will be held accountable for, the salespersons over whose activities the broker has failed to exercise reasonable care.

4. **Unlicensed Activity Violations**. Brokers and salespersons who do not renew their licenses on time must discontinue performing any activity that requires a real estate license. An individual who receives a commission for activities that require a real estate license without having a valid real estate license is subject to prosecution for committing a public offense punishable by a fine not exceeding $20,000, or by imprisonment in the county jail for a term not to exceed 6 months, or by both fine and imprisonment. Such an offense by a corporation shall be

punishable by a fine not exceeding $60,000. B&PC §10139. It is a misdemeanor, punishable by a fine not exceeding $100, for any person to pay a real estate commission to anyone who does not possess a valid real estate broker license. B&PC §10138.

5. **Misrepresentation Violations**. A misrepresentation violation can arise not only from a direct statement regarding a material fact that is untruthful or incorrect; it can also arise from the failure to disclose material facts that the licensee's principal should be made aware of.

6. **Criminal Conviction or Disciplinary Violations**. Individuals can be denied a license or disciplined for failing to disclose a criminal conviction on an application for a license. Furthermore, on January 1, 2012, a new section was added to the California Real Estate Law that compels real estate licensees to submit a report of any of the following to the CalBRE:

"(A) The bringing of an indictment or information charging a felony against the licensee.

(B) The conviction of the licensee, including any verdict of guilty, or plea of guilty or no contest, of any felony or misdemeanor.

(C) Any disciplinary action taken by any other licensing entity or authority of this state or of any other state or an agency of the federal government." B&PC §10186.2(a)(1).

The law requires that any such report must be made in writing within 30 days of the date of the bringing of the indictment or the charging of a felony, the conviction, or the disciplinary action, and that failure to make such a written report shall constitute a cause for discipline.

Key Terms for Chapter 17

business opportunity — involves the sale or lease of the assets of an existing business enterprise or opportunity, including the goodwill of the business or opportunity, enabling the purchaser or lessee to begin a business.

goodwill — an intangible asset derived from the expectation of continued public patronage.

Uniform Commercial Code (UCC) — a set of laws that established unified and comprehensive regulations for security transactions of personal property and that superseded existing laws in that field.

bulk sale — a sale, not in the ordinary course of the seller's business, of more than half of the value of the seller's inventory as of the date of the bulk sale agreement.

certificate of clearance — a certificate issued by the Board of Equalization to the buyer of a business that states that no taxes, interest, or penalties are due from the seller or from any previous owner of the business.

eLicensing — a system developed by the CalBRE that allows the examination application and the licensing process to be completed online.

Real Estate Commissioner — the chief executive officer of the CalBRE who is appointed by the governor and whose responsibility is to oversee and enforce the Real Estate Law and the Subdivided Lands Law and to issue regulations, known as the Regulations of the Real Estate Commissioner, that have the full force and effect of law.

Quiz for Chapter 17

1. The sale or lease of the business and goodwill of an existing enterprise or opportunity is
   a. a land contract
   b. an exclusive right to sell listing
   c. a real estate purchase agreement
   d. none of the above

2. Goodwill is
   a. a business opportunity
   b. an intangible asset derived from the expectation of continued public patronage
   c. a sale of more than half of the value of the seller's inventory
   d. none of the above

3. Public records usually disclose
   a. the condition of title to real property
   b. the condition of title to personal property
   c. both a and b
   d. neither a nor b

4. In a bulk sale situation
   a. more than half of the seller's inventory is sold not in the ordinary course of business
   b. the seller must give notice to the public of the proposed transaction at least 12 days before the sale is completed
   c. both a and b
   d. neither a nor b

5. The document issued by the Board of Equalization, stating that no taxes, interest, or penalties are due from the seller of a business, is called
   a. sales and use tax release
   b. certificate of clearance
   c. bulk sale clearance
   d. none of the above

6. Unless an applicant for a real estate salesperson license qualifies for some exemption, the applicant must complete how many college-level real estate courses?
   a. 8
   b. 5
   c. 3
   d. 2

7. Members of the California State Bar who wish to apply for a real estate broker license are exempt from
    a. the 8 college-level course requirement
    b. the 2-year experience requirement
    c. both a and b
    d. neither a nor b

8. A California real estate salesperson license is issued for how many years?
    a. 5
    b. 4
    c. 3
    d. 2

9. California real estate licensees are authorized to act as an agent for the sale of
    a. new, unregistered manufactured homes
    b. business opportunities
    c. both a and b
    d. neither a nor b

10. As a general rule, if real estate is involved as part of a transfer of a business opportunity
    a. a deed is prepared for the transfer of the real property
    b. a bill of sale is prepared for the transfer of the personal property
    c. both a and b
    d. neither a nor b

11. The Real Estate Commissioner is
    a. appointed by the Attorney General of the State of California
    b. elected by the California legislature
    c. appointed by the Board of Governors of the CalBRE
    d. none of the above

12. Among the five continuing education mandatory subjects is (are)
    a. Real Estate Principles
    b. Fair Housing
    c. both a and b
    d. neither a nor b

13. Real estate license renewal applications may be submitted
    a. any time prior to the expiration of the license
    b. any time within one year of the expiration of the license
    c. any time within six months of the expiration of the license
    d. none of the above

14. All salesperson and broker license renewals effective on or after July 1, 2011, must complete how many hours of approved continuing education prior to the expiration of the license?
    a. 45
    b. 40

    c. 35

    d. 30

15. An individual who receives a commission for activities that require a real estate license without having a valid real estate license is subject to prosecution for committing a public offense punishable by a fine not exceeding

    a. $60,000

    b. $20,000

    c. $15,000

    d. $10,000

Answers for Chapter 17 Quiz

1. d. A business opportunity involves the sale or lease of the assets of an existing business enterprise or opportunity, including the goodwill of the business or opportunity, enabling the purchaser or lessee to begin a business.

2. b. Goodwill is an intangible asset derived from the expectation of continued public patronage.

3. a. Unlike a deed, a bill of sale is not usually recorded; therefore, public records may not disclose the condition of title to personal property.

4. a. In a bulk sale, the buyer, not the seller, must give notice to the public of the proposed sale.

5. b. The purchaser of a business will be released from the obligation to withhold part of the sales price only upon receiving from the Board of Equalization a certificate (known as a certificate of clearance) stating that no taxes, interest, or penalties are due from the seller or from any previous owner of the business.

6. c. Unless an applicant for a California real estate salesperson license qualifies for some exemption, the applicant must complete 3 college-level real estate courses.

7. c. Members of the California State Bar are exempt from both the 8 college-level course requirement and the 2-year experience requirement.

8. b. Both salesperson and broker licenses are issued for 4 years.

9. b. California real estate licensees are not authorized to act as agents for the sale of new, unregistered manufactured homes.

10. c. As a general rule, if real estate is involved as part of a transfer of a business opportunity, a bill of sale is prepared for the transfer of all personal property, a deed is prepared for the transfer of the real estate, and the separate and concurrent transactions are processed by separate and concurrent escrows.

11. d. The Real Estate Commissioner is appointed by the governor.

12. b. The five mandatory continuing education subjects are: Ethics, Agency, Trust Fund Handling, Fair Housing, and Risk Management.

13. d. Real estate license renewal applications may be submitted no earlier than 90 days prior to the expiration of the license.

14. a. All salesperson and broker license renewals effective on or after July 1, 2011, must complete 45 hours of approved continuing education prior to the expiration of the license.

15.b. An individual who receives a commission for activities that require a real estate license without having a valid real estate license is subject to prosecution for committing a public offense punishable by a fine not exceeding $20,000, or by imprisonment in the county jail for a term not to exceed 6 months, or by both fine and imprisonment.

Examination Content and Practice Examination

Both the salesperson exam and the broker exam are intended to help ensure that licensees

- have a basic understanding of the principles of California real estate, such as the principles discussed in this textbook; and
- have a good working knowledge of the English language and of the arithmetic computational skills often used in real estate and business opportunity practices.

The salesperson exam consists of 150 multiple-choice questions. To pass the salesperson exam, the examinee must correctly answer at least 70% of the questions. The broker exam consists of 200 multiple-choice questions. To pass the broker exam, the examinee must correctly answer at least 75% of the questions.

Both the salesperson exam and the broker exam are comprised of 7 major areas of real estate subject matter. The CalBRE provides the following list of exam topics and the approximate percentage of questions on each topic that occurs on the salesperson exam and on the broker exam:

Area 1 — Property Ownership and Land Use Controls and Regulations (approximately 18% of sales exam & 15% of broker exam)

- Classes of property
- Property characteristics
- Encumbrances
- Types of ownership
- Descriptions of property
- Government rights in land
- Public controls
- Environmental hazards and regulations

- Private controls
- Water rights
- Special categories of land

Area 2 — **Laws of Agency** (approximately 12% of sales exam & 12% of broker exam)

- Law, definition and nature of agency relationships, types of agencies, and agents
- Creation of agency and agency agreements
- Responsibilities of agent to seller/buyer as principal
- Disclosure of agency
- Disclosure of acting as principal or other interest
- Termination of agency
- Commission and fees

Area 3 — **Valuation and Market Analysis** (approximately 12% of sales exam & 11% of broker exam)

- Value
- Methods of estimating value

Area 4 — **Financing** (approximately 13% of sales exam & 13% of broker exam)

- General concepts
- Types of loans
- Sources of financing
- How to deal with lenders
- Government programs
- Mortgages/deeds of trust/notes
- Financing/credit laws
- Loan brokerage

Area 5 — **Transfer of Property** (approximately 9% of sales exam & 10% of broker exam)

- Title insurance
- Deeds
- Escrow
- Reports
- Tax aspects
- Special processes

Area 6 — Practice of Real Estate and Mandated Disclosures (approximately 24% of sales exam & 27% of broker exam)

- Trust account management
- Fair housing laws
- Truth in advertising
- Record keeping requirements
- Agent supervision
- Permitted activities of unlicensed sales assistants
- CalBRE jurisdiction and disciplinary actions
- Licensing, continuing education requirements and procedures
- California Real Estate Recovery Fund
- General ethics
- Technology
- Property management/landlord-tenant rights
- Commercial/industrial/income properties
- Specialty areas
- Transfer disclosure statement
- Natural hazard disclosure statements
- Material facts affecting property value
- Need for inspection and obtaining/verifying information

Area 7 — Contracts (approximately 12% of sales exam & 12% of broker exam)

- General
- Listing agreements
- Buyer broker agreements
- Offers/purchase contracts
- Counteroffers/multiple counteroffers
- Leases
- Agreements

Practice Examination

The following practice exam contains 150 multiple-choice questions that are representative of the kinds of questions that often appear on the actual exams given by the CalBRE. Answers to the exam questions can be found immediately following the exam.

The actual CalBRE salesperson exam consists of 150 multiple-choice questions that must be completed in one session of 3 hours 15 minutes. The CalBRE broker exam consists of 200 multiple-choice questions and is given in two sessions totaling 5 hours: a morning 2½ hour session and an afternoon 2½ session.

1. Township A has a section numbered 24. What section number lies just east of Section 24?
   a. 13
   b. 23
   c. 19
   d. 25

2. Personal property is usually transferred by
   a. a deed
   b. an appropriation
   c. a bill of sale
   d. an emblement

3. If a deed restriction restricts something that the applicable zoning ordinances do not restrict
   a. the deed restriction, if legal, would control
   b. the zoning ordinances would override the deed restriction
   c. the zoning ordinances would not be enforceable
   d. the deed restriction would not be enforceable

4. The tests of a fixture include
   a. method of attachment, intent, adaptability, agreement
   b. relationship of the parties, adaptability, agreement, favorability
   c. agreement, relationship of the parties, intent, specificity

    d. none of the above

5. The Treaty of Guadalupe Hidalgo was signed in
    a. 1850
    b. 1822
    c. 1840
    d. none of the above

6. Which of the following can be terminated by extended nonuse?
    a. an easement created by grant
    b. an easement created by prescription
    c. an easement created by reservation
    d. both b and c

7. Remedies for the violation of a condition contained in a deed may include
    a. injunction
    b. forfeiture of the title to the deed
    c. *profit á prendre*
    d. either a or b

8. A person who makes an improvement to land in good faith and under erroneous belief that he or she is the owner of the land is called a
    a. trespasser
    b. licensee
    c. tenant
    d. none of the above

9. Mineral rights that are sold separately from the land
    a. are personal property
    b. are emblements
    c. carry an implied right to enter the land for extraction
    d. both a and c

10. Which of the following sets of words is best associated with riparian rights?
    a. reasonable, adjacent
    b. profit á prendre, reasonable
    c. reasonable, subjacent
    d. law of capture, subjacent

11. The term of a lease for agricultural land cannot exceed
    a. 89 years

    b. 75 years

    c. 51 years

    d. none of the above

12. The term of the lease for a city lot cannot exceed

    a. 49 years

    b. 51 years

    c. 89 years

    d. none of the above

13. A reversionary interest in real property often refers to

    a. a remainderman

    b. life estates

    c. fee simple absolutes

    d. both a and b

14. Real property may include

    a. mineral rights

    b. airspace

    c. natural vegetation

    d. all of the above

15. Which of the following concepts is least associated with the others?

    a. estate for years

    b. periodic tenancy

    c. life estate

    d. estate at will

16. The type of lease that lasts for a specific period of time is called a

    a. tenancy at will

    b. periodic tenancy

    c. tenancy for years

    d. none of the above

17. The characteristic(s) of a tenancy for years include

    a. continues for a definite term

    b. the term may not exceed 49 years

    c. has specific beginning and ending dates

    d. both a and c

18. A lease starting on a particular day and lasting for 33 days would describe

    a. periodic tenancy

    b. estate for years

    c. estate at will

    d. estate at sufferance

19. An estate at will can be terminated

    a. without notice

    b. only after a court orders eviction

    c. by either party at any time

    d. none of the above

20. A lease in real estate conveys to the tenant

    a. a nonexclusive right to possess

    b. an exclusive right to possess

    c. an irrevocable remainder

    d. a license

21. A minor

    a. is a competent grantor

    b. is a competent grantee

    c. is a person 18 years of age or younger

    d. both b and c

22. Which of the following deeds contain no warranties?

    a. quitclaim deed

    b. sheriff's deed

    c. grant deed

    d. both a and b

23. Acknowledgment is a requirement to

    a. make a deed valid

    b. record a deed

    c. make a will valid

    d. witness a will

24. Which of the following terms least belongs with the others?

    a. reliction

    b. accession

    c. prescription

    d. accretion

25. An executor

    a. is a person named in a will

    b. is appointed by a probate court

   c. is appointed by the beneficiaries

   d. either b or c but not both

26. Which of the following statements is incorrect?

   a. a quitclaim deed conveys no warranties

   b. answer d is incorrect

   c. a grant deed conveys after-acquired interests

   d. a devisee is one who acquires real property by a will

27. Recording a deed gives

   a. acknowledgment

   b. constructive notice

   c. public prescription

   d. both a and b

28. An instrument used to convey government land is a

   a. land patent

   b. homestead

   c. public grant

   d. public dedication

29. A statutory will

   a. is written entirely in the testator's handwriting

   b. is no longer valid in California

   c. must be signed by two competent witnesses

   d. none of the above

30. A recorded deed

   a. must have been acknowledged

   b. must have been signed

   c. must be free from outstanding liens

   d. both a and b

31. Jane and Bob acquire an undeveloped city lot as joint tenants. Jane marries Joe and conveys her interest in the joint tenancy to Joe without the knowledge or consent of Bob. Joe

   a. is a joint tenant with Bob

   b. is a tenant in common with Bob

   c. has no interest in the lot because Jane could not transfer her interest without Bob's approval

   d. none of the above

32. Which real estate owner usually has no personal liability in regard to property?
    a. a joint tenant
    b. a general partner
    c. a limited partner
    d. a tenant in common

33. The unities necessary to create a joint tenancy include
    a. freehold estate
    b. title
    c. relationship
    d. all of the above

34. Jane and Bob are joint tenants. Jane conveys one half of her interest to Susan. Ownership of the property is
    a. Jane, Bob, and Susan as joint tenants
    b. Jane and Susan as joint tenants; Bob as tenant in common
    c. Jane, Bob, and Susan as tenants in common
    d. Jane and Bob as joint tenants; Susan has no interest in the property

35. Jane and Susan own a condo as tenants in common. Susan dies having willed her interest to Joe.
    a. Jane owns the condo in severalty, free of Susan's debts
    b. Jane owns the condo in severalty, subject to Susan's debts
    c. Jane and Joe own the property as joint tenants
    d. none of the above

36. Jane and Bob are married. Bob may dispose by will
    a. a joint tenancy interest
    b. a tenancy in common interest that is not part of community property
    c. all of the community property
    d. both b and c

37. Sisters Jane and Susan inherit property from their parents. They might own the property as
    a. joint tenants
    b. tenants in common
    c. community property
    d. either a or b

38. The most important characteristic of joint tenancy is
    a. unity of time

b. right of survivorship

c. equal right to possession

d. equal right to convey

39. Joint tenants have all of the following except

a. right of survivorship

b. right to will good title to another

c. equal right of possession

d. right to sell their interest to another

40. While she was single, Jane owned a condo. After Jane and Bob marry and move into the condo, the condo is held as

a. community property

b. joint tenancy

c. separate property, unless otherwise agreed

d. community property with right of survivorship

41. Sally files a notice of cessation regarding the construction project on her property. Bob, a subcontractor, has how long to file a mechanics lien?

a. 30 days

b. 45 days

c. 60 days

d. 90 days

42. In order to be protected from liability, an owner of a property must post and record a notice of nonresponsibility within how many days of discovering a work of improvement on his or her property?

a. 15

b. 20

c. 30

d. none of the above

43. A mechanics lien can be terminated when

a. the lien debt is paid

b. the one who filed the mechanics lien pays all of his debts

c. the owner files a notice of completion

d. both a and b

44. A lawsuit can result in which kind of lien?

a. lis pendens

b. mechanics

c. construction

    d. none of the above

45. The order in which lien holders are paid is known as
    a. lender's priority
    b. priority of commencement
    c. lien priority
    d. judgment priority

46. A notice of completion must be recorded within how many days of the completion of a work of improvement?
    a. 10
    b. 15
    c. 20
    d. none of the above

47. Joe and Sally have worked for a subcontractor on a home remodeling project. Sally began working on June 1, and Joe on June 15. Both filed preliminary notices on time. After completion of the remodeling project, neither Sally nor Joe is paid by the subcontractor. Sally files for a mechanics lien 10 days after Joe but in time to obtain a valid mechanics lien. Between them, who will have priority if there is a foreclosure on the remodeled home?
    a. Sally because she began work before Joe
    b. Joe because he filed for the mechanics lien first
    c. both have the same priority
    d. Sally because she worked more days than Joe

48. Joe, who is 40, single, and lives alone, owns a home that has a fair market value of $400,000. He still owes $100,000 on a deed of trust against the house. Sally obtains a judgment lien against Joe for $175,000. The costs of foreclosure are $5,000. The amount that Joe will probably get from the foreclosure is
    a. $75,000
    b. $70,000
    c. $120,000
    d. $100,000

49. After a notice of cessation has been recorded, someone who furnished work and who was not a direct contractor with the owner has how long to file a mechanics lien?
    a. 10 days

  b. 30 days

  c. 60 days

  d. none of the above

50. A direct contractor must file a lis pendens within how many days of foreclosing on a mechanics lien?

  a. 10

  b. 20

  c. 30

  d. 60

51. A contract that has been fully performed is an

  a. executory contract

  b. executed contract

  c. unenforceable contract

  d. rescindable contract

52. Mutual consent is evidenced by

  a. a lawful object

  b. capable parties

  c. offer and acceptance

  d. a written document

53. The law that requires certain types of contracts be in writing in order for the contract to be enforceable is the

  a. Statute of Executed Contracts

  b. Statute of Limitations

  c. Statute of Frauds

  d. Statute of Enforceability

54. Which of the following is not an essential element of a valid contract?

  a. writing

  b. mutual consent

  c. consideration

  d. capable parties

55. After a certain time, a valid contract can become

  a. voidable

  b. unenforceable

  c. illegal

  d. void

56. A counteroffer by an offeree

    a. revokes the offeror's offer

    b. presents an offer to the offeror

    c. terminates the offeror's offer

    d. both b and c

57. A contract that, at the request of one party only, may be declared unenforceable, but is valid until it is so declared, is called

    a. an executory contract

    b. a void contract

    c. a voidable contract

    d. a unilateral contract

58. In California, the Statute of Limitations for written contracts generally is

    a. 1 year

    b. 2 years

    c. 4 years

    d. 10 years

59. Bob enters into an oral contract with Joe to rent Joe's apartment for 9 months. The contract is

    a. voidable because of the statute of frauds

    b. not void because of the statute of frauds

    c. void because of the statute of frauds

    d. illegal because of the statute of frauds

60. A contract that has been fully performed by all parties is called

    a. executory

    b. voidable

    c. unilateral

    d. executed

61. A broker's trust account need not be

    a. in the broker's name as trustee

    b. in an interest-bearing account

    c. in a California financial institution

    d. any of the above

62. A group boycott occurs when

    a. two or more brokers agree not to deal with another broker

    b. two or more brokers agree to divide the market geographically

    c. two or more brokers agree that they are going to raise their commission rates by 1%

d. all of the above

63. An interpleader is

a. a person who pleads the case of another

b. a form of agency by estoppel

c. a finder who introduces a buyer to a seller

d. none of the above

64. A selling agent can

a. represent the seller

b. represent the buyer

c. be a dual agent

d. all of the above

65. A dual agent need not

a. receive compensation from both the seller and the buyer

b. tell the seller that the buyer will pay a higher price than initially offered

c. tell the buyer that a dog next door barks day and night

d. both a and b

66. Broker Janet tells her salespersons not to take any listing that calls for less than 6% commission. Janet's action is

a. legal

b. price fixing

c. illegal group action

d. both b and c

67. A real estate salesperson may accept payment from

a. the employing broker

b. a builder to whom the salesperson merely introduces a prospective buyer

c. the seller

d. both a and b

68. A listing broker is not

a. usually a special agent

b. always an agent for the seller

c. neither a nor b is true

d. both a and b are true

69. An agency relationship cannot be created by

a. estoppel

    b. interpleader

    c. ratification

    d. implication

70. To avoid antitrust violations, agents should

    a. never discuss commission rates with other agents

    b. never make derogatory comments about other agents

    c. never discuss their business plans with other agents

    d. all of the above

71. Bob owns a three-acre rectangular lot and wishes to divide it into 5 lots, each having a depth of 70 yards. What would be the width of each of these lots?

    a. 41.49 feet

    b. 207.43 feet

    c. 124.46 feet

    d. none of the above

72. A building depreciates by 3% per year. How many years will it take for the building to be worth only 40% of its initial value?

    a. 20 years

    b. 18 years

    c. 15 years

    d. none of the above

73. As a general rule, a true mortgage has how many parties?

    a. 1

    b. 2

    c. 3

    d. 4

74. Leverage refers to

    a. the ability of a lender to foreclose if the borrower defaults

    b. the maximum amount the interest rate can go up during the life of a loan

    c. a method of multiplying gains or losses on investments

    d. none of the above

75. A straight note provides for

    a. installments consisting of an equal amount of principal and interest

    b. installment payments that pay off the entire loan gradually over the life of the loan

    c. periodic payments that consist of interest only

    d. none of the above

76. A mortgage under which all periodic installment payments are equal is called

    a. an adjustable rate mortgage

    b. a level payment mortgage

    c. a negative amortized loan

    d. none of the above

77. The federal act that made due-on-sale provisions a federal issue is

    a. the Garn-St. Germain Act

    b. the Truth-in-Lending Act

    c. the Real Estate Settlement Procedures Act

    d. the Federal Alienation Act

78. A loan under which payments are sufficient to pay off the entire loan by the end of the loan term is called

    a. a balloon payment loan

    b. a negative amortized loan

    c. a fully amortized loan

    d. an adjustable-rate loan

79. In an assumption,

    a. the seller remains personally liable on the loan, but the purchaser is not personally liable on the loan

    b. the buyer agrees to be primarily liable on the loan

    c. there is no prepayment penalty

    d. the lender agrees to subordinate the loan

80. A clause in a deed of trust that allows the beneficiary to declare the entire balance of the loan due and payable immediately if the borrower materially defaults on the loan is called a

    a. due-on-sale clause

    b. acceleration clause

    c. defeasance clause

    d. either a or b

81. In a deed of trust, what clause permits the trustee to sell the property if the borrower defaults

    a. alienation

    b. power of sale

   c. due-on-sale

   d. assumption

82. Which of the following terms least belongs with the others?

   a. deficiency judgment

   b. due-on-sale clause

   c. judicial foreclosure

   d. sheriff's sale

83. Junior loans are made

   a. by acceleration

   b. in the secondary mortgage market

   c. by subrogation

   d. none of the above

84. Preapproval typically

   a. does not involve verification of income

   b. does not involve verification of credit

   c. does not involve appraisal of the property

   d. all of the above are usually required for preapproval

85. The SAFE Act applies to

   a. individual condominium units

   b. mobile homes

   c. manufactured homes

   d. all of the above

86. Fannie Mae was originally created as

   a. Federal National Mortgage Administration

   b. Federal National Mortgage Association

   c. Federal National Mortgage Agency

   d. none of the above

87. Which of the following terms least belongs with the others?

   a. assets

   b. liabilities

   c. purpose of loan

   d. source of income

88. PMI would likely be included in

   a. front-end ratio

   b. back-end ratio

   c. HPA

    d. both a and b

89. Appraisal, preliminary title report, and property due diligence are components of
    a. property information assembled by a loan processor
    b. LTV
    c. PMI
    d. capacity to repay a loan

90. A house has a sale price of $520,000 and an appraised value of $500,000. If the LTV is 75%, what is the loan amount?
    a. $375,000
    b. $390,000
    c. $400,000
    d. none of the above

91. Conventional loans are not
    a. FHA-insured
    b. VA-guaranteed
    c. either a or b
    d. neither a nor b

92. Bob purchased a house appraised at $400,000 for $420,000 with a $350,000 loan. If the lender required PMI to cover the top 15% of the loan, the PMI coverage was
    a. $52,500
    b. $60,000
    c. $63,000
    d. $80,000

93. Subjective value is also known as
    a. market value
    b. residual value
    c. value in use
    d. none of the above

94. The capitalization approach to value is also referred to as the
    a. income approach
    b. cost approach
    c. straight-line method
    d. none of the above

95. The principle of competition states that

a. improvements made to a property will contribute to its value or that, conversely, the lack of a needed improvement will detract from the value of the property

b. the best use of a property in terms of value is the use most likely to produce the greatest net return (in terms of money or other valued items, such as amenities) over a given period of time

c. property values are in a constant state of flux due to economic, environmental, political, social, and physical forces in the area

d. none of the above

96. The estimated value of a property is $500,000; land value is $200,000; and accrued depreciation of the structure is $75,000. What is the replacement cost of the structure?

a. $300,000

b. $225,000

c. $325,000

d. $375,000

97. The most probable price that a property should bring in a competitive market in which buyers and sellers are acting prudently is referred to as

a. market price

b. value placed on property by a specific person

c. capitalization value

d. market value

98. Economic obsolescence generally is

a. obsolescence resulting from outdated equipment

b. obsolescence resulting from wear and tear of use

c. curable depreciation

d. incurable depreciation

99. A Self-Contained Report is also referred to as a

a. Form Report

b. Restricted Use Report

c. Summary Report

d. none of the above

100. The sales comparison approach most heavily relies on the

a. principal of substitution

b. principal of conformity

c. principle of balance

    d. principle of competition

101. To help ascertain estate and gift taxes and to help ascertain the basis for depreciation in regard to income producing properties are not
    a. tax related activities
    b. potential purposes of an appraisal
    c. both a and b
    d. neither a nor b

102. The cost-to-cure method of calculating depreciation
    a. estimates the cost to cure the curable depreciation and subtracts it from the value of incurable depreciation
    b. calculates the accrued depreciation by dividing the cost of the improvement by its useful life
    c. calculates the accrued depreciation by dividing the cost of the improvement by the estimated useful life of a typical such improvement
    d. none of the above

103. An escrow agent is
    a. an employee of an escrow company
    b. a corporation licensed by the Bureau of Real Estate
    c. a real estate broker who refers a client to an escrow company
    d. none of the above

104. A real estate broker who is not licensed as an escrow agent
    a. may advertise that he or she can conduct escrow for any real estate transaction
    b. may conduct escrow for any real estate transaction
    c. may not conduct escrow for any real estate transaction
    d. none of the above

105. A binding contract between a buyer and a seller may be
    a. a deposit receipt
    b. escrow instructions
    c. either a or b
    d. neither a nor b

106. As the term is used in reference to escrow accounts, a credit is any
    a. item payable by a party
    b. item payable to a party
    c. item deposited into an escrow

       d. none of the above

107. Verifying that the title policy is in place and sending the original policy to the borrower is an act typically performed by the
    a. buyer
    b. seller
    c. lender
    d. none of the above

108. In case a controversy arises between the buyer and seller as to what certain escrow instructions mean, the escrow agent may
    a. do what the seller wants
    b. do what the buyer wants
    c. do what the lender wants
    d. none of the above

109. Which of the following terms least belongs with the others?
    a. reserve account
    b. title insurance
    c. impound account
    d. loan servicing

110. Accepting escrow instructions that contain one or more blanks to be filled in after the signing of the instructions and failing to deliver at the time of signing any instruction a copy thereof to all persons signing the instructions are
    a. acts typically performed by escrow agents
    b. acts typically performed by lenders
    c. acts permitted by the CalBRE of real estate agents who act as escrow agents for real estate transactions that are they are involved in
    d. none of the above

111. A legal doctrine that states that a relationship exists between parties who hold interests in the same real estate is
    a. novation
    b. privity of contract
    c. privity of chattel real
    d. none of the above

112. A landlord may enter a leased residential unit after giving proper notice
    a. to make necessary or agreed repairs

    b. to ensure that the tenant is maintaining the premises in a neat condition

    c. either a or b

    d. neither a nor b

113. A lease that provides that the tenant will construct a building on the premises most likely is a

    a. net lease

    b. graduated lease

    c. ground lease

    d. percentage lease

114. A lease in a stripmall provides for rent payments based in part on a tenant's gross sales. The lease is a

    a. graduated lease

    b. net lease

    c. ground lease

    d. none of the above

115. A tenant who assigns his or her interest in a lease

    a. transfers the tenant's right to less than all of the premises

    b. transfers the entire premises for less than the entire remaining lease term

    c. neither a nor b

    d. either a or b

116. Bob's lease is a gross lease. What percent of the property taxes on the premises is Bob responsible for paying?

    a. all of the property taxes

    b. none of the property taxes

    c. some percentage of the property taxes as provided in the lease

    d. none of the above

117. If a tenant remains in possession of leased property after the expiration of the lease and the landlord accepts rent from the tenant, the tenancy is presumed to be

    a. an estate at will

    b. an estate at sufferance

    c. under a renewed lease

    d. a freehold interest

118. Constructive eviction arises from

    a. acts of government authorities

    b. breaches by a tenant

    c. breaches by a landlord

    d. any of the above

119. In the absence of a provision in the lease that states when rent is due, and in absence of a course of dealing between landlord and tenant, rent is due

    a. at the beginning of each month

    b. at the end of each month

    c. at the beginning of each week

    d. none of the above

120. Under the Costa-Hawkins Rental Housing Act

    a. there can be no rent restriction on rental units built after February 1, 1995

    b. there can be no control of rents for leases on single-family homes where the leases are entered into after January 1, 1996

    c. both a and b

    d. neither a nor b

121. "To declare a national policy which will encourage productive and enjoyable harmony between man and his environment" is one of the declared policies of the

    a. California Coastal Zone Conservation Act

    b. Rumford Act

    c. California Environmental Quality Act

    d. none of the above

122. If pursuant to the requirements of the California Environmental Quality Act a local agency determines that a development project will not have a significant adverse impact, the agency issues

    a. an environmental impact statement

    b. a negative declaration

    c. a negative impact statement

    d. none of the above

123. An estate in real property coupled with the right of occupancy for certain periods of time (such as one month per year) is a

    a. time-share estate

    b. time-share use

c. both a and b

d. neither a nor b

124. The preparation of a general plan includes
   a. collecting data on the local economy and local environmental conditions
   b. formulating community goals and development policies
   c. both a and b
   d. neither a nor b

125. A subdivision in which purchasers own or lease a separate lot, unit, or interest, and have an undivided interest or membership in a portion of the common area of the subdivision is a
   a. common interest development
   b. standard subdivision
   c. undivided interest subdivision
   d. none of the above

126. A stock cooperative is a
   a. corporation formed or availed of primarily for the purpose of holding title to improved real property either in fee simple or for a term of years
   b. residential unit owned in severalty, the boundaries of which are usually walls, floors, and ceilings, and an undivided interest in portions of the real property, such as halls, elevators, and recreational facilities
   c. development in which an undivided interest in the land is coupled with the right of exclusive occupancy of an apartment located thereon
   d. none of the above

127. The Civil Rights Act of 1866 was held to be constitutional in what landmark Supreme Court case?
   a. Johnson v. Virginia
   b. Jones v. Mayer
   c. Unruh v. Holden
   d. none of the above

128. For the physical development of communities, every city and county in California must adopt a
   a. general plan
   b. final map

c. community apartment project

d. none of the above

129. A community apartment project is a

a. development in which an undivided interest in the land is coupled with the right of exclusive occupancy of an apartment located thereon

b. common interest development

c. both a and b

d. neither a nor b

130. To help ensure that the purchaser will receive what he or she bargains for, a subdivider must demonstrate that

a. the buyer's security deposit will be protected

b. arrangements have been made to clear mechanics liens

c. proper title will be conveyed to the buyer

d. all of the above

131. As a general rule, for tax purposes the depreciable life of nonresidential properties is

a. 27 years

b. 27½ years

c. 39½ years

d. none of the above

132. If delinquent property taxes remain unpaid until the end of the fiscal year, the county tax collector publishes

a. a writ of possession

b. an intent to sell

c. a cease-and-desist order

d. none of the above

133. An installment sale is a sale in which the seller

a. receives at least one payment in a later tax period

b. may report part of the gain from the sale for the year in which a payment is received

c. both a and b must apply

d. neither a nor b

134. A buyer purchases a condo for $850,000, agreeing to pay $150,000 cash and to assume the seller's $700,000 outstanding loan on the house. Assuming that only the county (not the city) in which the property lies has a documentary transfer tax, how much would that tax be?

a. $165

b. $150

c. $935

d. $467.50

135. San Francisco has a documentary transfer tax

a. of $0.55 per $500 (or fraction thereof) of the transfer price

b. that varies depending on the sales price of the property

c. of $1.10 per $1,000 (or fraction thereof) of the transfer price

d. none of the above

136. The redemption period that begins after a tax collector publishes an intent to sell is

a. 5 years

b. 4 years

c. 3 years

d. 1 year

137. The two sources of passive income are

a. rental activity and salaries

b. rental activity and dividends

c. rental activity and gains on stocks and bonds

d. none of the above

138. Under a tax postponement program

a. repayment of all postponed taxes must be made when the property is sold

b. repayment of all postponed taxes must be made when the owner of the property reaches the age of 62

c. the postponed taxes need not be repaid if the owner reaches the age of 90

d. none of the above

139. It is possible to qualify as a 1031 exchange if an apartment building is exchanged for a property to be used as a

a. personal residence

b. vacation home

c. second home

d. none of the above

140. Proposition 13 states that the maximum ad valorem tax on real property shall be equal to what percent of the property's "full cash value"?

    a. 1%

    b. 2%

    c. up to 2%, as long as it does not exceed the CPI

    d. none of the above

141. Functional obsolescence results from

    a. out-dated styles or equipment

    b. over-improvements

    c. either a or b

    d. neither a nor b

142. A one and one-half story house is likely to

    a. be a French Provincial style house

    b. have dormers

    c. be a Southern Colonial style house

    d. none of the above

143. BTU refers to the

    a. ratio of the cooling capacity of a room air conditioner to power drawn

    b. amount of heat required to raise 1 pound of water from 39°F to 40°F

    c. measure of resistance of insulation to heat transfer

    d. none of the above

144. A roof with two sloping sides but not sloping ends is a

    a. hip roof

    b. mansard roof

    c. shed roof

    d. none of the above

145. In condominiums, bearing walls are typically

    a. owned by the individual condominium owners

    b. owned in common

    c. walls that do not support structures above them

    d. none of the above

146. To sell a business opportunity in California, a person

    a. must have a business opportunity license

    b. must have a real estate license

    c. both a and b

    d. neither a nor b

147. The transfer of a business opportunity usually involves preparation of a

    a. balance sheet

    b. profit and loss statement

    c. both a and b

    d. neither a nor b

148. In a bulk sale situation, how many business days before the sale is completed must the public be given notice of the proposed sale?

    a. 21

    b. 12

    c. 7

    d. 5

149. Sales and use tax results from

    a. the sale of real property

    b. the sale of tangible personal property

    c. both a and b

    d. neither a nor b

150. An applicant for a California real estate license must

    a. be a California resident

    b. prove legal presence in the United States

    c. both a and b

    d. neither a nor b

Answers to Practice Exam

1. c. Section 19 lies just to the east of section 24. You can see this by imagining another township lying just to the east of the one in Figure 1.2.

2. c. A bill of sale is a written document given by a seller to a purchaser of personal property.

3. a. If a deed restriction is legal and restricts something that applicable zoning ordinances do not, the deed restriction regarding that "something" would control.

4. a. The five tests of a fixture are (1) method of attachment, (2) adaptability of the attached item, (3) relationship of the parties, (4) intent of the person attaching the item, and (5) agreement between the parties.

5. d. The Treaty of Guadalupe Hidalgo was signed in 1848.

6. b. An easement created by prescription can be terminated by extended nonuse.

7. d. Remedies for the violation of a condition contained in the deed may include injunction or forfeiture of the title to the deed.

8. d. A good-faith improver is a person who, because of a mistake of law or fact, makes an improvement to land in good faith and under erroneous belief that he or she is the owner of the land.

9. c. Mineral rights that are sold separately from the land carry an implied right to enter the land for extraction of those minerals.

10. a. Riparian rights are the rights of a landowner to use water from a stream or lake adjacent to his or her property, provided such use is reasonable and does not injure other riparian owners' rights to the water.

11. c. The term of a lease for agricultural land cannot exceed 51 years.

12. d. The term of a lease for a city lot cannot exceed 99 years.

13. b. A reversionary interest in a life estate is an interest in the property that reverts to the grantor at the termination of the life estate.

14. d. In addition to land and buildings, real property may include mineral rights, airspace, and natural vegetation.

15.   c. An estate for years, a periodic tenancy, and an estate at will are less-than-freehold estates.

16.   c. A tenancy for years is a leasehold that continues for a definite fixed period of time, measured in days, months, or years.

17.   d. A tenancy for years is a leasehold that continues for a definite fixed period of time, which may exceed 49 years.

18.   b. A lease for 33 days is an estate for years because it is for a definite period.

19.   d. An estate at will can be terminated by the landlord upon giving a 30-day notice to quit.

20.   b. A lease in real estate conveys to the tenant an exclusive right to possess.

21.   b. A minor is a person under the age of 18 years. A minor is a competent grantee.

22.   d. Quitclaim deeds and sheriff's deeds contain no warranties.

23.   b. Acknowledgment is a requirement to record a deed but not to make a deed or a will valid.

24.   c. Reliction, accretion, and accession relate to the acquisition of land by natural means or, in the case of accession, possibly by human addition of fixtures or improvements made in error. Prescription refers to the acquisition of an interest in property by use and enjoyment for at least five years.

25.   a. An executor is a person named in a will to carry out the directions contained in the will.

26.   b. A devisee is one who acquires real property by will, so answer b is incorrect in that it claims answer d is incorrect.

27.   b. Recording a deed gives constructive notice of the deed.

28.   a. A land patent is an instrument used to convey government land.

29.   c. A statutory will must be signed by two competent witnesses.

30.   d. In order to record a deed, it must be acknowledged and signed, but it need not be free from outstanding liens.

31.   b. Joe is a tenant in common with Bob. A joint tenant may transfer his or her interest without the consent of other joint tenants.

32.   c. A limited partner generally has no personal liability vis-à-vis his or her ownership of real property.

33.   b. The four unities of joint tenancy are possession, title, interest, and time.

34.   c. Because the transfer destroyed the unities of time and interest, Jane, Bob, and Susan are tenants in common.

35.   d. Jane and Joe would own the property as tenants in common.

36.   b. Bob may dispose of a tenancy in common interest that is not part of community property. He may not dispose by will all of the community property.

37.   d. Jane and Susan can own the property as joint tenants or as tenants in common, but not as community property because they are not married.

38.   b. The most important characteristic of joint tenancy is considered to be right of survivorship.

39.   b. Because joint tenancy has right of survivorship, a joint tenant may not will his or her interest to another.

40.   c. Jane owned the property as separate property before marriage, and unless otherwise agreed, the property would remain her separate property following marriage.

41.   a. A subcontractor has 30 days in which to file a mechanics lien after the filing of a notice of cessation.

42.   d. In order to be protected from liability, an owner of a property must post and record a notice of nonresponsibility within 10 days of discovering a work of improvement on his or her property.

43.   a. A mechanics lien can be terminated when the lien debt is paid.

44.   d. A lawsuit can result in the award of a judgment lien.

45.   c. Lien priority is the order in which lien holders are paid.

46.   b. A notice of completion must be recorded within 15 days of the completion of a work of improvement.

47.   c. For a mechanics lien priority, the date of attachment of the lien is the date on which the work of improvement began — not the date on which the claimant began furnishing labor or materials for the work of improvement. Therefore, all mechanics liens relating to the same work of improvement have equal priority, and each mechanics lien holder is entitled to collect his or her pro rata (proportional) share of the work furnished.

48.   c. At the time of foreclosure, Joe has $300,000 equity in his home — $400,000 fair market value minus $100,000 trust deed lien. From that

$300,000 equity, $175,000 and $5,000 will be taken at the foreclosure, leaving $120,000 for Joe. Note that if Joe were 65 or older, he would have received $175,000 because of California's homestead law.

49.   b. After a notice of cessation has been recorded, someone who furnished work and who was not a direct contractor with the owner has 30 days in which to file a mechanics lien.

50.   b. A direct contractor must file a lis pendens within 20 days of foreclosing on a mechanics lien.

51.   b. An executed contract is a contract that has been fully performed. The term may also refer to a contract that has been signed by the parties to the contract.

52.   c. Mutual consent is evidenced by an offer and an acceptance.

53.   c. The statute of frauds is a law that requires certain types of contracts, including most real estate contracts, to be in writing and signed by the party to be bound in order for the contract to be enforceable.

54.   a. A valid contract does not have to be in writing.

55.   b. The statute of limitations requires particular types of lawsuits to be brought within a specified time after the occurrence of the event giving rise to the lawsuit.

56.   d. A counter offer by an offeree terminates the offeror's offer and presents a new offer to the offeror.

57.   c. A voidable contract is a contract that, at the request of one party only, may be declared unenforceable, but is valid until it is so declared.

58.   c. In California, the statute of limitations for written contracts generally is 4 years.

59.   b. In California, oral contracts to lease for a period of one year or less need not be in writing.

60.   d. An executed contract is a contract that has been fully performed by all parties.

61.   b. A broker's trust account must be in the broker's name as trustee and held in a California financial institution. Except under certain circumstances, the account should not be an interest-bearing account.

62.   a. A group boycott occurs when two or more brokers agree not to deal with another broker.

63.   d. An interpleader is an action that allows for a neutral third party (such as a real estate agent) to avoid liability to two or more claimants (such as

a seller and buyer) to the same money or property (such as an earnest money deposit) by forcing the claimants to litigate among themselves, letting the court determine who deserves what while not enmeshing the neutral third party in the litigation.

64.   d. A selling agent is a real estate agent who sells or finds and obtains a buyer for property, regardless of which party or parties to the transaction the agent represents.

65.   d. A dual agent need not receive compensation from both the seller and the buyer and must not tell the seller that the buyer will pay a higher price than initially offered unless the buyer explicitly permits such a representation.

66.   a. Janet's action is legal because a real estate agency is considered to be a single entity for most antitrust purposes, and it takes at least two entities to engage in price fixing.

67.   d. A real estate salesperson may accept payment from his or her employing broker and from a builder to whom the salesperson merely introduces a prospective buyer, but may not receive payment directly from the seller.

68.   c. A listing broker *is* usually a special agent and *is* always an agent for the seller. Be careful of questions such as this one where the question and answer involve a double negative.

69.   b. An agency relationship can be created by estoppel, ratification, or implication, but not by interpleader.

70.   d. To avoid antitrust violations, agents should never discuss commissions with other agents, never make derogatory comments about other agents, and never discuss their business plans with other agents.

71.   c. 3 x 43,560 ft.^{2} = 130,680 ft.^{2} as the area for the entire lot.
130,680 ft.^{2} ÷ 5 = 26,136 ft.^{2} per parcel.
26,136 ft.^{2} ÷ 210 ft. = 124.46 ft. width for each of the 5 parcels.

72.   a. It takes 60 ÷ 3 = 20 years to depreciate by 60%, leaving 40% value.

73.   b. As a general rule, a true mortgage has two parties, the borrower and the lender.

74.   c. Leverage refers to a method of multiplying gains or losses on investments, such as by using borrowed money to make the investments.

75.   c. A straight note provides for periodic payments that consist of interest only.

76.   b. A level payment mortgage is a mortgage under which all periodic installment payments are equal.

77.   a. The Garn-St. Germain Act is a federal law that made enforceability of due-on-sale provisions a federal issue.

78.   c. A fully amortized loan is a loan whereby the installment payments are sufficient to pay off the entire loan by the end of the loan term.

79.   b. In an assumption, the buyer agrees to be primarily liable on the loan.

80.   b. A clause in a deed of trust that allows the beneficiary to declare the entire balance of the loan due and payable immediately is called an acceleration clause, which can be violated by any material default, including nonpayment of taxes, hazard insurance, etc.

81.   b. A power of sale clause is a clause contained in most trust deeds that permits the trustee to foreclose on, and sell, the secured property without going to court.

82.   b. A judicial foreclosure is completed by a sheriff's sale and may result in a deficiency judgment being given to the creditor.

83.   d. Junior loans are made in the primary mortgage market.

84.   c. Preapproval usually involves verification of income and credit but not an appraisal of the property.

85.   d. The SAFE Act applies to loans primarily for personal, family, or household use secured by a residential structure that contains 1 to 4 dwelling units. The term "residential structure that contains 1 to 4 dwelling units" includes individual condominium units, cooperative units, mobile homes, manufactured homes, and trailers, if they are used as residences.

86.   a. Fannie Mae was created as the Federal National Mortgage Administration in 1938.

87.   c. Assets, liabilities, and source of income are primary determinants of the capacity of the potential borrower to repay the loan.

88.   d. PMI is a housing-related expense that would be included in both front-end and back-end ratios.

89.   a. Appraisal, preliminary title report, and property due diligence are components of property information assembled by a loan processor.

90.   a. The LTV is the ratio of the loan amount divided by the lesser of the sale price and the appraisal value.

91. c. A conventional mortgage is a mortgage that is not FHA insured or VA guaranteed.

92. a. 15% of $350,000 = $52,500.

93. c. Subjective value is also referred to as value in use.

94. a. The income approach to value is also referred to as the capitalization approach.

95. d. The principle of competition states that increased competition results in increased supply in relation to demand, and thereby to lower profit margins.

96. d. Replacement cost = $500,000 - $200,000+ $75,000 = $375,000.

97. d. Market value is the most probable price which a property should bring in a competitive and open market under all conditions requisite to a fair sale, the buyer and seller each acting prudently, knowledgeably and assuming the price is not affected by undue stimulus.

98. d. Economic obsolescence is usually beyond the control of a property owner and is therefore incurable.

99. d. A Self-Contained Report is also referred to as a Narrative Report.

100. a. The principle of substitution holds that buyers are generally unwilling to pay more for a property than for a substitute (a comparable with appropriate adjustments) property in the area.

101. d. Helping to ascertain estate and gift taxes and the basis for depreciation in regard to income producing properties *are* tax related and potentially purposes of an appraisal. [Be careful if the word "not" appears in questions.]

102. d. The cost-to-cure method calculates depreciation by estimating the cost of curing the curable depreciation and *adding* to it the value of the incurable depreciation.

103. d. An escrow agent is an impartial agent who holds possession of written instruments and deposits until all of the conditions of escrow have been fully performed.

104. d. A real estate broker not licensed as an escrow agent may serve as an escrow agent for any real estate transaction in which the broker represents the buyer or seller or is a party to the transaction and performs acts that require a real estate license.

105. c. A binding contract between a buyer and a seller can be in any legal form, including a deposit receipt or escrow instructions.

106.   b. As the term is used in reference to escrow accounts, a credit is any item payable to a party.

107.   d. Verifying that the title policy is in place and sending the original policy to the borrower is an act typically performed by the escrow agent.

108.   d. In case a controversy arises between the buyer and seller as to what certain escrow instructions mean, the escrow agent may petition a court through interpleader to decide the issue.

109.   b. Loan servicing often entails the establishment of a reserve account, which is also referred to as an impound account.

110.   d. Accepting escrow instructions that contain one or more blanks to be filled in after the signing of the instructions, and failing to deliver at the time of signing any instruction a copy thereof to all persons signing the instructions are acts that are prohibited by the CalBRE.

111.   d. Privity of estate is a legal doctrine that states that a legally enforceable relationship exists between the parties who hold interests in the same real property.

112.   a. Ensuring that the premises are being kept neat is not one of the acceptable reasons for landlord entry, regardless of notice.

113.   c. A ground lease is a lease under which a tenant leases land and agrees to construct a building or to make other significant improvements on the land.

114.   d. The lease is a percentage lease.

115.   c. An assignment of a lease transfers the tenant's entire interest in the leased premises for the duration of the lease term.

116.   b. A gross lease is a lease under which the tenant pays a fixed rental amount, and the landlord pays all of the operating expenses for the premises, including taxes.

117.   c. If a tenant remains in possession of the leased property after the expiration of the lease and the landlord accepts rent from the tenant, the lease is presumed to have been extended or renewed on the same terms and for the same time, not exceeding one month if the rent under the original lease is payable monthly, or in any case not exceeding one year.

118.   c. Constructive eviction is a breach by the landlord of the covenant of habitability or quiet enjoyment.

119.   d. In the absence of a provision in the lease that states when rent is due, and in the absence of a course of dealing between landlord and tenant,

rent is due at the termination of the successive lease periods, which may be different from a month.

120. c. Under the Costa-Hawkins Rental Housing act there can be no rent restriction on rental units built after February 1, 1995, and there can be no control of rents for leases on single-family homes where the leases are entered into after January 1, 1996.

121. d. "To declare a national policy which will encourage productive and enjoyable harmony between man and his environment" is one of the declared policies of the National Environmental Policy Act. A tipoff in this question lies in the phrase "national policy." As big as it is, California does not make national policy.

122. b. A negative declaration is a report issued by a state or local agency acting pursuant to the California Environmental Quality Act when the agency determines that a development project will not have a significant adverse environmental impact.

123. a. A time-share estate is an estate in real property coupled with the right of occupancy for certain periods of time.

124. c. The preparation of a general plan includes collecting data on the local economy and local environmental conditions, formulating community goals and development policies, preparing diagrams that reflect and support the formulated development policies, and deciding on measures to implement the general plan.

125. a. A common interest development is a subdivision in which purchasers own or lease a separate lot, unit, or interest, and have an undivided interest or membership in a portion of the common area of the subdivision.

126. a. A stock cooperative is a corporation formed or availed of primarily for the purpose of holding title to improved real property either in fee simple or for a term of years.

127. b. In 1968, the United States Supreme Court held in the landmark case *Jones v. Mayer* that the Civil Rights Act of 1866 was constitutional (based on the Thirteenth Amendment) and that it prohibited all racial discrimination, whether private or public, in the sale or rental of property.

128. a. California state law mandates that the legislative body of every city and county must adopt a comprehensive, long-term general plan for the

physical development of the county or city, and of any land outside its boundaries which in the planning agency's judgment bears relation to its planning.

129.   c. A common interest development is a subdivision in which purchasers own or lease a separate lot, unit, or interest, and have an undivided interest or membership in a portion of the common area of the subdivision, of which a community apartment project is a type.

130.   d. To help ensure that the purchaser will receive what he or she bargains for, the subdivider must demonstrate that the buyer's security deposit will be protected; arrangements have been made to clear mechanics liens; arrangements have been made to release the interest from any blanket mortgage lien; and proper title will be conveyed to the buyer.

131.   d. As a general rule, for tax purposes the depreciable life of nonresidential properties is 39 years.

132.   b. If delinquent real property taxes remain unpaid until June 30, the county tax collector publishes an "intent to sell" the property.

133.   c. An installment sale is a sale in which the seller receives at least one payment in a later tax period and may report part of the gain from the sale (as well as any interest received) for the year in which a payment is received.

134.   a. The documentary transfer tax is only applied to the cash paid and, therefore, in this case is $1.10 x 150 = $165.

135.   b. San Francisco, being both a county and a city, has a combined county/city documentary transfer tax that varies from $5.00 per $1,000 to $25.00 per $1,000, depending on the sales price of the property.

136.   a. The redemption period that begins after a tax collector publishes an intent to sell is 5 years.

137.   d. There are only two sources of passive income: (1) rental activity and (2) a business in which the taxpayer does not materially participate.

138.   a. Repayment of all postponed taxes has to be made when the property is sold or title transferred.

139.   d. To qualify as a 1031 exchange, the property must be of like kind. In general, this means that any property held for business use or investment can be exchanged for any other like-kind property held for business use or investment (for example, a farm can be exchanged for an apartment building).

140.   a. Basically, Proposition 13 places a maximum ad valorem tax on real property equal to 1% of the "full cash value" plus a maximum increase of the assessed value of up to 2% per year, as long as the annual increase does not exceed the Consumer Price Index (CPI).

141.   c. Functional obsolescence results (1) from deficiencies arising from poor architectural designs, out-dated style or equipment, and changes in utility demand, such as for larger houses with more garage space, and (2) from over-improvements, where the cost of the improvements was more than the addition to market value.

142.   b. A one and one-half story house is likely to have dormers to provide windows and additional headroom for the upper floor.

143.   b. BTU is a measure of heating (or cooling) capacity equivalent to the amount of heat required to raise the temperature of 1 pound of water 1° Fahrenheit (from 39°F to 40°F).

144.   d. A gable roof is a roof with two sloping sides but not sloping ends.

145.   b. A bearing wall supports structures (such as the roof or upper floors) above it. In condominiums, non-bearing walls are owned by the individual condominium owners, whereas bearing walls usually are property owned in common.

146.   b. Since 1966 when the merger of real estate and business opportunity licenses occurred, a real estate license has been required to negotiation to buy, sell, or lease a business opportunity or to negotiate a loan secured directly or collaterally by liens on a business opportunity.

147.   c. The transfer of a business opportunity requires certain documentation additional to the documentation necessary to transfer only real estate: a balance sheet showing the assets, liabilities, and net worth of the business; and a profit and loss statement showing the gross income, expenses, and net worth (gross income minus expenses) of the business during some period of time.

148.   b. In a bulk sale situation, the *buyer* (not the seller) must give notice to the public of the proposed transaction at least 12 business days before the sale is completed by recordation of a notice of intent to sell in bulk in each county recorder's office where any of the merchandise is located. Additionally, this notice must be published at least once and at least 12 days before the bulk sale is consummated in a newspaper of general circulation in the judicial district in which the property is located.

149. b. Sales and use tax results from the sale of tangible personal property.

150. b. An applicant for a California real estate license need not be a California resident but must prove legal presence in the United States.

Glossary

1031 exchange — under Internal Revenue Code section 1031, a tax-deferred exchange of "like kind" properties.

1031 exchange boot — cash and/or unlike property received in a 1031 exchange.

1099-S Reporting — a report to be submitted on IRS Form 1099-S by escrow agents to report the sale of real estate, giving the seller's name, Social Security number, and the gross sale proceeds.

30/360 day count convention — a convention for calculating interest or allocating expenses in which each month is considered to have 30 days, and each year is considered to have 360 days.

acknowledgment — a written declaration signed by a person before a duly authorized officer, usually a notary public, acknowledging that the signing is voluntary.

acknowledgment of satisfaction — a written declaration signed by a person before a duly authorized officer, usually a notary public, acknowledging that a lien has been paid off in full and that the signing is voluntary.

abandonment — failure to occupy or use property that may result in the extinguishment of a right or interest in the property.

abatement — a legal action to remove a nuisance.

abstract of judgment — a summary of the essential provisions of a court monetary judgment that can be recorded in the county recorder's office of the county or counties in which the judgment debtor owns property to create a judgment lien against such properties.

acceleration clause — a clause in either a promissory note, a security instrument, or both that states that upon default the lender has the option of declaring the entire balance of outstanding principal and interest due and payable immediately.

acceptance — consent (by an offeree) to an offer made (by an offeror) to enter into and be bound by a contract.

accession — the acquisition of additional property by the natural processes of accretion, reliction, or avulsion, or by the human processes of the addition of fixtures or improvements made in error.

accretion — a natural process by which the owner of riparian or littoral property acquires additional land by the gradual accumulation of soil through the action of water.

accrued depreciation — depreciation that has happened prior to the date of valuation.

acknowledgment — a written declaration signed by a person before a duly authorized officer, usually a notary public, acknowledging that the signing is voluntary.

acknowledgment of satisfaction — a written declaration signed by a person before a duly authorized officer, usually a notary public, acknowledging that a lien has been paid off in full and that the signing is voluntary.

active investor — an investor who actively contributes to the management of the business invested in.

actual agency — an agency in which the agent is employed by the principal, either by express agreement, ratification, or implication.

ad valorem — a Latin phrase meaning "according to value." The term is usually used regarding property taxation.

adjustable-rate mortgage (ARM) — a mortgage under which interest rates applicable to the loan vary over the term of the loan.

adjusted cost basis — the dollar amount assigned to a property after additions of improvements and deductions for depreciation and losses are made to the property's acquisition cost.

adjustment period — the time intervals in an adjustable-rate mortgage during which interest rates are not adjusted.

administrator — a person appointed by a probate court to conduct the affairs and distribute the assets of a decedent's estate when there was no executor named in the will or there was no will.

advance fee — a fee charged in advance of services rendered.

adverse possession — the process by which unauthorized possession and use of another's property can ripen into ownership of that other's property without compensation.

after-acquired interests — all interests in a property acquired subsequent to a transfer of the property.

age-life method — *see*, straight-line method.

agency — the representation of a principal by an agent.

agent — a person who represents another.

alienation clause — a due-on-sale clause

alluvium — addition to land acquired by the gradual accumulation of soil through the action of water.

ALTA policy — an extended title insurance policy developed by the American Land Title Association.

ambulatory instrument — a document that can be changed or revoked, such as a will.

amended public report — a report that a subdivider must apply for if, after the issuance of a final public report, new conditions arise that affect the value of the subdivision parcels.

Americans with Disabilities Act — a federal act that prohibits discrimination against persons with disabilities, where "disability" is defined as "a physical or mental impairment that substantially limits a major life activity."

amortization — in general, the process of decreasing or recovering an amount over a period of time; as applied to real estate loans, the process of reducing the loan principal over the life of the loan.

anchor bolt — a bolt inserted into concrete that secures structural members to the foundation.

annual percentage rate (APR) — expresses the effective annual rate of the cost of borrowing, which includes all finance charges, such as interest, prepaid finance charges, prepaid interest, and service fees.

appraisal — an estimate of the value of property resulting from an analysis and evaluation made by an appraiser of facts and data regarding the property.

appreciation — an increase in value due to any cause.

appropriation, right of — the legal right to take possession of and use for beneficial purposes water from streams or other bodies of water.

appurtenance — an object, right or interest that is incidental to the land and goes with or pertains to the land.

assignment — a transfer of a tenant's entire interest in the tenant's leased premises.

associate broker — a person with a real estate brokers license who is employed as a salesperson by another broker.

assumption — an adoption of an obligation that primarily rests upon another person, such as when a purchaser agrees to be primarily liable on a loan taken out by the seller.

attachment lien — a prejudgment lien on property, obtained to ensure the availability of funds to pay a judgment if the plaintiff prevails.

attorney in fact — a holder of a power of attorney.

automatic homestead —a homestead exemption that applies automatically to a homeowner's principal residence and that provides limited protection for the homeowner's equity in that residence against a judgment lien foreclosure.

avulsion — a process that occurs when a river or stream suddenly carries away a part of a bank and deposits it downstream, either on the same or opposite bank.

back-end ratio — the ratio of total monthly expenses, including housing expenses and long-term monthly debt payments, to monthly gross income.

balloon payment — a payment, usually the final payment, of an installment loan that is significantly greater than prior payments — "significantly greater" generally being considered as being more than twice the lowest installment payment paid over the loan term.

bankruptcy — a legal process conducted in a United States Bankruptcy court, in which a person declares his or her inability to pay debts.

base lines — in the Sections and Township method of land description, California has three sets of base lines, which are east-west lines, and meridians, which are north-south lines.

beam — a horizontal member of a building attached to framing, rafters, etc., that transversely supports a load.

bearing wall — a wall that supports structures (such as the roof or upper floors) above it. In condominiums, non-bearing walls are owned by the individual condominium owners, whereas bearing walls usually are property owned in common.

beneficiary — (1) the lender under a deed of trust, (2) one entitled to receive property under a will, (3) one for whom a trust is created.

bequeath — to transfer personal property by a will.

bequest — a gift of personal property by will.

bilateral contract — a contract in which a promise given by one party is exchanged for a promise given by the other party.

bill of sale — a written document given by a seller to a purchaser of personal property.

blanket mortgage — a mortgage used to finance two or more parcels of real estate.

blight — as used in real estate, the decline of a property or neighborhood as a result of adverse land use, destructive economic forces, failure to maintain the quality of older structures, failure to maintain foreclosed homes, etc.

blind ad — an advertisement that does not disclose the identity of the agent submitting the advertisement for publication.

blockbusting — the illegal practice of representing that prices will decline, or crime increase, or other negative effects will occur because of the entrance of minorities into particular areas.

board foot — a unit of measure of the volume of lumber, equivalent to the volume of lumber of 1 square foot and 1 inch thick; 144 cubic inches.

bona fide — in good faith; authentic; sincere; without intent to deceive.

book depreciation — a mathematical calculation used by tax authorities and accountants to determine a depreciation deduction from gross income.

book sale — a "sale" for accounting purposes regarding tax-delinquent property; this "sale" does not entail an actual transfer property.

bridge loan — a short-term loan (often referred to as a swing loan) that is used by a borrower until permanent financing becomes available.

broker — a person who, for a compensation or an expectation of compensation, represents another in the transfer of an interest in real property. A real estate broker must pass the CalBRE's brokers exam and be licensed as a real estate broker.

BTU (British Thermal Unit) — A measure of heating (or cooling) capacity equivalent to the amount of heat required to raise the temperature of 1 pound of water 1° Fahrenheit (from 39°F to 40°F).

bulk sale — a sale, not in the ordinary course of the seller's business, of more than half of the value of the seller's inventory as of the date of the bulk sale agreement.

bundle of rights — rights the law attributes to ownership of property.

business opportunity — involves the sale or lease of the assets of an existing business enterprise or opportunity, including the goodwill of the business or opportunity, enabling the purchaser or lessee to begin a business.

buyer's agent — a real estate broker appointed by a buyer to find property for the buyer.

California Association of Realtors® — the state organization of the National Association of Realtors®.

California Coastal Zone Conservation Act — a California state law that is intended to promote the preservation and protection of California's diverse coastal zone.

California Environmental Quality Act (CEQA) — a California state law that requires state and local agencies to consider and respond to the environmental effects of private and public development projects.

California Housing Finance Agency (CalHFA) — a California state agency that makes low-interest loans to "first-time homebuyers" from funds derived from the sale of tax-exempt bonds.

California Withholding Law — a California law that, with certain exceptions, requires the buyer of California real estate to withhold 3⅓% of the gross sales price from any individual seller.

CalVet loan — a loan made by the Farm and Home Loan Division of the DVA to eligible military veterans for the purchase of a home or farm in California.

capital asset — permanent, non-inventory assets held for personal or investment purposes, such as householders' homes, household furnishings, stocks, bonds, land, buildings, and machinery.

capital gain — the amount by which the net sale proceeds from the sale of a capital asset exceeds the adjusted cost value of the asset.

capitalization approach — *see*, income approach

capitalization rate — the annual net income of a property divided by the initial investment in, or value of, the property; the rate that an appraiser estimates is the yield rate expected by investors from comparable properties in current market conditions.

capture, law of — the legal right of a landowner to all of the gas, oil, and steam produced from wells drilled directly underneath on his or her property, even if the gas, oil, or steam migrates from below a neighbor's property.

carbon monoxide (CO) detector — a CO detector/alarm or a CO alarm combined with a smoke detector. As of January 1, 2013, CO detectors must be installed in all California dwelling units that contain a fossil fuel burning heater or appliance, a fireplace, or that have an attached garage.

Carbon Monoxide Poisoning Prevention Act — a California law that requires the installation of carbon monoxide alarms in most residential units.

carryover —under an adjustable-rate loan, an increase in the interest rate not imposed because of an interest-rate cap that is carried over to later rate adjustments.

Cartwright Act — the California legislative act that is the basis for California's antitrust laws.

caulking — a putty-like material used to seal cracks and joints to make tight against leakage of air or water, as in making windows watertight.

CC&Rs — an abbreviation of "covenants, conditions, and restrictions" — often used to refer to restrictions recorded by a developer on an entire subdivision.

certificate of clearance — a certificate issued by the Board of Equalization to the buyer of a business that states that no taxes, interest, or penalties are due from the seller or from any previous owner of the business.

certificate of discharge — a written instrument used to release a lien created by a mortgage.

Certificate of Eligibility — a certificate issued by the VA, certifying that the applicant is eligible for a VA-guaranteed loan of a certain amount.

Certificate of Reasonable Value (CRV) — a certificate issued by a VA-approved appraiser that certifies, pursuant to VA guidelines, the reasonable value of a property that is to be used as security for a VA-guaranteed loan.

chain of title — a complete chronological history of all of the documents affecting title to the property.

chattel real — personal property that contains some interest in real property, the most common example being a lease.

Civil Rights Act of 1866 — a federal law enacted during Reconstruction that stated that people of any race may enjoy the right to enforce contracts, to sue, be parties, and give evidence, to inherit, purchase, lease, sell, hold, and convey real and personal property, and to full and equal benefit of all laws.

Civil Rights Act of 1968 — a federal law (often referred to as the Fair Housing Act) that prohibited discrimination in housing based on race, creed, or national origin. An amendment to this Act in 1974 added prohibition against discrimination based on gender, and an amendment in 1988 added prohibition against discrimination based on a person's disabilities or familial status.

client — an agent's principal

closing — in reference to an escrow, a process leading up to, and concluding with, a buyer's receiving the deed to the property and the seller's receiving the purchase money.

CLTA policy — a standard title insurance policy developed by the California Land Title Association.

collar beam — a beam connecting pairs of opposite rafters well above the attic floor.

column — a circular or rectangular vertical structural member that supports the weight of the structure above it.

commercial acre — the buildable part of an acre that remains after subtracting land needed for streets, sidewalks, and curbs.

commingling — regarding trust fund accounts, the act of improperly segregating the funds belonging to the agent from the funds received and held on behalf of another; the mixing of separate and community property.

commission — an agent's compensation for performance of his or her duties as an agent; in real estate, it is usually a percent of the selling price of the property or, in the case of leases, of rentals.

common interest development (CID) — a subdivision in which purchasers own or lease a separate lot, unit, or interest, and have an undivided interest or membership in a portion of the common area of the subdivision.

community apartment project — a development in which an undivided interest in the land is coupled with the right of exclusive occupancy of an apartment located thereon.

community property — property owned jointly by a married couple or by registered domestic partners, as distinguished from separate property. As a general rule, property acquired by a spouse or registered domestic partner through his/her skills or personal efforts is community property.

community property with right of survivorship — property that is community property and that has a right of survivorship. Upon the death of a spouse or registered domestic partner, community property with right of survivorship passes to the surviving spouse or domestic partner without probate.

Community Redevelopment Law — a California state law that provides local governments with the authority to correct blighted conditions in areas within their jurisdictions.

comparable property — a property similar to the subject property being appraised that recently sold at arm's length, where neither the buyer nor the seller was acting under significant financial pressure.

compound interest — the type of interest that is generated when accumulated interest is reinvested to generate interest earnings from previous interest earnings.

concealment — the act of preventing disclosure of something.

condition subsequent — a condition written into the deed of a fee estate that, if violated, may "defeat" the estate and lead to its loss and reversion to the grantor.

conditional use — a zoning exception for special uses such as churches, schools, and hospitals that wish to locate to areas zoned exclusively for residential use.

condominium — a residential unit owned in severalty, the boundaries of which are usually walls, floors, and ceilings, and an undivided interest in portions of the real property, such as halls, elevators, and recreational facilities.

conduit — a (usually) metal pipe in which electrical wiring is installed.

conflict of interest — a situation in which an individual or organization is involved in several *potentially* competing interests, creating a risk that one interest *might* unduly influence another interest.

conforming loan — a loan in conformance with FHFA guidelines.

consideration — anything of value given or promised, such as money, property, services, or a forbearance, to induce another to enter into a contract.

conspiracy — in antitrust law, occurs when two or more persons agree to act and the agreed-upon action has the effect of restraining trade.

construction mortgage — a security instrument used to secure a short-term loan to finance improvements to a property.

constructive eviction — a breach by the landlord of the covenant of habitability or quiet enjoyment.

constructive notice — (1) notice provided by public records; (2) notice of information provided by law to a person who, by exercising reasonable diligence, could have discovered the information.

Constructors' State License Law — a California state law that, with certain exceptions, requires that every building contractor must be licensed by the Contractors' State License Board.

contingency — an event that may, but is not certain to, happen, the occurrence upon which the happening of another event is dependent.

conventional loan — a mortgage loan that is not FHA insured or VA guaranteed.

conversion — the unauthorized misappropriation and use of another's funds or other property.

cooperating broker — a broker who attempts to find a buyer for a property listed by another broker.

co-ownership — joint ownership

cost approach — an appraisal approach that obtains the market value of the subject property by adding the value of the land (unimproved) of the subject property to the depreciated value of the cost (if currently purchased new) of the improvements on subject property.

cost recovery — the recoupment of the purchase price of a property through book depreciation; the tax concept of depreciation.

Costa-Hawkins Rental Housing Act — a state law that places restrictions on local rent control laws.

cost-to-cure method — a method of calculating depreciation by estimating the cost of curing the curable depreciation and adding it to the value of the incurable depreciation.

counteroffer — a new offer by an offeree that acts as a rejection of an offer by an offeror.

coupled with an interest — an aspect of an agency that refers to the agent's having a financial interest in the subject of the agency.

covenant — a contractual promise to do or not do certain acts, the remedy for breach thereof being either monetary damages or injunctive relief, not forfeiture.

crawlspace — the space between the ground and the first floor that permits access beneath the building.

credit bid — a bid at a foreclosure sale made by the beneficiary up to the amount owed to the beneficiary.

credits — in reference to an escrow account, items payable to a party. This definition of a debit does not conform to its use in double-entry bookkeeping or accounting.

curable depreciation — depreciation that results from physical deterioration or functional obsolescence that can be repaired or replaced at a cost that is less than or equal to the value added to the property.

debits — in reference to an escrow account, items payable by a party. This definition of a debit does not conform to its use in double-entry bookkeeping or accounting.

declared homestead — the dwelling described in a homestead declaration.

deed — a document that when signed by the grantor and legally delivered to the grantee conveys title to real property.

deed in lieu of foreclosure — a method of avoiding foreclosure by conveying to a lender title to a property lieu of the lender's foreclosing on the property.

defeasance clause — a provision in a loan that states that when the loan debt has been fully paid, the lender must release the property from the lien so that legal title free from the lien will be owned by the borrower.

defendant — the one against whom a lawsuit is brought.

deferred maintenance — any type of depreciation that has not been corrected by diligent maintenance.

deficiency judgment — a judgment given to a lender in an amount equal to the balance of the loan minus the net proceeds the lender receives after a judicial foreclosure.

demand — the level of desire for a product.

deposit receipt — a written document indicating that a good-faith deposit has been received as part of an offer to purchase real property; also called a purchase and sale agreement.

depreciation — the loss in value due to any cause.

depreciation deduction — an annual tax allowance for the depreciation of property.

devise — (1) (noun) a gift of real property by will; (2) (verb) to transfer real property by a will.

devisee — a recipient of real property through a will.

disabled veteran's exemption — and exemption that can reduce the tax liability of a qualified veteran's principal place of residence.

discounted rate — a rate (also called a teaser rate) on an adjustable-rate mortgage that is less than the fully indexed rate.

discount points — a form of prepaid interest on a mortgage, or a fee paid to a lender to cover cost the making of a loan. The fee for one discount point is equal to 1% of the loan amount.

disintegration — the phase when a property's usefulness is in decline and constant upkeep is necessary.

divided agency — an agency in which the agent represents both the seller and the buyer without obtaining the consent of both.

documentary transfer tax — a tax imposed by counties and cities on the transfer of real property within their jurisdictions.

dominant tenement — land that is benefited by an easement appurtenant.

dormer — a projecting structure built out from a sloping roof that is used to provide windows and additional headroom for the upper floor.

drywall — prefabricated sheets or panels nailed to studs to form an interior wall or partition.

dual agent — a real estate broker who represents both the seller and the buyer in a real estate transaction.

due diligence — the exercise of an honest and reasonable degree of care in performing one's duties or obligations. A real estate agent's due diligence involves investigating the property to ensure that the property is as represented by the seller and to disclose accurate and complete information regarding the property.

due-on-sale clause — a clause in the promissory note, the security instrument, or both that states that the lender has the right to accelerate the loan if the secured property is sold or some other interest in the property is transferred.

duress — unlawful force or confinement used to compel a person to enter into a contract against his or her will.

DVA — the California Department of Veterans Affairs is a California state agency whose mission is to promote and deliver benefits to military veterans and their families who live in California.

dwelling house homestead — an automatic homestead.

earnest money deposit — a deposit that accompanies an offer by a buyer and is generally held in the broker's trust account.

easement — a non-possessory right to use a portion of another property owner's land for a specific purpose, as for a right-of-way, without paying rent or being considered a trespasser.

easement appurtenant — an easement that benefits, and is appurtenant to, another's land.

easement by necessity —arises as a creation of a court of law in certain cases were justice so demands, as in the case where a buyer of a parcel of land discovers that the land he or she just purchased has no access except over the land of someone other than from the person from whom the parcel was purchased.

easement in gross — an easement that benefits a legal person rather than other land.

Easton v. Strassburger — the 1984 landmark California court case that held that real estate agents have an "affirmative duty to conduct a reasonably competent and diligent inspection of the residential property listed for sale and to disclose to prospective purchasers all facts materially affecting the value of the property that such an investigation would reveal."

eaves — the overhang of a roof that projects over an exterior wall of a house.

economic life — the period of time that the property is useful or profitable to the average owner or investor.

economic obsolescence — *see*, external obsolescence.

EER and SEER — Air-conditioners have an efficiency rating that states the ratio of the cooling capacity (how many BTUs per hour) to the power drawn (in watts). For room air conditioners the ratio is the EER (energy efficiency ratio); for central air conditioners the rating is the SEER (seasonal energy efficiency ratio). The higher the EER or SEER, the greater the efficiency of the air-conditioning unit. Significant savings in electricity costs can be obtained by installing more efficient air-conditioning units.

effective age — the age of an improvement that is indicated by the condition of the improvement, as distinct from its chronological age.

effective demand — demand coupled with purchasing power sufficient to acquire the property from a willing seller in a free market.

effective gross income — income from a property after an allowance for vacancies and uncollectible rents is deducted from gross income.

ejectment — a legal action to recover possession of real property from a person who is not legally entitled to possess it, such as to remove an encroachment or to evict a defaulting buyer or tenant.

eLicensing — a system developed by the CalBRE that allows the examination application and the licensing process to be completed online.

emancipated minor — a minor who, because of marriage, military service, or court order, is allowed to contract for the sale or purchase of real property.

emblements — growing crops, such as grapes, avocados, and apples, that are produced seasonally through a tenant farmer's labor and industry.

eminent domain — right of the state to take, through due process proceedings (often referred to as *condemnation proceedings*), private property for public use upon payment of just compensation.

employee — a person who works for another who directs and controls the services rendered by the person.

employer — a person who directs and controls the services rendered by an employee.

encroachment — a thing affixed under, on, or above the land of another without permission.

encumber — To place a lien or other encumbrance on property.

encumbrance — A right or interest held by someone other than the owner the property that affects or limits the ownership of the property, such as liens, easements, licenses and encroachments.

Endangered Species Act — a federal law that is intended to provide a means whereby the ecosystems upon which endangered species and threatened species depend may be conserved, and to provide a program for the conservation of such endangered species and threatened species.

environmental impact report (EIR) — a report that the agency investigating the feasibility of a development project pursuant to the California Environmental Quality Act is required to make if it is determined that there is substantial evidence of the project would have a significant adverse environmental impact.

environmental impact statement (EIS) — a statement that certain agencies are required to make pursuant to the National Environmental Policy Act regarding development that might significantly impact the quality of the environment.

Equal Credit Opportunity Act (ECOA) — a federal law that prohibits a lender from discriminating against any applicant for credit on the basis of race, color, religion, national origin, sex, marital status, or age (unless a minor), or on the grounds that some of the applicant's income derives from a public assistance program.

equal dignities rule — a principle of agency law that requires the same formality to create the agency as is required for the act(s) the agent is hired to perform.

equilibrium — the period of stability when the property changes very little.

equitable title — the right to possess and enjoy a property while the property is being paid for.

escalator clause — a provision in a lease that provides for periodic increases in rent, often based on the Consumer Price Index.

escheat — a process whereby property passes to the state if a person owning the property dies intestate without heirs.

escrow — a neutral depository in which something of value is held by an impartial third party (called the escrow agent) until all conditions specified in the escrow instructions have been fully performed.

escrow activity report — a report that certain real estate brokers must file with the CalBRE if their escrow activities exceed a certain threshold.

escrow agent — an impartial agent who holds possession of written instruments and deposits until all of the conditions of escrow have been fully performed.

escrow holder — an escrow agent

escrow instructions — the written instructions signed by all of the principals to the escrow (buyers, sellers, and lenders) that specify all of the conditions that must be met before the escrow agent may release whatever was deposited into escrow to the rightful parties.

estate — the degree, quantity, nature, duration, or extent of interest one has in real property.

estate at sufferance — a leasehold that arises when a lessee who legally obtained possession of a property remains on the property after the termination of the lease without the owner's consent. Such a holdover tenant can be evicted like a trespasser, but if the owner accepts rent, the estate automatically becomes a periodic tenancy.

estate at will — a leasehold that has no specified duration, though it may only be terminated by the owner of the property upon giving proper notice. An estate at will arises when a tenant takes possession of a property while negotiating a lease or under a void contract or lease.

estate for years — a leasehold that continues for a definite fixed period of time, measured in days, months, or years.

estate from period to period — a leasehold that continues from period to period, whether by days, months, or years, until terminated by proper notice.

estate of inheritance — a freehold estate.

estoppel — a legal principle that bars one from alleging or denying a fact because of one's own previous actions or words to the contrary. Ostensible agency can be created by estoppel when a principal and an unauthorized agent act in a manner toward a third-party that leads the third party to rely on the actions of the unauthorized agent, believing that the actions are authorized by the principal.

exclusive agency listing — a listing agreement that gives a broker the right to sell property and receive compensation (usually a commission) if the property is sold by anyone other than the owner of the property during the term of the listing.

exclusive authorization and right to sell listing — a listing agreement that gives a broker the exclusive right to sell property and receive compensation (usually a commission) if the property is sold by anyone, including the owner of the property, during the term of the listing.

executed contract— a contract that has been fully performed; may also refer to a contract that has been signed by all of the parties to the contract.

executor — a person named in a will to carry out the directions contained in the will.

executory contract — a contract that has not yet been fully performed by one or both parties.

express contract — a contract stated in words, written or oral.

external obsolescence — depreciation that results from things such as (1) changes in zoning laws or other government restrictions, (2) proximity to undesirable influences such as traffic, airport flight patterns, or power lines, and (3) general neighborhood deterioration, as might result from increased crime.

Factory Built Housing Law — a California state law that regulates factory built housing.

factory-built home — a home specifically manufactured to conform to the local building codes of the site, transported on flatbed trucks rather than being built on a permanent chassis, and assembled on the site where it is affixed it to a permanent foundation.

Fair Employment and Housing Act — a California state law (also known as the Rumford Act) that prohibits discrimination in the sale, leasing, or financing of nearly all types of housing, except the rental to one boarder in a single-family, owner-occupied home or to accommodations operated by charitable, fraternal, or religious organizations. The Rumford Act specifically prohibits landlords from asking prospective buyers or tenants about race, color, religion, gender, sexual orientation, marital status, familial status, national origin, ancestry, or disability.

Fair Housing Act — *see*, Civil Rights Act of 1968

false promise — a promise made without any intention of performing it.

Fannie Mae — a U.S. government conservatorship originally created as the Federal National Mortgage Association in 1938 to purchase mortgages from primary lenders.

federally designated targeted area — federally designated locations where homeownership is encouraged and incentivized.

fee simple absolute estate — the greatest estate that the law permits in land. The owner of a fee simple absolute estate owns all present and future interests in the property.

fee simple defeasible estate — a fee estate that is qualified by some condition that, if violated, may "defeat" the estate and lead to its loss and reversion to the grantor.

FHA — the Federal Housing Administration is a federal agency that was created by the National Housing Act of 1934 in order to make housing more affordable by increasing home construction, reducing unemployment, and making home mortgages more available and affordable.

FHFA — the Federal Housing Finance Agency is a U.S. government agency created by the Housing and Economic Recovery Act of 2008 to oversee the activities of Fannie Mae and Freddie Mac in order to strengthen the secondary mortgage market.

FICO score — a credit score created by the Fair Isaac Corporation that ranges from 300 to 850 and is used by lenders to help evaluate the creditworthiness of a potential borrower.

fiduciary relationship — a relationship in which one owes a duty of utmost care, integrity, honesty, and loyalty to another.

final map —a final map that a planning commission must approve after consideration of a tentative map before regulated subdivided property may be sold.

final public report — a report that the Real Estate Commissioner issues after determining that a subdivision offering meets certain consumer protection standards.

finder — a person who merely introduces a buyer to a seller, but does nothing else to facilitate a transaction between the buyer and seller, such as rendering assistance in negotiating terms.

fire stop — a block or board placed horizontally between studs to form a tight closure of a concealed space, thereby decreasing drafts and retarding the spread of fire and smoke.

first mortgage — a security instrument that holds first-priority claim against certain property identified in the instrument.

fiscal year — in California, the fiscal year begins on July 1 and ends on June 30 of the following calendar year.

fixed lease — a gross lease

fixture — an object, originally personal property, that is attached to the land in such a manner as to be considered real property.

flashing — sheet metal or other material used in roof and wall construction to prevent water from entering.

flue — a channel in a chimney through which flame and smoke passes upward to the outer air.

footing — concrete poured on solid ground that provides support for the foundation, chimney, or support columns. Footing should be placed below the frost line to prevent movement.

foreclosure — a legal process by which a lender, in an attempt to recover the balance of a loan from a borrower who has defaulted on the loan, forces the sale of the collateral that secured the loan.

foreclosure consultant — any person who makes any solicitation, representation, or offer to any owner to perform for compensation or who, for compensation, performs any service which the person in any manner represents will in any manner stop or postpone the foreclosure sale; obtain any forbearance from any beneficiary or mortgagee; assist the owner to exercise the right of reinstatement; obtain any extension of the period within which the owner may reinstate his or her obligation; obtain any waiver of an acceleration clause contained in any promissory note or contract secured by a deed of trust or mortgage on a residence in foreclosure or contained that deed of trust or mortgage; assist the owner to obtain a loan or advance of funds; avoid or ameliorate the impairment of the owner's credit resulting from the recording of a notice of default or the conduct of a foreclosure sale; save the owner's residence from foreclosure; or assist the owner in obtaining from the beneficiary, mortgagee, trustee under a power of sale, or counsel for the beneficiary, mortgagee, or trustee, the remaining proceeds from the foreclosure sale of the owner's residence. Exempted from the definition of foreclosure consultant are licensed attorneys who render foreclosure consultant services to clients in the course of his or her practice as an attorney, licensed real estate brokers, and licensed real estate salespersons who work under the supervision of their employing broker.

foreclosure prevention alternative — a first lien loan modification or another available loss mitigation option.

Foreign Investment in Real Property Tax Act (FIRPTA) — a federal act that, with certain exceptions, requires the buyer in a real estate transaction to determine whether the seller is a non-resident alien; and if so, the buyer has the responsibility of withholding 10% of the amount realized from the sale and sending that 10% of the IRS.

Form Report — *see*, Summary Report.

four unities — refers to the common law rule that a joint tenancy requires unity of possession, time, interest, and title.

Freddie Mac — a U.S. government conservatorship originally created as the Federal Home Loan Mortgage Corporation in 1968 to purchase mortgages from primary lenders.

freehold estate — an estate in land whereby the holder of the estate owns rights in the property for an indefinite duration.

front-end ratio — the ratio of monthly housing expenses to monthly gross income.

fully amortized loan — a loan whereby the installment payments are sufficient to pay off the entire loan by the end of the loan term.

fully indexed rate — on an adjustable-rate mortgage, the index plus the margin.

functional obsolescence — depreciation that results (1) from deficiencies arising from poor architectural design, out-dated style or equipment, and changes in utility demand, such as for larger houses with more garage space, or (2) from over-improvements, where the cost of the improvements was more than the addition to market value.

gable roof — a roof with two sloping sides but not sloping ends.

gambrel roof — a roof sloped on two sides, each side having a steep lower slope and a flatter upper slope.

Garn-St. Germain Act — a federal law that made enforceability of due-on-sale provisions a federal issue.

general agent — an agent who is authorized by a principal to act for more than a particular act or transaction. General agents are usually an integral part of an ongoing business enterprise.

general lien — a lien that attaches to all of a person's nonexempt property.

general partnership — a partnership in which each partner has the equal right to manage the partnership and has personal liability for all of the partnership debts.

general plan — a comprehensive, long-term plan for the physical development of a city or county that is implemented by zoning, building codes, and other laws or actions of the local governments.

gift deed — a deed used to convey title when no tangible consideration (other than "affection") is given. The gift deed is valid unless it was used to defraud creditors, in which case such creditors may bring an action to void the deed.

Ginnie Mae — the Government National Mortgage Association is a wholly owned U.S. government corporation within HUD to guarantee pools of eligible loans that primary lenders issue as Ginnie Mae mortgage-backed securities.

good-faith improver — a person who, because of a mistake of law or fact, makes an improvement to land in good faith and under erroneous belief that he or she is the owner of the land.

goodwill — an intangible asset derived from the expectation of continued public patronage.

graduated lease — a lease that is similar to a gross lease except that it provides for periodic increases in rent, often based on the Consumer Price Index.

grant deed — the deed most commonly used in California. It has two implied warranties that are enforced whether or not they are expressly stated in the deed: the grantor has not transferred title to anyone else, and the property at the time of execution is free from any encumbrances made by the grantor, except for those disclosed.

grantee — one who acquires an interest in real property from another.

grantor — one who transfers an interest in real property to another.

gross income — total income from a property before any expenses are deducted.

gross income multiplier (GIM) — a number equal to the estimated value of a property divided by the gross income of the property.

gross lease — a lease under which the tenant pays a fixed rental amount, and the landlord pays all of the operating expenses for the premises.

gross rent multiplier (GRM) — a number equal to the estimated value of a property divided by the gross rental income of the property.

ground lease — a lease under which a tenant leases land and agrees to construct a building or to make other significant improvements on the land.

group action — in antitrust law, two or more persons agreeing to act in a certain way.

group boycott — in antitrust law, the action of two or more brokers agreeing not to deal with another broker or brokers.

heir — a person entitled to obtain property through intestate succession.

hip roof — a sloping roof that rises from all four sides of the house.

Holden Act — *see*, Housing Financial Discrimination Act.

holographic will — a will written, dated, and signed by a testator in his or her own handwriting.

home equity line of credit (HELOC) — a revolving line of credit provided by a home equity mortgage.

home equity mortgage — a security instrument used to provide the borrower with a revolving line of credit based on the amount of equity in the borrower's home.

homeowner's exemption — and exemption of $7,000 from the assessed value of a homeowner's residence.

Homeowner's Protection Act (HPA) — a federal law that requires lenders to disclose to borrowers when the borrowers' mortgages no longer require PMI.

homestead declaration —a recorded document that claims a particular dwelling (such as a house, condominium, boat, or mobile home) as the owner's principal place of residence and that provides limited protection for the claimant's equity in the dwelling.

homestead exemption — the amount of a homeowner's equity that may be protected from unsecured creditors.

Housing Financial Discrimination Act — a California state law (also referred to as the Holden Act) that prohibits redlining by making it illegal for financial institutions to consider the racial, ethnic, national origin, or religious composition of a neighborhood when determining whether to make loans or to provide financial assistance for housing in that neighborhood.

HUD-1 Uniform Settlement Statement — an escrow settlement form mandated by RESPA for use in all escrows pertaining to the purchase of owner-occupied residences of 1-4 dwelling units that use funds from institutional lenders regulated by the federal government.

implication — the act of creating an agency relationship by an unauthorized agent who acts as if he or she is the agent of a principal, and this principal reasonably believes that the unauthorized agent is acting as his or her actual agent.

implied contract— a contract not expressed in words, but, through action or inaction, understood by the parties.

implied easement — an easement arising by implication, as when a purchaser of mineral rights automatically acquires an implied right to enter the property to extract the minerals.

impound account — *see*, reserve account

Improvement Bond Act of 1915 — this act permits local governments to issue bonds to finance subdivision street improvements. Owners of the subdivisions bear the cost of redeeming the bonds.

inclusionary zoning — a zoning law that requires builders to set aside a specific portion of new construction for people of low to moderate incomes.

income approach — an appraisal approach that estimates the value of an income-producing property as being worth the present value of the future income of the property through a three-step process: (1) determine the net annual income, (2) determine an appropriate capitalization rate, and (3) divide the net income by the capitalization rate to obtain the estimate of value.

incurable depreciation — depreciation that results from (1) physical deterioration or functional obsolescence that cannot be repaired at a cost that is less than or equal to the value added to the property and (2) economic obsolescence (which is beyond the control of the property owner).

independent contractor — a person who performs work for someone, but does so independently in a private trade, business, or profession, with little or no supervision from the person for whom the work is performed.

index — under an adjustable-rate mortgage, a benchmark rate of interest that is adjusted periodically according to the going rate of T-bills, LIBOR, or the like.

individual building manager — a property manager who usually manages just a single large property.

individual property manager — a real estate broker who manages properties for one or more property owners.

installment note — a promissory note in which periodic payments are made, usually consisting of interest due and some repayment of principal.

installment sale — a sale in which the seller receives at least one payment in a later tax period and may report part of the gain from the sale for the year in which a payment is received.

integration — the growth and development stage of property.

interest — the compensation allowed by law or fixed by the parties for the use, or forbearance, or detention of money.

interest-rate cap —under an adjustable-rate mortgage, the maximum that the interest rate can increase from one adjustment period to the next or over the life of the entire loan.

interpleader — an action that allows for a neutral third party (such as a real estate agent) to avoid liability to two or more claimants (such as a seller and buyer) to the same money or property (such as an earnest money deposit) by forcing the claimants to litigate among themselves, letting the court determine who deserves what while not enmeshing the neutral third party in the litigation.

Interstate Land Sales Full Disclosure Act — a federal consumer protection act that requires that certain land developers register with the Bureau of Consumer Financial Protection if they offer across state lines parcels in subdivisions containing 100 or more lots. A regulated developer must provide each prospective buyer with a Property Report that contains pertinent information about the subdivision and that discloses to the prospective buyer that he or she has a minimum of 7 days in which to cancel a purchase agreement.

intestate — not having made, or not having disposed of by, a will.

intestate succession — transfer of the property of one who dies intestate.

involuntary lien — a lien created by operation of law, not by the voluntary acts of the debtor.

jamb — the vertical sides of a door or window that contact the door or sash.

joint ownership — ownership of property by two or more persons.

joint tenancy —a form of joint ownership which has unity of possession, time, interest, and title.

joist — one of a series of parallel heavy horizontal timbers used to support floor or ceiling loads.

Jones v. Mayer — a landmark 1968 United States Supreme Court case that held that the Civil Rights Act of 1866 was constitutional and that the Act prohibited all racial discrimination, whether private or public, in the sale or rental of property.

judicial foreclosure — a foreclosure carried out not by way of a power-of-sale clause in a security instrument, but under the supervision of a court.

judgment — a court's final determination of the rights and duties of the parties in an action before it.

jumbo loan — a mortgage loan the amount of which exceeds conforming loan limits set by the FHFA on an annual basis.

junior mortgage — a mortgage that, relative to another mortgage, has a lower lien-priority position.

land contract — a real property sales contract.

land installment contract — a real property sales contract.

lateral support — the support that soil receives from the land adjacent to it.

lease extension — a continuation of tenancy under the original lease.

lease renewal — a continuation of tenancy under a new lease.

leasehold estate — a less-than-freehold estate.

legatee — one who acquires personal property under a will.

lessee — a person (the tenant) who leases property from another.

lessor — a person (the landlord) who leases property to another.

less-than-freehold estate — an estate in which the holder has the exclusive right to possession of land for a length of time. The holder of a less-than-freehold estate is usually referred to as a lessee or tenant.

level payment note — a promissory note under which all periodic installment payments are equal.

leverage — a method of multiplying gains or losses on investments, usually by using borrowed money to acquire the investments.

license to use —a personal right to use property on a nonexclusive basis. A license to use is not considered an estate.

lien —an encumbrance against real property that is used to secure a debt and that can, in most cases, be foreclosed.

lien priority — the order in which lien holders are paid.

lien stripping — a method sometimes used in Chapter 13 bankruptcies to eliminate junior liens on the debtor's home.

life estate — a freehold estate the duration of which is measured by the life of a natural person — either by the life of the person holding the estate, or by the life or lives of one or more other persons.

limited liability partnership — a partnership in which there is at least one general partner and one or more limited partners. The limited partners have no liability beyond their investment in and pledges to the partnership.

lintel — a horizontal support made of wood, stone, concrete, or steal that lies across the top of a window or door and supports the load above.

liquidated damages — a sum of money that the parties agree, usually at the formation of a contract, will serve as the exact amount of damages that will be paid upon a breach of the contract.

lis pendens — (Latin for "action pending") a notice of pendency of action.

listing agreement — a written contract between a real estate broker and a property owner (the principal) stipulating that in exchange for the real estate broker's procuring a buyer for the principal's property, the principal will compensate the broker, usually with a percentage of the selling price.

loan modification — a restructuring or modification of a mortgage or deed of trust on terms more favorable to the buyer's ability (or desire) to continue making loan payments.

loan servicing — the administration of a loan from the time the loan proceeds are dispersed to the time the loan is paid off in full.

loan-to-value ratio (LTV) — the amount of a first mortgage divided by the lesser of (1) the appraised value of the property or (2) the purchase price of the property.

long-term capital gain — the capital gain on the sale of a capital asset that was held for a relatively long period of time, usually more than one year.

lot, block, and tract land description — (see "recorded map land description")

maker — the person who makes a promissory note.

manufactured home — a structure that was constructed on or after June 15, 1976 and built to HUD standards; transportable in one or more sections; eight body feet or more in width, or 40 body feet or more in length, in the traveling mode, or, when erected on site, is 320 or more square feet; built on a permanent chassis.

margin — a number of percentage points, usually fixed over the life of the loan, that is added to the index of an adjustable-rate mortgage to arrive at the fully indexed rate.

market allocation — in antitrust law, the process of competitors agreeing to divide up geographic areas or types of products or services they offer to customers.

market price — the price actually paid for a particular property.

market value — as defined for appraisal purposes by HUD/FHA is: "The most probable price which a property should bring in a competitive and open market under all conditions requisite to a fair sale, the buyer and seller, each acting prudently, knowledgeably and assuming the price is not affected by undue stimulus."

material fact — a fact that is likely to affect the decision of a party as to whether to enter into a transaction on the specified terms.

mechanics lien — a specific lien claimed by someone who furnished labor or materials for a work of improvement on real property and who has not been fully paid.

Megan's Law — a law that provides for the registration of sex offenders and for the making available to the public information regarding the location of these offenders.

Mello-Roos Community Facilities Act — this act provides for the construction or improvement of a wide variety of facilities and services. Because the property tax burden on Mello-Roos districts can be quite high, a seller of a residential structure consisting of 4 or fewer dwellings that is subject to a lien of a Mello-Roos district must make a good-faith effort to obtain from the district a disclosure notice concerning the special assessment and give notice of the disclosure to prospective purchasers.

menace — a threat to commit duress or to commit injury to person or property.

meridians — (see and compare "base lines")

metes and bounds land description — a method of describing a parcel of land that uses physical features of the locale, along with directions and distances, to define the boundaries of the parcel.

minor — in California, a person who is under 18 years of age.

mobile home — a structure that was constructed before June 15, 1976; transportable in one or more sections; eight body feet or more in width, or 40 body feet or more in length, in the traveling mode, or, when erected on site, is 320 or more square feet; built on a permanent chassis.

mobile home park — an area of land where two or more mobile home sites are rented, or held out for rent, to accommodate mobile homes used for human habitation.

moldings — patterned strips, usually of wood, used to provide ornamental finish to cornices, bases, windows, and door jambs.

mortgage banker — a primary lender that uses its own money in creating a mortgage loan.

mortgage broker — an individual or company that finds borrowers and matches them with lenders for a fee.

mortgagee — a lender or creditor to whom a mortgagor gives a mortgage to secure a loan or performance of an obligation.

Mortgage Forgiveness Debt Relief Act of 2007 — a federal law that allowed taxpayers to exclude from income debt that is canceled on their principal residence (not on a second home) through foreclosure, loan modification, or other form of debt cancellation. The amount of canceled debt that can be excluded from income is $2 million for a married couple filing jointly, or $1 million for individuals or married persons filing separately. After being extended several times, this Act expired at the end of 2013.

mortgage loan originator (MLO) — a person who takes, or offers to take, a residential mortgage loan application or offers or negotiates terms of a residential mortgage application for compensation or gain or in expectation of compensation or gain.

mortgagor — the borrower who gives a mortgage on his or her property to secure a loan or performance of an obligation.

mudsill — for houses built on a concrete slab, the wood sills that are bolted to all sides of the slab, providing a means of attaching portions of the framing for the house to the foundation.

multiple listing service — an organization (MLS) of real estate brokers who share their listings with other members of the organization.

mutual consent — refers to the situation in which all parties to a contract freely agree to the terms of the contract; sometimes referred to as a "meeting of the minds."

Narrative Report — *see*, Self-Contained Report.

National "Do Not Call" Registry — a registry established by the Federal Trade Commission to protect consumers from unwanted commercial telephone solicitations.

National Association of Real Estate Brokers — a real estate trade association whose members are called Realtists®.

National Association of Realtors® — the largest real estate trade association in the United States, founded in 1908, whose members are called Realtors®.

National Environmental Policy Act (NEPA) — a federal law intended to protect, and to promote the enhancement of, the environment.

negative amortization — a loan repayment scheme in which the outstanding principal balance of the loan increases because the installment payments do not cover the full interest due.

negative amortized loan (NegAm loan) — a loan by which the installment payments do not cover all of the interest due — the unpaid part of the interest due being tacked onto the principal, thereby causing the principal to grow as each month goes by.

negative declaration — a report issued by a state or local agency acting pursuant to the California Environmental Quality Act if the agency determines that a development project will not have a significant adverse environmental impact.

negative fraud — the act of not disclosing a material fact which induces someone to enter into a contractual relationship and that causes that person damage or loss.

net income — income from a property remaining after expenses are deducted from gross income.

net lease — a lease under which the tenant pays a fixed rental amount plus some of the landlord's operating expenses.

net listing — a listing agreement providing the broker with all proceeds received from the sale over a specified amount.

NMLS — the Nationwide Mortgage Licensing System and Registry is a mortgage licensing system developed and maintained by the Conference of State Bank Supervisors and the American Association of Residential Mortgage Regulators for the state licensing and registration of state-licensed loan originators.

nonconforming loan — a loan not in conformance with FHFA guidelines.

nonconforming use — a zoning exception for areas that are zoned for the first time or that are rezoned and where established property uses that previously were permitted to not conform to the new zoning requirements. As a general rule, such existing properties are "grandfathered in," allowing them to continue the old use but not to extend the old use to additional properties or to continue the old use after rebuilding or abandonment.

non-judicial foreclosure — a foreclosure process culminating in a privately conducted, publicly held trustee's sale. The right to pursue a non-judicial foreclosure is contained in the power-of-sale clause of a mortgage or deed of trust, which, upon borrower default and the beneficiary's request, empowers the trustee to sell the secured property at a public auction.

notice of cessation — a written form that notifies that all work of improvement on a piece of real property has ceased, and that limits the time in which mechanics liens may be filed against the property.

notice of completion — a written form that notifies that a work of improvement on real property has been completed, and that limits the time in which mechanics liens may be filed against the property.

notice of default (NOD) — a document prepared by a trustee at the direction of a lender to begin a non-judicial foreclosure proceeding.

notice of nonresponsibility — a written notice that a property owner may record and post on the property to shield the owner from any liability for a work of improvement on the property that a lessee or a purchaser under a land sales contract authorized.

notice of pendency of action — a notice that provides constructive notice to potential purchasers or encumbrancers of a piece of real property of the pendency of a lawsuit in which an interest in that piece of real property is claimed.

notice of sale — a document prepared by a trustee at the direction of a lender that gives notice of the time and place of sale of an identified foreclosed property.

novation — a substitution of a new obligation or contract for an old one, or the substitution of one party to a contract by another, relieving the original party of liability under the contract.

nuisance — anything that is indecent or offensive to the senses, or an obstruction to the free use of property, so as to interfere with the comfortable enjoyment of life or property.

nuncupative will — an oral will; nuncupative wills are no longer valid in California.

offer — a proposal by one person (the offeror) to enter into a contract with another (the offeree).

offeree — one to whom an offer to enter into a contract is made.

offeror — one who makes an offer to enter into a contract.

open listing — a listing agreement that gives a broker the nonexclusive right to sell property and receive compensation (usually a commission) if, but only if, the broker is the first to procure a buyer for the property.

option contract — a contract that gives the purchaser of the option the right to buy or lease a certain property at a set price any time during the option term.

option listing — a listing agreement in which the broker is given the right to sell the subject property or to purchase it at a specified price for a specified time.

ordinary interest — interest calculated by the 30/360 day count convention.

ostensible agency — an agency in which the principal intentionally, or by want of ordinary care, causes a third person to believe another to be his agent who was not actually employed by him.

parol evidence rule — a rule that prohibits the introduction of extrinsic evidence of preliminary negotiations, oral or written, and of contemporaneous oral evidence, to alter the terms of a written agreement that appears to be whole.

partial release clause — a clause in a blanket mortgage that allows a developer to sell off individual parcels and pay back, according to a release schedule, only a proportionate amount of the blanket loan.

partition —a court-ordered or voluntary division of real property held in joint ownership into parcels owned in severalty.

passive income — in general, income from either rental activity or from a business in which the taxpayer does not materially participate.

passive investor — an investor who does not actively contribute to the management of the business invested in.

patent, land — an instrument used to convey government land.

payee — the person to whom a promissory note is made out.

payment cap —under an adjustable-rate mortgage, the maximum amount that installment payments may increase from one adjustment period to the next or over the life of the loan.

percentage lease — a lease, often used in shopping centers, under which the tenant typically pays a base rent amount plus a percentage of the gross receipts of the tenant's business.

period of redemption — a period of time after a sheriff's sale in a judicial foreclosure proceeding during which the borrower may redeem his or her property by paying off the entire debt plus costs.

periodic tenancy — an estate from period to period.

physical deterioration — depreciation that results from wear and tear of use and from natural causes.

physical life — the period of time that the property lasts with normal maintenance.

pitch — the degree of inclination or slope of a roof.

plaintiff — the one who brings a lawsuit.

planned development (PD) — a development (other than a condominium, community apartment project, or stock cooperative) consisting of lots or parcels owned separately and areas owned in common and reserved for the use of some or all the owners of the separate interests.

planning commission — the city or county agency responsible for proposing a general plan for the city or county.

plaster — a mixture of lime or gypsum, sand, water, and fiber that is applied to walls and ceilings and that hardens into a smooth coating.

point of beginning — the fixed starting point in the metes and bounds method of land description.

points — see discount points.

police power — the power of a government to impose restrictions on private rights, including property rights, for the sake of public welfare, health, order, and security, for which no compensation need be made.

portfolio loans — loans that primary lenders retain in their own investment portfolios rather than sell into the secondary market.

post-dated check — a check dated with a date after the date the check is written and signed.

power of attorney — a special written instrument that gives authority to an agent to conduct certain business on behalf of the principal. The agent acting under such a grant is sometimes called an attorney in fact.

power-of-sale clause — a clause contained in most trust deeds that permits the trustee to foreclose on, and sell, the secured property without going to court.

preapproval —an evaluation of a potential borrower's ability to qualify for a loan that involves a credit check and verification of income and debt of the potential borrower.

preliminary notice — a notice sent by someone who furnishes work or materials for a work of improvement on real property that creates a right to file a mechanics lien against the property.

preliminary public report — a report that a subdivider may request that requires fewer disclosures than does a final public report and that only allows the subdivider to accept reservations from potential purchasers.

preliminary title report — a statement by a title insurance company of the condition of the title and of the terms and conditions upon which the company is willing to issue a policy.

prepayment penalty — a fee charged to a borrower for paying off the loan faster than scheduled payments call for.

prequalification — an initial unverified evaluation of a potential borrower's ability to qualify for a mortgage loan.

prescription — a method of acquiring an interest in property by use and enjoyment for five years.

prescriptive easement — an easement acquired by prescription.

price fixing — an agreement between competitors to set prices or price ranges.

primary financing — first mortgage property financing.

primary lender — lenders who originate mortgage loans.

primary mortgage market — the market where mortgage loans are originated.

principal — the one whom an agent represents.

principle of anticipation — principle that value is derived from a calculation of anticipated future benefits to be derived from the property, not from past benefits, though past benefits may inform as to what might be expected in the future.

principle of balance — principle that the maximum value of property, its highest and best use, is created and maintained when land use by interacting elements of production are in equilibrium or balance.

principle of change — principle that property values are in a constant state of flux due to economic, environmental, political, social, and physical forces in the area.

principle of competition — principle that increased competition results in increased supply in relation to demand, and thereby to lower profit margins.

principle of conformity — principle that the maximum value of land is achieved when there is a reasonable degree of social, economic, and architectural conformity in the area.

principle of contribution — principle that improvements made to a property will contribute to its value or that, conversely, the lack of a needed improvement will detract from the value of the property.

principle of four-stage life cycle — principle that property goes through a process of growth, stability, decline, and revitalization.

principle of progression — principle that the value of a residence of less value tends to be enhanced by proximity to residences of higher value.

principle of regression — principle that the value of a residence of higher value tends to be degraded by the proximity to residences of lower value.

principle of substitution — principle that the value of a property will tend toward the cost of an equally desirable substitute property.

principle of supply and demand — principle that the value of property in a competitive market is influenced by the relative levels of supply and demand: the greater level of demand in relation to the level of supply, the greater the value.

principle of the highest and best use — principle that the best use of a property in terms of value is the use most likely to produce the greatest net return (in terms of money or other valued items).

private mortgage insurance (PMI) — mortgage insurance that lenders often require for loans with an LTV more than 80%.

privity of contract — a legal doctrine that states that a legally enforceable relationship exists between the persons who are parties to a contract.

privity of estate — a legal doctrine that states that a legally enforceable relationship exists between the parties who hold interests in the same real property.

probate — a legal procedure whereby a superior court in the county where the real property is located or where the deceased resided oversees the distribution of the decedent's property.

profit á prendre — the right to enter another's land for such purposes as to drill for oil, mine for coal, or cut and remove timber.

promissory note — a contract whereby one person unconditionally promises to pay another a certain sum of money, either at a fixed or determinable future date or on demand of the payee.

property tax postponement program — a program in which the state pays all or part of the real property tax on a qualified senior's residence until he or she moves, sells the property, dies, or transfers title to the property. Repayment of all postponed taxes must be paid when the property is sold or title transferred.

Proposition 13 — an amendment to the California state Constitution that places a maximum ad valorem tax on real property equal to 1% of the "full cash value" plus a maximum increase of the assessed value of up to 2% per year, as long as the annual increase does not exceed the Consumer Price Index for that year.

Proposition 193 — this law extends Proposition 58 tax relief to certain transfers from grandparents to their grandchildren, but not transfers from grandchildren to their grandparents.

Proposition 58 — this law provides for an exclusion from reassessment when property is transferred between spouses. It also provides for an exclusion from reassessment of a transfer of a principal residence and transfers of the first $1 million of other real property between parent and child.

Proposition 60 — this law allows certain older persons to transfer the adjusted basis of their present principal residence to a replacement if the replacement is in the same county and is of equal or lesser value than the prior residence.

Proposition 8 — this law requires the county assessor to assess real property either at the property's Proposition 13 adjusted value or its current market value, whichever is less.

Proposition 90 — this law extends Proposition 60 to allow the purchase of a new residence in a different California county, but only if the county in which the new residence lies adopts Proposition 90.

proration — an adjustment of expenses that either have been paid or are in arrears in proportion to actual time of ownership as of the closing of escrow or other agreed-upon date.

public dedication — a gift of an interest in land to a public body for public use, such as for a street, a park, or an easement to access a beach.

public grant — public land conveyed, usually for a small fee, to individuals or to organizations, such as to railroads or universities.

puffing — the act of expressing a positive opinion about something to induce someone to become a party to a contract.

purchase money loan — a deed of trust or mortgage on a dwelling for not more than four families given to a lender to secure repayment of a loan which was in fact used to pay all or part of the purchase price of that dwelling, occupied entirely or in part by the purchaser.

pyramid roof — a hip roof that has no ridge.

quitclaim deed — a deed that contains no warranties of any kind, no after-acquired title provisions, and provides the grantee with the least protection of any deed; it merely provides that any interest (if there is any) that the grantor has in the property is transferred to the grantee.

rafter — one of a series of parallel sloping timbers that extend from the ridgeboard to the exterior walls, providing support for the roof.

ratification —the act of creating an agency relationship by a principal who accepts or retains the benefit of an act made by an unauthorized agent.

Real Estate Commissioner — the chief executive officer of the CalBRE who is appointed by the governor and whose responsibility is to oversee and enforce the Real Estate Law and the Subdivided Lands Law and to issue regulations, known as the Regulations of the Real Estate Commissioner, that have the full force and effect of law.

Real Estate Fund — a special account controlled by the California State Treasury into which real estate license fees are deposited.

real estate investment trust (REIT) — a company that invests in and, in most cases operates, income-producing real estate and that meets numerous criteria, such as the necessity of being jointly owned by at least 100 persons.

real estate owned (REO) — property acquired by a lender through a foreclosure sale.

real estate professional — a real estate investor who (1) materially participates for at least 750 hours during the tax year in the real estate business and (2) spends more than 50% of his or her personal services performed in all businesses during the tax year in the real estate business that he or she materially participates in.

Real Estate Settlement Procedures Act (RESPA) — a federal law designed to prevent lenders, real estate agents, developers, title insurance companies, and other agents (such as appraisers and inspectors) who service the real estate settlement process from providing kickbacks or referral fees to each other, and from facilitating bait-and-switch tactics.

Real Estate Transfer Disclosure Statement"("TDS") — a form that a seller of a residential real estate property of 1 to 4 units must complete, sign, and have delivered to a buyer. The TDS must also be completed in part by the agent representing the seller, stating whatever defects are discovered or known by the agent.

Real Property Loans Act — a California law that addresses abuses and loan charges on small loans secured by real property.

real property sales contract — an agreement in which one party agrees to convey title to real property to another party upon the satisfaction of specified conditions set forth in the contract and that does not require conveyance of title within one year from the date of formation of the contract.

Realtist® — a member of the National Association of Real Estate Brokers.

Realtor® — a member of the National Association of Realtors®.

reconciliation — the process of ascertaining value by comparing and evaluating values obtained from comparables or from different valuation approaches; the process of comparing what is in a trust fund account with what should be in the account.

reconveyance deed — a deed executed by the trustee of a deed of trust after the promissory note is paid off in full by the borrower and the lender instructs the trustee to so execute the reconveyance deed, which reconveys legal title to the borrower

recorded map land description — a method of land description that states a property's lot, block, and tract number, referring to a map recorded in the county where the property is located.

Recovery Account — a special account into which is credited some of the funds from the Real Estate Fund, which funds are used to reimburse members of the public who have obtained a civil judgment or criminal restitution order against a real estate licensee but have not been able to collect fully from the licensee through normal collection efforts.

redemption period — a period of time extending for 3 months after a sheriff's sale if the proceeds of the sale is enough to pay off the debt and all costs of foreclosure; it is 1 year if the proceeds of the sale are not enough to pay off the debt *and* the lender pursues a deficiency judgment. If the lender elects not to pursue a deficiency judgment, there is no right of redemption.

redlining — the illegal practice of refusing to make loans for real property in particular areas.

Regulation Z — the set of regulations that implement the Truth-in-Lending Act (TILA).

reinforced concrete — concrete poured around steel bars or metal netting to increase its ability to withstand tensile, shear, and compression stresses.

rejection — the act of an offeree that terminates an offer. An offer may be rejected (1) by submitting a new offer, (2) by submitting what purports to be an acceptance but is not because it contains a variance of a material term of the original offer, or (3) by express terms of rejection.

rejuvenation — the phase when a property is rebuilt, remodeled, or otherwise revitalized to a new highest and best use.

reliction — a natural process by which the owner of riparian or littoral property acquires additional land that has been covered by water but has become permanently uncovered by the gradual recession of water.

remainder — the residue of a freehold estate where, at the end of the estate, the future interest arises in a third person.

remainder depreciation — depreciation that will occur after the date of valuation.

remainderman — a person who inherits or is entitled to inherit property held as a life estate when the person whose life determines the duration of the life estate passes away.

replacement cost — the cost of replacing improvements with those having equivalent utility, but constructed with modern materials, designs, and workmanship.

reproduction cost — the cost of replacing improvements with exact replicas at current prices.

request for a reconveyance — an instrument that a lender sends to a trustee requesting that the trustee execute and record a deed of reconveyance that is then sent to the borrower.

rescission — the cancellation of a contract and the restoration of each party to the same position held before the contract was entered into.

reserve account — in reference to loan servicing, the escrow account from which the loan servicer typically pays, on behalf of the borrower, property taxes, hazard insurance, and any other charges (such as mortgage insurance) with respect to the loan.

resident manager — an individual who resides on the premises, is a "responsible" person, and has "charge" of the apartment building.

residential loan — a loan primarily for personal, family, or household use secured by a residential structure that contains 1 to 4 dwelling units. The term also includes a loan for an individual condominium unit, cooperative unit, mobile home, manufactured home, and trailer, if it is used as a residence.

residual value — an estimate of the reasonable fair market value of a property at the end of its useful life.

respondeat superior — in agency law, the doctrine that a principal is liable for the acts of an agent if those acts were performed within the scope of the agent's authority. (See, vicarious liability.)

Restricted Use Report — a type of appraisal report that is sometimes used when the client is familiar with the area and a report summarizing the data that supports the final estimate of value is not necessary. The Restricted Use Report must contain a notice that it is to be used only by the client for one particular purpose, not by potential buyers or lenders or others.

retaliatory eviction — an eviction action brought to retaliate against a tenant for making a habitability complaint or for asserting other of the tenant's legal rights.

return on investment (ROI) — an investor's cash flow (net income minus financing charges) divided by the investor's actual cash investment (as distinct from the purchase price).

reverse mortgage — a security instrument for a loan for homeowners over the age of 62 who have a large amount of equity in their homes, usually designed to provide such homeowners with monthly payments, often over the lifetime of the last surviving homeowner who either moves out of the house or dies.

reversion — the residue of a freehold estate where at the end of the estate, the future interest reverts to the grantor.

revocation — the withdrawal of an offer by the person who made the offer.

rezoning amendment — an amendment to a zoning ordinance that property owners may request if they feel that their area has been improperly zoned.

ridgeboard — a horizontal board placed on edge at the apex of a roof to which the upper ends of the rafters are attached.

right of first refusal — the right to be given the first chance to purchase a property at the same price, terms, and conditions as is offered to third parties if and when the property is put up for sale.

right of reinstatement — a borrower's right to, at any time within the period from the date of recordation of the notice of default until 5 business days prior to the date of sale, have his or her loan reinstated by paying all delinquent loan installments, foreclosure costs, and trustee's fees. No right of reinstatement exists after a trustee's sale, when the purchaser immediately acquires all rights held by the former owner, subject to the rights of holders of rights superior to the mortgage that was foreclosed.

right of survivorship — the right to succeed to the interest of a joint tenant or, if community property with right of survivorship, to succeed to the interest of a spouse or registered domestic partner. Right of survivorship is the most important characteristic of joint tenancy.

riparian rights — the rights of a landowner to use water from a stream or lake adjacent to his or her property, provided such use is reasonable and does not injure other riparian owners.

Rumford Act — *see*, Fair Employment and Housing Act

R-value — a measure of the resistance of insulation to heat transfer. The FTC requires sellers of new homes to disclose the R-value of each home's insulation. The higher the R-value, the greater is the effectiveness of the insulation.

SAFE Act — the Safe and Fair Enforcement for Mortgage Licensing Act of 2008 was designed to improve consumer protection and reduce mortgage fraud by setting minimum standards for the licensing and registration of mortgage loan originators.

safety clause — a clause in a listing agreement that protects the broker's commission for a sale that is consummated after the termination of the broker's listing agreement to a buyer who is found by the broker during the term of the listing agreement.

sales comparison approach — an appraisal approach that compares recent sales of similar properties in the area to evaluate the market value of the subject property.

salesperson — a natural person who is employed by a licensed real estate broker to perform acts that require having a real estate license.

salvage value — residual value.

sandwich lease — a leasehold interest that lies between a primary lease and a sublease.

sash — frames that contain one or more windowpanes.

scarcity — a lack of abundance.

scrap value — residual value.

second mortgage — a security instrument that holds second-priority claim against certain property identified in the instrument.

secondary financing — second mortgage and junior mortgage property financing

secondary mortgage market — the market where mortgages are sold by primary mortgage lenders to investors.

secret profit — any compensation or beneficial gain realized by an agent not disclosed to the principal. Real estate agents must always disclose any interest that they or their relatives have in a transaction and obtain their principals' consent.

section — one square mile, containing 640 acres.

sections and township land description — a method of land description based on a grid system of north-south lines ("ranges") and east-west lines ("tier" or "township" lines) that divides the land into townships and sections.

security instrument — the written instrument by which a debtor pledges property as collateral to secure a loan.

SEER — (see EER)

Self-Contained Report — a type of appraisal report that contains a complete description of the data relied on, including data about the neighborhood as well as the property; the reasons the appraiser used for his or her interpretation of the estimate of value; and pertinent maps, photographs, charts, and the plot plans.

self-help eviction — a landlord's denial of possession of leased premises to a tenant without complying with the legal process of eviction.

seller carry back loan — a loan or credit given by a seller of real property to the purchaser of that property.

Seller Financing Disclosure Law — a California law that requires the seller of real property who carries back a loan to give the purchaser loan disclosures similar to the disclosures required in conventional loans.

seller's agent — a real estate broker appointed by the seller to represent the seller.

selling agent — the real estate agent who sells or finds and obtains a buyer for the property in a real estate transaction.

senior mortgage — a mortgage that, relative to another mortgage, has a higher lien-priority position.

separate property — property that is owned in severalty by a spouse or registered domestic partner. Separate property includes property acquired before marriage or the registering of domestic partnership, and property acquired as a gift or by inheritance during marriage or registered domestic partnership.

servient tenement — land that is burdened by an easement.

settlement — *see*, closing

severalty — ownership of property by one person.

severance — the act of detaching an item of real property that changes the item to personal property, such as the cutting down of a tree. Also, the act of terminating a relationship, such as the act of partitioning by court order or the transfer of an interest that changes a joint tenancy into a tenancy in common.

sheriff's deed — a deed given at the foreclosure of a property, subsequent to a judgment for foreclosure of a money judgment against the owner or of a mortgage against the property. A sheriff's deed contains no warranties and transfers only the former owner's interest in the property.

sheriff's sale — a sale of property following a judicial foreclosure.

Sherman Act — the federal law passed in 1890 that prohibits agreements, verbal or written, that have the effect of restraining free trade.

short sale — a pre-foreclosure sale made by the borrower (usually with the help of a real estate agent) with lender approval of real estate for less than the balance due on the mortgage loan.

short-term capital gain — the capital gain on the sale of a capital asset that was held for a relatively short period of time, usually one year or less.

sill — the board or metal forming the lower side of the frame for a window or door; the lowest part of the frame of a house, resting on the foundation and providing the base for the studs.

simple interest — the type of interest that is generated only on the principal invested.

single agency — an agency in which a broker represents either the seller or the buyer, but not both.

single point of contact — an individual or team of personnel employed by a mortgage loan servicer, each of whom has the ability and authority to assist a borrower in assessing whether the borrower may be able to take advantage of a foreclosure prevention alternative offered by, or through, the mortgage servicer.

special agent — an agent for a particular act or transaction.

specific lien — a lien that attaches only to specific property.

specific performance — a court order that requires a person to perform according to the terms of a contract.

spot zoning — an improper use of zoning whereby a particular property is zoned differently from similar property similarly situated in the neighborhood.

standard subdivision — is a subdivision with no common areas of ownership or use among the owners of the subdivision parcels.

standby loan commitment — a commitment by a lender to make a take-out loan after construction on a property is completed

State Housing Law — a California state law that provides for minimum construction and occupancy requirements for housing.

statute of frauds — a law that requires certain types of contracts, including most real estate contracts, to be in writing and signed by the party to be bound in order for the contract to be enforceable.

statute of limitations — a law that requires particular types of lawsuits to be brought within a specified time after the occurrence of the event giving rise to the lawsuit.

statutory will — a pre-printed "fill-in-the-blanks" will provided by statute that must be signed in the presence of two competent witnesses.

statutory year — contrasted with a calendar year, a "year" period consisting of 360 days, with 12 months of 30 days (also referred to as a banker's year).

steering — the illegal practice of directing people of protected classes away from, or toward, housing in particular areas.

step-up lease — a graduated lease

stigmatized property — a property having a condition that certain persons may find materially negative in a way that does not relate to the property's actual physical condition.

stock cooperative — a corporation formed or availed of primarily for the purpose of holding title to improved real property either in fee simple or for a term of years.

straight note — a promissory note under which periodic payments consist of interest only.

straight-line depreciation — the expensing of a property by equal amounts over the useful life of the property, determined by subtracting from the cost of the property the estimated residual value of the property and dividing that amount by the useful life of the property measured in years.

straight-line method — a method of calculating annual depreciation of an improvement by dividing the cost of the improvement by the estimated useful life of a typical such improvement.

Street Improvement Act of 1911 — this act provides local governments with the authority to issue bonds to improve streets and make other improvements to specific areas. Assessments on properties are due in equal installments during the term of the bonds, which can run for decades.

studs — vertical wood or metal members in wall or partition framing that serve as the main support for upper floors or roof. Studs are usually placed 16 to 24 inches apart.

subagent — an agent of an agent.

Subdivided Lands Law — a California state law that requires subdividers to disclose certain pertinent information to the initial purchasers of parcels in subdivisions.

Subdivision Map Act — a California state law that gives local officials the authority to regulate subdivisions to ensure that they conform to local general plans.

subjacent support — the support that soil receives from land beneath it.

subject to — acquiring real property that is burdened by a mortgage without becoming personally liable for the mortgage debt.

subjective value — (also referred to as *value in use*) is value placed on the amenities of a property by a specific person.

sublease — a transfer of a tenant's right to a portion of the leased premises or to the entire premises for less than the entire remaining lease term.

subordination clause — a provision in a mortgage or deed of trust that states that the mortgage or deed of trust will have lower priority than a mortgage or deed of trust recorded later.

Summary Report — a type of appraisal report that typically consists of several pages of forms to be filled out by an appraiser that contain pertinent data about the subject property, along with photos, maps, and plans. This type of appraisal report is most often used by lending institutions, insurance companies, and government agencies.

supplemental tax assessment — an event that occurs upon the sale of real property or completion of new construction on real property when the county assessor determines the current market value of the transferred property or the newly constructed real property and subtracts the prior assessed value from the current assessed value to obtain the net supplemental value that will be enrolled as a supplemental assessment. The increase (or decrease) in assessed value is then reflected in a prorated supplemental tax bill that covers the period from the first day of the month following the transfer or completion of construction to the end of the fiscal year, which runs from July 1 to June 30.

take-out loan — a loan that provides long-term financing for a property on which a construction loan had been made.

tax assessor — the county or city official who is responsible for appraising property.

tax auditor — the county or city official who maintains the county tax rolls.

tax collector — the county or city official who is responsible for collecting taxes.

tax deed — the deed given to the successful buyer at a tax sale. A tax deed conveys title free and clear from private liens, but not from certain tax liens or special assessment liens, or from easements and recorded restrictions.

tenancy in common — a form of joint ownership that is presumed to exist if the persons who own the property are neither married nor registered domestic partners and they own undivided interests in property. Tenants in common may hold unequal interests; however, if the deed does not specify fractional interests among the tenants, the interests will be presumed to be equal.

tenancy in partnership — a form of joint ownership in which the partners combine their assets and efforts in a business venture.

tentative map — a map required pursuant to the Subdivision Map Act for subdivisions that create five or more parcels, five or more condominiums, a community apartment project containing 5 or more interests, or the conversion of a dwelling into a stock cooperative of 5 or more dwelling units. The tentative map, which is to be filed with the local planning commission, must include a legal description of the property; the location and description of all adjoining highways, streets, and waterways; the location and description of easements for roads, drainage, sewers, and other public utilities; proposed public areas; and proposed provisions for floods and other natural hazards.

testament — a will.

testator — one who dies leaving a will.

time-share estate — an estate in real property coupled with the right of occupancy for certain periods of time.

time-share use — a right to occupancy during certain periods of time, not coupled to an estate in real property.

title plant — a duplicate of county title records maintained at title insurance companies for use in title searches.

township — six square miles, containing 36 sections.

trade fixtures — objects that a tenant attaches to real property for use in the tenant's trade or business. Trade fixtures differ from other fixtures in that, even though they are attached with some permanence to real property, they may be removed at the end of the tenancy of the business.

transferability — the ability to transfer some interest in property to another.

Treaty of Guadalupe Hidalgo —the treaty that ended the Mexican-American war (1846-48), annexed California to the United States, and provided for the recognition of community property rights in California.

triggering term — any of a number of specific finance terms stated in an advertisement for a loan that triggers Regulation Z disclosure requirements in the advertisement.

triple net lease — a lease under which the tenant pays a fixed rent plus the landlord's property taxes, hazard insurance, and all maintenance costs.

trust deed — a three-party security device, the three parties being the borrower (***trustor***), the lender (***beneficiary***), and a third-party (***trustee)*** to whom "bare legal title" is conveyed.

trust fund overage — a situation in which a trust fund account balance is greater than it should be.

trust fund shortage — a situation in which a trust fund account balance is less than it should be.

trustee — a person who holds something of value in trust for the benefit of another; under a deed of trust, a neutral third-party who holds naked legal title for security.

trustor — a borrower who executes a deed of trust.

Truth-in-Lending Act (TILA) — a federal consumer protection law that was enacted in 1968 with the intention of helping borrowers understand the costs of borrowing money by requiring disclosures about loan terms and costs (in particular, the APR) and to standardize the way in which certain costs related to the loan are calculated and disclosed.

tying arrangement — occurs in antitrust law when the seller conditions the sale of one product or service on the purchase of another product or service.

underwriter — one who analyzes the risk of, and recommends whether to approve, a proposed mortgage loan.

undivided interest — an ownership interest in property in which an owner has the right of possession of the entire property and may not exclude the other owners from any portion by claiming that a specific portion of the property is his or hers alone.

undivided interest subdivision — a subdivision in which owners own a partial or fractional interest in an entire parcel of land. The land in an undivided interest subdivision is not divided; its ownership is divided.

unenforceable contract — a contract that a court would not enforce.

Uniform Commercial Code (UCC) — a set of laws that established unified and comprehensive regulations for security transactions of personal property and that superseded existing laws in that field.

unilateral contract — a contract in which one party gives a promise that is to be accepted not by another promise but by performance.

unity of interest — in reference to joint ownership, refers to each of the owners having equal interests in the property.

unity of possession — in reference to joint ownership, refers to each of the owners having an equal, undivided right to possession of the entire property.

unity of time — in reference to joint ownership, refers to each of the owners having acquired his/her interest in the property at the same time.

unity of title — in reference to joint ownership, refers to each of the owners having received ownership in the property from the same deed.

unlawful detainer — a legal action to regain possession of real property.

Unruh Civil Rights Act — a California state law that prohibits persons engaged in business from discriminating on the basis of race, color, religion, ancestry, national origin, gender, disability, medical condition, or age when providing products or services in California. In housing related activities, businesses are also prohibited from discriminating on the basis of marital status, familial status, sexual orientation, or source of income. This law applies to all real estate salespersons and brokers.

useful life — the estimated period during which a property generates revenue (if the property is an income property) or usefulness (if the property, such as a private residence, has value other than income value).

usury — the charging of interest in excess of that allowed by law.

utility — the usefulness of property; its ability to satisfy a potential buyer's need or desire, such as to provide shelter or income.

VA — the Department of Veterans Affairs is a federal agency designed to benefit veterans and members of their families.

Vacation Ownership and Time-Share Act of 2004 — a California state consumer protection law that regulates disclosures and representations made by time-share salespersons.

valid contract — a contract that is binding and enforceable in a court of law.

value — the present worth of all rights to future benefits, arising out of property ownership, to typical users or investors.

variance — an exception that may be granted in cases where damage to the value of a property from the strict enforcement of zoning ordinances would far outweigh any benefit to be derived from enforcement.

vendee — the purchaser in a real property sales agreement

vendor — the seller in a real property sales agreement.

veteran's exemption — and exemption of up to $4,000 from the assessed value of a qualified veteran's property.

vicarious liability — liability imposed on a person not because of that person's own acts but because of the acts of another. (See, respondeat superior.)

void contract — a purported contract that has no legal effect.

voidable contract — a contract that, at the request of one party only, may be declared unenforceable, but is valid until it is so declared.

voluntary lien — a lien obtained through the voluntary action of the one against whose property the lien attaches.

Vrooman Street Act of 1885 — this act provides local governments with authority to construct streets, sewers, and other improvements. Funds for these improvements are secured by the issuance of bonds, which are redeemed by assessing the properties benefited.

warranty deed — a deed in which the grantor warrants that the title being conveyed is good and free from defects or encumbrances, and that the grantor will defend the title against all suits.

warranty of habitability — mandated by both statutes and by common law, an implied warranty in any residential lease that the premises are suitable for human habitation.

will — a document that stipulates how one's property should be distributed after death; also called a testament.

writ — a court order commanding the person to whom it is directed to perform an act specified therein.

writ of attachment — a writ ordering the seizure of property belonging to a defendant to ensure the availability of the property to satisfy a judgment if the plaintiff wins.

writ of execution — a writ directing a public official (usually the sheriff) to seize and sell property of a debtor to satisfy a debt.

writ of possession — a court order that authorizes the sheriff or other eviction authority to remove a tenant and the tenant's possessions from leased premises.

zoning — laws of a city or county that specify the type of land-use that is acceptable in certain areas.

Index

Made in the USA
San Bernardino, CA
12 June 20